More praise for *In Search of the Racial Frontier*

"An absorbing chronicle. . . . Marshaling a wealth of primary source material, Taylor documents black Westerners' participation in all aspects of life in the American West and, in the process, reclaims an important dimension of African American history." —*Publishers Weekly*

"Those looking for a solid overview of the African-American presence in our region would do well to let Quintard Taylor be their guide." —John C. Walter, *Seattle Times*

"Taylor has given us the most comprehensive survey of his subject in a generation, and by far the most ambitious ever in scope and chronology. Clearly written, widely researched, and filled with vivid stories and details, this book demonstrates conclusively that blacks have played an important role in creating both the Old West and the New West."
—Donald Worster, University of Kansas

"Quintard Taylor, certainly a foremost historian of the Black West, significantly enriches and broadens our understanding of the black quest for freedom on the racial frontier. His dynamic and insightful history spans 400 years, clearing away mountains of debris born of age-old myths and stereotypes. *In Search of the Racial Frontier* adroitly reconstructs a black West that is, among other things, urban to the core. This is a major contribution to American history and to African American studies. It is not to be missed."
—Darlene Clark Hine, Michigan State University

"Thoroughly researched, lucidly written, and powerfully argued, *In Search of the Racial Frontier* is a stellar synthesis of black Western history. It corrects the usual Southern and Northern bias in our understanding of the African American experience. Scholars, teachers, public policy experts, and the general reader will remain indebted to Dr. Taylor deep into the twenty-first century."

—Joseph Trotter, Carnegie-Mellon University

"Quintard Taylor's gracefully written overview of the African American West challenges simple interpretations of 'frontier opportunity' and inaccurate black/white models of race in America. In a wide-ranging narrative that extends from the first explorations of northern New Spain to urban uprisings of the 1990s, Taylor describes a diverse cast of black western women and men in a variety of social relationships with other westerners. *In Search of the Racial Frontier* fills a long-neglected void in the histories of the American West and of U.S. race relations."   —Elizabeth Jameson, University of New Mexico

In Search of
the Racial Frontier

Also by QUINTARD TAYLOR:

THE FORGING OF
A BLACK COMMUNITY

In Search of the Racial Frontier

AFRICAN AMERICANS IN THE AMERICAN WEST

1528–1990

◆ ❧ ◆ ❧ ◆

Quintard Taylor

W·W·NORTON & COMPANY

New York   London

To

Grace and Quintard Taylor, the first historians I ever knew

Copyright © 1998 by Quintard Taylor

All rights reserved
Printed in the United States of America
First published as a Norton paperback 1999

Excerpt of "One-Way Ticket" from *Collected Poems* by
Langston Hughes. Copyright © 1994 by the Estate of
Langston Hughes. Reprinted by permission of Alfred A. Knopf, Inc.

For information about permission to reproduce selections from this book, write to
Permissions, W. W. Norton & Company, Inc.,
500 Fifth Avenue, New York, NY 10110.

The text of this book is composed in ITC New Baskerville
with the display set in Baskerville
Composition and manufacturing by the Maple-Vail Manufacturing Group.
Book design by Jacques Chazaud

Library of Congress Cataloging-in-Publication Data

Taylor, Quintard.
In search of the racial frontier : African Americans in the
American West, 1528–1990 / by Quintard Taylor.
p.   cm.
Includes bibliographical references (p.   ) and index.
ISBN 0-393-04105-0
1. Afro-Americans—West (U.S.)—History.   2. West (U.S.)—History.
I. Title.
E185.925.T39   1998
978′.00496073—dc21   97-14747
                                                                         CIP
ISBN 0-393-31889-3 pbk.
W. W. Norton & Company, Inc., 500 Fifth Avenue, New York, N.Y. 10110
www.wwnorton.com

W. W. Norton & Company Ltd., 10 Coptic Street, London WC1A 1PU

1 2 3 4 5 6 7 8 9 0

Contents

❖ ❀ ❖ ❀ ❖

Illustrations follow pages 96 and 224

Tables

◇ ✿ ◇ ✿ ◇

Maps

◊ ❀ ◊ ❀ ◊

Acknowledgments

◊ ❧ ◊ ❧ ◊

In Search of the Racial Frontier is the result of five years of reflecting, researching, collecting, consulting, and writing on the African American West. In many ways this effort has been a group project with dozens of people offering advice, critiques, and myriad forms of support. Without their help and encouragement this project would not have been completed. I want to thank a number of persons who rendered invaluable assistance.

Patricia Nelson Limerick was there almost from the genesis of the book. Her enthusiasm for this project led her to contact W. W. Norton on my behalf. Her action immediately provided me a publisher. More important, it made me much more aware of the value of this work to historians, students, and the general public.

Edwin Barber, my editor at W. W. Norton & Company, became involved in this project in 1992. Through numerous phone and E-mail conversations he led me through the labyrinth of the publishing world, constantly reminding me of my responsibility to remain focused and on task. His editorial suggestions in the final year of this project transformed ambiguity into clarity, creating a much stronger, richer, more readable manuscript.

A number of colleagues at the University of Oregon read all or portions of the manuscript and added their valuable insights and suggestions. I think in particular of Earl Pomeroy, Richard Maxwell

Brown, James Mohr, Jeff Ostler, Barbara Welke, Peggy Pascoe, and Daniel Pope. I received critiques from other campus colleagues, including Edwin Coleman, Sandra Morgen, Elizabeth Ramirez, Robert Proudfoot, Marshall Sauceda, Joe A. Stone, and Steven L. Stone.

The list of historians and other university scholars who assisted includes Sue Armitage, Washington State University; Alwyn Barr, Texas Tech University; Eugene Berwanger, Colorado State University; Albert L. Broussard, Texas A&M University; Thomas R. Buecker, Fort Robinson Museum; Lonnie Bunch III, Smithsonian Institution; Clarence Caesar, California Office of Historic Preservation; Suzanne Campbell, San Angelo, Texas; Robert Cherny, San Francisco State University; Garna Christian, University of Houston; Ronald G. Coleman, University of Utah; Willi Coleman, University of Vermont; Thomas Cripps, Morgan State University; Douglas Daniels, University of California, Santa Barbara; Lawrence B. de Graaf, California State University, Fullerton; Richard Etulain, University of New Mexico; Douglas Flamming, California Institute of Technology; Neil J. Foley, University of Texas; Jimmie L. Franklin, Vanderbilt University; Christopher Friday, Western Washington University; Larry Gerlach, University of Utah; Bruce Glasrud, Sul Ross State University; William H. Goetzmann, University of Texas; David Gutiérrez, University of California, San Diego; Ramón A. Gutiérrez, University of California, San Diego; Willie Hill, University of Colorado; Albert Hurtado, Arizona State University; William H. Issel, San Francisco State University; Elizabeth Jameson, University of New Mexico; Howard Jones, Prairie View A&M University; William M. King, University of Colorado; Paul Lack, McMurry University; William Lang, Portland State University; Rudolph Lapp, San Mateo, California; William and Shirley Leckie, Winter Springs, Florida; Daniel F. Littlefield, Jr., University of Arkansas at Little Rock; George Lipsitz, University of California, San Diego; James Locklear, University of Nebraska; Bradford Luckingham, Arizona State University; Charles H. Martin, University of Texas, El Paso; Delores N. McBroome, Humboldt State University; Shirley Ann Moore, California State University, Sacramento; Elizabeth McLagan, Portland; Dennis Mihelich, Creighton University; Darrell Millner, Portland State University; Kevin Mulroy, Gene Autry Museum; Gerald Nash, University of New Mexico; Merline Pitre, Texas Southern University; Howard Rabinowitz, University of New Mexico; John A. Ravage, University of Wyoming; Wilson Ed Reed, North Texas State University; William Richter, Tucson, Arizona; Glenda Riley, Ball State University; Ricardo Romo, University of Texas; James A. Ronda, University of Tulsa; Vicki Ruiz, Arizona State University; Frank N. Schubert, Army War College; Malik Simba, California State University, Fresno; Stephanie Smith, Ohio State University; Alonzo Smith, Smithsonian Institution; Clarence Spigner, University of Washington; Joe W. Trotter, Carnegie-Mellon University; William M. Tuttle, University of Kansas; David J. Weber, Southern Methodist University; Elliott West, University of Arkansas; Richard White, University of Washington; and Ruthe Winegarten, Austin, Texas.

Graduate students and now new Ph.D.'s across the nation also shared their own research, pointed out errors, and inevitably strengthened this book. I am particularly indebted to my graduate students Stuart McElderry and Ken Harlan at the University of Oregon. Stuart and Ken provided information on their respective projects, African American Portland and Los Angeles. I also want to thank other UO students, including Kevin Hatfield and Deborah Syrdal, for their contributions. Students across the country who assisted me include Saheed Adejumobi, University of Texas; James Brooks, University of Maryland; Angela Darlean Brown, Stanford University; Gary R. Entz, University of Utah; Todd Guenther, Lander, Wyoming; Lynn Hudson, California Polytechnic State University; Robert Franklin Jefferson, Wayne State University; James N. Leiker, University of Kansas; Gretchen Lemke-Santangelo, St. Mary's College; Dedra McDonald, University of New Mexico; Claire M. O'Brien, Southern Illinois University; David J. Organ, Auburn University; Stacey Shorter, National Parks Service; Ernest Obadelli Starks, Texas A&M University; Alan Thompson, Helena, Montana; and Matthew C. Whitaker, Arizona State University. I also want to acknowledge William A. Smith, a UO undergraduate who was a research assistant on this project.

My wide consultation notwithstanding, errors have undoubtedly occurred in this volume. They are my responsibility alone. Perhaps other historians will follow with their own accounts of the African American West, correcting mistakes and breaking new ground.

This project relied heavily on the support of the University of Oregon library staff. Space limitations prevent me from listing all those who helped, but I want to acknowledge the particular efforts of Aimee Yogi, interlibrary loan; Barbara Jenkins, Lawrence Crumb, and Jon Cawthorne, reference; Thomas Stave, government publications; Dennis Hyatt, law librarian; and Joy Halliwell, microforms.

I am grateful to librarians and historical society archivists across the region who gathered documents, papers, and photographs for the project. They include Judith Austin and Elizabeth Jacox, Idaho Historical Society; Charles Brown, St. Louis Mercantile Library; Bertha Calloway, Great Plains Black Museum; Richard H. Engeman, University of Washington Library; Barbara Foley, Colorado Historical Society; Susan Forbes, Kansas Historical Society; Prentice Gautt, historian, Big Eight Conference; Floyd M. Geery, Fort Bliss Museum; William W. Gwaltney, Fort Laramie National Historical Site; Moya Hansen, Colorado Historical Society; Bonnie Hardwick, Bancroft Library, UC-Berkeley; Cheryl Brown Henderson, The Brown Foundation, Topeka, Kansas; Steve Jansen, Watkins Community Museum, Lawrence, Kansas; Barbara Jenkins, University of Oregon Library; Rebecca Kohl, Montana Historical Society; John P. Langellier, Gene Autry Museum; Rebecca Lintz, Colorado Historical Society; Carolyn J. Marr, Museum of History & Industry, Seattle; William H. Mullane, Northern Arizona University; Orlando Romero and Arthur Olivas, Museum of New Mexico; Richard Ogar, Bancroft Library, UC-Berkeley; Susan Seyl, Oregon Historical Society; Nancy Sherbert and Paul Stewart, Black American West Museum, Denver, Colorado; Anne Taylor, Arizona Historical Society; Leeca Wright, Dodge City Community College Library; and Dina Young, Missouri Historical Society.

I want to thank Andrea Soule for creating the maps in this volume, Julieta Díaz Barrón for editing the Spanish text; and Cindy Routtu, Carol Foster, and Margaret Wooten White for clerical support. The University of Oregon Humanities Center provided crucial fellowship support for the fall term 1994. I want to thank my children, Quintard III, Jamila, and William, for patiently putting up with this ever-expanding project. I also thank others who gave support and encouragement, including Marvin Perry, Clarence and Jennifer Spigner, Eckard V. Toy, Lillian Whitlow, Joe Franklin, Junko and Bill Toll, Bettie Sing Luke, Art Cary, Wilson Ed Reed, Helen and Glenn May, Marcine Anderson, Elaine and Ralph Hayes, Laura Fair and Fuadi Hilal, Howard Shorr, Betty Mohr, Patricia Dawson, Evelyn and Billy Ray Flowers, Patricia Melson, Marietta and Robert Fikes, and Diane Taylor Brown. Finally this book is dedicated to the memory of millions of westerners who struggled for racial justice in an uncommon land.

Introduction

◇ ❀ ◇ ❀ ◇

There is room for only a limited number of colored people here. Overstep that limit and there comes a clash in which the colored many must suffer. . . . The few that are here do vastly better than they would do if their number were increased a hundredfold.

Seattle Daily Intelligencer, May 28, 1879

Your West is giving the Negro a better deal than any other section of the country. I cannot attempt to analyze the reasons for this, but the fact remains that there is more opportunity for my race, and less prejudice against it in this section of the country than anywhere else in the United States.

JAMES WELDON JOHNSON, NAACP national secretary, quoted in the *Denver Post,* June 24, 1925

The two statements above frame the central paradigm in the history of African Americans in the American West. Did the West represent the last best hope for nineteenth- and twentieth-century African Americans? Was it a racial frontier beyond which lay the potential for an egalitarian society? Or did the region fail to match the unobtainable promise imposed upon it by legions of boosters, to provide both political freedom and economic opportunity? Perhaps black Americans, in their desire to escape the repression of the East and South, simply exaggerated the possibilities in the region. Did western distinctiveness apply to race? Such questions defy easy, immediate answers.

Certainly evidence can be assembled that directs us to either conclusion suggested in the newspaper quotations. Colonial elites in seventeenth-century New Spain erected an elaborate racial classification system that was designed to ensure the maintenance of caste but that quickly disintegrated on its northern frontier, allowing persons of African ancestry remarkable social fluidity. African Americans in California and Oregon challenged antebellum discriminatory legislation. Often they received the support of prominent whites. Post–Civil War southern blacks benefited from overwhelming western support for their full and equal integration into the political life of the ex-Confederate states. Many of these white westerners were unwilling to extend comparable equality to African American residents in their own region. Twentieth-century African American westerners found both considerable support and opposition to their efforts to integrate the industrial workplace, residential neighborhoods, and public schools. Yet the very struggle itself reflects the fact that, as historian Duane Smith has argued, "The problem of black rights and citizenship was not limited to the South or Northern cities. The failure was that of the American people—not of a section or a particular generation."[1]

There is striking ambiguity about race in the West. Much of it stems from the presence of four groups of color—African Americans, Asian Americans, Latinos, and Native Americans—all of whom interact with Anglos in varied ways over the centuries and throughout the region. These groups also interacted both competitively and cooperatively among themselves. Few western blacks at any point in history lived or worked in communities where they were the only people of color. The presence of black people as members of multiracial, multiethnic eighteenth-century communities, such as Los Angeles, Santa Fe, and San Antonio, as much as the presence of Latinos in contemporary South Central Los Angeles (Watts now has a Latino majority) suggests that historians need to examine how these groups faced one another in the West. Indeed, the concept of "race" as generally advanced in the South and East has undergone reinterpretation and redefinition precisely because of the presence of the variety of groups in the West. Richard White argued in 1986 that "minority peoples should be at the heart of historical claims for Western distinctiveness." Without them, he wrote, the West "might as well be New Jersey with mountains and deserts."[2]

As important as such questions are to understanding the dynamics of the region, *In Search of the Racial Frontier* is not an analysis of western black-white social relations or a comparison of people of color. Rather its major purpose is to reconstruct the history of African American women and men in the nineteen western states on and beyond the ninety-eighth meridian—North Dakota to Texas westward to Alaska and Hawaii. Its chronological scope extends from the era of the first Spanish-speaking arrivals in the seventeenth century through the civil rights era of the 1960s. Its goals are threefold: first, to introduce and provide national visibility to the rich, diverse, complex tradition of black western history over the past five centuries; second, to illustrate both the black West's regional distinctiveness and its continuity with the legacy of African American history in the rest of the nation; and finally to establish conclusively the existence of multiple African American historical traditions. In examining the black West, the region least identified with the history of African Americans in the United States, this history follows the admonition of Roger Lotchin that ". . . the art and science of history progresses more from the literature that fills gaps in our knowledge than from the endless reinterpretation of well-known evidence."[3]

In Search of the Racial Frontier pursues themes of race, ethnicity, gender, and environment, against the background of the nineteenth and twentieth centuries. It is not primarily a study of colorful individuals, although some invariably will be discussed, as much as it is a collective biography, an examination of the African American quest for community in the West and the paradoxical consequences of that quest. It also seeks to locate the black West in the larger model of a regional history that defines the West as a place rather than a process.[4]

Our arrival at this juncture of western African American history has come after a long, controversial intellectual journey. Until the 1960s the images of the West centered on Frederick Jackson Turner's ideal of rugged Euro-American pioneers constantly challenging a westward-moving frontier, bringing civilization, taming the wilderness, and, in the process, reinventing themselves as "Americans" and creating an egalitarian society that nurtured the fundamental democratic values that shaped contemporary American society. This interpretation was reinforced by western paintings, by novels, and, most important, by movies and television programs, which cemented into our national consciousness, as no historical work could, the image of white settlers as "conquerors" who superimposed their will on a vast, virtually uninhabited virgin land. African Americans, according to this interpretation, were not an indigenous conquered group, and certainly they were not among the conquerors. Thus black westerners had no place in the region's historical saga. Walter Prescott Webb's 1957 comment that the West is defined by its scarcity of "water, timber, cities, industry and Negroes" reflected and influenced conventional wisdom about African Americans and the region.[5]

By the 1960s and early 1970s the first significant writing on the African American West had emerged. That writing reflected what

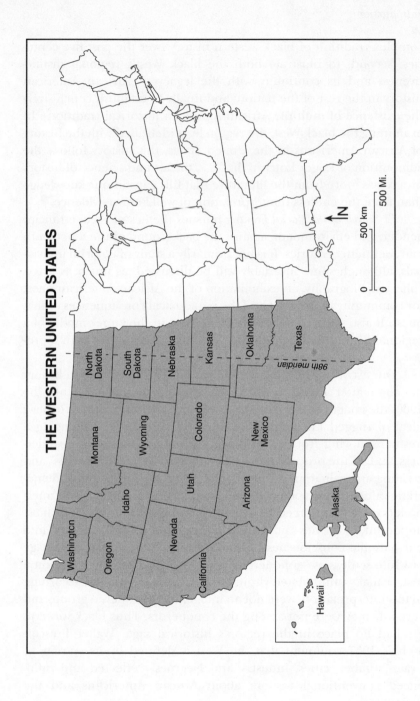

THE WESTERN UNITED STATES

North Dakota
South Dakota
Nebraska
Kansas
Oklahoma
Texas
98th meridian

Montana
Wyoming
Colorado
New Mexico

Idaho
Utah
Arizona

Washington
Oregon
Nevada
California

Alaska

Hawaii

500 km
500 Mi.
0
0
N

historian Lawrence B. de Graaf has called the recognition school, which posited that in simply acknowledging the presence of African American women and men in the western states and territories, historians had adequately fulfilled their primary mission of eliminating African American invisibility in the region. Kenneth W. Porter advanced that premise when he wrote his justification for pursuing black history in the American West. "Its thesis is simply: they were there," he declared in his 1971 edited volume *The Negro on the American Frontier.* "It does not intend, in overreaction to previous disregard or minimization of the frontier Negro, to present Negroes as the most important ethnic element on the American frontier. Negroes . . . could not . . . have played the same roles in the drama of the expanding frontier as did the dominant whites. What is surprising and significant . . . is that they were as important on the frontier as they were. . . ."[6]

In 1976 W. Sherman Savage's *Blacks in the West* appeared as the first survey of the West. It is a study in the classic Frederick Jackson Turner tradition, beginning with the Anglo-French fur-trading era and ending with the closing of the frontier in 1890. Savage excluded from his survey Texas but included Wisconsin, Minnesota, and Iowa. Since publication of *Blacks in the West* an enormous body of books and articles on African Americans in the region has appeared, making imperative a new interpretative historical survey.[7]

Despite the foundation provided by the recognition school, we must pursue the significance of the black presence in the West beyond simply locating African Americans on the scene. What does it mean, for example, when we assess the role of African American soldiers on the frontier that they protected as an emerging political order inimical to the interests of western Native Americans, who throughout the post–Civil War decades fought to defend their families, homes, and way of life? What of the role of black soldiers in quelling strikes by western white workers who struggled against powerful eastern-based corporations for decent wages and living conditions? How does one reconcile the dedication of African American soldiers who risked their lives to defend lands that would soon be populated by settlers determined to deny other blacks the similar opportunity to settle and prosper?[8]

In Search also addresses the void created by the paucity of black western urban history. Nearly half this volume is dedicated to examining the western urban black experience. The black urban West provides the striking example of continuity between the experiences of nineteenth- and twentieth-century African Americans in the region and those of black people in other sections of the United States. With the publication of a growing number of monographs, numerous articles, and some chapters that serve both as specific studies and as segments of larger urban histories, black western urban history can provide a prism through which to examine and reinterpret the meaning of African American city life in the entire nation.[9]

Any accurate portrayal of African Americans in the West thus must begin with the efforts of these women and men in places as disparate as Helena, Montana; Topeka, Kansas; Boulder, Colorado; San Francisco; Seattle; San Diego; and San Antonio to fashion a supportive world far from the major centers of black population. To what extent were these small urban enclaves different from and similar to the surrounding cities and the African American urban cultures of the East and South? How did segregation and exclusion shape black western urban life and what were the subregional, ethnic, racial, class, and gender considerations that impacted on such communities? Indeed, the differences within the West are often as striking as the differences between the West and other regions. The African American community of San Antonio, for example, was situated in former slaveholding and Confederate Texas, where "haciendas met the plantations." Black people there confronted a different set of racial norms and values from those that impacted upon African Americans who migrated to Seattle, which for all practical purposes never experienced an antebellum period or the Civil War.[10]

If historians who sought a "new" western history were dismayed by the persistence of the mythic West, those who write African American history in the West are equally distressed by the emergence of a more recently promoted parallel myth of the black cowboy, buffalo soldier, and "motherly but single" elderly black female pioneer who found their place in the West.[11]

In Search will not conclusively lay to rest the image of the West as a region inclusive of rowdy, rugged *black* cowboys, gallant *black* soldiers, and sturdy but silent *black* women, but it will forcibly challenge the stereotype of the black westerner as a solitary figure loosened from moorings of family, home, and community. As Eugene Berwanger reminds us, few of the twenty-five thousand western African Americans in 1870 lived such romantic lives on the rural frontier. Instead they resided in cities, generating a living and making lives for themselves while developing supportive community institutions and attempting, as much as possible, to integrate themselves into both the larger social and political lives of their cities and the cultural and political life of the national African American community.[12]

For all that has been written on the black West, and a prodigious amount has been published and continues to roll off the presses, we still know woefully little about large areas of the African American past in this region. *In Search* signals the opportunity to begin our reconstruction of that past.

In Search of
the Racial Frontier

1

◇ ✤ ◇ ✤ ◇

Spanish Origins,

1528–1848

African American life in the West began with nature's violence. In November 1528 a storm in the Gulf of Mexico washed ashore on the Texas coast two small boats, the only remnants of an ill-fated expedition. Spanish conquistador Pánfilo de Narváez's survivors included Esteban, a black slave owned by Captain Andrés Dorantes. Born half a world away in Azamor, Morocco, Esteban was the first African to set foot in what would become Texas and the western United States.[1]

Narváez's voyage began in Cuba in April 1528, when five ships and 400 adventurers set out from Havana to explore the North American mainland. On May 1 Narváez reached Tampa Bay, abandoned his ships, and, with 260 men, set forth into the interior. Native peoples warily watched this strange procession of breastplated soldiers, long-robed priests, and one servant, Esteban, for four months as it marched northwest under brightly colored plumes and banners. Despite repeated attacks that steadily reduced their ranks, the conquistadors pushed forward, driven by a search for riches and fame in the North American interior comparable to Cortés's discoveries in the Valley of Mexico a decade earlier. By July 1528 they reached Apalachee (near present-day Tallahassee), a village of forty thatched huts, instead of their anticipated city of gold. The Apalachee drove the invaders south toward the Gulf of Mexico until the now much depleted party reached St. Marks Bay. The wounded Narváez ordered construction of five crude barges and then, believing he was closer to Mexico than to Cuba, commanded his party to sail west. Three of the five boats, including Narváez's, sank in storms off the Texas coast. One storm deposited Esteban and others on a sandbar near Galveston. They named it the Island of Ill Fate.[2]

Sixteen stranded men endured a Gulf Coast winter on the island and then, in April 1529, moved onto the mainland where they were soon captured and enslaved for the next five years by the coastal Indians. By September 1534 only four still lived: Esteban, Dorantes, Alonso del Castillo Maldonado, and Álvar Núñez Cabeza de Vaca. They escaped from the Indians and fled into the interior, where friendlier Native Americans accepted them as medicine men. Because of his ability to "talk fluently with his hands in the language of the signs," Esteban became group interpreter, emissary, and diplomat with the natives. The disoriented survivors now began an arduous journey southwest. They crossed the Rio Grande and then, with the guidance of Shuman Apache, straggled over Chihuahua and Sonora. They finally reached Mexico City in July 1536, ending their eight-year fifteen-thousand-mile ordeal.[3]

Don Antonio de Mendoza, the viceroy of New Spain, failed to persuade Dorantes, Castillo, and Cabeza de Vaca to return to the northern frontier in pursuit of yet another legend of Indian wealth, the Seven (Golden) Cities of Cibola. Undaunted, Mendoza in 1539 organized an expedition led by a Franciscan friar, Marcos de Niza, who purchased Esteban to serve as his guide and interpreter. The expedition traveled steadily across the Sonora desert with the Moroccan-born slave moving well ahead, dispatching regular reports to Fray Marcos while gathering around him a retinue of three hundred Indian women and men, who believed him to be a powerful healer and medicine man. Surviving Indian accounts of this journey describe the approach of a black katsina (the rain spirit that represented the ancestral dead), large in stature and adorned with animal pelts, turquoise, bells, and feathers on his ankles and arms. Yet when Esteban attempted to enter the Zuni town of Hawikuh (just east of the present Arizona–New Mexico border) after being warned by town elders to stay out, he was killed.[4]

Esteban did not "discover" Arizona or New Mexico. The region had been inhabited for thousands of years. Yet the expedition that cost him his life profoundly changed the course of western history. His journey strengthened Spanish claims in the north, sparked exploration by the Spaniards, and encouraged the founding of such towns as Santa Fe, Los Angeles, and El Paso. Esteban's journey also initiated the tripartite meeting of Indian, Spanish, and Anglo cultures that was to shape much of the region's history. The journey also opened this northern frontier to subsequent dark-skinned settlers. For the next three centuries persons of African ancestry more likely moved north from Mexico rather than west from the Atlantic slope.[5]

Esteban's travels comprise the best account of an early African presence, but the historical records yield many examples of other Africans who accompanied Spanish explorers. When the Coronado expedition of 1540–42 retraced Esteban's route to the northern frontier, "upward of a thousand servants and followers, black men and red men, went with them." Most of these servants were Native Americans, but a number were Africans, including some who deserted with Indian members of the party. Moreover, a free black interpreter assisted Coronado expedition friar Juan de Padilla in 1541, when he chose to remain among the Kansas Indians. The Bonilla de Leyva–Antonio Gutiérrez de Humana Expedition of 1593, which attempted to establish a Spanish colony along the upper Río Grande near Santa Fe, had black members. So did the Juan de Oñate party that colonized New Mexico in 1598. Oñate's colonizers included at least five blacks and mulattoes, two of them soldiers, and three female slaves. The Juan Guerra de Resa Expedition of 1600, organized to strengthen Oñate's New Mexican colony, included several soldiers and their mulatto wives and children. Nearly a century later, in 1692, the Don Diego de Vargas Expedition, which reconquered New Mexico following the Pueblo Revolt, included Sebastián Rodríguez Brito from Angola. Other persons of African ancestry entered Texas with Spanish expeditions. In 1691 an unidentified black bugler accompanied the second Domingo Terán de los Ríos missionary expedition to the Indians of East Texas. Twenty-five years later a black man named Juan Concepción came with Domingo Ramón's seventy-five-person party to found the mission of Nuestro Padre San Francisco de los Téjas just east of the Neches River.[6]

Isabel de Olvera, a servant accompanying the Juan Guerra de Resa Expedition, expected that her rights as free woman would be protected under Spanish law. Upon joining the expedition, Olvera became the first free woman of African ancestry to venture into northern New Spain. Her appearance in Santa Fe in 1600 predates by nineteen years the arrival of twenty blacks in Jamestown, Virginia.

Concerned for her safety and status on the northern frontier, Olvera gave a predeparture deposition to Don Pedro Lorenzo de Castilla, the alcalde of Querétaro. She stated, "I am going on the expedition to New Mexico and have some reason to fear that I may be annoyed by some individual since I am a mulatto, and it is proper to protect my rights in such an eventuality by an affidavit showing that I am a free woman, unmarried and the legitimate daughter of Hernando, a negro, and an Indian named Magdalena. . . . I therefore request your grace to accept this affidavit, which shows that I am free and not bound by marriage or slavery. I request that a properly certified and signed copy be given to me in order to protect my rights, and that it carry full legal authority. I demand justice."[7]

We know little else of these early women and men except that their presence confirms the African contribution to the *raza cósmica*, the multiracial population that emerged in New Spain soon after the conquest of 1519–21. Although free black men accompanied Cortés, African slaves soon followed after 1521, and by 1570 the 20,000 black bond servants outnumbered the combined white and mestizo population. Nearly 200,000 Africans entered Mexico during the colonial period (1521–1821), a figure comparable to the 345,000 brought to British North America. Unlike the English-speaking mainland colonies, where racial boundaries were sharply drawn, New Spain produced a multiracial population through large-scale intermarriage. African women never comprised more than 25 percent of the black population in New Spain. Thus black men generally took Indian wives. Moreover, Spaniards and criollos often took mulattas as consorts and occasionally as wives, adding to the partly African population. The black-Indian and black-Spaniard population grew rapidly from 2,435 in 1570 to 369,790 by 1793. Mestizos demographically and culturally dominated Mexico after independence from Spain in 1821, but by the 1740s mulattoes outnumbered mestizos and constituted, after Indians and criollos, the largest "racial" group in New Spain.[8]

Cultural integration followed. Blacks and mulattoes adopted the religion, language, foods, clothing, and lifestyles of the *españoles* because both Europeans and Africans were racial minorities among a much-larger Indian population. Europeans and Africans integrated economically as well. Much of the Indian population maintained a self-contained, subsistence agricultural economy, but blacks and mulattoes alike, whether slave or free, like the Spaniards, criollos, and mestizos, served the economic interests of Spain. In British

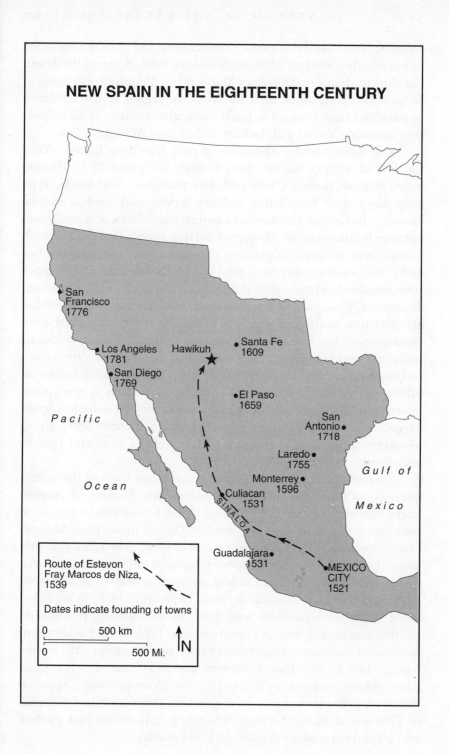

NEW SPAIN IN THE EIGHTEENTH CENTURY

San
Francisco
1776

Los Angeles
1781

San Diego
1769

Pacific

Ocean

Hawikuh

Santa Fe
1609

El Paso
1659

San
Antonio
1718

Laredo
1755

Monterrey
1596

Culiacan
1531

S I N A L O A

Gulf of

Mexico

Guadalajara
1531

MEXICO
CITY
1521

Route of Estevon
Fray Marcos de Niza,
1539

Dates indicate founding of towns

0   500 km

0   500 Mi.

N

colonial North America racial demography and slavery combined to encourage a distinct "African-American culture," as in the South Carolina lowlands or Tidewater Maryland and Virginia. Few areas of Mexico, however, other than the Veracruz region supported black populations large enough to foster cultural autonomy. In New Spain that autonomy rested with Indians rather than Afro-Mexicans.[9]

New Spain had few Spaniards of pure European lineage. Thus the task of settling the northern frontier fell primarily to Hispanicized Indians, mestizos, free and slave mulattoes, and blacks. Typically slaves were forced into military service and used as menial laborers. But many seventeenth-century free blacks and mulattoes became militiamen, an obligatory service for all free males. Both groups were assigned to garrison duty along the northern frontier and remained there as poorly paid civilian laborers at military garrisons, missions, or towns after their service was over. In 1760 Pedro de Labaquera, who traveled across Arizona to locate a site for a presidio, charged that most of the frontier soldiers he encountered were "mulattoes of low character, without ambition. . . ." After 1765 free mulattoes and blacks became professional soldiers when the crown established a regular army in New Spain. Nine years later a colonial official judged the population of northern New Spain to be so intermixed as to obliterate distinct racial antecedents. Nonetheless Spanish census records continued to note race or color until 1800, giving historians a fascinating glimpse into the role of class and race in assigning social status in New Spain.[10]

Spanish settlement in California reveals much about the consequences of forging a mixed-race population. Persons of African ancestry accompanied the naval and military expeditions that occupied San Diego and Monterey in 1769. One of them, Juan Antonio Coronel, was described as a *soldado de cuero* (leather-jacketed soldier), indicating he had joined the Spanish colonial militia. Friar Junípero Serra wrote of two mulatto sailors after his arrival at Monterey in 1771, and the Juan Bautista de Anza Expedition of 1775 included seven black soldier-settlers and their families among twenty-nine families emigrating to Alta California. The 1785 Santa Barbara census showed mulattoes comprising 19 percent of the town's 191 inhabitants, while in San Jose, Monterey, and San Francisco, five years later, the percentages were 24, 19, and 15 respectively. Approximately 55 percent of the Spanish-speaking population in California in 1790 was of mixed heritage, according to historian Jack Forbes, and 20 percent possessed some African ancestry.[11]

Population of New Spain, 1570–1790

	1570	%	1646	%	1742	%	1793	%
Indians	3,336,860	98	1,269,607	74	1,540,256	62	2,319,741	61
Europeans	6,644	0*	13,780	0	9,814	0	7,904	0
Criollos	11,067	0	168,586	10	391,512	16	677,458	18
Mestizos	2,437	0	109,042	7	249,368	10	418,568	11
Blacks	20,569	0	35,089	2	20,131	1	6,100	0
Mulattoes	2,435	0	116,529	7	266,196	11	369,790	10
Total	3,380,012	100	1,712,615	100	2,477,277	100	3,799,561	100

*Less than 1 percent is represented by 0. All percentages may not total 100 percent.

Source: Colin M. MacLachan and Jaime E. Rodríguez O., The Forging of the Cosmic Race: A Reinterpretation of Colonial Mexico *(Berkeley: University of California Press, 1980), p. 197.*

Castas: Racial Classification System in Colonial New Spain

Male	Female	Offspring
Spaniard	Indian	Mestizo
Spaniard	Negro	Mulatto
Spaniard	Mestiza	Castizo
Spaniard	Mulatta	Morisco
Morisco	Española	Chino
Chino	Indian	Salto atrás
Salto atrás	Mulatta	Lobo
Lobo	China	Gibaro
Gibaro	Mulatta	Alborazado
Alborazado	Negro	Cambujo
Cambujo	Indian	Zambaigo
Zambaigo	Loba	Calpamulatto

Source: Leslie B. Rout, Jr., The African Experience in Spanish America *(Cambridge: Cambridge University Press, 1976), 130.*

Black and biracial settlers founded Los Angeles in 1781. When Spanish colonial officials chose to locate a settlement between the Mission San Gabriel and the Presidio of Santa Barbara, they recruited families from the province of Sinaloa. Twelve families, mainly from Rosario, a village two-thirds mulatto, left Sinaloa in February 1781 under a military escort for their five-hundred-mile land and sea journey to Alta California. Seven months later, on September 4, they reached what would become Nuestra Señora la Reina de Los Angeles de Porciuncula. Colonial records detail the races and places of birth of most of these settlers. They included Luis Quintero, a fifty-five-year-old black native of Guadalajara his mulatta wife, María Petra Rubio, forty, and their five children; José Moreno, twenty-two, and María Guadalupe Gertrudis, nineteen, a recently wed mulatto couple; Antonio Mesa, a thirty-eight-year-old black man born in Alamos, Sonora, his mulatto wife, Ana Gertrudis López, twenty-seven, and their two children; and forty-two-year-old José Antonio Navarro, a mestizo, his forty-five-year-old mulatto wife, María Rufina Dorotea, and their three children. Twenty-six of the forty-six original settlers of Los Angeles, soon to be Alta California's largest settlement, were of African or part African ancestry.[12]

Surviving evidence suggests a similar pattern in Texas. Fray Antonio Olivares disdainfully described the seventy-two people who founded San Antonio de Bexar in 1718 as "mulattoes, lobos, coyotes, and mestizos, people of the lowest order, whose customs are worse than those of the Indians." Sixty-three years later another priest, Fray Agustín Morfi, described San Antonio's town council as "a ragged band of men of all colors." An informal 1777 census of San Antonio de Béxar confirmed his assessment. Among its population of 2,060 lived 151 blacks and mulattoes. The 1789 census of Laredo showed similar ethnic and racial diversity. Of the 708 residents, 45 percent were Spanish, 17 percent mestizos, and 17 percent mulattoes. Indians constituted another 16 percent of the population. The official census of Texas in 1792 confirmed the pattern in San Antonio and Laredo, where it recorded 34 blacks and 414 mulattoes, who made up 15 percent of province's population.[13]

Occasionally the records reveal some idea of black status and of relationships that crossed race, class, and gender boundaries. In 1735 Antonia Lusgardia Ernandes, a free mulatta in San Antonio, sued her former employer, Don Miguel Núñez Morillo, for custody of their son. Ernandes admitted that she "suffered so much from lack of clothing and from mistreatment" that she left Morillo and sought shelter with her two children in the home of Alberto López. When Morillo seized their son, "the only man I have and the one who I hope will eventually support me," Ernandes appealed to the court to "make use of all the laws in my favor. . . ." Miguel Núñez Morillo admitted paternity but argued that Ernandes had voluntarily relinquished custody of the boy to his wife. The court found otherwise and awarded custody to the biological mother on the condition that she give her son a "proper home."[14]

No reliable statistics exist for New Mexico's population comparable to those of California and Texas, but impressionistic evidence again points to a multiracial population. The region received its first permanent non-Indian inhabitants in 1598, when Don Juan de Oñate led 129 soldier-colonists into the Upper Rio Grande Valley, where they settled among the Pueblo Indians. One of the Oñate party, Francisco de Sosa Penalosa, brought "three female negro slaves, one mulatto slave, and other men and women servants." The Spanish population grew slowly to 750 in 1630 and 2,900 in 1680. It also grew more diverse, including not only criollos but mestizos, New Mexican and Mexican Indians, mulattos and blacks, prompting Fray Estevan de Perea to characterize the region's colonists in 1631 as "mestizos, mulattos, and zambohijos." Persons of African ancestry joined the various competing political factions that emerged in the region. During the 1640–43 civil war in New Mexico the faction that supported Governor Luis de Rosas was reportedly comprised of mestizos and mulattos, while Rosas's successor was supported primarily by "mestizos and sambahigos [sic], sons of Indian men, and Negroes, and mulattos."[15]

Persons of African descent may in fact have moved to New Mexico to escape the discrimination they faced in central Mexico. Historian Dedra McDonald profiles the lives of two such men. Sebastián Rodríguez Brito, the Angolan-born free son of African slaves, rose from servant to soldier and landholder in the late seventeenth century and eventually married Isabel Olguin, an *española* widow in 1692. José Antonio, a Congo-born slave brought to El Paso del Norte in 1752, married Marcela, an Apache maid in a neighboring household eight years later. Such marriages, and the highly ritualized witnessing ceremonies that accompanied them, featuring Indians, mestizos, mulattoes, and Spaniards, suggested that certain social networks transcended racial and class boundaries.[16]

Racial identification within colonial populations on the northern frontier, as in much of Latin America, was a matter of social class as much as physical appearance. In 1783 Spain's King Charles III began to issue documents called *cédulas de gracias al sacar* to "cleanse" persons of "impure origin," principally Indians and Africans. Such cleansing afforded legal, if not social, equality to certificate holders. By 1795 such certificates were sold rather than simply conferred upon worthy individuals. Few blacks could afford the seven hundred pesos required to change their racial status from *pardo* (half black–half Indian) to *quinterón* (one-eighth black–seven-eighths white) and the one thousand pesos to move from *quinterón* to white. Even so, official recognition of the ability to purchase a new racial identity encouraged others to assert a higher status and allowed Spanish officials to ignore or blur the various categories. Pedro Huízar is one such example. A native of Aguascalientes, Huízar came to San Antonio de Béxar around 1778, where he was soon employed as a sculptor at Mission San José. A man of numerous talents, Huízar became the mission carpenter, and in the 1790s he helped survey surrounding mission farmlands. By 1798 Huízar was the appointed justice at Mission San José, bearing the honorific title of Don. Don Huízar's racial status rose accordingly. First listed as a mulatto in the 1779 census, by 1793 he had become an *español*.[17]

Color, then, presented no insurmountable barrier to fame, wealth, or new ethnoracial status on the northern frontier. Some mulattoes near San Antonio owned both land and cattle. The mulatto Francisco Reyes, who arrived in Los Angeles from central Mexico in 1781, eventually became its alcalde while the descendants of Santiago de la Cruz Pico, a mestizo, and his mulatto wife, Jacinta, became prominent political leaders and wealthy ranchers in early-nineteenth-century California. In 1807 Felipe Elua, a black native of Louisiana, settled on an estate just outside San Antonio, where he grew sugar and cotton.[18]

Even so, color mattered in New Spain, for it still defined political and social class. As Jesús de La Teja has written, racial mixture notwithstanding, the stain of mixed blood attached to mestizos and the additional stigma of slavery attached to mulattos in colonial society reached the frontier. Throughout the colonial period the quintessential mark of status was to be considered *español* rather than mulatto, mestizo, Indian, or black. When San Antonio resident Antonio de Armas called Francisco Rodríguez's wife a mulatta, Rodríguez did not immediately defend his spouse. Instead he declared that should the charge be true, he would end the marriage, "for I married her in the faith that she was Spanish." Given such attitudes, few Spanish speakers of Texas, New Mexico, and California openly alluded to their African heritage.[19]

For three centuries Spanish colonial policies promoted, however inadvertently, upward social and political mobility among the *castas*. The Mexican War of Independence theoretically enshrined social equality in the constitution and laws of Mexico. That political revolution began in September 1810, when Fray Miguel Hidalgo y Costilla led mestizo, mulatto, black, and Indian masses in a brief but furious campaign to destroy the caste system and Spanish rule. Hidalgo's *Grito de Dolores* called for the abolition of slavery and the equality of all Mexican citizens before the law. The war continued fitfully for ten years without either side winning decisively. Then in 1821 Agustín de Iturbide, the Spanish military commander, joined rebel leader Vicente Guerrero in issuing the *Plan de Iguala*, a new proposal for independence. While much more conservative than the *Grito de Dolores*, the *Plan de Iguala* nonetheless reiterated the guarantees of social equality and the abolition of slavery, and it affirmed the right of all races to hold office. With an army of former enemies and the support of criollo conservatives, Iturbide forced the surrender of Spain's colonial armies. Although subsequent political regimes sought to curtail the promises, Mexico had legally committed itself to liberty and political equality for all its citizens.[20]

Fugitive slaves and free blacks "from the States" soon took note of those promises. Texas, the Mexican province most accessible to African Americans from the United States, became the principal area of settlement and a "political and cultural frontier." Beginning in the 1820s, a small number of African Americans came to east Texas. Many were fugitive slaves, but the immigrants also included free blacks determined to live under Mexican liberty instead of American tyranny. Samuel H. Hardin, for example, wrote that he and his wife had moved to Texas because Mexico's laws "invited their emigration" and guaranteed their right to own property. Virginian John Bird came because he believed he and his son, Henry, "would be received as citizens" under Mexico's colonization laws "and entitled as such to land."[21]

Other free blacks shared these aspirations. William Goyens, a North Carolinian, settled near Nacogdoches in 1820 and became a blacksmith, freighter, trader, land speculator, and slaveowner. At his death in 1856 Goyens had amassed nearly thirteen thousand acres in four East Texas counties. Lewis B. Jones and Greenbury Logan, who arrived in 1829 and 1831 respectively received land grants in the Stephen F. Austin colony, while Jean Baptiste Maturia of Louisiana was awarded a land grant directly from the Mexican government. Although there appears to be no evidence of land grants held in their names, single black women also participated in the migration to Texas. Harriet Newell Sands, a "free woman of color," emigrated from Michigan in 1834 and worked as a housekeeper. Zelina Husk, a Georgia native, and Diana Leonard, who came from "the States," were employed as washerwomen near San Jacinto in 1835. Fanny McFarland of Harris County "by industry, prudence, and economy" bought and sold small plots of real estate.[22]

However, the South Carolina–born Ashworth brothers, William, Aaron, Abner, and Moses, became the largest free black family in antebellum Texas and perhaps the wealthiest. The four brothers migrated to southeast Texas between 1831 and 1835. Two of the Ashworths were apparently wealthy enough to avoid military service in the Texas revolution, sending substitutes instead. Eventually the brothers acquired nearly two thousand acres in southeast Texas, and Aaron Ashworth owned twenty-five hundred head of cattle, the largest herd in Jefferson County. In 1850 Aaron Ashworth was the only resident of the county wealthy enough to afford a tutor for his children.[23]

Some free black immigrants in Mexican Texas openly appreciated such racial tolerance. When the American abolitionist Benjamin Lundy visited San Antonio de Béxar in 1833, he met a former slave from North Carolina who had become a blacksmith. The blacksmith said "the Mexicans pay him the same respect as to the other laboring people, there being no difference made here on account of color." Impressed by the prospects of freedom in Texas for former slaves, Lundy launched a program to purchase 138,000 acres of land and colonize 250 families within two years.[24]

The Mexican government never endorsed Lundy's efforts. Nonetheless liberal politicians, such as Vice-President Valentín Gómez Farías, did support the relocation of former slaves in Mexico. Responding to Philadelphia abolitionist Samuel Webb's 1833 inquiry about black colonization, Gómez Farías wrote: "[I]f they [black slaves] would like to come, we will offer them land for cultivation, plots for houses where they can establish towns, and tools for work, under the obligation [that they will] obey the laws of the country and the authorities already established by the Supreme Government of the Federation."[25]

Euro-American immigrants, however, hoped to transform Texas into an empire for slavery. In 1821 Mexican Texas had only thirty-two hundred non-Indian inhabitants. Concerned that Texas might be seized by the United States, France, or Great Britain, the Spanish government in 1821 granted Moses Austin permission to settle a colony of American-born immigrants loyal to Spain along the Brazos and Colorado rivers. When Austin died later that year, Stephen F. Austin, his son, inherited his colonizing enterprise. By the time Austin reached San Antonio, Mexico had become independent but nonetheless encouraged American settlement. The prospect of free land lured thousands of Euro-Americans across the Sabine and Red rivers. By 1823 three thousand U.S. citizens had entered Texas illegally, joining approximately seven hundred legitimate settlers. Seven years later the seven thousand Euro-American settlers had surpassed the three thousand Mexican residents, and by 1835 the American population stood at thirty-five thousand, including three thousand black slaves.[26]

The Texas revolution of 1835–36 is often presented as a contest between liberty-loving Anglos and Tejanos confronting a despotic Mexican government. That image belies a central motive in the campaign for independence: an Anglo desire to preserve slavery. That motive was to have a profound impact on Texas's free blacks. Although slavery had been introduced into Texas by the Spaniards, it was insignificant before the *norteamericanos* came. Nacogdoches, the largest settlement in east Texas, had thirty-three black slaves in 1809 while San Antoino de Bexar and La Bahía (Goliad) combined had a mere nine slaves in 1819.[27]

All this changed in the early 1820s. Jared E. Groce, who reached central Texas in January 1822 from Georgia, brought with him ninety bondsmen and established the Bernardo cotton plantation on the Brazos River. Groce, like many subsequent arrivals, insisted that the cash crop, the labor system, and the social relations of the U.S. South, all resting on black slavery, could be replicated with ease along the Colorado and Brazos rivers.

Through the 1820s both Texas settlers and Mexican political and military leaders warily skirted the slavery issue. The Mexican government, committed constitutionally to black freedom, nonetheless desired economic development on its northern frontier. It vacillated, compromised, and occasionally defied slaveholder wishes. For their part Anglo settlers never confronted Mexican political sensibilities on black bondage. But they did exploit local and national political rivalries and official indecision to increase the number of slaves and the security of slaveowning in the region.

The contract labor system, introduced in 1828, proved an insidious subterfuge for slavery by redefining bondspeople as "indentured servants for life." United States immigrants took their slaves before a Mexican public official and drew up a contract with each bond servant. Theoretically freed by the contract, the laborer nonetheless owed his value and the expenses of moving to the new country to his "former" slaveowner, who recovered those costs by appropriating his labor. The contract between Marmaduke D. Sandifer and Clarissa, "a girl of color," before the alcalde at San Felipe de Austin on Christmas Day 1833 was typical. Clarissa agreed to "conduct & demean herself as an honest & faithful servant, renouncing and disclaiming all her right and claim to personal liberty for & during the term of ninety-nine years." In return Sandifer promised to furnish her "food, lodging, and medical care and, should she be disabled, to support her in a decent and comfortable manner." Such arrangements kept blacks in slavery by another name.[28]

As the American population rapidly outgrew its Spanish-speaking counterpart, some Tejanos openly supported the growth of slavery. Emboldened, many Anglo settlers sought to remove the subterfuge of the contract labor system and establish slavery outright. Indeed Texans such as James W. Fannin, Jr., Monroe Edwards, and Major Benjamin Fort Smith, impatient for additional bond servants, began to import slaves from Africa through Cuba. One historian of the trade suggests that by 1836 one in five Texas slaves came directly from Africa or the Caribbean.[29]

Most southern-born white settlers, who could not imagine Texas being developed without slave labor, would have agreed with S. Rhoads Fisher of Pennsylvania. Writing in response to Stephen Austin's short-lived proposal to encourage free white northern labor to emigrate to Texas, Fisher asked, "Do you believe that cane and cotton can be grown to advantage by a sparse white population? We must either abandon the finest portion of Texas to its original uselessness or submit to the acknowledged, but lesser evil of slavery." Three years later Austin was persuaded: "I have been adverse to the principle of slavery in Texas. I have now . . . changed my views of the matter; though my ideas are the same as to the abstract principle.

Texas *must* be a slave country. Circumstances and unavoidable necessity compels it. It is the wish of the people there, and it is my duty to do all I can, prudently, in favor of it."[30]

By 1835 Texas slaveholders had duplicated the U.S. slave system. Fully 10 percent of English-speaking Texans were slaves. Slaveholders now demanded protection of their property and open commerce in human beings. Texas and Mexico were on a collision course. African Americans, free and slave, would soon be caught in the middle of these contesting sides. For many Texas slaves Mexico's flag represented liberty. As early as 1833 Juan N. Almonte, a Mexican government representative, arrived in Texas to inform the slaves of their liberty under Mexican law and to promise them land as freedmen. Three years later, and one month before his siege of the Alamo, General Antonio López de Santa Anna, president of Mexico and commander of the Mexican Army, queried government officials in Mexico City about freeing the slaves. "Shall we permit those wretches to moan in chains any longer in a country whose kind laws protect the liberty of man without distinction of cast or color?" Santa Anna received a response that placed the Mexican government unequivocally on the side of black freedom. Minister of War José María Tornel wrote Santa Anna on March 18 to reaffirm that "the philanthropy of the Mexican nation" had already freed the slaves. Santa Anna was simply to grant their "natural rights," including "the liberty to go to any point on the globe that appeals to them," to remain in Texas or another part of Mexico.[31]

The Mexican Army, which included some black infantrymen and servants, was poised to become a legion of liberation. As the army crossed the Colorado and Brazos rivers and moved into the region heavily populated by slaves, the boldest of the bondspeople fled to their lines. Soon after the Alamo fell, Brazoria's slaveholders were quoted as saying that "their negroes . . . were on the tip-toe of expectation, and rejoicing that the Mexicans were coming to make them free."[32] Fourteen slave families fled to the command of General José de Urrea near Victoria on April 3. In May thirteen blacks left Matagorda to join the Mexican troops. Countless others took flight toward Santa Anna's forces both when they marched into Texas and when they retreated. In return for Mexican protection, these fugitives served as spies, messengers, or provocateurs for their liberators. Even after Santa Anna had been captured and signed his battlefield surrender on April 22, Texas found Mexican commanders loath to return fugitive slaves. Lieutenant Colonel José Enrique de la Peña, for example, personally intervened in one case when he disguised a soon-to-be reenslaved black as a Mexican soldier and sent him to safety in Matamoros.[33]

For most white Texans the prospect of a servile insurrection instigated by the Mexican Army proved far more frightening than black flight to Santa Anna's lines. In October 1835 the Matagorda Committee of Safety and Correspondence, acknowledging Santa Anna's preparations for suppressing rebellious Texans, declared that a "merciless soldiery" was advancing on Texas, "to give liberty to our slaves, and to make slaves of ourselves." Residents of the Colorado River region were alarmed by the false rumor of an amphibious assault force of two thousand troops under the command of General Martín Perfecto de Cos poised to ascend the river and incite a servile insurrection. Later that month nearly one hundred black slaves on the Brazos did attempt a revolt although it is unclear whether they received any direct assistance from Mexican forces. Anglo troops from Goliad suppressed the revolt and hanged or whipped to death its leaders. Uprising fears intensified days after the fall of the Alamo. A Safety and Correspondence Committee at Brazoria announced that the advancing Mexican Army sought "a general extermination" of the people regardless of age or sex and claimed that the "treacherous and bloody enemy" intended to recruit black slaves "as instruments of his unholy and savage work . . . thus lighting the torch of war in the bosoms of our domestic circles."[34]

While the Texas War of Independence cannot be called a "race war," racial and ethnic tensions that lurked beneath the surface before 1835 became distressingly evident once the fighting began. The mostly southern-born Anglo Texans of the 1820s and 1830s, who applied white supremacy arguments to justify black slavery and Native American removal, easily projected their racialist views onto the Spanish-speaking population they encountered. In an appeal for U.S. support William H. Wharton, one of the more radical agitators for independence, declared: "The Justice and benevolence of God, will forbid that . . . Texas should . . . be permanently benighted by the ignorance and superstition . . . of Mexican rule. The Anglo-American race are destined to be forever the proprietors of this land . . . Their laws will govern it, their learning will enlighten it, their enterprise will improve it."[35]

Racial differences made the break with Mexico easier than the U.S. struggle to free itself from Great Britain sixty years earlier. Whereas Americans had broken their political allegiance with the

British, a people of "kindred blood, language, and institutions," wrote one Texan to the *Telegraph and Texas Register* in December 1835, "we separate from a people one half of whom are . . . different in color, pursuits and character."[36] Stephen Austin spoke for many Anglos when he declared the revolution a contest between the barbarism of a "mongrel Spanish-Indian and negro race, against civilization and the Anglo-American race," while James W. Fannin demanded that Texans take up arms to prevent the violation of "the Fair daughters of chaste white women" by the oncoming Mexican Army. Such sentiments became a fountainhead of racist imagery that extended well beyond the end of the fighting and constituted a profound "reversal of fortune," according to historian Paul Lack, for Tejanos and black Texans who were ostracized and segregated after the Texas revolution. A delegate to the Texas Constitutional Convention of 1845 justified this nexus between black and brown Texans when he declared, "In their taste and social instincts, they [the Mexicans] approximated the African. The difference between them and the Negro is smaller, and is less felt, I believe, than that between the Northern and Southern European races. . . . Notice how [the peons] meet [the slave] on an equality. They do not intermarry with the white population; they form their connections among the slaves."[37]

For every slave that fled to the Mexican lines, far more took advantage of the confusion and turmoil of the fighting to make good their escape. Recently arrived Africans seemed particularly adept at flight, often persuading American-born bondsmen to flee with them. The Africans developed such a reputation for fierce resistance that they moved at will in the interior Colorado River region. Other slaves fled to the sparsely populated region south of the Nueces River or toward an already well-established colony of fugitive slaves at Matamoros. Planters who sent or traveled with their slaves into east Texas or Louisiana during the "Runaway Scrape," the mass flight of Texas settlers before the march of Santa Anna's army, frequently told of black fugitives who fled north toward the Red River or west into Comanche country. Such slaves were willing to risk the possibility of acceptance and freedom with Native Americans or the advancing Mexican Army rather than face the prospect of continued bondage in Texas.[38]

Only a handful of the 150 free black Texans voluntarily supported the revolutionary cause. Most realized that their status, and possibly their collective fate, would change dramatically with a victory by Anglo Texans. Some, however, chose the independence campaign because of personal friendships, vague promises of land, or because they were persuaded that some grievances against Mexico were justified. Samuel McCullough, Jr., was influenced by all of these ideas when he volunteered to fight at Goliad on October 9, 1835. He became "the first whose blood was shed in the War of Independence" when a wound in the shoulder cost him the use of his arm. During the assault on Mexican forces at San Antonio, Greenbury Logan was wounded and disabled for life. Pennsylvania native Peter Allen, one of the few black volunteers from the United States who served in the independence campaign, joined the ill-fated command of James W. Fannin, which was captured and executed by Mexican forces in the Goliad Massacre. William Goyens served as an interpreter between Sam Houston and various Indian nations in the successful effort to prevent an alliance between Mexico and Native Americans.[29]

The Texas revolution set in motion political forces that in the next decade added all of Mexico's northern frontier to the United States. But it also initiated the decline in status of the indigenous Afro-Mexican population of Texas and the free blacks who sought refuge there. The new constitution graphically spelled out their status in independent Texas, giving citizenship rights to all persons except Africans, the descendants of Africans, and Indians, and declared that "no free persons of African descent . . . shall be permitted to reside permanently in the republic without the consent of the Texas Congress." The constitution announced that "All persons of color who were slaves for life previous to their emigration to Texas, and who are now in bondage, shall remain in the like state of servitude." Furthermore, it denied future Texas Congresses the power to prevent U.S. emigrants from bringing their slaves into the republic or emancipating slaves. Newly independent Texas had fixed African slavery as its predominant economic and social system and simultaneously stripped citizenship from its free black inhabitants.[40]

Disabled by his war wounds and fearing the loss of his property to back taxes, Texas revolutionary war veteran Greenbury Logan petitioned the Texas Congress in 1841 for assistance. Reacting to the sweeping changes ushered in by the War of Independence, Logan said, "I love the country and did stay because I felt myself mower [sic] a freeman then in the states . . . but now look at my situation. Every privilege dear to a freeman is taken away."[41] The future of slaves, however, was certain. With the guarantee of state protection to the "peculiar institution" impossible under Mexican hegemony, the three thousand African American "servants" held in bondage

in 1835 rapidly grew to a quarter of a million slaves three decades
later.

Far fewer blacks entered California between 1821 and 1848, and
none are known to have arrived in New Mexico during the period.
As with African Americans in Texas, black emigrants to California
correctly concluded that both Spanish and Mexican rule offered
fewer racial restrictions than in the United States. Yet California's
vast distance from concentrated black settlement in the American
South precluded it from becoming a major destination of English-
speaking African Americans.

Unlike Texas or New Mexico, however, California's political
leadership included some individuals of African ancestry such as
Andrés and Pío Pico, descendants of one of the most successful
Californio families. The two grandsons of Santiago and Jacinta de la
Cruz Pico became influential in Mexican-era California politics. Pío
Pico, consummate politician and "revolutionist," challenged three
California governors and subsequently became governor twice during the twenty-five years of Mexican rule in California, first in 1831
and again in 1845–46, when he served as the last governor of Mexican California. Pío Pico, who eventually became part of the political
elite in Anglo-dominated post-1848 California, could not rally Mexican support for California resistance to the American occupation
forces. Andrés Pico, a wealthy landowner, served as a military commander in the Mexican California militia, and in 1846 he defeated
American General Stephen Watts Kearny at the Battle of San Pas-
cual. In January 1847 he represented California at the signing of the
Treaty of Cahuenga (with U.S. Commander John C. Frémont), which
ended the Mexican War in California. After the American occupation Pico mined gold at Mokelumne and served in the California
legislature in 1851 and again in 1860–61.[42]

California's other prominent official of African ancestry, Lieutenant Colonel Manuel Victoria, served briefly as governor in 1831.
Before his arrival in Alta California, Victoria had earned a reputation
for honesty and efficiency while *commandante* of Baja California. But
he soon ran afoul of the local political elite, including Pío Pico, who
unflatteringly described Victoria as "very dark, thin, beardless . . .
gruff and despotic." In November 1831 a group of influential
Californios, including Pico, issued a pronunciamento, a declaration
of insurrection against Victoria. Rebel leaders confronted Victoria's

forces at Cahuenga Pass near Los Angeles. Governor Victoria was seriously wounded in the ensuing confrontation, forcing his surrender. The rebels declared their victory and placed Victoria on a ship bound for Mexico.[43]

The ambiguity of California's fluid racial order confused and irritated English-speaking visitors, such as Richard Henry Dana, who condemned the society as far too free of racial distinctions for his tastes. Shortly after his arrival in California in 1835, he wrote: "Generally speaking, each person's caste is decided by the quality of the blood, which shows itself, too plainly to be concealed, at first sight. Yet the least drop of Spanish blood, if it be only of quadroon or octoroon, is sufficient to raise them from the rank of slaves and entitles them . . . to call themselves Espanolos. . . ."[44]

The ambiguity that distressed Dana proved naturally attractive to some English-speaking African Americans who began arriving after 1810. The first English-speaking African Americans to enter California were seafarers who jumped ship while in the province's various ports. A seventeen-year-old African American known only as Bob was one of the first when he deserted a New England vessel, *Albatross,* in 1816 and three years later was baptized in Santa Barbara as Juan Crístobal. William Warren left his ship when it landed in the San Francisco Bay in 1828 and settled near San Jóse. John Caldwell, a cook on the frigate *California,* deserted in Monterrey in 1832 and took refuge in the San Jóse home of John Burton, a former Massachusetts ship captain.[45]

Of the black sailors who settled in California before 1848, Allen Light became the most prominent. Light was a crew member of the *Pilgrim* along with Richard Henry Dana, whose *Two Years before the Mast* chronicled the ship's voyage to California. Light deserted the ship at Santa Barbara in 1835, acquired Mexican citizenship, and became a leading otter hunter along the southern California coast. In 1839 Governor Juan Bautista Alvarado appointed Light *comisario general* to serve as "principal representative of that national armada" assigned to halt illegal otter hunting of California's coastal waters. Light thus became the first U.S.-born black to serve as a Mexican official.[46]

West Indian–born William A. Leidesdorff was Mexican California's most prominent African American. Leidesdorff, of Danish-African ancestry, left the West Indies as a young man and became a successful merchant captain in New York and then New Orleans before arriving in Yerba Buena (San Francisco) in 1841. Soon after his arrival he sailed his commercial schooner *Julia Ann* on regular voyages between Honolulu and California. He also operated the *Sitka*, the first steam-powered vessel on San Francisco Bay. By 1844 Leidesdorff had become a Mexican citizen and received a thirty-five-thousand-acre land grant along the American River. Despite his adopted nationality, Leidesdorff's commercial ties with the United States led to his appointment as American vice-consul in 1845 by President James K. Polk, who was unaware of the California's African ancestry. Leidesdorff was thus involved in the diplomatic maneuverings of the American explorer John C. Frémont, whom he entertained in his Yerba Buena home in 1846 and escorted to Monterey to meet American Consul Thomas Oliver Larkin. As one of the most prominent businessmen in the city Leidesdorff was elected to the town council in 1847 and helped establish its school system. The following year he became city treasurer.[47]

Leidesdorff's business transactions with another prominent pre–gold rush Californian, Captain John A. Sutter, reveal his incorporation into the local elite and his acceptance of the Spanish and Mexican enslavement of Native Americans. Between 1844 and 1846 Sutter had run up a debt to Leidesdorff of $2,198, a third of which he liquidated by supplying Leidesdorff with Indian slaves. In the spring of 1846 Sutter promised ten or twelve "selected Indians . . . which will be of some service to you" along with "two Indian Girls, of which you will take which you like the best. . . ." Sutter then added, "As this shall never be considered an article of trade [I] make you a present with the girl."[48]

Leidesdorff's death in April 1848, coming just months after the two cataclysmic events that changed western history, symbolized the end of an era for African Americans who searched for freedom and security in northern Mexico. The Treaty of Guadalupe Hidalgo, signed on February 2, 1848, at the conclusion of the Mexican War, officially reduced Mexico by half when it transferred California, Nevada, Utah, New Mexico, Arizona, and parts of Colorado, Kansas, and Oklahoma to the jurisdiction of the United States.

The gold rush initiated by the discovery of the precious metal near Sutter's Fort in January 1848, was to have an equally profound influence. The gold rush rapidly "Americanized" the population of California and encouraged settlement of the vast region between Missouri's western border and the Pacific Ocean. African Americans would now settle in a West completely under the jurisdiction of the United States and be susceptible to racially restrictive legislation already well entrenched east of the Mississippi River.

Much of the pre-1846 exploration and early settlement in western North America took place on Mexico's northern frontier. However, after 1788 smaller numbers of English-speaking blacks entered the region claimed by Great Britain and the United States, first by sea and after 1806 overland. They preceded hundreds of other men of various races and nationalities who came to the Louisiana Territory and the Oregon country to trap and trade for "a wealth of furs not surpassed by the mines of Peru."[49] Some arrived by ship and entered the Pacific Northwest through the Columbia River valley corridor into the interior. Their overland counterparts followed the Missouri or Arkansas rivers west toward the Rocky Mountains.

Like their more numerous white counterparts, African American traders and trappers chose this solitary life in the western mountains primarily for the profits derived from trading or trapping. But the frontier afforded freedom from racial restrictions typically imposed by "settled" communities. Moreover, unlike the sailors who jumped ship or members of earlier overland exploring parties, the fur trappers embraced the region by choice rather than circumstance, and they reinforced that decision by forging ties with the Native Americans among whom they traded. They often adopted native dress and customs and usually took Indian wives, although the motives for such marriages were political and economic as well as personal since marriage into Indian communities assured military allies and a steady supply of furs. At least one African American trapper, Edward Rose, actually crossed the cultural frontier and was permanently accepted into Native American society.[50]

Two English-speaking African American men, Jacob Dodson and York joined major overland expeditions that traversed the West and helped open the region to settlement much as Esteban had three centuries earlier. York, the personal servant—and slave—of Captain William Clark, accompanied Lewis and Clark in 1804–06 as they became the first Americans to journey overland from St. Louis to the Pacific coast. York proved essential, serving as a hunter, an explorer, a trader, and a scout. He frequently bartered with Native Americans for the expedition's food and supplies and voted on crucial decisions, such as the site of the winter camp when the party reached the Pacific Ocean. Clark freed York when the expedition returned to St. Louis, and the former slave married and settled into a comfortable life operating a dray service between Louisville, his home, and Nashville, Tennessee.[51]

Thirty-seven years later in 1843, Jacob Dodson, an eighteen-year-old freeborn resident of Washington, D.C., volunteered to accompany John C. Frémont on his second western expedition. The seventeen-person party, which included Kit Carson, traveled from Westport, Missouri, to Fort Vancouver in the Oregon country on the route that became the Oregon Trail. The party moved south into western Nevada and California's Central Valley on a return route that took them through Utah, Colorado, and Kansas. Dodson was also on the third expedition (1845–46), when the explorers participated in the American occupation of California. He returned to Washington, D.C., in 1848 and worked for the remainder of his life as a messenger for the U.S. Senate.[52]

York and Dodson were brief visitors in the West. Two other African Americans, Edward Rose and James Beckwourth, committed their lives to the region. Rose, the son of a white trader and a black-Cherokee woman, grew up near Louisville, Kentucky. He traveled to New Orleans as a keelboat deckhand, then moved north to St. Louis in 1805. In the following year he joined the Manuel Lisa fur trading expedition to the Bighorn River in present-day Wyoming. During his first winter in the West Rose lived and traded with the Absaroka (Crow) Indians, eventually becoming a trusted leader, proving himself in battle against rival Indian nations. Although Rose periodically left the Absaroka to work as a guide, hunter, and trapper for various fur-trading companies, he inevitably returned to Indian society.[53]

Unlike other "mountain men" who married Native American women but remained white, Rose joined two aboriginal societies. The Absaroka nation along the Wyoming-Montana border accepted him as a tribal member around 1807, and the Arikara, in what is now South Dakota, adopted him in 1820. Rose learned the languages and customs of these two native peoples and used his association with the trading companies to secure goods for the tribes. Viewing the Upper Missouri region as a political and social sanctuary, Rose allied himself with the Native Americans against potential enemies. The Absaroka and Arikara in turn deemed Rose a crucial link with the trader's world and a skilled fighter.

Rose's encounter with the overland Astorian Expedition in 1811 illustrated his loyalties. When the Absaroka entered the Astorians' camp near Powder River (in present-day northeastern Wyoming) on August 31, Rose was an interpreter between their chiefs and the expedition leader, Wilson Price Hunt, as they exchanged goods and information. Hunt, however, soon grew suspicious of Rose, whom he described as "a very bad fellow full of daring," who "planned to desert us . . . taking with him as many of our men as he could seduce, and steal our horses." Facing what he considered a major threat to the success of the expedition, Hunt watched Rose carefully and chose to bribe him into leaving the Astorians. Whether Rose actually planned any of the actions Hunt feared is unclear. Rose in any case took the offer of a half year's wages, a horse, beaver traps, and trade goods and left with the Absaroka. Two days later Rose and the Absaroka returned, this time to direct the Astorians safely across the Bighorn Mountains after the expedition had become stranded on a treacherous mountain passage.[54]

Edward Rose spent the remainder of his life with the Absaroka. In 1832, twenty-five years after his introduction to Indian life, he was seen at one of their villages by another trapper, Zenas Leonard, who offered this description: "He has acquired a correct knowledge of their manner of living and speaks the language fluently. He has rose to be quite a considerable character, or chief in their village; at least he assumes all the dignities of a chief, for he has four wives with whom he lives alternately. This is the custom of many of the chiefs."[55]

Edward Rose was the only black trapper known to have crossed the cultural frontier. Other African Americans, however, figured prominently in the fur trade era, the most famous and controversial being James Beckwourth, who lived and worked in the West for nearly sixty years. Born in Virginia in 1798 of a slave mother and white father who brought his "family" to St. Charles, Missouri, in 1810, Beckwourth worked as a hunter and lead miner until he joined the Ashley fur-trapping expedition in 1824. With one brief interlude to fight in the Seminole Indian War in Florida in 1836–37, he spent the rest of his life in the West. Beckwourth lived twice with the Absaroka Indians in Montana and during that time took two Native American wives. He later also married Luisa Sandoval, a "young Spanish girl," in Santa Fe in 1840 and Elizabeth Lettbetter, an African American woman, in Denver in 1860.[56]

Discounting the exaggerations that pepper his 1856 autobiography, Beckwourth lived a remarkable life. He trapped at the foot of the Rocky Mountains in 1826 and two years later along the Snake River in Idaho and Wyoming. In 1835 he joined the Thomas Smith expedition, following the Old Spanish Trail from Utah to southern California. Shortly after Beckwourth obtained the only position of responsibility in his peripatetic career. He supervised trading operations at Fort Vázquez, New Mexico, for Luis Vázquez. In 1839 he returned to California with Smith, as part of a gang of horse thieves who plundered ranches between Santa Barbara and San Luis Obispo. Despite his reputation in California, Beckwourth joined the rebel forces of Juan Bautista Alvarado and fought in the Battle of Cahuenga Pass in 1845 against Governor Manuel Micheltorena in an abortive attempt by Californiòs to gain independence from Mexico. In 1847 he returned to New Mexico in time to help the Americans defeat Mexican forces in the region.[57]

Ever on the move, Beckwourth entered California as a gold-seeking forty-niner and discovered the wagon train trail through the Sierra Nevada Mountains that now carries his name. He took a land claim on the California side of Beckwourth Pass and built a combined hotel and store that supplied California-bound emigrants. This business anchored the town eventually named after him. Sixty-one years old in 1859, Beckwourth moved to Denver, where he managed a store for his New Mexico fur-trapping employer Luis Vázquez. In November 1864 Beckwourth was hired as a guide for the Third Regiment of Colorado Volunteer Cavalry under Colonel J. M. Chivington, which carried out the notorious Sand Creek Massacre, during which more than five hundred Cheyenne men, women, and children were slaughtered. In testimony before a military commission established to investigate Sand Creek, Beckwourth claimed that the massacre was unnecessary and it "revolted him." He subsequently abandoned his property and job in Denver and returned to Montana as a trapper. Though he lived a dangerous life, James Beckwourth died quietly of natural causes a month after returning to the Crow Indian country in 1866.[58]

As these two lives attest, African American mountain men had little in common beyond race and a desire to trap or trade for furs. Edward Rose felt so comfortable with native people that he embraced their societies, while maintaining some participation in the Euro-American commercial world that drove the fur trade. James Beckwourth, however, moved freely among Indian, Anglo, and Hispanic communities, as evidenced by the varied choices of his business partners, military allies, and wives. If Rose lamented the decline of the trade and the Indian societies that constituted a crucial component of that western economy, Beckwourth eagerly exploited the opportunity presented by the rapidly expanding settlement in the far West. Yet Rose, Beckwourth, and other traders and trappers achieved, through their varied roles in the West, a degree of liberty seldom accorded free blacks during that era and certainly more than the thousands of African Americans who were to follow them to the region after the demise of the fur trade.

2

◇ ❖ ◇ ❖ ◇

Slavery in
the Antebellum West,
1835–65

Few western historians link slavery with the youngest of the nation's regions. When the Civil War began in 1861, only four western states—Texas, Kansas, California, and Oregon—had been admitted to the Union, and the Euro-American inhabitants of the vast territories considered themselves physically and psychologically removed from slavery's debate. The West's claims of innocence on slavery, however, are muted by the presence of black bond servants in virtually every state and territory prior to the Civil War and by the intense local debates about its suitability in Oregon, California, Utah, and "bleeding" Kansas, where political discourse gave way to armed conflict in the 1850s. The ninety-eight meridian, which stretched across the plains from Dakota Territory to central Texas, represented the farthest advance of plantation agriculture. It did not, however, bar some mutation of the servile institution in the West. The region was saved from slavery by the demands of white free-soil farmers, who were always more numerous than proslavery advocates and slaveholders, rather than by geography or westerners' commitment to universal liberty.[1]

Before 1861 most African Americans came West as slaves. Yet in such a large, diverse region the importance of slavery in the states and territories differed markedly. Texas, where the Old South met the western frontier, had by far the largest slave population. The

1860 U.S. census reported 182,556 bondspeople, 30 percent of the state's total population. With the influx of "refugeed" slaves from neighboring states during the Civil War, Texas's total servile population surpassed 250,000 by April 1865.[2]

Texas was the exception in the West because its economic and political elite embraced a slave-based economy and society before 1836. But slavery emerged in other western areas. The Five Nations like Texas, had an economy that rested largely on slave labor. Indian Territory in 1860 had seven thousand slaves, who constituted 14 percent of the total population. Slavery was legal in one other territory, Utah, although only twenty-nine of its fifty-nine black inhabitants were slaves in 1860. Slavery was outlawed in the remainder of the states and territories. Yet the historical record is replete with accounts of bond servants held from Washington Territory to New Mexico.[3]

The discussion of slavery in the West begins in Texas, the heart of the region's slave regime. After the Texas war of independence slave-holding Anglo-Americans poured into the republic. Slaveholders unapologetically proclaimed both the agricultural need for black labor and their right to own their fellow human beings. "I have no doubt," District Court Judge C. A. Frazier told an Upshur County grand jury in 1860, "of the right of a civilized and Christian nation to capture the African wherever he may be found and subject him to labor, enlightenment and religion, than I have of one of our people to capture a wild horse on the prairies of the West, and domesticate and reduce him to labor." Austin's *Texas State Gazette* editor, John Marshall, was more direct. Arguing that slavery was growing too slowly in Texas, Marshall in 1858 called for the reopening of the African slave trade. "Until we reach somewhere in the vicinity of two million slaves," declared Marshall, "such a thing as too many slaves in Texas is an absurdity."[4]

Slaves resided in virtually all of Texas's 105 counties in 1860, but they were concentrated in three regions of the state. The oldest slaveholding area, the Austin colony, extended inland from the Gulf Coast along the cotton-, rice-, sugarcane-producing lowlands of the Brazos and Colorado rivers. Slaveholders also favored southeast Texas, around San Augustine County, and the northeastern corner of the state near the Arkansas and Louisiana borders. Some of these counties quickly obtained black majorities. In 1850 six predomi-

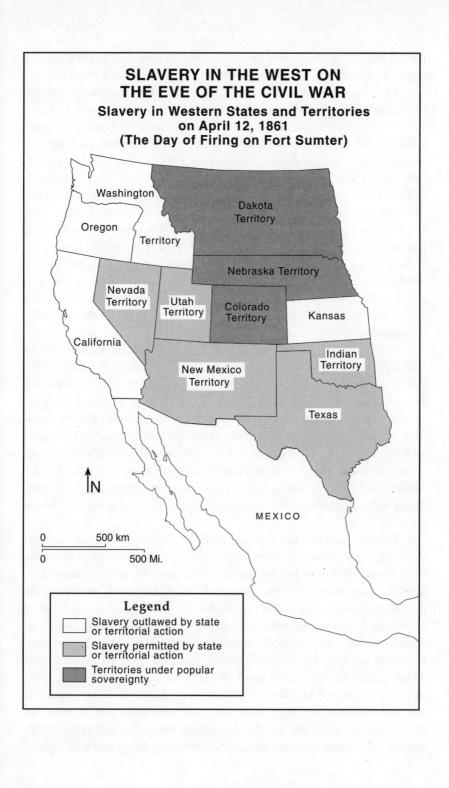

SLAVERY IN THE WEST ON THE EVE OF THE CIVIL WAR

Slavery in Western States and Territories
on April 12, 1861
(The Day of Firing on Fort Sumter)

Washington

Oregon

Territory

Dakota
Territory

Nebraska Territory

Nevada
Territory

Utah
Territory

Colorado
Territory

Kansas

California

New Mexico
Territory

Indian
Territory

Texas

MEXICO

N

| 0 | 500 km |
| 0 | 500 Mi. |

Legend

Slavery outlawed by state
or territorial action

Slavery permitted by state
or territorial action

Territories under popular
sovereignty

nantly black counties stretched along the Brazos and Colorado. Ten years later thirteen Texas counties were predominantly black.[5]

This labor system produced a harsh daily physical routine described by one former Texas slave as work from "can see to can't see." There was little division of labor based on gender or age. Women, men, and children alike harvested the crops, picking cotton, pulling corn, or cutting sugarcane, and performed the numerous chores associated with nineteenth-century farming. Slave men handled the heaviest work of plowing, felling trees, and digging ditches; female slaves planted corn and cotton, drove horses, and hoed cotton, corn, and vegetable gardens. Children began with such jobs as gathering firewood, hauling water, and knocking down old cotton stalks and, as they grew older, assumed responsibilities for tending livestock. Just as some male slaves were allowed to develop special skills, such as blacksmithing and carpentry, or became carriage drivers and butlers, some slave women specialized as cooks, laundresses, maids, seamstresses, and spinners.[6]

Much of the work routine of Texas slaves paralleled that of bondspeople east of the Sabine River, but some slaves worked in the state's emerging cattle industry. African slave stock grazers from the cattle-raising region of the Gambia River in West Africa were part of the expansion of the livestock industry in colonial South Carolina, passing their herding skills down through generations and steadily across the Gulf Coast states to Texas. These skills and those acquired from Mexican vaqueros themselves descendants of colonial-era mestizo, mulatto, black, and Indian cattle herders, gave Texas slaves considerable cattle-growing experience on the southwest frontier.[7]

Usually assigned the task of catching and tending wild cattle in the Gulf Coast brush country, slave cowboys used lariats to produce long trains of steers led by oxen and trailed by baying dogs. The Civil War governor of Texas, Francis Richard Lubbock, relied on his five bondsmen to tend the two thousand cattle on his ranch near Houston. Lubbock allowed one of them, a man named Willis, to acquire cattle and horses while still a slave so that he could purchase freedom for himself and his family. James Taylor White, the first Texas "cattle baron," used black drovers for the thousands of head of cattle he owned in Liberty County, while Amanda Wildy reported her dependence on black slave cowboys when she told a court in 1854, that "it will require the service of the principal part of the horses and negroes to take care of and manage [her] stock of cattle."

African Americans constituted the majority of cowboys in Texas by the early 1850s, according to one historian, and in an activity that foreshadowed the famous post–Civil War cattle drives to Kansas, they trailed herds of cattle to Mexico and New Orleans.[8]

Plantation life for Texas slaves demanded the harshest, least remitting toil under the most oppressive social pressures, but it also afforded the greatest opportunity for the development of family life. Familial ties provided love, individual identity, and a sense of personal worth from people like themselves rather than from anglo Texans. In 1839 Albert, one of Ashbel Smith's slaves, strenuosly objected to even briefly leaving his family. Smith's plantation overseer, M. S. Tunnel, reported to his employer: "Albert got home, safely, on Monday night. He takes the separation from his family to heart considerably." "I haven't forgot you nor I never will forget you as long as the world stands, even if you forget me," wrote Fannie, a Harrison county slave woman, in 1862 to her husband, Norfleet, who was away with his owner, a Confederate officer. "If I never see you again, I hope to meet you in Heaven."[9]

Plantations set the norm for much of antebellum Texas society, but 54 percent of the state's slaves lived on farms with fewer than twenty bondspeople, and one-fourth of the slaveholders owned only one slave. Significant sections of east and central Texas considered unsuitable for cotton cultivation developed an agricultural economy centered on small-scale wheat and corn production. Slaves on these farms fared no better. Their material condition depended upon the affluence of their owners. Slaves of impoverished farmers shared the poverty of their masters. Although masters and slaves often worked side by side, such slaveowners were no more and no less considerate of the welfare of their slaves than the planters.[10]

Unless they lived in plantation country, small farm slaves had few opportunities to mingle with other African Americans. Those on the frontier saw few other people, black or white. In such settings black slaves and their white owners developed a mutual dependence born of necessity. The much-feared Comanche made no distinction between black and white frontier settlers. As Kenneth W. Porter remarked, the Comanche saw people dressed similarly, using identical tools and weapons, living in comparable houses and often in the same house. Because of their basic lifestyle and cultural similarity, the Comanche regarded whites and blacks with antipathy and contempt and killed men and captured women and children with scant regard to color. Conversely, many black slaves (and free blacks),

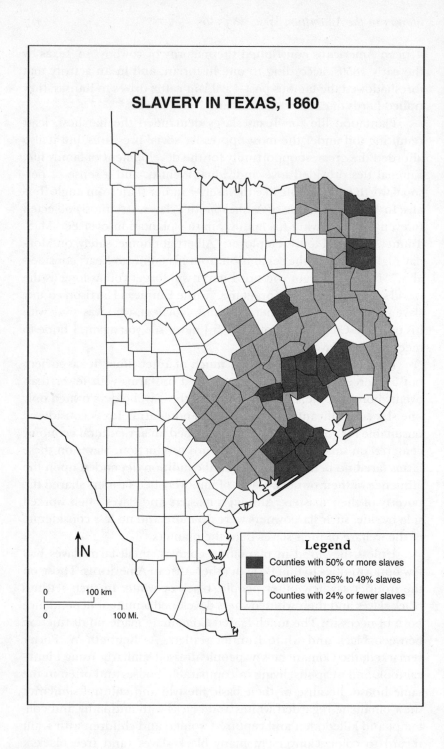

SLAVERY IN TEXAS, 1860

N

0   100 km

0   100 Mi.

Legend

Counties with 50% or more slaves

Counties with 25% to 49% slaves

Counties with 24% or fewer slaves

embraced a hatred and fear of the plains raiders with as much fervor as white frontier settlers.[11]

Urban slaves, although only 6 percent of Texas bondspeople, nonetheless formed a distinct population. Galveston and Houston, the largest cities in antebellum Texas, each had more than 1,000 black slaves while several hundred lived in Austin and San Antonio. The urban black slave population grew proportionately with the cities. Occasionally these urban populations established churches and other community institutions. Galveston slaves, for example, founded Baptist and Methodist churches housed in substantial buildings seating 350 worshipers. The majority of these slaves were house servants, but others worked on farms outside the cities or as cooks, teamsters, hotel waiters, carpenters, bricklayers, and boatmen. A small number of skilled slaves worked in flour mills, sawmills, and brickyards. The growth of the skilled slave artisan class prompted white groups, such as the Houston Mechanics Association, to adopt a resolution in 1858 declaring their opposition to "the practice adhered to by some, of making contracts with the negro mechanics to carry on work, as a contractor."[12]

Most white urban Texans worried more about the social latitude black people assumed in the cities than their occupations. One Austin ordinance enacted in 1855 granted the "city marshal and his assistants . . . control and supervision of the conduct, carraige [*sic*], demeanor and deportment of any and all slaves living, being, or found within the city limits," and another forbade "any white man or Mexican" from "making associates" of black slaves. City laws called for slave patrols, the regulation of assemblies, and the prohibition of gambling or the possession of liquor and weapons. Yet some urban slaves openly flouted these bans, prompting one Austin newspaper editor in 1854 to declare in disgust that he "almost imagines himself in the land of amalgamation, abolition meetings, and woman's rights conventions." Other slaves challenged the limits of their servile status by openly defying whites. Urban slaves, according to historian Paul Lack, commonly disregarded the groveling courtesies demanded by "polite" racial etiquette and instead used loud and profane language and engaged in insubordination and disorderly conduct. One bondsman was quoted in an Austin paper: "[L]et any white man tell him to stop his mouth, and see if he would not give him hell." Describing his visit to Houston in 1863, a British observer was surprised to see "innumerable Negros and Negresses parading about the streets in the most outrageously grand costumes." Galveston's slaves celebrated the city's May Day parade by driving their owners' carriages and riding their horses.[13]

Most Texas slaves were not openly defiant, but many sought every opportunity to escape. The problem was far more acute than in the Old South. Texas was bordered on three sides by sparsely populated regions that offered the possibility of escape: Indian Territory to the north, the western frontier, and Mexico. Of the three border regions Mexico posed the greatest concern to slaveholders. "Sometimes someone would come 'long and try to get us to run up North and be free," declared San Antonio slave Felix Haywood. "We used to laugh at that. There was no reason to run up North. All we had to do was to walk . . . south, and we'd be free as soon as we crossed the Rio Grande." Haywood's view confirmed Mexico's image as a haven for fugitive slaves dating back to the Texas war of independence. Many blacks fled with the retreating Mexican Army and settled just below the Rio Grande in Matamoros. A colony of former slaves on the international border prompted other blacks to strike out south for freedom. If they reached the Rio Grande, Mexicans often helped their river crossing.[14]

Four thousand fugitives lived south of the Rio Grande by 1855. Mexico welcomed them because officials believed they and Native Americans discouraged further American incursion. The symbol of this black-Indian-Mexican nexus was the border settlement created by the Seminole Indian chief Wild Cat, who led a band of 200 Indians and blacks into Coahuila in 1850. The Mexican government allowed this band to create a colony in the Santa Rosa Mountains eighty miles southwest of the Rio Grande border community of Piedras Negras. There Wild Cat welcomed other fugitives from Texas and Plains Indians. South Texas slaveholders demanded an end of the colony. Mexico has "long been regarded by the Texas slave," according to the San Antonio Ledger in 1852, "as his El Dorado for accumulation, his utopia for political rights, and his Paradise for happiness." After a series of meetings in San Antonio and other South Texas towns, slaveholders raised twenty thousand dollars for an expedition to recapture runaways. In October 1855 they sent Texas Ranger Captain James H. Callahan and 130 men to Mexico ostensibly to "chastise hostile Indians" but in fact to attack Wild Cat and his followers and return as many fugitive slaves as possible to Texas. The expedition failed when a combined Mexican-Indian-black force drove the intruders out of the region.[15]

Mexican opposition to slaveholder efforts to retrieve fugitives generated reprisals against Tejanos. With their loyalty to Texas already suspect, it took very little "evidence" to persuade slaveholders that Tejanos were abolitionists. In September 1854, when Anglo citizens learned that transient Tejanos near Seguin were enticing bondsmen to run away, they quickly passed a resolution declaring that no peon could enter or live in Guadalupe County. Austin residents took similar action. In October 1854, after a "respectable citizen" had observed a Mexican camp where slaves and tejanos "smoked, drank, gambled and made love," the local citizens in a resolution declared that Mexican laborers instilled "false notions of freedom," and made slaves "discontented and insubordinate." The city subsequently expelled all Tejanos except those identified by "respectable citizens." Colorado and Matagorda counties drove out their Mexican populations two years later, when county officials linked Tejanos to an abortive insurrection. In all, the Mexican "abolitionist" scare affected more than ten counties in south-central Texas.[16]

The Civil War ended black bondage in Texas but not before its servile population grew dramatically during the conflict. While black southerners from Virginia to Louisiana were gaining their freedom with the approach of Union armies after January 1, 1863, Texas instead received nearly seventy thousand additional bondspeople during the last years of the war as slaveholders from throughout the Confederacy fled to the state. "It looked like everybody in the world was going to Texas," ex-slave Allen Manning recalled as he described mothers carrying children on their backs and fathers tending wagons and livestock. "We would have to walk along side all the time to let the wagons go past, all loaded with folks going to Texas."[17]

The refugee flight, which continued into 1865, only delayed the inevitable. On June 19, 1865, Union forces landed at Galveston, where Major General Gordon Granger issued General Order No. 3 ending slavery in the last state of the former Confederacy. The day of Texas emancipation was from that point called Juneteenth. As news of emancipation spread throughout Texas, the reactions were predictable. "Soldiers, all of a sudden, was everywhere—coming in bunches, crossing and walking and riding. Everyone was singing. We was all walking on golden clouds," recalled Felix Haywood of San Antonio. Many newly freed slaves, however, were sobered by an uncertain future. As Haywood succinctly put it, "We knowed freedom was on us, but we didn't know what to do with it . . . Freedom could make folks proud but it didn't make them rich." Yet few former slaves wished for the return of slavery. H. C. Smith spoke for many of them in 1867: "Freedom, in poverty . . . and tribulations, even amidst the most cruel prejudice, is sweeter than the best fed or the best clothed slavery in the world."[18]

Indian Territory comprised the second-largest slaveholding region in the West. The Cherokee, Creek, Choctaw, Chickasaw, and Seminole entered the region after the Indian removal treaties of the 1830s, and they brought slaves with them. Of the five hundred Indian nations that inhabited the United States, the Five Nations were virtually the only Indians holding blacks in bondage. Moreover, only a minority in each tribe were slaveholders. Yet for this minority, which often was each tribe's political and economic elite, slavery was a profitable labor system and a proud source of identification with the planter culture of the Old South. Slavery in much of Indian Territory was a microcosm of the peculiar institution in the United States, differing only in that the owners were "red" rather than "white." However, that is not the entire story. Slaveholding varied among the five tribes. The Cherokee, with their stringent slave codes, regulations on free blacks, and laws against black-Indian intermarriage, exhibited "the strongest color prejudice of any Indians." Black slaves among the Seminole had wide latitude of action and considerable influence within tribal society.[19]

Slavery among Native Americans predated European arrival on the North American continent. Numerous Indian people regularly enslaved other native people from opposing tribes. By the 1600s the Cherokee, Creek, and other southeastern Indians welcomed runaway black slaves because initially neither group harbored suspicions about the racial inferiority of the other. Moreover, the black newcomers brought important skills. Fugitive slaves served as interpreters and negotiators with whites; they also knew how to repair guns and traps, to shoe horses, to improve agricultural methods, to spin and weave, to make butter, and to build houses, barns, and wagons.[20]

By the 1670s white traders had become permanent residents among the Cherokee, Creek, Choctaw, and Chickasaw. Although the traders learned the Indian languages, adopted some native customs, and took wives from among their hosts, they also created the first plantations and purchased black slaves to work them. The biracial children of the traders inherited the plantations and became the first generation of prominent mixed-blood landholders. These people were far less sympathetic to fugitives from neighboring white plantations.

By 1800 the Cherokee and Creek had established plantation agriculture and its labor system, black slavery, both of which challenged the traditional Indian values of communal property and wealth sharing. Alexander McGillivray, a Creek chief, set the pattern of large-scale landholding when he developed a plantation that by 1793 included 60 slaves and three hundred head of cattle. In 1802 a visitor to the Cherokee Nation described large plantations worked by black slaves. One early northwest Georgia plantation, Chieftains, owned by Major Ridge, a full-blooded Cherokee, had a spacious two-story eight-room house with front and back verandas and a brick fireplace at either end. His 30 slaves, acquired "to do the harder work about the premises," cultivated three hundred acres of corn, cotton, tobacco, wheat, and oats and an orchard of seventeen hundred fruit trees. By 1810 the total population of the Cherokee Nation stood at 12,395, including 583 bondspeople.[21]

Slavery had become so fixed in Cherokee and Creek society by 1819 that various laws, remarkably similar to those of the white South, were devised to regulate black behavior and protect the institution. In 1819 the Cherokee General Council adopted the first slave codes. These laws prohibited slaves from purchasing liquor or engaging in unsupervised trade. The council also established patrols to monitor the slave community. In 1824 the council outlawed marriage between blacks and Indians, but not between Indians and whites. Creek laws, which first appeared in 1824, were less draconian than the Cherokee statutes, but they also provided a legal foundation for slavery and discrimination. One law barred slaves from owning property while another banned marriages between blacks and Indians. Slaves could not be educated or become citizens of the nation. Censuses in 1833 for the Creek and 1835 for the Cherokee, the last enumerations taken when the majority of the tribes still resided in the East, revealed 22,694 Creek with 902 slaves and 16,542 Cherokee who possessed 1,592 black slaves. The Cherokee and Creek had chosen slaveholding as the path toward social progress.[22]

This path, however, did not assure these native people security in their ancient lands. In 1829, according to one account, a black slave found a gold nugget in northwest Georgia, touching off the first gold rush of the nineteenth century and ultimately precipitating the events that removed the Cherokees and four other southern tribes to Indian Territory. When President Andrew Jackson refused to uphold the U.S. Supreme Court ruling in *Worcester v. Georgia,* he opened Cherokee territory to thousands of gold seekers and land speculators. The subsequent policy of relocating the Cherokee to Indian Territory eight hundred miles to the West made possible an orderly and dignified retreat.[23]

The saga of the Trail of Tears is too well known to be recounted here. Less well known is that among the native people who emigrated were hundreds of black slaves, including 175 who perished on the journey with the Cherokee. Slaves who traveled along the Trail of Tears performed labor that reduced the suffering experienced by slaveholding Indians during the removal. They hunted game, worked as teamsters, cooks, and nurses, tended livestock on the trail, and guarded the camps at night. After arrival they cleared and fenced fields, built houses and barns, constructed docks, and planted crops. With slave labor, Indian planters cleared more acreage and made more improvements on their lands than did their impoverished kinsfolk. Seventy thousand Indians and their bond servants migrated to a vast new domain of woodland and prairie "west of Arkansas," where the newcomers overwhelmed the indigenous "wild tribes," pushing them into the western part of the territory. This rich land, protected from white intrusion by the federal government, evolved into a plantation society that, like the Old South, was politically and culturally dominated by a minority of affluent Indian landowners. Typical of this dominant group was George Lowery's family. The Lowerys left their "comfortable" estate in northwest Georgia in September 1838 with 30 slaves. Five months later the family settled eight miles south of Tahlequah, the capital of the Western Cherokee Nation, and their slaves soon had several hundred acres under cultivation. In time Lowery built a "substantial house" on the land he now called Greenleaf Plantation. Benjamin Marshall, a Creek, took his family of 8 and 19 slaves from central Georgia to Indian Territory in December 1835. Five years later Benjamin Love, a Chickasaw from Holly Springs, Mississippi, emigrated west leading a party that included 340 slaves, 95 of whom he owned.

Slaveholding Indians held a tremendous advantage in reestablishing their prosperity and wealth in the new land. Josiah Gregg, a trader who frequently crossed Indian Territory on his way to Santa Fe, remarked on the contrast between the "occasional stately dwelling, with an extensive farm attached, and the miserable hovels of the indigent, sometimes not ten feet square, with a little patch of corn, scarce[ly] large enough for a garden." Gregg also noted: "Most of

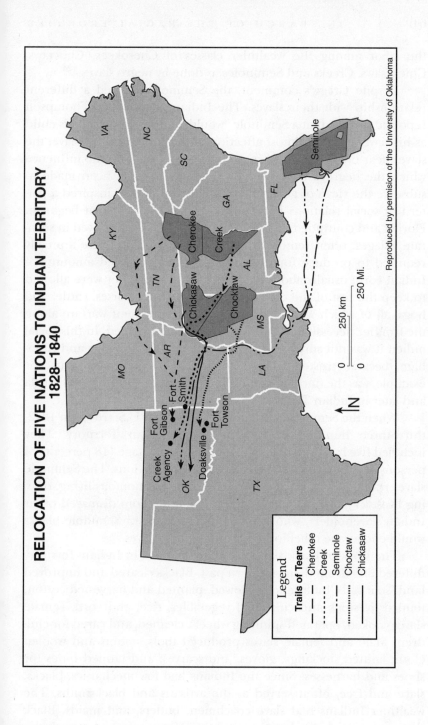

RELOCATION OF FIVE NATIONS TO INDIAN TERRITORY 1828–1840

Legend

Trails of Tears
- Cherokee
- Creek
- Seminole
- Choctaw
- Chickasaw

N

the labor among the wealthier classes of Cherokees, Choctaws, Chickasaws, Creeks and Seminoles, is done by negro slaves."[24]

Despite Gregg's comment, the Seminoles devised a different relationship with their slaves. The Indian agent Wiley Thompson reported in 1835 that a Seminole "would almost as soon sell his child as his slave. . . . The almost affection of the Indian for his slave, the slave's fear of being placed in a worse condition, and the influence which the negroes have over the Indians, have all been made to subserve the views of government." This "influence" inspired a pattern of social relations between master and servant that began in Florida and continued in Indian Territory. Black slaves lived in separate villages, often remote from their owners. They were annually required to produce for their masters predetermined amounts of Indian corn, usually about ten bushels. In return they were allowed to keep the rest of the crop along with stocks of horses, cattle, and hogs, all of which were their property. The frequent warfare along the frontier necessitated that the blacks remain armed. In this social milieu it was not surprising that two blacks, John Caesar and Abraham, became trusted advisers to Seminole chiefs. Abraham, for example, was the uncle-in-law of Principal Chief Micanopy in Florida and later in Indian Territory.[25]

When the Seminole were finally defeated by U.S. troops in 1842, thirty-three hundred were removed to Indian Territory. They included five hundred blacks, the largest percentage (18 percent) of persons of African ancestry in any of the Five Nations. The Seminole slaves resumed in the West their pattern of autonomous living, owning livestock, and carrying weapons. Such freedom dismayed other Indian slaveholders, who feared the demeanor of Seminole blacks would encourage rebelliousness among their slaves.[26]

The work of black slaves for other nations in Indian Territory differed little from their southern past. Blacks cleared and improved land, split rails, built fences, plowed, planted and harvested cotton, tended livestock and cultivated vegetables, rice, and corn. Female slaves cooked, operated spinning wheels, cleaned, and cared for children. Male and female slaves produced tools, cotton and woolen cloth; knitted stockings, gloves, and scarves; and tanned hides for shoes and harnesses. Since the Indians had few mechanics, blacks, slave and free, often served as the artisans and blacksmiths. The wealthier Indians had slave coachmen, butlers, and maids. Black slaves were used as saltworks operatives, ferrymen, and stevedores, who loaded and unloaded steamships and flatboats. One group of

Slave Population in Indian Territory, 1860

Tribe	Total Population	Slave Population	Percentage
Cherokee	13,821	2,511	15
Choctaw	13,666	2,349	14
Chickasaw	4,260	975	18
Creek	13,550	1,532	10
Seminole	2,630	1,000*	29

*The Seminole forbade a census enumeration of their black population. The figure above is an estimate provided by Michael F. Doran.

Source: Michael F. Doran, "Population Statistics of Nineteenth Century Indian Territory," Chronicles of Oklahoma 53:4 (Winter 1975), 501.

Cherokee slaves constituted the majority of the crew of Joseph Vann's steamboat *Lucy Walker*.[27]

Indian Territory slaves developed one special skill: They were language translators. John Cowaya, a Seminole slave, spoke Spanish, English, and Seminole. He was the interpreter for several Seminole chiefs in Florida, Indian Territory, and Mexico between 1835 and 1860. An unnamed African American woman in 1832 translated for Washington Irving and Charles Latrobe when they visited the home of a Cherokee farmer. One commentator wrote of another black female interpreter for the Cherokee: "The spectacle seems strange . . . no doubt, the coal black girl speaking both English and Cherokee and keeping the old woman informed as to what was being said."[28]

To give a "sense of the white man's meaning" suggests that many African American slaves moved comfortably between the worlds of red and white. But some African American slaves, having lived among Indian people for generations, knew no other language and culture. They adopted Indian dress, followed the Indian diet, used native medicine, carried tomahawks and club axes, and practiced Indian modes of agriculture. These blacks even celebrated Indian holidays and festivals, attended "ball plays" and "bangas" (dances), and on occasion participated in syncreatic church services. At North Fork Town (Creek Nation) in January 1842, Lieutenant Colonel Ethan Allen Hitchcock observed Creek, mixed-bloods, and blacks in prayer and psalm singing. His description of the service revealed an odd mixture: The language was Creek, the music typical of Southern Baptist or Methodist services, and the lyrics were those of an old slave spiritual. Another observer described Chickasaw slaves in 1837 as "picturesque looking Indian negroes, with dresses belonging to no country but partaking of all."[29]

As in the Old South, many slaves resisted their Indian masters. This resistance became evident soon after Indian Removal. The most famous fugitive from Indian Territory, Henry Bibb, fled upon the death of his Cherokee owner. Bibb eventually arrived in Michigan, where he wrote *The Life and Adventures of Henry Bibb,* a popular nineteenth-century slave narrative. Other black slaves exploited both the journey west and unsettled frontier conditions to make their escapes. Some fugitives went north to Kansas Territory; others took their chances with Plains Indians. The greatest opportunities lay in the vast Indian Territory itself. Slaves of the Creek, Cherokee, Choctaw, and Chickasaw fled to the Seminole Nation, at the center of the territory. Other fugitives sought temporary refuge within their own sparsely populated nations, often joining runaway groups from neighboring Missouri, Arkansas, and Louisiana. "Our country is traversed," lamented the *Cherokee Advocate* in 1846, "by numbers of slaves who have escaped from their rightful owners, either of the Nation, or the State[s] or the Creek Country."[30]

Slaves also rebelled against their owners. The Cherokee Nation saw three uprisings in 1841, 1842, and 1850. The 1842 "revolt" eventually included Creek and Choctaw slaves as well as Cherokee bondspeople. In November 1842 about two dozen slaves from Cherokee plantations attempted a mass escape. At a predetermined hour and on the signal of a particular song, the insurrectionists took horses, mules, several rifles, ammunition, food, and supplies and started for Mexico, spurred on by the "rumor" that there was a settlement of free blacks along the Rio Grande. Indian officials blamed the rumor on "some renegade Mexican [who claimed] that far away over the setting sun was a country where slavery did not exist and was not tolerated by law." That settlement did exist at Matamoros, but the slaves would never reach it. They headed southwest toward New Mexico, then part of the Mexican nation, pursued by forty Cherokee slave catchers.[31]

When the fugitives entered the Creek country, other slaves joined them, bringing the total number to thirty-five. Creek slave catchers, meanwhile, joined the Cherokee pursuers and caught the fleeing party just south of the Canadian River. The blacks fought off their pursuers although two were killed and twelve captured. Driven off, the Creek and Cherokee pursuing parties returned for reinforcements. Fifteen miles beyond the battle site the fugitives encountered Choctaw slave traders with eight recently captured runaways, including five children. They killed the slave catchers and brought the Choctaw runaways into their group. Recognizing the potential for general unrest, the Cherokee Council dispatched a force of one hundred men to capture the slaves and return them to the Cherokee Nation. On November 26 the Cherokee militia overtook the slaves on the plains three hundred miles from their former plantations and seven miles north of the Red River. Two fugitives escaped, but the remaining thirty-one surrendered to the Cherokee militia.[32]

On the eve of the Civil War Indian people held 7,367 black slaves.[33] African slavery was firmly established among these nonwhite peoples. In contrast with Texas, however, their liberation came quickly in the war. Three Indian nations, the Cherokee, Creek, and Seminole, sent soldiers to fight for both the Union and the Confederacy, engulfing the territory in the national conflict while pitting Indian against Indian in an intratribal warfare that historian Alvin Josephy called the "little civil war." By the fall of 1861 two Confederate Cherokee Indian regiments were created, one commanded by Stand Watie and the other under John Drew. Before the end of the year Drew and most of his regiment, nearly a thousand men, joined the Union forces, which accepted "all persons, without reference to color . . . willing to fight for the American flag . . . and the Federal Government." The Indian "Federals" in fact attracted nearly one thousand fugitive slaves, primarily from the various nations but also from neighboring Confederate states. Indian Territory freedman Chaney McNair remembered Union troops gathering up "four or five hundred" slaves in the territory to take to Kansas. When the group arrived, "most all the negro men folks joined the Northern Army and the women were put to work in the fields." Fugitives from the territory joined the First Kansas Colored Infantry and fought against their former masters at Honey Springs and Cabin Creek. Meanwhile loyal Cherokee met on February 21, 1863, to issue an emancipation proclamation, making them the only tribe to end slavery before 1865.[34]

The horrific impact of the war on Indian Territory, where proportionately more lives were lost and more refugees created than in any Union or Confederate state, ironically accounted for more slaves gaining their freedom than the Cherokee proclamation. Several

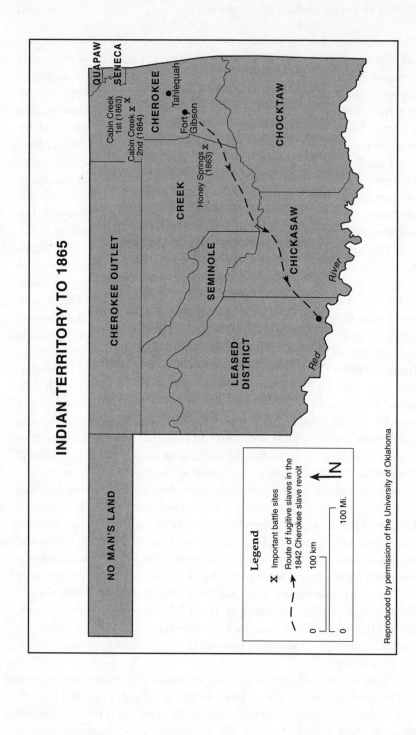

INDIAN TERRITORY TO 1865

NO MAN'S LAND

CHEROKEE OUTLET

QUAPAW

SENECA

CHEROKEE

Tahlequah

Fort Gibson

Cabin Creek 1st (1863) x x
Cabin Creek 2nd (1864)

CHOCKTAW

CREEK

Honey Springs (1863) x

SEMINOLE

CHICKASAW

River

LEASED DISTRICT

Red

Legend

x   Important battle sites

----   Route of fugitive slaves in the 1842 Cherokee slave revolt

N

| 0 | 100 km |
| 0 | 100 Mi. |

Reproduced by permission of the University of Oklahoma

hundred African Americans fled north with loyal Indians, such as the Creek chief Opothlayahola, who led three thousand Union supporters to safety in Kansas in 1861 after fending off numerous attempts by white and Indian Confederate soldiers to capture the refugee party. Far more slaves escaped from pro-Confederate Indians en route to Texas or the southern part of the Choctaw and Chickasaw nations to protect their property. Other slaves fled owner-abandoned farms and plantations for nearby woods and hills until Confederate forces rounded them up and transferred them to Fort Gibson. As the war continued, these refugees "piled in[to Fort Gibson] from everywhere" according to freedwoman Rochelle Ward. Living conditions deteriorated rapidly, and by 1863 blacks were "cooking in the open, sleeping most anywhere, making shelter . . . out of cloth scraps and brush, digging caves along the river bank to live in." When Union officials occupied the fort in 1863, they found five hundred black refugees. Unable to persuade the blacks to leave the area for Kansas and bound by the Emancipation Proclamation to free them, the U.S. Army provided supplies for the remainder of the war. Given the chaotic conditions in the Indian nations, few blacks remained in bondage when the fighting ended in 1865.[35]

Utah was the only other territory to legalize slavery. When Brigham Young led 143 Mormon men, 3 women, and 2 children into the Salt Lake Valley to establish "Zion," the party included 2 black slave Mormons—Green Flake and Hark Lay—and another slave, Oscar Crosby, who was baptized into the church two weeks after the party's arrival. They and other black slaves who came later ensured that the national debate over slavery would extend into the Salt Lake Valley.[36]

Utah Territory in 1850 counted only twenty-six black slaves and twenty-four free blacks. In fact the slave population declined over the rest of the decade. Yet slaveholding and race shaped the Mormon experience in profound ways as the Latter-day Saints sought in the 1830s and 1840s to reconcile their spiritual beliefs with the varied sensibilities of their neighbors in Ohio, Illinois, and Missouri. The Mormons could not evade the tension over slavery in Utah in the 1850s even as their leaders carefully charted a course between the northern and southern interests competing for control of the national government.[37]

Plagued by persecution and anti-Mormon violence across Ohio, Illinois, Missouri, and Iowa, church leaders in 1845 made the fateful decision to move westward beyond white settlement. Despite the announcement of their impending departure, the Mormons were expelled from Nauvoo the following year and fled to winter quarters near Omaha, Nebraska. On April 17, 1847, Brigham Young's party left Winter Quarters, and three months later, on July 22, the first Mormon wagons entered the Salt Lake Valley.[38]

Green Flake returned east with Brigham Young on August 16. Lay and Crosby went about the myriad tasks of the new colony, constructing shelters for the coming winter, preparing land for cultivation, building dams for irrigation, in addition to preparing for the arrival of their owners the following year, a practice that appeared common for many of the first slaves arriving in the Salt Lake Valley. Lay and Crosby were joined by ten other blacks, who arrived with later Mormon parties by the end of 1847, including Mississippian Robert Smith's slave, Bridget ("Biddy") Mason. A single mother of three daughters, Mason was in charge of herding the livestock for the Smith-led emigrant party from Mississippi to Utah and walked virtually the entire distance of seventeen hundred miles in seven months. By 1848 approximately fifty blacks were among the seventeen hundred settlers in the Salt Lake Valley. Most of these arrivals were part of a contingent called the Mississippi Saints—white slaveholders and their black bondspeople—who settled in the Holladay-Cottonwood area of the valley. Frontier conditions strained the resources of the initial colony, forcing whites and blacks to share rationed food and live in crude dugout shelters until log cabins could be constructed.[39]

By the spring of 1849 the Great Basin Zion could accommodate a growing number of emigrants, including additional slaves. Although most of the blacks were agricultural workers, others worked as teamsters, carpenters, or store laborers for their merchant slaveowners. One woman, Hannah Smith, was midwife to white and black Holladay-Cottonwood settlers. By 1850 the valley's slaves regularly congregated in a small building in Salt Lake City, where they socialized, developed relationships, and, according to one former bondsman, discussed their common condition. A musical group known simply as the African Band grew out of this social exchange and provided entertainment for the bondspeople and for white Mormons.[40]

The Mormons, like most nineteenth-century Christians, found justification for both slavery and black racial inferiority in their interpretation of the Scriptures. Brigham Young, leader of the church after the assassination of Joseph Smith, believed, for example, that black people had descended from the "seed of Canaan" and were thus condemned to be the "servant of servants." He welcomed individual Mormon slaveholders to Utah, but he refused to own slaves and believed the Great Basin Zion could develop without the servile institution. Indeed Utah slaves, believing they had a sympathetic friend, frequently took their grievances against their masters directly to the Mormon church president and sometimes sought refuge in his home.[41]

Once territorial status was granted, Young and other church leaders began to address slavery publicly. In 1852 Young proposed that the territorial legislature enact An Act in Relation to Service. Apparently church leaders felt the necessity legally to recognize slavery in the Great Basin to appease important slaveholders in the territory, including William H. Hooper, a prominent Mormon merchant who later became Utah's territorial delegate to Congress, and Abraham O. Smoot, the second mayor of Salt Lake City. Young's recognition of slavery may have also been driven by his perceived need to gain the support of proslavery representatives in Congress.[42]

The Utah act was the most complete elaboration of Mormon views regarding slaveholding. Unlike southern slave codes, the Utah law set forth more regulations of slaveholders than of slaves. Utah slaveholders had to present proof that their black servants had come into the territory "of their own free will and choice." One provision detailed the obligations of masters to provide their slaves adequate food, clothing, shelter, and recreation opportunities and urged that they work "reasonable hours." Another provision restricted the punishment meted out to servants. Slaves could be bought and sold only with their consent. Utah owners were required to send their bond servants to school. Finally slaveholders who violated the prohibition against sexual intercourse with their slaves were fined up to one thousand dollars and ran the risk of losing their property upon conviction.[43]

Brigham Young spoke for many Saints in 1863 when he assessed the Civil War raging in the East: "One portion of the country wish [*sic*] to raise their ... black slaves and the other wish [*sic*] to free them, and apparently, to almost worship them. ... Who cares? ... Ham will continue to be the servant of servants, as the Lord has decreed, until the curse is removed." However, the outcome of the war was a vital matter for the twenty-nine Utah slaves, like Sam Bankhead, who continually inquired about the progress of the fighting and who on one occasion said, "My God, I hope de Souf get licked." Liberation officially came for those slaves in the spring of 1862, when Congress passed an emancipation act for the territories. It is unclear, however, if Utah owners immediately complied with the legislation. By 1865 they had no choice, and slavery died quietly in its only foothold west of the Rocky Mountains.[44]

Slavery was never legal in other western states and territories, but its advocates envisioned black servitude expanding to the Pacific and worked to institute it in New Mexico, Oregon, and California. Yet these proslavery advocates could never overcome political, institutional, and social barriers to African slavery in their regions. Black slavery failed in New Mexico, for example, because the landholding aristocracy had other sources of coerced labor: Mexican American peons and Indian slaves.

The origin of New Mexico's coerced labor system lay in the two centuries of Spanish control and two decades of Mexican rule, but it was reinforced with the American occupation in 1846. Prior to that occupation New Mexico's political economy resembled the plantation South. A small aristocracy controlled most tillable land and used debt peonage to attach landless agricultural workers to their estates. Peonage involved an indebted agricultural worker who indentured himself, or a member of his family, to meet his obligation. The debt became a de facto lifetime bondage as expenses invariably exceeded the worker's earnings. One New Mexican father in 1850 indentured his sixteen-year-old daughter to pay a five-dollar debt.[45]

Native Americans, however, were subject to slavery. They were captured in wars and then sold as house servants in southwestern settlements. By the beginning of the nineteenth century slave trading had become a regular and profitable activity for the Navaho and Ute, who sold captives for fifty to one hundred dollars each. New Mexicans began conducting their own slave raids in the 1830s into Utah, Arizona, and California. Occasionally slave raiders captured and sold Mexican Americans to other Indian peoples or to New Mexican settlers, as when Navaho appeared in Santa Fe in 1852 hoping to sell three Mexicans they held as slaves, or when Comanche attempted to sell several Mexican children captured near Durango. In 1854 Juan Felipe Salazar of Abiqui, New Mexico, was forced to surrender a fourteen-year-old boy he had purchased from Ute Indians because U.S. authorities deemed it illegal for any "white person" to be held as property. Although the vast majority of Indian slaves were held by *ricos* (wealthy Hispanos), U.S. born residents and military officials quickly embraced the practice. J. R. Bartlett, a federal official in charge of the Mexican border survey in 1852, recommended that any expedition sent to fight Indians should kill all the warriors but turn the women and children "and such men as fall into our hands" over to the Mexicans. "Trading in captives has been so long tolerated in this territory," reported James S. Calhoun, the territory's first governor, in 1850, "that it has ceased to be regarded as wrong . . . ." In 1850 the three thousand enslaved Indians in New Mexico constituted 4.8 percent of the population.[46]

Despite the exploitation of Indian and Mexican American peasant labor, some black slaves entered New Mexico Territory. Most of the forty blacks accompanied the territory's southern-born first chief justice. African slavery became a political issue in 1856, when the territorial legislature limited free blacks entering New Mexico. The measure was designed to prevent runaway Texas slaves from entering New Mexico or from being brought in by sympathetic groups, such as the Cumancharus (Comancheros). Two free blacks, Harriet Brown in 1859 and John Winters in 1861, were expelled from the territory under its provisions. In 1859 Miguel Otero, the New Mexican delegate to Congress, persuaded the territorial legislature to enact a slave code that restricted slave travel, prohibited slaves from testifying in court, and limited the owners' right to arm slaves except when necessary in defense against Indian raids.[47]

New Mexico's black slaves were freed when Congress banned slavery in the territories. The war also initiated the liberation of thousands of Indian slaves and Mexican American peons. Since the Thirteenth Amendment outlawed slavery *and* involuntary servitude, in 1867 Massachusetts Senators Charles Sumner and Henry Wilson pushed through Congress legislation designed to end New Mexican peonage. Another three decades passed, however, before this labor system disappeared from New Mexico.[48]

Slavery intruded upon the politics of Oregon, prompting bitter debate and elaborate legal and legislative maneuvering during the 1850s. The first provisional government of Oregon used the language of the Northwest Ordinance of 1787 to prohibit slavery. Nonetheless a small number of blacks brought to the Pacific Northwest between 1840 and 1860 were slaves in fact if not in name. Surviving accounts of two Oregon ex-slaves, Amanda Johnson and Lou

Black Population in Western States and Territories, 1860

Black	Population	Population	Total Percentage
States			
California	379,994	4,086	1.1%
Kansas	107,994	627	0.6
Oregon	52,465	128	0.2
Texas	604,215	182,921	30.3
Territories			
Colorado	34,277	46	0.1
Dakota	4,837	0	0.0
Indian Territory	58,594	8,376*	14.2
Nebraska	28,841	82	0.3
Nevada	6,857	45	0.7
New Mexico	93,516	85	0.09
Utah	40,273	59	0.1
Washington	11,594	39	0.3

*This estimated figure is based on the hand count of the manuscript census schedules for the population "west of Arkansas," as Indian Territory was designated in 1860. They appear in Michael F. Doran, "Population Statistics of Nineteenth Century Indian Territory," *Chronicles of Oklahoma* 53:4 (Winter 1975), 501. The figures do not take into account the unknown number of free blacks and fugitive slaves from the surrounding states who illegally resided in the region.

Sources: *U.S. Bureau of the Census,* Eighth Census of the United States, 1860 *(Washington, D.C.: Government Printing Office,1864), iv; U.S. Bureau of the Census,* Negro Population in the United States, 1790–1915 *(Washington, D.C.: Government Printing Office, 1918), 44; and Michael F. Doran, "Population Statistics of Nineteenth Century Indian Territory,"* Chronicles of Oklahoma 53:4 (Winter 1975), 501.

Southworth, pointed to the existence of slavery. Johnson, born in Clay County, Missouri, in 1833, was brought to Oregon in 1853 by her owner, Nancy Wilhite. She remembered crossing the plains that year in a wagon train that included two other bond servants, Lou Southworth and Benjamin Johnson, who left brief narratives of their bondage in Oregon. The most persuasive evidence of human bondage in Oregon came in 1857, one month after the territory's voters had overwhelmingly approved a ban on slavery. William Allen, a representative from Yamhill County, listed slaves in Benton, Lane, Polk, and Yamhill counties in his unsuccessful attempt to obtain legislation to protect slave property.[49]

Some Oregon blacks resisted slavery either through the legal process or by flight. Their actions undermined slavery in the Pacific Northwest. The major legal challenge to slavery in Oregon was *Holmes v. Ford*. In 1844 Nathaniel Ford, a Missouri farmer, brought a slave couple, Robin and Polly Holmes, to Oregon. Before leaving Missouri, Ford promised freedom to the Holmes family upon arrival. Settling in the Willamette Valley, Ford built a small cabin for the Holmeses. Although allowing them limited travel and the right to sell some of the agricultural produce, he still denied the family its promised freedom.

In 1849 Ford manumitted Robin and Polly and their newborn son but refused to free their four other children, three of whom had been born in Oregon Territory. Robin and Polly moved to Salem and opened a nursery. Harriet, one of the children still held by Ford, died on a visit to her parents in 1851. Realizing that Ford would not voluntarily free the surviving children and blaming him for Harriet's death, Holmes brought suit in the Polk County district court the following year to gain custody of his children.[50]

The *Holmes v. Ford* case languished in various courts for eleven months. Finally, in July 1853, George A. Williams, recently arrived chief justice of the territorial supreme court, placed it at the head of his docket. Williams, a free-soil Democrat from Iowa, ruled against Ford, declaring that slavery could not exist in Oregon without specific legislation to protect it. He said: "[I]n as much as these colored children are in Oregon, where slavery does not legally exist, they are free."[51] The Holmes case was the last attempt by Oregon's proslavery settlers to protect slave property through the judicial process.

Slavery in California was also illegal despite the best efforts of proslavery advocates. In 1849 California adopted an antislavery constitution and less than one year later was admitted to the Union as a free state. Yet state officials were unable or unwilling to challenge slaveholders who continued to bring their bond servants to the state until the outbreak of the Civil War. Slaveholders interpreted the silence of the state's leading officials on slavery as tacit support for the institution. Robert Givens admitted as much when he wrote to his father in Kentucky in 1852 that although the law made it impossible to hold a slave ... longer than the present year," he did not consider it a risk because "no one will put themselves to the trouble of investigating the matter." By 1852 an estimated three hundred slaves worked in the goldfields, and an undetermined but sizable number were house servants in California cities. California had by far the largest number of bond servants west of Texas.[52]

Slaveholders, however, did not anticipate the small group of black and white abolitionists who would challenge their designs. The white abolitionists included the prominent attorneys Joseph W. Winans, Cornelius Cole, Joseph C. Zabriskie, Edward D. Baker, Edwin Bryan Crocker (brother of Charles Crocker), and the merchants Caleb Fay and Mark Hopkins. Often the antislavery legal activists found sympathetic jurists, such as Judge Benjamin Hayes of Los Angeles, who established important legal precedents while freeing black men and women in cases before their courts.[53]

California slavery was also undermined by an African American community willing to employ both legal and extralegal means to ensure the freedom of black slaves. Some of these black abolitionists were well known. Mary Ellen Pleasant became famous in San Francisco's black community in 1858, when she sheltered the fugitive slave Archy Lee. Peter Lester, a Philadelphian, who arrived in San Francisco in 1850, invited black slaves into his home to lecture them on their rights. "When they left," he declared, "we had them strong in the spirit of freedom. They were leaving [slavery] every day." Less well known were two black sailors, William Freeman and Charles Moreno, and boardinghouse owner William R. Mathews who tried physically to prevent the return of a Maryland slave in 1859. Often black opponents raised funds to mount legal challenges on behalf of individual slaves. In 1851 members of the San Francisco black community retained attorney Samuel W. Holladay to defend a slave known as Frank, who was being detained in preparation for his return to Missouri. The active role of blacks in challenging slavery prompted a contemporary German observer to remark, "The wealthy California Negroes . . . exhibit a great deal of energy and intelligence in saving their brethren."[54]

California's abolitionists faced slavery virtually every day. Slaveholders and antislavery activists lived in the same urban communities or worked almost side by side in the mining fields. The close proximity of slave and abolitionist exposed the bond servant to direct contact with his champions, a position virtually impossible in the eastern United States. Vigilant free blacks, such as Robert Owens in Los Angeles, Elizabeth Flake Rowan in San Bernardino, Peter Lester in San Francisco, or the unidentified Oakland abolitionists who rescued Hannah and Pete, two Berkeley slaves, in 1859, challenged an institution in their midst.[55]

The role of antislavery activists was clearly evident in the Perkins case in 1852, the first major legal confrontation of slavery in California, and the Archy Lee case, the last legal challenge in 1857. However, the Biddy Mason case affected the largest number of people. Mason claimed freedom for herself and her extended family of thirteen women and children. Mason, the slave of Mississippi Mormon Robert Marion Smith, migrated to San Bernardino, California, from Utah in 1851. Smith and other Mormon slaveowners took their servants to help establish the San Bernardino colony despite Brigham Young's warning that "there is little doubt but [the slaves] will all be free as soon as they arrive in California." The trip to San Bernardino undermined Mason's fear of her owner and the legal system that supported slavery. She and another Smith slave, Hannah, conversed with Elizabeth Flake Rowan and her husband, Charles H. Rowan, free blacks who were also part of the 150-wagon caravan from Utah to southern California. The couple quietly urged them to contest their servile status in California. After her arrival Mason met Robert and Minnie Owens, former Texas slaves who operated a prosperous Los Angeles corral that employed ten Mexican vaqueros. By 1855 Owens's son had developed a romantic relationship with Biddy Mason's seventeen-year-old daughter, prompting the Owens family to take a personal interest in Biddy's fear that Smith planned to relocate her family to Texas. When Owens and Elizabeth Flake Rowan told local officials that Smith was illegally holding black slaves, the Los Angeles county sheriff, along with Owens, his son, another African American cowboy, Manuel Pepper, and Owens's vaqueros, swooped down on the Smith camp in the San Bernardino Mountains to prevent Smith's departure. The Masons were placed "under the charge of the Sheriff for their protection."[56]

Mason now petitioned for freedom for herself and her family. After three days of hearings in January 1856 Los Angeles District Court Judge Benjamin Hayes handed down his decision. Citing California law that prohibited both slavery and involuntary servitude, he ruled that "all of the said persons of color are entitled to their freedom and are free forever."[57] The *Mason* decision was propitious. One year later the U.S. Supreme Court in its *Dred Scott* decision overruled

Hayes's interpretation of the rights of slaveowners to hold blacks in bondage in free states.

As events in New Mexico, Oregon, and California illustrate, the West was not a natural geographic, economic, or cultural barrier to the expansion of slavery. Slavery spread easily from the Old South into the Indian nations and Texas. Moreover, as in Texas and California, it could adapt to new forms of economic activity, including ranching and mining. Since both activities existed in virtually every western state, slavery might well have become a significant labor system for the region.

Historians later wrote of the "natural limits" of slavery east of the ninety-eighth meridian. However, nineteenth-century proslavery advocates from New Mexico to Oregon saw no such restriction. Slavery failed in the West because of political decisions: the Missouri Compromise, the Kansas-Nebraska Act, the promulgation of antislavery constitutions in California and Oregon, the war in "bleeding Kansas," and the Civil War itself, which destroyed the institution throughout the nation.

3

✧ ❀ ✧ ❀ ✧

Freedom in
the Antebellum West,
1835–65

For much of the nineteenth century African Americans viewed the West as a place of economic opportunity and refuge from racial restrictions. The first public expression of that sentiment appeared in 1833 at the Third Annual Convention for the Improvement of the Free People of Color. The convention met in Philadelphia, far removed from the region under consideration, but it nonetheless endorsed western settlement, especially the emigration of blacks to Mexican Texas, over a return to Africa. "To those who may be obliged to exchange a cultivated region for a howling wilderness," declared its resolution, "we recommend, to retire into the western wilds, and fell the native forest of America, where the ploughshares of prejudice have as yet been unable to penetrate the soil."[1] This resolution reflected the steady erosion of black rights more than familiarity with western conditions. Even so, the delegates subscribed to a widely held American belief that migrating offered a chance to start anew.

Such faith proved elusive. White western settlers rapidly constructed familiar racially based political and economic restrictions. Texas, which in the 1820s offered hope to many African Americans, entered the Union in 1845 as a slave state. By 1860 Texas had 355 free blacks and 182,000 slaves, clear proof that Anglo Texas liberty and black freedom had become incompatible. California's 4,000

African Americans, all nominally free, constituted 75 percent of the free black population in the West. Yet successive antebellum California legislatures built what historian Malcolm Edwards calls "an appallingly extensive body of discriminatory laws." These laws denied voting rights, prohibited African American court testimony, and banned black homesteading, jury service, and marriage with whites. Territorial legislatures in Oregon, Kansas, Utah, and Nebraska enacted similar restrictions.[2]

Despite their small numbers, African American westerners challenged these restrictions. Occasionally an individual simply moved himself and his family from harm's way. Missouri farmer George Washington Bush, like thousands of others in the 1840s, caught "Oregon fever." In 1844 he uprooted his wife and six children, and with four other families set out on an eight-month, two-thousand-mile journey to the Pacific Northwest. On September 5, 1844, near Soda Springs in present-day Idaho, Bush confided to fellow traveler John Minto that "he should watch when we got to Oregon, what usage was awarded to people of color." Bush resolved that "if he could not have a free man's rights, he would seek the protection of the Mexican Government in California or New Mexico." The Bush party eventually reached Oregon, but unlike the majority of white settlers who spread out over the Willamette Valley south of the Columbia, he chose the sparsely populated area north of the river. A recently passed black exclusion law would be difficult to enforce in that area. Bush's decision initiated migration north of the Columbia and led to the organization of Washington Territory.[3]

On other occasions a lone voice protested evolving discrimination. In 1851 Abner Hunt Francis reported to the country's abolitionists through articles in *Frederick Douglass' Paper* the impact of Oregon Territory's black exclusion law on its one hundred African American residents. Abner's brother, O. H. Francis, a successful Portland merchant, had been arrested under the provisions of the law. Although Abner Francis railed against the statute, which allowed "the colored citizen [to be] driven out like a beast in the forest" and vowed to "suffer severely" if it helped bring about the law's repeal, he also noted that many Portland citizens had petitioned for his brother's exemption from the law and its eventual repeal.[4]

Organized political and legal action, however, dominated resistance tactics, especially in California, where a small but articulate

African American community confronted racially discriminatory legislation. In the process they initiated the first civil rights campaign in the West. California's antebellum black population comprised the first voluntary African American migrants to the West. In an 1854 letter to Frederick Douglass, black San Franciscan William H. Newby aptly described his new city of thirty-five thousand inhabitants: "San Francisco presents many features that no city in the Union presents. Its population is composed of almost every nation under heaven. Here is to be seen at a single glance every nation in miniature." Newby depicted the entire population, but his words applied equally to the diverse array of African Americans gathered in the golden state. In 1850 California had nearly one thousand blacks from north and south of the Mason-Dixon Line as well as a foreign-born population of Afro–Latin Americans from Mexico, Peru, and Chile and a significant population of Jamaicans. California was the only state where freeborn women and men from such northern states as Massachusetts, New York, Illinois, and Ohio rubbed shoulders with slaves from Georgia, Alabama, Tennessee, and Texas. That mix, particularly with its leadership drawn disproportionately from New England abolitionist circles, produced a community capable of protecting its interests.[5]

Most black migrants trekked the main route from Westport, Missouri, through the Rocky Mountains, across the Great Basin, and over the Sierra Nevada range to northern California or the southern route from New Orleans or Fort Smith, Arkansas, across Indian Territory, Texas, northern Mexico, Arizona, and the Mojave Desert into southern California. Both routes tested the endurance and stamina of the strongest men and women regardless of their race.

There is no record of an overland company (as the wagon trains to California were called) composed solely of African Americans. Yet these companies usually had some black members. Typical was a forty-niner group that included "105 men, 15 Negroes and 12 females." Sometimes the migrants traveled alone. Margaret Frink described a black female she encountered in 1850 near the Humboldt Sink, the desert just east of the Sierra Nevada. Frink recalled the woman "tramping along through the heat and dust, carrying a cast iron bake stove on her head with her provisions and a blanket piled on top—all she possessed in the world—bravely pushing on for California." For some the trail proved fatal. One overland traveler wrote that "a white woman and a colored one died yesterday of the cholera."[6]

Most African Americans moved to California for economic reasons, pursuing the promise of quick wealth in the goldfields or in burgeoning San Francisco and Sacramento. The costs exacted by migration selected out only those African Americans with means or with access to credit. For the intrepid, the effort seemed well worth the dangers. The *New Bedford* (Massachusetts) *Mercury* in September 1848 described an encounter between a black man walking near the San Francisco docks and a white gold seeker just off a ship. When the newcomer called on the black man to carry his luggage, the African American responded with an indignant glance and turned away. Having walked a few steps, he turned toward the newcomer, drew a small bag from his bosom, and said, "Do you think I'll lug trunks when I can get that much in one day?" The sack of gold dust was estimated by the newcomer to be worth over one hundred dollars.[7]

Three years later Peter Brown described his new life as a gold miner to his wife, Alley, in Ste. Genevieve, Missouri: "I am now mining about 25 miles from Sacramento City and doing well. I have been working for myself for the past two months . . . and have cleared three hundred dollars. California is the best country in the world to make money. It is also the best place for black folks on the globe. All a man has to do, is to work, and he will make money."[8]

Such reports of opportunity in the goldfields ensured a steady flow of African Americans to California. By 1852 the black population had doubled to 2,000 women and men. As with all mining frontiers, it was overwhelmingly male. Of the 952 blacks counted in the 1850 census, only 9 percent were women. Ten years later, when black California numbered 4,086 inhabitants, black women constituted only 31 percent of the total population.[9]

Slightly more than half of California's African Americans in the early 1850s headed for the mother lode country, a band of gold-mining communities stretching south along the western slope of the Sierra Nevada from the Trinity River for four hundred miles to the Tuolumne River. A hundred thousand miners from five continents lived there. A few black gold seekers found wealth. An African American sailor known only as Hector in 1848 deserted his naval squadron ship, *Southampton,* at Monterey, went to the mother lode, and returned a few weeks later with four thousand dollars in gold. Another black man, known only as Dick, mined a hundred thousand dollars in gold in Tuolumne County in 1848 only to lose it at San Francisco gambling tables. While his was one of the largest discoveries by any miner, the average black miner made five to six dollars per day.[10]

African American miners usually worked in integrated settings, preferring the company of Chinese, Latin American, European, or white New Englander miners, all less prejudiced than southerners and midwesterners. On occasion black miners grew numerous enough to support a community. In 1852 a small predominantly black community called Little Negro Hill grew up around the lucrative claims of two Massachusetts-born black miners working along the American River. A store and boardinghouse became the nucleus for a concentration of African American residences. Little Negro Hill attracted Chinese and Portuguese miners and eventually American-born whites. By 1855 it was described as a settlement of four hundred, with "scores of hardy miners making good wages." Other integrated mining settlements evolved as well: a second Negro Hill near the Mokelumne River, Union Bar along the Yuba River, and Downieville, one of the few permanent settlements in the mother lode. Downieville was founded in 1849 by a Scotsman, William Downie, who led a party of nine miners, including seven blacks, to the site where the town now stands.[11]

Initially African American miners encountered little difficulty. J. D. Borthwick, an Englishman who spent three years in the goldfields, came to that conclusion in 1851, when he wrote: "In the mines the Americans seemed to exhibit more tolerance of negro blood than is usual in the states...."[12] The popularity of black-owned boardinghouses and restaurants in the gold country, the apparent ease of African Americans in establishing mining claims, the relaxed racial etiquette of the saloon and gambling house, where multiracial patrons casually interacted with little tension, attest to the appealing idea that racial barriers had fallen as all men and women had become, to quote a popular gold rush–era poem, "to gold a slave." Such equality did not last. As frontier conditions quickly gave way to settlement, first in San Francisco and Sacramento and by 1860 in the gold country itself, traditional racial parameters were soon established.

The population center of antebellum black California was in the mother lode, but its political, intellectual, and cultural centers emerged in San Francisco and Sacramento. The 1852 state census listed 464 African Americans in the state's principal seaport and 338 in the state capital. Such figures, however, underestimate the significance of the two cities as points of arrival for newcomers destined for the goldfields, as winter quarters, as entertainment centers for black miners, and as potential areas of retirement for both successful and unsuccessful argonauts. Eventually the cities claimed the residential allegiance of most blacks.

Most African Americans in gold rush California, including many community leaders, were free and from eastern cities. Typical of such San Francisco leaders were James P. Dyer of New Bedford, Massachusetts, and former Philadelphians Mifflin Gibbs and Peter Lester, while Sacramento claimed former Baltimorean the Reverend Darius Stokes. Even ex-slaves from rural backgrounds, such as Georgia-born Mary Ellen Pleasant and former North Carolinian James R. Starkey, found western urban life far more congenial.

Antebellum urban California blacks pursued a range of occupations similar to those available in eastern cities, although the gold-enriched economy provided significantly higher wages for the most menial positions. Black stewards on river steamers earned $150 a month during the 1850s. At the top of this employment hierarchy stood the cook. Of the 464 blacks in San Francisco in 1852, 67 were cooks. Sacramento, with 338 black residents, had 51 African American cooks. The designation *cook,* however, obscured the vast range of incomes African Americans received in this occupation. Mary Ellen Pleasant's reputation as a cook had preceded her when she arrived in the city in 1852, and she was besieged at the wharf by men anxious to employ her. She ultimately selected an employer who promised $500 a month, a gold miner's average income. Next came barbers and stewards. San Francisco in 1852 had 22 black stewards and 18 black barbers, Sacramento 8 and 23 respectively. Yet most African American men and women worked at unskilled positions—"whitewashers," porters, waiters, maids, and servants—in businesses and private homes.[13]

A few fortunate African Americans in San Francisco became wealthy business owners. Mary Ellen Pleasant, perhaps the most celebrated black property owner in antebellum California, owned three laundries and was involved in mining stock and precious metals speculation. John Ross operated Ross's Exchange, a used-goods business, while James P. Dyer, the West's only antebellum black manufacturer, began the New England Soap Factory in 1851. Former slave George Washington Dennis managed a successful livery business in the city.

Mifflin W. Gibbs, who arrived in San Francisco in 1850 with ten cents and initially worked as a bootblack, in 1851 formed a partnership with fellow Philadelphian Peter Lester to operate the Pioneer Boot and Shoe Emporium, a store that eventually had "patrons extending to Oregon and lower California." By 1854 black San Francisco could proudly boast of "two black-owned joint stock companies with a combined capital of $16,000, four boot and shoe stores, four clothing stores, two furniture stores, two billiard saloons, sixteen barbershops, and two bathhouses . . . 100 mechanics, 100 porters in banking and commercial houses, 150 stewards, 300 waiters, and 200 cooks." Much of black California's wealth stemmed, however, from rapidly appreciating urban real estate. During the first statewide Colored Convention in 1855, delegates listed assets of $750,000 for California's population.[14]

The goldfields proved a temporary home for African American miners, but black urban residents created permanent communities. San Francisco's black community was the first indication of this permanency. Between 1849 and 1855 most African American residents settled near the waterfront and expanded slowly from there. The eastward-facing slope of Telegraph Hill was home to most blacks in a larger mixed community of color that evolved in a section derisively termed Chili Hill because of the concentration of Latin Americans. Occupying the same neighborhood of tents, shacks, saloons, hotels, and gambling houses, Mexican American, Chilean, and African American sailors, miners, and laborers pooled resources in one of the earliest examples of cooperation among people of color. In 1854, for example, Mexican Americans and African Americans organized a pre-Christmas masquerade ball.[15]

Middle-class African Americans lived throughout the city, often on the premises of their shops. For them the parameters of the black community were cultural rather than physical. They created institutions that brought together blacks from throughout the city for spiritual and social support. As usual the church became the first permanent institution. The first African American church in California was St. Andrews African Methodist Episcopal (AME), organized by the Reverend Bernard Fletcher in Sacramento in 1851. The following year the Reverend John Jamison Moore, a former slave, founded the AME Zion Church of San Francisco; four years after its founding the church occupied a brick building and had a Sabbath school with fifty pupils and a library of 250 books. The Third Baptist Church was also organized in 1852 by thirteen congregants led by

Joseph Davenport. Later in the year came Bethel AME church, led by a white clergyman, the Reverend Joseph Thompson, before the arrival of the Reverend (later Bishop) Thomas M. D. Ward in 1854. Also in 1854 the Reverend Fletcher arrived from Sacramento to organize St. Cyprian AME Church, which quickly became the largest church in the city as well as the site of the first public school for black children in California. The role of these churches as moral and spiritual base in an underdeveloped urban society was important in its own right, but they also assumed other responsibilities. The congregations supported orphans and widows with food and money, aided victims of such natural disasters as the 1861 Sacramento flood, raised money to assist the sick and wounded soldiers of the all-black Fifty-fourth Massachusetts Regiment during the Civil War, and aided both California Indians and southern freedmen immediately after 1865.[16]

Antebellum California urban African Americans promoted cooperative endeavor and community building. In December 1849 thirty-seven black San Francisco men, mostly ex-New Englanders, formed the West's first black self-help organization, the Mutual Benefit and Relief Society, to assist newcomers and encourage other African Americans to emigrate to California. This society was succeeded four years later by the San Francisco Atheneum, a two-story men's club housing a first floor saloon for social gatherings, but whose second story, called the Atheneum Institute, soon became a center of black intellectual life. Former New Englanders, New Yorkers, and Pennsylvanians organized the institute, electing Jacob Francis, a Rochester, New York, native and an associate of Frederick Douglass, as its first president. Within a year the institute had eighty-five dues-paying members who raised two thousand dollars to support an eight-hundred-book library. The Atheneum hosted community debates over abolitionist political activity and emigration to Latin America or Africa. It also housed strategy sessions on the various legal challenges to slavery and to California's antiblack laws. Later the institute led the campaign for a statewide African American newspaper, *Mirror of the Times,* which in 1856 became the first antebellum African American newspaper west of St. Louis.[17]

The black population of Sacramento also grew rapidly during the early 1850s. Most blacks were cooks, barbers, and boardinghouse keepers. In the last category the Hackett House, owned by a former Pennsylvanian, J. Hackett, was considered the largest African American business in the city and the center of social and political life for black Sacramento. A second, smaller hotel, the St. Nicholas, was distinctive for the period in that it employed three Chinese men. The black population was concentrated in residences along the banks of the Sacramento River, sharing its neighborhood with Mexican and Chinese settlers. All three groups were subject to random attacks by "rowdy young men and boys" who vandalized black- and Chinese-owned businesses. Because of its proximity to the mother lode, black Sacramento had a large transient male population and few religious and cultural institutions. By 1860 it claimed the only two African American doctors in the far West and its only engineer. Yet its African American residents were less wealthy and educated and far more likely to be southern-born former slaves than San Francisco blacks. The diverging trajectories of the two communities was best seen in their population increases. In 1860 San Francisco had 1,176 African Americans compared with 394 in Sacramento.[18]

Marysville, Grass Valley, Placerville, and Stockton were the only other cities in antebellum northern California that had any sizable black presence. Marysville and Stockton attracted ex-miners seeking permanent occupations. Many of them typically became barbers, porters, laborers, and male and female servants. Stockton, however, reflecting its importance as an agricultural community, listed a few African Americans as farmers and vaqueros. Histories of the region

Black Population in Antebellum California Cities

	1850	1852*	1860
San Francisco	NA	464	1,176
Sacramento	191	338	394
Marysville	NA	NA	118
Stockton	NA	NA	93
Placerville	21	NA	67
Los Angeles	12	NA	66
Grass Valley	6	NA	62

* California state census.

Source: U.S. Bureau of the Census, Seventh Census of the United States, 1850 (Washington, D.C.: Robert Armstrong, Public Printer, 1853), 970–71; U.S. Bureau of the Census, Eighth Census of the United States, 1860, Population (Washington, D.C.: Government Printing Office, 1864), 29–32. Governor's Message and Report of the Secretary of State on the Census of 1852 (Sacramento: George Kerr, State Printer, 1853), 6–55.

and era occasionally provide glimpses into community life in these towns. Marysville's 118 African American residents in 1860 maintained a community centered on the Mount Olivet Baptist Church. Founded in 1853, the church was supported not only by parishioners but also by committees of churchwomen who conducted fund-raising "Ladies' Festivals" featuring baked goods and knitwear popular with white residents. Similar female-organized fund-raising activities also sustained small AME churches in Placerville, Grass Valley, and Stockton.[19]

Los Angeles had the only significant black population in southern California. Most black Angelenos were ex-slave servants brought to California by white officers during the Mexican War. Typical of this group was Peter Biggs, a former Missouri slave who became the city's first barber and bootblack. Biggs married a Mexican woman, Juana Margarita, and during the 1860s had a monopoly on the barbering trade in this city of forty-three hundred. The small black Angeleno population also included the Owens family, which rode the post–Civil War southern California real estate boom to become the wealthiest African American family in the state by the end of the century. The Owens family saga began in Texas, where Robert Owens first earned his freedom and then worked to purchase, in turn, his wife, Minnie, and his children, Charles, Sarah Jane, and Martha. After bringing his family from Texas to Los Angeles in 1850 by an ox-drawn wagon, Robert held odd jobs and Minnie took in washing until he received a government contract to supply wood for local military installations. By 1860 the Owens family had a flourishing livery business employing ten Mexican vaqueros to break wild horses and supply cattle for sale to newly arriving settlers. The Owens homestead became the center of community life in 1854, when the family invited other blacks to attend religious services in its residence. The family reputation was enhanced when the Owenses assisted Biddy Mason's family in its legal battle to obtain its freedom. Afterward the two families merged through marriage of the eldest children. Their descendants played prominent roles in Los Angeles's African American community through the end of the century.[20]

The four statewide California Colored Conventions proved the greatest example of the political sophistication of antebellum black California. These all-male conventions, designed to present political grievances and chronicle black success, evolved out of a tradition of black collective leadership dating from the second decade of the nineteenth century, when the first national Colored Convention was held at Philadelphia in 1817. By the 1830s smaller statewide conventions were meeting in Ohio, Michigan, and Illinois. Black Californians held four conventions between 1855 and 1865. The first two were in Sacramento in 1855 and 1856. The third was held in San Francisco in 1857. Black Californians returned to Sacramento for the last Convention in 1865.

State convention leaders, such as Henry M. Collins, Jonas Townsend, Jeremiah B. Sanderson, Frederick Barbadoes, Peter Lester, Jacob Francis, David W. Ruggles, and Mifflin W. Gibbs, had been prominent abolitionists and convention supporters before migrating to California in the 1850s. They maintained their links to the national movement by subscribing to *Frederick Douglass' Paper,* and by contributing articles to that and other abolitionist journals, including the *National Anti-Slavery Standard* and the *Pennsylvania Freeman.*[22]

Black protest was inspired by high principle, but it also was driven by indignity and, on occasion, by physical danger. That point was made clear in an 1851 incident involving San Francisco's leading African American business, Lester and Gibbs's Pioneer Boot and Shoe Emporium. During an argument a white customer beat Lester with his cane and left the store without paying for a pair of boots. Since the assault occurred without white witnesses, Lester could not prosecute his attacker. The following year Mifflin Gibbs, William Newby, and Jonas Townsend organized an unsuccessful petition campaign to repeal the discriminatory sections of the testimony statute. The First State Convention of the Colored Citizens of the State of California evolved three years later from that campaign.[23]

Forty-nine delegates representing ten of California's twenty-seven counties attended the convention at St. Andrews AME Church in Sacramento. Twenty-eight of them represented San Francisco and Sacramento. The other delegates spoke for Sierra, Yuba, El Dorado, Nevada, and other mother lode counties as well as San Joaquin, Contra Costa, and Santa Clara counties. Once assembled, the delegates debated the testimony prohibition. They empowered a committee to organize another petition campaign urging repeal of California's onerous law and voted to raise twenty thousand dollars to fund the campaign. Fully conscious of their history-making gathering, Sacramento delegate Jeremiah B. Sanderson proclaimed the convention "the most important step on this side of the Continent." After describing the accumulated wealth of black Californians, the convention called on the state's urban African Americans to turn to farming. The convention concluded with an eloquent statement aimed at white California: "You have been wont to multiply our vices, and never to see our virtues. You call upon us to pay enormous taxes to support Government, at the same time you deny us the protection you extend to others; the security of life and property. . . . [Y]ou receive our money to educate your children, and then refuse to admit our children into the common schools. . . ." It concluded with the appeal that "justice may be meted out to all, without respect to complexion . . . and that the shield of wise, wholesome and equal laws, extend all over your great state." Five thousand copies of the convention proceedings circulated among black Californians and their supporters.[24]

Two conventions followed in 1856 and 1857. While both continued to call attention to the testimony law, the 1856 convention assumed publication of *Mirror of the Times* as "the State Organ of the colored people of California." It also voted a special tribute to the African American women who had organized the Mirror Association to support the fledgling newspaper. The 1857 convention, the last till 1865, condemned the U.S. Land Office's prohibition on black homesteading of public lands and protested the exclusion of black children from public schools in rural counties. When the Democratic-controlled state legislature proved increasingly intransigent on the testimony prohibition and introduced a measure to outlaw black immigration to the state, some four hundred disillusioned black Californians (about 10 percent of the state's population), including political leaders Mifflin Gibbs and Peter Lester, emigrated to British Columbia in 1858.[25]

Leland Stanford's election in 1862 as California's first Republican governor proved encouraging. Sensing growing popular support, San Francisco blacks created the Franchise League in 1862 to campaign for voting rights and an end to testimony restrictions. Meanwhile the Republican-dominated legislature partly obliged them by removing discriminatory barriers in education. But the crowning achievement was the elimination of the testimony restriction. In 1863 the Republican-dominated legislature repealed the antiblack provision of the testimony statute. However, it maintained the prohibition against "Indian, Mongolian, and Chinese" testimony.[26]

In the Civil War years California's African Americans also challenged segregated public transportation in successful lawsuits. On May 26, 1863, San Franciscan William Bowen was ejected from a streetcar operated by the North Beach and Mission Railroad. He filed a civil suit for $10,000 in damages. The case eventually ended in district court, where on December 21, 1864, a jury awarded him $3,199 in damages. The Charlotte Brown case began a month earlier than Bowen's on April 17, 1863, when she was ejected from a San Francisco streetcar operated by the Omnibus Company. She filed suit for $200 in damages in county court. The case first came before Judge Maurice C. Blake, who reminded the jury that California law prohibited the exclusion of blacks from streetcars. Nonetheless the jury awarded Brown five cents in damages (the cost of the fare). Three days after the trial she was again ejected from an Omnibus streetcar and once again filed suit, this time in Twelfth District Court for $3,000 in damages. Her second suit ended on January 17, 1865, when a jury awarded her $500 in damages. These victories, however, did not abolish streetcar exclusion. In 1868 the California Supreme Court reversed on appeal lower court judgments in favor of Mary E. Pleasant and Emma J. Turner, who had brought similar suits against the North Beach and Mission Railroad. The campaign for unfettered access to public transportation continued in San Francisco, as elsewhere in the West. In California black access to both public transportation and accommodations was assured only in 1893 with the enactment of an antidiscrimination law.[27]

When the Emancipation Proclamation took effect on January 1, 1863, local black leaders marked the event with public speeches and festivals. The black San Francisco poet James Madison Bell captured the new spirit of optimism and promise with "A Fitting Time to Celebrate," a poem written for the occasion. After emancipation African Americans in the state's largest city began to participate in the general community, raising hundreds of dollars for the Sanitary Fund, the forerunner of the American Red Cross, and taking part in Fourth of July celebrations.

Much of this optimism was promoted by a new newspaper, the *Pacific Appeal.* Founded by Philip A. Bell and Peter Anderson in 1862, the *Appeal* established a long tradition of journalistic activism. Bell was one of the most experienced newspaper editors and political activists in the nation when he arrived in San Francisco in 1858. A graduate of the African Free School in New York, a leading antebellum educational institution, Bell counted among his classmates the actor Ira Aldridge and the abolitionists Alexander Crummell, Henry Highland Garnet, and Samuel Ringgold Ward. After editing New York's *Weekly Advocate* in 1837, he became one of four coeditors of the *Colored American*, the most successful African American newspaper of the period. Peter Anderson had less journalism experience but was a former correspondent for eastern black newspapers and one of the founders of *Mirror of the Times*. Dissatisfied with Anderson's moderate editorial policy at the *Pacific Appeal*, Bell left the paper in 1865 to begin the *Elevator*. Although their editorial styles varied and Anderson was more politically conservative, both spoke eloquently for black Californians.[28]

As Civil War–inspired political changes swept through California, the state's African American leaders organized the fourth statewide political convention at Bethel AME Church in Sacramento in October 1865. This convention, more optimistic about the African American future in the West, "devise[d] ways and means for obtaining . . . the right for elective franchise." Invoking the specter of international concern over local discrimination, the convention called suffrage denial "unwise," considering the soon-to-be-established trade with the "copper-colored nations of China and Japan." Although the delegates addressed old problems, such as the exclusion of black students from rural public schools, they also urged the "colored people of the Pacific States and Territories, to secure farms and homesteads [and] to seek unsettled lands and pre-empt them, as is the right of every American citizen." Mindful that construction would soon begin on the transcontinental railroad linking Omaha to Oakland, the convention urged the hiring of forty thousand freedmen to lay its tracks. Finally, the delegates placed black California on record as being sympathetic to "the oppressed of all nations, every race and clime," and willing to "extend our aid to every effort to free themselves from bondage, whether it is personal servitude or political disfranchisement." The resolution specifically mentioned the Poles and Hungarians then attempting to gain their independence from Russia and Austria. Finally, in a surprising resolution, given the rivalry between black and Irish workers, the convention declared support for the Irish independence campaign against the British Empire.[29]

Kansas had the only other significant concentration of free black westerners prior to 1865. Black Kansas was virtually created by the Civil War itself. The late 1850s battle for "bleeding Kansas" ended in a victory for free-state partisans. Yet the territory by 1860 attracted only 627 African Americans. By 1865, however, more than 12,000 blacks resided in Kansas, comprising 9 percent of the population. This population explosion came from a combination of politics and geography. "Free" Kansas posed an enticing destination to the large Missouri slave population.

During the 1850s Kansas attracted abolitionists, who set up Underground Railroad stations. Moreover, although only a minority of Kansas whites approved of their actions, antislavery partisans, such as James H. Lane, James Montgomery, Charles Jennison, and John Brown, who resided briefly in Kansas, led bands of Jayhawkers into Missouri in the late 1850s, raiding for slaves they escorted back across the border, creating what one historian of Missouri slavery describes as the "golden age of slave absconding." John Brown, known primarily for the revengeful terror he inflicted on proslavery settlers in the Pottawatomie Creek massacre, is also remembered by local blacks and abolitionists for his dramatic "rescue" of eleven slaves from a Missouri plantation on Christmas Night 1858. He and his relatives concealed the women in a frontier home and the men in corn shacks for more than a month in Kansas while slave catchers searched in vain. If northern black and white abolitionists lectured against slavery and occasionally protected fugitives who fled the South, white Kansans entered a slaveholding state to rescue black men and women from bondage.[30]

Slaves also acted on their own, fleeing for the Kansas-Missouri border and then on to Lawrence, "the best advertised anti-slavery town in the world." Missouri slaves learned quickly which people and places in Kansas Territory to seek out or to shun. Many fugitives sought the branch of the Underground Railroad that extended from western Missouri into Lawrence and Topeka, through Nebraska Territory, Iowa, Chicago, and finally to Canada. While Kansas abolitionists and Missouri slaveholders exaggerated the numbers of escaped slaves, clearly western Missouri, isolated from other slaveholding regions and close to free western territories, proved susceptible to servile flight.[31]

Opportunities for flight increased dramatically in 1861. Kansas entered the Union on January 29, 1861, barely five weeks before Lincoln's inauguration and one month after South Carolina's secession. The first state legislature chose two U.S. senators, one of whom, James H. Lane, was to play a crucial role in the fate of African Americans in this border region. A passionate, volatile abolitionist, Lane fused his military responsibilities and his antislavery goals. The Kansas senator envisioned a powerful slave-liberating southern expeditionary force that would march from Kansas through Indian Territory to Texas. He never completely abandoned this goal, but his immediate task, to defend Kansas from Missouri secessionists, prompted him to raise a regiment of twelve hundred troops to repulse an expected invasion by Confederate General Sterling Price. The invasion did not occur, and Lane's forces instead marched into southwest Missouri in August 1861. News of his presence encouraged fugitive slaves to seek out his camp near Springfield. Without authorization from higher military or civilian authorities, Lane enlisted male fugitives into his command and sent the women and children to Kansas "to help save the crop and provide fuel for the winter." This impetuous and largely symbolic act created the first African American troops in the Union army during the Civil War.[32]

In early September Lane dispatched his 3 chaplains to lead 218 refugees out of Missouri to Fort Scott, Kansas. The Reverend Hugh Dunn Fisher, placed in charge of the party, armed 30 black males with "almost useless guns" and sent out advance and rear scouts to warn the caravan of Confederate attack. When the refugees finally reached Kansas, Fisher ordered silence and then under "the open heavens, on the sacred soil of freedom . . . proclaimed that they were forever free." When word of Lane's action as a "liberator" spread, other Missouri slaves and refugees from Arkansas and Indian Territory made their way toward Kansas. In a speech before the New York Emancipation League in June 1862, Lane boasted that 5,000 fugitives from Missouri and Arkansas were in Kansas and that he had personally "aided 2,500 in their escape." He also claimed command of 1,200 black soldiers in Kansas. Although he grossly exaggerated his impact on the black freedom, numerous fugitives sought refuge in Kansas.[33]

The enormous scale of the flight from slaveholding Missouri becomes evident when one examines the slave population statistics for the period. Between 1860 and 1863 Missouri's slaves declined from 114,931 to 73,811. Some Missouri slaveholders sent or carried their slaves south to Arkansas, Indian Territory, and Texas. Other slaves fled across the Mississippi River to Illinois or north to Iowa. But many of them made the perilous dash west. Henry Clay Bruce, the brother of future Mississippi Senator Blanche K. Bruce, recounted in his autobiography how he and his fiancée escaped from Missouri to Kansas in 1863. Bruce strapped around his waist "a pair of Colt's revolvers and plenty of ammunition" for the run to the western border. "We avoided the main road and made the entire trip

Esteban, ca. 1539. *David J. and Carol Bryant Weber Collection*

York in the Camp of the Mandans, 1805. *Montana Historical Society*

James P. Beckwourth.
Nevada Historical Society

Negroes for sale. *Center for American History, University of Texas at Austin*

NEGROES FOR SALE.—I will offer for sale, in the
City of Austin, before Stringer's Hotel, on the
1st day of January next, to the highest bidder, in
Confederate or State Treasury Notes, the following
lot of likely Negroes, to wit. Three Negro Girls
and two Boys, ages ranging from 15 to 16 years.
The title to said Negroes is indisputable.
  dec25-2t*   SQUIRE S. CONNETT.

Frontier family in Brewster County, Texas. *Southwest Collection, Texas Tech University*

Green Flake, among the first party of settlers to reach the Salt Lake Valley in 1847. *Utah State Historical Society*

Abner Hunt Francis mercantile store, Portland, Oregon, 1858. *Oregon Historical Society*

Black and white gold miners near Spanish Flat, California, 1852. *California State Library, Sacramento, California*

African Methodist Episcopal
Zion Church, San Francisco,
1864. *California Historical Society*

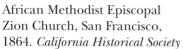

Mary Ellen Pleasant at
eighty-seven. *Bancroft
Library, University of California, Berkeley*

First Kansas Colored Volunteers, ca. 1863.
Kansas Historical Society

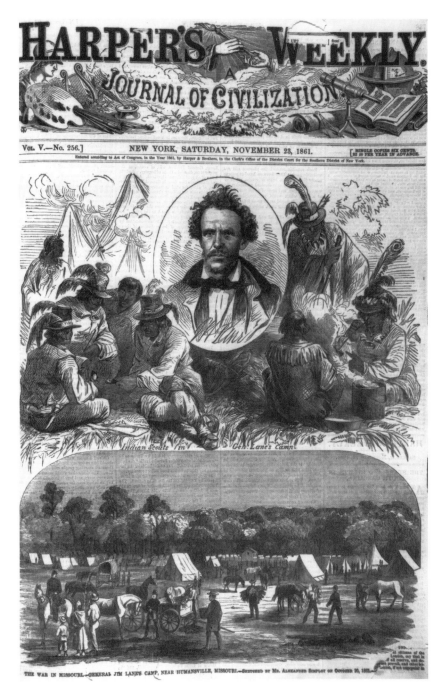

General James Lane (*Harper's* illustration), 1861.
Kansas Historical Society

William Jefferson Hardin in the Wyoming Territorial Legislature, 1882. *Wyoming Division of Cultural Resources*

A Creek freedman's home, ca. 1880. *Western History Collection, University of Oklahoma Library*

Freedwomen washing laundry along creek near Circleville, Texas, ca. 1866. *Austin History Center, Austin Public Library*

Nicodemus street scene, ca. 1885. *Kansas Historical Society*

Benjamin Singleton and S. A. McClure, Negro emigrants leaving Nashville, Tennessee, for Kansas, April 15, 1876. *Kansas Historical Society*

Moses Speece family, Custer County, Nebraska, 1888. *Nebraska State Historical Society*

Family and dugout home near Guthrie, Oklahoma Territory, 1889.
Western History Collection, University of Oklahoma Library

Edwin P. McCabe.
Western History Collection, University of Oklahoma Library

Oliver T. Jackson, founder of Dearfield. *City of Greeley Museums, Greeley, Colorado*

Black cowboy roping steer, ca. 1880. *American Heritage Center, University of Wyoming*

African American cowboys near Bonham, Texas, 1909. *Amon Carter Museum, Fort Worth, Texas*

Captain Dodge's Colored Troops to the rescue, 1891. *Frederic Remington Art Museum, Ogdensburg, New York*

K Troop, Ninth Cavalry on the Pine Ridge, Dakota Territory. *Nebraska State Historical Society*

African American cavalrymen in Montana, 1894. *Montana Historical Society*

Buffalo soldiers and wives near Fort Keogh, Montana, ca. 1890. *Montana Historical Society*

Buffalo soldier and Indian wife. *Buehman Collection, Arizona Historical Society*

Tenth Cavalry prisoners, Carrizal, Mexico, 1916. *Fort Bliss Museum*

Court-martial of 24th Infantry, Fort Sam Houston. *Mike Kaliski, San Antonio, Texas*

... without meeting anyone.... We crossed the Missouri River on a ferry boat to Fort Leavenworth, Kansas. I then felt myself a free man."[34]

The Civil War influx swelled the state's black population to 12,527 in 1865. The migrants concentrated in three counties, Leavenworth, Douglas, and Wyandotte, which had 56 percent of the total black population. Moreover, two Kansas towns—Leavenworth with 2,400 blacks, and Lawrence with nearly 1,000—contained 72 percent of the state's urban black population. From the beginning of the war Senator Lane and other abolitionists envisioned an exchange of black labor for black freedom. The fugitive slaves who arrived in the state were dispersed through rural counties to cultivate and harvest crops. Very little machinery was available to grow wheat, a principal crop in the 1860s, and since most white males were in the Federal army, black laborers were especially welcomed and were credited with producing the bountiful harvest of 1863. The *Fort Scott Bulletin* in 1862 observed that almost every farm in the Neosho River valley "was supplied with labor in the shape of a good healthy thousand dollar Contraband, to do the work while the husbands, fathers and brothers are doing the fighting." Even Senator Lane employed former slaves to grow cotton on his Douglas County farm.[35]

Other refugees depended upon work and charity in towns and cities. John B. Wood of Lawrence wrote Boston abolitionist George L. Stearns in November 1861, warning that the thousands of black wheat field workers would soon be unemployed and sure to gather in Lawrence. Fearing their plight would overwhelm the town, Wood requested financial assistance from the "friends of humanity at the East," to feed and clothe the ex-slaves. Wood's fears proved groundless. Most of the migrants found or created work, and thus, according to Richard Cordley, "very few, if any of them, became objects of charity."[36]

If most Lawrence blacks avoided charity, the type of work they performed and the skills they brought from their slave experience guaranteed that they were never far from that condition. The state census of 1865 showed 349 employed blacks in Lawrence. Of these, 95 men were listed as soldiers, while 85 were day laborers, the second largest occupational category. Of the 92 female workers, 49 were domestics, 27 were washerwomen, and 7 worked as housekeepers, 6 as servants and 3 as cooks. Thus 177 blacks, half of the town's total, worked as unskilled laborers. Of the one-fifth who were skilled, 23 were teamsters, 8 were blacksmiths, and 4 barbers. Lawrence also had 1 black saloonkeeper, 1 carpenter, 1 shoemaker, 1 printer, and 1 preacher.[37]

After 1862 Lawrence's residents began to recognize a permanent black settlement. "The Negroes are not coming. They are here. They will stay here," asserted abolitionist Richard Cordley, "They are to be our neighbors, whatever we may think about it, whatever we may do about it." White Lawrence citizens supported efforts to teach ex-slaves literacy. While black children attended public schools during the day, adults joined a night school that met for two hours five nights a week. Classes were taught by volunteer teachers, including future Mississippi Senator Blanche K. Bruce, who instructed approximately 125 pupils. The refugees themselves founded Freedmen's Church on September 28, 1862. The first black church in Lawrence was described as a "comfortable brick [building] . . . filled with an attentive congregation of 'freedmen'—all lately from bondage, and all neatly dressed as a result of their short experience of free labor."[38]

Leavenworth, the oldest and largest Civil War–era Kansas town, also had a sizable African American population, 2,455 in 1865, 16 percent of the population. Like most black newcomers to Kansas, Leavenworth's African Americans were mostly fugitives who had arrived "wholly destitute of the means of living." Leavenworth's civic leaders met with members of the First Colored Baptist Church in February 1862, to "take into consideration measures for the amelioration of the condition of the colored people. . . ." Whites at that meeting included Colonel Daniel R. Anthony (brother of women's suffrage advocate Susan B. Anthony), Dr. R. C. Anderson, and Richard J. Hinton, a prominent abolitionist and journalist. African American community leaders included the Reverend Robert Caldwell of the Baptist Church, Lewis Overton, a teacher in a black community-sponsored school, and William Mathews, destined to become one of the first black officers in the Union army. Hinton proposed the founding of the Kansas Emancipation League, whose object was to "assist all efforts to destroy slavery" and to provide help for the freedpeople arriving in the Leavenworth area.[39]

Leavenworth African Americans found employment in a variety of occupations. Some worked on farms during the spring and summer, but a much larger number were employed as teamsters, hotel waiters, porters, cooks, maids, and manual laborers. The Emancipation League's Labor Exchange and Intelligence Office, in Dr. R. C. Anderson's drugstore, became an informal employment agency for local blacks. Yet the rapid influx of fugitive slaves, their few skills, and the small size of the town ensured that their employment prospects remained circumscribed. From 1862 to 1865 the Emancipation League, the Baptist Church, and interested black and white individuals continued to provide support for the fugitives.[40]

Not all black Kansans welcomed the ex-slaves. Freeborn blacks in Leavenworth derisively termed the Missourians "contrabands," and by 1865 they were attempting to exclude the wartime migrants from their organizations and social circles. Ex-slave ministers Jesse Mills and Moses White were denied permanent churches in Kansas even though both were able preachers and White had founded the African Methodist Episcopal Church in Leavenworth. Yet since the newcomers were the overwhelming majority of the population, they supplanted the political and social leadership of the tiny prewar population. African American women in Lawrence organized the Ladies Refugee Aid Society to collect food, clothing, and money and to assist destitute ex-slaves. The society foreshadowed the Kansas Federation of Colored Women's Clubs and provided a model for self-help activities that extended well into the twentieth century.[41]

"Soldiering" led all occupations among black males in Lawrence, Leavenworth, and the rest of the state. The reason is readily apparent. Fugitive slaves saw the Civil War as a struggle for emancipation. Many wanted a role in freeing relatives and friends who remained behind. Western Union army commanders had few reservations about recruiting and incorporating black or Indian soldiers. Senator James Lane set the tone in a speech in Leavenworth in January 1862, declaring that "if negroes attached to his army secured guns, he did not intend to punish them for killing 'traitors.' " Official support for recruiting black soldiers in Kansas came in July 1862, when Brigadier General James G. Blunt, a Lane political ally and the commander of the Department of Kansas, wrote to Colonel William Weer, authorizing him to accept "all persons, without reference to color," who were "willing to fight for the American flag . . . and the Federal Government." Thirty-five-year-old Blunt, a former frontier doctor and abolitionist, had helped John Brown spirit slaves to Canada. He seized the opportunity to make the military contest in the West a war for black liberation. The following month Lane informed Secretary of War Edwin Stanton that the state would furnish two regiments of black soldiers.[42]

Lane presented a carefully crafted public image as a courageous leader dedicated to black liberation much like his hero, John Brown.

But Lane in fact exhibited a callous disregard for the people he vowed to free from bondage. Arriving at Leavenworth on August 3, 1862, he announced that all able-bodied African American males between the ages of eighteen and forty-five could join the First Kansas Colored Infantry Regiment of the "Liberating Army." He called for a thousand volunteers at a black mass meeting and then added, "We have been saying that you would fight, and if you won't, we will make you." Moreover, Lane ignored charges that his recruiters "unlawfully restrained persons of their liberty" and paid cash bonuses for seized Missouri slaves who were delivered to Kansas recruiting stations.[43]

Such practices continued even after Lee's surrender at Appomattox. In June 1865 Captain H. Ford Douglas, the highest-ranking African American officer in Kansas, took the extraordinary step of requesting that the Kansas Independent Battery of the U.S. Colored Light Artillery under his command be immediately mustered out of service. Douglas told of black Kansans being beaten and dragged from their wives and children in midwinter, starved until sheer exhaustion, and then compelled to join the U.S. Army. Seventy-five percent of the men under his command that June were "victims of a cruel and shameless conscription . . . in opposition to all civil and military law." Following an investigation by the War Department, the men were mustered out on July 22, 1865.[44]

Most African Americans, however, eagerly fought against the Confederacy. Senator Lane promised ten dollars per month as well as "good" quarters, rations, and clothing. In addition to the pay and provisions, certificates of freedom were issued to each black enlistee and his immediate family. By September 12, 1862, the "colored" regiment was six hundred strong. Captain George J. Martin reported that "the men learn[ed] their duties with great ease and rapidity" and were "delighted with the prospect of fighting for their freedom." On October 17, 1862, the First Kansas Colored Infantry was organized near Fort Lincoln in Bourbon County.[45]

The First Kansas Colored was soon sent to secure Federal control of the northeastern part of Indian Territory. The regiment became part of the Army of the Frontier, a unit remarkable in the annals of U.S. military history. This triracial force of three thousand soldiers included loyal Indian regiments, white regiments from the western states and territories, and now the First Kansas Colored. While stationed in Indian Territory, the First Kansas Colored undertook a number of military assignments. It fought Confederate guerrilla leader Colonel William C. Quantrill in 1863 and the following year faced Colonel Stand Watie, the Cherokee commander of Confederate Indian forces. The regiment suffered a humiliating defeat at the hands of Confederates at Flat Rock in September 1864.[46]

On July 17, 1863, the First Kansas Colored fought in the largest single Civil War engagement in Indian Territory, the Battle of Honey Springs. Confederate troops, eager to drive Union occupying forces from Indian Territory, launched an attack on the Federal lines at Honey Springs. Posted in shoulder-high prairie grass, 500 black soldiers, flanked on each side by Cherokee Indian and dismounted white Colorado cavalry units, held the crucial center of the Union line. Arrayed against this forward position of the Army of the Frontier were 6,000 Confederates. The battle commenced with a dawn artillery exchange, followed at 10:00 A.M. by an order for Union forces to advance. Confederate artillery bombarded the advancing troops, particularly the First Kansas Colored, "tearing huge gaps in the Union line." Nonetheless Union units advanced until forty yards from the Confederate front line held by the Twenty-ninth Texas Infantry. Then Union and Confederate troops fired simultaneous volleys. Thinking the Union forces had retreated after the initial volley, Confederate commander Charles DeMorse ordered his troops to charge the Union lines, which fired another volley. The "first rank of the Twenty-ninth simply disappeared," and the remaining Confederate troops retreated. After the battle the First Kansas Colored soldiers discovered strewn among the abandoned Confederate supplies shackles that were to be used to chain the captured black soldiers. Eight days after the Battle of Honey Springs, General Blunt wrote in his report that the soldiers of the First Kansas Colored Regiment "fought like veterans, with a coolness and valor that is unsurpassed. They preserved their line perfect throughout the whole engagement and, although in the hottest of the fight, they never once faltered." By June 1863 a second Kansas "colored" regiment had been formed under Colonel Samuel J. Crawford, a future governor of the state. The Lane and Crawford regiments and a smaller brigade brought together 2,083 African American men for the Union cause, one-sixth of the African American population in Kansas in 1865.[47]

In October 1863 twenty-three delegates representing approximately seven thousand black Kansans gathered in Leavenworth for the first Kansas State Colored Convention. Most delegates, and the people they represented, had been in Kansas less than three years.

Nonetheless they pledged their future to Kansas. The delegates praised the help black Kansans received from sympathetic whites but then called for more self-reliance. "It does not follow, because so much is being done for us, that we can do nothing for ourselves." They called for universal male suffrage, access to public education, and federal pay for soldiers of the First Kansas Colored Regiment for their time in the army before January 1863. The convention opposed colonization of blacks abroad and urged the new Kansans to become farmers. It reiterated the necessity of black suffrage ". . . as in architecture, that building is most secure whose base is broadest, so in politics, that government is most permanent, whose base rests on the broadest foundations of liberty and justice." Finally it declared to white Kansas "our misery is not necessary to your happiness. . . . Your rights can never be secure whilst ours are denied."[48]

The October meeting was the first of a series of annual conventions of African American Kansans. Subsequent gatherings agitated for an amendment to the Kansas Constitution to guarantee black male voting rights. Black Kansans also demanded the right to serve in the state militia and on juries and called for an end to discriminatory practices in public transportation and public accommodations, initiating a century-long struggle to extend the prewar promise of freedom for slaves into the post–Civil War prospect of equal rights for all of the state's citizens.[49]

Voluntary pre–Civil War black migration was limited by slavery, which held 90 percent of African Americans in its grip. It was also discouraged by discriminatory legislation in California, Oregon, Kansas, and most western territories. However, the Thirteenth Amendment, which terminated slavery in 1865, also opened the West to tens of thousands of African American emigrants. They and their descendants were to place a profound social and cultural imprint on the region.

4

◇ ❀ ◇ ❀ ◇

Reconstruction in
the West,

1865–75

In February 1863, while the eastern United States fought the Civil War and the Emancipation Proclamation was less than two months old, Peter Anderson wrote an editorial in the *Pacific Appeal* that fused the destiny of the ex-slaves with the West. Anderson called on "our leading men in the east" to initiate a "system of land speculation west of Kansas, or in any of the Territories, and endeavor to infuse into the minds of these freedmen the importance of agriculture, that they may become producers. By this means they can come up with the expected growth of the Great West. . . ."[1]

Anderson envisioned a great march of freedpeople westward, urged on by "our leading men in the east," the federal government, and "our white friends who have been battling in the cause of freedom." But the great march did not come. Most freedpeople in the late 1860s saw their destiny in an economically and politically "reconstructed" South. The promise was so alluring that it briefly drew some westerners back East. San Francisco minister John Jamison Moore, former *Mirror of the Times* editor Jonas H. Townsend, and Mifflin W. Gibbs, British Columbia's first black officeholder, all moved to the South, casting their lot with the freedpeople. Their return prompted another San Francisco editor, Philip A. Bell, of the *Elevator*, to conclude in 1868: "The tide of travel is reversed. Our representative men are leaving us, going East, some never to return."[2]

The African American Population in
Western States and Territories, 1860–70

	1860	1870	Total Population 1870
Arizona Territory	u	26	9,658
California	4,086	4,272	560,247
Colorado Territory	46	456	39,864
Dakota Territory	u	94	14,181
Idaho Territory	u	60	14,999
Indian Territory	8,376	6,378	68,152
Kansas	627	17,108	364,399
Montana Territory	u	183	20,595
Nebraska	82	789	122,993
Nevada	45	357	42,491
New Mexico Territory	85	172	91,874
Oregon	128	346	90,923
Texas	182,921	253,475	818,579
Utah Territory	59	118	86,786
Washington Territory	30	207	23,955
Wyoming Territory	u	183	9,118

u—unorganized, part of a larger territory.

Sources: U.S. Bureau of the Census, Negro Population in the United States, 1790–1915 (Washington, D.C.: Government Printing Office, 1918), 43, 44; U.S. Bureau of the Census, Statistics of the Population of the United States, 1870 (Washington, D.C.: Government Printing Office, 1872), 3.

Bell proved as wrong as Anderson, for a steady trickle of blacks pushed westward. By 1870, 284,000 African Americans lived in the sixteen states and territories of the region and comprised 12 percent of the total population. The great concentrations were in Texas and Indian Territory, the major antebellum slaveholding areas. California and Kansas were the only other states with more than 4,000 black residents. Caution must be used in interpreting low figures elsewhere in the West. Blacks avoided some places, anticipating scant economic opportunity. Few African Americans, for example, migrated to Idaho and the Dakotas during this period, and the nineteenth-century African American population of Nevada peaked at 488 in 1880 and declined to 134 during the next two decades.[3]

Before the West could become secure for African American settlement, the various states and territories had to extend political rights to African Americans. The debate over those rights lasted from the end of the Civil War to the enactment of the Fifteenth Amendment in 1870. Reconstruction thus became not simply a conflict between the federal government and ex-Confederate states over their restoration to the Union but a larger national debate over the relationship between federal and state power.[4]

Black westerners paid attention to Reconstruction. They were understandably anxious that Reconstruction in the ex-Confederate states ensure suffrage and civil rights for the ex-slaves, but they also understood their own political disabilities. Denial of the rights to vote and to serve in the militia; exclusion from public schools, the jury box, and public transportation and accommodations; and prohibition of interracial marriages were painful reminders of the limitations on black freedom in the West. Thus Reconstruction meant black westerners' obtaining full citizenship within their states and territories.[5]

Despite a history of antiblack legislation in the West, by the 1860s some Euro-Americans began to speak on behalf of African American rights. John Martin, editor of the *Atchison* (Kansas) *Champion,* wrote in January 1865: "Give the negro a chance to make a man of himself. . . . Treat him as a human being and he will quickly assert by his own capacities and exertions his right to be regarded as one." Occasionally attitudes changed. Jesse Applegate of Oregon reminded Federal Judge Matthew P. Deady in 1865 that "it is not right to indulge prejudices of creed or race. . . ." Recalling Deady's prominent role in instituting Oregon's 1857 black exclusion clause, Applegate believed the judge had become a "wiser and better man" in abandoning his prejudices regarding blacks.[6]

Post–Civil War Texas, however, remained closer to the old South than the New West. Union General Gordon Granger's occupation force of eighteen hundred soldiers reached Galveston on June 19, 1865, initiating Texas Reconstruction. Granger immediately issued General Order No. 3, the Texas emancipation proclamation, which established "an absolute equality of personal rights and rights of property between former masters and slaves." However, he advised the freedpeople to sign labor contracts and remain with their old masters.[7]

Shortly after General Granger's proclamation, the Freedmen's Bureau was organized in Texas to assist ex-slaves in adjusting to their new legal and social status. Education for the freedpeople led the way. By 1870 forty-six bureau-sponsored schools were operating in the state, with the largest of these in Galveston, Houston, San Antonio, and Brownsville. The bureau reported 5,182 black pupils were attending those schools, compared with only 11 African American children enrolled in schools throughout the entire state ten years earlier.[8]

Emancipation fueled every emotion. Some former slaves, such as the people set free on the James Davis plantation in San Jacinto County, were disoriented and confused. "There was lots of crying and weeping," reported one ex-slave observer, "because they knew nothing and had nowhere to go." To others emancipation meant "no more whippings." After the local sheriff read Granger's proclamation in Austin, Harriet, a domestic slave, thinking more of her new baby's changed status than her own, ran home to her child and threw her in the air, crying "Tamar, you are free."[9]

Numerous slaves tested their freedom by leaving east Texas and Gulf Coast plantations. Some, brought to the state during the Civil War, immediately headed eastward, hoping to reunite with family members in the Old South. Others moved to Galveston, Houston, Austin, San Antonio, and other Texas cities. As one ex-slave remarked, they wanted "to get closer to freedom, so they'd know what it was—like a place or a city." Many ex-slaves sought out the cities because federal garrisons there offered protection from the racist violence that continued from emancipation until the end of the century.[10]

Many slaves were driven off plantations by angry landowners. Often such actions were taken in concert as dozens of planters in a county sought to punish the blacks for their freedom. In the fall of 1865 white citizens in Freestone County, for example, resolved to hire no blacks and to whip any freedman who tried to sign a labor contract with a white employer. Whites who violated the resolution were to be warned on the first offense and whipped or hanged on the second. Other owners were so disturbed by emancipation that they poisoned water wells or shot slaves who persisted in proclaiming their freedom. When future Texas Governor Oran M. Roberts called for the colonization of the freedpeople in west Texas, one Houston newspaper disingenuously argued that placing blacks among the Comanche and Apache, "the most savage of all the savages of America, [would] excite among them the most relentless fury. . . . It pleases us amazingly." Such extreme measures went against the economic interests of white employers as well as ex-slaves, but they indicated ex-Confederate resistance to the postwar political order.[11]

As in the Old South, moves to maintain white supremacy came long before the elected Reconstruction government of white and black Unionists assumed power in 1870. Ex-Confederates dominated the 1866 constitutional convention called to reestablish state government. Emboldened by President Johnson's lenient reconstruction policies, the convention accepted the end of slavery but not black suffrage. Instead it restricted black legal testimony, required racially segregated schools, called for dismantling the Freedmen's Bureau, and repudiated the recently enacted Civil Rights Act.[12]

The first postconvention legislature added railroad passenger segregation and black exclusion from service on juries or public officeholding. Reflecting the frontier status of much of the state, the legislature also enacted a "whites only" Texas Homestead Act that granted up to 160 acres of free land in west Texas. This measure alone did not prevent blacks from buying land, but coupled with the widespread opposition to land sales to the freedpeople, it froze most ex-slaves into a landless peasantry.[13]

However, the black codes enacted by this legislature constituted the cornerstone of the postwar social order orchestrated by the ex-Confederates. One code, a child apprenticeship law, allowed white employers to control the labor of black children until they were twenty-one or married. The contract labor code bound entire families to their employers, who could impose fines on any worker guilty of disobedience or unapproved absence. In fact laborers who missed three days of work forfeited an entire year's wages. Texas, like other ex-Confederate states, promulgated a vagrancy law to pressure blacks into accepting labor contracts. Another law established Texas's notorious convict leasing system. Those serving time in city or county jails for petty crimes could be hired out to railroads, iron foundries, ore mines, and public utilities. When a northern newspaper correspondent asked a white Texan if using prison labor to build a railroad through Rusk County was a safe practice, he was assured, "Of course, [the prisoners] haven't done anything very bad." The Texan's reassurances were all too accurate. At that time one black male convict was serving three years for stealing a twenty-five-cent can of sardines.[14]

The Texas black codes and similar measures in other ex-Confederate states generated a backlash in the North. Union objectives won on the battlefield were about to be sacrificed in the effort to reestablish civilian government in the South. Consequently northern voters in 1866 elected a huge Republican majority that halted temporarily the racial caste system evolving in Texas and other ex-Confederate states. In March 1867 Congress passed the first of three Reconstruction Acts. It divided the ex-Confederate states into five military districts and returned civil government to provisional status subject to military command. Each state was now required to call a new constitutional convention to be elected by all eligible male voters. The other acts denied voting rights to ranking ex-Confederates and stipulated that commanding generals supervise voter registration. The commanders were empowered to remove or suspend anyone in state government who blocked federal programs. Angry ex-Confederates and their sympathizers soon stepped up their campaign of terror and economic intimidation while white Unionists and newly enfranchised blacks moved to participate in a more democratic government.

Heeding a call from Texas Unionists, approximately 20 white and 150 black delegates met in Houston on July 4, 1867, to form the Texas Republican party. They selected Elisha M. Pease as chairman. Later that month Pease was appointed provisional governor of Texas after General Philip Sheridan, the regional military commander, removed Governor James Throckmorton. In 1868 another constitutional convention met this time with African Americans constituting 10 of the 90 delegates. For a brief period in the early 1870s black Texans had a strong voice in state government. They were led by decidedly different politicians, George T. Ruby of Galveston and Matthew Gaines of Washington County, who were elected to the state senate in 1869. Ruby and Gaines were the highest-ranking black elected officials in Texas during Reconstruction.

George Thompson Ruby, a freeborn native of New York City, had been educated in Maine. Prior to the Civil War he worked in Boston as a correspondent for the *Pine and Palm,* a newspaper edited by the British abolitionist James Redpath. Ruby spent two years (1860–62) in Haiti as part of Redpath's short-lived effort to promote African American immigration to that Caribbean nation. He returned to the United States, arriving in Louisiana shortly after

Union forces occupied New Orleans. Ruby served as a schoolteacher for the freedpeople for the next four years before moving to Texas in 1866 to become the Freedmen's Bureau agent for Galveston. There he edited a newspaper, the *Freedman,* which appeared intermittently in Galveston and Austin. Ruby, as president of the Galveston Union League and the Colored National Labor Convention, a black Galveston dockworkers' union, built a formidable political organization. He also aligned with white Unionist Edmund J. Davis, the first elected governor under the new constitution. Ruby remained a Davis confidant and supporter even when other African American politicians began to question the governor's commitment to equal rights. Young, educated, articulate, ambitious, Ruby exhibited all the characteristics Texas conservatives most feared Reconstruction would produce in the freedpeople.[15]

Matthew Gaines, in contrast, spoke for the rural freedpeople. Born a slave in Louisiana around 1840, Gaines was sold to a Robertson County cotton planter in 1859. In 1863 Gaines attempted an escape to Mexico. Working his way west, he arrived at Fort McKavett, an abandoned frontier outpost in Menard County, where he was captured by Texas Rangers. Inexplicably, Gaines was not returned to Robertson County and instead worked as a blacksmith and sheepherder in west Texas for the remainder of the war. By 1866, however, he had moved back to Texas plantation country, settling in Washington County. By 1869 Gaines had become both a minister and a Republican party activist when he was elected to the Texas senate.[16]

Gaines soon developed in the senate what his biographer called a "critical, emotional and apocalyptic style" in politics. During an era when partisan political loyalty was revered, Gaines challenged fellow Republicans, including his colleague George T. Ruby, as easily as Democrats. When the legislature proposed a bureau of immigration to encourage settlers from the northern United States, western Europe, and Great Britain, Gaines offered an amendment to dispatch agents to Africa. His amendment was voted down, eighteen to four, with Ruby among its opponents. When conservative legislators opposed creation of a state police force to address the rampant political violence against the freedpeople, Gaines declared on the floor of the senate, "It is not so much the idea of placing . . . great power in the hands of the [governor] but the idea of gentlemen of my color being armed and riding around after desperados." He again broke ranks with many of his black and white colleagues when he called for integrated public schools. After listening to days of attacks by Democrats and some Republicans, an exasperated Gaines, directing his comments at the opponents, said if they objected to whites sitting next to blacks, they should resign their posts in the legislature and go home. He then added, "They talk about separating them. It can't be done . . . my children have the right to sit by the best man's daughter in the land."[17]

Texas had the third-smallest black population of the former Confederate states, a fact reflected in the state legislature. The 14 blacks who served in 1870–71 were the largest number elected during the nineteenth century. Black Texans made up 30 percent of the state's population, but they never exceeded 12 percent of the 120-member legislature. Thus Radical Reconstruction programs depended on the partnership of white Unionists and newly enfranchised black voters. Radical Unionists, primarily from the western part of the state, followed Edmund Davis of Corpus Christi, who formed a unit of Texas Union cavalry during the Civil War and in 1870 gave Texas its only elected Republican administration of the nineteenth century.[18]

Conservatives abhorred Texas Unionists such as Davis, whom they deemed responsible for the "antiwhite" politics of the Reconstruction era. Yet Texas Unionists never agreed on black political participation and civil rights. Few wanted to exclude all black voters, but some, such as Andrew Jackson Hamilton, clearly wanted restrictions placed on African American suffrage. Other Unionists, including Davis, and German immigrants, such as Edward Degener, Julius Schutz, and Louis Constant, pushed for full rights for the ex-slaves. Yet most white citizens of the state viewed such activities by fellow white Texans as racial treason. Little wonder that during the gubernatorial election of 1869 the *San Antonio Daily Herald* openly wished Davis and Ruby hanged. "Oh, what a happy pair they would be, upon a tree together."[19]

When conservatives boycotted the election of delegates to the 1868 constitutional convention and the 1869 gubernatorial election, black and white Unionists temporarily dominated Texas politics. George Ruby and Matt Gaines went to the state senate, and twelve African American men gained seats in the house of representatives. By 1898 forty-two black men had served in that body at different times. African American politicians assumed other offices as well. Walter Burton, who served four terms in the state senate in the 1880s, was twice elected sheriff of Fort Bend County between 1869 and 1874. Matt Kilpatrick was elected treasurer of Waller County.

Norris Wright Cuney, who never ran for a major political office, nonetheless led the Texas Republican party from Edmund Davis's death in 1883 until 1896.[20]

Despite a Republican majority, Texas's first interracial legislature failed to repeal the black codes. Moderate Republicans joined Democrats to maintain most contract labor provisions, the convict labor system, the vagrancy statute, and the child apprenticeship law. Practically, however, these laws became moot as planters and freedpeople increasingly adopted sharecropping and tenancy, thus eliminating the landowner's need to "control" black labor. The new legislature ratified the Fourteenth and Fifteenth Amendments, outlawed bribery or intimidation of voters, prohibited discrimination on public transportation, centralized (but did not desegregate) the public schools, passed a gun control law, reestablished the state militia, and organized the Texas State Police. Directly under the governor's control, this mounted police force was authorized to pursue criminals across county lines and to arrest offenders in those counties where "authorities [were] too weak to enforce respect, or indisposed to do so." Freedmen constituted a majority of the 3,500-man militia. The 257-member state police included whites and Mexican Americans but was 40 percent black.[21]

The state police, however, could not prevent the reign of Reconstruction-era terror in the state. The Texas Ku Klux Klan murdered numerous freedmen, including former state legislator Goldstein Dupree, who was killed in 1873 while campaigning for the reelection of Governor Davis. Antiblack violence was exacerbated by a frontier mentality, if not frontier conditions, which condoned settling disputes by force. Moreover, a highly romanticized "social banditry" rising from antipathy toward the Davis administration and toward freedpeople spawned unusually callous violence. When a Red River County Freedmen's Bureau agent asserted that whites killed blacks "for the love of killing," he described a one-sided racial war that engulfed Texas for the rest of the century. Whites killed blacks for celebrating their emancipation, for refusing to remove their hats when whites passed, for refusing to be whipped, for improperly addressing a white man, and "to see them kick." The sheriff of De Witt County shot a black man who whistled "Yankee Doodle." Some Texas outlaws, including a Limestone County desperado known only as Dixie and the infamous John Wesley Hardin, who bragged in his autobiography about his killing of several black state policemen, were often shielded from authorities by sympathetic whites. Ignoring the potential consequences, some freedmen defended themselves against these outlaws. Merrick Trammell, for example, killed the notorious Dixie and gained Limestone County a respite from the terror campaign.[22]

Despite both the violence and discriminatory legislation, freedpeople in Texas created lives independent of the shadow of slavery. The U.S. Congress legalized slave marriages in March 1865. After Union occupation began three months later, thousands of Texas women and men who had lived together during slavery, gained an important measure of self-respect when their marriages were formally recognized. Moreover, after 1865 thousands of other couples obtained licenses and took vows in civil or religious ceremonies to establish or renew their commitments. Other freedpeople attempted to reunite families separated during slavery, with some black Texans travelling as far as South Carolina and California to retrieve their children. Census figures in 1870 confirm the desire of freedpeople to maintain families. Whether in such cities as Galveston, Austin, and Houston or such rural counties as Matagorda, Fayette, and Grayson, black marriage ratios ran only slightly behind those of whites. In Fayette County, for example, 90 percent of the households included husband and wife in comparison to 96 percent for Anglos.[23]

Postwar black Texans also asserted their new freedom by founding churches. Soon after emancipation black Texans voluntarily withdrew from white churches, partly to escape prejudice and partly to control their own institutions. Black Baptists in Waco in 1866 created the New Hope Baptist Church, which first met in an abandoned foundry. In the same year, the first Methodist Church of Austin lost its black members, when the latter created the Austin Methodist Episcopal Church. By 1870 at least 150 black churches operated in the state, and the numbers increased dramatically during the rest of the century. As one historian describes it, church separation "represented as much an assertion of freedom as the practice of leaving the old plantation."[24]

Black churches were usually the first institutions in the emerging African American communities. They were places of worship and community centers, where social events, political meetings, and sporting events took place. Churches in Galveston, Houston, and Corpus Christi also served as sites for the first Freedmen's Bureau schools in the state. The long relationship between the state's African American churches and colleges was established during this period when the African Methodist Episcopal Church Conference established Paul Quinn College in Austin in 1872 (it moved to Waco in 1881). In 1873 the Methodist Episcopal Church established Wiley College in Marshall. However, Tillotson College of Austin, the oldest black college in the state, was founded in 1867 by the racially integrated Congregational Church.[25]

Often black churches were the anchors of distinct African American neighborhoods. As freedpeople flocked to dozens of communities, usually called freedman towns, across the state, they created shantytowns usually on the edges of established communities. Austin had two post–Civil War black communities. The first, Pleasant Hill, was an impoverished area of shacks and tents founded in 1865. By the early 1870s ex-slave Griffin Clark had developed Clarksville, which became a segregated enclave in West Austin. With the help of former Texas Governor Elisha M. Pease, these freedpeople built or purchased homes and created a village separate from white Austin. The voluntary separation often expressed in the creation of independent black churches and in distinct neighborhoods occasionally extended to separate communities. By 1875 black Texans had created thirty-nine separate towns and villages in fifteen Texas counties to escape white political and economic control. Kendleton in Fort Bend County, Shankleville in Newton County, and Board House in Blanco County all attested to their desire to give lasting meaning to the concept of emancipation.[26]

Texas's brief interlude of interracial democracy began to crumble in 1872, when conservative Democrats regained control of the state legislature. The Democrats immediately abolished the Texas State Police over Governor Davis's veto, replacing it with the all-white Texas Rangers, until then primarily a frontier and border defense force. Moreover, the Democrats denied the governor the authority to declare martial law. The following year Davis was defeated in the gubernatorial election by ex-Confederate Richard Coke, and the freedpeople lost their major political ally in the effort to democratize Texas government. Conservatives in 1875 wrote a new constitution that, although acknowledging black suffrage, included measures that reestablished white supremacy. Yet reimposed white rule could not entirely erase the progress black Texans had made in creating their own institutions, in gaining access to education, and in asserting in crucial ways their dignity and self-worth. Building upon that foundation, they were to sustain a growing campaign that in the twentieth century successfully challenged their status as second-class citizens.[27]

Reconstruction in Indian Territory, the home of the Cherokee, Creek, Choctaw, Cherokee, and Seminole people, also occurred against a backdrop of heightened tension between Native Americans and their ex-slaves. Yet Reconstruction in Indian Territory also set in motion the process by which both Native Americans and African Americans became politically marginalized in the Five Nations by the end of the nineteenth century.

The federal government reallocated land from Indians to the freedpeople, a crucial reform that it was unable or unwilling to require in the states of the former Confederacy. Each tribe was required to relinquish control of the sparsely settled portions of its lands west of the ninety-eighth meridian. This region, eventually called Oklahoma Territory, was opened to settlement by other Indian tribes and, in 1889, to non-Indians. Moreover, the nations were compelled to grant rights-of-way to railroad companies crossing their lands, a concession that exposed Indian Territory to successive waves of uninvited outsiders.[28]

The genesis of this policy can be traced to the report of Union officer John Sanborn. In October 1865 Congress appointed Brevet Major General John Sanborn special commissioner to investigate conditions among the freedpeople in Indian Territory. Sanborn visited every nation between November 1865 and April 1866. He reported to Congress that both the Indians and the freedpeople were eager for the ex-slaves to remain in the territory but "upon a tract of country by themselves." He urged that such a tract, "large enough to give a square mile to every four persons," be set aside and that it "should be the most fertile in the territory as the freedmen are the principal producers." Anticipating opposition from the nations, Sanborn called on the federal government to grant the land quickly and resolutely. "When the tribes know that this policy is determined upon by the government," he argued, "they will submit to it without any open resistance . . . and the freedmen will rejoice that . . . they have a prospect of a permanent home for themselves and their children."[29]

Sanborn also reported Indian sentiment toward the freedpeople. The Seminole and Creek favored incorporation of their former slaves into their tribes, the Cherokee were divided on the issue, and

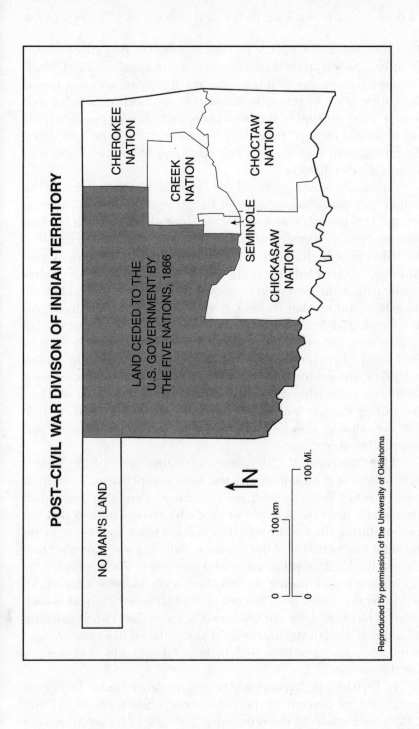

POST–CIVIL WAR DIVISON OF INDIAN TERRITORY

NO MAN'S LAND

CHEROKEE NATION

CREEK NATION

CHOCTAW NATION

SEMINOLE

CHICKASAW NATION

LAND CEDED TO THE U.S. GOVERNMENT BY THE FIVE NATIONS, 1866

N

0 — 100 km
0 — 100 Mi.

the Chickasaw and Choctaw exhibited "a violent prejudice" toward their freedpeople, punctuated by assaults and murders. The Chickasaw, for example, would not permit any freedman who had joined the Union army to return to the nation. Sanborn concluded that since a "large portion of the [Chickasaw and Choctaw] people [did] not admit any change" from the prewar status of masters and slaves, the government had to place federal troops in the two nations to protect the freedpeople.[30]

Sanborn's report predicted the course of Reconstruction in the Indian nations. Citing widespread Indian support of the Confederacy, the U.S. government nullified all previous treaties with the Five Nations. New treaties negotiated in 1866 abolished slavery, required the tribes to cede the western half of their lands to the federal government, and called for reorganized tribal governments. After emancipation the government allowed each nation to decide individually if, and in what manner, it would incorporate the freedpeople. Creek and Seminole Indians made their former slaves tribal citizens with full civil and political rights. Tribal emancipation in 1863 freed Cherokee slaves, but only those who lived in the nation in 1866 or who returned within six months of the treaty signing were eligible for citizenship. Consequently some Cherokee slaves who had fled during the war but returned after 1867 were declared "intruders," even though they might be husbands, wives, children, and parents of Cherokee citizens.[41]

The Choctaw and Chickasaw argued that none of the former slaveholders of the Confederacy had been compelled to share their land or other property with their ex-slaves. Thus they refused to incorporate their freedpeople or take back those who had fled the nations during the war. Instead they enacted black codes to regulate the labor and behavior of the ex-slaves, including a vagrancy act that allowed the local sheriff to arrest and hire out to the highest bidder any ex-slave found moving about without a job. Moreover, for a brief period in the 1860s the Choctaw and Chickasaw mounted a campaign of terror to drive out unwanted Texas ex-slaves who settled on tribal lands. Indian vigilantes seized and whipped blacks not known in the area, destroyed their settlements, and forced most of them to flee the nations.[32]

In 1870 Indian Territory had 68,152 residents. Native Americans constituted 87 percent of the population, while 6,378 blacks and 2,407 whites made up the remainder. The 6,000 African Americans were fewer than the 8,000 counted ten years earlier. However, some freedpeople from neighboring states had settled in Indian Territory without authorization. In 1868 Chickasaw officials bitterly complained of former black soldiers from the United States residing illegally in the western section of their nation.[33] Yet most African Americans in the territory in 1870 were former slaves of the various Indian nations. Their fate was determined by the actions of individual Indian nations and the federal government.

All five tribes extended certain privileges, and each allocated farmland. As Sanborn had urged in 1866, Creek and Seminole ex-slaves received allotments along the river bottoms—choice parcels for cotton production. Theoretically the new tribal constitutions guaranteed freedpeople the protection of person and property as well as civil and criminal protection in the courts. But local prejudice among the Cherokee, and the failure of the Choctaw and Chickasaw to adopt their freedpeople as citizens, limited those liberties. With the exception of the Choctaw-Chickasaw vigilante activity of 1865–67, however, freedpeople were not subject to terroristic campaigns, as were former slaves in Texas and the Old South. Even in the Choctaw and Chickasaw nations, where tribal leaders called for their removal, the freedpeople resided without molestation after 1870 in an uneasy accommodation with their former owners.[34]

The Seminole and Creek Nations allowed their former slaves to participate fully in tribal government. By 1875 the forty-two member National Council, the Seminole legislative body, included six freedmen representing two of the fourteen towns of the Seminole Nation. The House of Warriors, the larger of the two branches of the annually elected Creek legislature, had two or more members (out of eighty-three), representing the three towns populated by freedpeople—North Fork Colored, Arkansas Colored, and Canadian Colored—almost continuously from 1868 until its last session in 1905. Sixteen freedmen served in the 1887 legislature, three in the House of Kings, and thirteen in the House of Warriors. The Creek Nation had the largest and most consistent black political representation anywhere in the West during the last three decades of the nineteenth century. Moreover, in the Arkansas River country, where they were numerically dominant, Creek freedmen were elected judges and district attorneys in tribal courts and district officials for the tribal government. One freedman, Jesse Franklin, was elected justice of the tribal supreme court in 1876. By the mid-1870s "the negroes," according to Angie Debo, "held the balance of power in Creek politics."[35]

Cherokee freedmen voted in their nation's elections but not without opposition. William P. Boudinot, the influential Cherokee attorney and editor of the *Cherokee Advocate*, later defended freed-people in their citizenship claims. In 1878, however, he wrote an editorial attacking black officeholding: "It was not complimentary or just . . . to instill the fatally mischievous idea that [an] element has distinct rights to hold office in proportion to its numbers and irre-spective of qualifications." George W. Johnson, Boudinot's successor at the *Advocate*, was more blunt. He wrote in 1879, "We shall at all times object to having our colored citizens sitting in our Council to legislate for us. We know of none that has the capacity to make laws for us." Nonetheless, beginning with the election of Joseph Brown in 1875, six freedmen served as councillors in the lower house of the Cherokee legislature during the remainder of the century.[36]

For most Cherokee freedmen, however, citizenship for "intrud-ers," not electoral office, was the major political question of the day. Many ex-slaves returned in time to become citizens under the provis-ions of the 1866 treaty. Others, including those carried off by slave-holders to neighboring states, were unaware of the treaty's provisions or without means to return to the nation. As years passed, these former slaves straggled back into the nation and lived with relatives who were legal citizens. These noncitizens had no rights to the improvements on the lands they made after returning to the nation and could not vote or otherwise participate in Cherokee politics. Further complications arose when blacks from "the State," believing marriages entitled them to tribal citizenship (as did the marriage of whites to Cherokee), married into the freedpeople families. The extent of the problem became evident after an 1870 census of the Cherokee Nation. Approximately fifteen hundred former slaves had been declared citizens, while seven hundred were intruders. More-over, the Cherokee National Council in 1869 created special courts to determine individually the cases of intruders and, if necessary, expel them. For many ex-slaves the issue was not simply land or rights as Cherokee citizens but identification with the only home they had known. "I am one of those unfortunates. I came too late," confessed freedman Joseph Rogers to Cherokee ex-slaves at a Delaware District emancipation celebration on August 24, 1876. Continuing his speech to the freedpeople and addressing, indirectly, the Cherokee political establishment, which determined citizenship, he declared: "Born and raised among these people, I don't want to know any other. The green hills and blooming prairies of this Nation look like home to me . . . I look around and I see Cherokees who in the early days of my life were my playmates . . . and in early manhood, my companions, and now as the decrepitude of age steals upon me, will you not let me lie down and die your fellow citizen?"[37]

Cherokee leaders were divided over adopting the intruders. Chief Lewis Downing and his successor, William P. Ross, favored adoption. In his first council address in 1873 Ross asked for the adoption of the freedmen who had returned too late "as a measure humane in its spirit, liberal in its character and expedient in result." He also requested repeal of all discriminatory statutes. But William P. Boudinot and George W. Johnson, editors of the *Cherokee Advocate*, and Chief Justice James Vann of the Cherokee supreme court opposed adoption. They argued it would unfairly reduce the land and money remaining in the common heritage of the tribe. "We say to our colored friends that . . . if the treaty of 1866 is . . . not in their favor, there is no hope for them; they cannot live in this nation as citizens. No Cherokee denies them their treaty rights, if the treaty gives them any . . . We admit, their case is a hard one, but it is not our fault." Vann's role on the supreme court in determining intruder status was particularly discouraging to freedpeople. In 1871 the court rejected 131 of 136 claims for citizenship.[38]

The Allen Wilson case reflected the complexities of the citizenship issue for the freedpeople, the Cherokee, and the federal government. Born a slave in the old Cherokee Nation, Allen Wilson came west on the Trail of Tears. During the Civil War he was stranded in the Choctaw Nation after his owner died in 1865. With a large family to support, Wilson farmed to obtain enough money to return to the Cherokee Nation. He returned to the Cherokee Nation in the fall of 1867, seven months after the treaty deadline. Unsure of his status, Wilson went to Cherokee leaders, who told him to begin farming. Wilson's family built a house on a sixty-acre farm about nine miles east of Fort Gibson. They planted an orchard and nursery and by 1879 had 350 bearing apple trees, 1,000 peach trees, and twelve acres planted in wheat. The family's industry, however, proved of no avail. When he appeared before a citizenship commission in 1879, Wilson's claim was rejected and the *Cherokee Advocate* published a notice of the sale of his farm improvements valued at two thousand dollars.

Wilson was undaunted. When some Cherokee citizens offered

to buy his improvements and let him work for them, he declared he would rather sell out and leave the nation. He did neither, and instead hired attorney William P. Boudinot, who argued that his client was a "pattern of industry." Boudinot appealed to Secretary of the Interior Carl Schurz, who suspended the sale and in turn told U.S. Attorney General Charles Devens to rule on three legal questions: the Cherokee right to determine their citizenship, the right of Cherokee freedpeople to tribal lands under the 1866 treaty, and the responsibility of the federal government to protect Cherokee lands from intruders. The attorney general's decision declared that the United States was not bound to regard Cherokee law as the final word in intruder cases. The attorney general's ruling made it virtually impossible for the nation to remove Wilson and other ex-slave intruders. But it also opened the nation and ultimately all Indian Territory to much larger numbers of non-Indian intruders who cared nothing about Indian law, culture, or sovereignty.[39]

The Chickasaw and Choctaw freedpeople had no rights in their nations, but they were not without influence in Washington, D.C. They sent their political leaders, James Squire Wolf, Squire Butler, Isaac Anderson, and Anderson Brown, to Washington, to represent their interests. They also obtained the removal of the Chickasaw and Choctaw Indian agent George T. Olmstead, whom they held responsible for the attempt to block their tribal rights. They skillfully made their appeals couched in references to their loyalty during the Civil War, reminding their supporters that many of the dispossessed were U.S. Army veterans. Unlike Cherokee freedpeople, they linked their fate to that of blacks from the States. Thus the real thrust of their political incorporation was no longer toward the Indian nations but toward the larger African American community. Some Indian leaders surmised as much. When Chickasaw Governor Benjamin Overton in his annual message of 1876 again urged the legislative council to withhold citizenship from the freedpeople, he declared: "If you [extend citizenship], you sign the death-warrant of your nationality . . . for the negroes will be the wedge with which our country will be rent asunder and opened up to the whites . . ." Overton was partly right. As Chickasaw and Chocktaw freedpeople saw their political and economic interests increasingly diverge from those of their former owners, they campaigned to open the territory to whites and "state negroes." In the process they weakened Indian control over the nations.[40]

Outside of Texas and Indian Territory western Reconstruction focused on black male suffrage.* The *San Francisco Elevator* was speaking as much about California as about South Carolina in 1868 when it called upon the nation to honor its debt not only to black soldiers who fought for the Union during the Civil War but also to "loyal" voters who were necessary to sustain the national Republican administration in Washington. "The Negroes who have rendered . . . signal service in the conflict on the field and at the ballot box," it declared, "expect the simple recognition of their political rights in every portion of the land."[41]

The first indication of congressional concern about black male suffrage occurred when Congress created Montana Territory in 1864. While debating the organic act that authorized the new territory, Minnesota Senator Morton S. Wilkinson introduced an amendment to strike the word *white* from the section of voter qualifications, prompting a sharp rebuttal from Senator James R. Doolittle of Wisconsin, who erroneously believed no blacks lived in Montana and thus claimed the amendment was meaningless. Senator Charles Sumner conceded the issue was an abstraction, but he nonetheless insisted on the change as a matter of principle. The Senate supported the Wilkinson amendment, but the two houses of Congress compromised by restricting the vote to U.S. citizens, leaving blacks temporarily without suffrage rights on the far western mining frontier. Nonetheless the debate served notice that African American suffrage would no longer be left to the territories.[42]

Between 1867 and 1869 Congress enacted three measures that enfranchised black males throughout the nation. In January 1867 the vote was granted first to black men in the District of Columbia. Days later Congress passed the Territorial Suffrage Act, which extended the privilege to western territories. Two months later the first Reconstruction Act extended suffrage to freedmen in the former Confederacy. In 1869 Congress passed the Fifteenth Amendment ratified by two-thirds of the states by January 1870, the amendment enabled black men throughout the nation to vote.

---

*Much like African American political leaders in the rest of the nation, black westerners sought the right to vote for black men. Apparently few black western women called for suffrage to be extended to them, and there is little evidence they were active in either black male campaigns or in woman suffrage efforts led by white women. African American women, however, did gain suffrage rights in western states and territories, beginning with Wyoming in 1869, and thus voted years before most of their southern or eastern counterparts.

If one measures the number of persons affected, the Territorial Suffrage Act had the least impact on black voting. It enfranchised only about eight hundred African Americans, far fewer, for example, than in the District of Columbia. Yet its enactment over Democratic and conservative Republican objections symbolically pointed to the inevitability of national black male suffrage. Speaking before an audience in Virginia City in September 1867 and using the Territorial Suffrage Act as a harbinger of future trends, Nevada Republican Senator William Stewart warned, "It is too late to war against negro suffrage." Two years later Stewart's state was the first to ratify the Fifteenth Amendment. Leland Stanford, California's first Republican governor, writing to U.S. Senator-elect Cornelius Cole, characterized the Civil War as an "incomplete revolution," which could end only with full suffrage for all citizens—all women as well as black men. Support for black suffrage also came from the far northwest corner of the West. The *Olympia Commercial Age* in the capital of Washington Territory declared in 1870, soon after the ratification of the Fifteenth Amendment, that the measure "does not particularly affect us in this Territory, as the colored folks have been voters among us for sometime already."[43]

Despite their small numbers, western African Americans conducted the suffrage campaign with determined energy and courage. In 1865 African Americans from Virginia City, Gold Hill, and Silver City, Nevada, formed the Nevada Executive Committee to "petition the next Legislature for the Right of Suffrage and equal rights before the Law to all the Colored Citizens of the State of Nevada." Dr. W. H. C. Stephenson chaired the committee and became the principal spokesman in the campaign for civil rights. During the January 1, 1866, anniversary celebration of the Emancipation Proclamation, he told his predominantly white Virginia City audience, "It is for colored men to . . . fearlessly meet the opponents of justice . . . . Let colored men contend for 'Equality before the Law.' Nothing short of civil and political rights."[44]

Kansas African Americans were equally determined to campaign for their rights. A convention of black men in Lawrence, Kansas, in 1866 challenged the widely held idea that black voting was a privilege the white male electorate could confer or reject at its pleasure. "The right to exercise the elective franchise is an inseparable part of self-government. . . . No man, black or white, can justly be deprived of this right. [It] is not merely a conventional privilege, . . . which may be extended to or withheld from any class of citizen at the will of a majority, but a right as sacred and inviolable as the right of life, liberty or property." Then the convention issued this warning to Kansas whites: "Since we are going to remain among you, we believe it unwise or inhuman to . . . take from us as a class, many of our dearest natural and justly inalienable rights. Shall our presence conduce to the welfare, peace, and prosperity of the state, or . . . be a· cause of dissension, discord, and irritation [?] We must be a constant trouble in the state until it extends to us equal and exact justice."[45]

Black westerners resorted to a long-standing protest weapon, the petition. In California, Nevada, Kansas, and Colorado Territory, between 1865 and 1867 they petitioned state and territorial governments for black male suffrage. They also held conventions to urge repeal of other discriminatory laws. Even though their campaigns came in states and territories then dominated by Republicans, all their entreaties were ignored. Daniel Wilder, editor of the *Leavenworth Conservative,* described popular opinion on equal suffrage in Kansas when he claimed Republicans "talk for it, vote agin it." His terse comment succinctly summarized the attitudes of many throughout the region.[46]

Yet blacks could claim one important victory in Colorado Territory. Between 1864 and 1867 Colorado's 150 African Americans waged a relentless campaign to delay statehood for the territory until their suffrage rights were guaranteed. Colorado's black males began campaigning in 1864, when the territorial legislature limited voting to white males. African American men angrily denounced the measure, claiming it denied them a right they had exercised since 1861. In July 1864 they sent a delegation to the state constitutional convention, where it lobbied unsuccessfully for equal male suffrage. When the entire constitution was rejected by the voters in 1865, a second convention again proposed the amendment and submitted the suffrage question to the voters. They narrowly approved the revised constitution by 155 votes but rejected black male suffrage by 4,192 to 476.[47]

African-American Coloradans refused to accept the decision. Three Denver barbers, Edward Sanderlin, Henry O. Wagoner, and William Jefferson Hardin, urged the U.S. Congress to delay Colorado's statehood until black male suffrage rights were assured. Kentucky-born Hardin, who had arrived in Denver in 1863, quickly assumed the leadership of this effort, writing Massachusetts Senator Charles Sumner, Ohio Representative James Ashley, and Horace Greeley, editor of the *New York Tribune,* to outline the grievances of the territory's African Americans. Hardin issued an ominous warning in his February 1866 missive to Senator Sumner: "Slavery went down in a great deluge of blood, and I greatly fear, unless the american [sic] people learn from the past to do justice now & in the future, that their cruel & unjust prejudices will, some day, go down in the same crimson blood." Greeley responded to Hardin's request by insisting that black suffrage, while desirable, should never be a condition of statehood. Senator Summer, however, declared his opposition to statehood because of the suffrage restriction after reading aloud the black Coloradan's telegram before the U.S. Senate.[48]

Hardin also targeted territorial political leaders. In December 1865 he presented to Territorial Governor Alexander Cummings a petition signed by 137 Colorado African Americans, 91 percent of the territory's black population, calling for repeal of the suffrage restriction. To deny equal suffrage, the petition asserted, was to disregard "the bloody lessons of the last four years." Governor Cummings forwarded the petition to Secretary of State William Seward for presentation to Congress. In January, Hardin, Henry O. Wagoner, and four other African Americans presented a second petition to Cummings, who forwarded it to the territorial legislature with his own appeal for equal suffrage. The legislature ignored both the petition and the governor's message.[49]

Black Coloradans' efforts seemed a failure. The territorial legislature felt no compulsion to respond to their demands, and the U.S. Congress actually voted in April 1866 to admit Colorado only to see the admission blocked by a veto by President Andrew Johnson. The president, who was certainly no advocate of black suffrage, gave as his reason for the veto the small population of the territory. But the debate over black suffrage restrictions in Colorado generated an unanticipated development. On the day that President Johnson issued his veto, Representative Ashley, chair of the Committee on Territories, introduced a bill regulating territorial government.Included in its provisions was a measure to give all male residents (Indians excepted) the right to vote. The bill passed the House of Representatives but died when the Senate failed to act on the measure.[50]

In January 1867, while the Senate debated black voting in Colorado, Ohio Senator Benjamin Wade resurrected Ashley's bill, arguing that it would solve the problem of equal suffrage in all the territories. He successfully maneuvered the bill through the Senate on January 10 and that afternoon rushed it to the House, where it was approved within two hours. The Territorial Suffrage Act became law without President Johnson's signature on January 31, 1867. Consequently black males in Colorado and other territories achieved voting rights at least three years before ratification of the Fifteenth Amendment ensured similar rights in northern and western states.[51]

Black males in western territories quickly exercised their newly won suffrage rights. Two hundred black men cast ballots in the Montana territorial election of 1867, although not without challenge. Pro-Democratic gangs circulated throughout Helena on election day in 1867 to intimidate black voters; Sammy Hays was killed by a gang of Irish toughs. However, most blacks recorded their votes and left the polling places without incident. Six black voters, men and women, who intended to cast ballots in South Pass City, Wyoming Territory, in 1869, faced an angry mob of mostly Democratic gold miners who blocked their route to the town's polling place. Only the timely intervention of the territory's Republican-appointed U.S. marshal, Church Howe, saved the day. Howe marched to the polls beside the voters, gun in hand, threatening to shoot anyone who got in the way.[52]

Despite rumors of possible mob action against Colorado blacks during 1867 municipal elections in Denver and Central City, no violence occurred. Instead Colorado Republicans courted the newly enfranchised voters. Republican newspaper editor D. C. Collier flattered black voters by claiming that though he believed most southern freedmen were incapable of voting wisely, "in Colorado, negro suffrage is intelligent suffrage. . . . We believe the negro in this Territory is fully capable of exercising the franchise." Such flattery soon proved crucial. In the 1868 election of the territory's congressional delegate, Denver's 120 black votes secured the victory for Republican candidate Allen Bradford in his 17-vote margin over his Democratic opponent, David Belden. Republicans publicly acknowledged their debt. When one maverick Republican proposed the temporary disfranchisement of blacks, party leaders immediately dismissed the idea. "We would lose our Republican majority," said one, while another wrote, "[W]ithout the colored vote Bradford would never have been elected. Now it is proposed to take the right of voting away from the men who saved the Republican Party."[53]

Suffrage for African American males in western states other than Texas (which was covered under the Congressional Reconstruction Act of 1867) came with the ratification of the Fifteenth Amendment. In those states black efforts focused on securing ratification of

the amendment. Of the five western states that considered ratification, three, Kansas, Nebraska, and Nevada, endorsed the measure.
Nebraska, as a condition of its admission in 1867, already allowed
black suffrage, while Nevada held the distinction of being the first
state in the Union to ratify the Fifteenth Amendment because its
senator, William Stewart, was a principal congressional sponsor.
Democratic-controlled legislatures in California and Oregon, however, adamantly opposed black voting. Oregon's legislature called it
an unconstitutional "change forced upon the states by the power of
the bayonet."[54]

The Kansas ratification was the most surprising since it occurred
three years after a bitter campaign that pitted supporters of black
male suffrage against woman suffrage advocates. The white male
electorate overwhelmingly rejected both black and female suffrage,
undermining Kansas's claim to be the "the most radicalized state in
the Union." The campaign began in 1862, when African American
political leaders petitioned the state legislature for the right to vote.
Although the campaign was supported by sympathetic white men,
including Daniel Wilder, the editor of the *Leavenworth Conservative*,
Charles H. Langston, an African American farmer and grocer from
Lawrence, emerged as its leader. Born a slave on a Virginia plantation in 1817, Charles and his younger brother, John Mercer Langston, another antebellum abolitionist who became a U.S.
representative from Virginia in 1889, were freed and educated at
Oberlin College in Ohio. In 1848, already an experienced political
activist, Charles Langston as an Ohio delegate attended the National
Negro Convention (where he joined Frederick Douglass in enrolling
other delegates). In 1859 Langston was arrested for violating the
terms of the Fugitive Slave Act when he helped John Price escape to
Canada. Although his brother returned to Virginia after the Civil
War, Charles Langston emigrated west to Kansas in 1862 to teach
and work among the freedpeople.[55]

The Kansas legislature at first refused to take action on the
black male suffrage petition, claiming that such a weighty measure
could not be decided while the state's soldiers were fighting the Civil
War. When petitions were again presented in 1866, the legislature
delayed until Governor Samuel Crawford recommended a statewide
referendum on the issue. The legislature subsequently drafted the
measure, scheduled for the November 1867 election, which removed
the word *white* from the state suffrage law. However, Republican legislator Samuel N. Wood added a second provision calling for removal

of the word *male.* Wood had opposed all previous measures broadening suffrage to include anyone other than white males. Thus many black suffrage supporters concluded that his real intent was to defeat both reforms.

The coupling of voting rights for black males and all women revealed the complexities of race and gender and the difficulty of maintaining coalitions in the face of varied opposition. The white male electorate divided into four camps. Some supported equal suffrage for all men and women, while advocates of gender or racial equality selfishly promoted their own reform at the expense of the other. Opponents of both reforms concluded that neither women nor black men were worthy of suffrage and urged defeat of both proposals. At the height of the Kansas campaign Thomas Hartley, a conservative Republican, published a pamphlet, *Universal Suffrage— Female Suffrage,* which argued that giving votes to women and to black men would invite demagogues into office by placing political power in the hands of "children" who would be swayed by emotion rather than serious intellectual reflection.[56]

Undaunted by such arguments, and refusing to accept the "black vote first" approach of most reformers of the era, national and state woman suffrage advocates seized the opportunity provided by the Kansas referendum to gain their first statewide victory. National suffrage leaders, such as Lucy Stone, Susan B. Anthony, Elizabeth Cady Stanton, and the Reverend Olympia Brown, campaigned throughout Kansas, accompanied by state leaders, such as Clarina Nichols and Sallie Brown.[57]

African American men in Kansas marshaled no comparably known national leaders to campaign for their suffrage. It fell to Charles H. Langston, Daniel Wilder, and other supporters to carry the campaign. Despite creation of the Impartial Suffrage Association to support both reforms (with Governor Crawford as honorary president), woman suffrage and black suffrage advocates were soon hurling charges against each other. "Negroes of Kansas and their friends are claiming rights which they are not willing to give to mothers, wives, sisters and daughters of the state," declared Samuel Wood. Speaking before an audience in Fort Scott, Kansas, the Reverend Olympia Brown "disclaimed against placing the dirty, immoral, degraded negro before a white woman," while Sallie Brown warned that "if the negroes get the ballot [before women] there will be no chance for us . . ."[58]

African American leaders were more circumspect in their public comments on women's suffrage. "I have no dispute with you . . ." Langston wrote to Samuel Wood, "there shall be no antagonism between me and the friends of woman suffrage." However in private correspondence with Wood two months earlier, a clearly furious Langston wrote: "I feel that you are responsible . . . for all the . . . unnecessary and embarrassing notions . . . in connection with the question of negro suffrage. I am not alone in this feeling . . . . If the measure is defeated, by these frivolous, extraneous, and distinctive motions, we the negroes shall hold you responsible." Indeed Langston was not alone in his feelings. One month before the election he persuaded a reluctant black convention meeting in Doniphan County to pass a resolution denying any rivalry between advocates of black and woman suffrage. White Republican leaders such as state Attorney General G. W. Hoyt and future Senator Preston B. Plumb exercised no similar restraint: They openly opposed woman suffrage while supporting black male suffrage. When the votes were counted, both measures went down to defeat. Black suffrage failed by 19,421 to 10,438, and woman suffrage collapsed under a slightly wider margin, 19,857 to 10,070. Three years later Kansas Republicans, concluding that the Fifteenth Amendment was the only means of gaining black suffrage, urged rapid ratification before legislative opposition could mount. That opposition did appear, but the national momentum toward ratification swept the amendment through the Kansas legislature in January 1870.[59]

Western African Americans celebrated the passage of the Fifteenth Amendment with "unrestrained elation" unmatched since the Emancipation Proclamation. Philip Bell proclaimed: GLORIA TRIUMPHE! WE ARE FREE! from the pages of the *Elevator* as his newspaper reported celebrations in California, Oregon, and Nevada. Black citizens of Helena, Montana Territory, assembled on the south hill overlooking the city to announce "to the wide world that we are free men and citizens of the United States—shorn of all those stigmatizing qualifications which have made us beasts." They then thanked God and the Congress of the United States and fired a thirty-two-gun salute. Nevada blacks at opposite ends of the state, in Virginia City and Elko, celebrated. The Elko residents had proposed to fire a cannon salute. Upon discovering there were no cannon in the town, they settled instead on hammering "two large anvils for that purpose." A procession of 150 black Nevadans paraded from Virginia

City to neighboring Gold Hill, "playing popular patriotic airs" and flying a "fine silk flag" made by the black women of Virginia City for the occasion and inscribed with the words *Justice is slow, but sure.* Portland African Americans staged a "Ratification Jubilee." The celebrants, marching to the music of the Twenty-third U.S. Infantry Band, staged a torchlight procession to the courthouse, where they were addressed by seven orators, including local African American businessman George P. Riley and prominent Republicans Elisha Applegate, a founder of the party in Oregon, and ex-Governor Addison C. Gibbs. Black Portlanders solemnly declared their loyalty to the nation, "should our country need us."[60]

One consequence of black voting was officeholding. By the end of the nineteenth century African Americans held office in Texas, Kansas, Colorado, Washington, and Wyoming. African Americans such as Edwin McCabe, the Kansas auditor in 1881, and "Colonel" John Brown, the Shawnee County, Kansas, clerk in 1889, successfully competed against whites for local office. Some African American politicians achieved national prominence. John Lewis Waller served as ambassador to Madagascar in the 1890s. However, few were as interesting as William Jefferson Hardin. By 1873 Hardin had moved to Cheyenne, Wyoming Territory, after a personal scandal cost him his position at the Denver Mint. He resumed his trade as a barber and in 1879 entered state politics and was elected to two terms in the territorial legislature.[61]

Politics of course would not resolve all the issues facing black communities in the West any more than elsewhere in the nation. Some late-nineteenth-century leaders, such as Booker T. Washington, criticized the inordinate energy and resources devoted to obtaining elective and appointive office particularly in the face of the poverty and marginalization of African American communities. Yet with voting rights permanently assured for black men throughout the region except in Texas and the Chickasaw and Choctaw Indian Nations and for black women in Wyoming by 1869 and other western states by the 1890s, western African Americans could proudly echo Peter Anderson's call for blacks to see their economic destiny in the "Great West."[62]

Nineteenth-Century Black Western Legislators, 1868–1900

Colorado

John T. Gunnell	1881–83
Joseph H. Stuart	1895–97

Indian Territory

Creek Nation

Sugar George	1868–74, 1882–85, 1887–89, 1892, 1894–95
Simon Brown	1868
Charles Foster	1869, 1873
Isom Marshall	1871
Harry Island	1872
Ned Robbins	1872, 1875, 1887, 1890
Robert Grayson	1872, 1875, 1883, 1885, 1887, 1893, 1900
Jesse Franklin	1872, 1873, 1881
Benjamin McQueen	1872, 1873
Scipio Sancho	1872–73, 1882
Thomas Bruner	1872, 1875, 1886
Toby McIntosh	1872–73
William McIntosh	1872
Samson Hawkins	1875
Monday Durant	1875
Simon Brown	1875
Jeffrey Smith	1875
Daniel Miller	1875
Pardo Bruner	1875, 1887, 1889–90, 1895
Ben Barnett	1875
Jack McGilbra	1875
Sandy Perryman	1875
Tom Richards	1875
Snow Sells	1882–83, 1895
William Peter	1882, 1889
Gabriel Jameson	1883–85, 1887–89, 1894
J. P. Davison	1883, 1885, 1887, 1890, 1899
H. C. Reed	1884, 1887–88, 1894–95

Joshua Tucker	1884
Manuel Warrior	1885
Manuel Jefferson	1885
Abraham Prince	1885
Simon Rentie	1885, 1890–91
Isom Jameson	1885
Stepney Colbert	1885
Dan Miller	1887
Moses Jameson	1887, 1894
Eli Jacobs	1887
Solomon Franklin	1887, 1890
Robert Walker	1887
Green Jackson	1887
Morris Sango	1887
Tony Sandy	1887
John Meyers	1887
Isaac Manual	1888
Warrior A. Rentie	1893, 1895, 1899
Alec Davis	1893
Stepney Durant	1893
Kellop Murrell	1895
Dan Tucker	1895
Joe Primus	1895
P. A. Lewis	1899
Alec H. Mike	1899
A. G. W. Sango	1899–1900
Lewis B. Bruner	1900
Wiley McIntosh	1900

Cherokee Nation

Joseph Brown	1875–77
Frank Vann	1887–89
Jerry Alberty	1889–91
Stick Ross	1893–95
Ned Irons	1895–97
Samuel Stidham	1895–97

Seminole Nation

| Ben Bruner | 1868–79 |
| William Noble | 1868–89 |

Nineteenth-Century Black Western Legislators, 1868–1900 (*Cont.*)

Caesar Bruner	1880–1900
Joe Scipio	1890
Joe Davis	1891
Dosar Barkus	1892–1900
Kansas	
L. W. Winn (Senate)*	1879
Alfred Fairfax	1889–91
Nebraska	
Dr. Moses O. Ricketts	1892–96
Oklahoma Territory	
Green Jacob Currin	1890–92
D. J. Wallace	1892–94
Texas	
George T. Ruby (Senate)	1870–71, 1873
Matthew Gaines (Senate)	1870–71, 1873
Walter M. Burton (Senate)	1874, 1876, 1879, 1881
Walter Riptoe (Senate)	1876, 1879
Mitchell M. Kendall	1870–71
D. W. Burley	1870–71
Richard Williams	1870–71, 1873
Henry Moore	1870–71, 1873
Richard Allen	1870–71, 1873
R. Goldstein Dupree	1870–71
John Mitchell	1870–71
Silas Cotton	1870–71
Sheppard Mullins	1870–71
Benjamin Franklin Williams	1870–71, 1879, 1885
Jermiah J. Hamilton	1870–71
David Medlock	1870–71
Shack R. Roberts	1873, 1874, 1876
Henry Phelps	1873
James H. Washington	1873
Allen Wilder	1873, 1876

*Appointed to fill unexpired term.

Edward Anderson	1873
David Abner, Sr.	1874
Edward J. Brown	1874
Thomas Beck	1874, 1879, 1881
Jacob E. Freeman	1874, 1879
John Mitchell	1874
Henry Sneed	1876
William H. Holland	1876
R. J. Evans	1879, 1881
B. A. Guy	1879
Harriel G. Geiger	1879, 1881
Elias Mayes	1879, 1889
Andrew L. Sledge	1879
Robert A. Kerr	1881
D. C. Lewis	1881
R. J. Moore	1883, 1885, 1887
George W. Wyatt	1883
James H. Stewart	1885
H. A. P. Bassett	1887
Alexander Ashberry	1889
Edward A. Patton	1891
Nathan H. Haller	1893, 1895
Robert L. Smith	1895, 1897

Washington

William Owen Bush	1889–91

Wyoming

William Jefferson Hardin	1879–84

Sources: Rebecca Lintz, reference librarian, Colorado Historical Society, to author, April 28, 1994; Daniel Littlefield to author, February 1, 1996; Kevin Mulroy to author, August 9, 1996; Thomas C. Cox, Blacks in Topeka, Kansas, 1865–1915: A Social History *(Baton Rouge: Louisiana State University Press, 1982), 122–23; Works Projects Administration,* The Negroes of Nebraska *(Lincoln: Woodruff Printing Company, 1940), 28; Oklahoma Historical Society to author, October 27, 1995; Emmet Starr,* History of the Cherokee Indians *(Millwood, N.Y.: Kraus Reprint Company, 1977), 277–83; Barry A. Crouch, "Hesitant Recognition: Texas Black Politicians, 1865–1900,"* East Texas Historical Journal *31:1 (Spring 1993), 53–56; Barton's Legislative Hand-Book and Manual of the State of Washington, 1889 (Tacoma: Thomas Henderson Boyd, 1889), 224; and Eugene Berwanger,* The West and Reconstruction *(Urbana: University of Illinois Press, 1981), 183–84.*

5

❖ ✧ ❖ ✧ ❖

Migration
and Settlement,
1875–1920

In his speech at the First State Convention of the Colored Citizens
of the State of California in 1855, the San Francisco minister Darius
Stokes proclaimed to the world that African Americans, were destined to stay in California and the West. "The white man came, and
we came with him; and by the blessing of God, we shall stay with him,
side by side. . . . Should another Sutter discover another El Dorado
. . . no sooner shall the white man's foot be firmly planted there,
than looking over his shoulder he will see the black man, like his
shadow, by his side." Stokes spoke of the gold rush era, but his words
applied equally to the post–Civil War West. African Americans by
1870 inhabited every state and territory of the region. From Fort
Benton, Montana Territory, where roustabouts unloaded the river-
boats along the headwaters of the Missouri River, to soldiers stationed at Fort Huachuca, Arizona, or Fort Davis, Texas, blacks were
no mere proverbial "shadow." Often they led the way for subsequent
settlers. None of this is surprising. Since the eighteenth century,
when blacks ventured north from central Mexico to California, New
Mexico, Texas, and other remote outposts of New Spain, African
Americans have sought out the region.[1]

African American entry into the region differed from the image
of westward migration. Few blacks crossed the plains and mountains
in wagon trains. Instead those traveling from the South were likely to

The African American Population in
Western States and Territories, 1880–1900

	1880	1890	1900
Arizona Territory	155	1,357	1,848
California	6,018	11,322	11,045
Colorado	2,435	6,215	8,570
Idaho	53	201	293
Kansas	43,107	49,710	52,003
Montana	346	1,490	1,523
Nebraska	2,385	8,913	6,269
Nevada	488	242	134
New Mexico Territory	1,015	1,956	1,610
North Dakota	113	373	286
Oklahoma Indian Territory	NA	18,636	55,684*
Oregon	487	1,186	1,105
South Dakota	288	541	465
Texas	393,384	488,171	620,722
Utah	232	588	672
Washington	325	1,602	2,514
Wyoming	298	922	940

NA—not available.
*Combined total for Indian and Oklahoma territories. Separate black population figures for Indian and Oklahoma territories are 36,853 and 18,831 respectively.

Source: U.S. Bureau of the Census, Negro Population in the United States, 1790–1915 (Washington, D.C.: Government Printing Office, 1918), 43, 44; Michael D. Doran, "Population Statistics of Nineteenth Century Indian Territory," Chronicles of Oklahoma 53:4 (Winter 1975), 501; and U.S. Bureau of the Census, Twelfth Census of the United States, 1900, vol. 1, Population, part 1 (Washington, D.C.: U.S. Census Office, 1901), 537, 553.

come by railroad or steamboat. Many more took the transportation naturally available to a newly freed people: They walked. Most settlers came westward into Texas, Indian Territory, and Kansas from the Old South. Texas wages of twenty dollars per month, double those of Virginia, North Carolina, and Tennessee, encouraged a steady stream of freedpeople westward. The hundreds of North Carolina freedpeople who migrated to Texas in 1879 pursued goals similar to those of the much larger Exoduster movement to Kansas. Prevented from claiming public lands by the provisions of the Texas Homestead Act and discouraged from owning farms elsewhere in the state, these former North Carolinians settled in cotton-growing areas, becoming agricultural workers or sharecroppers much like their counterparts in the states east of the Sabine. By the 1890s many of them had joined John B. Rayner, Melvin Wade, and other ex-Republicans in the state's major nineteenth-century political insurgency, the Populist party.[2]

African Americans also moved to Indian Territory mainly from Arkansas and Tennessee. They became farmers, but on lands they could not possess until 1889 and in areas where their status as intruders subjected them to removal. Kansas absorbed twenty-five thousand black emigrants during the 1870s and early 1880s. As the closest western state to the Old South in the 1870s that allowed black homesteading, it became the destination for a particularly intrepid group of migrants. Most of these newcomers were from neighboring Missouri, but other border states, such Kentucky, Tennessee, and Virginia, and Deep South states, such as Mississippi and Louisiana, were also increasingly represented.

Kansas loomed large in the minds of many African American southerners. The state offered potential homesteaders access to vast tracts of undeveloped farmland. The 1862 Homestead Law, which applied to Kansas and other western states and territories, was uncomplicated and unambiguous. The federal government provided 160 acres of free land to any settler, regardless of race or sex, who paid a small filing fee and resided on and improved the land for five years. However, the settler could choose to purchase the land for $1.25 per acre after living on it for six months.[3]

The Republican party dominated Kansas politics, no small consideration for those who saw their rights quickly erode after Democrats returned to power in the former Confederacy by 1877. Moreover, Kansas carried a powerful abolitionist tradition. Here John Brown had first struck to free slaves, and here the first black soldiers had joined the Union army. Kansas had applauded the Emancipation Proclamation and been among the first states to ratify the Thirteenth Amendment. "I am anxious to reach your state," wrote a black Louisianian to the governor of Kansas in 1879, "not because of the great race now made for it but because of the sacredness of her soil washed by the blood of humanitarians for the cause of black freedom." Numerous Quakers, Presbyterians, and Congregationalists moved to the state after the Civil War, proudly embracing their "sense of mission toward the Negro." With their help Kansas became to the freedperson what the United States was to the European immigrant: a refuge from tyranny and oppression.[4]

African American migrants also anticipated fertile farmlands. George Marlowe, who represented a black emigration agency in Louisiana, wrote a glowing report after an eight-day visit in 1871: "What is raised yields more profit than elsewhere, and it is raised at less expense. The weather and roads enable you to do more work than elsewhere. . . . The country is well watered . . . [and] produces 40–100 bushels of corn and wheat to the acre and the corn grows 8 to 9 5-feet high." Such enticements drew thousands of black settlers, including young George Washington Carver, to west Kansas. In 1886 Carver claimed 160 acres of land in Ness County, built a modest sod house, and raised corn and vegetables for two years before leaving the area to continue his education in Iowa.[5]

Most African Americans who moved to Kansas came, like Carver, as individuals or in families, but some arrived through various emigration agencies. Of the groups, the Tennessee Real Estate and Homestead Association, founded by Benjamin ("Pap") Singleton, was the most successful. Born a slave near Nashville, Tennessee, in 1809, Singleton spent much of his life as a cabinetmaker. Sold off to the Deep South, he escaped to Detroit, where he operated a boardinghouse that often harbored fugitive slaves. After the war he returned to Nashville and became a carpenter. Convinced that the salvation of southern blacks lay in farm ownership rather than in sharecropping or wage labor, Singleton by 1871 had turned to Kansas, where homesteaded land could be acquired for $1.25 per acre.

In 1878 Singleton led his first emigrants, a party of two hundred settlers to the east bank of the Neosho River in Morris County, where he established the Dunlop colony, taking up residence there himself in 1879 and 1880. The colony illustrated both the prospects and the problems of Kansas colonization by the freedpeople. From 1846 to 1872 the colony's land was part of the Kansa Indian Reservation, which originally covered 256,000 acres. Under pressure from settlers, the federal government in 1859 reduced the reservation to 80,000 acres and in 1872 removed the last of the Kansa Indians to Indian Territory. Two years later Joseph Dunlop, a former trader with the Kansa, laid out the town and built the colony's first store near the Missouri, Kansas, and Texas Railroad. By 1878, when Singleton and his followers arrived, most of the best river and creek bottom farmland belonged to speculators and the railroad. The remainder, priced at $7 per acre, was still considered too expensive for the emigrants. Nonetheless, persuaded by exaggerated claims of the local boosters that the Neosho River valley was an idyllic agrarian environment, Singleton settled for the less fertile uplands, where colonists could purchase 80-acre homesteads for $1.25 to $2 per acre. In all, the colonists bought 7,500 acres of land to grow wheat, corn, vegetables, and other cash crops on land used today for cattle grazing.[6]

Had the colony remained agricultural, those who first arrived might have prospered. Events in Topeka, however, soon overtook the colony. The 1879 Exodus brought thousands of blacks to Kansas in a matter of months and prompted Governor John St. John to establish the Kansas Freedmen's Relief Association (KFRA) to "aid destitute freedmen, refugees, and emigrants." Encouraged by what they interpreted as sympathy and support, additional exodusters concentrated in the Kansas capital. Facing the prospect of clothing, housing, and feeding these thousands of exodusters, the KFRA chose to resettle them in rural Kansas, on the already established Dunlop colony. Four hundred new settlers arrived in the colony, built makeshift homes, and worked, when possible, for local ranchers.[7]

The relocation effort soon became an example of good intentions gone awry. KFRA moved the refugees onto impractically small homesteads. The association subdivided the 240 acres into twenty-eight lots with either 5 or 10 acres of land. The average white farmer in the area had 160 acres, most of the original colonists still had 80-acre homesteads, but the Exodusters often cultivated about 2 acres of their 5- to 10-acre "farms" and owned little livestock. None of the farms were self-sufficient; exodusters survived mainly by work on ranches, on larger farms, and in neighboring towns through or subsidies from local charities. The Dunlop colony population peaked at one thousand in the early 1880s and declined to less than five hundred by the end of the century as many colonists or their children moved to the cities.[8]

Benjamin Singleton was the most famous Kansas emigration leader. Yet he played no role in founding Nicodemus, Kansas's best-known black community. That distinction goes to six men—W. H. Smith, Benjamin Carr, president and vice-president respectively of the Nicodemus Town Company, Jerry Allsap, the Reverend Simon Roundtree, Jeff Lenze, and William Edmonds—who envisioned a black agricultural community west of the hundredth meridian near what was in 1877 the west Kansas frontier. They named their community Nicodemus after a legendary African slave prince who purchased his freedom. They chose to locate Nicodemus on the Solomon River. They also decided to recruit settlers from among their former friends and neighbors in central Kentucky.[9]

In July 1877, 30 colonists arrived at Nicodemus from Topeka, followed by 150 in March 1878. Additional settlers arrived later that year from Kentucky, Tennessee, Missouri, and Mississippi. Nothing in their experience prepared them for life in western Kansas. Graham County had 75 residents, primarily cattlemen, when the first colonists arrived. The flat, barren, windswept high plains, known for blazing summer heat and bitter winter cold, were better suited to growing cactus and soapweed than corn and wheat. Willianna Hickman, a settler in the 1878 migration to Nicodemus, wrote excitedly of navigating across the plains by compass. Finally she heard fellow travelers exclaim: "There is Nicodemus!" Expecting to find buildings on the horizon, she said, "I looked with all the eyes I had. 'Where is Nicodemus? I don't see it.' " Her husband responded to her query by pointing to the columns of smoke coming out of the ground. "The families lived in dugouts," she dejectedly recalled. "We landed and struck tents. The scenery was not at all inviting and I began to cry."[10]

By 1880, 484 African Americans, 11 per cent of the total population, lived in Graham County, while 258 blacks and 58 whites resided in Nicodemus and the surrounding township. The separation between town dweller and farmer was inexact because many townspeople were waiting for their opportunity to homestead land. Even Nicodemus boardinghouse owner Anderson Boles by 1881 had 75 acres of wheat under cultivation. The Graham County migrants were better prepared for homesteading than the Dunlop colonists. After initially difficult years most settlers by 1881 had planted 10 to 15 acres to wheat and corn and began to acquire some livestock. The first settlers had little farm equipment and faced drought, prairie fires, crop failures, and grasshopper swarms. Nonetheless many of them succeeded. R. B. Scruggs, a self-described "ole green boy, never 'way from home," before settling in Nicodemus in 1878, supplemented his meager farm income by driving a freight wagon and working as a railroad section hand during his first years in the West. His perseverance paid off; his original 120-acre homestead grew to a 720-acre farm.[11]

Nicodemus Township emerged as a briefly thriving community that served a surrounding countryside once described by a local newspaper as so flat "that you can see what your neighbors are doing in the next township." The Boles House, operated by Anderson Boles, and the Myers House, owned by J. M. Myers, and Eliza Smith's Gibson House all provided food and accommodations to visitors. Smith, a former Denverite, was unusual in the community not for her gender but because she emigrated to Nicodemus from farther west. John W. Niles opened the first livery stable in 1880 near John Lee's blacksmith shop. Z. T. Fletcher, the town postmaster, also operated a succession of businesses, the most prominent of which was the St. Francis Hotel, established in 1885. Two white residents were responsible for the town's only newspapers. Arthur G. Tallman established in 1886 the *Nicodemus Western Cyclone*, which had a brief newspaper monopoly until Hugh K. Lightfoot founded the *Nicodemus Enterprise* one year later. Two other prominent white businessmen integrated themselves into the economic and political life of Nicodemus. A former New Yorker, S. G. Wilson, erected the first two-story stone building in 1879, when he established the general store. C. H. Newth, a European-born physician, operated the drugstore for Nicodemus. "Nicodemus," wrote *Cyclone* editor Lightfoot, "is the most harmonious place on earth. . . . Everybody works for the interest of the town and all pull together. . . ." By 1886 Nicodemus had Baptist, Free Methodist, and African Methodist Episcopal churches and a new schoolhouse, considered one of the finest buildings in the town. Nicodemus's residents celebrated the Fourth of July, September 17 (the town founding day), and West Indian Emancipation Day, August 1, all of which included a community celebration of "speeches, dancing, a carnival, and . . . a great variety of food served under the trees of R. B. Scruggs' grove."[12]

Nicodemus's success attracted other African Americans, including Edwin P. McCabe. A Troy, New York, native born in 1850, McCabe worked on Wall Street before moving to Chicago in 1872, where he was appointed a clerk in the Cook County office of the federal Treasury. He arrived in the Nicodemus settlement in 1878 and, after advertising himself as an attorney and land agent, began surveying land and locating settlers on their claims. When Governor John P. St. John established Graham County in April 1880, McCabe was appointed temporary county clerk, beginning a long career of officeholding. In November 1881 McCabe was elected to a full-term as clerk, and the following year, at the age of thirty-two, he became the highest-ranking African American elected official outside the South when Kansas voters chose him as state auditor. Nicodemus

had other black elected officials, including John DePrad, who succeeded McCabe as county clerk; Daniel Hickman, who chaired the
Graham County Board of Commissioners; and W. L. Sayers, a prominent Hill City lawyer who was county attorney.[13]

As the first predominantly black western town to receive
national attention, Nicodemus became an important symbol of the
African American capacity for self-governance and economic enterprise. Yet the town's prospects, always precarious, had gone into
steady decline by the end of its first decade. First the weather struck.
The winter blizzards of 1885 destroyed 40 percent of the township's
wheat crop, prompting an exodus. Two years later town leaders
placed their hopes and sixteen thousand dollars in railroad bonds,
in unsuccessful efforts to attract the Missouri Pacific, the Santa Fe,
and the Union Pacific railroads to their town. When all three railroads bypassed Nicodemus, its fate was sealed. After 1888 local boosters ceased trying to lure additional settlers, and prominent citizens,
including most notably Edwin McCabe, left the area.[14]

The settlement of a few hundred blacks in Morris and Graham
counties presaged a much larger influx of southern African Americans into Kansas in the spring and summer of 1879. Named the
Exodus, this movement swept some six thousand blacks from Louisiana, Mississippi, and Texas into Kansas. As earlier in the decade,
southern hardships pushed the migration as much as Kansas opportunity pulled it. Although the "Kansas fever" generated images of a
leaderless millenarian movement of impoverished freedpeople,
driven by blind faith toward a better place, it was, as Nell Painter has
shown, a rational response to a hopeless condition in the South.
When Kansas critics called for barring impoverished Exodusters, one
emigrant had this rejoinder: "That's what white men go to new coun-
tries for, isn't it? You do not tell them to stay back because they are
poor. Who was the Homestead Act made for if it was not for poor
men?" An unidentified black woman's response was more succinct.
When a *St. Louis Globe* reporter asked the woman with a child at her
breast if she would return to the South, she replied, "What, go back!
. . . I'd sooner starve here."[15]

John Solomon Lewis's family saga embodied the movement.
The Lewis family lived in heavily black Tensas Parish, Louisiana, on
the west bank of the Mississippi River. There they and other African
Americans suffered grinding poverty. Lewis, however, challenged the
local landowner: "It's no use, I works hard and raises big crops and
you sells it and keeps the money . . . so I will go somewhere else and

try to make headway like white workingmen." When Lewis's angry landlord threatened to have him shot for his defiance, he and his wife and their four children fled to the woods for three weeks, waiting for a riverboat to take them away. The Lewis family reached Kansas a few weeks later with other black Exodusters who solemnized their entry into the state with a meeting to offer prayers of thanksgiving. "It was raining but the drops fell from heaven on a free family, and the meeting was just as good as sunshine. . . . I asked my wife did she know the ground she stands on. She said, 'No.' I said 'it is free ground' and she cried like a child for joy."[16]

Reactions to the influx of southern blacks was predictably varied. The *New West*, a journal that promoted settlement in Kansas, suggested that the freedpeople would have a chance for advancement denied them in the South. "Whatever befalls them in Kansas they at least have a chance to rise and fall on their own merits." The *Topeka Colored Citizen* celebrated the exodus and added: "Our advice . . . to the people of the South, Come West, Come to Kansas . . . in order that you may be free from the persecution, and cruelty, and the deviltry of the rebel wretches. . . . If they come here and starve, all well. It is better to starve to death in Kansas than be shot and killed in the South." But the newspaper also cautioned the Exoduster: "Remember that in Kansas everybody must work or starve. This is a great state for the energetic and industrious, but a fearful poor one for the idle or lazy man." However, Republican Mayor Michael C. Case spoke for many Topekans when he refused to spend municipal funds to aid the Exodusters. Moreover, the money spent by the KFRA to house and feed the Exodusters, he suggested, would be better used for returning them to the South. The oppression by the southern Democrats was, according to the mayor, a just reward for blacks "who were always talking politics."[17]

Without assistance from the city, state, or federal government (where Kansas Senator John Ingalls and Ohio Representative James A. Garfield both introduced unsuccessful relief bills), the burden fell to the Kansas Freedman's Relief Association. It hired two people to direct the relief efforts. John M. Brown, an African American schoolteacher from Mississippi, was made general superintendent of KFRA properties, primarily the Barracks, a shelter erected along the Kansas River as the temporary home of most Exodusters. Brown also headed the resettlement efforts. Laura Haviland, a white Quaker philanthropist from Michigan, became the organization's secretary and solicited relief supplies and donations. In response to a national appeal, black and white religious and civic organizations sent assistance. Edwin McCabe, then residing in Chicago, brought a boxcar of food and clothing and a check for $2,000, which he presented to Governor St. John. John Hall, a Philadelphia Quaker, donated $1,000, and Chicago meat-packer Philip D. Armour collected $1,200 from local businessmen. Laura Haviland reported in 1881 that the KFRA had received more than $70,000 in supplies and cash, $13,000 from England. Even William Lloyd Garrison, who publicly questioned the Exodus, directed Boston-area relief efforts from his home. These national efforts spurred the local community. St. John gathered sixty prominent citizens at the Opera House to form the Central Relief Committee. It raised $533 that night.[18]

Despite Mayor Chase's fears, many Exodusters found work in Topeka and other cities as mechanics, teamsters, laborers, and maids. Some worked as agricultural laborers or ranch hands in rural Kansas; others moved to black agricultural settlements, such as the Dunlop colony and Nicodemus, where they had mixed success as homesteaders. Robert Athearn poignantly described these impoverished black farmers who battled nature with their bare hands. "More than one of the Exodusters tried to dig out little circles of sod with hand shovels," he wrote, "and to plant potatoes in the unfriendly soil below." Most black newcomers ultimately adjusted and many became successful farmers, tradespeople, and mechanics.[19]

The Kansas Exodus ended almost as suddenly as it had begun, not because of white opposition or the advice of "representative colored men," such as Frederick Douglass, that blacks remain in the South. Neither the suffering Exodusters experienced on the banks of the Mississippi and Kansas rivers nor the machinations of numerous swindlers who preyed on the gullibility of the freedpeople could arrest the movement. However, word filtered back that little free land remained in Kansas and that many Exodusters remained destitute a year after their arrival. Blacks in the South realized Kansas was not the "promised land." Migration continued from Mississippi, Louisiana, and Texas after 1880, but it never matched that of the spring and summer of 1879.[20]

Oklahoma Territory was the other major area for black emigration. The territory was created out of the western half of the Five Indian Nations lands returned to the federal government by the 1866 treaties. Between 1866 and 1885 various Indian tribes, including the

Iowa, the Sac and Fox, the Comanche, the Cheyenne, and the Apache, were placed on reservations in Oklahoma Territory. Pressure from prospective settlers persuaded the federal government to reduce those reservations and open the "surplus lands" to homesteaders, resulting in the famous "run" for land claims on April 22, 1889. The subsequent opening of other former Indian lands in Oklahoma was one of the last opportunities for large-scale homesteading on public lands. A black territorial newspaper, the *Langston City Herald,* called it "the last chance for a free home."[21]

For many African Americans, Oklahoma Territory was more than a homesteading opportunity. It represented a concerted effort to create towns and colonies where black people would be free to exercise their political rights without interference. In a nation of growing racial segregation and restriction, successful settlement in Oklahoma seemed a rare opportunities for African Americans to control their destiny in the United States. Kansans William Eagleson and Edwin P. McCabe became the two leaders in this movement. Eagleson, the editor of the *Topeka American Citizen,* was himself an emigrant to Kansas. By 1888 he had shifted his recruitment efforts to Oklahoma. In 1889 he founded the Oklahoma Immigration Association, headquartered in Topeka but with agents in the major cities of the South, where he hoped to attract a hundred thousand black settlers. Eagleson promised economic opportunity and freedom from racial restrictions: "Oklahoma is now open for settlement . . . the soil is rich, the climate favorable, water abundant and there is plenty of timber. Make a new start. Give yourselves and children new chances in a new land, where you will not be molested and where you will be able to think and vote as you please. . . . Five hundred of the best colored citizens have gone there within the last month . . . there is room for many more."[22]

Eagleson's effort met with some success. R. F. Foster, an association representative in the South, reported in April 1890 that seventeen hundred African American settlers had already left Atlanta for Oklahoma. In August a committee of three, representing some three hundred blacks from Mississippi, visited the territory to investigate immigration prospects, and in February 1891, forty-eight black Arkansans arrived in Guthrie, followed by two hundred prospective settlers from Little Rock. By the spring of 1891, when blacks from the South arrived in Oklahoma on "almost every train," the territory had seven African American settlements.[23]

Edwin P McCabe, came to symbolize the Oklahoma emigration

movement. Through most of the 1880s McCabe was committed to his adopted Kansas. After serving two terms as auditor, McCabe failed to win nomination for a third term. He nonetheless continued to support the Republican party and was closely aligned with Kansas Senators John Ingalls and Preston Plumb. When McCabe failed in his 1889 election bid for register of the Kansas Treasury, he moved to Washington, hoping to obtain an appointment from President Benjamin Harrison. During his months in Washington both friends and foes accepted the rumor that McCabe was campaigning to be appointed the first governor of Oklahoma Territory. Although Harrison was not impressed with the Kansas politician, McCabe allowed the rumor to persist. Employing the typical language of Oklahoma boosters, he declared the territory "the . . . paradise of Eden and the garden of the Gods." But to the blacks growing restless under southern segregation and lynch law, he added a special enticement: "Here the negro can rest from mob law, here he can be secure from every ill of the southern policies."[24]

The idea of a predominantly black Oklahoma inspired ridicule and condemnation outside the African American community. Oklahoma's Democrats used the McCabe plan to brand all Republicans dangerous and unworthy of white support. When the territory's Democrats met in convention at Kingfisher in 1892, they declared that a vote for a Republican was a vote for "negro domination, race mixing and race war." The *Vinita Indian Chieftain*, a Native American newspaper, condemned the scheme to colonize Oklahoma with African American settlers, which it claimed was hatched by Kansas Senator Plumb during a visit to Guthrie in 1889. The newspaper commented on the irony of white "Oklahomaists" scheming to "take the land from the Indians only to have negroes take it from them." But Republicans issued the worst rebuke. One angrily declared "if the negroes try to Africanize Oklahoma they will find that we will enrich our soil with them." Another declared that if McCabe were appointed governor, he "would not give five cents for his life."[25]

Undaunted, McCabe and his wife, Sarah, arrived in Oklahoma in April 1890 and joined Charles Robbins, a white land speculator, and Eagleson in founding Langston City, an all-black community about ten miles northeast of Guthrie, then the capital of Oklahoma Territory. Langston City was named after the Virginia black representative who supported emigration to Oklahoma and pledged support for a black college in the town. The McCabes owned most of the town lots and immediately began advertising for prospective purchasers through their contacts in the territory and through the *Lang-ston City Herald*'s readers in Kansas, Arkansas, Texas, Louisiana, Missouri, and Tennessee. "Langston City is a Negro City, and we are proud of that fact," proclaimed McCabe in the *Herald*. "Her city officers are all colored. Her teachers are colored. Her public schools furnish thorough educational advantages to nearly two hundred colored children." The *Herald* also touted the Oklahoma prairie's potential for growing superior cotton, wheat, and tobacco. "Here too is found a genial climate, about like that of southern Tennessee or northern Mississippi, a climate admirably suited to the wants of the Negro from the Southern states. A land of diversified crops where . . . every staple of both north and south can be raised with profit." Edwin and Sarah McCabe's promotions blended their political and economic objectives. A large black population in Oklahoma ensured McCabe's political influence and the couple's profit.[26]

By 1891 Langston City had two hundred people, including a doctor, a minister, and a schoolteacher. "People who scoffed at the idea of Negroes being able to build a town of their own," the *Herald* reminded the skeptics in 1892, "[must] acknowledge that they were mistaken." McCabe and other immigration promoters scrupulously encouraged prosperous blacks to settle in Langston City. For nearly a year between 1891 and 1892 the *Herald* ran a column titled "Come Prepared or Not at All." The paper called for "active, energetic men and women with some money" who were "prepared to support themselves and families until they could raise a crop." The *Herald* told the poor, "If you come penniless you must expect it to get rough."[27]

African Americans comprised 6 percent of Logan County's population in 1890. Thus McCabe realized that Langston City's fate depended largely upon homesteading of nearby lands, starting with the Sac and Fox Reservation, opening on September 22, 1891. The *Langston City Herald* and Oklahoma Immigration Association agents spread the word throughout the South nearly a year prior to the opening. The *Herald* published advice on homesteading procedures: "Wherever you can find it, get 40, 80, or 100 acres of land and claim that as your homestead. As evidence that you do claim it, you must make some visible improvements. Drive a stake with your name on it, cut timber to lay the foundation of a house, do a little plowing or some other act that will show to others that you have occupied that particular piece of land." The *Herald* urged these initial improvements be followed by more permanent ones and called on the prospective settlers to file claims promptly with the land office.[28]

Hundreds of blacks reached Langston City in time for the opening. Many of them were armed and reputedly ready to secure a home "at any price." Their presence in the Cimarron Valley agitated local white cowboys and the Fox Indians, who threatened violence. Nonetheless prospective black homesteaders surged in. On September 21 five hundred black Texans stepped from a train in Guthrie and headed for the border of the new lands nine miles away. Half of them traveled by foot. On the day of the run some two thousand armed African Americans assembled at Langston City. Tensions mounted. Some whites on the northern line drove away would-be black settlers, and four miles south of Langston City black settlers exchanged gunfire with white cowboys. While checking on the progress of some prospective settlers, McCabe was fired upon by three white men, who ordered him to leave. He was rescued when armed blacks came to his assistance. Despite this violence, an estimated one thousand black families made successful claims on the Sac and Fox lands.[29]

Thousands of blacks raced for the opening of the Cheyenne-Arapaho lands in 1892 and for the Cherokee Strip the following year. A day before the Cheyenne-Arapaho run, many of them massed on the sandbars besides the Cimarron River and along the ninety-eighth meridian, carrying their children and belongings on their backs. Just before the Cherokee Strip was opened, the *Langston City Herald* advised its readers: "Everyone that can should go to the strip . . . and get a hundred and sixty, all you need . . . is a Winchester, a frying pan, and the $15.00 to file." A number of blacks did make the run on the strip and established the town of Liberty. One Oklahoma African American summarized the openings by declaring that "the whole Indian Territory will have been swallowed by the white man [but] many black men helped in the swallowing."[30]

Black settlement in rural Oklahoma was much more extensive than in Kansas. By 1900 African American farmers in the territory owned 1.5 million acres valued at eleven million dollars. Many of these landowners were freedpeople or "state negroes" married to former slaves who acquired allotments in Indian Territory after the Dawes Act terminated communal landholding among the Five Nations. But an equal number of blacks gained homesteads in the various runs in Oklahoma between 1889 and 1895. W. G. Taylor, for example, arrived in 1892, claimed 160 acres, and, in accordance with homesteading requirements, received a deed to his property after living on the land for five years. Taylor and his wife, like many of their neighbors, lived in a dugout, grew vegetables, and raised chickens well into the 1930s. Roscoe Dungee arrived in Oklahoma from Minnesota in 1892 and found that "most everybody lived in dugouts." Even after the initial settlement years the Dungee family and other farmers retained their dirt homes because of the safety they offered during tornadoes. The Dungees survived on vegetables, supplemented by prairie chicken, deer, rabbit, and quail.[31]

Eventually a thriving farming population arose that supported business owners and professionals. Blacks in Muskogee, Guthrie, Ardmore, Tulsa, and Oklahoma City operated cafés, grocery stores, saloons, rooming houses, and barber and blacksmith shops. They also occasionally owned clothing stores, jewelry shops, butcher shops, carriage stables, banks, and cotton gins. Black wheat and cotton buyers purchased crops from African American farmers while black doctors, dentists, lawyers, and druggists provided their varied services to numerous patrons.[32]

Yet the success of black farmers in Oklahoma and elsewhere in the region rested on a tenuous foundation of ample credit and rain. The absence of either could quickly spell disaster. Gilbert Fite did not have black farmers in mind when he wrote: "Rather than . . . establishing [sic] a successful farm and living a happy, contented life . . . [farmers] were battered and defeated by nature and ruined by economic conditions over which they had no control." African American agriculturists knew well the conditions he described. Moreover, in Oklahoma Territory and elsewhere in the West their poverty precluded acquiring sufficient land to ensure success. By 1910 black landownership in Oklahoma had already peaked. Statistics tell the story: In 1910, 38 percent of black farmers had less than fifty acres, as opposed to 18 percent of white farmers. The average size of white farms was 50 percent greater than black holdings. Early-twentieth-century African Americans, like all Americans, were enticed by city life, but small landholdings in a region where large landholding was a necessity ensured an early exit from many western farms.[33]

African American migration to the Twin Territories (Indian and Oklahoma) produced thirty-two all-black towns. Generally settlers believed residence in these communities ensured economic and political control over their destinies. All-black communities were not unique to the twin territories. Historian Kenneth Hamilton has identified forty-six black towns in five western states and territories in the late nineteenth and early twentieth centuries. These towns grew out of the desire of southern black emigrants to find some respite from racism. As one argued, "we are oppressed and disenfranchised. . . . Times are hard and getting harder every year. We as a people believed that Africa is the place but to get from under bondage we are thinking Oklahoma as this is our nearest place of safety."[34]

The first black towns date back to antebellum times, when Seminole slaves settled in autonomous communities. After the Civil War, Creek and Cherokee freedpeople settled in such communities as North Fork and Canadian, which in time became attractive to blacks from neighboring states. Boley, however, became the most noted all-black town in the Twin Territories. Boley was founded in the former Creek Nation in 1904 by two white entrepreneurs, William Boley, a

Black Towns in the West

California	Chase	Tatum
Abila	Clearwater	Tullahassee
Allensworth	Ferguson	Vernon
Bowles	Forman	Wellston Colony
Victorville	Gibson Station	Wybark
Colorado	Grayson	*Texas*
Dearfield	Langston City	Andy
Kansas	Lewisville	Board House
Nicodemus	Liberty	Booker
New Mexico	Lima	Cologne
Dora	Mantu	Independence Heights
Blackdom	Marshalltown	Kendleton
El Vado	North Fork Colored	Mill City
Oklahoma	Overton	Oldham
Arkansas Colored	Porter	Roberts
Bailey	Red Bird	Shankleville
Boley	Rentiesville	Union City
Booktee	Summit	
Canadian Colored	Taft	

Adopted from Kenneth Marvin Hamilton, Black Towns and Profit: Promotion and Development in the Trans-Appalachian West, 1877–1915 *(Urbana: University of Illinois Press, 1991), 153.*

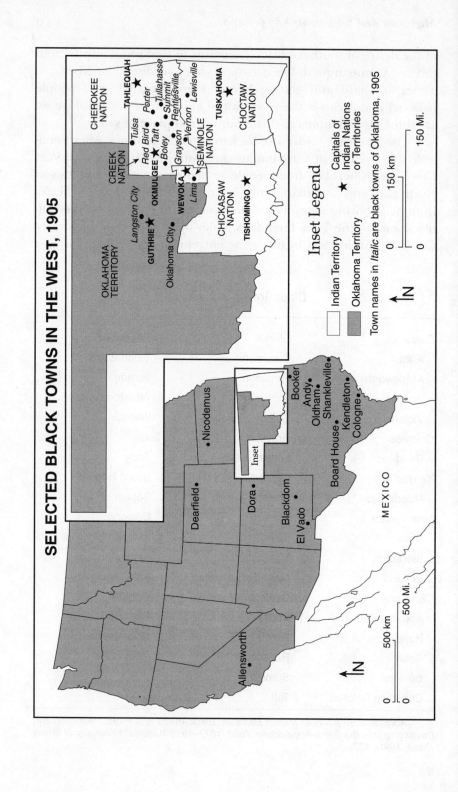

SELECTED BLACK TOWNS IN THE WEST, 1905

Inset Legend

☐ Indian Territory

▧ Oklahoma Territory

★ Capitals of Indian Nations or Territories

Town names in *Italic* are black towns of Oklahoma, 1905

0   150 km

0   150 Mi.

CHEROKEE NATION

★ TAHLEQUAH

Tulsa

Red Bird

Porter

Tullahasse

Summit

Taft

Rentiesville

CREEK NATION

★ OKMULGEE

Boley

Grayson

Vernon

Lewisville

SEMINOLE NATION

Langston City

★ GUTHRIE

Oklahoma City

OKLAHOMA TERRITORY

WEWOKA ★

Lima

★ TUSKAHOMA

CHOCTAW NATION

CHICKASAW NATION

★ TISHOMINGO

0   500 km

0   500 Mi.

N

Dearfield ●

Nicodemus ●

Dora ●

Blackdom ●

El Vado ●

Allensworth ●

Booker ●

Andy ●

Oldham ●

Shankleville ●

Board House ●

Kendleton ●

Cologne ●

Inset

MEXICO

railroad manager, and Lake Moore, a former federal officeholder. They hired Tom Haynes, an African American, to handle town promotion. Fortunately Boley was located on the Fort Smith & Western Railroad in a timbered, well-watered prairie that easily supported agriculture familiar to most prospective black settlers. Still, the frontier character of the town was evident from its founding. Newcomers lived in tents until they could clear trees and brush to construct houses and stores. In 1904 Creek Indians and Creek freedmen frequently rode through Boley's streets on shooting sprees. Several people died by gunfire until T. T. Ringo, a peace officer, killed some native "pranksters" outside a Boley church. Boley's reputation for lawlessness persisted. In 1905 peace officer William Shavers was killed while leading a posse after a gang of white horse thieves who terrorized the town.[35]

By 1907 Boley had a thousand people, with two thousand farmers in its surrounding countryside. Churches, a school, restaurants, stores, fraternal lodges, women's clubs, and a literary society attest to the economic and cultural development of the town. Booker T. Washington, in a town visit in 1908, explained its symbolic meaning for African Americans: "Boley . . . is striking evidence of the progress made in thirty years . . . . The westward movement of the negro people has brought into these new lands, not a helpless and ignorant horde of black people, but land-seekers and home-builders, men who have come prepared to build up the country. . . ."[36]

Boley's spectacular growth was over by 1910. When the Twin Territories became the state of Oklahoma in 1907, the Democratic-dominated state legislature quickly disenfranchised black voters and segregated public schools and accommodations. Oklahoma was no longer a place where African Americans could escape Jim Crow. Black men continued to vote in town elections, but political control at the local level could not compensate for powerlessness at the courthouse or the state capital controlled by unsympathetic officials.

Moreover, after the initial years of prosperity, declining agricultural prices and crop failures gradually reduced the number of black farmers who supported the town's economy. Even under ideal conditions, Boley and other black towns faced a challenge rampant throughout the rural United States: the lure of the city. The dreams of autonomy and prosperity that propelled an earlier generation to create Boley now encouraged the second generation to leave the town.[37]

No western state or territory held the emotional and economic appeal of Kansas or a potential for homesteads equal to Oklahoma Territory. Yet some black homesteaders ventured into the Dakotas, Nebraska, and Colorado. The *Cleveland Gazette* in 1883 reported that a colony of Chicago blacks organized under a "Mr. Watkins," a Chicago firefighter, acquired "several thousand acres of land at Villard, in McHenry County," Dakota Territory. A number of black agricultural colonies appeared in Nebraska between 1867 and 1889. The largest, a group of two hundred former Tennesseans, tried homesteading in Harlan County. On New Year's Day 1884 one successful homesteader, I. B. Burton, wrote to a Washington, D.C., black news-

African American Farms in the West, 1900, 1910

	1900		1910	
	Number	Value	Number	Value
Arizona Territory	15	$ 65,969	12	$ 62,630
California	135	497,802	159	2,276,941
Colorado	58	150,359	81	505,135
Idaho	9	23,166	13	62,706
Kansas	1,782	3,757,904	1,532	8,452,975
Montana	21	46,672	29	206,533
Nebraska	78	278,091	96	582,076
Nevada	3	40,719	6	113,551
New Mexico Territory	14	32,275	48	344,544
North Dakota	18	94,994	22	214,307
Oklahoma	6,353	7,313,156	13,209	30,347,738
Oregon	14	38,417	27	201,726
South Dakota	17	89,496	50	1,617,893
Texas	65,472	56,180,207	69,816	111,853,611
Utah	11	20,675	11	105,963
Washington	55	131,227	77	572,129
Wyoming	2	3,108	19	148,988
Percentage of U.S. Total	*10*	*14*	*9.5*	*14*

Source: U.S. Bureau of the Census, Negro Population, 1790–1915 *(Washington, D.C.: Government Printing Office, 1918), 592.*

paper from his new home near Crete, Nebraska, where another group of black settlers had bought land. He described how the settlers had pooled their resources, and he urged others to follow their example. "A large company can emigrate and purchase railroad lands for about half of what it would cost single persons, or single families. . . . Windmills are indispensable in the far west, and one windmill could be made to answer four or five farmers—each having an interest in it."[38]

Burton's call went largely unanswered until the Kinkaid Homestead Act of 1904 threw open thousands of acres in the sand hills of northwestern Nebraska. Recognizing the land's aridity, the federal government provided larger homestead claims of 640 acres. The first African American to file a claim, Clem Deaver, arrived in 1904. Other blacks, primarily from Omaha, soon followed, and by 1910, 24 families claimed 14,000 acres of land in Cherry County. Eight years later 185 blacks claimed 40,000 acres around a small all-black community near present-day Brownlee, originally named Dewitty for a local black business owner but later called Audacious. "The Negro pioneers worked hard," recalled Ava Speese Day, who wrote of her childhood in the sand hills. "It was too sandy for grain so the answer was cattle. . . . We [also] raised mules [which] brought a good price on the Omaha market." Yet in a pattern much like Oklahoma and Kansas, black farm families by the early 1920s had begun leaving for Denver, Omaha, or Lincoln. "Looking back, it seems that getting our [land] was the beginning of the end for us in Nebraska," Day remembered. "There was one thing after another. . . . In March 1925, we left the Sand Hills for Pierre, South Dakota."[39]

Dearfield, Colorado, was the last major attempt at agricultural colonization on the high plains. Dearfield was the idea of Oliver Toussaint Jackson, an Ohio-born caterer and messenger for Colorado governors. Jackson arrived in the state in 1887 and worked in Boulder and Colorado Springs as well as Denver. Inspired by Booker T. Washington's autobiography, *Up from Slavery,* Jackson believed successful farm colonies were possible in Colorado. His faith in rural western settlement as racial uplift was shared by many prospective Dearfield settlers. One of them told a *Denver Post* reporter in 1909: "We realize the negro has little . . . chance in competition with the white race in the ordinary pursuits of city life. We want our people to get back to the land, where they naturally belong, and to work out their own salvation from the land up."[40]

In 1910 Jackson and his wife, Minerva, filed a "desert claim" for

320 acres in Weld County, where the Dearfield colony was established. The claim attracted other investors, including Denver physician J. H. P. Westbrook, who suggested the name Dearfield. In late
summer of 1910 forty-eight-year-old Jackson and his first recruit for
the colonization venture, sixty-two-year-old construction worker
James Thomas, set out from Denver by wagon. Seven hundred mostly
middle-aged Denver women and men followed them to Dearfield
over the next decade. The female and male settlers included former
laborers, teamsters, janitors, coal miners, teachers, barbers, porters,
maids, and waiters. Although they had little capital and virtually no
experience in agriculture, all hoped to become dryland farmers.
Jackson recalled the first settlers as "poor as people could be when
they took up their homesteads. Some who filed on their claims did
not have the money to ship their housegoods or pay their railroad
fare. Some of them paid their fare as far as they could and walked
the balance of the way to Dearfield. . . . Some of us were in tents,
some in dugouts and some just had a cave in the hillside."[41]

Settlers' fortunes slowly improved. By 1915 the colonists had
filed claims on eight thousand of the available twenty thousand acres
in Weld County. One farmer optimistically wrote in 1915: "We
planted oats, barley, alfalfa, corn, beans, potatoes of all kinds, sugar
beets, watermelons, cantaloupes, and squash. Everything came up
fine, then came the grasshoppers that almost cleaned us out. . . . We
were not discouraged, however and last fall did some clearing for
hay ground. . . . If we have no bad luck this year, our people will be
self supporting by next fall."[42]

Dearfield prospered during World War I. By 1917 Jackson had
stopped recruiting settlers from Denver because all available land
had been homesteaded. Record high agricultural prices generated a
prosperity that many of the first settlers could not have imagined
seven years earlier. "Dearfield . . . has laid a great foundation for the
building of the wealthiest Negro community in the world," wrote
Oliver Jackson with both pride and typical booster hyperbole. A year
later he added in a nationwide letter advertising the town, "There is
no better location in the United States than Colorado to try on the
garment of self government."[43]

However, like Nicodemus, Boley, and other western agricultural
settlements that preceded it, Dearfield eventually slid into oblivion.
The colony's population peaked at seven hundred in 1921 and fell
sharply during the postwar agricultural depression. The lure of jobs
in Denver, the colony's inability to obtain water for irrigation, and

the bleak countryside (one former resident recalled that "it was always the same—a lot of wind blowing—bad wind") all contributed to the colony's demise. By 1946 Dearfield's only residents were Oliver T. Jackson and his niece Jenny, who had recently moved from Denver to care for him.[44]

Oscar Micheaux of Gregory County, South Dakota, became the most famous black homesteader on the northern plains, in part because he left accounts of his activities in autobiographical fiction, *The Conquest* and *The Homesteader,* the first of his seven novels. Born in 1884 on a farm near Murphysboro, Illinois, Micheaux worked as a Pullman porter before homesteading. When the federal government opened the eastern part of the Rosebud Indian Reservation to non-Indian settlement in 1904, Micheaux moved west from his Chicago home. He missed the spring lottery that distributed the lands (the federal government, learning from its experience in Oklahoma, decided to avoid a land rush) but nonetheless acquired a farm. "I concluded . . . [that] if one whose capital was under eight or ten thousand dollars, desired to own a farm in the great central west," wrote Micheaux, "he must go where the land was . . . raw and undeveloped."[45]

In 1913 Micheaux published *The Conquest,* a thinly veiled autobiography, followed four years later by his personal history of high plains farming, *The Homesteader.* After *The Homesteader* appeared, Micheaux lost interest in farming. By 1918 he had created the Micheaux Film and Book Company, which transformed *The Homesteader* into an eight-reel film. Micheaux left South Dakota for Chicago to film *The Homesteader* in the Selig Studio and never again lived in the state. He had launched the career that established him as the nation's most prolific black filmmaker between the 1920s and 1940s, producing forty-five movies before his death in 1951 in Charlotte, North Carolina.[46]

Oscar Micheaux homesteaded and then turned away from the West, but the histories of two homesteaders, Robert Ball Anderson of Nebraska and James Edwards of Wyoming, provide a glimpse into the world of successful African American settlers. Robert Ball Anderson, born a slave in Green County, Kentucky, in 1843, joined the Union army in 1864 and spent three years of his enlistment in the West. In 1870 he homesteaded 80 acres of land in southeastern Nebraska. Low crop prices, drought, and grasshopper infestations forced him temporarily out of farming in 1881. After working as a Kansas farmhand, Anderson, now forty-one, moved to the Nebraska panhandle to start over. He took one of the first homestead claims in Box Butte County, where he built a two-room sod house for shelter. Despite the agricultural depression of the 1890s, Anderson continued to add to his holdings. By the end of the century he had acquired 1,120 acres of wheat and grazing land. "I lived alone, saved, worked, hard, lived cheaply as I could," recalled Anderson in his autobiography, *From Slavery to Affluence.* By 1918 Anderson, now the owner of 2,080 acres, was by far the largest black landholder in Nebraska, and one of the most prosperous farmers in the state. Nine years later he wrote: "I am . . . old now, and can't do much work. I have a good farm . . . and money in the bank to tide me over my old age when I am unable to earn more. . . . I am a rich man today, at least rich enough for my own needs."[47]

James Edwards, born in Ohio in 1871, reached Wyoming in 1900, traveling west with his father to work as a coal miner near Newcastle. When he and his father were driven from the mines by Italian miners, Edwards herded sheep on a Niobrara County ranch. By 1901 Edwards had taken his first homestead claim, a ninety-acre parcel that became the center of a ten-thousand-acre ranch with two hundred cattle and one thousand sheep. Except for his skin color, Edwards looked and acted the part of the "classic Old West cowboy." Tall, athletic, mustached, lanky, Edwards rolled Bull Durham cigarettes and, despite his wife's disapproval, "got drunk" on whiskey on his visits to town.[48]

Like Anderson, Edwards lived in an overwhelmingly white community. His stock brand was the "sixteen bar one" representing, he claimed, the ratio of white men to black men in Niobrara County. Yet both farmers provided valuable work experience for black youth from as far away as Denver, Minnesota, Oklahoma, and Arkansas. Moreover, each in his own way earned the respect of neighbors. One neighbor wrote of Edwards: "All in all . . . he was a good man, and was liked in the community. . . . I have a lot of respect for any black man who invades a white territory, makes a living for himself, and builds a home as elaborate as his was on the prairie."[49]

An influential minority of westerners made ranching their exclusive economic activity, giving rise to the twentieth-century image of the region as the nearly exclusive domain of cattlemen and cowboys. Sixty-one thousand ranchers, herders, and drovers worked in the range cattle industry in 1890. However, they comprised only 2 percent of the three million workers in western states and territories. By comparison the West had nearly nine hundred thousand farmers.[50]

If historians have exaggerated the number and influence of western cowboys, they have also erred in their estimates of African Americans in the industry. Early estimates placed the numbers of blacks in ranching at nine thousand. The 1890 census, however, listed the total number of black, Asian, and Native American stock raisers, herders, and drovers in the western states and territories at sixteen hundred. Black Texas cowboys, who were more numerous than in any other western state or territory, nonetheless constituted 4 percent of the total of Texas herders in 1880 and 2.6 percent by

Stock Raisers, Herders, Drovers, 1890

	Total	Total Nonwhite*
Arizona Territory	2,712	148
California	5,978	293
Colorado	5,297	21
Idaho	1,553	28
Kansas	1,565	28
Montana	4,458	34
Nebraska	1,619	10
Nevada	1,049	118
New Mexico Territory	6,832	333
North Dakota	693	1
Oklahoma Territory	378	2
Oregon	3,105	55
South Dakota	886	21
Texas	17,819	473
Utah	2,418	8
Washington	1,044	26
Wyoming	4,147	32

*Also included Chinese, Japanese, Indians.

Source: U.S. Bureau of the Census, Population of the United States, 1890, Part II (Washington, D.C.: Government Printing Office, 1897), 532–626.

African American Stock Raisers, Herders, Drovers, 1910

	Stock Raisers	Stock Herders, Drovers
Arizona Territory	5	16
California	17	31
Colorado	4	7
Idaho	1	1
Kansas	10	17
Montana	1	9
Nebraska	3	9
Nevada	0	3
New Mexico Territory	6	21
North Dakota	0	0
Oklahoma	14	32
Oregon	4	6
South Dakota	6	3
Texas	48	406
Utah	1	17
Washington	1	3
Wyoming	5	23

Source: U.S. Bureau of the Census, Negro Population, 1790–1915 (Washington, D.C.: Government Printing Office, 1918), 513–16.

1890. Overall, black cowboys were about 2 percent of the total in the West.[51]

While the number of black cowboys was smaller than previously assumed, census data nonetheless show them throughout the region. Numerous vignettes in newspapers, journals, biographies, and histories that briefly mentioned or described African Americans corroborated their presence in the range cattle industry. Typical of such accounts was J. Frank Dobie's description of Pete Staples. A former Texas slave, Staples after the Civil War worked along the Rio Grande with vaqueros, in both northern Mexico and west Texas, married a Mexican woman, and joined the first cattle drives to Kansas. For two decades Jim Perry was one of a number of black employees of the three-million-acre XIT Ranch in the Texas Panhandle. He once declared, "If it weren't for my damned old black face I'd have been boss of one of these divisions long ago." Charlie Siringo recalled a visit to Texas cattle baron Abel ("Shanghai") Pierce's headquarters near Matagorda in 1871. "There were about fifty cowboys at the headquarter ranch," Siringo wrote, including "a few Mexicans and a few negroes. . . . The negro cook . . . drove the mess-wagon. . . ." Mississippi-born slave Bose Ikard was lifted from anonymity by the fulsome praise given him from his employer, Texas cattleman Charles Goodnight. "Ikard surpassed any man I had in endurance and stamina," wrote Goodnight. "He was my detective, banker, and everything else in Colorado, New Mexico, and the other wild country I was in. . . . We went through some terrible trials during those four years on the trail. . . . [He] was the most skilled and trustworthy man I had." Print Olive, a transplanted Texan in western Nebraska, left no flowing tribute for his employee and constant companion James Kelly but was equally grateful. Olive, wounded three times in an Ellsworth, Kansas, saloon by Texas cowboy Jim Kennedy, was about to be killed when Kelly shot Kennedy.[52]

One black cowboy's brief personal narrative has survived. Daniel Webster (80 John) Wallace, born near Inez, Texas, in 1860, eventually became the state's most successful black rancher. Before his ascent into the ranks of cattlemen, Wallace was a west Texas cowboy who started working at the age of sixteen in Lampasas County. By 1881 he had begun working for rancher Clay Mann, who originated the "80" brand, the basis of Wallace's nickname. Wallace described life on the cattle frontier, where everyone "slept on the ground in all kinds of weather with our blankets for a bed . . . a saddle for a pillow . . . and gun under his head." He recalled standing guard on stormy nights "when you couldn't see what you were guarding until a flash of lightning," or where a rattlesnake might be "rolled up in your bedding" or where cowboys were awakened by the "howl of the wolf or holler of the panther."[53]

We don't know if Wallace participated in the post–Civil War cattle drives, but other African Americans trailed longhorns from central Texas to railheads in Abilene, Dodge City, Denver, Cheyenne, or northern pastures in Montana. William G. Butler in 1868 drove a herd of cattle to Abilene with a crew of fourteen that included three Chicanos, nine whites, and two black drovers, Levi and William Perryman. R. F. Galbreath arrived in Kansas in 1874 leading a crew of four whites and three blacks, while Jim Ellison went up the trail in the same year with an all-black crew. In 1885 Lytle and Stevens sent north a herd of two thousand steers bossed by a black Texan, Al Jones.[54]

Since the trail drives began during the Reconstruction era, it would be naive to assume no racial tension existed between black and white Texans. The cowboys' trail drive rosters usually included names for white drovers but made references to "nigger" or "colored" hand for African Americans. During an 1878 Texas to Kansas trail drive, Poll Allen, the principal drover, directed a black cowboy to eat and sleep away from the rest of the crew. Finally Allen ran the man off by shooting at him. Instances of outright exclusion from the trail herd were rare, but discrimination in work assignments was common. John M. Hendrix, a white rancher and former drover, inadvertently described that discrimination in an early tribute to African American cowboys. Blacks "were usually called on to do the hardest work around an outfit," such as "taking the first pitch out of the rough horses . . ." recalled Hendrix. "It was the Negro hand who usually tried out the swimming water when a trailing herd came to a swollen stream, or if a fighting bull or steer was to be handled, he knew without being told that it was his job." On cold, rainy nights blacks would stand "a double guard rather than call the white folks. . . . These Negroes knew their place, and were careful to stay in it."[55]

Yet such nostalgia often obscured complexities and contradictions of the racial order on the high plains. Interdependence on the trail undermined arrogant displays of racial superiority or overt discrimination. Men on trail drives spent long hours facing common dangers. Black and white wages were equal although vaqueros were paid one-third to one-half the wages of the other cowboys. The workplace racism that permeated plantations in east Texas or the Old South did not exist on the plains.[56]

Nor were racial sentiments openly expressed in the most famous end-of-the-trail town, Dodge City, Kansas. Kansas's reputation for racial toleration and the promise of hundreds of black cowboys spending wages in the saloons, restaurants, hotels, brothels, and other businesses along notorious Front Street encouraged social mixing in this raw new town, founded in 1875. White and black drovers shared hotel rooms, card games, café tables, and on occasion jail cells. One attempt to exclude blacks from a hotel was recalled years later precisely because of its failure. When a hotel clerk in the Dodge House told a black cowboy that no rooms were available, the drover drew what the frightened clerk described as the "longest barreled six-shooter he had ever seen" and waved it in his face, saying, 'You're a liar!' " The clerk quickly rechecked his roster and found a suitable room.[57]

Texas's enormous African American population, coupled with its role in founding the nineteenth-century range cattle industry, guaranteed the state the largest black cowboy population. But African American cowboys worked elsewhere in the West. In 1883 Theodore Roosevelt admired the skills of a Texas-born Dakota Territory drover known only as Williams who broke horses on a neighboring ranch. Four African American cowboys in eastern New Mexico found themselves embroiled in the infamous Lincoln County range war of 1878, which introduced William Bonney, or Billy the Kid, to the American public. Three cowboys, George Washington, George Robinson, and Zebrien Bates, sided with the supporters of Alexander McSween and Bonney, who styled themselves Regulators, while John Clark worked for businessman-rancher Lawrence Murphy. New Mexico trail drover George McJunkin, who became a ranch foreman in Union County, is remembered primarily for his 1908 accidental discovery of the Folsom archaeological site that established the presence of humans on the North American continent during the ice ages. In neighboring Arizona Territory, John Swain and John Battavia worked for former Texas rancher John Slaughter, who had established a new ranch near Tombstone in 1884. Men such as Thornton Biggs, who worked in northern Colorado, and Henry Harris, another former Texan who became a foreman on the Elko County ranch of Nevada Governor John Sparks at the turn of the century are examples of black range workers throughout the West.[58]

Some African American cowboys were lifted from obscurity by irresponsible behavior or untimely death. In 1870 a black cook from Texas "shot up" Abilene, Kansas, while celebrating the end of a successful trail drive. He obtained the dubious distinction of becoming the first occupant of the new city jail and its first escapee when fellow drovers rescued him. Another black man, an innocent observer of a gambler's quarrel, was the first person killed in Dodge City. His death and subsequent murders prompted town merchants to form a vigilance committee and to hire a series of marshals, of whom Wyatt Earp and Bat Masterson were the most famous. The *Trinidad* (Colorado) *Daily Advertiser* reported in 1883 that a San Miguel, New Mexico Territory, black drover, George Withers, "wantonly and without provocation shot and killed George Jones (colored)," another ranch hand on the Canaditas cattle ranch, and then fled for Texas, pursued by a "posse of cowboys." The violent death of a black cowboy in Trinidad, Colorado, in 1887 elicited editorial comment from *Field and Farm,* a Denver journal: "Lawson Fleetwell . . . a bad man from the Indian nation, was shot and killed by an officer in Trinidad on Monday night. Fleetwell was in a gambling institution and got up a gun play in which he himself was killed. The cowboy seems to be keeping up his reputation this year as well as ever, and the mortuary reports are as entertaining as usual. It's generally the cowboy that gets the worst of the racket and he is not such a successful bad man as he has been pictured."[59]

A chasm separated the "cattleman" and his "cowboy" employees. Yet a few African Americans bridged that divide to become successful ranchers. Soon after the Civil War a Texan, Felix Haywood, and his father rounded up unbranded cattle along the San Antonio River for a white rancher who paid them in land that became the Haywood ranch. Henry Hilton and Willis Peoples owned ranches near Dodge City in the 1870s while Ben Palmer became "one of the heaviest taxpayers of Douglas County, Nevada," in the same decade. Isaac and Lorenzo Dow, two brothers born into slavery in Arkansas, arrived in Nevada in 1864 and acquired cattle ranches near Caliente, which they worked until 1900. The most successful western cattleman, however, was Daniel Webster ("80 John") Wallace, who made his first land purchase in Mitchell County, Texas, in 1885 while working as a cowboy. By the time of his death in 1939 the Wallace ranch had grown to 10,240 acres.[60]

Philip Durham and Everett Jones offered a succinct reason for the twentieth-century invisibility of nineteenth-century black drovers: "When the West became a myth . . . the Negro became the invisible man. . . . There was no place for him in these community theatricals. He had been a real cowboy, but he could not easily pretend to be one." This statement offers a partial explanation. Without doubt early Wild West shows, dime novels, and later more substantive literature, such as Owen Wister's 1902 novel *The Virginian,* established the white Anglo-Saxon as the cowboy archetype of the imagined West. Hundreds of subsequent books, films, and television episodes, advertising strategies, and toys reinforced the stereotype. But the "whitening" of the cowboy actually occurred in the late nineteenth century with the careful manipulation of the image by drovers and ranchers themselves, who extolled the virtues of white supremacy and racial purity.[61]

Theodore Roosevelt's description of the cowboys he worked

with in the 1880s, for example, simultaneously exposed both the multicultural dimensions of the range cattle work force and the prejudices (including his own) toward those who were not white: "Some of the cowboys are Mexicans who generally do the actual work well enough but are not trustworthy ... they are always regarded with extreme disfavor by the Texans in an outfit, among whom the intolerant caste spirit is very strong. Southern-born whites will never work under them and look down upon all colored or half-caste races. One Spring I had with my wagon a Pueblo Indian, an excellent rider and roper, but a drunken, worthless, lazy devil; and in the summer of 1886 there were with us a Sioux half-breed, a quiet, hard-working, faithful fellow, and a mulatto, who was one of the best cow-hands in the whole round-up."[62]

The elevation of one group often occurred alongside the denigration of others who at the time were significant elements in the drover work force. "The Greasers are the result of Spanish, Indian and negro miscegenation," wrote Joseph McCoy in 1872 in his assessment of the vaquero, "and as a class are unenterprising, energy-less and decidedly at a stand-still so far as progress, enlightenment, civilization, education, or religion is [sic] concerned."[63] Despite the considerable skill, dedication, and innovation they brought to the range cattle industry, it was increasingly clear even in the 1870s and 1880s that the racial dynamics of the period precluded the entry of black, brown, or red drovers into the pantheon of cowboy heroes.

"The process of moving" wrote George W. Pierson in 1973, "alters the stock, temperament, and culture of the movers, not only by an original selection but on the road as well as also at journey's end."[64] Pierson's words apply particularly to the nineteenth-century black western migrants. Their migration initiated the process of their own self-transformation. They adapted to the new physical environment, new customs, and new neighbors. But these settlers, full of hope, expectation, and promise, also modified their new region. Convinced that the political culture in the post–Reconstruction South offered no hope for equitable citizenship, late-nineteenth-century African Americans summoned all their energies to fight discrimination in their new homes. If they failed, the prospect for creating better lives for themselves and their children was lost forever.

6

⬦ ⬤ ⬦ ⬤ ⬦

Buffalo Soldiers
in the West,
1866–1917

No group in black western history has been more revered or reviled than the buffalo solders, some twenty-five thousand men who served in four regiments, the Ninth and, Tenth cavalries and the Twenty-fourth and Twenty-fifth infantry regiments, between 1866 and 1917. Along with black cowboys, these troops were the first African American western historical figures to capture public attention in the 1960s, when the nation grew to accept black heroes. Yet African Americans had long derived considerable pride from the soldiers' role as the "sable arm" of the U.S. government. Some African American soldiers consciously embraced that role. "We made the West," boasted Tenth Cavalry Private Henry McCombs; "[we] defeated the hostile tribes of Indians; and made the country safe to live in." William Leckie, the first biographer of the cavalry regiments, echoed that view, writing in 1967 that "the thriving cities and towns, the fertile fields, and the natural beauty [of the West] are monuments enough for any buffalo soldier." By the 1970s, however, historians such as Jack Forbes began to probe the moral dilemma posed by their soldiering. Were they not instruments in the subjugation of native peoples for a society that went on to "erect thriving *white* cities, grow fertile *white* fields and leave no real monuments to the memory of brave, but denigrated-in-their-lifetime soldiers"?[1]

The buffalo soldier's legacy is enveloped in controversy, but his origin is beyond dispute. The Civil War established African Americans in the nation's military. The Fifty-fourth Massachusetts Infantry Regiment, organized on the day the Emancipation Proclamation took effect, January 1, 1863, was the first officially recognized U.S. African American military unit. However, as early as 1861 General James Lane incorporated black men into his Kansas defense forces. By the end of the Civil War 180,000 African Americans had worn the uniform of the U.S. Army and had proved their courage from Fort Wagner on the Atlantic Ocean to Honey Springs in Indian Territory.[2]

After the war the U.S. Army was quickly reduced from 1.5 million troops to its prewar total of 16,000. The possibility of intervention in Mexico and of intensified warfare with Native Americans as the postwar nation turned westward prompted Congress in 1866 to increase the army's authorized strength to 54,000. Budgetary constraints, recruiting difficulties, and desertion, however, kept the size of the army in the West at 25,000 men in ten cavalry regiments and twenty-five infantry regiments. Black soldiers, led by white officers, made up the Ninth and Tenth Cavalry and Twenty-fourth and Twenty-fifth Infantry.[3]

Most assignments of the post–Civil War army related to frontier defense, so black units, like other regiments, were organized in the East and quickly stationed in western military outposts. Unlike white regiments, which expected to be rotated between the frontier and more populated areas, all four black units stayed in the West from 1869 until the Spanish-American War. The War Department rationalized that decision by arguing that their presence in eastern states and particularly in the South would prompt racial violence. "However senseless and unreasonable it may be regarded," wrote General C. C. Augur, commander of the Department of the South, in 1879, ". . . a strong prejudice exists at the South against colored troops." Troop assignment in Texas, the only state that experienced both Reconstruction-era violence and frontier warfare, illustrated the role of race in determining assignments. By the end of 1865 federal military power in Texas grew to thirty-two thousand troops, including the XXV Corps, twenty thousand African American veterans of the fighting in Virginia. These black troops, sent to the Rio Grande Valley ostensibly to "seal off the Mexican border from refugees and bandits," were in fact part of a U.S. show of force against Emperor Maximilian's French troops occupying Mexico. Some discharged black troops, in fact, crossed the Rio Grande to join Mexican resistance leader Benito Juárez.[4]

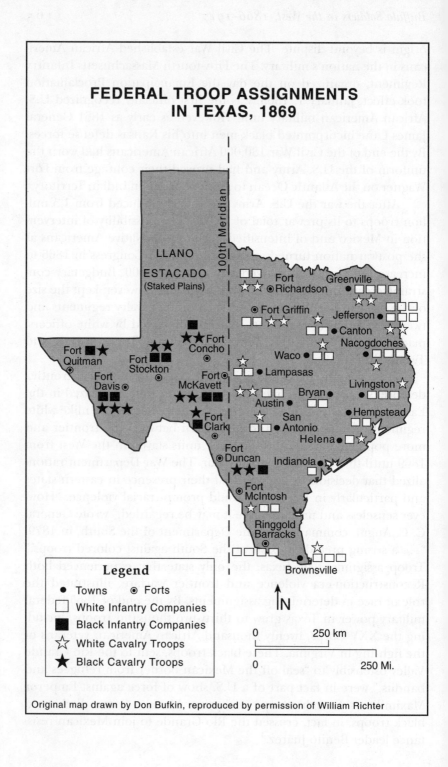

FEDERAL TROOP ASSIGNMENTS
IN TEXAS, 1869

LLANO
ESTACADO
(Staked Plains)

100th Meridian

Fort
Richardson

Greenville

Fort Griffin

Jefferson

Canton

Nacogdoches

Fort
Concho

Waco

Fort ■★
Quitman

Fort ■■
Stockton

Fort ◉
McKavett

Lampasas

Livingston

Fort
Davis ◉

Bryan

Austin

Hempstead

San
Antonio

Helena

Fort
Clark

Fort
Duncan

Indianola

Fort
McIntosh

Ringgold
Barracks

Brownsville

Legend

● Towns   ◉ Forts

□ White Infantry Companies

■ Black Infantry Companies

☆ White Cavalry Troops

★ Black Cavalry Troops

N

0   250 km

0   250 Mi.

Original map drawn by Don Bufkin, reproduced by permission of William Richter

Nonetheless black troops in Texas epitomized the hated "occupation" of the state, generating animosity with white civilians that lasted decades. The *Bellville Countryman,* for example, concluded that "the idea of a gallant and highminded people being ordered and pushed around by an inferior, ignorant race is shocking to the senses." Opinion evolved into attack in 1866. Two privates from the Eightieth U.S. Colored Infantry ventured into Jefferson, Texas, for a drink of water only to be killed by Deputy Town Marshal Jack Phillips as they passed him. Phillips was not arrested by military authorities because, as General Philip Sheridan, military commander of Union forces in the Southwest, concluded, "the trial of a white man for the murder of a freedman in Texas would be a farce." Although African American soldiers comprised nearly half the federal garrison in Texas during Reconstruction, the racial prejudices of white Texans had forced them, by 1869, to be assigned to the west Texas frontier rather than east Texas, where antiblack violence reigned.[5]

Two African American cavalry regiments were organized in 1866 under officers with impressive credentials. Colonel Benjamin Grierson, famous for his six-hundred-mile, sixteen-day Union cavalry raid through Mississippi in April 1863, was selected to command the Tenth Cavalry. After George Armstrong Custer refused the rank of lieutenant colonel with the Ninth, Colonel Edward Hatch, a highly decorated Civil War general, headed that regiment. The first commanding officer of the Twenty-fourth Infantry was Lieutenant Colonel William R. Shafter, who later achieved fame in the Spanish-American War. The Twenty-fifth Infantry was led by Colonel George L. Andrews. One promising junior officer who served at various times with black troops was John Joseph Pershing, who in 1917 commanded the American Expeditionary Force in France during World War I. Pershing's strong regard for the Tenth Cavalry began with his assignment to the regiment in Fort Assiniboine, Montana, in 1896. It was atypical of the officer corps of the era but common among those commanding black soldiers. Pershing wrote of his surprise at the number of complaints leveled at black troops by his fellow officers and concluded that he "would make the same appeal to them as to any other body of men. Most men, of whatever race, creed, or color, want to do the proper thing and they respect the man above them whose motive is the same." Pershing's respect for his troops earned him the racist nickname Nigger Jack, later softened to Black Jack when he was briefly assigned to West Point in 1897.[6]

The few African American officers faced more than racist nicknames. All three nineteenth-century African American graduates of West Point, Lieutenants Henry O. Flipper (1877), John Hanks Alexander (1887), and Charles Young (1889), served in western outposts with the four black regiments, as did the chaplains Allen Allensworth, Henry Plummer, George Prioleau, Theopolis Gould Steward, and William Anderson. Each officer faced ostracism from his colleagues. White officers at Fort Duchesne, Utah, and Fort Robinson, Nebraska, complained, for example, that they were discriminated against by the army because it assigned the only two black line officers, Alexander and Young, to the Ninth Cavalry. The War Department responded that since no vacancies existed in the other all-black regiments, reassignment of Young, the more recent West Point graduate, would have meant his joining a white regiment.[7]

The reaction of the black officers to this discrimination varied with their social and regional backgrounds. During the 1886 Senate debate over his nomination for a commission, Allen Allensworth made it clear to Georgia Senator Joseph E. Brown that "my Southern training has taught me enough to know how to appreciate . . . those who are my superiors. . . . I am prepared to guard against allowing myself . . . to give offense." Captain Henry Plummer, by contrast, plunged into black nationalist activities. In 1894 he proposed to the War Department that he lead an expedition of one hundred black soldiers to seize Central Africa before Europeans colonized the entire continent. Charles Young devoted so much energy to pleasing his superiors, even as they regularly upbraided him for "tactical errors," that he rarely fretted over his social isolation.[8]

Two officers' careers reflect the range of success and failure among these men. Chaplain Allen Allensworth expanded the educational role of the army, establishing an innovative program at Fort Bayard, New Mexico Territory, where enlisted men became teachers of other soldiers. His booklet describing the program, *Outline of Course of Study, and the Rules Governing Post Schools of Ft. Bayard, N.M.*, became standard on army posts. He retired in 1907 as a colonel, then the highest rank achieved by any black officer. In contrast, Henry O. Flipper, the first black graduate of West Point, was court-martialed in 1882 at Fort Davis, Texas, for accounting irregularities as a commissary officer. After leaving the army, Flipper worked for the next thirty-seven years as a mining engineer in New Mexico and

Mexico, becoming the first black American to gain prominence in the profession. In 1913 he worked as a consultant for New Mexico Senator Albert B. Fall's Sierra Mining Company, and from El Paso he dispatched reports on the Mexican Revolution to Washington, D.C.[9]

The first black enlisted men in the cavalry and infantry regiments were mostly eighteen- and nineteen-year-olds, too young to have served in the Civil War. They represented a cross section of black America. William Christy and George Gray were ex-farmers from Pennsylvania and Kentucky. Washington Wyatt was a former Virginia slave. Nineteen-year-old Emanuel Stance, scarcely five feet tall, from East Carroll Parish, Louisiana, joined the Ninth Cavalry when the regiment was two months old. Stance enlisted in F Troop in 1866 and four years later became the first post–Civil War African American soldier to win a Congressional Medal of Honor. Black soldiers' motives for joining the army varied as much as their backgrounds. Former slave Reuben Waller joined the Tenth Cavalry in 1867 to fight in "the Indian war that was then raging in Kansas and Colorado." Sergeant Samuel Harris wanted to see the West and believed his military service would help him get a good government job. The possibility of education sparked the interest of others. "I felt I wasn't learning enough," recalled Mazique Sanco, "so I joined." George Conrad, Jr., recalled how he did not learn to read and write until he joined the army in 1883. "I got tired of looking mules in the face from sunrise to sunset," recalled Private Charles Creek. "Thought there must be a better livin' in this world." Private George Bentley, the illegitimate son of a black woman and a white man, joined the army to escape an overbearing mother and brother. Others included cooks, waiters, painters, bakers, and teamsters, who eagerly enlisted for five years at thirteen dollars a month.[10]

African American soldiers faced hazardous duty almost immediately in west Texas and central Kansas in 1867. By the summer of that year the all-black Thirty-eight Infantry Regiment, which had already fought in a number of western engagements with Indian warriors, assisted the Seventh Cavalry in defending Fort Wallace, Kansas, against a Cheyenne attack led by Chief Roman Nose. Elizabeth Custer, the wife of Colonel George Custer, recalled that battle and the strange sight of a mule-drawn wagon full of black infantrymen firing at the Cheyenne while it raced to the skirmish line. When they reached their destination, all the soldiers jumped out of the wagon and began firing again. "No one had ordered them to leave their picket station," she remembered, but "they were determined that no soldiering should be carried on in which their valor was not proved."[11]

The newly organized Tenth Cavalry arrived in Kansas, where they guarded settlers and Kansas Pacific Railroad construction crews, during the 1867 war against the Comanche, Kiowa, Southern Cheyenne, and Arapaho. On August 1 one of the camps was attacked by Cheyenne Indians, who killed 7 workers. A 34-man troop followed the raiders into an ambush. Forced to dismount, they fought off 80 warriors in a six-hour battle, killing 6 of them. The ambush, however, cost the life of Sergeant William Christy, the first of hundreds of black soldiers to die in various western military engagements during the next five decades. Between August 21 and 24 approximately 800 Kiowa and Cheyenne led by Roman Nose and Satanta trapped a company of Tenth Cavalry and a regiment of Eighteenth Kansas Volunteer Cavalry in a ravine near the Nebraska border. The 164 troopers heard taunts directed at the white soldiers. "Come out of that hole, you white sons of bitches; we don't want to fight the niggers; we want to fight you white sons of bitches." Yet in the ensuing battle blacks and whites fought with equal intensity, and the Indians showed no particular mercy toward any soldiers.[12]

African American soldiers defended the region's inhabitants, usually white settlers. On occasion, however, they guarded Native Americans in Indian Territory from other Indians. Chickasaw, Cherokee, and Creek farmers suffered as much from Comanche or Kiowa raids as did white farmers in neighboring states. Sometimes the soldiers protected Indian people from white attack as in 1879, when Tenth Cavalry troops defended Kiowa women and children from Texas Rangers who had invaded their village intent upon killing and scalping its occupants and in 1887, when units of the Ninth protected Ute Indians from Colorado militiamen determined to enter their reservation in pursuit of their tribal leader, Colorow.[13]

Settler protection meant pursuing elusive Indian horsemen much more familiar than they were with the countryside. In the summer of 1869, when the Kiowa and Comanche raided as far east as Fort Worth and San Antonio, units of the Ninth Cavalry were ordered to intercept all nonreservation Indians. In 1869, 95 troopers of the Ninth left Fort McKavett, Texas, on a grueling forty-two-day, six-hundred-mile pursuit of Comanche who had attacked ranches near San Saba. Six years later Colonel William Shafter led 220 officers and men from the Tenth Cavalry and Twenty-fourth and Twenty-fifth Infantry on a six-month sweep of the Llano Estacado to destroy Comanchero, Apache, and Comanche camps. The expedition, which covered more than twenty-five hundred miles, crisscrossed the remote high plains in Texas and New Mexico. Between July 1879 and March 1880, Company C, Ninth Cavalry, chased a small band of Mescalero Apache over two thousand miles through west Texas and eastern New Mexico.[14]

One example of the danger of such missions occurred in May 1880, during the campaign against the Apache band led by Victorio. When warned of an impending attack by Victorio on the tiny settlement of Tularosa, New Mexico, Sergeant George Jordan led twenty-four soldiers of the Ninth Cavalry on an all-night ride to the settlement. Upon arriving, the soldiers turned a corral and an old fort into a defensive stockade and gathered the frightened settlers into it. Soldiers and citizens fought off repeated attacks by the Apache, who then tried to capture the town's horses and cattle. Anticipating their plan, Jordan sent ten troopers to assist two soldiers and a herder who had been earlier assigned to protect the livestock. Jordan's decisive leadership and bravery earned him the Congressional Medal of Honor.[15]

One decade later Ninth Cavalry troopers endured a South Dakota winter as they supported the last major military operation against native people, the Ghost Dance campaign of 1890–91. When the messianic Ghost Dance religion appeared to attract a large following on the Sioux Indian reservations at Pine Ridge and Rosebud, the War Department in November 1890 placed 1,400 soldiers on the two reservations. A tense peace held for the next month until December 29, when 350 Sioux men, women, and children awoke at their camp on Wounded Knee Creek to find themselves surrounded by 500 Seventh Cavalry troopers. Colonel James Forsyth ordered his soldiers to disarm the Sioux. In a subsequent confrontation between an Indian and a soldier, a rifle discharged, prompting both sides to begin firing. When it ended, more than 250 Sioux (including women and children) and 25 soldiers lay dead at Wounded Knee.[16]

In the ensuing campaign the Seventh and Ninth cavalry pursued frightened Sioux survivors. Hampered by internal divisions, separated from supplies, encircled by a slowly contracting ring of soldiers, and facing the prospect of fighting in the middle of winter, the Sioux were ill prepared to resist the army. On January 15 the

Sioux leader, Kicking Bear, surrendered to General Nelson A. Miles. As the other army units quickly evacuated the Pine Ridge Reservation, four companies of Ninth Cavalry were left to guard the Sioux. The men endured a bitterly cold winter with only canvas tents and were not relieved until March. The Sioux faced even greater privation. Private W. H. Prather, who shared the anti-Indian bias of many black and white soldiers of the era, nonetheless asked why both Indians and blacks seemed abandoned to a harsh Dakota winter with record snowfalls and temperatures as much as thirty degrees below zero. "The Ninth, the willing Ninth," he lamented, "[who] were the first to come, will be the last to leave, we poor devils, and the Sioux are left to freeze."[17]

The duty of a buffalo soldier entailed pursuing outlaws of any race or nationality. A report by Colonel Benjamin Grierson at Fort Sill, Indian Territory, in 1870 suggested their activities as a frontier police force. In 1869 soldiers under Grierson's command tracked and returned over 250 stolen animals, turned over twenty alleged thieves to civil authorities, and killed several suspects who resisted arrest or tried to escape. A terse report on the Tenth Cavalry at Fort Davis, Texas, in 1881 summarized one example of such duty: "Sgt. Winfield Scott and Pvt. Augustus Dover wounded in the line of duty while attempting to arrest desperado on military reservation—desperado W. A. Alexander was killed resisting arrest."[18]

Occasionally police duty involved civilian disputes. In December 1877 Colonel Edward Hatch led Ninth Cavalry troops into El Paso to end the Salt War, a conflict seething with overtones of racial tension between the tiny Anglo minority of the city and its Latino majority. The "war" was precipitated by Judge Charles Howard's attempt to control the nearby saltworks, previously available to any resident. Howard's actions and his subsequent murder of Luis Cardis, a local political leader, prompted Latino leaders to demand his arrest. When a company of twenty Texas Rangers intervened to protect Howard, the Mexican American population rose in anger. On Thursday, December 13, they surrounded the ranger headquarters, where Howard and other Anglos had retreated for safety. In a one-week battle three Rangers were killed and two wounded. The commander surrendered, and Howard was arrested and quickly executed by a firing squad.

The violence prompted Governor Richard B. Hubbard to call

for U.S. military intervention. Colonel Hatch arrived in El Paso on December 19 with fifty-four troopers and declared that federal troops were in the city to "protect the lives and property of all the citizens." He also vowed that "outrages in the name of . . . the law and by those who ought to be its representatives and guardians will not be tolerated." Hatch's statement was intended equally for the Latino leaders who had executed Howard and for the Texas Rangers, who had arrested and subsequently shot two Latinos in reprisal for their humiliating defeat. In an era when black men themselves increasingly became the victims of violence, the African American troops of the Ninth Cavalry stood between white and brown men in one of the worst ethnic and political feuds in nineteenth-century west Texas.[19]

In 1890 Ninth Cavalry troopers found themselves enmeshed in a civilian dispute in Johnson County, Wyoming. In 1890 small ranchers in Wyoming protested the territory's 1884 law that allowed the major cattle ranches to claim all unbranded cattle. Unable to get the law amended in a legislature dominated by powerful cattlemen, the small ranchers resorted to claiming unbranded cattle. The Wyoming Stock Growers' Association, which represented the large ranchers, immediately labeled its opponents "rustlers." In 1892 it hired twenty-five gunmen to drive small ranchers out of northern Wyoming. Local law enforcement officials, however, supported by the Sixth Cavalry, arrested both the cattlemen and their hired guns for the death of two alleged rustlers near Casper. Angered that the troops and civilians had thwarted its plans, the association wired Wyoming's U.S. senator Joseph M. Carey, on June 1, 1892, with specific demands: "We want cool level-headed men whose sympathy is with us. . . . Send six companies of Ninth Cavalry from [Fort] Robinson to [Fort McKinney]. The colored troops will have no sympathy for Texan thieves, and these are the troops we want."[20]

The Wyoming Stock Growers' Association relied on both old animosities and a new role that black troops would assume in industrial disputes. The old animosities stemmed from long-standing tensions between white Texans and black soldiers. The new role arose from the belief that the white working-class racism toward African Americans ensured that black soldiers would harbor little sympathy for small ranchers. Subsequent events bore out that assumption.

Two weeks after Senator Carey received the stock growers' telegram, 314 Ninth Cavalry troops were transferred from Fort Robinson to Johnson County, Wyoming. On June 13 the troops established

Camp Bettens near the town of Suggs and almost immediately encountered hostility from local residents. Black troopers of course were long accustomed to verbal insults and rebuffs from townspeople, but when Privates Abraham Champ and Emile Smith were chased out of Suggs by townspeople on June 16, most troopers realized this new assignment posed more than "normal" hazards. On the night of June 17, 20 black soldiers vowed to avenge the attack on their fellow troopers. Disobeying orders, they "penetrated the centre of [Suggs], fired one volley in the air, and then commenced firing through the streets and at some of the houses." The gunfire exchange with townspeople left Private Willis Johnson dead. Two companies of the Ninth arrived in town to disarm and arrest fellow troopers.[21]

Immediately after the Suggs incident, John M. Schofield, commanding general of the army, ordered the troopers responsible for the attack on Suggs turned over to civilian authorities for trial and barred the remaining troops from contact with civilians until they returned to Fort Robinson. Yet Ninth Cavalry's Colonel James Biddle's fear for the safety of the troopers at the hands of local authorities prompted the army to try the soldiers at Fort Robinson, where they were given minor punishments.[22] Unlike El Paso, where troop presence reduced tension between warring factions, their introduction into the cattlemen's dispute by the Wyoming Stock Growers' Association was cynical ploy calculated to exacerbate racial tension. The death of Private Willis Johnson was the tragic but not surprising result of the association's actions.

Civilian animosity posed danger for African American soldiers nearly comparable to their confrontations with Native Americans or desperadoes. Unlike the South, where defenseless blacks could not retaliate against racial violence, the troopers seemed eager to extract revenge for every perceived injustice. The 1867 vigilante lynching of three African American infantrymen at Fort Hays, Kansas, drew retaliation by black soldiers that culminated in a thirty-minute gun battle in the center of town. In 1885 a black soldier was lynched near Sturgis, Dakota Territory. Soon after, approximately twenty soldiers of the Twenty-fifth Infantry returned to town and fired on two saloons, killing a civilian.[23]

Such impetuous acts, regardless of provocation, only intensified civilian-soldier animosity. The Sturgis (Dakota Territory) Weekly

Record recognized that black soldiers harbored resentment over the recent lynching. Nonetheless it argued that murder of the trooper did not justify their attack. "Here are soldiers whom we help support [and who] are placed at the post for our supposed protection. . . . They take the guns that we bought, march calmly out of the post and mob our town. . . . What difference can there be between that and an Indian raid?" The *Black Hills Daily Times* of Deadwood added, "Never has any people been visited by a more horrible murder. . . . Men who think of life so lightly are fit subjects for a cannibal island, and only such a place. . . ."[24]

Some anti–black soldier hostility stemmed not from any particular act by troopers against civilians but from sheer racism. The editor of the *Las Cruces* (New Mexico Territory) *Thirty-Four* expressed the frustration of many westerners at the inability of the army to capture or defeat Indian raiders when he wrote in 1879, "The experiences . . . which the people of Southern New Mexico have passed during the past two months are sufficient to convince any sane man that the portion of the United States Army known as the Ninth Cavalry is totally unfit to fight Indians. . . . Let the Ninth be . . . disbanded [so that its members] might contribute to the nation's wealth as pickers of cotton and hoers of corn, or to its amusement as a travelling minstrel troupe. As soldiers on the western frontier they are worse than useless—they are a fraud and a nuisance."[25]

Hostility against black soldiers was most entrenched among Reconstruction-era Texans. Their animosity toward all U.S. troops who represented the victorious Union and the hated Republican administrations in Washington and Austin was exacerbated when the federal troopers were African American. Local civilian juries rarely convicted outlaws captured by black soldiers or civilians accused of murdering African American troopers. In 1870 John Jackson, a civilian near Fort McKavett, murdered Private Boston Henry, then as he fled, killed Corporal Albert Marshall and Private Charles Murray, who were part of the unit sent to capture him. When Jackson was finally apprehended and brought to trial, a jury set him free. Five years later two soldiers were killed when a five-man patrol was ambushed by vaqueros near Rio Grande City, Texas. A grand jury indicted nine men for the murders, but the only one brought to trial was quickly acquitted. In 1878 cowboys and buffalo hunters in a San Angelo, Texas, saloon humiliated a black sergeant by removing his stripes. Angry troopers from nearby Fort Concho stormed the saloon in retaliation and in the subsequent gunfight killed one of the hunters. Nine troopers were indicted for murder, and one, William Mace, was condemned to death. But when sheepherder Tom McCarthy killed unarmed Tenth Cavalry Private William Watkins in a San Angelo saloon in 1881, he was indicted for murder, transferred to Austin for trial, and promptly acquitted.[26]

No citizen-soldier clashes occurred in the West between 1885 and 1899. Still, segregation and racial violence increased the chasm between soldiers and civilians. When the Salt Lake City Tribune urged the War Department to station the Twenty-fourth Infantry someplace other than nearby Fort Douglas, Infantry Private Ernest A. Thomas wrote to the paper: "We object to being classed as lawless barbarians. We were men before we were soldiers, we are men now, and will continue to be men after we are through soldiering." Lieutenant Charles Young, speaking before a Stanford University audience in 1903, repudiated the views of Booker T. Washington, suggesting that submission in the face of growing racial oppression would gain nothing. Instead, he argued, black Americans should be allowed to use their abilities without interference from society. "All the Negro asks is a white man's chance," concluded Young, "Will you give it?" The answer soon came with the Brownsville raid and its aftermath.[27]

In May 1906 the War Department ordered two battalions of the Twenty-fifth Infantry stationed at Fort Niobrara, Nebraska, to transfer to Fort Brown, near Brownsville, Texas. En route they were scheduled for joint maneuvers with Texas national guardsmen. Chaplain Theophilus Gould Steward, recalling the conflict between white and black soldiers during joint maneuvers with the Texas Guard at Fort Riley, Kansas, in 1903, urged cancellation of the military exercise because "Texas, I fear, means a quasi battleground for the Twenty-fifth Infantry." He may also have been troubled by other incidents. In 1899 a Tenth Cavalry troop train transporting Spanish-American War veterans between Huntsville, Alabama, and their new post near San Antonio was fired upon in Meridian, Mississippi, and Harlem, Texas. Later that year armed citizens of Rio Grande City, Texas, confronted Ninth Cavalry troops stationed at Fort Ringgold, who responded by firing on the town. In 1900 Twenty-fifth Infantry soldiers temporarily on assignment near San Antonio and El Paso fought townspeople. In the El Paso conflict a white policeman and a black corporal were killed. Colonel Chambers McKibbin, a white officer sent to El Paso to investigate the episode, observed that black soldiers were arrested for offenses that, when committed by whites, were overlooked, and he added that African Americans were abused even when they behaved "with perfect propriety." "There is unquestionably a very strong prejudice throughout all of the old slave states against colored troops," McKibbin concluded. "It is not because the colored soldier is disorderly—for as a rule, they behave better than white soldiers . . . but because they are soldiers." Heeding Steward's warning and McKibbin's report, the War Department cancelled the maneuvers and sent the black soldiers directly to Fort Brown.[28]

Most soldier-civilian clashes involved white-black racial violence. Yet conflicts at Rio Grande City, Laredo, Brownsville, and other south Texas border towns reflected black-Latino tensions. The origins of these black-brown tensions can be traced to the immediate post–Civil War era, when both south Texas Anglos and Latinos supported the Confederacy and faced a mostly black Union occupying force along the lower Rio Grande. Open disdain of blacks by postwar Texas state officials and the Texas Rangers increased the distance between soldiers and civilians. But impoverished Latinos developed other reasons for opposing black troops. Throughout the late nineteenth century Texas buffalo soldiers pursued Mexican "bandits" and revolutionaries who were often viewed as folk heroes by the local population. On other occasions they maintained order as in 1899, when Tenth Cavalry troopers suppressed rioting Latinos in Laredo. Moreover, in Texas's racial hierarchy, Latinos resented African Americans occupying positions of authority. Lieutenant Colonel Cyrus Roberts deduced after investigating the Rio Grande City incident that Latinos "consider themselves their [black troops'] superiors, whereas with white troops they accept their inferiority."[29]

Like most Rio Grande border towns, Brownsville had a Latino majority, 80 percent of this community of seven thousand, with Anglo residents comprising most of the rest of the population. Only ten black families lived in the town. As the center of the lower Rio Grande Valley range cattle industry, Brownsville was "filled with rough, rootless, violent men, living in a community as much frontier and western as it was racist and southern." Anglo Brownsvillians maintained a rigid segregation against their Latino neighbors, and both groups opposed the presence of the Twenty-fifth Infantry.

Three incidents in July 1906, soon after the first three companies of the Twenty-fifth arrived, suggested the future. Two privates, James W. Newton and Frank J. Lipscomb, out for a Sunday stroll, met a party of women escorted by Fred Tate, a federal customs official. When the two privates attempted to pass the women by walking on the inner part of the sidewalk rather than stepping temporarily into the street, Tate struck Newton with his revolver, knocking him unconscious, while Lipscomb fled. One week later several soldiers were returning from a visit to Matamoros, Mexico, just across the Rio Grande, when the inspector of customs, A. Y. Baker, claiming Private Oscar W. Reed, was drunk, rude, and disorderly, allegedly pushed the soldier into the river. As investigators later reported, "the facts in these two cases were exaggerated on both sides and increased the bitter feeling between soldiers and citizens."[30]

The third incident proved more serious. A man later identified as a black infantryman attacked Mrs. Lon Evans. When she screamed, the assailant fled. The *Brownsville Daily Herald* recounted the event in lurid detail under the headline NEGRO SOLDIER INVADED PRIVATE PREMISES LAST NIGHT AND ATTEMPTED TO SEIZE A WHITE LADY. The town mayor, Frederick J. Combe, persuaded the post commander, Major Charles Penrose, to confine all soldiers to the fort to preclude racial violence in the aftermath of the assault. Nonetheless on August 13, 1906, approximately fifteen unidentified men gathered across from Fort Brown and began firing into buildings along the alley and adjacent Thirteenth Street. Before they stopped ten minutes later, Frank Natus, a bartender, was dead. The wounded included M. Ygnacio Domínguez, a police lieutenant, and Paulino S. Preciado, editor of the Spanish-language newspaper *El Porvenir.*[31]

The Brownsville raid quickly polarized national public opinion. A Brownsville citizens' committee, appointed by the mayor, concluded after a two-day investigation that black soldiers had staged the raid and telegraphed President Theodore Roosevelt on August 15, asking him to replace the Twenty-fifth Infantry with white troops. President Roosevelt sent Major Augustus P. Blocksom, assistant to the inspector general, to Brownsville to ascertain responsibility. Within two days of his arrival Blocksom conceded that although the raid was provoked by civilian mistreatment of the soldiers, African American troops were responsible for the shooting. He recommended immediate removal of all black soldiers from the lower Rio Grande Valley. The president complied, and the War Department transferred the infantry to Fort Reno, Oklahoma. Texas Rangers, however, acting on behalf of local civil authorities, arbitrarily selected eleven soldiers and 1 civilian as the most likely responsible parties, in effect holding them as judicial hostages until they or other troopers were specifically implicated by fellow soldiers. When no other soldiers stepped forward to acknowledge responsibility for the raid, Texas authorities reluctantly released the prisoners. President

Roosevelt, however, discharged 167 men, arguing that his action would teach blacks that they should not "band together to shelter their own criminals."[32]

Roosevelt's action generated a fire storm of protest from the African American press. Interracial organizations, such as the Constitution League, protested, and some major northern newspapers sent reporters to Brownsville. The *New York World* called the president's action "executive lynch law," and the *New York Times* declared, "Not a particle of evidence is given . . . proving the guilt of a single enlisted man." African Americans felt particularly betrayed by Roosevelt. Many of them remembered his high praise of the Tenth Cavalry during his campaign for governor of New York. "I don't think any rough rider," he declared, recalling the role of black troops in his charge up San Juan Hill in 1898, "will ever forget the tie that binds us to the Ninth and Tenth Cavalry." Most African Americans considered that tie severed by the president's decision to discharge the 167 soldiers.[33]

Eleven years later it was the Twenty-fourth Infantry's turn. In this instance the price for the soldiers, for Houston, and for American race relations was much higher. In July 1917, 654 enlisted men and 8 officers of the Third Battalion, Twenty-fourth Infantry, arrived in Houston, then a city of 130,000 (including 30,000 African Americans), to assume guard duty around Camp Logan, a military training facility then under construction. The Twenty-fourth knew well the experience of the Twenty-fifth at Brownsville. The men also were aware of the state's long history of lynching (Texas ranked third in the nation in that grisly statistic). Only two months before the black soldiers arrived in Houston, a mob of 200 whites had hanged a black man in nearby Galveston.[34]

Most soldiers of the Twenty-fourth, realizing the well-entrenched pattern of segregation and racial subordination in Houston, obeyed the law. Many local white Houstonians, eager to maintain lucrative federal contracts, followed the pronouncement of the chamber of commerce that "in a spirit of patriotism, the colored soldiers would be treated right." Some soldiers tested the city's Jim Crow policies, sitting in the front seats on public trolleys or removing Colored Only signs, which they kept as "souvenirs."[35]

The greatest tension was between the soldiers and the Houston police. On August 18 two policemen chased, beat, and then arrested two black soldiers when they protested the officers' brutal handling of a black youth. Later that day two other soldiers were assaulted by police for objecting to being called "nigger." The following day a Harris County deputy sheriff pistol-whipped a soldier for resisting arrest when the officer found him in the white-only section of a streetcar. These incidents were prelude to the Houston riot of August 23, 1917, the worst interracial violence in the city's history. Earlier that day, in 102-degree heat, two mounted Houston police officers, Rufus Daniels and Lee Sparks, arrested Private Alonzo Edwards of Company L for interfering in the arrest of a black housewife. Later in the afternoon Corporal Charles Baltimore, the provost guard, tried to obtain information from the police officers about Edwards's arrest. Sparks struck the corporal with his pistol and then fired at him as Baltimore fled. Sparks and Daniels caught Baltimore in an unoccupied house, beat him, and placed him in jail.

News of the attacks, embellished by the false rumor that Baltimore had been killed, reached the Twenty-fourth Infantry camp just outside the city. Several soldiers vowed to avenge Edwards and Baltimore and to "burn down the town" even as the white officers tried to calm the men with promises of an official investigation. As Major Kneeland S. Snow pleaded with one group of soldiers to remain calm and loyal, Private Frank Johnson slipped to the rear of the assembled body and yelled, "Get your guns, boys! Here comes the mob!" The frightened men grabbed arms and ammunition and began fifteen minutes of indiscriminate firing. The officers could not regain control over the company as mutiny leaders, shouting, "Stick by your own race," and "To hell with going to France, get to work right here," gained the allegiance of most of the men. Their leader, Sergeant Vida Henry of Company I, commanded the mutineers to "get plenty of ammunition and save one for yourself because there will be no Third Battalion . . . We are in it now . . . [and] have to go." Most of Company I, joined by some men from other companies, about a hundred soldiers in all, marched out of the camp at 9:00 P.M., headed for Houston.[36]

Intent on exacting their vengeance on the police officers who had attacked their associates, the soldiers bolted through the heavily black San Felipe district, where they confronted both Lee Sparks and Rufus Daniels. Daniels and three other policemen were killed while Sparks escaped. The soldiers then disagreed on their next course of action. Sergeant Henry called on them to attack the police station. Most of them refused and began to make their way back to Camp Logan. One group took refuge in the homes of black Houstonians, where they were captured the following day by policemen and other black soldiers. The death toll in the one-night orgy of violence was twenty: fifteen whites (including five policemen), one Mexican American, and four black soldiers, including insurrection leader Vida Henry. The Houston mutiny and riot became the second-deadliest racial confrontation of the year, exceeded only by the East St. Louis race riot on July 2, in which thirty-nine people died.[37]

Eight black participants agreed to testify against the others, and the first 65 of the 118 soldiers arrested were brought to trial in three separate court-martials in San Antonio and El Paso between November 1917 and March 1918. The combined trials became the largest court-martial since the Mexican War. The verdicts: 13, among them Corporal Charles Baltimore, sentenced to death on November 30 and executed at dawn on December 11; 41 others given life in prison. The army later tried the remaining 53 in December and February and sentenced 16 to hang and 12 to serve life terms. Of the others, 7 soldiers were acquitted, while the remainder received prison sentences ranging from two to fifteen years.[38]

The consequences of the Houston riot extended far beyond Texas and 1917. Calls rose for the elimination of African Americans from military service. While the soldiers' supporters in Congress prevented outright dissolution of the units, the War Department limited the four regular black regiments to menial labor, thus excluding most black soldiers from combat in World War I. Congress's decision, viewed as a temporary response to the misconduct of some black soldiers, removed the four buffalo soldier regiments from combat roles until World War II. The buffalo soldiers as distinct units would never again fight under the flag of the United States.

But the mutiny itself both reflected and inspired a growing militancy among African Americans. Many African Americans disagreed with the impulsive, destructive actions of the soldiers in Houston, but they lauded the troopers' refusal to succumb to second-class citizenship. Eventually black Americans were to transform the soldiers' defiance of segregation laws and customs into a larger, more controlled civil rights movement. The New Negro of the post–World War I period—assertive, decisive, and proud—was the younger cousin of the black soldier.[39]

Most soldiers, black and white, spent their time at remote military outposts. Living conditions through the 1870s ranged from poor to deplorable. Congress rarely allocated funds for military outposts that would be abandoned with the rapidly shifting frontier. Black troopers, however, occupied the west Texas outposts, the oldest forts in the region. Troopers differed on the worst posts, but the problems at Fort Davis were typical. Colonel George Andrews, commander of the Twenty-fifth Infantry, described conditions there in 1875: "I have visited the . . . quarters several times during the past summer to find everything saturated with rain, the dirt floor full four inches deep of mud, and the men sitting at meals while their heads and backs were being defiled with ooze from the dripping dirt roof."[40]

Conditions improved in the 1880s. One black enlisted man captured the beauty and hardship of frontier posts in his description of Fort Washakie, Wyoming. Located in the Rocky Mountains, 150 miles from the nearest railroad station, Fort Washakie was for him a place of scenic wonder. "Here, with our trees and grass and flowers, with a cool river at our feet, we live the life of the free and healthy mountaineer." However, when the snows came, the men were isolated and "lonesome during the long winter evenings." Twenty-fourth Infantry troopers at Fort Grant, Arizona Territory, in 1890 had access to a gymnasium, a billiard parlor, and two bowling alleys as well as a library, where they read black newspapers and other "race" publications. By the early twentieth century the wide-ranging cultural and recreational activities included boxing, football, basketball, and baseball. One chaplain reported that "the men seem to have their minds so employed now with baseball . . . that they do not get drunk." Activities also included lectures by Mrs. Henry Highland Garnet, widow of the abolitionist clergyman, and the Reverend Jesse Moorland, international secretary of the YMCA, who spoke at Fort Robinson, Nebraska. Matthew Henson, the black explorer who accompanied Admiral Robert Peary to the North Pole, described his experiences to men of the Twenty-fifth Infantry at Fort Wright, just outside Spokane, Washington. On occasion enlisted men, such as Corporal Joseph Wheelock and Private Beverly F. Thornton, both at Fort Robinson, offered orations on subjects such as "race consciousness" and "black economic development."[41]

Black soldiers occasionally were stationed near a western city such as El Paso, Spokane, or Salt Lake City, providing respite from isolation. The soldiers of the Twenty-fourth Infantry and their wives and children welcomed the opportunity in 1896 to serve at Fort Douglas, Utah. Located outside Salt Lake City, just east of the University of Utah campus, Fort Douglas was considered an attractive post-

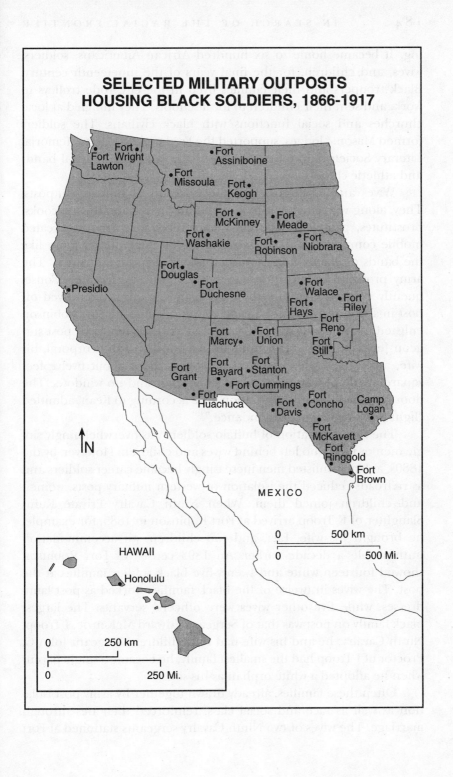

SELECTED MILITARY OUTPOSTS
HOUSING BLACK SOLDIERS, 1866-1917

Fort Lawton
Fort Wright
Fort Missoula
Fort Assiniboine
Fort Keogh
Fort McKinney
Fort Meade
Fort Washakie
Fort Robinson
Fort Niobrara
Fort Douglas
Fort Duchesne
Presidio
Fort Walace
Fort Hays
Fort Riley
Fort Reno
Fort Marcy
Fort Union
Fort Still
Fort Grant
Fort Bayard
Fort Stanton
Fort Cummings
Fort Huachuca
Fort Davis
Fort Concho
Camp Logan
Fort McKavett
Fort Ringgold
Fort Brown

N

MEXICO

0   500 km
0   500 Mi.

HAWAII

Honolulu

0   250 km
0   250 Mi.

ing. It became home to six hundred African Americans, soldiers, wives, and children, for the final years of the nineteenth century. Black troopers and their families lived in the city, rode trolleys to work, and sent their children to local schools. They mingled at local churches and social functions with black civilians. The soldiers formed Masonic lodges, supported the Frederick Douglass Memorial Literary Society, and joined local African American musical bands and athletic clubs.[42]

Wives and children eased the isolation of military outposts. They, along with single black women and men—laundresses, cooks, prostitutes, gamblers, laborers who trailed after troops—created mobile communities that resembled a "traveling village, more like the bands of Plains Indians who inhabited the same territory." The army provided on-post housing only for officers' families. Consequently enlisted men and their wives and children often lived off post in sheds and shanties. Living conditions for one Fort Robinson enlisted man's family were described in an 1889 report by post surgeon Jefferson Kean. This unidentified Ninth Cavalry corporal, his wife, and their child lived in a one-room shack about twelve feet square, made of waste timber with one door and no windows. The door provided the only ventilation and, according to Kean, admitted "light and dust in equal abundance."[43]

The first generation of buffalo soldiers was overwhelmingly single men or men who left behind wives and children. However, by the 1880s, as black enlisted men increasingly became career soldiers and as railroads reduced the isolation of western military posts, women and children joined them. When Ninth Cavalry Private Rufus Slaughter of K Troop arrived at Fort Robinson in 1885, for example, he brought his wife, Ella, and two children, an accommodation unthinkable a decade earlier. An 1893 census of Fort Robinson showed fourteen white and twenty-five black soldier families at the post. The wives in twelve of the black families worked as post laundresses, while five other wives were officers' servants. The largest black family on post was that of Sergeant Edward McKenzie, I Troop, Ninth Cavalry; he and his wife had four children. Sergeant John C. Proctor of I Troop had the smallest family; he became a single parent when he adopted a white orphan as his son.[44]

Often these families, already drawn together by army post isolation as well as race and social class, reinforced their ties through marriage. The wives of two Ninth Cavalry sergeants stationed at Fort

Robinson in the 1890s were sisters, while another cavalry wife was the daughter of a buffalo soldier and had been born at Fort Ringgold, Texas, in 1875. Both daughter and mother resided at Fort Robinson. The daughter spent her entire life with the Ninth Cavalry. Three Tenth Cavalry wives, stationed at Fort Robinson after the Spanish-American War, had similar backgrounds; all had been born in the West Indies. One was from Cuba, and the other two were sisters from Kingston, Jamaica. Still another Tenth Cavalry wife, Sallie Conley, who married regimental cook Beverly Thornton, was the sister of Quartermaster Sergeant Paschal Conley. Such close-knit communities banned together to protect those in need. When Tenth Cavalry First Sergeant James Brown froze in a blizzard near Fort Assiniboine, Montana, another sergeant informed his widow that she "ain't going to want for bread while the 10th Cav. has a ration left." Despite military regulations that called for her departure, Mrs. Brown remained at the post.[45]

Married and single troopers faced a constant mix of danger and boredom, accentuated by rigid military discipline. The strain extracted a toll. While alcoholism, suicide, and desertion were far more prevalent among white troops, they did occur with black regulars. Two Ninth Cavalrymen, James Nelson and William Burns, deserted Fort Cummings, New Mexico Territory, in 1880. Joining fellow deserter Henry Burks from Fort Union, they made their way to Trinidad, Colorado, before being apprehended by the local sheriff and returned to Fort Marcy for trial. Perhaps they should have gone to Las Vegas, New Mexico Territory, since a detachment of troops led by Lieutenant Matthias W. Day, found it impossible to apprehend deserters there because of the resistance of approximately ninety black civilians. "The whole colored population here seem to be in league with [deserters]," wrote Day, "and spy around to find out everything I do."[46]

African American soldiers more often vented their anger and frustration in attacks on fellow troopers. Frank N. Schubert has profiled the internal violence at one outpost, Fort Robinson, Nebraska. Between September 1886 and December 1887 three soldiers were murdered at Fort Robinson, all at the hands of other troopers. One of the victims was Sergeant Emanuel Stance, a twenty-one-year, battle-hardened, medal-winning veteran of the Ninth Cavalry. Stance's verbal and physical assaults on his men, which he justified as necessary discipline for black soldiers, contributed to his brutal death, leading Schubert to conclude that "rank was a more divisive force than the bonds of race could overcome."[47]

By the 1890s black soldiers in the West had assumed a new responsibility in the growing labor struggles of the region. That role was anticipated in an 1892 *St. Louis Republic* editorial that coupled the Suggs incident with the evolving role of black troops in suppressing western labor unrest: "As a stamping ground for buffalo soldiers, the new states of Idaho and Wyoming may safely be set down as a howling success. They have had great fun chasing enterprising white pioneer cattle farmers in Wyoming and are now amusing themselves suppressing labor unions in Idaho."[48]

Corporate and political leaders realized the army could be invaluable in labor disputes. First, the army theoretically represented national interests, a claim neither labor organizers nor corporate managers could make. The army operated simultaneously in a number of states, providing centralized coordination against nationwide labor-capital confrontations, such as the railway strikes of 1877 and 1894. Moreover, local law enforcement officers were overwhelmed by the scale of strike-related disorders and occasionally were sympathetic to or intimidated by strikers, whereas army regulars rarely identified with the workers they faced. This was especially true for African American soldiers, who were aware of organized labor's well-known racial exclusivity,[49]

Many army officers welcomed their new role as the nation's police force because it afforded new opportunities and responsibilities. "The red savage is pretty well subdued," editorialized the *Army and Navy Register* in 1892, "but there are white savages growing more numerous and dangerous as our great cities become greater." Most officers shared the class background and fears of class warfare that permeated the nation's economic elite by 1900. Twenty-fourth Infantry Chaplain Theophilus Gould Steward embraced the officer corps's disdain for striking workers. "A great strike ... not to be accompanied by violence," Steward wrote in an article for the *Independent* while his regiment was assigned to suppress labor unrest in northern Idaho, "is an impossibility in fact, and an absurdity in idea ... violence, if unorganized, is riot, and if organized, war!"[50]

African American troops played no role in the national railway strike of 1877, which set the pattern for multistate labor action and for federal intervention. They were however, crucial in the next wave of western strikes, beginning with Idaho's Coeur d'Alene mining district in 1892. Their theater of action was the northern Idaho panhandle towns of Wallace, Gem, Burke, Mullan, Kellogg, and Wardner, created to service the silver and lead mines and house thousands of miners. Most of these towns, situated in a narrow gorge less than a mile across, were unlike the prairies and plains so familiar to black troops. These towns of mostly immigrant miners from Ireland, Sweden, Austria, Poland, and Finland proved a formidable assignment.

In the spring of 1892 the miners of the Coeur d'Alene region went out on strike. The Bunker Hill and Sullivan Company, the mineowners, subsequently locked out the strikers, imported strikebreakers, and hired armed guards and union-busting Pinkerton spies, the most famous being the former Texas cowboy Charlie Siringo. On July 11 striking miners opened fire on the entrance of the largest mine near Gem, blew up the nearby ore smelter, and drove both strikebreakers and guards out of the valley. Fully aware of the volatility of the situation, particularly in light of the ongoing Homestead, Pennsylvania, steel strike, Governor Norman B. Willey quickly asked President Benjamin Harrison to send in troops. On July 14 the first federal troops, four companies of the Fourth Infantry, moved east into the valley from Fort Sherman on Coeur d'Alene Lake, while three companies of the Twenty-fifth Infantry traveled west from Fort Missoula.[51]

For the next four months the Coeur d'Alene district was under martial law. Soldiers were to prevent further violence or destruction of property. Moreover, they assisted the Shoshone County sheriff and the U.S. marshal in making arrests and detaining suspected union members and sympathizers. Eventually six hundred miners were arrested. Since no town jails had such capacity, federal officials commandeered used storehouses and warehouses in Wardner and Wallace, constructing high fences around them that prisoners and their sympathizers soon labeled "bullpens."

Reaction to the soldiers, and particularly to the black troops, formed along predictable lines. Mineowners and managers, strikebreakers and their families, and townspeople who viewed labor protests as impending anarchy welcomed the troops. They invited off-duty soldiers to dances and baseball games. The troops reciprocated by staging band concerts, amateur theatrical presentations, and civic activities like sanitary cleanups around the towns. One Sunday evening in July a quartet from the Twenty-fifth Infantry "charmed visitors by singing ... gospel hymns," according to the *Spokane*

Spokesman Review. Incarcerated miners and local union supporters of course did not share the mutual cordiality between soldiers and some townspeople. The policy of mass arrest, engineered by the mineowners and carried out by state and federal officials, was meant to crush the union. It had the opposite effect, driving the workers into a radical regionwide union, the Western Federation of Miners, and setting the stage for Idaho's next confrontation between management and labor in the district in 1899.[52]

Violence flared again in the Coeur d'Alene district in April 1899. By that date the Western Federation of Miners had organized every mine and ore mill except the largest, the Bunker Hill and Sullivan, near Wardner. Company officials, anticipating a confrontation with the union, fortified the mine and silver ore mill with an army of private guards. On April 29, a thousand miners from surrounding towns arrived in Wardner, disarmed most of the guards, and then dynamited the plant. In the ensuing fight two company guards were killed. Governor Frank Steunenberg declared "an insurrection in Shoshone County" and requested that President McKinley send five hundred federal troops into the Coeur d'Alene. The first troops, six companies from the Twenty-fourth Infantry and two from the Fourth Cavalry, arrived in Wardner on May 2. The following day Governor Steunenberg imposed martial law.[53]

As in 1892, martial law created the opportunity for Steunenberg to break the WFM. The governor ordered the arrest of every known union member and sympathizer in Shoshone County. Troops began making mass arrests. By May 4, when most of the Twenty-fourth had finally arrived in the Coeur d'Alene, seven hundred people were in custody. Special deputies, mostly from the ranks of nonunion mine employees, assisted the soldiers, spreading out across the district and the surrounding hills in search of fugitives. *Harper's Weekly* described a sweep in Burke: "Two companies of soldiers . . . did the work with uncommon thoroughness. . . . Guards were stationed on the walls of the gorge to prevent escape of the fugitives and then the soldiers made a house-to-house search. At the shafts soldiers . . . [seized] miners as they came off their shift. In the business [district] merchants and clerks were taken from their shops. Cooks and waiters were captured in the kitchen, and guests as they sat at table. The postmaster, the superintendent of the public schools, doctors and lawyers, were all alike 'rounded up'—a grand total of two hundred and forty-three persons."[54]

By May 7, when the prisoner total reached a thousand, the incarcerated men were crammed in a two-story grain storage warehouse, and the overflow placed in stationary railroad box cars. State Attorney General Samuel H. Hays reflected the grim, determined mood of state officials when he said, "We have the monster by the throat and we are going to choke the life out of it. . . . It is a plain case of the state or the union winning, and we do not propose that the state be defeated." The Western Federation of Miners was outlawed by Governor Steunenberg, and state officials notified the army that mineowners were forbidden to employ miners until they obtained work permits, which were to be issued only after workers had denounced the union.[55]

Surviving evidence reveals tremendous civilian animosity toward Twenty-fourth Infantry troopers, who were the main military force occupying the Coeur d'Alene district. Incarcerated miners claimed soldiers forcibly separated them from visiting relatives, threatened them by bayonet, and stole personal property. White soldiers arresting strikers, conducting house-to-house searches for other workers and guarding detainees without trial in a makeshift prison camp would have been resented by union supporters. That black soldiers carried out these duties aroused particular contempt. Fortunately the Twenty-fourth Infantry, first to arrive at the beginning of May, also became the first regiment to leave at the end of the month. Other federal troops remained on duty until April 1901.[56]

The buffalo soldiers' last major assignment came in March 1916, when General John J. Pershing led eleven thousand troops on a "punitive expedition" against Mexican revolutionary Francisco ("Pancho") Villa, who had raided Columbus, New Mexico. The expedition included infantry and artillery support regiments, such as the Twenty-fourth Infantry. However, the Seventh and Tenth Cavalry regiments were assigned to find Villa's forces. The expedition was a strange mixture of nineteenth- and twentieth- century armies. Pershing believed the horse soldiers could capture or punish Villa. But he also foresaw that the expedition offered the last opportunity to repeat nineteenth-century cavalry pursuits of Indians and outlaws. This new cavalry, however, carried mobile machine guns, was supported by military aircraft, and its commander traveled in a Dodge touring car rented from a Mormon missionary. Lieutenant George S.

Patton, who had orchestrated a temporary transfer from the Eighth Cavalry to Pershing's staff, led a cavalry charge against Villa's forces in an automobile.[57]

Although no strangers to desert tracking and warfare, neither regiment could catch the elusive Villa. Moreover, Pershing's troops encountered a diplomatic minefield. Expedition orders were to inflict punishment on Villa's forces alone, but increasingly U.S. forces encountered opposition from the troops of Venustiano Carranza, whose government President Woodrow Wilson supported. Pershing's worst Mexican defeat came in June 1916, when fighting broke out between seventy-nine Tenth Cavalry soldiers and four hundred Carrancista cavalry in the town of Carrizal. Tenth Cavalry Captain Charles T. Boyd, stubbornly determined to lead his forces past the Mexican *federales,* provoking a battle between the U.S. and Mexican soldiers. After an hourlong fight, fourteen cavalrymen, including Captain Boyd, were dead. Ten troopers lay wounded, and twenty-four black soldiers and one white Mormon scout were prisoners. Thirty Mexican soldiers, including the commanding officer, Géneral Félix Gómez, were killed. The Carrizal incident nearly triggered a full-scale war between the United States and Mexico as officials of both nations negotiated for the release of the prisoners while mobilizing thousands of troops for the expected invasion of Mexico. Briefly the soldiers' race was minimized as newspapers throughout the United States demanded their release to restore American honor. "Though the captured men were negroes," wrote one El Paso resident, "they were United States soldiers and had gallantly upheld the honor of their nation on a foreign battlefield."[58]

One week after the confrontation at Carrizal, President Carranza released the prisoners, who returned to a hero's welcome in El Paso. Thereafter passions cooled. In July both nations met in a joint commission to negotiate an end of American intervention. While the commission deliberated, an uneasy truce held throughout Chihuahua. By February 1917, as both the public and the Wilson administration turned to World War I, the last expedition troops quietly returned to the United States. Two months later General Pershing sailed for France as commander of the American Expeditionary Force.[59]

Both nineteenth- and twentieth-century African Americans were proud of the buffalo soldiers, who joined the still-small pantheon of African American heroes. "[Black soldiers] are possessed of the notion," wrote Chaplain George M. Mullins of the Twenty-fifth Infantry in 1877, "that the colored people of the whole country are more or less affected by their conduct in the Army." The *Langston* (Oklahoma) *Daily Herald* called them "a brave and courageous company of men of whom the race may well feel proud." Years later historian Rayford Logan remarked that African Americans "had little, at the turn of the century, to help sustain our faith in ourselves except the pride that we took in the Ninth and Tenth Cavalry, the Twenty-fourth and Twenty-fifth Infantry. . . . They were our Ralph Bunche, Marian Anderson, Joe Louis and Jackie Robinson." Considering the racism these soldiers stoically faced, the horrible living and working conditions they experienced, and the violence they inflicted on others and themselves, this small group of black men paid a dear price in their bid to earn the respect of the nation. Thus Rayford Logan's understandable pride must be tempered by W. E. B. Du Bois's poignant eulogy for the first thirteen soldiers executed following the Houston mutiny: "Thirteen young, strong men; soldiers who have fought for a country which never was wholly theirs; men born to suffer ridicule, injustice and, at last, death itself."[60]

7

❖ ❖ ❖ ❖ ❖

The Black
Urban West,
1870–1910

Today most African American westerners live in the region's cities. The origins of these contemporary communities lie with the rise of the nineteenth-century African American urban population. In 1885, as black cowboys trailed cattle from Texas to Dodge City, or black homesteaders grew wheat in west Kansas soil, far more black women and men moved to Denver, San Francisco, Seattle, and Los Angeles in search of the jobs available in the urban economy. These contrasting images of black cowboys, homesteaders, and urban workers remind us that "multiple" Wests often existed side by side.

The nineteenth-century black urban community expanded in the larger cities and in smaller towns, such as Salt Lake City, Utah; Topeka, Kansas; Virginia City, Nevada; Helena, Montana; Yankton, South Dakota; and Pocatello, Idaho. In large and small cities, churches, fraternal organizations, social clubs, even fledgling civil rights organizations established the pattern of community life. Black urban populations in Helena and Yankton did not survive into the twentieth century, but Houston, Dallas, Oakland, Denver, and Los Angeles became the final destination for tens of thousands of hopeful migrants.[1]

Our fascination with the rural West often obscures this urban life. As early as 1870 most African American westerners (outside Texas and Indian Territory) resided in cities and towns. African

African American Urban Population in the West, 1880–1910
Black Population in Cities of 100,000 or More in 1910

	1880		1900		1910	
	Black Population	Total Population	Black Population	Total Population	Black Population	Total Population
Denver	1,046	35,629	3,923	133,859	5,426	213,381
Los Angeles	102	11,183	2,131	102,479	7,599	319,198
Oakland	595	34,555	1,026	66,960	3,055	150,174
Omaha	789	30,518	3,443	102,555	4,426	124,096
Portland	192	17,557	775	90,426	1,045	207,214
San Francisco	1,628	233,959	1,654	342,782	1,642	416,912
Seattle	19	3,533	406	80,671	2,296	237,194
Spokane	NA	350	376	36,848	723	104,402

Sources: U.S. Bureau of the Census, Population of the United States, 1880, *vol. 1 (Washington, D.C.: Government Printing Office, 1883), 416–25, and U.S. Bureau of the Census,* Twelfth Census of the United States, 1900, *vol. 1,* Population, *part 1 (Washington, D.C.: United States Census Office, 1901), 609–46; U.S. Bureau of the Census,* Negro Population, 1790–1915 *(Washington, D.C.: Government Printing Office, 1918), 95–105.*

Americans in Colorado, California, Utah, Montana, and Nevada mostly lived in cities from the beginning of their settlement. Even in Kansas, a state destined to become the home of thousands of black farmers, more than half its 17,108 African Americans in 1870 lived in four cities: Atchison, Lawrence, Leavenworth, and Wyandotte (Kansas City). These nineteenth-century urbanites were influential far beyond their numbers as the organizations and institutions they created, the values they shared, the goals they sought through politics and civil rights influenced successive generations well into the twentieth century.[2]

The combined African American population of the five largest western cities in 1910—San Francisco, Los Angeles, Seattle, Denver, and Portland—totaled only 18,008, slightly more than one fifth the total of the largest black urban community at the time, Washington, D.C. Such small numbers, however, did not prevent western urban blacks from organizing a rich social and cultural life or battling against racial injustice. That battle had to be waged in a particularly local fashion. Willard Gatewood's description of late-nineteenth-century San Francisco as a place where antiblack prejudice "was always ambiguous, [and] where respect and support coexisted with antipathy" could well apply to most western cities.[3]

Western black urban communities shared numerous characteristics. Local and subregional economies might differ, but African Americans in every western city performed surprisingly similar work: Both men and women were personal servants for wealthy households, while black males worked as hotel waiters, railroad porters, messengers, cooks, and janitors. Some entrepreneurial blacks operated barbershops, restaurants, and boardinghouses. By the 1890s most western urban black communities had a few doctors and lawyers and newspaper editors, who, along with ministers and schoolteachers, comprised the "elite." Intraracial class distinctions were far less apparent than in the nation's older eastern cities. Even so, some African Americans, alarmed and embarrassed by the ways of the impoverished and uneducated, followed the advice of one Kansas newspaper editor to "make a line, and keep within it . . . to ostracize them from our society."[4]

Despite their small numbers, black urban westerners established churches, fraternal organizations, social clubs, newspapers, and literary societies. These fledgling nineteenth-century institutions and organizations immediately addressed the spiritual, educational, social, or cultural needs of the local inhabitants. But "race organizations" also provided African Americans with a respite from a hostile world, a retreat where, according to historian Douglas Daniels, blacks could loose their anonymity and gain some control over their lives. While such desires were hardly peculiar to black westerners, the small size of the region's population and the vast distances between major cities and from the South increased the importance of these organizations. As early as 1862 the *San Francisco Pacific Appeal* called on its readers to create political, religious and moral organizations "wherever there are half a dozen Colored people." Forty-four years later the *Montana Plaindealer* in Helena reiterated that view: "The greatest hope for the ultimate solution of the problems . . . of our race is our ability to get together . . . and we are glad that even in this section with a scattering population of our people, they are abreast . . . in their efforts to solidify their interests. . . ."[5]

This network of organizations did not end at a city's boundaries. Instead it linked small, isolated populations with the larger African American world. The sixty-eight-member African Methodist Episcopal (AME) Church Conference for Kansas included small black churches from as far away as Montana and Colorado. The Puget

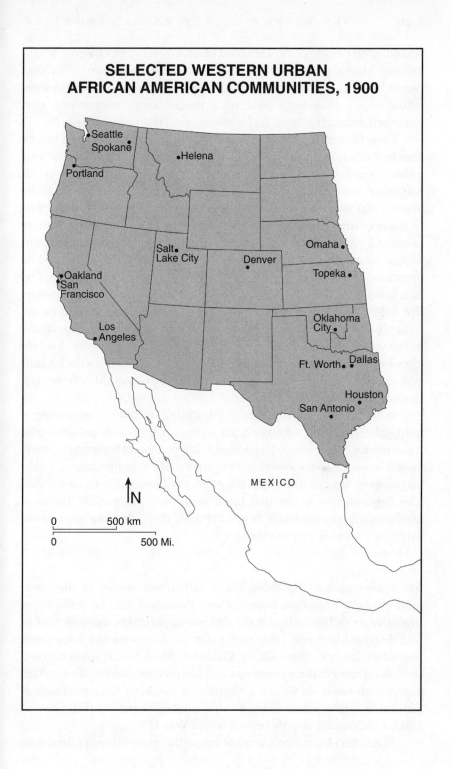

SELECTED WESTERN URBAN
AFRICAN AMERICAN COMMUNITIES, 1900

Seattle
Spokane
Portland
Helena
Oakland
San
Francisco
Salt
Lake City
Denver
Omaha
Topeka
Los
Angeles
Oklahoma
City
Ft. Worth Dallas
Houston
San Antonio

MEXICO

N

0   500 km

0   500 Mi.

Sound AME Conference embraced black churches in Oregon, Washington, Alaska, Idaho, and British Columbia. Both served as vital reminders that however isolated African Americans might be in individual cities, they were part of a much larger community that stretched across the West and encompassed the entire nation.[6]

Even protest forged bonds of community. Western urban blacks attacked school segregation and discrimination in employment and public accommodations. While these challenges illustrated racial prejudice throughout the region, they also generated connections among blacks at the state and national levels. The most important of these connections was the National Association for the Advancement of Colored People (NAACP), which appeared throughout the region soon after its founding in New York in 1909, while earlier organizations such as the Afro-American League, with chapters in San Francisco, Seattle, Denver, Topeka, Helena, and other cities in the 1890s, integrated small black communities into a nationwide struggle for racial justice. Western African American newspapers were crucial, providing information on protest struggles and leaders elsewhere, articulately expressing indignation, defending their small communities and the race, and encouraging responsible challenges to discrimination and exclusion.[7]

Whether the activity involved building a church, mounting a political campaign, organizing a women's club, or protesting a lynching locally or in the Deep South, black urban Westerners generated a sense of cooperation and shared destiny impossible to establish among African American trappers, cowboys, soldiers, or miners. The urbanites were the first black westerners who could be accurately called a community. It was through them that the contemporary black West began to take shape.

San Francisco had the oldest black urban community in the West. Following the gold rush influx of one thousand African Americans, the number of blacks in the city did not appreciably increase and in fact declined between 1890 and 1910, as numerous black residents moved to the city's first suburb, Oakland. Black San Francisco nonetheless remained the epitome of organized community life for African Americans from British Columbia to southern California and as far east as Utah. San Francisco ruled unchallenged until the rise of black Los Angeles shortly before World War I.[8]

Black San Francisco's reputation as the most cosmopolitan and sophisticated community in the West stemmed from various sources. First it could uniquely lay claim to antebellum antecedents. Moreover, with northern and southern blacks as well as a foreign-born population, the city was far more diverse than other communities in the region. The foreign-born population constituted 13 percent of the city's blacks in 1860 and 11 percent in 1900, second only to New York City. West Indians and particularly Jamaicans dominated. But San Francisco's black foreign-born also included Canadians, Latin Americans, and immigrants from Africa's Cape Verde Islands. These blacks, whose first language was Spanish, Portuguese, or French, lent an international ambiance to the city. One example from the 1880 U.S. census is instructive. José Seminario, a black cook from Peru, lived at 522 Broadway with his Panamanian wife, their four children (all but one born in Panama), and a Mexican boarder who was designated as a mulatto. Also in the building were a black Panamanian named Cajar and two Mexican black women with Spanish surnames. The building's other tenants included Chileans and Irish, Italians, and Germans.[9]

San Francisco had two of the oldest black newspapers in the West, the *Pacific Appeal* and the *Elevator.* Both had regional readerships. "Your paper is the only comfort we have to pass away the sad evening moments," wrote an Idaho Territory correspondent for the *Appeal* in 1863. "It is to us, in this far-off Territory, like the *Union* and *Bulletin* to the whites." The editors, Philip Bell of the *Elevator* and Peter Anderson of the *Pacific Appeal,* were bitter rivals. The rivalry stemmed partly from intense competition for a limited market. But the editors also held different views that anticipated twentieth-century debates between black intellectuals and political activists. Bell urged African Americans to organize race-specific groups to build black pride and work for equality. Anderson, conveniently ignoring his editorship of a black newspaper, argued that blacks should avoid self-segregation and confront the world as confident individuals, demanding justice for each person regardless of race. Those who advocated separate organizations, he believed, worked in opposition to full equality.[10]

Black San Francisco's leadership also flowed from its wealth. The resources of businesswoman Mary Ellen Pleasant are well known. Her wealth, however, should be viewed as the leading example of a remarkable group of resourceful entrepreneurs. The gold rush generated short-lived prosperity for a few fortunate black miners, but true wealth lay in successful real estate and stock speculation in a booming local economy. By the 1870s Richard Barber, William E. Carlisle, Peter H. Joseph, Henry M. Collins, and Salina Williams all had acquired modest fortunes. Despite his occupation as a porter, Barber's seventy thousand dollars in real estate made him the city's richest African American in 1870. Williams, a steamer stewardess, saved her meager salary and invested in real estate as well; by 1870 she owned twelve thousand dollars in property. It was George Washington Dennis's Horatio Alger story, however, that inspired blacks far beyond San Francisco. Arriving in California as a slave in 1849, Dennis purchased his (and his mother's) freedom while a janitor at the El Dorado, San Francisco's largest gold rush gambling saloon. After 1865 Dennis operated a variety of businesses while buying and selling property. By 1890 his holdings were worth fifty thousand dollars.[11]

Black San Francisco's prosperity rested precariously on a weak economic foundation. Most of the city's black residents survived on the margin of the urban economy. San Francisco in 1910 offered the same types of service jobs as in 1860. Most black workers were coachmen, butlers, cooks, maids, and porters. If the city's black sailors, ship stewards, and dockworkers indicated a more diverse workforce than most western urban communities, their meager wages did little to raise overall prosperity.[12]

Restricted opportunity for blacks in San Francisco rested primarily on employer and white worker prejudices. Major employers preferred white and Asian workers to African American laborers. The pattern of large-scale use of Chinese labor, for example, began with the construction of the Central Pacific Railroad. Irish and German workers by sheer numbers produced an informal network of relatives and friends who rapidly alerted them about jobs. European immigrant workers dominated both skilled trades and the general laborer market. Indeed the most intense competition for jobs in post–Civil War San Francisco was between the Irish and the Chinese. The Workingmen's party of California arose in the 1880s to use political clout on behalf of the city's Irish and German workers. The WPC, led by Irish-born Denis Kearney, generated much of the anti-Chinese sentiment that eventually resulted in the 1882 Exclusion Act. San Francisco's African Americans were at best mere spectators in these developments.[13]

African American San Franciscans were left with few employment options. One of them was in food service. San Francisco's booming economy, with its multitude of hotels, restaurants, saloons, and private clubs, should have offered numerous opportunities. But black workers were challenged even in this arena. In 1875 San Francisco's most exclusive luxury hotel, known simply as the Palace, offered nearly two hundred service positions to black workers. Besides the good wages and prospect for handsome tips, these workers basked in the prestige of employment in the most elegant hotel west of the Mississippi River. That pride showed in an 1875 banquet honoring General Philip Sheridan. The staff for the evening were portrayed by one spectator as "an army of waiters in swallow-tailed coats and white . . . gloves, flitting noiseless to and fro."[14]

Fourteen years later, however, the black Palace waiters were abruptly replaced by whites, a move that presaged the elimination of most African Americans from the city's hotel and restaurant industry. The genesis of this change could be traced to July 1883, when white waiters formed the Cooks and Waiters Union of the Pacific Coast and went on strike to bar future hotel and restaurant employment of black and Asian waiters. The strike did not eliminate black workers, but the CWU gained the support of such allied labor groups as the bakers' and confectioners' unions. In 1888 the San Francisco local again struck and succeeded in eliminating all nonunion labor in "the places were colored help is employed." One of those places was the Palace. Many black San Franciscans shared the conclusion of an editorial in one of the city's major newspapers, the *Daily Alta California:* "The object of this movement is to do away with colored help altogether and to have only white men in the kitchen and dining room."[15]

African American San Francisco found little succor in local politics. Some white Republicans had helped the city's African Americans in their Civil War–era civil rights campaigns. The apex of nineteenth-century black political influence, however, may well have been reached with Newton Booth's election as governor in 1871. Booth, a Republican, won the statewide election by a slim majority of four thousand votes. San Francisco's African Americans provided seventeen hundred of them. Governor-elect Booth lived at Mary Ellen Pleasant's boardinghouse. She boasted that "he was elected from my house," after Booth gave an impromptu victory speech to an interracial crowd gathered in front of the residence. The governor-elect declared that he stood squarely for political equality, a theme repeated at his Sacramento inaugural address: "All badges of distinction that are relics of the slave holding era of our national history should pass away with the system they commemorate." After

Booth's two-year term, however, San Francisco Republicans fell away from egalitarian principles. African American San Franciscans' continued support for the Republican party yielded few patronage jobs. One anonymous politico declared in 1873 that Republicans "descant . . . with oiled tongues . . . on equal rights, equal privileges, and equal spoils. . . . Children as we were, our faith was great. We went the whole ticket blind. We swallowed several bitter pills. . . ."[16]

Yet the source of black political failure in the city was more complex than Republican perfidy. Nineteenth-century black San Franciscans constituted 0.05 percent of the city's population and were dispersed throughout the city. By the mid-1870s city control had fallen to the Democrats, who assembled a coalition of working-class Irish, German, Italian, and Jewish supporters. Except for brief interludes when the Workingmen's party of California in the late 1870s and the Union Labor party in the first decade of the twentieth century controlled City Hall, the Democrats dominated San Francisco politics through this era.[17]

In 1894 a *San Francisco Chronicle* reporter noted "several shapely Afro-American young ladies [who] rode to the [Midwinter] Fair grounds on their bicycles . . . jauntily attired in knickerbocker costumes." The women, if they read the description, would have been pleased, for much of black San Francisco prided itself on its style, dress, and manners. African Americans joined societies and clubs to acquire or further refine social skills and poise. Whether learning the "fine art of dancing" for three dollars a month at Seales Hall in 1865 or exhibiting a flair for Shakespearean acting at the Charles H. Tinsley Drama Club four decades later, these urbanites saw successful citizenship as linked to standards of Victorian civility. If few black San Franciscans could quote the classics, many sought through reading, "refinement," and knowledge of the world to garner the respect of their fellow citizens. The drive for civility sometimes invaded surprising quarters. Peter Jackson, the West Indian–born San Francisco boxer who won the heavyweight championship of the British Empire in 1884, was lionized by the San Francisco press because of his "quick wit," his avoidance of coarse language, and his skill as a "clever, well-informed conversationalist."[18]

Fraternal orders, cultural associations, social clubs, and literary societies abounded. They included the Young Men's Union Beneficial Society, the Prince Hall Masons, the West Indian Benevolent Association, the Amateur Literary and Drama Association, and the Elliott Literary Institute. But much of urban life was centered in the

Comparative Black Populations
of San Francisco and Oakland, 1860–1910

Year	San Francisco		Oakland	
	Total	Black	Total	Black
1860	56,776	1,176	1,543	11
1880	233,959	1,628	34,555	593
1900	342,782	1,654	66,960	1,026
1910	416,912	1,642	150,174	3,055

Sources: U.S. Bureau of the Census, Eighth Census of the United States, 1860, Population (Washington, D.C.: Government Printing Office, 1864), 29–32; U.S. Bureau of the Census, Population of the United States, 1880, vol. 1 (Washington, D.C.: Government Printing Office, 1883), 416–25; and U.S. Bureau of the Census, Twelfth Census of the United States, 1900, vol 1, Population, part 1 (Washington, D.C.: U.S. Census Office, 1901), 609–46; and U.S. Bureau of the Census, Negro Population, 1790–1915 (Washington, D.C.: Government Printing Office, 1918), 95–105.

city's churches. The three largest in 1880 were the Powell Street (formerly St. Cyprian) African Methodist Episcopal, the African Methodist Episcopal Zion Church and the Third Baptist Church. The Powell Street AME Church, could seat four hundred in a "stately building . . . with gothic piers and handsome gilding." The rival AME Zion Church was slightly less ornate but more commodious, seating eight hundred parishioners. Church interior furnishings usually matched their elaborate facades. Carpets, bells, cushioned seats, and an artificial pool for baptism in the Third Baptist Church suggested a sophistication that surprised visitors. New Yorker William P. Powell, who attended the Powell Street AME in 1874, was moved to remark, "Well, I never! In all my travels I never saw the like—colored worshipers *rung* to church and *bell'd* to prayers."[19]

Faced with the high cost of housing, nineteenth-century black San Franciscans settled in Oakland and other East Bay communities, becoming early suburbanites and commuters. Oakland, founded in 1852, first attracted African Americans after the completion of the transcontinental railroad in 1869. Many of the initial settlers were railroad construction and repair workers lured to the city, the terminus of the Central Pacific, Southern Pacific, and Western Pacific railroads. But the Oakland settlers also included Pullman porters, who emerged following the Pullman Company's 1869 decision to require an African American male porter on each of its cars. Some black sailors, notably William T. Shorey, the Barbados-born captain of a whaling vessel, also sought out the East Bay city in the 1880s because of its lower housing costs. By the 1890s many newcomers had settled in Oakland rather than San Francisco, and subsequently black businesses also located or relocated there as East Bay residents now comfortably utilized ferries and trolleys to travel between communities. The 1906 earthquake, which made thousands of San Franciscans temporarily homeless, accelerated the trend; in 1910 nearly twice as many African Americans lived in Oakland as in San Francisco. Yet African Americans on both sides of the San Francisco Bay were confronted with such job restrictions that their black populations lagged behind those of Omaha, Denver, and other western metropolises. This paucity of jobs discouraged black population growth until well into the twentieth century.[20]

Denver's black community emerged as the first western rival to San Francisco, and sometime in the 1880s its population exceeded the Bay Area metropolis. Black Denver grew from 237 in 1870 to 5,426 in 1910, as the entire population expanded from 4,700 to 213,000. Violence characterized frontier Denver's first decade. In 1859 gambler Charles Harrison shot an unidentified African American for claiming to be "as good as a white man." This murder led to the fledgling city's first vigilance committee and town marshal. Five years later retired mountain man James Beckwourth won praise from Denverites when he killed William Paine, an African American who had terrorized local residents. If Beckwourth's gunplay symbolized a fading era in the region's past, the activities of other black residents signaled its future. Edward J. Sanderlin, William J. Hardin, Barney Ford, and Henry O Wagoner all arrived immediately before or during the Civil War, opened successful businesses, and simultaneously became active in civil rights campaigns. In 1866 they were joined by Frederick Douglass's sons, Lewis and Frederick, Jr. Lewis opened a night school for adult blacks, and both brothers campaigned for integrated public schools at a time when most Denverites were more distressed about the plains wars with Native Americans than about public school segregation.[21]

Colorado's African Americans were concentrated in Denver, where as early as 1870 they were 56 percent of the state's black population. These mostly male settlers included Barney Ford, a Virginia native who had worked as a Chicago barber and a steward on a Nicaragua steamer in the 1850s before coming to Denver in 1860. After brief periods as a successful barber, restaurant owner, and boarding-house owner, Ford in 1874 built the Inter-Ocean Hotel, which "for some years . . . was the aristocratic hostelry of Denver." Later in the decade Ford accepted the invitation of Cheyenne businessmen to build a hotel in the Wyoming territorial capital.[22]

A number of other African Americans followed Ford's initial trade, barbering, because it offered both status and relative financial independence. The 1870 census reported that Denver-area black barbers made up 65 percent of the territory's barbers. By the 1880s fast-growing Denver attracted far more laborers and construction workers. These mostly single black Denverites lived throughout the city in its earliest decades. By the 1890s, however, a small number of middle-class African American families had begun to concentrate in the Five Points district, creating a stable, if increasingly segregated, community northeast of the city's downtown core. Black Denverites took pride in their growing community. "Our people are settling around Five Points very rapidly," boasted Joseph D. D. Rivers, editor of the *Colorado Statesman.* "In a few years this will be an aristocratic colored neighborhood."[23]

Rivers had much to boast about. Despite the limited job prospects, black Denver evolved into a permanent community. Three African American newspapers, the *Star,* the *Argus,* and the *Statesman,* were published during the late nineteenth century. By 1900 the community was supporting nine churches, one hotel, various restaurants, saloons, a funeral home, and a drugstore. Its professional class included two doctors, three lawyers, and numerous professional musicians. Moreover, a number of women were involved in dress-making, catering, storekeeping, and mining. The Bonita Silver and Gold Mining Company, founded in 1896, was controlled by two women, president Mary E. Phelps and secretary Mrs. L. K. Daniels. The community also included by 1906 an enterprising former Louisi-anian, Sarah Breedlove, who married a local newspaper reporter, Charles J. Walker. Mrs., or "Madame," C. J. Walker marketed hair care products door to door and in 1907 opened a business and man-ufacturing headquarters in Denver while promoting her "Walker System" throughout the East. She eventually became the most successful African American cosmetics manufacturer in the United States and the first black female millionaire. By the 1890s black Denver could boast of its cultural and social organizations, such as the Young Men's Literary Association and the Young Men's Social Club, and within two decades it was to use its location at the foot of the Rockies to organize children's nature camps; bicycle, gun, and automobile touring clubs; and mountain resorts.[24]

West Indian Emancipation Day led local African American celebrations. As early as 1865 it was observed with a march past the governor's mansion, a Cherry Creek picnic, an oration at the Denver Theater, and finally a "gay and brilliant ball and sumptuous dinner." Denver's black community had already achieved notoriety by gaining voting rights in 1867. During the 1870s the Black Republican Club and the Central Political Equal Rights League fought to preserve those rights and encourage regular black political participation. By 1880 they had been joined by the Colored Ladies Legal Rights Association, a group of middle-class black women who denounced racial discrimination, such as African American exclusion from the Tabor Opera House. The political acumen of black Denver led to Henry O. Wagoner's serving as Arapaho County deputy sheriff between 1865 and 1875, Isaac Brown as the city's first black policeman in 1880, and Beatrice Thompson as an employee of the county treasurer's office twelve years later. But the high point of black Denver's political success came in 1892 with the election of Joseph H. Stuart to the state legislature.[25]

Nineteenth-century black Denver, however, faced serious problems. Although State Representative Stuart successfully sponsored an 1895 civil rights bill, most Denver blacks still could not enter local restaurants, hotels, and theaters. Black parents' poverty forced most children out of school and into the work force at an early age. Those who did not work gravitated toward juvenile gangs. By 1897 black Denver's Ragged Lovan gang rivaled its more notorious white counterpart, the Klondike Kids. In a city famed for its healthy climate, the black mortality rate was 20 percent higher than for whites because most African Americans were denied access to city hospitals and sanitariums. Even black self-help efforts failed. Ada McGoway's Colored Home and Orphanage closed three years after it was founded in 1899. The plight of black Denver moved J. N. Walker, editor of the *African Advocate,* to call for a movement back to Africa. In 1899 Walker created the short-lived Colorado African Colonization Society in a futile attempt to effect that goal.[26]

In 1910 Omaha's 4,426 blacks constituted the third-largest African American population among the major cities in the West. Most Omaha blacks worked as janitors, maids, and porters, but at least some held jobs in railroad construction, the city's stockyards, and meat-packing industry. Major firms used African American workers as part of the "reserve army" of strikebreakers. The Union Pacific introduced black strikebreakers into the region during the 1877 railroad strike. Seventeen years later the major packing companies— Swift, Hammond, Cudahy, and Omaha—also used blacks to break a strike. Not all African Americans were antiunion, however. Black Omaha barbers, for example, organized the first African American labor union in the city in 1887 and went on strike because they deemed it "unprofessional to work beside white competitors." In a city where race and ethnicity defined worker solidarity as much as did class, such a development was not surprising.[27]

Black Omaha slowly generated community institutions. St. John's African Methodist Episcopal Church was organized in 1867, followed by the African Baptist Church in 1874. Zion Baptist, which dates to 1884, had become the city's largest African American church by the first decade of the twentieth century. By 1890 Omaha's community of forty-five hundred had a Colored Women's Club and the state's first black hotel. On July 3–4, 1894, Omaha blacks held the nation's first Afro-American fair, featuring exhibits mounted by Nebraska's urban and rural residents.[28]

Omaha blacks have been politically active since Nebraska's admission to the Union in 1867. Political leadership in the city fell to recently arrived southern-born migrants, such as Cyrus D. Bell, a newspaper employee, and E. R. Overall, a postal worker, until Dr. Moses O. Ricketts spoke for the community as president of the Colored Republican organization. In 1884 Ricketts became the first African American to graduate from the University of Nebraska College of Medicine. Eight years later, in 1892, he entered the Nebraska legislature, where he served two terms.[29]

Omaha's nineteenth-century black community was residentially dispersed. Josie McCulloch, who grew up in the city in the 1870s and 1880s, recalled the "Swedish, Bohemian, Italian, Irish and Negro children" who played together and "contributed to the process of Americanization." Residential integration, however, did not eliminate racial antipathy. In 1891 a black man, Joe Coe, was accused of assaulting a five-year-old white child, Lizzie Yates. After hearing an erroneous report that the girl had died, a mob of several hundred people overwhelmed the police force at the county jail, seized Coe, and beat him as they dragged him through the streets. Coe was probably already dead when his body was hung from an electric trolley wire in downtown Omaha. Mayor Richard C. Cushing condemned the lynching as "the most deplorable thing that has ever occurred in the history of the county," but no members of the mob were brought to trial.[30]

In 1910 Los Angeles ranked second in size to San Francisco among the West's cities. Its African American population of 7,599, however, was the largest black urban concentration west of Texas. Modern black Los Angeles, according to historian Lawrence B. de Graaf, began with the land boom of the late 1880s, which propelled the black population from 102 in 1880 to 1,258 ten years later. The boom increased the entire city's populace from slightly over 11,000 to 47,000, allowing a few early settlers to profit immensely from the increase. Among the most successful was Bridget ("Biddy") Mason, the midwife who purchased her family homestead between Spring Street and Broadway for $250 in 1866 and sold part of her property for $1,500 eighteen years later. Mason founded and operated the first nursery for orphans and deserted children. She also established the First African Methodist Episcopal Church in 1872, the oldest black church in the city, and single-handedly supported it and its minister, the Reverend Jesse Hamilton, during the crucial first years by paying all taxes and expenses "to hold it for her people." Mason's descendants continued to profit from the growing value of southern California real estate. Her son-in-law, Charles Owens, owned valuable parcels in downtown Los Angeles, and her grandson, Robert C. Owens, constructed a six-story $250,000 building in 1905 on the site of the original Mason homestead. Owens, whom the *Colored American Magazine* in 1905 called "the richest Negro west of Chicago," became a friend and confidant of Booker T. Washington's and a major contributor to Tuskegee Institute.[31]

The prosperity of the Mason/Owens family, however, did not affect most nineteenth-century black Angelenos. Many newcomers found typical jobs as construction and repair workers for the Southern Pacific and Santa Fe railroads or as porters, cooks, waiters, and maids. Former Governor Pío Pico, for example, recruited one hundred black workers for his Pico House in the mid-1880s. J. Max Bond described late-nineteenth-century black Angelenos as "without leadership . . . poor . . . scattered [but] with no restrictions against them." Like their counterparts in San Francisco, Denver, and Omaha, African Americans were not residentially segregated, but their employment prospects were limited by biased employers and all-white unions.[32]

African American Los Angeles grew rapidly in the first decade

of the twentieth century. The population jumped from 2,131 in 1900
to 7,599 in 1910. In 1903 the Southern Pacific Railroad brought in
nearly 2,000 black laborers to break a strike by Mexican American
construction workers, doubling the size of the community and initiating an intense ethnic rivalry between the largest non-Anglo
groups in the region that continued long after the strike ended.
Independent of the SP's recruiting efforts, hundreds of black Texans
migrated to the Los Angeles area, enticed by their naive belief that
"there [was] no antagonism against the race." Familial networks
encouraged migration. "We came here back in 1902," declared a
Tennessee couple in a 1934 interview. "We were doing pretty well, so
we sent back home and told cousins to come along. When the cousins got here, they sent for their cousins. Pretty soon the whole community was made up of Tennessee people." Others were no doubt
influenced by urban boosters like E. H. Rydall, who wrote in 1907:
"Southern California is more adapted for the colored man than any
other part of the United States [because] the climate of Southern
California is distinctively African. . . . This is the sunny southland in
which the African thrives." At least one historian claims, however,
that Harrison Gray Otis, the powerful antiunion founder of the *Los
Angeles Times,* exploited organized labor's antiblack bias by encouraging African American workers to come and by financing such
organizations as the local Afro-American League. The first black residential concentration began to evolve along Central Avenue just
south of downtown L.A. Black Los Angeles absorbed this huge influx
of mainly southwestern-born migrants who by 1920 gave the southern California metropolis the West's second-largest (after Houston)
black urban population.[33]

Early-twentieth-century black Angelenos also established organizations and institutions that defined and defended the community.
By 1910 there were twelve churches, seven major fraternal organizations, the Union Literary Society in Boyle Heights, and the
Sojourner Truth Industrial Club, founded by African American
women in 1904 to "establish a . . . safe refuge" for the hundreds of
young working women streaming into the city. The Women's Day
Nursery, building on Biddy Mason's earlier efforts to assist poor families, provided day care facilities for children of working parents.
Although black women did not yet have the right to vote, their voices
were prominently heard in the Women's Civic League, which sponsored candidate debates and held rallies for office seekers they
endorsed. Three newspapers, the *Los Angeles New Age,* the *Liberator,*

and the *California Eagle,* served the community with the last paper
destined to be published until 1966. The *Eagle* (called the *Owl* until
1892) was founded by Texas native John J. Neimore, who arrived in
the city in 1879.[34]

In 1903 J. E. Edwards, pastor of First AME Church, Jefferson
Lewis Edmonds, editor of the *Liberator,* and Frederick Roberts, an
attorney, created a local civil rights organization known simply as
the Forum. The organization, open to "any man or woman of good
character," was predicated on two strategies. (1) to incorporate or, if
necessary, ostracize new residents who might damage the reputation
of the local community and (2) to challenge those in the white community who chose to discriminate. The organization, which theoretically included all black Angelenos, provided scholarships for
ambitious community youth, and collected money for a variety of
causes, including relief funds in 1906 for the victims of the San Francisco earthquake and the Atlanta race riot. That year Ruth Temple,
who became the first black female doctor on the West Coast, received
a scholarship from the Forum. The organization was also a vehicle
for the discussion of community issues. One of those issues was
crime. In 1909 the Forum worked with the chief of police, black
police officers, churches, and newspapers in an attempt to close
vice dens in black neighborhoods. Until its demise in 1942 the
Forum was one of the premier political organizations in black Los
Angeles.[35]

The nineteenth-century black urban West spread far and wide across
the region's urban landscape. From Dodge City to Virginia City African American women and men pursued varied economic activities
and contributed to the ambiance of the western town. Often the
most vibrant African American communities thrived in smaller cities
and towns, such as Topeka, Lawrence, and Manhattan, Kansas;
Houston, Dallas, and San Antonio, Texas; Helena, Montana; Salt
Lake City, Utah; Roslyn, Washington; and Yankton, South Dakota.
When black communities were enclaves of towns or cities, their fates,
not surprisingly, rested with the destiny of the larger community. As
Houston grew, its African American community expanded accordingly, eventually becoming one of the largest in the nation. Con-
versely, the once-dynamic late-nineteenth-century communities of
Roslyn and Helena barely survived into World War I.[36]

The Texas cities—San Antonio, Houston, Dallas, and Fort

Worth—constitute an anomaly in the discussion of the black urban West. In 1910 because no Texas city exceeded 100,000 inhabitants, they were not among the region's largest urban centers. Yet the Texas cities' combined African American populations totaled 65,949, and Houston's 23,929 residents exceeded the combined black population of the five largest cities in the West. Nineteenth-century black urban Texas emerged in the shadow of slavery. The first significant numbers of blacks to arrive in post–Civil War Texas cities were newly freed slaves from nearby plantations, who began an intrastate rural to urban migration in the summer of 1865 that continues to this day. Former slaves from Brazos River plantations, for example, entered Houston from the southwest by way of the San Felipe Road and settled in the first part of the town they encountered, an area they named Freedmantown, the nucleus of the city's oldest black enclave, Fourth Ward. "They traveled mostly on foot, bearing heavy burdens of clothing, blankets, etc, on their heads," recalled one witness to this spontaneous human hegira; "they arrived tired, foot sore, and hungry."[37]

Most of these urban newcomers to Houston, Dallas, Fort Worth, and San Antonio had been tenant farm and sharecropper families of east and south-central Texas, seeking wider economic opportunity in the closest city. The ex-slaves who settled in Houston's Freedmantown or Dallas's Deep Ellum usually found work as domestic servants, manual laborers for railroads, or on numerous building construction projects and, in Houston, as dockworkers. They created churches, such as Antioch Baptist in Houston in 1866, and, with the assistance of the Freedmen's Bureau, opened the first schools for their children. Houston's sizable post–Civil War population supported numerous black politicians, including Richard Allen, who was elected to the state legislature in 1869, and three black city council members by 1872. The return of the Democrats to power in 1874 interrupted black officeholding in Texas cities until well into the twentieth century.[38]

Segregation overwhelmingly characterized Texas cities, distinguishing them from other western urban centers and tying them to the South. In virtually every regard blacks and whites existed in separate worlds, prompting the term *city within a city* to describe the social milieu. Schools of course were segregated. Black Texas parents at first relied on northern philanthropy to support African American schools or taxed themselves a second time to educate their children after paying into the general education fund utilized for white pupils. Beginning with the efforts of Houston churches in 1872, black citizens also raised money to purchase parks for their children. By 1891 state legislation segregated railroads, and by 1905 city ordinances segregated local public transportation and public accommodations. Custom and law separated blacks from whites in city hospitals and jails and excluded the former from libraries and swimming pools. African Americans in Texas's largest cities derived some solace from the segregated environment that generated opportunities for business owners and professionals—doctors, lawyers, and numerous schoolteachers—but they also realized the Jim Crow social order must be dismantled. They began that process in the twentieth century.[39]

Salt Lake City, Utah; Helena, Montana; and Topeka, Kansas, all had more typical African American communities in small western cities. Salt Lake City's community grew from a colony of black Mormons who accompanied Brigham Young to Utah in 1847. By the 1890s, however, non-Mormons predominated, most attracted to the city by railroads and mining. An African Methodist Episcopal church was formed in 1890, followed by a Baptist church in 1896. Between 1895 and 1910 African American Salt Lake City had six newspapers. The largest, the *Utah Plain Dealer*, edited by William W. Taylor, ran from 1895 to 1909, while its principal rival, the *Broad Ax*, was published by Julius F. Taylor from 1895 until 1899, when he moved it to Chicago. While both editors were active in Salt Lake City, they maintained a rivalry similar to the *Elevator–Pacific Appeal* competition in San Francisco. William Taylor, a St. Louis native, was active in the Republican party and was the GOP candidate for a seat in the Utah house of representatives in 1896. Julius Taylor, who arrived from Chicago in 1895 because of his wife's health problems, quickly became involved in local politics, urging Utah's blacks to support the Democratic party. The unusual activity of the black press in a community of fewer than three hundred people in 1900 no doubt helped William Taylor become president of the Western Negro Press Association in 1899 and Salt Lake City to host its 1900 convention. Black Salt Lake City, with its two churches, its Masonic lodges, social and literary clubs, political organizations, and newspapers, maintained a remarkably vibrant community far from other black population centers.[40]

Helena, like Salt Lake City, also developed a small African American community. Its black population grew from 71 inhabitants in 1870, 2.3 percent of the city's residents to a peak of 420 in 1910, or

3.4 percent of the city's 12,515 population. African Americans had lived in the area before the city was founded. Accounts of the first settlers in the Prickly Pear Valley included an unidentified African American male, one of three who first discovered gold deposits in the Helena area in August 1862. Other African Americans followed as gold miners, servants, cooks, cowboys, and soldiers. Although many were transient, a core of residents established a comfortable community centered on religious, social, and cultural organizations. In 1867 several black families organized a church society that prospered through the next decade. In 1888, however, the Reverend James Hubbard from Kansas established the St. James African Methodist Episcopal Church. St. James eventually developed a library, a literary society, and a ladies' benevolent association. In 1894 the church hosted the annual convention of the Kansas Conference of AME Churches.[41]

Although St. James was the cultural and religious center of community by the 1890s, black Helena also had five fraternal lodges (two for women), as well as the Manhattan Social Club, which sponsored local dances and boasted a reading room, billiard parlor, and private dining room at its Main Street location. Flourishing small businesses included a grocery store, a cleaning establishment, a beauty shop, a "physical culture club" for women, two saloons, a local all-black band, and a debating society. Black Helena also had an underside of gamblers, prostitutes, pimps, and hustlers who congregated in the saloons along Clore Street. After a highly publicized trial of an African American prostitute accused of murdering a black soldier during an argument, local newspaper editor Joseph B. Bass declared in frustration: "Give us credit for what we do . . . we are lawabiding. The moral degenerates are the weight upon us as they are upon your race, and this is no fault of the whole race. . . ." Despite Helena's seamy underworld, many of the city's African American residents participated in civic life. In 1888, for example, William C. Irvin was appointed to the city's police force, where he remained for the next two decades. In 1894 Helena's first black newspaper, the *Colored Citizen,* edited by Ohio-born photographer J. P. Ball, Jr., campaigned for the city's selection over Anaconda as the state capital.[42]

Black Helena's prosperity continued into the first decade of the twentieth century, benefiting from the powerful voice of Joseph B. Bass, editor of the *Montana Plaindealer,* from 1906 to 1911. Bass arrived in the city from Topeka to edit the paper and quickly emerged as the black populace's most articulate spokesman and defender and its most successful business owner. Influenced by the ideas of Booker T. Washington, Bass helped form the Helena chapter of the Tuskegee educator's National Negro Business League in 1907 and a year later the Afro-American Building Association "for the purpose of buying real estate and erecting buildings." Yet Bass rejected Washington's accommodationist approach to politics, calling Democratic State Senator Charles S. Muffly "the Ben Tillman of the Northwest" for proposing in 1907 a bill to ban interracial marriages. When the measure became law in the second attempt in 1909, Bass declared in a front-page editorial that "Montana has joined the Jim Crow Colony alongside of Mississippi, South Carolina, Texas, and Arkansas. God help us!" One month later the editor and other Helena blacks formed the Afro-American Protective League to defend black rights. Passage of the antimarriage legislation, although a symbolic indication of changing racial views, nonetheless meant less than the region's declining economy. By 1910 Helena's prosperous mining days had passed. The town's population declined by five hundred between 1910 and 1920, but the African American community shrank by half and fell as sharply again during the decade of the 1920s.[43]

Nineteenth-century black Topeka, like Helena and Salt Lake City, evolved in a small-town setting. However, it shared little else. By 1870 black Topeka's population of 473 had already eclipsed the Montana capital's peak population in 1910. Moreover, the 1870 population represented 8 percent of Topeka's inhabitants. Ten years later 3,648 black Topekans were 23 percent of the population. Black Topeka continued to grow, and by 1900 its population had reached 4,807, although now only 14 percent of the city's inhabitants.[44]

Black Topeka began in 1852, when Clement Shattio, a Missouri-born farmer, settled one mile west of the site that became Topeka. Shattio was white, but his wife, Ann Davis Shattio, was a free black woman from Illinois. Their daughter and son were among the first non-Indian children born in the territory. The Civil War initiated the influx of blacks into Topeka. In 1865 there were 83 African Americans, and five years later 473. Most African Americans lived next to the Atchison, Topeka, & Santa Fe or Kansas Pacific railroad yards, where unskilled men found employment as porters, construction workers, and brakemen. Other African American men and women worked on nearby farms or became small business owners. The first black church, the Freedmen's Church, was organized in 1863. Two years later the First African Baptist Church issued its first call to worship under a "brush arbor," and in 1868 sixteen men and women who came together to hold religious services in a rented barn created the St. John AME Church. By 1889 black Topeka was served by twenty-five churches.[45]

In 1879 black Topeka's population exploded as thousands of Exodusters arrived in the city. Southern blacks poured in at a rate of three hundred per month through much of 1879, sorely taxing the economic resources of all of the town's citizens. Although the migration affected the entire state, Topeka became the destination of many of the newcomers because it was the state capital and the center of the region's rail and river transportation network. It was also home of the Kansas Freedmen's Relief Association (KFRA), which provided assistance for indigent migrants. The KFRA built a temporary shelter called the Barracks, which in January 1880 housed four hundred men, women, and children.[46]

The influx of nearly three thousand blacks into an African American community that three years earlier had had only seven hundred African American residents ushered in profound, permanent changes. It created a black business district on Kansas Avenue and spurred the growth of a professional class of doctors, lawyers, and teachers. Black Topeka was served by six newspapers, the earliest of which was William L. Eagleson's *Colored Citizen* which he relocated in 1878 from Fort Scott, Kansas, and published for two decades. The influx also exposed class divisions expressed in church and social club membership.

The new citizens turned to politics, electing black Topekans to numerous local offices. Alfred Kuykendall, for example, in 1879 was elected constable, a post he held for ten years, while Wesley I. Jameson was justice of the peace in 1888, and "Colonel" John Brown became Shawnee County clerk in 1889. Beginning in 1897, Fred Rountree represented the Fifth Ward in the Topeka City Council. Black Topeka had in 1897 five policemen, ten firemen, and one postman, a patronage success rate that rivaled the nation's largest African American urban communities. Its crowning achievement in this area came in 1891, when President Benjamin Harrison appointed local attorney and political activist John L. Waller U.S. consul to Madagascar.[47]

The activity of Topeka's black women is particularly noteworthy. African American women led numerous religious, social, and cultural organizations, such as the Women's Benevolent Society, a coalition of church and privately sponsored social welfare groups, the Interstate Literary Association, and the Shakespeare, Handel, and

Beethoven clubs. The Coterie was a women's club whose activities ranged from whist parties and church suppers to sponsorship of an 1893 lecture by Ida B. Wells titled "The Evils of Lynching." Black Topeka women organized the Colored Women's Suffrage Association in 1887 to join the national crusade to obtain voting rights. The women of Topeka could boast among their ranks Lutie Lytle, a policeman's daughter, who was also the second black female attorney in the nation, and a Populist party campaigner, Sarah Malone, who supervised the all-black Florence Crittenton Home for Unwed Mothers, and Lizzie Reddick, one of the two founders of the Kansas Industrial and Educational Institute, known locally as the Western Tuskegee.[48]

The Kansas Industrial and Educational Institute began in 1895 as a kindergarten, sewing school, and reading room. It was founded by Reddick and Edward Stephens, two elementary school teachers, and located in Mud Town, a poor neighborhood on the city's far south side. With funds raised from supporters, Reddick and Stephens purchased a small building on Kansas Avenue in 1898, in the heart of the black community's business district. One year later the institute received its first state appropriation of fifteen hundred dollars. Booker T. Washington, on a visit to Topeka in 1897, specifically endorsed the efforts of Reddick and Stephens in initiating the institute. When a newly formed board of managers assumed control in 1900, Washington sent a Tuskegee graduate, William Carter, to supervise operations. Carter became its first principal, and the school developed facilities for the teaching of industrial arts to black Topekans and scientific agriculture to African American farmers throughout the state. The Tuskegee connection was reinforced when Washington supporter Andrew Carnegie contributed fifteen thousand dollars between 1908 and 1911 to fund the construction of buildings on the campus.[49]

In 1903 the institute purchased a farm of 105 acres outside the city and relocated to the site, which had "one of the most commanding views in the state." The institute's agricultural extension service, which sponsored the Sunflower State Agricultural Association, became an important link to black communities throughout Kansas. From the institute's founding its administrators and faculty were African Americans, as were most of the members of the board of managers. No records showing student enrollment survive, but newspaper accounts imply that the student body came from throughout the state and some neighboring states and that the institute appealed to both poor and middle-class black families.[50]

The institute's Tuskegee connection continued after the death of Booker T. Washington in 1915. In 1917 George Bridgeforth, formerly director of the agricultural department at Tuskegee, replaced William Carter as principal. Bridgeforth solicited the support of Kansas politicians, including Governor Arthur Capper, to establish a hospital and nursing school for the institute. By 1919 the state had become the major supporter of the institute, and in that year the legislature assumed full control and renamed the school the Kansas Vocational Institute.[51]

Even as they took pride in the Kansas Industrial and Educational Institute, black Kansans and other African American westerners opposed segregated education, which by 1900 had evolved in most states of the West. In March 1882 an angry Park City, Utah, African American mother wrote to her local newspaper about an incident involving her children in the public school: "The school is free to all whether white or black, rich or poor. I sent my two little girls to school and because of this a white brother has taken his children out of school. My children's skin may be a shade darker than his but in all other respects they are equal. . . ."[52]

This unidentified black woman's concern over school segregation reflected the determination to challenge it in the most isolated settings. That determination was constructed on the fervent belief in education as the premier weapon in the campaign for both economic advancement and racial equality. "Nothing will free the colored race from all disabilities," wrote black Kansan Fred Scott in 1889, "and cause their general recognition on an equal [level] with whites so fast as education." Simeon O. Clayton, editor of the *Parsons* (Kansas) *Blade*, added that "we must educate or we must perish."[53]

Although exclusion, segregation, and integration constituted the three major approaches of white school officials in the West toward black education, African American westerners were in fact subject to a complicated array of school policy regarding access to the common schools. A survey of school policy among the six western states admitted to the Union by 1870 provides an indication of the variety of approaches. Texas Democrats wrote a constitution in 1875 that mandated segregated education. California separated black, Indian, and Asian pupils from white enrollees once the number of nonwhites reached ten students. Neighboring Nevada enacted similar legislation although it did not specify the number of "colored" students necessary to establish a separate school. Nebraska and Oregon permitted individual cities to separate pupils by race. Kansas enacted legislation in 1868 to "organize and maintain separate schools for the education of white and colored children."[54]

Yet school segregation laws were infinitely malleable, subject as they were to shifting public opinion, population demographics, local economics, federal laws and Supreme Court decisions, and the concerted efforts of ardent segregationists and integrationists. Kansas school policy is a case in point. The Kansas constitution of 1859 called for separate schools for whites and blacks. In 1874, however, the legislature passed a civil rights law that prohibited state educational institutions from making distinctions based on race. Four years later the legislature passed and state voters ratified a constitutional amendment striking the word *white* from the educational code, eliminating separate schools. Yet in 1879 the legislature reversed itself and allowed cities of ten thousand or more to establish separate primary schools but not secondary schools or colleges, a policy that remained in force until the 1954 U.S. Supreme Court ruling in *Brown v. Board of Education of Topeka.*[55]

Kansas school policy shifts reflected division among whites. The Kansas State Teachers Association, meeting in Lawrence in July 1866, resolved "to use our best endeavors to overcome the unreasonable prejudice existing in certain localities against the admission of colored children upon equal terms with white children." Atchison newspaper editor and future governor John A. Martin admitted that separate schools were not equal and told fellow Kansans to "give the colored children equal school privileges. . . . Let us have one system, one school, for all children of the great human brotherhood." Yet other Kansans, such as "X" from Leavenworth, opposed efforts of "demented white men" to legislate "social equality. . . ." Topeka newspaper editor J. Clarke Swayze warned that if the legislature attempted to integrate the schools, "we shall not be disappointed to see the excellent system now in operation in Kansas left to the negroes . . . while independent institutions . . . will educate the whites."[56]

Many African American westerners resisted segregation with the meager resources they could summon. "We hear of no Irish schools, no German schools, no Swedish schools. No, not one," declared *Topeka Colored Citizen* editor William Eagleson. "All the children in the city are at liberty to attend the school nearest them, except the poor child that God . . . chose to create with a black face instead of a white one. . . . We say to every colored man and woman in the city to come together and resolve that you will no longer submit to unjust discrimination on account of your color. This thing has gone on long enough and now if it can be stopped, let's stop it."[57]

Occasionally African Americans won antisegregation and anti-exclusion campaigns as when Virginia City, Nevada, in 1872 enrolled black children in state-supported schools for the first time. One year later Lewis and Frederick Douglass, Jr., led the effort to integrate Denver's public schools. Peter Anderson, editor of the *Pacific Appeal,* and the black Stockton educator Jeremiah Sanderson figured prominently in the thirty-year campaign to desegregate public schools in California by 1880. But more often they were unsuccessful, as in Kansas. Black parents in the Sunflower State brought a number of lawsuits throughout the state in the 1880s that resulted in only slight relief and culminated in an 1890 Kansas Supreme Court decision in *Reynolds v. Board of Education of Topeka,* that held the state's segregation law constitutional. Segregation in Texas and Oklahoma were so well entrenched that few legal challenges were mounted in the nineteenth century. Conversely, segregation came late in the far Southwest. Arizona's territorial legislature, for example, enacted its first statute in 1909, in response to the growing black population in Phoenix and Tucson. In one particularly appalling application of the new law, schools that had only one black pupil were required to mount "a screen around the desk of a Negro child." By 1910 African American parents from Beaumont to Yuma campaigned for "fair" appropriation of resources to all-black schools. Nonetheless they and indeed most western black parents anticipated the day when separate schools would be eliminated.[58]

Wichita, Kansas, provides an example of an initially integrated school system that embraced racial segregation "for the good of the colored community." From its beginnings in 1870, Wichita had a small African American population of 5 percent or less that was residentially dispersed throughout the city. Through the 1880s black and white children attended the same schools without distinction. In 1889 a delegation of black Wichitans, concerned about growing segregation of African American pupils in Kansas City and Topeka schools, persuaded State Senator O. A. Bentley, who represented the city in the legislature, to enact a law specifically prohibiting Wichita from segregating its children by race. Despite the legislation, their fears remained and were publicly expressed in a series of resolutions adopted at a mass meeting at St. Paul's African Methodist Episcopal Church in January 1891.[59]

In 1902 the *Wichita Eagle,* which had previously been silent on school segregation, announced that the Topeka Board of Education had constructed an all-black school. The paper then noted that "prejudice is something which neither laws nor courts can control ... and the colored man makes a mistake whenever he tries to enforce social recognition through legal channels." In 1905 the *Eagle* concluded that separate schools were best for blacks because they bolstered racial self-esteem. "The colored people take more interest in their separate schools than they do in the mixed schools, because they feel that they belong to them."[60]

In 1906 the Wichita school board adopted school segregation over the objections of black parents. African American students were to be educated in the west wing of Park School, and a portion of the school playground was set aside for their exclusive use. African American parents continued their resistance. In a episode that foreshadowed *Brown v. Board of Education of Topeka* nearly a half century later, Sallie Rowles, in September 1906, attempted to enroll her thirteen-year-old daughter, Fannie, in Emerson School, only four hundred feet from the family home. When Fannie was turned away, her mother filed a lawsuit against the Wichita Board of Education. The case reached the Kansas Supreme Court, which in July 1907 upheld the plaintiff. Local politicians struck back. During the 1909 legislative session State Senator H. H. Stewart, who represented Wichita, responding to a petition of five thousand local residents calling for school segregation, pushed through a bill that allowed the Wichita Board of Education to segregate students. In 1911 Wichita citizens voted three to one to approve school bonds of sixty thousand dollars for the construction of two schools expressly for black students. In the face of such overwhelming sentiment for segregation, black leaders accepted the inevitable, named the schools Toussaint L'Ouverture and Frederick Douglass, and eventually embraced the black teachers hired for the schools. However, some local residents remained intensely aware of their second-class status as reflected in the separate schools and continued a pattern of legal protest that finally desegregated the schools in the 1960s.[61]

Segregation was well entrenched in Oklahoma and Texas, where there were sizable African American communities, much greater racial tension, and a seldom challenged philosophy of racial inferiority. Segregationist ideology was so overwhelmingly supported by the white populace that African American leaders were reduced to arguing for equitable appropriations for separate facilities that seemed somehow never to equal white schools. African Americans faced severe difficulties, in Texas, where because of white taxpayer opposition to building and supporting all-black public schools, more than two-thirds of the facilities for African American pupils in the 1880s were in churches, barns, and other rented buildings. Virtually all the high schools for blacks, such as Dallas's Colored High School, founded in 1892, were in the state's largest cities, further restricting educational opportunity for the state's mostly rural populace.[62]

The African American urban West spawned one distinctly female social activity, the black women's clubs. African American western women were concentrated heavily in western towns and cities. In 1900 they formed the majority of blacks in Los Angeles, Denver, Kansas City, and small towns, such as Topeka, Pasadena, and Berkeley. Middle-class black western women assumed leadership of all African American women and promoted respectability and reform. Clubwomen eagerly sought self-education, cultural and intellectual improvement, and mutual self-help and support. But the clubs also engaged in "racial uplift," which usually meant encouraging education and moral rectitude among lower-class black women. Invoking the geographical symbol of the region, the president of the Colorado Association of Colored Women's Clubs, in her address at the sixth annual convention in 1909, called on the state's black clubwomen to lift "a downtrodden race above the rockies [*sic*] of prejudice." For all of their outward-directed activity, these clubs also offered western black women the opportunity for self-expression and informal education while linking them to the national network of African American women's organizations. Most important, these women took charge of their collective lives and fates and avoided victimization by the world around them. As the Kansas Federation of Women's Clubs stated in its motto, they were "rowing, not drifting."[63]

African American women's clubs sprang up in virtually every western community that had a concentration of black women. They established day care centers, nurseries, and industrial schools or led campaigns to close pool halls and gambling dens. Their history is long and illustrious. The Ladies' Refugee Aid Society, the first black women's club in the West, was organized in Lawrence, Kansas, to assist fugitive slaves entering the area from Missouri, Arkansas, and Indian Territory. The Heart's Ease Circle of King's Daughters, organized in Austin, Texas, in 1894, created a home for the elderly that served the community for nearly a century. The Fanny Jackson Coppin Club, the "mother club" of the black women's club movement in California, was founded in Oakland in 1899 to provide accommodations to blacks visiting the East Bay. In 1904 black women in Cheyenne, Wyoming, formed the Searchlight Club in response to the lynching of an African American male, while their counterparts in Los Angeles organized the Sojourner Truth Industrial Club to provide shelter for single women entering the city. An alliance of Denver clubs supported the Colored Orphanage and Old Folks Home in Pueblo, Colorado, through the first decade of the twentieth century. The Dorcas Charity Club was founded in Seattle 1906 to care for abandoned babies.[64]

Western African American women quickly realized that affiliation of the individual clubs strengthened their standing and influence locally and regionally. To that end the various clubs formed statewide federations. Kansas women's clubs came together in 1900; Colorado followed in 1903, Texas and Nebraska in 1905, and California in 1906. The clubs in Oklahoma formed a statewide federation in 1910. Over the next fifteen years state federations were created in Oregon (1912), Arizona (1915), Washington (1917), Montana (1912), New Mexico (1923), and Wyoming (1925).[65]

The Kansas Federation was typical of the statewide organizations in the West. From an initial group of ten clubs in five cities in 1900, the federation quickly grew to fifty-one clubs in sixteen cities by 1913. The delegates who attended the annual meetings presented artwork, read papers on domestic science, raised money and collected clothing for charities and scholarships, and protested discriminatory movie theaters and other public accommodations. The black Kansas women equivocated on one of the major controversies at the national level; their exclusion from white clubs. Lucy B. Johnson, state president of the white women's federation, praised the state's black women for working in their own communities and for their refusal to follow the example of eastern black women who sought admission to white clubs. One unidentified black clubwoman responded to Johnson, stating that they refused to "thrust ourselves in where we are not wanted." She added, however, that Kansas segregation was neither just nor inevitable. "In localities where women are estimated by their intelligence, refinement and ability to do good club work, it may be [a] common sight to see a colored woman a member of a white woman's club, but it is not at all likely that we will see such a sight as that in Kansas soon." Historians who view the black women's clubs only in terms of their promotion of Victorian standards of behavior fail to recognize that African American women in Kansas and the West saw uplift in their communities not as an end in itself but as preparation for the eventual elimination of all individious racial distinctions.[66]

By 1910 the parameters of black urban settlement in the West were fixed. African American communities existed in all the cities of the region and were poised to grow with the general population of the cities and of the West. The African American communities in the region differed from one another—black Houston was a segregated "city within a city" that grew from a nearby rural population while black San Francisco evolved from a population of globally diverse origins—yet as the twentieth century progressed, such differences receded. Western urban blacks now fought for greater economic opportunity, political influence, and educational access. Those battles were to ally black westerners with sympathetic whites and other people of color. They also incorporated the region's blacks into the national struggle for racial justice.

8

❖ ❖ ❖ ❖ ❖

The Black
Urban West,
1911–40

In 1913 W. E. B. Du Bois embarked on a promotional tour through
Texas, California, and the Pacific Northwest. The tour signaled recognition of the West's crucial role in the burgeoning campaign for
racial justice and equality. Du Bois assured his audiences that the
NAACP was committed to fighting injustice locally, regionally, and
nationally. The black West would not be ignored.[1]

Du Bois's tour also recognized the importance of western urban
African American communities. By the second decade of the twentieth century the center of African American life in the West was
urban. African American urbanites outnumbered rural residents in
every western state except Texas and Oklahoma. Even there the
political, economic, and cultural center of black life lay in Houston
and Dallas, Oklahoma City and Tulsa long before most black Texans
or Oklahomans became urbanites. The fate of the average twentieth-
century black westerner would be determined on city streets.

Black Los Angeles emerged during this period as the largest
urban black western community in California. By the second decade
of the twentieth century it had eclipsed San Francisco and Oakland
as the center of black politics and business in California, a transition
symbolized by the 1918 election of Frederick M. Roberts as the first
African American assemblyman in the state and by the rise of the

African American Urban Population in the West, 1920–40
Black Population in Cities of 250,000 or More in 1940

	1920		1930		1940	
	Black Pop.	Total Pop.	Black Pop.	Total Pop.	Black Pop.	Total Pop.
Dallas	24,023	158,976	38,742	260,475	50,407	294,734
Denver	6,075	256,491	7,204	287,861	7,836	322,412
Los Angeles	15,579	576,673	38,894	1,238,048	63,774	1,504,277
Houston	33,960	138,276	63,337	292,352	86,302	384,514
Oakland	5,489	216,261	7,503	284,063	8,462	302,163
Portland	1,556	258,288	1,559	301,815	1,931	305,394
San Antonio	14,341	161,379	17,938	231,542	19,235	253,854
San Francisco	2,414	506,676	3,803	634,394	4,846	634,536
Seattle	2,894	315,312	3,303	365,583	3,789	368,302

Sources: U.S. Bureau of the Census, Fourteenth Census of the United States, *vol. 2,* Population, 1920 *(Washington, D.C.: Government Printing Office, 1922), 47, and U.S. Bureau of the Census,* Sixteenth Census of the United States, 1940, Population, *vol. 2,* Characteristics of the Population *(Washington, D.C.: Government Printing Office, 1943), part 1, 629, 636, 657, 787; part 5, 1041; part 6, 1026, 1044, 1053; part 7, 400.*

state's largest black business, the Golden State Mutual Insurance Company. African American communities in Houston and Dallas rivaled Los Angeles in size, if not in fame. Denver's black community continued its steady growth, while a World War I–era influx of African American migrants from the South doubled Omaha's black population.[2]

African Americans moved to other western cities, notably Seattle and Portland in the Pacific Northwest; Phoenix, Tucson, and San Diego in the far Southwest; and Wichita, Oklahoma City, and Tulsa on the southern plains. Black Tulsa's rapid growth during World War I, prompted by oil discoveries in the region, gave rise to an enterprising, successful population that chafed under southern-inspired racial restrictions. Their success heightened black-white tensions and sparked the Tulsa race riot of 1921, an orgy of white violence on June 1 that took thirty lives and destroyed eleven hundred homes and most businesses in Deep Greenwood, Tulsa's African American district.[3]

Nineteenth-century urban employment patterns continued virtually unchanged until World War II. In 1930 most African American males in San Francisco, Oakland, Denver, Portland, and Seattle were servants. Only in Houston did male workers in manufacturing out-number those in domestic service. For black women in the largest western cities, domestic service dominated, with percentages rang-ing from a low of 83 percent in Seattle to a high of 93 percent in Dallas. This employment concentration prompted the *Northwest Enterprise,* Seattle's black newspaper, to declare in 1927: "Colored men should have jobs as streetcar motormen and conductors. [Black women] should have jobs as telephone operators and stenographers. . . . Black firemen can hold a hose and squirt water on a burning building just as well as white firemen. We want jobs, jobs, after that everything will come unto us."[4]

C. L. Dellums, vice-president of the Brotherhood of Sleeping Car Porters, recalled work opportunities soon after he came to the San Francisco Bay Area from Texas in 1923. "I had been around here long enough to realize there wasn't very much work Negroes could get." African American workers could either "go down to the sea in ships or work on the railroads." Fourteen years later Kathryn Bogle discovered similar limitations when she began to search for employ-

Percentage of Black Workers in Major Occupational Categories in Western Cities of 250,000 or More, 1930

	Manufacturing		Trade		Professional Service		Domestic Service	
	Men	Women	Men	Women	Men	Women	Men	Women
Dallas	32.3	2.2	11.0	.7	3.7	2.8	33.6	93.3
Denver	17.3	3.4	10.3	1.3	4.3	3.4	57.2	88.8
Houston	40.7	4.8	11.2	1.1	2.8	3.9	19.0	89.1
Los Angeles	21.8	4.7	7.7	1.5	5.2	4.5	39.7	86.7
Oakland	22.1	8.6	3.9	1.4	3.3	2.4	52.6	83.4
Portland	11.8	2.6	3.5	1.3	4.6	3.6	66.9	88.3
San Francisco	16.4	5.5	3.8	1.0	2.6	2.7	58.0	88.9
Seattle	19.5	4.9	5.3	1.4	5.1	6.8	51.0	83.0

Source: U.S. Bureau of the Census, Fifteenth Census of the United States, 1930, Population, *vol. 4,* Occupations by States *(Washington, D.C.: Government Printing Office, 1933), 199–210, 244–46, 1370–72, 1585–87, 1593–96, 1709–11.*

Women of the Owens and Mason families on porch of Biddy Mason's home, ca. 1875. *UCLA Special Collections*

African American cyclists along the South Platte River, Denver, ca. 1900. *Colorado Historical Society, Lillybridge Collection (w294), Gift of John Werness*

Second Baptist Church of Bismarck, North Dakota, ca. 1920. *Historical Society of North Dakota*

Second Baptist Church baptism, San Antonio River, 1914. *Institute of Texan Cultures, University of Texas at San Antonio*

Womens' Progressive Club, San Antonio, Texas, ca. 1895. *Institute of Texan Cultures*

First meeting of Montana Federation of Colored Women's Clubs, Butte, Montana, 1924. *Montana Historical Society*

Black longshoremen working along the Houston Ship Channel, 1922.
Houston Metropolitan Research Center

Waiters, Portland Hotel, ca. 1925. *Oregon Historical Society*

Deliverymen for Bryant's Department Store, Albuquerque, New Mexico, ca. 1925. *Center for Southwest Research, University of New Mexico*

Tulsa race riot, 1921. *Oklahoma Historical Society*

African American Auto Club, Tucson, Arizona, 1923. *Arizona Historical Society*

Interior of Creole Palace. *San Diego Historical Society*

WPA road paving crew, Oakland, California, 1937. *Oakland History Room, Oakland Public Library*

George Morrison Orchestra. *Denver Public Library, Western History Department*

Hotel Somerville (later the Dunbar Hotel). *Miriam Matthews Collection*

Richmond shipyard, ca. 1943. *Richmond Museum of History, Richmond, California*

First African American family moves into Carver Park, Las Vegas, 1943. *Henderson Public Library Collection, Special Collections Department, UNLV Library*

Nightclub scene, Salt Lake City, ca. 1943. *Utah Historical Society*

Lena Horne at Fort Huachuca, 1943.
Fort Huachuca Museum

Ninety-fifth Engineers working on Sikanni Chief River Bridge, Alcan Highway, 1942. *U.S. Army Corps of Engineers*

Restricted housing tract, Los Angeles, ca. 1948. *Southern California Library for Social Studies & Research*

Houston Negro Chamber of Commerce, 1946. *Courtesy Houston Metropolitan Research Center, Houston Public Library*

Richmond, California, war housing, 1949. *Richmond Museum of History, Richmond, California*

The Reverend Oliver Brown (middle, standing), ca. 1954. *Oliver Brown Family Collection, University of Kansas Libraries*

Civil Rights demonstration, Oklahoma City, 1964. *Oklahoma Historical Society*

Tracy Simms at the San Francisco Auto Row demonstrations, 1964. *Ted Streshinsky*

103d Street, Watts uprising, 1965. *UCLA Special Collections*

Bobby Seale and Huey Newton in front of Panther headquarters, Oakland, 1967. *San Francisco Examiner*

SNCC demonstration, Texas Southern University, Houston, 1967. *Houston Metropolitan Research Center, Houston Public Library*

Ten thousand Seattleites in memorial march for Dr. Martin Luther King, Jr., April 1968. *Seattle Times*

ment after graduating from a Portland high school. "I visited large and small stores. . . . I visited the telephone company; both power and light companies. I tried to become an elevator operator in an office building. I answered ads for inexperienced office help. In all of these places I was told there was nothing about me in my disfavor except my skin color." Bogle then described how several employers who refused to hire her downtown offered her work, "as a domestic . . . where her color would not be an embarrassment."[5]

One occupation—motion-picture actor—was exclusively western. By the second decade of the twentieth century the motion-picture industry centered in Hollywood, California, as Los Angeles–area studios gained nationwide control over production and distribution of films. African Americans had been film actors in the pre-California days of motion pictures and often had sensitive, nonstereotypical roles in pre–World War I films. They hoped to continue working in the industry after it concentrated in southern California. But film moguls relegated black employees to service jobs and black actors to roles that reflected their subservient status in the work force. From 1915 to 1920 roughly half the black roles reviewed by *Variety* were maids, butlers, and janitors. In the 1920s menial roles reached 80 percent and remained there until the 1930s, when such performers as Lena Horne, Cab Calloway, and Louis Armstrong played themselves in films directed toward black audiences. Art ruthlessly imitated life in the nation's film capital.[6]

Virtually no one inside the studios challenged these early stereotypes forcing black actors to accept demeaning roles to "build ourselves into" the movie industry, as law school student–turned–actor Clarence Muse described it. A few actors, such as Paul Robeson, pursued careers abroad, while Louise Beavers and Hattie McDaniel plunged into community service or sponsored lavish parties to distance themselves from their portrayals as faithful servants. Yet the most successful film performer of the period, Stepin Fetchit, personified Hollywood's negative characterizations of African Americans.[7]

Born Lincoln Theodore Monroe Andrew Perry in 1902 in Key West, Florida, Stepin Fetchit (the stage name derived from a vaudeville comedy team he formed with Ed Lee called Step and Fetch It) arrived in Hollywood in the early 1920s. When a Fox talent scout spotted him, he was given a successful screen test, and his career began. By the end of the 1920s he alone among African American actors had achieved feature billing and regular work. Between 1929 and 1935 he appeared in twenty-six films. Regardless of the script or setting, Fetchit's character was usually a shuffling, superstitious, subservient black man. Many white moviegoers easily accepted Fetchit's portrayals as African American "comic relief" in action-oriented films. Black audiences, however, were deeply ambivalent about his success. Many admired Fetchit's wealthy lifestyle, symbolized by his multiple homes and servants and his champagne pink Cadillac, which regularly cruised Central Avenue. Yet off-screen antics, such as insisting reporters publish his interviews "in my dialeck," indicated his failure to distinguish between his film portrayals and real-life persona. By the end of the 1930s Fetchit's extravagant lifestyle had bankrupted him, and NAACP criticism of his portrayals ended his career.[8]

Meanwhile hundreds of black extras seeking careers in film lived precariously. Unlike Fetchit, these actors had no agents and did not haunt casting offices. Instead they clustered along Central Avenue, waiting for a casting director to drive by and choose an especially attractive woman or man to try out as an extra—often a slave in a plantation musical or a native in a jungle adventure. The prospect of earning up to $3.50 per day in a feature film drew hundreds of bit players into motion pictures ranging from D. W. Griffith's *The Birth of a Nation* through David O. Selznick's *Gone with the Wind*. As film historian Thomas Cripps notes, white actors were sometimes defeated by this system, but blacks never won.[9]

African American professionals and entrepreneurs served working-class residents in every western city. By 1915 nearly four hundred black Houston businesses served an all-black clientele. Black Los Angeles had fewer but more high-profile businesses, which generated enormous pride among the city's African Americans and occasional comment from outsiders. Chandler Owen, Harlem resident and editor of the *Messenger*, declared Central Avenue a "veritable little Harlem in Los Angeles," after a 1922 speaking tour. His assessment was based on the concentration of businesses and fashionable homes on "the Avenue." Along a twelve-block section of Central Avenue could be found black-owned theaters, including the Angelus, which advertised itself as "the only show house owned by Colored men in the entire West," savings and loan associations, automobile dealerships, newspaper offices, and retail businesses. The "Avenue" was also home to the Golden State Mutual Life Insurance Company and the Hotel Somerville (later the Dunbar Hotel), which became nationally famous after NAACP delegates stayed there during the organization's 1928 national convention. Four stories tall, the Somerville, at Forty-first Street and Central Avenue, had one hundred rooms, sixty with private baths. In 1929 Dr. H. Claude Hudson, a prominent dentist and president of the local NAACP, built the Hudson-Liddell Building also at Forty-first and Central. The building, designed by African American architect Paul Williams, soon became the "symbol to black Angelenos of what was possible in Los Angeles."[10]

In cities with small African American populations, such as Denver, Seattle, and San Francisco, black businesses struggled against intense competition from other people of color. In Seattle, for example, those blacks who resented white storeowner attitudes were eagerly courted by Asian entrepreneurs. Japanese and Chinese restaurants welcomed working-class black customers. One Asian restaurant owner developed a specialized menu of soul food to entice black porters and ship stewards. Occasionally Asian and black stores vied for the support of black community residents in a contest that pitted ethnic loyalty against perceptions of superior service. Margaret Cogwell, a black Seattle grocery store owner who lost her competition with an Asian grocer across the street, bitterly remarked: "The Negroes were always coming to the Japanese right across from me, and they'd go there and buy the same milk and bread . . . from the Japanese. Mine wasn't good enough even though it was delivered the same time and everything." Cogwell closed her store and left Seattle in 1919. Cogwell's Japanese competitor had access to a regional distribution network that included Japanese wholesalers, other Japanese grocers, and Japanese farmers. Nonetheless her loss was painful when it appeared race disloyalty was responsible for the store's failure.[11]

The Great Depression ravaged Western black communities throughout the 1930s. In Houston in 1931 black unemployment approached 40 percent compared with 17 percent for white workers. One of every three black workers in Los Angeles was unemployed in 1931, and one of every four in Denver and Seattle. The unemployment burden African American workers assumed prompted the *Colorado Statesman* to ask in 1933: "Is [the Negro] not an American citizen and entitled to share and share alike? . . . Although he is perfectly willing to take his chances, he is not given a chance. . . . He is, in truth and deed, the forgotten man. . . ."[12]

Statistics cannot completely convey the sense of loss and

despair. Seattleite Sara Oliver Jackson remembered that during the early 1930s, "There wasn't any particular jobs you could get, although you knew you had to work. So, you got a domestic job and made $10.00 a month, 'cause that was what they were paying, a big 35 cents a day. . . ." William Pittman, a San Francisco dentist unable to continue his practice, worked for eighty dollars per month as a chauffeur. His wife, Tarea, a 1925 University of California graduate, concluded that race discrimination added to the family's declining economic fortunes. "I am unable to find work," wrote Tarea Pittman, ". . . on account of my race." One unidentified Portland woman recollected, "We were without work for well over a year. I did a number of things to help bring in money, and my husband worked for fifty cents a day shoveling snow down at the [Portland] Hotel. . . . People were just . . . trying to make it."[13]

Black westerners turned to community self-help projects. Churches from Texas to Washington collected clothing and food and provided the homeless with temporary shelter. Father Divine and Daddy Grace helped some of Los Angeles's destitute. When Phoenix relief agencies refused to aid impoverished African Americans, local blacks formed the Phoenix Protective League, which joined forces with black fraternal orders to provide assistance. In 1931 black churchwomen in Houston organized soup lines and dispensed food while in Richmond, California, Beryl Gwendolyn Reid single-handedly cooked "big pots of beans" to "feed all the people who were hungry." Denver politician and nightclub owner Ben Hooper organized groups of World War I veterans to hunt jackrabbits, which were then distributed as food to needy families. Despite such valiant efforts, in 1931 many black community leaders agreed with Seattle Urban League director Joseph S. Jackson, who reported to New York that "blacks had supported themselves as long as they were able. . . ." They, and the nation, increasingly looked to the local, state, and federal government to address their plight.[14]

Even New Deal agencies did not guarantee public employment or relief. Willis Johnson, an unemployed black worker, moved to Houston from Louisiana during the Great Depression. He told an interviewer, "Relief is the only thing that I know anything about, and about all I know about that is that I have never been able to get any of it." Johnson's view was confirmed by Lorena Hickok, a "confidential investigator" for FDR's adviser Harry Hopkins. Traveling across the nation in 1934, Hickok gave firsthand accounts of relief efforts. She reached Houston in April and wrote: "At no time . . . since taking

Unemployment in the Black Urban West, 1931, 1937

	% Black Unemployed, 1931	% Black Unemployed, 1937
Denver	25.7	19.0
Houston	39.6	15.5
Los Angeles	33.1	34.1
San Francisco	18.3	26.8
Seattle	23.7	21.9

White unemployment in Seattle, 1937, 10.1

Sources: U.S. Bureau of the Census, Fifteenth Census of the United States: 1930, Unemployment, vol. 2 (Washington, D.C.: Government Printing Office, 1932), ch. 5, "The Special Census of Unemployment, January 1931," Table 2; U.S. Bureau of the Census, Census of Unemployment, 1937: Final Report on Total and Partial Unemployment, vols. 1, 3 (Washington, D.C.: Government Printing Office, 1938), Table 1. Gainful worker totals for 1931 were used to determine 1937 unemployment rates. Unemployment percentages for 1937 are based on the combined "totally unemployed" and "emergency workers" categories as percentage of population, 1930, age fifteen to seventy-four.

this job, have I been quite so discouraged as I am tonight. Texas is a Godawful mess . . . relief in Houston is a joke." New Deal agencies operating in Texas, including the National Recovery Administration, the Civil Works Administration, and the Works Progress Administration, discriminated against local blacks, prompting the *Houston Informer*, at first a supporter of the New Deal, to conclude in 1936, "Texas Negroes don't benefit much one way or the other whether Roosevelt or Landon is in."[15]

The one exception in the otherwise dismal treatment blacks received from New Deal relief agencies was the state's National Youth Administration programs under twenty-seven-year-old Lyndon B. Johnson, who was selected as the first state director in September 1935. Johnson resisted pressure from national NYA officials to integrate the state advisory board, declaring that if he followed such a course, he would be "run out of Texas." However, he did appoint an all-black advisory board and carefully weighed their suggestions. Moreover, he covertly reallocated funds from white to more needy black programs and created the Freshman College Center, a forerunner of Upward Bound, which brought to college campuses impoverished but academically capable students. Fifteen of the twenty programs in the state served black youth, giving them the support and incentive to enter college. Johnson's efforts on behalf of black youth in a conservative state won accolades from African American government officials, including Mary McLeod Bethune and Robert C. Weaver. Bethune, director of the NYA Office of Negro Affairs and the ranking black appointee in the Roosevelt administration, condemned Johnson's refusal to place an African American on the state NYA Advisory Board. Nonetheless she praised his other efforts and predicted, "He's going to go places. He'll be a big man in the country." Weaver (whom President Johnson would appoint, in 1965, the first black cabinet officer) declared the young Texas NYA director ". . . was shocking some people up on [Capitol] Hill because he thought that the National Youth Administration benefits ought to go to poor folks. . . . To make matters worse, he was giving a hell of a lot of this money to Mexican-Americans and Negroes." The future president did not act out of political expediency, since few blacks in Texas in the 1930s could vote. Instead his efforts demonstrated a genuine commitment to extend to blacks their share of the National Youth Administration allocations.[16]

Generally other western blacks fared better than Texas's African Americans in getting federal support. Of Phoenix's blacks, 51 percent (as opposed to 59 percent of the Mexican Americans and 11 percent of the Anglos) were on relief in 1933, a statistic revealing both easier access to government assistance than their Texas counterparts and the level of African American poverty. In December 1933, 160 black men earned eighteen dollars per week while working on the South Platte River flood control project sponsored by the Public Works Administration, prompting the *Colorado Statesman* to declare, "The Negro population cheerfully relishes their portion of the employment."[17]

California's blacks also fared well in their access to relief. San Franciscans received a disproportionate amount of relief or public employment. Women used public works programs to upgrade their skills away from domestic service. Black workers throughout the state were particularly successful with the Works Progress Administration and the National Youth Administration. Much of the success stemmed from the activities of Vivian Osborne Marsh, who headed the state's Division of Negro Affairs. Marsh, a friend of Mary McLeod Bethune, used the network of the California Federation of Colored Women's Clubs to attract more than two thousand black youths into the NYA between 1935 and 1941. Her efforts allowed four hundred African American college and graduate students to complete their education. Moreover, over one thousand women and men received training in sheet metal, machine, and radio and aircraft production and repair that served them well in the state's World War II defense plants.[18]

The Great Depression encouraged leftist activism, which in turn assisted black westerners. The political left, including Communist-inspired popular front organizations, such as the Unemployed Citizens League, League of Struggle for Negro Rights, National Negro Congress, and International Labor Defense, mounted civil disobedience campaigns to confront racial discrimination in the region's cities. In March 1930 500 mostly black women and men descended on Houston's city hall in a Communist-organized demonstration to demand emergency unemployment relief and the abolition of racist legislation. Two years later in Phoenix the International Defense League and the Afro-American League sponsored a march to the state capitol to demand an end to discriminatory pay scales for black state workers and direct relief for needy families. In July 1932 Communists in Denver organized 150 African Americans to desegregate Smith Lake in South Denver, a public swimming area. In 1934, 700 Dallas activists organized an eleven-day city hall "sit-in" protesting cuts in federal WPA jobs for the area. Such demonstrations rarely gained their immediate objectives. They did introduce small western communities to "direct action" and brought together working-class people of various races over social justice issues.[19]

Like eastern black voters, Depression-era African American westerners embraced the Democratic party. This transition was encouraged by white liberal politicians, such as the members of the Washington and Oregon Commonwealth federations, which represented the left-liberal wing of the Democratic party. The WCF sponsored black Democratic clubs and opposed discriminatory state laws, while the OCF pushed for a state civil rights act in the 1930s. In a 1938 letter to NAACP Executive Director Walter White, Edgar Williams, a Portland branch official, declared the OCF "the only group of any political importance which has interested itself in [African American] problems. . . ."[20]

California's black voters gravitated toward the Democratic party in the late 1920s through political organizing by Titus Alexander, John W. Fowler, and Dr. J. Alexander Somerville. In 1934, when Republican Frederick Roberts, who had served sixteen years in the state assembly, was defeated by a twenty-seven-year-old Democrat, Augustus Hawkins, a new political era began in the state. Hawkins represented the south-central Los Angeles assembly district until

1962, when he became the first African American member of Congress from California. With his ties to unions and leftist politicians, Hawkins personified an emerging political nexus of liberals, labor, and blacks in the Roosevelt coalition. Colorado's black voters, however, were attracted to the Democrats by Denver saloon owner Ben Hooper, the "Mayor of Five Points." Hooper forged an alliance with popular Denver Mayor Benjamin F. Stapleton in the early 1920s and through traditional big-city patronage dominated political life in Denver's African American community during most of the interwar years.[21]

Most Texas and Oklahoma Democratic leaders remained steadfastly white supremacist in the 1930s and thus attracted little black support. San Antonio Representative Maury Maverick, who favored antilynching legislation and abolishing the poll tax, was the one notable exception. Maverick's progressive stand began to attract the attention of African Americans across the state. However, his opposition to black San Antonio political boss Charles Bellinger kept Maverick from getting the support of the only major black Texas voting constituency in pre–World War II Texas. Bellinger, a real estate entrepreneur and gambler, in the 1920s forged a deal with San Antonio's Latinos and the white-led political machine. In exchange for increased public services—parks, water lines, and street paving—Bellinger delivered a bloc of approximately eight thousand votes. As one historian claims, "Bellinger was able to secure from the . . . machine what could not be obtained through a democratic system crippled by racism." Unique in Texas at the time, Bellinger's machine demonstrated how blacks and Latinos could achieve leverage in a hostile political system. Elsewhere in the state Antonio Maceo Smith and Reverend Maynard H. Jackson, Sr., of Dallas organized the Progressive Voters League, which challenged the all-white primary system and developed a black constituency in the Democratic party. No white Oklahoma Democratic politician spoke out against racial injustice in the 1930s as Maury Maverick had in Texas, but influential African Americans, such as A. J. Smitherman, editor of the *Tulsa Star,* and Isaac W. Young, president of Langston University, began in the 1920s to persuade blacks to support Democratic candidates. By 1932 most African American voters in the state had made the transition.[22]

Despite economic difficulties a number of western African American urbanites purchased homes. Compared with the Northeast and Mid-

Black Home Ownership Rates in Selected Cities

	Percentage of African Americans in Owner-Occupied Homes, 1910–40		
	1910	*1930*	*1940*
Western Cities			
Portland	23.4%	42.6%	41.1%
San Antonio	25.9	41.4	34.2
Omaha	15.5	32.0	33.0
Denver	20.2	38.4	31.8
Los Angeles	36.1	33.6	29.7
Seattle	27.0	38.8	29.2
Oakland	29.9	34.5	28.4
Houston	20.1	31.4	21.6
Oklahoma City	24.0	27.3	23.8
Dallas	14.1	24.9	20.7
San Francisco	16.3	13.6	9.2
Midwestern and Eastern Cities			
Minneapolis	18.6	25.7	25.2
Detroit	17.2	15.0	17.1
Cleveland	10.9	8.3	10.5
Chicago	6.4	10.5	7.4
Milwaukee	5.1	5.5	5.6
New York	2.4	5.6	4.1

Sources: *U.S. Bureau of the Census,* Negro Population, 1790–1915 *(Washington, D.C.: Government Printing Office, 1918), 471–501;* Fifteenth Census of the United States: 1930. Population, *vol 6,* Families, *156–57, 194, 1098, 1270, 1402;* Sixteenth Census of the United States: 1940, Housing, *vol. 2,* General Characteristics, *part 2, 214, 327; part 4, 809; part 5, 274, 731. No figures were available for 1920.*

west, western cities (with San Francisco the notable exception) usually had high levels of black homeownership. Los Angeles led the way with a "bungalow boom" during the first two decades of the twentieth century. Along Central Avenue four or five-bedroom "California cottages" advertised for nine hundred to twenty-five hundred dollars and usually sold for one hundred dollars down with monthly payments of twenty dollars. Promotional ads occasionally described suburban areas such as Sierra Madre, where those who wanted a "splendid chance . . . for steady work [and a] fine climate" could purchase half acre lots or Eureka Villa, near Saugus, which advertised building lots for as little as seventy-five dollars. L. G. Robinson, a city custodian and Georgia migrant who arrived in Los Angeles in 1912, bought several lots on the edge of the city that he sold for a profit of several thousand dollars. Gracie Hall, a female domestic, proudly described the purchase of her first residential lot in a 1914 letter to Booker T. Washington. One anonymous black woman explained the success of her husband and herself as real estate entrepreneurs in a 1934 interview: "My parents were slaves and didn't leave us anything but the desire to get ahead in life. We now own eight houses. How did we get so much property? Why, we worked for it. I ran a hand laundry and my husband worked for the city." By 1924 black realtors proudly advertised Los Angeles as having one of the nation's highest percentages of homeowners. The claim would "broadcast to Colored Americans everywhere," according to California Realty Board attorney Hugh McBeth, "the opportunities, the welcome, the hope . . . which free California, its hills and valleys . . . and always sunshine offer to the American Negro."[23]

Some black Angelenos gravitated to the independent community of Watts, seven miles southeast of downtown Los Angeles. Established in 1903, the town soon became attractive to white working-class families, who were drawn to its low rents and housing prices. However, Watts was unique among Los Angeles suburbs; from its founding black, Latino, and white migrants purchased houses and small farms. By 1920, 14 percent of Watts was African American, the highest percentage in any California community. Arna Bontemps, whose family arrived in 1906 from Alexandria, Louisiana, recalled the integrated setting that greeted early black migrants. "We moved into a house in a neighborhood where we were the only colored family. The people next door and up and down the block were friendly and talkative, the weather was perfect . . . and my mother seemed to float about on the clean air." Bontemps's grandparents bought several acres of farmland north of Watts and built a house, a summer house, and a barn. One 1913 newspaper advertisement offered houses for two hundred to five hundred dollars in cash or for ten dollars down and five dollars per month. By the 1920s Watts was an attractive, increasingly African American suburb whose reputation had reached the East. When the leading black Los Angeles realtor Sidney P. Dones relocated in this southern suburb in 1923, the *Pittsburgh Courier* announced, "Watts . . . is the coming Negro town of California." The African American population of the community continued to grow after the town was annexed to Los Angeles in 1926, and by World War II it had become mostly African American. Both before and after annexation Watts remained, according to Lawrence B. de Graaf, "a lonely island in an otherwise white southeast Los Angeles."[24]

Although some suburban home opportunities existed in Watts, Pasadena, Santa Monica, and Sierra Madre, most blacks resided in the Central Avenue district. African American Angelenos, like their counterparts across urban American, faced restrictive covenants that ensured residential segregation. Such covenants prohibited blacks, Asians, Native Americans, Latinos, and on occasion Jews from occupying certain neighborhoods. One Los Angeles resident in 1917 described these agreements as "invisible walls of steel. The whites surrounded us and made it impossible for us to go beyond these walls." A 1927 covenant covered the residential area between the University of Southern California and the suburb of Inglewood, placing it off limits for people of color for ninety-nine years with the words "no part of any of the . . . lots and parcels . . . shall be sold or rented to any person other than those of the White or Caucasian race." In order to ensure convenient domestic help, the covenant exempted "domestic servants, chauffeurs, or gardeners [who live] where their employer resides." The California Supreme Court in 1928 upheld such agreements and ruled that even when blacks lived in neighborhoods before the restrictions were established, they must vacate properties under covenants. An occasional challenge succeeded, as in 1917, when Homer Garrett, a black policeman, appealed an order to remove him from a recently purchased house. The court, however, did not declare such agreements illegal. The most celebrated case of residential exclusion involved the family of realtor Booker T. Washington, Jr., who in the 1920s retained their home in the San Gabriel Valley.[25]

Restrictive covenants emerged in other western cities. Covenants created African American communities on Omaha's North Side and in the industrial suburb of South Omaha. By 1940 Houston covenants (reinforced by a state law enacted in 1927) produced several all-black enclaves throughout the city, "like islands set apart," according to urban historian Blaine Brownell. The 1942 *WPA Guide to Dallas* claimed that Oak Cliff, Deep Ellum, and other segregated communities that housed the city's forty-three thousand African

Americans "grew through the natural tendency of these people to live among their kind." The evidence points to a pattern of segregation punctuated by violence against those who sought to live elsewhere. The *Dallas Express* reported a dozen bombings in 1940 against blacks who moved into all-white neighborhoods. Such violence prompted Mayor Woodall Rogers to write letters advising black residents not to relocate in white residential areas and to white homeowners urging them not to sell to African Americans. Ultimately the city bought property in "sensitive areas" to prevent residential integration.[26]

Restrictive covenants enforced residential segregation in Denver, as Claude DePriest, a black fireman, discovered when he attempted in 1920 to buy a house just beyond Five Points, the city's black district. The Clayton Improvement Association warned him that "if you continue to reside at your present address, you do so at your own peril." Soon afterward 250 whites demonstrated in front of the DePriest home. The harassed family moved. A year later the home of postal worker Walter R. Chapman was bombed to protest his arrival in a previously all-white neighborhood. When restrictive covenants were challenged in Oklahoma City in 1933, the state's governor, Alfalfa Bill Murray, segregated the city by executive order, declaring, "I don't have the law to do this, but I have the power.[27]

Virtually all Phoenix African Americans were restricted to the southwestern section of the city, a "cesspool of poverty and disease . . . permeated with the odors of a fertilizer plant, iron foundry, a thousand open privies, and the city sewage disposal plant." Most black Phoenicians lived in shacks where "babies were born without medical care," and "often died because of the extreme temperatures (up to 118 degrees) in the summer or froze to death in the winter." San Francisco blacks avoided such squalor, but they nonetheless faced widespread restrictive covenants which prompted the *San Francisco Spokesman* to declare in 1927: Residential Segregation is as real in California as in Mississippi. A mob is unnecessary. All that's needed is a neighbor[hood] meeting and agreement in writing not to rent, lease, or sell to blacks, and the Courts will do the rest.[28] The campaign against residential segregation was to consume much of the time, energy, and resources of western black urbanites through the World War II period.

African Americans who migrated from Texas and Oklahoma to the West Coast thought they would encounter vastly different racial standards. Yet no region of the United States had completely avoided the burden of race. Houston, Dallas, or Oklahoma City blacks encountered segregation and discrimination via city ordinance or state law. Their counterparts in Los Angeles, Omaha, Denver, Seattle, and Phoenix were limited by private agreements. Segregated movie theaters and swimming pools were as common in Denver and Los Angeles as in Oklahoma City or Dallas. Most western blacks faced de facto public school segregation, but in Texas, Oklahoma, and Arizona the separation was de jure. Separate colleges were mandated in Texas and Oklahoma, but African Americans in public institutions throughout the west faced varying degrees of discrimination. Between 1913 and 1950 African American athletes in the Big Six Conference schools, such as the University of Kansas and the University of Nebraska, were banned from intervarsity competition because of the objections of the University of Missouri and the University of Oklahoma.[29]

Yet racial discrimination in the West was inconsistent. Most Portland and Seattle African Americans in 1920s and 1930s listed employment bias as their most serious challenge. Blacks in Phoenix worried about job discrimination and segregated schools. Houston and Dallas blacks noted similar limitations in 1928, but they also faced voting restrictions and segregated public accommodations. Houston's segregation received national attention in 1928, when white Texas Democrats, hosting their party's national convention, separated black delegates and spectators by a chicken wire fence. In Dallas as late as 1936 only twenty-seven of the city's four thousand acres of parkland were open to African Americans. Moreover, although lynching of African Americans was not unknown in California, Kansas, Nebraska, North Dakota, and Oregon during this period, western blacks outside Texas and Oklahoma noted the absence of white mob violence used to intimidate blacks into accepting second-class citizenship. As one black Phoenix resident remarked in 1916 after living in Georgia, "At least they don't lynch you here, like they did back there."[30]

While grievances differed, responses were strikingly uniform. Community after community organized branches of the NAACP. Founded in New York City in 1910, the association arrived in the West in 1912, when Houston blacks organized a branch. By 1919 eleven branches existed in Texas. The largest was the twelve-hundred-member San Antonio branch. Oklahoma City and Seattle formed branches in 1913, with Denver, Portland, Albuquerque, and

Omaha creating others the following year. In 1915 a Topeka branch was organized with Kansas Governor Arthur Capper a founding member. By 1919 branches had been established in Salt Lake City and Boise. Arizona was a particular area of early NAACP activity. Phoenix had the state's first branch, but by 1922 statewide membership exceeded one thousand blacks and whites operating in Tucson, Flagstaff, Bisbee, and Yuma.[31]

The Los Angeles and northern California branches of the NAACP soon became the largest in the West. Los Angeles's chapter was inspired by Du Bois's 1913 visit, and a letter from E. Burton Ceruti (who less than six years later became the first westerner to sit on the association's national board) to the national NAACP described housing restrictions and Jim Crow practices in southern California; "Problems and grievances arise constantly demanding attention. . . . We feel . . . the necessity of an organization such as yours. . . . Please advise." Before the end of the year the NAACP branch was under way in Los Angeles.[32]

The northern California NAACP also began with Du Bois's 1913 tour. The *Crisis* editor noted rigid patterns of segregation were absent in San Francisco. But he concluded, "The opportunity of the San Francisco Negro is very difficult; but he knows this and he is beginning to ask why." When Oakland and San Francisco blacks petitioned for chapters in 1915, the national NAACP office urged them to combine their efforts into a Northern California branch headquartered in Oakland. Within two years of its founding the branch had 1,000 members.[33]

NAACP branches in the West, like the national organization, focused their initial efforts on D. W. Griffith's film *The Birth of a Nation*, Hollywood's first "epic" motion picture. The twenty-five million people who viewed *The Birth of a Nation* within one year of its 1915 release saw the first film to utilize a complex story line, a variety of Southern California locations, the pan shot, artificial lighting, night photography, and split screens. Griffith's epic also employed far more black "extras" than any previous film, as hundreds of California African Americans portrayed soldiers, townspeople, and, of course, slaves. But the brief employment opportunities for African Americans in *The Birth of a Nation* could not compensate for its racist message of black incompetence and villainy during Reconstruction. That message generated the most extensive organized protest ever conducted against a feature film. The protest campaign was orchestrated by the NAACP national office, but local branches in such western cities as Seattle, Portland, Denver, Dallas, Wichita, and Topeka took independent action. The California branches led the way.[34]

The newly formed Northern California NAACP immediately sought to block showing of the film. Appealing to the San Francisco Board of Supervisors, it argued that the film was a "malicious misrepresentation of colored people, which create[d] enmity and hatred . . . disorder and race riots." It appealed directly to Oakland Mayor Frank K. Mott, San Francisco Mayor James Rolph, and Governor Hiram Johnson. Of the three, only Rolph appeared sympathetic. At his urging the San Francisco Moving Picture Censor Board reviewed the film and advised the removal of certain racially inflammatory scenes involving physical contact between white women and black men "to make the picture less offensive to all sides." NAACP leaders had hoped to prevent the film's showing. They settled for this limited censorship. The film continued to play in Bay Area theaters until 1921.[35]

The Los Angeles NAACP's protest began, and ended, earlier than the Bay Area effort. In February 1915, just days before the film's New York premiere, black Angelenos attacked Griffith's epic. The NAACP attempted unsuccessfully to get Los Angeles city officials to block its showing while the *California Eagle* kept up a barrage of attacks on both the film and the theaters that presented it. Moreover, the NAACP praised San Francisco city leaders for exhibiting more concern than Southern Californians over the movie's potential impact on local race relations. Yet by March it was clear that the local efforts would fail. NAACP board member Arthur B. Spingarn admitted the film was a "masterpiece" and, "from an artistic point of view, the finest thing of its kind I have ever witnessed."[36]

Spingarn's comments exposed a dilemma posed by *The Birth of a Nation*. Clearly the film harmed race relations. Yet many liberals, normally committed to civil rights issues, thought the NAACP's calls for banning the film unacceptable censorship. Thus, even as the campaign provided a crucial impetus to the fledgling association, the protest isolated the organization from potential allies. W. E. B. Du Bois reflected as much in a *Crisis* commentary, quoting at length from a white North Carolina newspaper that argued Griffith was a "mighty genius" against whom protest was pointless. Du Bois endorsed the paper's view, urging African Americans to forget "the cruel slander upon a weak and helpless race" and instead create their own aesthetic tradition.[37]

Individual NAACP branches responded to other issues. In 1915

Oklahoma City's NAACP, led by newspaper editor Roscoe Dungee, provided crucial assistance in *Guinn v. United States,* the national organization's challenge to Oklahoma's grandfather clause. The San Francisco branch (San Francisco seceded from the Northern California branch in 1923) investigated complaints of police brutality and public accommodations discrimination. It also raised money for the Scottsboro Defense Committee and brought suit against a segregated movie theater in Fresno. Both the San Francisco and Oakland branches fought the local Universal Negro Improvement Association (UNIA), which one Northern California NAACP official in 1922 claimed "had much to do with retarding our progress."[38]

The Texas branches' legal campaign over black participation in the state Democratic primary was the longest effort of any NAACP chapters during the interwar period. Texas, which levied a poll tax, never barred African Americans from voting in general elections, but most black voters were effectively disfranchised because they were denied access to the Democratic primary in a one-party state. In January 1921 the Houston City Democratic Executive Committee passed a resolution expressly prohibiting blacks from voting in the coming primary election. In response Charles Norvell Love, editor of the *Texas Freedman,* filed suit against the Harris County Democratic party.[39]

This opening salvo in the legal war between black Texans and leaders of the state Democratic party led to four U.S. Supreme Court decisions between 1927 and 1944. Shortly after Love lost his lawsuit, the 1923 Texas legislature enacted the Terrell Law, which expressly said: "In no event shall a Negro be eligible to participate in a Democratic primary election . . . in . . . Texas." The law prompted another suit by El Paso dentist Lawrence A. Nixon, who quickly emerged as the symbol of the Texas suffrage campaign.[40]

Lawrence Aaron Nixon moved to El Paso from Marshall, Texas, in 1910 and five years later helped found the city's NAACP branch. In 1924 NAACP Field Secretary William Pickens visited El Paso and announced that the NAACP intended to test the constitutionality of the Terell Law. Pickens asked for volunteers to file a lawsuit. "We are looking for someone who is not afraid," he said, and Nixon stepped forward. On Saturday, July 26, Nixon presented himself to local election officials. "The [election] judges were friends of mine," he recalled. "They inquired about my health, and when I presented my poll-tax receipt, one of them said, 'Dr. Nixon, you know we can't let you vote.' " "I know you can't," Nixon responded and then added, "but I've got to try."[41]

NAACP attorneys from the local branch and the national office won *Nixon v. Herndon* before the U.S. Supreme Court in 1927. Subsequently the Texas legislature modified the exclusion statute to satisfy the Court, but in 1928, having been denied a Democratic primary ballot, Nixon again filed suit. The High Court in *Nixon v. Condon* (1932) again ruled in favor of the plaintiff, concluding that the state Democratic party convention rather than the legislature had the power to bar blacks from voting in the primary.[42]

For twelve years the Texas Democratic party tried to limit the impact of the Supreme Court rulings while African Americans fought to widen their scope. Local leaders, such as James M. Nabrit and Carter W. Wesley of Houston, C. A. Booker of San Antonio, and Richard D. Evans of Waco, all pursued various legal strategies against county Democratic organizations. El Paso party officials allowed only two black city residents, Nixon and a pharmacist, M. C. Donnell, to vote in the July 1934 primary, providing them with ballots marked "colored." Black Texas voters received an additional setback the following year, when the U.S. Supreme Court in *Grovey v. Townsend* upheld the Democratic party's right to limit its membership.[43]

In 1941 the NAACP launched a final assault. Pressured by the Houston branch and working under Thurgood Marshall's leadership the NAACP found a test case. Harris County election Judge S. E. Allwright denied a primary ballot to Dr. Lonnie Smith, a Houston physician. In *Smith v. Allwright* the U.S. Supreme Court voted eight to one in January 1944 to declare the all-white primary unconstitutional. The NAACP had won the greatest legal victory of its thirty-four-year history.[44]

The NAACP remained dominant in the West, but two other organizations, the National Urban League and the Universal Negro Improvement Association (UNIA), had moderate success organizing black westerners during this period. These organizations stood on either side of the NAACP. The National Urban League, founded in New York City in 1911, sought employment for urban blacks and helped rural migrants adjust to city life. The UNIA, formed by Marcus A. Garvey in 1914 in Kingston, Jamaica, and relocated two years later in Harlem, advanced three black nationalist aims: African independence, worldwide black political unity, and economic self-sufficiency.[45]

The National Urban League grew slowly in the West, adding affiliates in Omaha in 1928, Seattle and Los Angeles in 1930, and Lincoln, Nebraska, in 1931. Although the Urban League is often described as a conservative rival to the NAACP, in western cities their membership overlapped as middle-class blacks divided their activities into NAACP "protest" and Urban League "uplift." In Seattle the league, under the leadership of Joseph S. Jackson, confronted social and economic problems, sponsoring community recreation and health programs and vocational training sessions. The Lincoln affiliate built a thirty-five-thousand-square-foot, sixteen-room community center that became the nucleus for the city's African American activities for the next three decades. The league accumulated statistics on the education, health, and employment of African Americans in all the cities it served.[46]

The Universal Negro Improvement Association was the only organization to challenge NAACP leadership. The UNIA's program proved popular among western African Americans skeptical of the NAACP's integrationist thrust. By 1926 UNIA divisions operated in nine of the seventeen western states. Indeed the small size and isolation of African American western communities enhanced the UNIA's appeal. Divisions, which required only seven members, sprang up in Mesa, Arizona; Colorado Springs, Colorado; Coffeyville, Kansas; Mill City, Texas; and Ogden, Utah, symbolizing a desire to interact with the larger black world. Emory Tolbert has used the term *outpost Garveyism* to describe the UNIA's attraction in small black communities. In California, for example, the association functioned in Bakersfield, Durante, Fresno, Wasco, and Victorville before it reached Los Angeles or San Francisco. By 1926 it had divisions in Omaha, Denver, Dallas, Kansas City, Oklahoma City, Tulsa, Portland, San Francisco, San Diego, Phoenix, and Oakland.[47]

African American Los Angeles was the center of western Garveyism. Black Angelenos had long supported black nationalist activity centered on the efforts of John Wesley Coleman. From the time of his arrival in the city in 1887 from Austin, Texas, Coleman had been active in the People's Independent Church and the Los Angeles Forum. In 1920 he founded the National Convention of Peoples of African Descent, an enigmatic organization that, with its parades, race unity rhetoric, and interest in Pan-Africanism, paralleled Garvey's UNIA. As Coleman learned of the larger Garvey movement, he dissolved the convention and, along with the Reverend John Dawson Gordon and the editors of the *California Eagle*, Charlotta and Joseph

Bass, founded Division 156 of the UNIA in 1920. A year later the division's thousand members made it the largest UNIA branch west of Chicago. The first UNIA president was newspaper writer and former Tuskegee Institute employee Noah Thompson. Subsequent presidents included two women, Charlotta Bass and Rosa Jones. The full extent of UNIA influence could be gauged in 1922 during Garvey's first Southern California visit. The welcoming parade down Central Avenue drew ten thousand spectators, almost half of the region's black population. Seated next to Garvey in the automobile was Frederick Roberts, the state's only black assemblyman. The parade ended at Trinity Auditorium, where the UNIA founder addressed a gathering of a thousand people following a welcoming speech by a representative of Mayor George Cryer.[48]

The UNIA did not survive the Depression. Yet during its heyday numerous working-class western black urbanites were drawn to its race consciousness. Seattle Garveyites Samuel and Maudie Warfield welcomed the opportunity to attend, with other Garveyites, the day-long Sunday UNIA meetings or to participate in the annual Memorial Day and Fourth of July parades of the paramilitary men's unit, the African Legion, and the women's auxiliary, the Black Cross Nurses. "They were trying to teach us about Africa," recalled Juanita Warfield Proctor, "that we should know more about Africa. . . ." The UNIA's focus in the West and throughout much of the black world was on political and economic empowerment, but to many Garveyism symbolized racial pride. Juanita Proctor explained Garvey's influence on her father and by extension on her. "My father [told] us we should be proud of Africa. . . . He used to say, 'Be proud of your race. . . .' We were never ashamed to be called Black. . . . That's why [now] I'm not ashamed of people calling me black . . . my parents taught me differently."[49]

The economic and political nationalism embraced by many early-twentieth-century black westerners paralleled a western-based literary tradition. Sutton E. Griggs, a black Texan, wrote a series of novels between 1899 and 1906 urging African American political and economic autonomy. In *Imperium in Imperio* (1899), his most influential work, Griggs portrayed Texas as an all-black state, a refuge for African Americans fleeing southern political terror. In subsequent novels, such as *Unfettered* (1902) and *Pointing the Way* (1906), he criticized racial discrimination and proposed a national organization to defend black rights that anticipated the founding of the NAACP.[50]

Drusilla Dunjee Houston explored black life as a historian. Born in Harpers Ferry, Virginia, and the sister of Roscoe Dunjee, the civil rights activist and founder of the *Oklahoma City Black Dispatch*, Houston lived most of her life in Oklahoma and Arizona. She operated the McAlester Seminary, a private school for African American students in McAlester, Oklahoma. In 1926 she published *The Wonderful Ethiopians of the Ancient Cushite Empire*, the first of a projected series on African civilization. The *Wonderful Ethiopians*, which examined ancient Egypt and Ethiopia, was widely reviewed in most of the African American newspapers and journals of the day. Mary White Ovington of the NAACP criticized the book's lack of footnotes and bibliography while acknowledging its "exciting influence" upon her perception of European history. Upon publication of her *Astounding Last African Empire*, Houston became the first African American woman to complete a multivolume history of blacks in antiquity. That she could accomplish such a feat in an intellectual milieu dominated by black men and far from the major eastern research sources prompted NAACP leader William Pickens to remark: "If her race were . . . economically able to buy her books, what an historic foundation she could lay for them. . . . Perhaps some day we will build her a statue, or name a university after her, when we have finished starving her to death. . . ."[51]

Langston Hughes, considered the greatest contributor to the Harlem Renaissance, also started in the West. Born in Joplin, Missouri, in 1902, Hughes spent his childhood years, from 1903 to 1915, in Lawrence and Topeka, Kansas. He was part of a prominent, if poor, family; his maternal grandfather, Charles Langston, led the post–Civil War black suffrage campaign in Kansas. Hughes's early writing reflected this upbringing. His first novel, the semiautobiographical *Not without Laughter* (1930), describes a young man's early years in a Kansas town. Many of Hughes's poems and short stories evoke his images of the West. In "One Way Ticket" he suggests the region's possibilities for "freedom."

> *I pick up my life*
> *And take it on the train*
> *To Los Angeles, Bakersfield,*
> *Seattle, Oakland, Salt Lake,*
> *Any place that is*
> *North and West*[52]

Hughes's Harlem Renaissance contemporary Wallace Thurman also drew inspiration from his native West. Thurman, who was born in Salt Lake City, spent time in Boise, Omaha, and Pasadena before settling in Los Angeles. While enrolled at the University of Southern California, he wrote poetry and briefly edited a literary magazine, the *Outlet*, which he hoped would encourage a West Coast renaissance similar to Harlem's. While at the university, Thurman met another rising literary star, Arna Bontemps. By 1925, however, Thurman had abandoned his efforts to establish a western "New Negro" Movement and joined Bontemps and Hughes in Harlem. Thurman's essays ranked him the major satirist of the Renaissance, but his novel *The Blacker the Berry* (1929) reflects the author's western origins as it focuses on an African American heroine native to Boise who moves to Harlem.[53]

Hughes, Thurman, and Bontemps were the contemporaries or precursors of Ralph Ellison, Taylor Gordon, Melvin Tolson, Sr., J. Mason Brewer, and other African American writers who explored black life through the prism of their western experiences. Despite their efforts, a regional literary aesthetic did not emerge. The small African American population, its recent arrival in the region, its scant identification with the rural West, which was at that time the principal focus of regional writing, and the absence of regional outlets for black writers all weighed heavily against a western African American literary tradition. Only Los Angeles nurtured a fledgling western renaissance. Langston Hughes, Arna Bontemps, and other writers periodically visited this "ever enlarging artistic colony," where Fay Jackson's *Flash Magazine* (1928–29) supplanted Wallace Thurman's short-lived *Outlet* as the second black literary journal in the West. Local artists and national writers mingled at the Twenty-eighth Street YMCA, near Central Avenue, where they read poetry and discussed their work. Los Angeles became the setting for Arna Bontemps's Depression-era novel *God Sends Sunday* (1931), which focuses on the hope and despair southern migrants found on Central Avenue, the "Beale Street of the West." Despite these efforts, black Los Angeles's major literary contribution lay in the future.[54]

Western African American musicians fared better than writers. They thrived in Kansas City, Los Angeles, Seattle, Dallas, Oklahoma City, and Denver and in the process helped shape the evolving national jazz culture of the 1920s and 1930s. Urban jazz grew from a variety of musical traditions, including southern blues, ragtime, and boogie-woogie, the last originating in western mining and lumber camps. Encouraged by the proliferation of Prohibition-era night-clubs, cabarets, and speakeasies, hundreds of black bands criss-crossed the region, freely borrowing and changing musical styles. Many of these nightclubs and cabarets were in African American urban communities, but even when they were not, they offered jobs to black musicians, who provided a colorful alternative to vaudeville, the concert stage, and legitimate theater.[55]

Most music historians no longer describe jazz as originating in New Orleans and flowing up the Mississippi to Chicago and the rest of the nation. Black musicians played jazz or its precursor in various African American communities from San Francisco to New York before New Orleans musicians began to migrate north. As early as 1907 indigenous black San Francisco performers "improvised" their music. Denver musician George Morrison claims to have played jazz music in 1911 and appropriated the name for his newly formed band, George Morrison and his Jazz Orchestra. By 1913 the word *jazz* appeared not in New Orleans but in a San Francisco newspaper description of local African American artists. Four years later a Honolulu newspaper advertised visiting San Francisco musicians as the "So Different Jazz Band."[56]

In the 1920s Kansas City emerged as a vital center of jazz. Black musicians from Kansas, Oklahoma, Texas, and Colorado made their way to Kansas City's nearly five hundred nightclubs, taverns, caba-rets, and honky-tonks to join local artists. This dynamic music scene rivaled Harlem and Chicago's South Side. "Work was plentiful for musicians, though some of the employers were tough people. . . ." recalled jazz vocalist Mary Lou Williams. "I found Kansas City to be a heavenly city—music everywhere in the Negro section of town, and fifty or more cabarets rocking on Twelfth and Eighteenth Streets."[57]

The southwestern origins of most of the jazz musicians who migrated to Kansas City generated the city's distinct musical style, which historian Ross Russell describes as "grassroots . . . retaining its earthy, proletarian character . . ." because it drew inspiration from folk songs, ragtime, and blues. "Don't let anyone tell you there's a 'Kansas City style' " wrote a *Down Beat* reporter in 1941. "It isn't Kan-sas City—it's Southwestern. The rhythm, and fast-moving riff figures, and emphasis on blues, are the product of musicians of the South-west—and Kansas City is where they met and worked it out. . . ."[58]

The African American communities in Houston, Dallas, San Antonio, Fort Worth, El Paso, Oklahoma City, Denver, and Omaha provided the first audiences for little-known but ambitious jazz artists, eager to introduce their particular musical style to the wider world. Dallas's Deep Ellum, for example, "swarmed with blues singers, boogie woogie pianists and small combos" that constantly formed and dissolved acts that played the clubs and bars of the city.[59]

Jazz bands also went on the road. The Oklahoma City—based Blue Devils' circuit took them through Kansas, Nebraska, Missouri, Arkansas, Texas, Colorado, and New Mexico. Often bands traveled hundreds of miles between engagements with as many as ten performers crammed into a single automobile, one or two of them standing on the running board. "Maybe we'd go from [Omaha] to Sidney, Nebraska," Walter Harrold recalled; "then we'd go from there to North Platte, we'd have an engagement the next night. . . . Then we had to go to Norton, Kansas, we had a four-day fair to play there." The circuit Harrold described encompassed Nebraska, Colorado, Kansas, South Dakota, and Wyoming and could involve travel of fifty thousand miles a year.[60]

These "territorial bands" operating west of Kansas City fell into two broad categories. Some played in Texas and Oklahoma, where their audiences were African American patrons of cabarets, ballrooms, taverns, and saloons. Representative examples include the Troy Floyd Orchestra in San Antonio, the Blues Syncopaters of El Paso, Clarence Love's Band in Tulsa, and Henry ("Buster") Smith's Blue Devils of Oklahoma City, which included at various times Lester Young, Count Basie, and vocalist Jimmy Rushing. Dallas contributed the Clouds of Joy and the Alphonso Trent Orchestra. Trent's musicians played gold-plated instruments, made $150 a week, wore silk shirts and camel hair overcoats, and drove Cadillacs as they performed from New York's Savoy Ballroom to roadhouses in Deadwood, South Dakota. In 1925 the Trent band was the first black ensemble to play regularly at the Adolphus, a white Dallas hotel, and the first black group outside New York City to broadcast over radio.[61]

Other black jazz artists played for white audiences farther north and west. George Morrison, a classically trained musician who aspired to conduct a symphony orchestra, gave his name to the band he organized in Denver in 1911. The George Morrison Jazz Orchestra appeared regularly at Denver's Albany Hotel and traveled a circuit that included Colorado, New Mexico, and Wyoming. The orchestra was the official band for the Cheyenne Frontier Days rodeo, beginning in 1912, and was popular on the southwestern college circuit. Hattie McDaniel, who later won an Oscar for her performance in *Gone with the Wind,* was the band's vocalist. Albuquerque-born John Lewis, who eventually became the pianist with the Modern Jazz Quartet, recalled the band's visit to New Mexico as his introduction to African American dance music. Omaha, in the shadow of Kansas City, developed a jazz tradition with the World War I black migration and by the 1920s had produced a number of musicians, including Fletcher Henderson, Lloyd Hunter, and vocalist Victoria Spivey. Salina, Kansas, was the home to Art Bronson's Bostonians, the state's leading band in the 1920s. In 1925 Bronson hired sixteen-year-old saxophonist Lester Young, who had previously worked with his father's band on the medicine show and minstrel circuit from Arizona to the Dakotas. Young later recalled that playing "music was better than blacksmithing," a reminder of limited opportunities even for gifted musicians.[62]

The West Coast's jazz culture rivaled the Southwest. Los Angeles, Portland, Seattle, San Francisco, and Oakland all drew on a complex mixture of local and imported influences. Many New Orleans jazz musicians migrated to the West Coast around World War I, enhancing the protojazz styles that evolved earlier with local artists. New Orleans performers Wade Whaley, Will Johnson, and Edward ("Kid") Ory helped shift the center of West Coast jazz from San Francisco to Los Angeles by 1920. The "Creoles" remained important through the mid-1920s, but growing numbers of Texans, Oklahomans, and midwesterners, including Lionel Hampton and Charlie Lawrence, challenged their dominance in Los Angeles.[63]

This new generation of Los Angeles musicians produced a sophisticated style featuring danceable arrangements that eventually inspired the swing era of the 1940s but that, unlike the Kansas City–southwestern style, did not emphasize blues. Moreover, the Los Angeles artists had more diverse performance opportunities than their counterparts to the east. Central Avenue had become by 1925 the vital pulse of West Coast jazz with its "hot-colored" nightclubs: the Kentucky Club, the Club Alabam (known in the 1920s as the Apex), the Savoy. The Cotton Club in Culver City attracted white and black celebrities: Mae West, Orson Welles, Joe Louis, and William Randolph Hearst. Radio also featured black artists. After the advent of sound films some bands played "mood music" for movie studios or appeared in movies directed toward black audiences. As the studios recognized the market for these black-oriented films, such performers as Louis Armstrong, Lena Horne, Bill ("Bojangles") Robinson, and Duke Ellington supplemented their incomes by arranging local club dates, while aspiring actresses, such as Carolynne Snowden and

Mildred Washington, sang and danced in the clubs "between roles."[64]

West Coast jazz, however, was not synonymous with Los Angeles. San Diego's Creole Palace nightclub had become by the 1930s the most famous West Coast cabaret outside Los Angeles. Built along with the Douglas Hotel in 1924 by black entrepreneurs Robert Lowe and George Ramsey, the Palace in the 1930s became well known in the national black community of entertainers. It employed black and Latino band members, show girls, waiters, cooks, and busboys and attracted Duke Ellington, Lionel Hampton, and Joe Louis as well as local black, white, and Latino patrons.[65]

Like their southwestern counterparts, these musicians traveled a circuit that included Honolulu, the major West Coast ports, and southwestern cities, such as Phoenix and Albuquerque, in the 1920s but that had expanded by the 1930s to embrace Yokohama, Shanghai, Hong Kong, and Manila. The Seattle-based Earl Whaley Band, for example, played in Shanghai clubs between 1934 and 1937, and most of the band members were imprisoned by the Japanese Army during its occupation of the city.[66]

Most black West Coast musicians worked closer to home. Seattle's Jackson Street had the Alhambra, the Ubangi, and the Black and Tan Club. Doubling as restaurants in the day and early-evening hours, these clubs flouted law and custom by allowing gambling, after-hours drinking, and interracial mingling. As Robert Wright, the nephew of a leading black nightclub owner, recalled, "In 1935 and 1936 you could see as many white people on 12th and Jackson at midnight, as you'd see on 3rd and Union in midday." Interracial mingling was not confined to whites and blacks. Up and down the coast black musicians played in Asian and Latino clubs. Baton Rouge–born Joe Darensbourg performed in Mexican and Filipino cabarets in Los Angeles and Asian clubs in Seattle. Seattle's jazz scene was particularly noted for the extensive camaraderie between Asian Americans and African Americans. The Chinese Gardens and the Hong Kong Chinese Society Club were leading venues for local jazz and regularly hired black musicians. African American and Filipino bands alternated in the dance halls of Little Manila, while struggling black musicians lived at the Tokiwa Hotel and ate at local Japanese restaurants. As Julian Henson recalled, "Most of the musicians who lived at the Tokiwa owed [the owners] money, but they wouldn't put you out." Added Marshal Royal: "They were a different type of people up in Seattle. . . . They were nice, they were cordial.

I'm not just speaking of black people, I'm talking about the Chinese guys. . . . They were our buddies."[67]

Seattle's jazz scene was unique in another respect. Female bandleaders were among the first jazz artists in the city. Indeed Lillian Smith's Jazz Band, which played at a Seattle NAACP benefit fund raiser on July 14, 1919, gave the first documented jazz performance by local musicians in the city's history. In the mid-1920s the Freda Shaw Band (which often played on the Seattle-based cruise ship SS *H. F. Alexander*), the Evelyn Bundy Band, and the Edythe Turnham Orchestra were considered three of the city's leading jazz acts. Other black women, such as Lillian Goode, Zelma Winslow, and Evelyn Williamson, became performers in local club acts.[68]

The rise of an active jazz network in western cities symbolized white recognition of black influence on popular entertainment. But it also indicated black western urbanites' identification with national cultural patterns. This process affected all westerners; urbanization rapidly homogenized the entire nation. But the African American population was urbanizing faster than most other regional ethnic and racial groups. These western urban communities defined the political issues, responded to the economic challenges, and created the social and cultural milieu that greeted much larger numbers of black migrants by World War II.

9

❖ ❀ ❖ ❀ ❖

World War II and
the Postwar Black West,
1941–50

World war changed forever the African American West. The region's black population grew by 443,000 (33 percent) during the forties and redistributed itself toward the West Coast. Oklahoma lost 23,000 African Americans, 14 percent of its black population, while California alone gained 338,000, a 272 percent increase. The three Pacific coast states and Nevada led the nation in the percentage of black population growth. Most of these newcomers concentrated in five major metropolitan regions: Seattle-Tacoma, Washington, and Portland, Oregon–Vancouver, Washington, in the Pacific Northwest; the San Francisco Bay Area, comprising San Francisco, Oakland, and smaller cities such as Berkeley and Richmond; the Los Angeles–Long Beach area; and San Diego. These metropolitan regions saw black population increases ranging from 798 percent for San Francisco to 168 percent for Los Angeles. Las Vegas, although three hundred miles inland, grew much like the coastal cities. Between 1940 and 1950 its African American population exploded from 178 to 2,888, a 1,522 percent increase. The numbers were less dramatic in Denver, Omaha, Phoenix, Tucson, and Honolulu, but these cities also saw surging black populations.[1]

If expanding populations indicated change, so did expanding work opportunities. After decades of menial labor thousands of black workers entered the region's factories and shipyards, a process historian Joe Trotter has described as the proletarianization of the African American work force. Thousands more African American military personnel were stationed in the West. Black military personnel frequently ended their enlistments at western bases, sent for family members, and settled permanently. Marilynn Johnson's conclusion that World War II–era migration made the East Bay Area population "younger, more southern, more female, and noticably more black" than ever before applies equally to western communities from Omaha to San Diego.[2]

African Americans working in defense industries had to overcome the bias of many employers and union leaders. Worker shortages, however, and pressure from the Fair Employment Practices Committee (FEPC) soon opened numerous western workplaces previously closed to African Americans as well as white women and other people of color. The FEPC proved a powerful ally. Although black leaders criticized its caution, many African Americans recognized it as the one federal agency sympathetic to their grievances. As Katherine Archibald remarks in her study of wartime Bay Area shipyards, "There was a feeling that the law, at least—if not . . . justice—was on the side of the black man. . . ."[3]

Without doubt the migration strengthened civil rights organizations, such as the NAACP, and encouraged antidiscrimination legislation in a number of western states. Washington, Oregon, New Mexico, and California all passed state fair employment practices statutes between 1949 and 1959, prefiguring the 1964 Civil Rights Act. But the migration also increased overcrowding in black western communities, accelerating the physical deterioration of the residential neighborhoods that had begun in the interwar years. All western cities were overcrowded since virtually no private housing was built during the war. But African Americans faced long-standing restrictive covenants that, coupled with population increases, meant unprecedented concentration. Fillmore in San Francisco, Logan Heights in San Diego, the Central District in Seattle, West Oakland, North Richmond, South Berkeley, and Las Vegas's West Side all joined the disreputable roll of crowded western black urban ghettos such as Los Angeles's Central Avenue, Dallas's Deep Ellum, and Houston's Fourth Ward.

Black wartime migration to the West occurred within a larger white influx to the region. In the 1940s, 8 million people moved west of the Mississippi, nearly half to the Pacific coast. California received 3.5 million newcomers, who accounted for the single largest addi-

Western Black Population Growth, 1940–50

	1940		1950		Black % Inc.
	Black Pop.	Total Pop.	Black Pop.	Total Pop.	
Arizona	14,993	499,261	25,974	749,587	73
California	124,306	6,907,387	462,172	10,586,223	272
Colorado	12,176	1,123,296	20,177	1,325,089	66
Idaho	595	524,873	1,050	588,637	76
Kansas	65,138	1,801,028	73,158	1,905,299	12
Montana	1,120	559,456	1,232	591,024	10
Nebraska	14,171	1,315,834	19,234	1,325,510	36
Nevada	664	110,247	4,302	160,083	548
New Mexico	4,672	531,818	8,402	681,187	80
North Dakota	201	641,935	257	619,636	28
Oklahoma	168,849	2,336,434	145,503	2,233,351	− 14
Oregon	2,565	1,089,084	11,529	1,521,341	349
South Dakota	474	642,961	727	652,740	53
Texas	924,391	6,414,820	977,458	7,711,194	6
Utah	1,235	550,310	2,789	688,862	126
Washington	7,424	1,736,191	30,691	2,378,963	313
Wyoming	956	250,742	2,557	290,529	167
Totals:	1,343,930	27,035,677	1,787,214	34,009,255	33
	4.9%		5.2%		

Total black regional population increase: 33%

Total regional population increase: 26%

Sources: U.S. Bureau of the Census, Sixteenth Census of the United States: 1940; Population, vol. 2, Characteristics of the Population, part 2 (Washington, D.C.: Government Printing Office, 1943), table 22; U.S. Bureau of the Census, Census of Population: 1950, vol. 2, Characteristics of the Population, part 1, United States Summary (Washington, D.C.: Government Printing Office, 1953), table 59.

tion to a state's population in one decade in the nation's history. The entire West grew by 26 percent during the 1940s. Because blacks were a segment of a much larger migration, resentment toward newcomers did not apply exclusively to them. When Portland Mayor Earl Riley warned, "Undesirables—white or colored—are not wanted and if they fail to obey our laws, will be unceremoniously dealt with," he

Population Growth in Six West Coast Cities, 1940–50

	1940			1950				
	Total Pop.	Bl. Pop.	% of Total	Total Pop.	Bl. Pop.	% of Total	Total % Inc.	Black % Inc.
Seattle	368,302	3,789	1.0	467,591	15,666	3.3	27.0	313.5
Portland	305,394	1,931	0.6	373,628	9,529	2.5	22.3	393.5
San Francisco	634,536	4,846	0.8	775,357	43,502	5.6	22.2	797.7
Oakland	302,163	8,462	2.8	384,575	47,562	12.4	27.3	462.1
Los Angeles	1,504,277	63,774	4.2	1,970,358	171,209	8.7	31.0	168.5
San Diego	203,341	4,143	2.0	334,387	14,904	4.5	64.4	259.7

Source: U.S. Bureau of the Census, Sixteenth Census of the United States, 1940, Population, vol. 2, Characteristics of the Population, parts 1, 5, 7 (Washington, D.C.: Government Printing Office, 1943), tables 31, 35; Census of the Population, 1950, vol. 2, Characteristics of the Population, parts 5, 37, 47 (Washington, D.C.: Government Printing Office, 1952), tables 34, 53.

articulated concerns that transcended the race of the newcomers.[4]

Even so, race became a powerful component of that opposition. The possibility of racial violence prompted Seattle Mayor William F. Devin in February 1944 to form the Seattle Civic Unity Committee. The mayor set the tone of urgency in a speech at the University of Washington in July 1944: "The problem of racial tensions is . . . going to affect us not only during the War, but also after the War, and it is our duty to face the problem together. If we do not do that, we shall not exist very long as a civilized city or as a nation."[5]

The five West Coast metropolitan areas—Seattle, Portland, San Francisco–Oakland, Los Angeles, and San Diego—collectively absorbed 70 percent of the increase in the region's African American population during the decade. These areas were heavily affected by rapidly expanding defense industries. San Diego became an aircraft production center. Portland and San Francisco–Oakland developed shipbuilding facilities. Los Angeles and Seattle excelled in both categories. Black migration, however, was not uniformly consistent throughout the decade or proportionately divided among the cities. Los Angeles attracted half the West Coast–bound migrants between 1940 and 1943, receiving a record twelve thousand in June of the latter year. Black Los Angeles, which had seen its population double each decade between 1900 and 1940, was accustomed to huge population increases. The same could not be said for the other Pacific coast metropolitan areas. Between 1943 and 1945 other West Coast cities saw influxes that overwhelmed their prewar populations. Los Angeles and Seattle continued to attract newcomers between 1945 and 1950, San Diego, and San Francisco saw their populations increase modestly, and Portland's black population fell from twenty-two thousand in 1945 to ninety-five hundred in 1950.[6]

Migrants went west for work in shipbuilding and aircraft production. Three Los Angeles shipbuilders—Consolidated Steel, California Ship (Cal Ship), and Western Pipe and Steel—employed more than 60,000 workers at the height of wartime production in 1944. Cal Ship, the largest, had 7,022 black employees at the end of 1944, 15 percent of the work force. African Americans found work in seven Bay Area shipbuilding facilities: Marinship near Sausalito, Moore Drydock and Bethlehem-Alameda in Oakland, and four Kaiser Company shipyards in Richmond. At peak production the Kaiser Richmond yards employed 90,000 people, including 18,000 African Americans. Kaiser also had three shipbuilding facilities in the Portland area. Two yards, Oregon Shipbuilding and Kaiser–Swan Island, were in the city; a third, Kaiser-Vancouver, was on the north bank of the Columbia River in neighboring Vancouver, Washington. The Portland area shipyards eventually employed more than 7,700 African Americans in 1944. They were 9 percent of the overall work force but 96 percent of all the black workers in the city. No single shipbuilding employer dominated production in Seattle. Twenty-nine yards in the city and neighboring Bremerton employed 4,000 African Americans.[7]

By 1944, 7,186 African Americans worked at four Los Angeles–area aircraft companies: Lockheed-Vega in Santa Monica, Douglas in Long Beach, North American Aviation in Inglewood, and Consolidated-Vultee in Los Angeles. These black employees comprised from 3.2 to 7.2 percent of the workers in the various firms. By 1945, 1,200 black Boeing workers were 3 percent of the Pacific Northwest's largest work force. Consolidated Aircraft employed 1,000 of the 1,200 black San Diego aircraft employees at the height of war production in 1945.[8]

Local African Americans fought to obtain defense plant jobs long after President Franklin Roosevelt issued Executive Order 8802 to prevent racial discrimination. Leaders of the Aero-Mechanics Local 751, which represented the Boeing work force, voiced their displeasure with the opening of jobs even temporarily to African

Americans. "We rather resent that the war situation has been used to alter an old established custom," declared International Association of Machinists representative James Duncan, "and do not feel it will be helpful to war production." By 1942 acute labor shortages in the West Coast cities required the mobilization of all able-bodied workers—women as well as men, Asians, Native Americans, Latinos, and blacks, even prisoners and the handicapped. A boilermakers' union publication claimed that the new Kaiser recruits represented "a bottom of the barrel" assortment of "shoe clerks, soda jerks, professors, pimps, and old maids." Nonetheless continuing labor shortages forced the shipbuilders to turn eastward to tap the national labor pool.[9]

With War Manpower Commission (WMC) assistance, defense employers began to recruit workers. Kaiser's efforts were typical. The company targeted dozens of southern and midwestern cities with "surplus" labor, dispatching 170 recruiters to the East. Between 1942 and 1943 Kaiser brought nearly thirty-eight thousand workers on "liberty" trains that originated as far east as New York City. Another sixty thousand paid their own way to the West Coast. "There's a job of vital importance to your country waiting for you in the Richmond shipyards," declared one Kaiser pamphlet. "You can learn a trade, get paid while you're learning, and earn the highest wages for comparable work anywhere in the world." Wartime migration soon assumed a momentum independent of Kaiser's recruiting efforts. Black workers wrote home describing the high wages, the mild climate, and greater freedom. A 1943 WMC survey indicated that nearly 75 percent of the black migrants to the Bay Area came west without any direct contact with recruiters.[10]

Four states—Arkansas, Louisiana, Texas, and Oklahoma—contributed a disproportionate number of newcomers. Moreover, 53 percent were female, and most of them were married. Getting to the Pacific coast was the first task. Many migrants followed hot, dusty stretches of U.S. Highways 80 and 60 and Route 66, made famous by the Dust Bowl migration a decade earlier, across Texas, New Mexico, and Arizona. They came with their "mementos, histories and hope, all tied to the top of a car." Since few hotels along the route accommodated black people, migrants took turns driving and camped by roadsides. On occasion they stayed in African American homes along the route in Amarillo, Albuquerque, Flagstaff, Phoenix, or Barstow.[11]

Train travelers faced three to four days in crowded, uncomfortable cars. Edwin Coleman accompanied his parents on their 1943 journey from El Dorado, Arkansas, to Alameda, California. Even segregated seating for blacks was unavailable since white soldiers and passengers filled the "colored" section. Coleman, his mother, and his sister stood in the vestibule of the train practically all the way to Salt Lake City. Another Arkansan, Ruth Gracon, carrying a baby in her arms, rode in a Jim Crow car until she reached Kansas City, where the Pullman porter "said that I could sit anyplace now." Bertha Walker, who left Houston in October 1943, rode "out of Texas on the Jim Crow car . . . packed with military people." In El Paso she changed trains and shortly afterward a soldier who rose to give her his seat said, "You can relax now, because we're at the Mason-Dixon line. . . ."[12]

"Getting there" proved relatively easy compared with challenges of the new workplace. All shipyard workers had to adjust to the regimen of prefabricated shipbuilding. Using techniques developed in building Boulder Dam, West Coast shipbuilders assembled whole sections of a ship's structure. Boilers, double bottoms, and deckhouses were preassembled elsewhere and lifted into place by huge cranes. This technique allowed these yards to assemble vessels in record time. The *Robert E. Peary* was built in four days in November 1942. Since workers performed specific, repetitive tasks, training went rapidly. But these workers faced a bureaucratized environment. For the first time in their lives they used security badges, got company-sponsored health care, reported to timekeepers, and received their paychecks (with income tax withheld) from pay windows. The Richmond yards were laid out in a grid system of numbered and lettered streets. One worker described the nine hundred acres of shipyards: "It was such a huge place. . . . People from all walks of life, all coming and going and working, and the noise. The whole atmosphere was overwhelming to me."[13]

West Coast shipyards pioneered new production techniques and labor-management relations, but they also embraced old stereotypes. Chinese women performed detail-oriented electrical work considered suitable for their skills. White women held welding jobs, considered the easiest position on the yards, while black women were relegated to scaling (cleaning), sweeping, and painting ship hulls. Portland shipyard worker Beatrice Marshall described her job as a painter's helper: "We had to crawl on our hands and knees and carry our light on an extension cord . . . because it was pitch dark. We . . . scraped the rust off the bottom of the boat where they had to paint. . . . We had to wear masks, there [was] so much rust in there . . . you could hardly breathe."[14]

Wartime labor demands guaranteed black women and men would work; they did not guarantee equitable treatment. Throughout the war black workers, shipyard managers, and union officials engaged in a triangular struggle over workplace segregation and worker assignments. In the bewildering order of job allocation by the shipyard unions and managers, black workers could build ships but not repair them; clean ships but not paint them; or weld steel plates but not pipes. Doris Mae Williams, originally a Kaiser-Vancouver shipyard welder, took a job as a laborer rather than suffer continued abuse from her supervisor and coworkers, who refused to accept her credentials. "I am now scaling. [It is] hard labor," Williams wrote to the FEPC. "Our crew is mixed, we are all treated alike. Why couldn't the same be said for skilled workers?" Eventually labor shortages and production demands broke down this arcane racial classification, but most black workers remained in unskilled work for the rest of the war.[15]

Two barriers were rarely breached. Black women and men, regardless of education or experience, did not become clerical workers or supervisors. Katherine Archibald recounted the story of an unidentified African American schoolteacher from Texas who worked at Oakland's Moore Dry Dock as "matron of a women's rest room." Despite clerical experience, the woman was denied the office job she sought "because of my race." We don't know why the woman refused a more lucrative position in the yards, but according to Archibald, "She bore herself with the dignity of a duchess at her tea table." Shipyard managers allowed blacks to head all-black crews but never to supervise whites. One Bay Area shipyard personnel director declared, "We wouldn't ask white people to work under a Negro and we shouldn't expect them to."[16]

African American workers, native and migrant alike, concluded that the International Brotherhood of Boilermakers (AFL) accounted for much of their difficulty. Until 1937 the boilermakers excluded black workers. However, facing escalating CIO competition and the prospect that shipyards would hire black workers, the union at its 1937 convention reversed its policy and created all-black "auxiliary" locals. Had the boilermakers remained one of a number of unions competing for shipyard jurisdiction, their impact on black workers would have been minimal. The rival CIO-affiliated Industrial Union of Marine and Shipbuilding, for example, was racially integrated. But in 1941 the boilermakers negotiated a closed shop agreement with the Kaiser company. Other shipbuilders followed, giving the boilermakers jurisdiction over 65 percent of the U.S. shipyard workers and all those in West Coast yards except Seattle. By 1944 thirty-two thousand black employees were forced into auxiliary unions A-26 in Oakland, A-32 in Portland, A-92 in Los Angeles, and A-41 in Sausalito.[17]

Membership in an auxiliary entailed restrictions not faced by white union members. Once hired, black employees had to secure approval of white locals before they could seek promotion. Furthermore, an auxiliary, unlike a regular local, could be abolished at any time by the international's officials. Testifying before a congressional committee, Fred Jones, a member of A-92, demonstrated the absurdity of auxiliary unions because when he initially claimed to be Hindu, he was granted full membership. Then, when he told union officials he was African American, they immediately reassigned him to the auxiliary union. "We pay our dues but what do we get?" declared Joyce R. Washington, a Cal Ship worker, in 1943. "Nothing but to be discriminated against and segregated."[18]

Most West Coast African Americans adamantly disagreed with a boilermaker official's view of auxiliary unions as an "internal union matter." Shipyards were by far the largest employers of African Americans on the Pacific coast. Boilermaker policies directly affected these workers from Portland to Los Angeles. FEPC representative James H. Wolfe, chief justice of the Utah Supreme Court, reached that conclusion after a 1943 West Coast fact-finding visit when he declared boilermaker discrimination "the biggest question [the FEPC] will . . . handle during its whole existence. . . . The problems presented by the West Coast situation are national in import and must be solved on the national level. . . ."[19]

That solution came in the summer of 1943, when West Coast shipyards, at the boilermakers' insistence, fired black workers for protesting the auxiliary scheme. In rapid succession two hundred workers were dismissed at Marinship in Sausalito, 100 at Moore Dry Dock in Oakland, 300 workers at Cal Ship in Los Angeles, and 350 at the three Kaiser shipyards in Portland. Among the dismissed Marinship workers was Joseph James, president of the San Francisco NAACP. Shipyard workers in each community immediately mounted legal challenges. In Portland and Los Angeles black workers requested FEPC action on shipyard discrimination. In response the federal agency held its first West Coast hearings in Portland on November 15 and 16 and in Los Angeles on November 19 and 20. On December 9 the FEPC directed the boilermakers and shipbuilders to end discrimination and abolish the auxiliary system. Shipyard companies complied with the ruling, but the boilermakers resisted, arguing that the FEPC's directives "alienate[d] the goodwill of organized labor and its support of the war effort." Black workers, emboldened by the FEPC ruling, filed lawsuits against the union in Portland, Los Angeles, and San Francisco. Joseph James's suit against Marinship reached the California Supreme Court in 1944. The court ruled in *James v. Marinship* that the union's "asserted rights to choose its own members does not merely relate to social relations; it affects the fundamental right to work for a living." It ordered the boilermakers to dismantle their auxiliary structure in the state. A U.S. district court in Portland ruled much the same, and in 1946 the California Supreme Court in *Williams v. International Brotherhood of Boilermakers* reaffirmed and extended the earlier *James* opinion. Following the *James* decision, the union abolished auxiliaries but retained other discriminatory practices until 1946. Such questions of discrimination appeared moot when thousands of workers—black and white—were laid off at the end of the war. Even so, the legal challenges affirmed Katherine Archibald's 1946 assessment that "the white worker . . . may still come to the table first and take the best seat, but now the Negro sits there too."[20]

West Coast aircraft makers were the second largest employer of African American labor during the war. At first, however, they excluded black workers. In 1940 W. Gerald Tuttle, director of industrial relations at Vultee Aircraft in Southern California, wrote the National Negro Congress stating, "I regret to say that it is not the policy of this company to employ people other than of the Caucasian race. . . ." The president of North American Aircraft in Inglewood, California, was equally blunt. "Regardless of their training as aircraft workers, we will not employ Negroes in the North American plant. It is against company policy."[21]

In 1942 Executive Order 8802, severe labor shortages, and occasional public pressure had ended the exclusion. In July 1942 several hundred black women marched on the Los Angeles office of the U.S. Employment Service, vowing to make the room look like "little Africa" until the agency opened aircraft production jobs. One protester, Mrs. Lou Rosser, declared, "This is our war [but] we cannot win it in the kitchen, we must win it on the assembly line." Their demonstration was unnecessary. Aircraft companies were already moving to employ black workers. Boeing hired its first African American production worker, Dorothy West Williams, a sheet metal worker, in May 1942. By July 1943, 329 blacks worked at Boeing. That number peaked at 1,600 by 1945. In June Consolidated Aircraft in San Diego and Lockheed-Vega in Los Angeles began placing black workers. By August 1942 Lockheed-Vega employed 400 blacks, including 50 women, among its 41,000 workers. By early 1943 the company had 2,500 black workers.[22]

The West Coast aircraft industry thus quickly rose above its past. One Watts resident recalled those days: "Man, we were all there the first day. We didn't know what we were applying for or what kind of job they had; some of us . . . had jive-time jobs as porters [or] janitors . . . and some of us hadn't worked in months. . . . Man, I didn't know what a P-38 or a B-17 was, but I wanted to learn, I wanted an opportunity. When the personnel officer asked me if I had ever worked on an assembly line or as a technician to produce a B-17, I was honest and I told him I didn't know if he were talking about a gun, a battleship, or a plane."[23]

Once in the aircraft plants African American employees encountered individual problems: an unwarranted pay deduction or transfer, antiblack remarks by supervisors or coworkers, or social segregation, as recalled by Fanny Christina Hill. "They did everything they could to keep you separated," declared Hill. "They just did not like for a Negro and a white person to get together to talk." But black workers in the aircraft plants were not relegated to auxiliary unions, work in segregated buildings, or lunch in separate cafeterias. Nor did any West Coast plants label jobs "white" and "colored" in advertisements, as happened in Texas and Oklahoma. For thousands of black women and men hired in skilled jobs, the wartime aircraft factory work changed the quality of their lives. Fanny Christina Hill was hired at North American Aviation in Inglewood in 1943 and worked there until her retirement in 1980. "The War made me live better," recalled Hill, "Hitler was the one that got us out of the white folks' kitchen."[24]

Las Vegas was the western city most dramatically affected by World War II's black influx. Its African American population surged from 178 in 1940 to approximately 3,000 in 1943. In 1950 blacks made up

11 percent of the total population, the largest percentage west of Fort Worth. Most blacks arrived after 1941 to work at Basic Magnesium Incorporated (BMI), a huge magnesium-processing facility in the southern Nevada desert. Nearly 3,000 African Americans, primarily from Louisiana and Arkansas, moved (along with white migrants) into shacks, shanties, and tents near the site before permanent housing went up in Las Vegas or at Carver Park, a wartime housing project for BMI workers. Henry Lee Lisby, who arrived there in 1942, recalled conditions for the black migrants. In the summer "it was hot. . . . Lay down and sleep awhile and get up and get wet; get in a tub of water . . . There were no coolers . . . a shoe box top was about all the fan I can remember." Another migrant, Sarah Ann Knight, recalled that "there were very few houses . . . it was mostly tents and shacks . . . and a lot of people were sleeping on lawns."[25]

The newcomers quickly formed churches, clubs, and community organizations reminiscent of their former homes. They also created a branch of the NAACP to protest discrimination at BMI, including segregated work crews, lunch facilities, water fountains, and toilets. When 186 black workers walked out of the plant in October 1943, the resulting FEPC investigation persuaded BMI to end "the practice of segregation on the job site." By November 1944 dwindling demand for magnesium caused BMI to close its facility. Nonetheless most of the ex-BMI male workers found work in hotels and the women as domestic servants.[26]

No other western cities saw population increases similar to the West Coast influx. Denver's population doubled during the 1940s, but Omaha, Wichita, Kansas City (Kansas), Phoenix, and Tucson saw only modest increases in their wartime African American populations. The black communities in urban Texas and Oklahoma also barely grew even as the cities became war production centers. Aircraft firms in Dallas, Fort Worth, and Tulsa and shipbuilding companies in Houston hired few black workers. In May 1943 the *Dallas Express* claimed that "26 major war plants in Dallas do not employ Negroes in skilled jobs." Only concerted protest by local African American leaders, manpower shortages, and pressure from the FEPC eventually forced North American Aviation in Dallas and Consolidated-Vultee in Fort Worth to hire black workers in skilled positions. Much the same pattern held in Houston. With the exception of the Hughes Tool Company, which had hired its first black workers in 1918, few manufacturing plants in the city employed African Americans. The *Houston Informer* reported in December 1942 that

Population Growth in the Interior West, 1940–50

	1940			1950			Total	Black
	Total Pop.	Bl. Pop.	%	Total Pop.	Bl. Pop.	%	% Inc.	% Inc.
Albuquerque	35,449	547	1.5	96,815	613	0.6	173.1	12.0
Dallas	294,734	50,412	17.1	432,970	57,825	13.3	46.9	14.7
Denver	322,412	7,836	2.4	415,786	15,214	3.6	289.6	94.1
Fort Worth	177,662	25,254	14.2	277,585	35,905	12.9	56.2	42.1
Houston	384,514	86,302	22.4	596,163	124,760	20.9	55.0	44.5
Kansas City (KS)	121,458	21,033	17.3	129,320	26,590	20.5	6.4	26.4
Las Vegas	8,422	165	1.9	24,624	2,725	11.0	192.3	1,551.5
Phoenix	65,414	4,263	6.5	106,818	5,280	4.9	63.2	23.8
Oklahoma City	204,424	19,344	9.4	242,085	20,890	8.6	18.4	7.9
Omaha	223,844	12,015	5.3	251,117	16,200	6.4	12.1	34.8
Salt Lake City	149,934	694	0.4	181,700	1,135	0.6	21.1	63.5
San Antonio	253,854	19,235	7.5	407,335	28,495	6.9	60.4	48.1
Tacoma	109,408	650	0.5	143,280	3,205	2.2	30.9	393.0
Tulsa	142,157	15,151	10.6	182,705	17,110	9.3	28.5	12.9
Wichita	114,966	5,686	4.9	166,980	7,925	4.7	45.2	39.3

Source: U.S. Bureau of the Census, Sixteenth Census of the United States, 1940, Population, Vol. 2, Characteristics of the Population, Part 1 (Washington, D.C.: Government Printing Office, 1943), tables 30, 31, 35; Census of the Population, 1950, Census of the Population, vol. 2, Characteristics of the Population, Parts 3, 6, 16, 27, 28, 31, 36, 43, 44, 47 (Washington, D.C.: Government Printing Office, 1952), tables 34, 53.

the Houston Shipbuilding Company, the largest employer in the city, "refuse[d] to hire qualified and competent skilled workers who are colored." Skilled black workers walked the streets in Texas cities through much of the war while defense contractors decried the shortage of workers. Ultimately many black Texas workers joined the migration to the West Coast.[27]

Thousands of African American women and men came West in uniform. Fort Huachuca in the Arizona desert had the largest concentration of black soldiers in the nation after the army decided in 1942 to create the U.S. 93d Infantry Division by combining the 25th, 368th, and 369th regiments with various field companies and battalions. Fort Huachuca had been home to the 10th Cavalry when it patrolled the U.S.-Mexican border in World War I. It was now expanded to accommodate fourteen thousand soldiers, who comprised the only all-black division in the U.S. Army. Unlike the buffalo soldiers, who had been led by white officers, the 93d had nearly three hundred African American officers.[28]

By December 1942 the 32d and 33d companies of the Women's Army Auxiliary Corps (WAAC) had joined the men of the 93d in the desert. These women were postal clerks, stenographers, switchboard operators, motor truck drivers, and typists, releasing the men for combat. Their officers included Irma Jackson Cayton, wife of the noted scholar Horace R. Cayton. Muriel Fawcett, a former West Virginia State College professor, exuded the confidence of the women on post when she said that "each WAAC is bursting with pride that she made the grade. If the men doubt that we can do the job efficiently, they will soon change their minds."[29]

Other African American soldiers were stationed at military facilities remote from any communities. The men of the 93d, 95th, 97th, and 388th engineers regiments worked in minus-seventy-degree temperatures while building the Alcan Highway through Alaska and the Canadian Northwest. Black soldiers and sailors patrolled ammunition depots at Hawthorne, Nevada, and Hastings, Nebraska. At other times African American soldiers were stationed at military bases near African American communities. The five thousand soldiers and sailors at Seattle's Fort Lawton, Fort Lewis near Tacoma, or the naval base at Bremerton visibly increased the black presence in the Puget Sound region. Comparable concentrations of servicemen and women in the San Francisco Bay Area, Los Angeles, San Diego, Denver, and San Antonio all had similar effect.[30]

Yet discrimination followed African American soldiers throughout the West. Businesses in towns as diverse as San Bernardino, Walla Walla, El Paso, and Tucson posted WE CATER TO WHITE TRADE ONLY signs. Favorable treatment of German and Italian prisoners of war was particularly offensive to African American soldiers. Lloyd Brown recalled a Salina, Kansas, restaurant owner who told him and other black troops, "You boys know we don't serve colored here," while German prisoners of war were eating at the lunch counter. In 1944 African American soldiers at Fort Lawton in Seattle rioted over their exclusion from clubs that served Italian prisoners of war.[31]

But black soldiers also saw their status enhanced in unanticipated ways. In Los Angeles in early 1942 Humphrey Bogart, Rosalind Russell, Lena Horne, Eddie ("Rochester") Anderson, and other actors welcomed members of the 369th New York National Guard Regiment (the Harlem Hellfighters), who manned antiaircraft guns in the backyards of Hollywood actors. Bogart invited the troops to use his home and gave them the keys to do so. Sometimes other people of color helped ease the adjustment to a new environment. Many of Honolulu's Asian Americans overcame their initial fears and stereotypes of black soldiers and welcomed them into the local community. Thousands of other black military women and men throughout reaped a gradual, grudging gratitude from other westerners. Regardless of the response of civilians, black servicemen and women made the double V campaign—victory over fascism abroad and racism at home—more than a slogan. African American troops in World War II fought for the opportunity to create a democracy, not to save a democratic society.[32]

On one occasion the Port Chicago mutiny, that commitment was purchased in blood and "dishonor." The Port Chicago Naval Base, completed in 1942 thirty-five miles northeast of San Francisco, quickly became a major supply conduit to the Pacific Theater. African American naval personnel dominated the work force. On the evening of July 17, 1944, about half the facility's black stevedores were loading two ammunition ships, *Quinalt Victory* and *E. A. Bryan,* when an explosion destroyed the ships and much of nearby Port Chicago. In the explosion 320 men, including 202 African Americans, died.[33]

Three weeks later 328 surviving stevedores at nearby Mare Island refused an order to load ammunition ships. Through threats and persuasion navy officials convinced all but 50 stevedores to resume work. The remaining men were arrested. Joe Smalls, one of the 50, recalled his reasoning years later: "I wasn't trying to shirk work. . . . But to go back to work under the same conditions, with no improvements, no changes . . . we thought there was a better alternative, that's all." When Chaplain J. M. Flowers urged the men to return to work to help "the men in the foxholes," an unidentified sailor replied, "In the foxholes a man has a chance to fight back."[34]

The navy's decision to arrest and prosecute the stevedores as mutineers initiated the longest and largest mutiny trial in naval history. The trial quickly took on racial overtones. The national African American press took note of the court-martial, as did the NAACP, which sent Thurgood Marshall to observe the proceedings. The military tribunal judged all the defendants guilty and sentenced each to fifteen years' detention and dishonorable discharge. In January 1946 the sentences were quietly reduced, and the men released from prison. The Port Chicago men were not, however, released from the navy. Instead they were divided into small groups and sent overseas to the South Pacific for a "probationary period." The former prisoners now became part of an involuntary navy experiment in racial integration on the high seas.[35]

The quest for housing united African Americans throughout the urban West. A Portland Urban League official spoke for them in 1945 when he declared: "A Man who must crowd his wife and children into an unsafe and unsanitary home . . . becomes an unstable citizen." Housing of course was scarce for all westerners, but restrictive covenants exacerbated the problem for African Americans. In Denver 89 percent of blacks in 1950 resided in the Five Points district, where they crowded into houses and apartments constructed in the nineteenth century. Virtually all of Omaha's 1950 black population of sixteen thousand lived on the North Side in neighborhoods that had hardly expanded despite a 36 percent population increase over the last decade. In Dallas, Houston, or Phoenix, cities with relatively modest wartime population increases, the story remained one of growing concentration.[36]

West Coast cities, however, saw the worst overcrowding. As thousands of migrants entered these communities in 1943 and 1944, Los Angeles, San Francisco, and Oakland housing officials described conditions to a 1944 congressional committee investigating congested areas. "I urge that your committee take enough time to walk through the former Little Tokyo," declared Los Angeles Deputy Mayor Orville R. Caldwell before the committee. "Here you will see

San Francisco Bay Area Black Population Growth, 1940–50

City	1940	1950	% Increase
Alameda	249	5,312	2,033
Albany	4	1,768	44,100
Berkeley	3,395	13,289	291
Oakland	8,462	47,562	462
Richmond	270	13,374	4,853
San Francisco	4,846	43,502	798
Vallejo	438	1,513	245

Source: U.S. Bureau of the Census, Sixteenth Census of the United States, 1940, Population, vol. 2, Characteristics of the Population, part 1 (Washington, D.C.: Government Printing Office, 1943), tables 31, C-35, F-36; Census of the Population, 1950, vol. 2, Characteristics of the Population, part 5 (Washington, D.C.: Government Printing Office, 1952), table 34.

life as no human is expected to endure it." Howard L. Holtezendorff, a Los Angeles Housing Authority official, described conditions in Little Tokyo: "[Our] records . . . show families piling up to . . . four, five, and six persons to a bedroom. In one case a family of five was living in a dirt-floored garage with no sanitary facilities whatsoever. In an abandoned storefront . . . twenty-one people were found to be living—and paying approximately $50 a month for these quarters."[37]

San Francisco's black newcomers piled into the Fillmore district and the former Japantown. Although Fillmore's population increased by 500 percent during the war, the geographical area of the black community grew by only 20 percent. Three-story houses became apartments and boardinghouses for war workers. City zoning ordinances were completely ignored as auto-repair shops, cafés, record shops, beauty parlors, and laundries peppered neighborhoods of once-pleasant houses and apartment buildings. This 2.5-square-mile area had seventy-one bars and forty-five liquor stores. In this setting crime and disease flourished. Fillmore became a center of prostitution, gambling, loan sharking, and other illegal activities. The juvenile delinquency rate was the highest in the city, and Fillmore soon stood second only to Chinatown in the incidence of tuberculosis and other chronic respiratory diseases.[38]

Much the same pattern evolved in Oakland. Prewar black Oaklanders lived primarily in West Oakland, a once-fashionable middle-class "Pullman Car colony" that grew at the western terminus of the transcontinental rail lines. West Oakland grew from 16 percent black in 1940 to 62 percent ten years later. Moreover, the black community expanded north into Berkeley. The federal government's war housing policy intensified residential segregation. In a pattern that was duplicated throughout the West, the Oakland Housing Authority built all-black projects—shipyard ghettos—on the periphery of West Oakland. This transformation generated ambivalence. Prewar Oakland black residents, such as Royal Towns, lamented the loss of "fellowship that we had with the foreign people." Yet the influx created a bustling African American commercial district along Seventh Avenue.[39]

Most of the 170,000 blacks in wartime Los Angeles lived in three distinct communities; the Central Avenue district, Watts, and West Adams. The Central Avenue district south of downtown was the oldest and largest of these communities and home to most black businesses in the city. About 65 percent of the city's African Americans lived there. Central Avenue received the largest number of migrants, about 14,000, and expanded in two directions available to it: south, toward Watts, and north to encompass Little Tokyo, the former home of 7,500 now-interned Japanese.[40]

Watts, seven miles south of downtown Los Angeles, was about equally divided among whites, blacks, and Latinos in 1941. During the war years twelve thousand migrants arrived, making it a predominantly black community. Watts's story is less one of "white flight," than of black influx. During the war only sixteen hundred whites and Latinos moved out. Nonetheless for the first time African Americans were the majority in the schools and stores along 103d Street and in every neighborhood. The rapid change in Watts's racial geography stiffened the resistance of neighboring white communities to any black newcomers. White suburbs south, west, and east of the community, including notably Compton, refused to accept black residents. As Arna Bontemps, one of the area's first black residents, wrote, "Watts awakened to the fact that it was a ghetto and a slum. That was the end. . . . All who could get away, fled. Those who remained—trapped—sank into indifference and then despair. . . ."[41]

West Adams, five miles southwest of downtown, housed middleclass black Angelenos as well as the entertainment elite, including Hattie McDaniel, Louise Beavers, and Eddie ("Rochester") Anderson. Although mostly black, the area had some middle-class Asian and white residents. West Adams received six thousand black newcomers. However, its boundaries expanded west to include the most prestigious residential areas available to African American Angelenos.[42]

Other West Coast communities shared the experiences of Los Angeles and the Bay Area on a smaller scale. Portland's prewar African American population of nineteen hundred was overwhelmed by twenty thousand new black defense workers. Albina, a narrow neighborhood of homes running north along Williams Avenue, quickly became overcrowded with migrant families. Both Seattle and San Diego had housing shortages, but the small number of African American newcomers (fewer than ten thousand in each city) and their relatively late arrival in 1944 and 1945 reduced the most pressing problems associated with the West Coast influx. Black migrants to Seattle moved into the Central District, a residential area between downtown and Lake Washington. San Diego's Logan Heights, southeast of downtown, received almost all of that city's African American newcomers. By 1950 both Logan Heights and the Central District still had significant numbers of Latinos, working-class whites, and most of the cities' Asian population. Nonetheless the concentration of black migrants in public housing and the conversion of older houses into apartments produced conditions similar to those in San Francisco and Los Angeles.[43]

Housing segregation proved a greater challenge for black westerners than did employment discrimination. An unidentified San Francisco homeowner expressed that sentiment in 1943: "I wouldn't even want Marian Anderson as a neighbor." Racial prejudice and fear of declining property values ensured a white opposition that was widespread and occasionally violent. When two African American families moved into Maywood, a Los Angeles suburb, in 1942, the local newspaper, the *Maywood-Bell Southeast Herald,* urged stronger restrictive covenants. "If you are interested in . . . keeping Maywood Caucasian . . . then you will help win the fight which immediately confronts us. . . . Within the next few weeks one section of the community is threatened with the moving in of undesirables. . . . After they are once in, it will take the moving of heaven and earth to remove them." Two years later the Arlington-Jefferson Property Owners Association in Los Angeles raised two thousand dollars to extend local covenants through January 1, 1990. The housing dispute brought fatalities in 1945. O'Day and Helen Short bought five acres of land in Fontana, a steel-manufacturing town sixty miles east of Los Angeles, and constructed a house on their property. One week after receiving threats from local whites, Helen and the two Short daughters died in a fire of mysterious origin. O'Day died from his burns one month later.[44]

Housing segregation generated widespread protest throughout the West but most effectively in Los Angeles. Restrictive covenants barred 95 percent of the World War II–era housing to blacks. Middle-class African American Angelenos who shared the city's enthusiasm for homeownership, and had the financial means to initiate lawsuits, led the national campaign to eliminate covenants. Between 1945 and 1948 the city's black residents filed more lawsuits contesting covenants than the rest of the nation combined. Many of these lawsuits were filed by Loren Miller, an NAACP attorney who developed a national reputation through his legal work against housing discrimination.[45]

The Bay Area influx was proportionally larger and more rapid than in Los Angeles. Consequently many African American migrants relied on public housing. For them, finding any shelter at all took precedence over integrated housing. Prior to World War II federal housing officials followed "local custom" to determine whether housing projects were integrated or segregated. In Bay Area housing, however, Washington imposed racial segregation without regard to past custom, creating shipyard ghettos. Oakland's Harbor Homes, constructed next to the Moore shipyards, for example, were racially divided even though nearby neighborhoods were integrated. The housing authority director in Alameda rejected integrated housing projects because they constituted "a form of discrimination against whites." Richmond housing officials concentrated black residents in projects near the shipyards and railroads, while all-white units rose near downtown. Codornices Village, which straddled the Berkeley-Albany border, situated black residents toward the Southern Pacific railroad tracks, while white units faced San Pablo Avenue, a major city thoroughfare. The consequences of this policy grew evident soon after the war. Whites left the projects for city or suburban housing. Blacks, blocked by restrictive covenants, remained concentrated in these enclaves.[46]

Housing shortages, job competition, black demands for political participation, white apprehension over challenges to "traditional" racial structures, and anxiety over the war itself all heightened tensions among whites, Latinos, Asian Americans, and blacks. On Thanksgiving night 1942 three black soldiers died during a riot against Phoenix police. Numerous smaller confrontations flared between black and white soldiers in Honolulu, Seattle, Camp San Luis Obispo, California, Fort Bliss, Texas, and Camp Phillips, Kansas. White and black shipyard workers clashed in Portland and Los Angeles in 1943, and black civilians and white sailors in fought in Oakland in 1944.[47]

The Beaumont, Texas, riot in 1943, however, was the largest wartime racial clash in the West and the third most violent in the nation after Harlem and Detroit. Beaumont became a war production center in the early 1940s, when Pennsylvania Shipyards, Inc., began building Liberty ships. Between 1940 and mid-1943 the city grew from fifty-nine thousand to eighty thousand. On the afternoon of June 15, 1943, the wife of a white shipyard worker reported to police a story of rape by a black man. As word of the incident spread, approximately two thousand shipyard workers dropped their tools and marched on the two black residential districts in the city. The rioting and looting ended twenty-four hours later only after the arrival of eighteen hundred Texas national guardsmen, contingents of Texas Rangers, and neighboring police and sheriff's deputies. Three black residents and one white resident lay dead, four hundred people were injured, and most of Beaumont's African American businesses and dozens of homes destroyed. Twenty-five hundred blacks fled the city by foot or auto, many never to return. The day after the rioting ended medical examiners proved the woman had had no sexual intercourse during the twenty-four-hour period surrounding the alleged assault. Beaumont's riot was the last confrontation of the century in which white Americans were the primary aggressors and black Americans the victims.[48]

Black and white remained the primary colors in American racial conflict. Yet black newcomers soon found themselves in a multiracial environment where they faced other people of color. In Seattle, Portland, and San Francisco African Americans came into contact with sizable Asian populations (excepting the Japanese, who had been interned). In Los Angeles they faced Asians and Latinos, while in San Diego, Phoenix, Denver, and the Texas cities the group was Latino. Despite some prewar efforts at political coalition building, employment rivalry, language, and culture often hampered effective cooperation.[49]

Los Angeles proved a crucible for wartime multiethnic relations. With 1940 populations of two hundred thousand Chicanos, sixty-four thousand blacks, and thirty thousand Asians, Los Angeles was already a multiethnic, multiracial metropolis. Geography separated as much as did language and culture: East Los Angeles was Chicano, Central Avenue was black, and Little Tokyo, Japanese, Chinese, and Filipino. But World War II brought them together in shipyards and aircraft factories. By 1944 California Shipbuilding, for example, employed thirteen hundred Mexican American workers and twelve hundred African Americans.[50]

Such contact demolished walls of parochial distrust. Black political activists in Los Angeles recognized the concerns of Chicanos. As early as 1942 the Los Angeles Urban League invited Spanish-speaking people onto its advisory board and "championed the cause of Negroes, Mexicans, and Orientals" in its campaign to integrate aircraft firms and the vocational schools. Some African Americans addressed police brutality toward Chicanos, as in the 1942 Sleepy Lagoon case, in which twenty-four young men were arrested and placed on trial for the murder of José Díaz. Charlotta Bass, State Assemblyman Augustus Hawkins, and actors Hattie McDaniel and Lena Horne supported efforts of the Citizens' Committee for the Defense of Mexican American Youth, formed by the actor Anthony Quinn and Josephine Fierro de Bright of the Spanish-Speaking People's Congress. Far more African American activists spoke out against anti-Chicano violence following the zoot suit riot in 1943.[51]

Finally, young blacks and Chicanos crossed cultural boundaries in wartime nightclubs and cabarets. Chicanos eagerly embraced black dances such as the jitterbug, and clothing styles like the zoot suit, while African American jazz and rhythm and blues musicians drew inspiration from pachuco dances and music. Writing her boyfriend in 1941, one Chicana declared she would "get a black finger tip coat, and when you come home we can go to the Orpheum when the Duke comes with his band . . . and everybody's jiving in his seat . . . so keen, so swell." The "borrowing" of music and fashion was the most overt manifestation of a network of cultural exchanges and interchanges ranging from "graffiti writing . . . car customizing . . . and festivals . . . to sports and slang."[52]

The interaction with Asian Americans proved particularly bittersweet. Blacks moved into recently evacuated Japanese communities in virtually every West Coast city and refused to relinquish these communities following the war, often forcing the returning Japanese to seek other housing. World War II migrant Maya Angelou recalls the transformation of San Francisco's Japantown into "San Francisco's

Harlem" in a matter of months. "The Yamamoto Sea Food Market quietly became Sammy's Shoe Shine Parlor. . . . Yashigira's Hardware metamorphosed into La Salon de Beaute owned by Miss Clorinda Jackson. . . . Where the odors of tempura, raw fish and *cha* had dominated, the aroma of chitlings, greens and ham hocks now prevailed. . . ." Racial understanding reached before the war between blacks and Japanese Americans in Seattle, Los Angeles, and San Francisco gave way to migrant-dominated communities that, without the benefit of prior contact, often refused to acknowledge Asian grievances. "No member of my family and none of the family friends ever mentioned the absent Japanese," said Angelou. "It was if they never owned or lived in the houses we inhabited. . . . The Japanese were not white folks . . . since they didn't have to be feared, neither did they have to be considered."[53]

Yet no major confrontation developed between the returning Japanese and the black migrants. In Los Angeles an ad hoc group of whites and blacks called Friends of the American Way found housing and jobs to ease the return of Japanese internees. A January 1945 Conference on Interracial Cooperation in San Francisco saw African American, Filipino, and Korean leaders pledge to "safeguard the rights and liberties of returning evacuees." The conference repudiated demagogic attacks on the Japanese and vowed to support the resettlement process. One month later, in a San Diego speech, the Reverend Clayton Russell of the Negro Victory Committee warned a predominantly African American audience of a "sinister campaign . . . in Los Angeles to incite hostility between members of Negro and Nisei minority groups" for housing and warned: "Those same forces which would take property away from Japanese Americans [in Little Tokyo] would in turn take your property away from you."[54]

Western African Americans shared the nation's joy on V-E Day 1945. Yet the celebration soon turned to anxiety. By war's end the federal government and western industrialists were scaling back war-related production and employees. Kaiser shipyards in Richmond shrank employment from forty-seven thousand workers in December 1944 to nine thousand by March 1946, a pace matched by other defense plants and shipyards. In 1947 thousands of African Americans who had been "essential workers" only two years before roamed the streets of Los Angeles, Oakland, and Portland. In 1947 black Oaklanders comprised half those applying for indigent relief although they were only 10 percent of the city's population. Nearly half the four thousand blacks in Vallejo, California, were unemployed. The prospects for postwar employment in Portland were so dismal that the black population declined by 50 percent (eleven thousand) between 1944 and 1947.[55]

Other black westerners prospered in the postwar period. In San Francisco black representation in unions and in the skilled occupations they controlled grew appreciably between 1945 and 1950. By the latter date nine thousand black unionists were 9 percent of the membership of seventy-six San Francisco locals. Large numbers of black males entered the construction trades and transportation, and a few men obtained white-collar jobs in banks, insurance firms, and utilities, such as Pacific Gas and Electric. Progress was slower for black women. In 1950 nearly 53 percent remained concentrated in domestic service (down from 65 percent in 1940), but a few black women had begun to work as clerks, stenographers, and secretaries.[56]

Postwar black Seattle suffered no economic downturn. Boeing's work force continued to grow because of the emerging Cold War dependence on air power and the growing demand for commercial airplanes. Thus the city proved attractive to blacks, drawing another five thousand between 1945 and 1950. In 1948 the median income of African American families in Seattle was $3,314, 53 percent above that of blacks nationally and only 14 percent below that of white Seattle families. The median income of blacks in Seattle was only 4 percent below that of white families nationally, prompting the *Chicago Defender*, the nation's largest African American newspaper, to urge blacks to leave the East and Midwest and move to that city.[57]

Postwar black westerners continued to campaign for adequate housing. The war's end further concentrated blacks in the shipyard ghettos. By 1949 blacks were the majority of public housing residents in Oakland, Richmond, Vallejo, and Berkeley. Conversely, white migrants often became the new suburbanites in residential areas closed to black home buyers. Seventy-five thousand building permits were issued for private dwellings in Bay Area cities between 1949 and 1951, yet only six hundred of those residences were open to African American purchase. "The Negro does not think of temporary housing units as temporary," remarked W. Miller Barbour, an East Bay Urban League official, in 1952. "He knows that very little housing is available to him and the reasons it will not be provided."[58] African American concentration in public housing generated an array of consequences. New cleavages developed in western urban politics. As blacks became identified with public housing and the government programs that assisted its residents, white city and suburban homeowners opposed public housing and other programs that assisted the poor. Race and property ownership became the dividing line in postwar urban politics, eclipsing prewar class divisions and wartime rivalry between newcomers and old residents.[59]

But the housing battles forged stronger alliances between prewar black residents and newcomers. As African Americans were forced to live together in public housing enclaves divisions between blacks disappeared. Margaret Starks, a Richmond NAACP official, spoke for many: "Where you were born wasn't the issue, but where you could go was the problem." Consequently migrants and old settlers joined forces to protect their interests. In 1943 Earl Mann of Denver was elected to the Colorado legislature. Five years later Berkeley pharmacist W. Byron Rumford went to the California assembly, where he joined Augustus Hawkins of Los Angeles. In 1950 attorney Charles Stokes, who had arrived in Seattle only in 1944, became the first African American to serve in the twentieth-century Washington legislature while Hayzel Daniels and Carl Sims became the first blacks in the Arizona legislature. A postwar political coalition of San Antonio blacks and Latinos elected Gus García and George Sutton to the local school board in 1948. Sutton was the first black elected official in Texas since the nineteenth century. Although San Francisco's African American community did not see a black officeholder until 1964, Thomas Fleming, a local political leader, recalled the postwar period as a time when the Fillmore district was alive with political activism and local political optimism was at its pinnacle. Voter registration drives and street corner political meetings became part of the Fillmore's daily life.[60]

Black voters supported liberal politicians who embraced their civil rights agenda. The postwar domination of Bay Area politics by California Democrats hinged upon the new migrant vote, a pattern common throughout much of the urban West. In Texas the black electorate grew dramatically after the Supreme Court's 1944 *Smith v. Allwright* ruling, which eliminated the all-white primary. African American groups, such as the Progressive Voters League and the United Citizens for Democracy, began to challenge conservative Democratic party leadership. The growing black electorate also changed old political practices. Texas Representative Wright Patman's initial response to *Smith* was a public declaration that blacks would vote in his district "over my dead body." Two years he was shaking hands at African American church picnics in Fort Worth. Lyndon Johnson's courting of new black voters helped in his eighty-seven-vote victory in the Senate primary election in 1948. Robert Tucker led liberal Houston politicians who now openly sought African American voters. He promised a black audience in a 1949 political rally to "show as much zeal in protecting your rights as I do those of any other group. We are going to build together."[61]

Black Western popular culture soon brought changes to literature and music. Chester Himes's novel *If He Hollers Let Him Go* was the first to capture the wartime migrant experience. But the greatest impact could be heard in bars and clubs and eventually on radios and in concert halls. Los Angeles's Central Avenue became the fountainhead of new jazz music styles, such as bebop, pioneered by newcomers Charlie Parker, Dizzy Gillespie, and Coleman Hawkins, and the "cool jazz" of Nat King Cole, who teamed with such local musicians as Dexter Gordon, Charles Mingus, and Eric Dolphy. Central Avenue's numerous nightclubs and after-hours bars stretched seven miles from downtown to Watts, rivaling New York's famed Fifty-second Street. "Our music was catching on," wrote local musician Hampton Hawes, "drawing . . . the white middle-class chicks, the rebels who were . . . pulled by . . . the excitement and hipness of the atmosphere." Yet Patricia Willard, a Central Avenue patron, challenged the characterization that whites who frequented such clubs were "slumming." She recalled that she and her friends went to the clubs "because we cared about the music. . . . You heard Wardell Gray and Dexter Gordon doing 'tenor sax battles' competitions. The greatest musicians and singers of the day were [on Central Avenue]."[62]

For all its innovation and appeal, West Coast jazz now competed with other musical genres. Urban blues, gospel, rhythm and blues, which began in Los Angeles, and even zydeco—a combination of blues and Cajun music imported from Louisiana with World War II migrants—joined the region's traditional music forms. World War II brought to the West Coast southern blues musicians, such as Jimmy McCracklin, Lowell Fulson, and Johnny Fuller, who played a "chitlin circuit" of nightclubs from Seattle to San Diego. Moreover, gospel music began to spread westward with the growth of African American churches. Gospel group names, such as the Singing Shipbuilders

Quartet, the Oakland Silvertones, and the Golden West Singers, often concealed the southern origins of their members as much as they revealed their new identification with region and workplace. In 1946 Texas-born Bob Geddins, a Kaiser shipyard worker, became a leading cultural entrepreneur of both blues and gospel when he formed Big Town Records, one of the first black-owned recording companies in the Bay Area. "Up here they was starving for blues, so the first [record] I put out they jumped on the bandwagon."[63]

In 1945 Lawrence D. Reddick invoked a western metaphor when he declared the World War II black migration had produced a "race relations frontier." The surge of African Americans into the far West, he argued, would determine the future of race relations in the region and the nation. Reddick's metaphor was inaccurate in failing to account for other racial groups—Native Americans, Latinos, Asian Americans—that had been in the region for centuries. Moreover, the African American presence in the West extended back to the sixteenth century. Yet Reddick correctly concluded that the influx of black migrants into the region's cities altered the dynamics of racial discourse. Many of these newcomers had sought out the racial frontier, hoping the West would allow their hopes and dreams to flourish. But the newcomers soon realized that they would have to join the region's established residents in fighting racial discrimination, demanding their citizenship right and defying those who would block the way to a better life.[64]

10

❖ ✿ ❖ ✿ ❖

The Civil Rights
Movement in the West,
1950–70

During World War II, nearly half a million African Americans migrated to the West. They joined 1.3 million other black westerners in defense industries or the military as part of the double victory campaign to defeat the Axis and racial discrimination. When half the double V campaign ended with the Allied victory in 1945, the other half, the struggle for civil rights, continued almost without interruption. The West offers a particular vantage point for reexamining the civil rights era. Historians of the period have focused on national legislation, such as the Civil Rights Act of 1964, or on efforts in the South to confront Jim Crow. Civil rights activities in the West suggest a third alternative. Direct-action protests, though often inspired by southern campaigns in Birmingham or Selma, had different goals in the West. Westerners confronted job discrimination, housing bias, and de facto school segregation. Thus the civil rights movement was national in scope, its western version integral to the effort to achieve a full, final democratization of the United States.[1]

Western civil rights activity began long before World War II. Nineteenth-century black parents fought school segregation in California, Colorado, Kansas, and Montana. Yet by the 1950s an urgency grew, born of the World War II promise of democracy, a rapidly growing African American population, and the flowering of postwar liberalism, when white politicians embraced civil rights issues. Moreover,

Western Black Population Growth, 1960–70

	1960		1970		Black
	Black Pop.	Total Pop.	Black Pop.	Total Pop.	% Inc.
Alaska	6,858	226,167	8,911	300,382	23.0
Arizona	43,585	1,302,161	53,344	1,770,900	18.3
California	880,486	15,720,860	1,400,143	19,953,134	37.1
Colorado	39,554	1,753,925	66,411	2,207,259	40.4
Hawaii	4,694	632,772	7,573	768,561	38.0
Idaho	1,694	667,191	2,130	712,567	20.5
Kansas	91,027	2,178,618	106,977	2,246,578	15.0
Montana	1,460	674,767	1,995	649,409	26.8
Nebraska	29,648	1,411,330	39,911	1,483,493	25.7
Nevada	13,424	285,278	27,762	488,738	51.6
New Mexico	17,109	951,023	19,555	1,016,000	12.5
North Dakota	899	632,446	2,494	617,761	64.0
Oklahoma	154,662	2,328,284	171,892	2,559,229	10.0
Oregon	18,225	1,768,675	26,308	2,091,385	30.7
South Dakota	1,181	680,514	1,627	665,507	27.4
Texas	1,185,476	9,581,512	1,399,005	11,196,730	15.3
Utah	4,172	890,627	6,617	1,059,273	37.0
Washington	47,904	2,853,214	71,308	3,409,169	32.8
Wyoming	2,156	330,066	2,568	332,416	16.0
Totals:	2,544,214	44,869,450	3,416,531	53,528,471	34.2
	5.6%		6.4%		

Total black regional population increase: 34.2%

Total regional population increase: 19.2%

Source: U.S. Bureau of the Census, Census of Population, 1960, *vol. 1,* Characteristics of the Population, *parts 4–49 (Washington, D.C.: Government Printing Office, 1963), table 15;* 1970 Census of the Population, *vol. 1,* Characteristics of the Population, *parts 4–49 (Washington, D.C.: Government Printing Office, 1973), table 17.*

many Westerners had been sensitized to twentieth-century racial injustice through the recent Japanese internment, the zoot suit riot, and the black-white confrontations in shipyards and military bases. The 1950s in fact marked an optimism about the region's racial future. William Mahoney, a white civil rights activist in Phoenix, said as much in 1951: "The die is . . . cast in the South or in an old city like New York or Chicago, but we here [in Phoenix] are present for creation. We're making a society where the die isn't cast. It can be for good or ill." The African American minister Roy Nichols, pastor of racially integrated Downs Memorial Methodist Church in Berkeley, shared this optimism during his 1959 campaign for a city council seat: "What other race in the twentieth century is going to have such a great experience?"[2]

Civil rights activity in the West took two distinct forms. The legal campaign used the courts to desegregate public schools, which many black westerners came to view as central to economic and political advancement. But black westerners also engaged in direct-action protests: demonstrations, sit-ins, boycotts, and other civil disobedience activities to eliminate discrimination. The legal effort reached its apogee with the 1954 Supreme Court decision *Brown v. Board of Education of Topeka*. However, direct action from Seattle to Austin preceded and followed *Brown*.

After 1965 the black power movement challenged both the tactics and goals of the civil rights movement. The Watts uprising of 1965 illustrated to the region and the nation the inability of nonviolent protest alone to address the concerns of millions of urban blacks trapped by inner-city poverty. Watts reminded the nation that while the ghettos of the West seldom resembled Harlem's brownstone tenements or Chicago's high-rise public housing, they shared a foundation of poverty, alienation, and anger. One year after Watts, western African American communities in Oakland and Los Angeles produced the Black Panther party and US (United Slaves), which formulated the two distinct brands of black nationalism, revolutionary and cultural, that eventually swept through African American communities throughout the nation.

Brown v. Board of Education is often called the beginning of the modern civil rights movement. Yet Phoenix blacks won a major legal victory over de jure segregation one year before the Topeka case. Encouraged by successful legal attacks on Mexican American school segregation in California and Arizona, state Representative Hayzel Daniels in 1951 introduced a bill to give local school districts authority to desegregate their school voluntarily. The bill passed, and Tucson and other Arizona communities quickly desegregated their schools. However, the Phoenix electorate voted two to one to maintain separate schools. Daniels and Stewart Udall in June 1952 filed a lawsuit on behalf of plaintiffs Robert B. Phillips, Jr., Tolly Williams, and David Clark, Jr., who had been refused admission to Phoenix Union High School. (One of the principal financial supporters of the suit was Phoenix City Council member Barry Goldwater, who contributed four hundred dollars.) The case came before Maricopa County Court Superior Court Judge Frederic C. Struckmeyer, Jr., who ruled that Arizona's segregation laws were invalid, adding, "A half century of intolerance is enough." Soon afterward Daniels filed suit against the Wilson Elementary School District in Phoenix before County Court Judge Charles E. Bernstein, who ruled that segregated elementary schools were unconstitutional.[3]

As Struckmeyer and Bernstein rendered their decisions, the *Brown* case moved through the courts. In 1951 a group of African American parents, supported by the local NAACP, sued Topeka's Board of Education, claiming segregated schools symbolized the second-class citizenship of black Topeka. By 1951 slightly more than a hundred thousand people, including seven thousand African Americans, lived in the Kansas capital. Few African Americans, however, shared in Topeka's prosperity. Approximately one hundred black professionals worked as teachers, ministers, doctors, and lawyers. Nearly all other local blacks were janitors, maids, porters, laundresses, cooks, and charwomen. "You'd look up and down Kansas Avenue [the city's main thoroughfare] early in the morning," recalled Charles Scott, one of three black attorneys in the city, "and all you could see were blacks washing windows. . . . There was no chance . . . to become a bank teller, store clerk or brick mason. . . . A lot of hopes got dashed.[4]

Segregated schools anchored this Kansas apartheid. Topeka had no all-black neighborhoods. Nonetheless the city maintained eighteen elementary schools for white pupils and four for blacks. Topeka High School had always been integrated, and the city's junior high schools had been desegregated after a 1941 lawsuit, *Graham v. Board of Education of Topeka.* Yet school administrators presided over segregation in an integrated setting. Topeka High had separate athletic teams, cheerleaders, and pep squads. Black students, excluded from the "regular" student government, had a separate advisory council and attended a separate school assembly. Black and white school administrators maintained social segregation, searching the cafeteria, for example, to detect interracial tables.[5]

Thirteen parent plaintiffs representing their twenty children participated in the lawsuit. The Reverend Oliver L. Brown headed the list of plaintiffs, suing on behalf of his daughter Linda. His role in the lawsuit was accidental. The thirty-two-year-old Brown, a welder for the Santa Fe Railroad and assistant minister at the St. John African Methodist Episcopal Church, was not a member of the NAACP and had no history of political activism. He was, however, one of only two males among the thirteen parents and a respected minister in the African American community. The NAACP assumed his name as lead plaintiff would lend credibility to the case. Some contemporaries remember Brown as "a good citizen . . . [but] not a fighter." Yet the NAACP viewed his timidity as an asset. Here was an ordinary man rather than a "militant" who "was no longer willing to accept second-class citizenship."[6]

In September 1950 African American elementary schoolchildren in Brown's neighborhood, including his daughter, were expected to travel one mile to attend the all-black Monroe Elementary School. White neighborhood children traveled only four blocks to the all-white Sumner Elementary School. NAACP officials directed Brown and the other parents to walk their children to the nearest white school on the day of enrollment. Oliver and Linda Brown and the others walked to Sumner and, as expected, were turned away by the principal, setting the conditions for the lawsuit.[7]

Brown v. Board of Education was argued for five weeks beginning on June 25, 1951, before a three-judge federal panel headed by Walter Huxman and including Arthur J. Mellott and Delmas Carl Hill. Robert Carter and Jack Greenberg represented the national NAACP. The local NAACP contributed Charles Bledsoe and the brothers Charles and John Scott, who were World War II veterans, grandsons of exodusters, and sons of the state's most prominent African American attorney. Lester Goodell, former prosecuting attorney of Shawnee County (Topeka), argued for the Board of Education. The court heard testimony from all the plaintiffs, including Silas Hardrick Fleming, who provided the most compelling rationale for desegregation. The lawsuit "wasn't to cast any insinuations that our teachers are not capable of teaching our children because they are. . . . But . . . I and my children are craving light—the entire colored race is craving light, and the only way to reach the light is to start our children together in their infancy and they come up together."[8]

In August 1951 the judges ruled unanimously against the plaintiffs, citing the equality of school facilities as technically within the parameters of existing law. The Kansas panel's decision, however, cited the expert testimony of Arnold M. Rose, a University of Minnesota sociologist, and Louisa Pinkham Holt, a psychology professor at the University of Kansas. Borrowing the language of the academic experts, the judges wrote: "Segregation of white and colored children in public schools has a detrimental effect upon the colored children. The impact is greater when it has the sanction of law. . . ." The decision, as the judges apparently intended, pushed the matter to the U.S. Supreme Court. However, the language, and the ideas that informed their decision, were incorporated into the Supreme Court's ruling reversing the Kansas judges three years later.[9]

The Supreme Court's unanimous decision on May 17, 1954, striking down de jure segregation came too late to affect many of the plaintiff's children. That fall Linda Brown entered Curtis Junior High School, which was already desegregated. However, millions of others across the nation were, and remain, affected by the ruling. The decision denied the legal basis for segregation in Kansas and twenty other states and inspired countless court challenges of school segregation. As Cheryl Brown (Henderson), Oliver Brown's youngest daughter, wrote four decades after the decision, *Brown* "would forever change race relations in this country." From a small prairie fire of Kansas civil rights activism, the *Brown* decision soon grew into a fire storm that engulfed the nation.[10]

The *Brown* victory bolstered the NAACP's legal strategy. Yet many western civil rights activists thought civil disobedience or direct action protest a necessary supplement to the court campaign. By World War II small interracial groups of westerners had initiated direct action efforts. The Congress of Racial Equality (CORE), soon to be one of the largest civil rights organizations, formed chapters in Denver and Colorado Springs in 1942 after a visit from national leader Bayard Rustin. By 1947 CORE had chapters in Lawrence, Kansas City, and Wichita, Kansas; Omaha and Lincoln, Nebraska; and Los Angeles, Berkeley, and San Francisco, California. CORE sponsored demonstrations throughout the West, the first a 1943 protest of a segregated Denver movie theater. Another early success came when the De Porres Club of Omaha, a Creighton University CORE group, through boycotts and picketing forced a number of local businesses to end job discrimination.[11]

Kansas CORE activists, however, failed in their first major civil disobedience campaign. On April 15, 1948, thirty University of Kansas students, including ten blacks from the university's year-old CORE chapter, staged a four-hour "sit-down" protest at the all-white Brick's Café. Lawrence police officers on the scene stood aside while KU football players tossed male CORE members onto the sidewalk. Many KU students roundly condemned the CORE demonstration. One student told the campus newspaper that white students "insist on policies of segregation that [business owners] enforce." Without support from other students, the community, or the state NAACP, the protest ended.[12]

CORE was not involved in the decade's most successful direct action campaign, the desegregation of restaurants near the University of New Mexico. In September 1947 the campus newspaper, the *New Mexico Lobo*, published an article describing how George Long, an African American university student, had been denied service at a nearby café, Oklahoma Joe's. In response the Associated Students of the University of New Mexico, not having the power to prohibit discrimination in private establishments off campus, enacted a resolution: "If any student of the University is discriminated against in a business establishment on the basis of race, color or creed, I will support a student boycott of that establishment." The resolution gave the ASUNM Judiciary Committee the authority to investigate cases of discrimination and, if necessary, to "declare a student boycott." The boycott measure passed in a university-wide student referendum on October 22, 1947, by a three to one margin. Approximately 75 percent of the students cast ballots. Shortly afterward students boycotted Oklahoma Joe's and forced the management to change its policy. Three months later the students mounted a similarly successful boycott against a downtown Walgreen drugstore. Such widespread student antipathy to discrimination led to the university's first NAACP chapter with Herbert Wright as its president.[13]

Building on the boycott momentum, Long, now a university law student, and Wright wrote the Albuquerque civil rights ordinance and persuaded sympathetic members of the city commission to introduce the measure in October 1950. The ordinance passed on Lincoln's Birthday 1952. Three years later the state legislature enacted a similar statute, nine years before the Civil Rights Act was passed by the U.S. Congress. George Long and Herbert Wright had formed a remarkable coalition of students and sympathetic off-campus organizations, including the NAACP, several churches, and

Latino organizations, to achieve the first civil rights ordinance in the intermountain West.[14]

Ten years after the failed Lawrence demonstration a new group of Kansas students challenged segregation through direct action. On Saturday, July 19, 1958, Ron Walters, a Wichita State College freshman and head of the Wichita NAACP Youth Council, led ten African American high school and college students in a four-week sit-in at the Dockum drugstore lunch counter. The students won their battle when the regional vice-president of the Dockum chain arrived and ordered, "Serve them, I'm losing too much money." The students quickly targeted other Wichita lunch counters over the remainder of the summer and desegregated most of them. Wichita's students drew on the support of a much larger African American community, local churches, and the Wichita NAACP. They were also inspired by the *Brown* decision, the Montgomery bus boycott, and the Little Rock school desegregation effort.[15]

Oklahoma City followed. On August, 19, 1958, Clara M. Luper, the adviser to the local NAACP Youth Council, led thirteen black teenagers into Katz's drugstore. The protesters occupied virtually every soda fountain seat for two days until they were served as police remained close by to prevent violence. The day after the victory at Katz's the teenagers marched to Kress, which agreed to serve them only after removing all counter seats. Brown's drugstore, the third of the five targeted downtown businesses, offered far more resistance. When the protesters arrived at Brown's lunch counter, they found every seat occupied by white youths, who relinquished them only to other white customers. When a white youth assaulted a black demonstrator, the youth became the first person arrested during the Oklahoma City protests.[16]

When the Youth Council suspended demonstrations on September 1, it had in two weeks desegregated four of the five targeted downtown Oklahoma City businesses. Barbara Posey, fifteen-year-old spokeswoman for the council, also claimed success with at least a dozen other restaurants in the city. The first victories were also the easiest. Most Oklahoma City restaurants and public facilities remained segregated, prompting a six-year campaign, led principally by Luper but involving thousands of demonstrators and expanding from sit-ins to protest marches to a boycott of all downtown stores, and high-level negotiations with Governor J. Howard Edmondson. The Oklahoma City campaign attracted Hollywood celebrities, such as Charlton Heston, who walked a picket line in May 1961. Finally, on

Western Cities with the Largest Black Populations, 1970
(Ranked by Size of the African American Population in 1970)

	1960			1970			Total	Black
	Total Pop.	Bl. Pop.	%	Total Pop.	Bl. Pop.	%	Total % Inc.	% Inc.
Los Angeles	2,479,015	334,916	13.5	2,816,061	503,606	17.8	13.5	50.3
Houston	938,219	215,037	22.9	1,232,802	316,551	25.6	31.3	47.2
Dallas	679,684	129,242	19.0	844,401	210,238	24.8	24.6	62.6
Oakland	367,548	83,618	22.7	361,561	124,710	34.4	-1.6	49.1
San Francisco	740,316	74,383	10.0	715,674	96,078	13.4	-3.3	29.1
Fort Worth	356,268	36,440	10.2	393,476	78,324	20.0	10.4	114.9
Compton	71,812	28,283	39.3	78,611	55,781	71.0	9.4	97.2
San Diego	573,224	34,435	6.0	696,769	52,961	7.6	21.5	53.8
Oklahoma City	324,253	37,529	11.5	366,481	50,103	13.6	13.0	33.5

San Antonio	587,718	41,605	7.0	654,153	50,041	7.6	11.3	20.2
Denver	493,887	30,251	6.1	514,678	47,011	9.1	4.2	54.9
Seattle	557,087	26,901	4.8	530,831	37,868	7.1	-4.7	40.7
Beaumont	119,175	34,883	29.2	115,919	35,553	30.6	-2.7	1.9
Tulsa	261,685	22,489	8.6	331,638	35,277	10.6	26.7	56.8
Kansas City, KS	121,901	28,134	23.0	162,213	34,345	21.1	33.0	22.0
Richmond, CA	71,854	14,388	20.0	79,043	28,633	32.6	10.0	99.0
Phoenix	439,170	20,919	4.7	581,562	27,896	4.7	32.4	33.3
Berkeley	111,268	21,850	19.6	116,716	27,421	23.4	4.8	25.4
Sacramento	191,667	12,103	6.3	254,413	27,244	10.7	32.7	125.1
Wichita	254,698	19,861	7.7	276,554	26,841	9.7	8.5	35.1

Source: U.S. Bureau of the Census, Census of Population, 1960, *vol. 1*, Characteristics of the Population, *parts 4, 6, 7, 18, 38, 45, 49 (Washington, D.C.: Government Printing Office, 1963), table 21*; 1970 Census of the Population, *vol. 1*, Characteristics of the Population, *parts 4, 6, 7, 18, 38, 45, 49 (Washington, D.C.: Government Printing Office, 1973), table 23*.

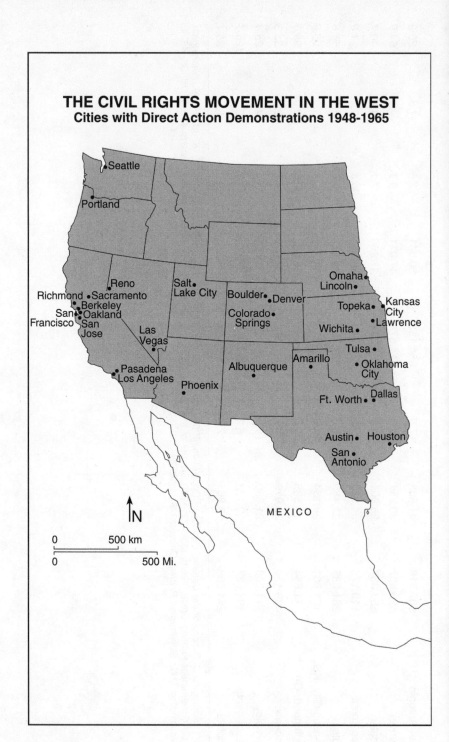

THE CIVIL RIGHTS MOVEMENT IN THE WEST
Cities with Direct Action Demonstrations 1948-1965

Seattle

Portland

Reno
Richmond • Sacramento
Berkeley
San • Oakland
Francisco San
Jose

Salt
Lake City

Omaha
Lincoln

Boulder • Denver

Colorado
Springs

Topeka • Kansas
City
• Lawrence

Wichita

Las
Vegas

Pasadena
Los Angeles

Phoenix

Albuquerque

Amarillo

Tulsa •
• Oklahoma
City

Ft. Worth • Dallas

Austin • Houston

San •
Antonio

N

0   500 km
0   500 Mi.

MEXICO

June 2, 1964, the Oklahoma City Council passed a public accommodations ordinance that forbade operators of public establishments from refusing to serve anyone because of "race, religion, or color."[17]

The Oklahoma City desegregation campaign was one of the longest in the West. But civil disobedience demonstrations against exclusion from public accommodations, job discrimination, housing bias, or school segregation occurred in dozens of other western cities. Merchants who refused to hire African American sales personnel drew protests in Denver and San Diego. Houston and San Antonio African Americans concentrated on restaurant exclusion while Salt Lake City and Portland protests addressed housing discrimination. Reno and Las Vegas African Americans challenged the state's gambling and hotel industry, which excluded blacks as casino patrons and hotel guests. Even celebrity performers, such as Sammy Davis, Jr., Nat King Cole, and Lena Horne, could not stay in the hotels where they performed. In 1963 demonstrators sat in at the California state capitol and the Colorado governor's mansion over civil rights issues. Direct action campaigns covered the West, as Seattle activist the Reverend John H. Adams recalled: "By 1963 the civil rights movement had finally leaped the Cascade Mountains."[18]

The San Francisco Bay Area became the focal point of civil disobedience campaigns between 1963 and 1965. San Francisco was familiar with civil rights protest. Its CORE chapter, formed in 1948, had launched successful demonstrations against employment discrimination in the Fillmore district. Nonetheless many employers and apartment owners in San Francisco and other Bay Area cities drew the color line. San Francisco blacks were confined to two segregated residential districts, Fillmore, west of downtown, and Hunter's Point, a World War II housing project built on a small peninsula jutting out into the bay. Even the rich and famous were not immune, as baseball star Willie Mays learned in 1957, when the baseball Giants left New York for San Francisco. Mays purchased a house in an affluent San Francisco neighborhood only after the personal intervention of Mayor George Christopher. Similarly, Oakland and Berkeley were divided by a "Maginot line" that confined most of the black community to the flatlands while affluent whites lived in the Oakland and Berkeley hills. Moreover, Black Oakland had an unemployment rate of nearly 25 percent in 1961. At least one of every three African American youths in Oakland was an unemployed high school dropout, and every predominantly black high school had a police patrol.[19]

In 1962 Wilfred Ussery, the new chairman of the San Francisco CORE, who later became national chairman, launched campaigns against de facto segregation and employment discrimination in downtown stores. He promised "an eyeball to eyeball confrontation with the white power structure of the city." One year later Oakland CORE embarked on an anti-employment discrimination campaign against Montgomery Ward and gained a victory after two weeks of picketing. Montgomery Ward agreed to provide statistical data on hires by race and launched special recruitment drives that eventually opened hundreds of jobs to people of color. The CORE–Montgomery Ward settlement proved a model for other fair employment agreements with retailers.[20]

In 1963 James Baldwin addressed a San Francisco civil rights protest march and rally that drew more than thirty thousand supporters. Both the rally and his remarks indicated that local and national civil rights goals had merged. The march was ostensibly to support the Birmingham campaign led by Martin Luther King, Jr. However, marchers followed a banner that read, "We March in Unity for Freedom in Birmingham and Equality of Opportunity in San Francisco." Baldwin pursued that theme: "We are not trying to achieve . . . more token integration [or] teach the South how to discriminate northern style. We are attempting to end the racial nightmare, and this means immediately confronting and changing the racial situation in San Francisco."[21]

Four months after the San Francisco rally a CORE chapter was formed on the University of California, Berkeley campus. The chapter's first target: the local branch of Mel's drive-in restaurant, later famous in the film American Graffiti. Although Mel's had black employees in menial positions, it refused to hire African Americans as waitresses, carhops, and bartenders. Ninety-two demonstrators were arrested in the first protest. After the second demonstration Mel's relented and began hiring blacks in the more visible staff positions.[22]

After the success of the Mel's drive-in demonstrations eighteen-year-old Tracy Simms, a Berkeley High School student; Roy Ballard, of San Francisco CORE; and Mike Myerson, a member of the UC-Berkeley radical student party, Slate, formed the Ad Hoc Committee to End Discrimination. Slate and CORE escalated Bay Area direct action protests. In February 1964 they challenged the Lucky grocery chain, specifically targeting the store on Telegraph Avenue in Berkeley with "shop-ins." Two weeks after the protests began, San Francisco Mayor John F. Shelly mediated an agreement between the Bay Area CORE chapters and Lucky management.[23]

Four days later the Ad Hoc Committee moved against the Sheraton Palace Hotel for its refusal to hire African Americans. The campaign became the largest civil rights protest in the far West. Picketing began on a small scale but escalated when 123 demonstrators were arrested. Within a week approximately 1,500 demonstrators ranging from working-class youth to university professors joined the picket lines. Hundreds filled the hotel lobby and sat down, leaving a small passageway for reporters and television photographers covering the event. The following day Tracy Simms, holding a megaphone, mounted a marble table and declared to the demonstrators who had spent the night in the lobby, "The Sheraton Palace has once again shown bad faith. They have refused to sign an agreement they . . . proposed. Are you ready to go to jail for your beliefs?" Demonstrators shouted their approval and then sang "We Shall Overcome" after deciding to block all hotel doorways. When Willie Brown, one of two attorneys for the Ad Hoc Committee, proposed that the demonstrators avoid arrest by switching from blocking the doorways to holding a lobby sleep-in, they announced, "We are going to jail." Eventually 167 demonstrators, including Mario Savio, a future leader of Berkeley's Free Speech Movement, went to jail. But 600 demonstrators remained in the hotel until later that afternoon, when Tracy Simms announced that Mayor Shelly had negotiated an agreement with the Sheraton Palace that was binding on all the city's major hotels. That agreement generated nearly 2,000 jobs for people of color.[24]

Meanwhile the San Francisco NAACP organized demonstrations against car dealerships on auto row along Van Ness Avenue. Two hundred protesters entered the Cadillac showroom to protest the dealership's discriminatory hiring policy. One hundred and seven of them were arrested. Again Mayor Shelly intervened. This time he requested civil rights leaders call a moratorium on civil disobedience demonstrations while he appointed a committee to promote the settlement of all racial disputes by "conciliation and mediation." Now, however, some political leaders lashed back at the demonstrators. Dr. Thomas Burbridge, leader of the auto row demonstration, was sentenced to nine months in prison, prompting James Farmer, national director of CORE, to declare, "As far as civil rights sentences . . . are concerned, San Francisco is the worst city in the country."[25]

Some Bay Area protests, such as picketing of the *Oakland Tribune*, continued into late 1964, but the civil rights momentum began to fade partly because of the passage of the national Civil Rights Act in June 1964 and partly because white civil rights activists turned their attention to the UC-Berkeley Free Speech protests, which began after the arrest of campus CORE member Jack Weinberg while he solicited funds for civil rights organizations. Angry students converged on the squad car holding Weinberg. Mario Savio, president of Campus Friends of SNCC and a teacher the previous summer in a Mississippi Freedom School, mounted the top of the trapped squad car and urged the two thousand protesters to continue their resistance. One unidentified protester mused, "A student who has been chased by the KKK in Mississippi is not easily scared by academic bureaucrats." For that student, Savio, and other protesters the Free Speech demonstrations were a continuation of the civil rights struggle in the South and the Bay Area.[26]

In terms of strategy, tactics, and objectives most western protests paralleled those waged east of the Mississippi River. However, many of these protests occurred in a milieu where African Americans were only one of a number of groups of color. The region's multiracial population moved civil rights beyond "black and white." The movement in Seattle and San Antonio reflects that complexity. San Antonio's huge Chicano population created a different racial atmosphere from that of Houston, Dallas, and Forth Worth, the other major Texas centers of civil disobedience. In 1960 Mexican Americans constituted 40 percent of the population as opposed to blacks' 7 percent. Although there had been some attempts at political alliances between the two groups, they lived on separate sides of San Antonio in largely separate worlds. "Our roots are different," explained the local dentist and civic leader Dr. José San Martín. "Our problems have been different, our solutions have been different. Therefore our philosophy is different." One of the differences was the level of discrimination. San Antonio public accommodations regularly excluded blacks. Yet a 1941 city ordinance prohibited discrimination against "anyone . . . merely because of his racial origin from one of the [Latin American] Republics."[27]

Despite the ordinance, Anglo San Antonians considered Latinos nonwhite and widely discriminated against them. A few Chicano activists, recognizing their commonality with African Americans, joined the black direct action protests that began in March 1960.

Leonel Javier Castillo and Perfecto Villareal, for example, organized sit-ins at San Antonio theaters that involved black, brown, and white volunteers. Moreover, black civil rights groups remembered San Antonio Congressman Henry B. González, who had led an unsuccessful effort to outlaw racial segregation while a state senator in the 1950s. Yet much of the Chicano population represented a paradox to black activists. Their presence in the city deflected prejudice from African Americans. But because they suffered less discrimination than blacks, most Chicanos, their leaders, and their organizations remained silent on discrimination, prompting San Antonio NAACP leader Claude Black to declare, "It's like having a brother violate [your] rights. You can hate the brother much more than you would the outsider because you expected more from the brother."[28]

For African American Seattle, the Asian Americans were the other group of color. Asian Americans, especially Japanese Americans, had been the largest racial minority in the city and the focus of most white prejudice before World War II. The wartime incarceration of the Japanese and the influx of African Americans to work in shipyards and aircraft plants made black Seattle the largest postwar population of color. However, Seattle's Asians made much greater postwar educational and economic progress than blacks, which, in turn, affected white attitudes toward them. One white homeowner opposed to a 1963 city ordinance banning housing discrimination declared, "Well, Orientals are O.K. in some places, but no colored."[29] Most Japanese American organizations and leaders were neutral, and some were openly hostile to African American efforts to end housing discrimination despite their appeals for black voter support to repeal the Anti-Alien Land Act, a leading symbol of anti-Japanese prejudice. As with Chicanos in San Antonio, many Asian Americans rested comfortably with the milder discrimination they faced in comparison to black Seattleites, or feared white anger if they identified too closely with civil rights activism.

Individual Asian Americans, however, did support local civil rights efforts. Wing Luke, the first Asian American to serve on the Seattle City Council, sponsored a controversial 1963 open housing ordinance. Philip Hayasaka, executive director of the Seattle Human Rights Commission, and Donald Kazama, chair of the Human Relations Committee of the Japanese American Citizens' League, criticized local Japanese leaders for not supporting the black civil rights movement. A Japanese American activist, the Reverend Mineo Katagiri joined the local movement, becoming the only Asian American member of the Central Area Civil Rights Committee, an otherwise all-black organization that coordinated the direct action protests of the NAACP, CORE, and other civil rights organizations. Asian American activists, such as Bernie Yang and Jim Takisaki, helped coordinate sit-ins and protest marches in Seattle. They and other young Asian Americans, like many white students of the era, genuinely identified with African American demands, which they believe stemmed from legitimate grievances. But they also believed the success of the civil rights campaign meant the end of anti-Asian discrimination. Despite the commitment of these individuals, Asian Americans and African Americans traveled different routes in seeking full-fledged citizenship in Seattle.[30]

De jure school segregation in Texas and Oklahoma and de facto segregation elsewhere in the region united African American parents from Houston to Seattle. The issue was hardly new. Nineteenth-century African American parents in Portland, San Francisco, Oakland, Denver, Helena, Wichita, and Topeka had waged campaigns to have their children attend integrated public schools. Segregation, however, became more acute after World War II with the rapid growth of the western urban African American population. As all-black neighborhoods emerged in western cities, school administrators allowed segregated schools to develop. After the *Brown* ruling in 1954, many western school boards moved slowly to desegregate facilities. Yet black parents were determined to gain for their children the educational advantages they believed were bestowed on white children. As one African American parent said in 1962, "I moved to San Francisco over ten years ago in hopes of improving the future of my children. I've had enough of promises from white politicians and school officials. Our children need to be taught in integrated schools in a city that refuses to perpetuate discrimination. My neighbors and I have had enough, we want change . . . we no longer accept empty promises."[31]

The 1960s desegregation campaigns of African American parents in two western cities, conservative Houston and liberal Berkeley, illustrate the complexity of the effort to eradicate school segregation. Moreover, these campaigns reveal the enormous difference between "desegregation" and "integration." The former term indicated the placing of children of various races and socioeconomic backgrounds in the same school although not necessarily in the same classes. The latter suggested that all students would have equal opportunities to learn and excel regardless of their racial or socio-economic backgrounds. Houston and Berkeley, and indeed most public schools in the United States, desegregated in the 1960s and 1970s. Many of those schools are still grappling with integration.

In 1960 the Houston Independent School District (HISD), with 177,228 students, maintained the nation's largest legally segregated school system. The first legal challenge to its segregated schools came in December 1956, when a lawsuit was filed in federal district court on behalf of nine-year-old Delores Ross and fourteen-year-old Beneva Williams. The most immediate effect of the lawsuit was the election to the seven-member local school board of a six-member antidesegregation majority that defiantly vowed to do everything in its power to prevent "race mixing," which it equated with communism.[32]

By 1959 the NAACP's chief attorney, Thurgood Marshall, had joined the Houston attorneys who initiated *Ross v. Houston Independent School District.* Nonetheless little progress was made until March 1960, when student activists at Texas Southern University launched sit-ins at the nearby Weingarten grocery store lunch counter. The demonstrations continued for a month until negotiations opened between Chamber of Commerce President Leon Jaworski and twenty-eight-year-old Eldewey Sterns, a TSU law student who was also president of the Progressive Youth Association, a coalition of student activists from TSU, Rice University, and all-black Erma Hughes Business College. When negotiations collapsed, the students resumed their protests and won significant concessions from various businesses by September 1, 1960.[33]

These student protests never targeted the Houston school system, but their impact, and the desire to avoid a Little Rock–style confrontation, prompted business and political elites to seek a peaceful solution to the desegregation crisis. Houston's business establishment did not wish desegregation in either public accommodations or schools, but in order to maintain a healthy business climate—its highest priority—it supported change. Federal Judge Ben C. Connally promoted its goal when he ruled in August 1960 that the district implement a grade-per-year desegregation plan that was to begin the following September. First grader Tyronne Raymond Day took his seat with twenty-nine white classmates on September 8, 1960, and became the first African American to attend a desegregated school in Houston.[34]

Celebrations of Houston school desegregation proved premature. School officials implemented strict academic criteria, effectively limiting the number of black students attending formerly all-white schools. By 1964 only 3 percent of Houston's thirty-nine thousand African American students attended desegregated schools. Consequently attorney Barbara Jordan and the Reverend William Lawson founded People for Upgraded Schools in Houston (PUSH) and called for a boycott of the city's black high schools. On May 10, 1965, 90 percent of Houston's black high school students stayed away from classes while two thousand demonstrators sponsored by PUSH and the local NAACP marched in front of HISD offices. The boycott and demonstration immediately prompted the school district to accelerate its timetable for desegregation of the sixth, seventh, and tenth grades. Conversely, both school district and federal court–implemented integration plans persuaded middle-class white parents to withdraw their children from local public schools. Black and Mexican parents, viewing this large-scale white flight, concluded that desegregation efforts were futile. By 1970 black and brown parents opposed busing and various other programs to promote desegregation. With the departure of middle-class whites (and, by the 1970s, blacks), integrated education seemed as remote in 1970 as it had ten years earlier.[35]

Berkeley's liberal image was also tested by de facto segregation. That city's school crisis evolved from the rapid growth of the city's African American population. Blacks were 4 percent of the city's population in 1940, 12 percent in 1950, 20 percent in 1960, and 23 percent in 1970. Virtually all the newcomers were working-class women and men drawn by the prospect of wartime shipyard employment and by the city's reputation for good schools. However, black

Houston School District Enrollment by Ethnicity, 1960–93

Year	Total Enrollment	Black %	Latino %	White %	Indian/Asian %
1960	177,228	23	na*	77	na
1970	241,138	36	14	50	na
1980	194,043	45	28	25	2
1993	200,613	36	49	12	3

*The school district counted Latino students as white until 1970.

Source: William Henry Kellar, "Make Haste Slowly: A History of School Desegregation in Houston, Texas" (Ph.D. dissertation, University of Houston, 1994), 326, 353, 371.

Berkeleyites quickly became part of a multicity ghetto of public housing projects that stretched along the flatlands. As one 1967 survey on school integration concluded, "segregation by race had been superimposed upon segregation by class. . . ."[36]

Residential segregation supported school segregation. In 1960 the city's public school enrollment was 56 percent white, 32 percent black, 8 percent Asian, and 4 percent Latino. Berkeley High, the only high school in the city, was desegregated, but 92 percent of the African American elementary school students attended six of the city's fourteen neighborhood schools. As historian W. J. Rorabaugh observes, the Berkeley school district "ran two separate school systems, one by and for educated, affluent whites in the hills, the other for poor blacks in the flatlands."[37]

By the time they reached one of Berkeley's two junior high schools (the third junior high drew its students almost exclusively from the hills), African American students began to note the differences in education. Although they attended the same schools, blacks had little contact with whites and Asian Americans because most African American students entered the two lower tracks of the four-track education system. Moreover, black students, often from homes where parents had rudimentary southern educations, had few academic demands placed upon them by teachers and administrators. White middle-class parents, teachers, and peers pushed white and Asian American children harder. Not surprisingly, many black students were among the 25 percent of Berkeley's students who scored in the bottom 10 percent on national standardized achievement tests while one third (mostly white Berkeley hills students) tested in the top 10 percent.[38]

Berkeley High School was hardly better for African American students since the tracking system continued the informal segregation of blacks from white and Asian American students. School activities also separated the races. Black youths were allowed to use the school swimming pool only on Friday night. Few African American students worked on the student newspaper or joined the selective school clubs that were often precursors to fraternity and sorority admission at the University of California, Berkeley and other prestigious colleges and universities. Many African American students dropped out or joined the military. Those who did graduate faced grim prospects. They were unskilled, unemployable, and unprepared for college, even though educated in the shadow of one of the nation's most prestigious universities.[39]

In 1958 some black parents began to challenge this de facto segregation system. The Reverend Roy Nichols raised the issue with the school board while representing the local NAACP. Three years later he became the first African American elected to the board, joining three other members to constitute a four to one liberal majority. In 1963 the school district proposed a ten-year desegregation program that required busing to aid desegregation. When the school board announced that junior high schools would be desegregated in September 1964, angry white parents created the Parents Association for Neighborhood Schools (PANS) which immediately tried and failed to recall the entire school board in October 1964. Following that defeat, the conservative *Berkeley Citizens United Bulletin* urged many white busing opponents to leave the city. "If you don't want to know the Negro mind," declared the paper, "then it is time for you to move over the hill."[40]

In September 1964 Berkeley put in place the first non-court-ordered busing plan in the United States. It called for a three-year busing program that involved a ride of no more than three miles each way. The program gave most of the city's elementary and junior high schools a rough balance between black and white students with Asian American students making up the balance. Despite elaborate planning and preparation by school officials, which included parental visits to schools their children were to attend, prebusing exchanges of white and black students, and "race relations" training for teachers, the plan continued to engender virulent opposition. One antibusing advocate said of African American children, "They're happy where they are!" Another suggested a gradual approach, waiting another generation, which prompted a black parent to reply, "What do you mean—it'll come? By magic? There ain't gonna be no magic!. We've gotta do it ourselves." Another black woman said, "We've been waiting since the Civil War. We can't wait any longer!" The Berkeley school superintendent, Neil V. Sullivan, a veteran of Virginia's desegregation troubles, remarked that "the only difference between white attitudes in Berkeley and Virginia was that in Berkeley, people were 'more polite.' "[41]

Parental fear and anxiety quickly transferred to the students, who were confused by the mixed signals they received. Desegregation worked well at most of the elementary and junior high schools. But Berkeley High became a caldron of racial tension. In the early 1960s white students ridiculed black students about their race and lower-class background. After 1965 African American students, influenced by the black power movement, raged against whites and Asian Americans regardless of their pro- or anti-integration views. Many white teachers and students were assaulted and humiliated in the halls and classrooms of the school. African American students formed the Black Student Union (BSU), which demanded and got more black counselors, curriculum materials, and "soul food" in the cafeteria. The BSU also served as monitor of the new racial divide, making it difficult for blacks and whites to maintain school friendships. Blacks dominated the football team, prompting a decline in white attendance. After 1965 virtually no whites attended postgame dances.[42]

Ultimately, as historian W. J. Rorabaugh explains, "black hope met white fear." Before 1965 most of Berkeley's African American parents believed the racial isolation of their children guaranteed failure because it denied them access to the best teachers, facilities, and equipment and ensured their marginalization once they did arrive at Berkeley High School. Yet after 1965 many African American parents began to reconsider desegregation as the sole tool to guarantee their children quality education. Those parents, influenced by black nationalists and radicals, called for control over neighborhood schools. By 1969 many of them had become as adamantly opposed to busing as were their white and Asian American counterparts. Despite Berkeley's reputation as one of the most liberal cities in the nation, antibusing advocates remained a sizable force in local politics. Thus school integration was challenged by various racial and political groups pursuing their own uncompromising agendas.[43]

As the campaigns in Houston and Berkeley illustrate, school desegregation without the concomitant neighborhood residential integration usually generated white fear and flight from the public schools, if not the city itself, and ultimately resegregation. Moreover, the decades-long public controversy over desegregation poisoned goodwill among all groups—whites, blacks, Asians, and Latinos—prompting the last three to vie among themselves for control of shrinking school districts. By 1980 many public school systems in western cities had failed to integrate their classrooms, and some were giving up on desegregation efforts, leaving students of color isolated in increasingly impoverished districts.

On August 11, 1965, in a predominantly African American neighborhood near Watts, California Highway Patrolman Lee Minikus stopped twenty-one-year-old Marquette Frye, who had reportedly been driving dangerously. Frye failed a roadside sobriety test and was arrested. His mother, Rena Frye, appeared from the family home nearby. A crowd gathered, and more highway patrol and Los Angeles police arrived on the scene. Bottles were thrown, answered by tear gas. The Watts riot began with this incident. It became the largest African American civil uprising in the nation's history. When the conflict was over, thirty-four people were dead: twenty-nine blacks, three Latinos, one Asian American, and one white. Behind such statistics were names: Charles Fitzer, Rena Johnson, Joe Maiman, Ramón Hermosillo, Eugene Simatsu, Ronald Ludlow, four-year-old Bruce Moore, the youngest, all killed in the disturbance, and twenty-seven others. The uprising of 1965 was not confined to Watts proper; it spread throughout south central Los Angeles encompassing an area as large as San Francisco or Manhattan. Even though the riot zone was larger than the community itself, after 1965 the name Watts symbolized anger, alienation, and resentment. Watts also represented in its poverty and, by 1965, its violence the possibility of a disturbing future for urban America.[44]

Watts proved rich in irony. Residents who lived in bungalows and low-rise housing projects on sun-drenched, palm tree–line streets were not considered likely candidates for urban rioting in 1965. African American Californians had voting rights, public accommodations access, and theoretically integrated schools. They seemed far removed from the conditions that sparked major civil rights confrontations in Birmingham or Selma. Even Marquette Frye, the catalyst for the uprising, came from a background that belied the Watts image. Although born in Lima, Oklahoma, Frye had been reared in Hannah, Wyoming. "People [in Wyoming] were much better," he recalled after his arrest. "The school curriculum was better. The kids' vocabularies were better. When I came to California, the kids here resented my speech, they resented my intelligence. . . . In Wyoming . . . there were only about eight Negroes in school . . . and we were accepted by the whites. When we came to California, we got into an all-Negro school. . . . I made 'A's and 'B's back in Wyoming. But here I kept getting suspended for fighting. . . ."[45]

The origins of the confrontation in August 1965 are rooted in developments that evolved in Watts from the 1920s through the 1960s. From its founding in 1903 Watts had been a portal through which laborers entered the Southern California economy and its homeowning class. It was unique among Los Angeles suburbs; from its beginning black, Latino, and white migrants purchased houses and small farms. By 1940 African Americans comprised 31 percent of the community's nearly seventeen thousand residents. The arrival of twelve thousand African Americans during World War II gave the community a black majority for the first time.[46]

The new residents entered Watts as tenants and job seekers rather than aspiring homeowners. Black newcomers doubled up in single-family dwellings or aging apartments. Neighboring suburban communities, such as Lynwood and Compton, continued their opposition to residential integration, prompting Robert C. Weaver to write in 1945 that Watts had assumed "the characteristics of a racial island." However, Arna Bontemps captured the psychological as well as physical boundaries of this evolving ghetto: "A crushing weight fell on the spirit of the neighborhood when [Watts] learned that it was hemmed in, that prejudice and malice had thrown a wall around it."[47]

Watts steadily declined into a slum. In 1950 the city of Los Angeles placed three of its eleven new public housing projects—Jordan Downs, Nickerson Gardens, and Imperial Courts—in Watts. The three projects housed nearly ten thousand people in a community of less than twenty-six thousand. Because of eligibility requirements for public housing residents, nearly all the residents were on some form of public assistance, unfortunate families that other communities either could not or would not accommodate. New residents arrived in the community when middle-class black families, no longer confined to Watts by restrictive covenants, began moving into West Los Angeles. Their departure increased the concentration of low-income, poorly educated residents in Watts. With no black elected officials at the city or county level in Los Angeles and no organizational voice, Watts interacted with the rest of Los Angeles in the 1950s primarily through menial work, welfare agencies, and the police.[48]

By 1960, 85 percent of Watts's 28,732 residents were African American. In the 1950s unemployment in Los Angeles declined; it increased in Watts. By the beginning of the 1960s, 15 percent of the residents were without jobs, including a growing number of "long-term unemployed," and 45 percent of the community's families were below the poverty level, earning under four thousand dollars annually. Watts residents had the lowest educational and income levels among African Americans in the city. By the 1960s many other black Angelenos treated this community with contempt. Eldridge Cleaver recalled how the name Watts became an insult, "the same way as city boys used 'country' as a term of derision. . . . The 'in crowd' . . . from L.A. would bring a cat down by saying he was from Watts. . . ."[49]

Watts, however, was not all of black Los Angeles. Only 9 percent of the city's African American residents lived there in 1960. The overwhelming majority of African American Angelenos resided in various working- and middle-class neighborhoods known collectively as South Central Los Angeles, while Baldwin Hills stood at the apex of the African American socioeconomic spectrum in Los Angeles. Although virtually every other African American community in the region had similar class division, in no other western black community was the separation so stark. Black median income in Baldwin Hills in 1960 was $12,000, well above the citywide median of $5,325 or the black median of $3,618. That separation manifested itself in the differing goals of African American leaders in the early 1960s. Many black Angeleno leaders invested heavily in the early 1960s campaign for political representation in city government, an effort that diverted considerable organizational energy and skill to local politics from civil rights activity or antipoverty efforts and may have prematurely led many middle-class and working-class Angelenos outside Watts to embrace the illusion that significant progress was being made. The emphasis on political power persuaded the direct action champion Dr. Martin Luther King, Jr., who in 1962 met with Tom Bradley, the Reverend H. H. Brookins, and other local leaders to plan strategy to elect an African American to the Tenth Council District. Throughout the affluent west side integration was the watchword for the area's upwardly mobile African Americans. For them the weapon of choice was the ballot box.[50]

As 1963 began, black Los Angeles had no representation at the city or state level and only one federal representative, Augustus Hawkins. Before the year ended, the city's African Americans mounted a remarkable campaign that elected three city council members (out of thirteen). Billy Mills represented the Eighth Council District, Gilbert Lindsay, the Ninth district, and Tom Bradley was elected in the Tenth district. These council members represented distinct constituencies. Mills and Lindsay were part of the Jesse Unruh–Mervyn Dymally political machine. Mills's predominantly black working-class district was the heart of South Central Los Angeles. Lindsay's Ninth District was predominantly Latino and had formerly been represented in the city council by Edward Roybal, who in 1962 became the member of Congress from East Los Angeles.

Tom Bradley meanwhile represented a district noted for its black and Jewish middle-class political reformers who opposed the Unruh machine. Robert Ferrell, who was to represent the Eighth District in 1974, characterized the class differences between the Eighth and Ninth districts and the Tenth as "cotton socks vs. silk stockings."[51]

Ten months after the Watts uprising the cry "black power" was first heard during a Canton, Mississippi, speech by Stokely Carmichael. Yet those words and what they symbolized were as applicable to post-1965 South Central Los Angeles or West Oakland as to any Mississippi community. Those two California communities produced the organizations that articulated the demands and aspirations of the two major streams of black power consciousness for the entire nation. Within a year of the Watts uprising Maulana Ron Karenga founded United Slaves (US), extolling cultural nationalism, while Huey Newton and Bobby Seale created the Black Panther party, epitomizing revolutionary nationalism.[52]

On the night of Marquette Frye's arrest in 1965, twenty-three-year-old Maulana Ron Karenga taught a Swahili class at Fremont High, Frye's high school. Karenga, born in 1941 in Parsonburg, Maryland, as Ronald McKinley Everett, was enrolled in the Ph.D. program in political science at UCLA while employed as a Los Angeles County social worker and part-time teacher at Fremont. Following the Watts uprising, Karenga emerged as the most prominent black nationalist in Los Angeles. In February 1966 he organized the first Watts Summer Festival, to honor the dead and recast the "riot" as a revolt. The festival attracted 130,000 people. Karenga also formed the Sons of Watts and the Simbas (young lions), which recruited former gang members, while his Community Alert Patrols monitored police activity in African American neighborhoods. Karenga was a major promoter of "Freedom City," a proposal to allow Watts and other sections of black Los Angeles to become independent. In the fall of 1966 Karenga and Tommy Jacquette were hired by the Westminster Neighborhood Association (WNA), which had received eight hundred thousand dollars in federal antipoverty funds. Jacquette recruited unemployed male youths into the program, which paid them twenty dollars per week for taking courses in remedial English, math, reading, and African American history. Karenga was the principal program instructor, teaching the history courses and Swahili-language classes. By the end of the year the WNA with 350 student-workers was "the largest employer in Watts."[53]

Karenga was secretive about the founding of United Slaves (US), allowing only that it was established soon after the Watts uprising. However, he promoted his views in a series of 1966 interviews with national newsmagazines. In an interview with John Gregory Dunne, Karenga dismissed the civil rights movement's goals: "Why integrate? Why live where we are not wanted? . . . You've got to get power of your own, because power listens to power. . . . By setting an example of fearlessness, education, pride and culture, we give the black man something to fight for." To Andrew Kopkind he reported, "Blacks should control their own communities. . . . We are free men. We have our own language. We are making our own customs and we name ourselves. Only slaves and dogs are named by their masters." With his ability to gain media attention and his profile in black Los Angeles, Karenga soon eclipsed all rivals except Imamu Amiri Baraka of Newark as the leading black nationalist in the nation.[54]

The origins of the Black Panther party in Oakland reveal a similar repudiation of the civil rights struggle. The Panthers' Marxism, however, cast them as "the greatest threat to the internal security of the country," according to FBI Director J. Edgar Hoover. Black Panther founders, Huey P. Newton and Bobby Seale, conducted their first meeting at a West Oakland clubhouse on October 15, 1966. The two had histories much like those of thousands of black Oakland residents, whom the new party vowed to defend. Born in Monroe, Louisiana, Newton came west to Oakland with his family in 1945, when he was three. Seale was born in Dallas, Texas, in 1936 but grew up in Codornices Village, the sprawling housing project that straddled the Berkeley-Albany border. Newton and Seale were members of the generation of black westerners who, unlike their shipbuilding parents, could not secure places in the postwar Bay Area economy. They were uninspired in school. Newton later wrote bitterly of his years in the Oakland public schools: "Not one instructor ever awoke in me a desire to learn more or question or explore the worlds of literature, science, and history. . . . They [tried] to rob me of my . . . worth . . . and nearly killed my urge to inquire." Moreover, Newton and Seale found little employment as teenagers and had numerous conflicts with the local police. In 1961 they met at Oakland City College and were drawn together by their mutual admiration for Malcolm X, "street brothers," and socialist theories.[55]

The Panthers embraced a philosophy that immediately placed

them in opposition with cultural nationalist groups such as US. Like all post-Watts nationalist organizations, they denounced the civil rights movement and predicted that only violent revolution would eliminate racism and oppression from African American life. However, the Panthers called for armed self-defense of black communities, urged African Americans to embrace Marxism, and espoused alliances with other U.S. radicals and with revolutionary governments throughout the world. They believed that direct confrontation with police across the United States would hasten the revolutionary struggle they and their allies were destined to win.[56]

Before May 1967 the BPP had only twenty members and was unknown outside Oakland. Most of its members, like its first recruit, sixteen-year-old Bobby Hutton, were "street blacks." One new member, *Ramparts* writer Eldridge Cleaver, provided an intellectual core to the Panther program as well as valuable connections to wealthy white liberals and radicals. Yet a Panther protest in Sacramento propelled this small party into international prominence. On May 2, 1967, virtually the entire membership arrived at the state capitol in Sacramento armed and dressed in the Panther uniform of black leather jacket, beret, turtleneck sweater, and pants. Alarmed capitol employees quickly retreated from the unexpected visitors, and Governor Ronald Reagan, giving a speech on the capitol lawn, was hustled away by security agents. Ostensibly there to protest a recently introduced bill that would have prohibited the carrying of firearms in public places, the Panthers inadvertently entered the state assembly chamber before a barrage of reporters and photographers who made them the most recognized "black militants" in the nation.[57]

Panther membership rose quickly after this media event and information on their philosophy became known. By 1968 the BPP had twelve hundred members in chapters throughout the nation. They also launched highly publicized but short-lived alliances. The first was with the Student Nonviolent Coordinating Committee (SNCC), "drafting" its leader, Stokely Carmichael, into their organization with the rank of field marshal and giving him the responsibility for "establishing revolutionary law, order, and justice" east of the Continental Divide with the Panthers holding authority west of the Rocky Mountains. The Panthers also linked themselves with the mostly white Peace and Freedom party (PFP), founded by Robert Scheer, Michael Lerner, Tom Hayden, and Jerry Rubin. In 1968 the party ran Eldridge Cleaver and Jerry Rubin as its presidential and vice-presidential candidates.[58]

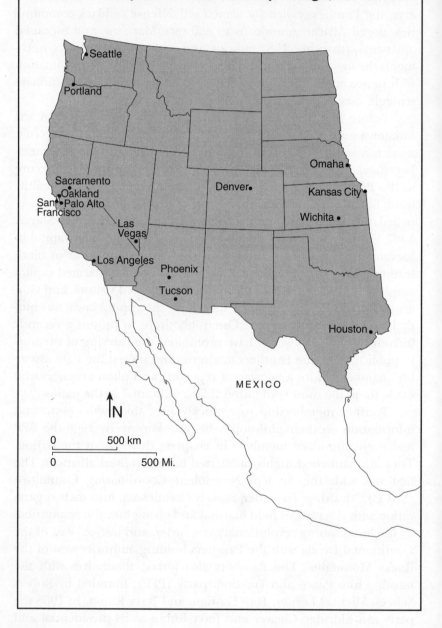

URBAN UNREST IN THE WEST
Cities That Experienced Urban Uprisings, 1965-1970

Seattle

Portland

Omaha

Sacramento
Oakland
San Palo Alto
Francisco

Denver

Kansas City

Wichita

Las
Vegas

Los Angeles

Phoenix

Tucson

Houston

MEXICO

N

0   500 km

0   500 Mi.

With success came increasing scrutiny and harassment by local, state, and federal authorities. Between 1967 and 1969 Panthers across the nation confronted police in clashes that left ten BPP members and nine police officers dead. They gained the attention of J. Edgar Hoover's FBI, which initiated the COINTELPRO campaign to disrupt them and other radical organizations. The increased harassment also brought notoriety, as evidenced by the huge "Free Huey" rallies staged after Newton was arrested and tried for the killing of the Oakland police officer John Frey. One rally before the Oakland courthouse where Newton was jailed attracted three thousand in a rainbow coalition of Newton supporters, including Whites for the Defense of Huey Newton, the Asian American Political Alliance, whose members held *Free Huey* signs in Mandarin Chinese, Japanese, and Tagalog, and young Latinos who appeared in tan bush jackets and brown berets anticipating the rise of the Brown Berets. Celebrities such as Yale president Kingman Brewster, Leonard Bernstein, Marlon Brando, Jane Fonda, Harry Belafonte, Jessica Mitford, James Baldwin, Ossie Davis, Susan Sontag, Norman Mailer, and Candace Bergen all supported various Panther efforts.[59]

The Panthers never found common ground with Maulana Ron Karenga's US. Both the BPP Southern California chapter and US operated in South Central Los Angeles and drew from the same constituency of impoverished, alienated black youth. To appeal to these men, many of whom had gang backgrounds, both organizations promoted their street-wise bravado, which quickly devolved into a series of ganglike street confrontations culminating in a bloody 1969 shoot-out on the UCLA campus that left Los Angeles Panthers Alprentice ("Bunchy") Carter and John Huggins dead in a dispute over the first director of the campus's new Afro-American Studies Center.[60]

The Black Panther party and United Slaves left an ambiguous legacy. A Panther-led political insurgency in Oakland helped elect Lionel Wilson the city's first black mayor in 1981. The party's free breakfast and education programs generated renewed interest in pre-adolescent nutrition and education for urban children. The Panthers borrowed from and inspired parallel defense organizations, including the American Indian Movement (AIM), the Brown Berets, the Puerto Rican Young Lords, and the Red Guards of San Francisco's Chinatown. Maulana Ron Karenga's US provided the foundation for the largest African American identification with Africa since the Garvey era. Both the current popularity of the end-of-year celebration Kwanzaa, which Karenga created in 1965, and Afrocentricity, which he influenced, are part of the US legacy. Both organizations also encouraged the rise of black (or ethnic) studies programs on university campuses with the first black studies program at San Francisco State College in 1968, following almost a year of violent confrontation between the Third World Liberation Front, a coalition of black, Asian, Latino, and Native American students, and campus administrators, led by college president S. I. Hayakawa.[61]

Neither US nor the Panthers achieved the transformation of black urban America they envisioned as counterinsurgency campaigns and federal and local authorities reduced their ranks and undermined their confidence. By 1970 Karenga, Newton, Seale, and Cleaver were incarcerated or in exile. Internal conflicts over philosophy and discipline also took a toll on both organizations. Neither the Panthers nor US developed significant middle-class African American support to offset the loss of their "natural constituency," young black males who by the early 1970s were destroyed by drugs or lulled into nihilistic violence and political apathy.

Nor could the Panthers or US successfully address the problem of gender equality. Both groups extolled the role of progressive black women in the coming revolutionary struggle. However, neither could fashion a program that promoted gender equality while many organization leaders and members insisted on maintaining male prerogatives that reinforced traditional gender roles. US embraced a mythical African cultural past that allowed no gender equality. The Panthers wrestled with the issue and alternated between progressive and reactionary stands. Certainly by the 1970s women outnumbered men in the party and, following Elaine Brown's assumption of leadership, had significant roles in its programs. But ultimately Brown and many other women left the Panthers because of male resentment of their impact on party programs and its image.[62]

Secondly, both groups made their appeal almost exclusively to "street blacks," the men and women of a rapidly growing black underclass. The Panthers, US, and virtually all post-Watts nationalist organizations made this lumpen proletariat the new political icon. The pre-1965 civil rights movement avoided championing the cause of blacks with criminal records. Post-1965 nationalists recruited gang members, drug dealers, pimps and prostitutes, thieves and murderers, calling them revolutionaries if they died in confrontations with police and political prisoners, if they landed in jail. These street fighters were "authentic" revolutionaries, their criminality dismissed as quasi-revolutionary activity and their confrontations with police hailed as challenges to racist oppressors. All blacks, regardless of background, were encouraged to emulate these street brothers as the revolutionary vanguard and follow their leadership.[63]

Some African Americans criticized the new orthodoxy. In an editorial following the slayings of Carter and Huggins at UCLA, the *Sentinel,* a black Los Angeles newspaper, challenged the claims of the cultural and revolutionary nationalists to speak for the African American community. "The whole problem-solving process in this community has been captured by a small, aggressive body of people whose self-sustainment needs preclude them from . . . making fair decisions in the name of the community. They will claim noble intentions but in the final analysis they mean to rule by any means feasible. That includes from the barrel of a gun." African American opinion never coalesced around nationalist visions of power and "authenticity." Nonetheless the image of street "outlaws" as a potential revolutionary force had, and continues to have, an enormous impact on African America.[64]

Black nationalism swept the West and the nation following Watts and the rise of US and the Black Panther party, ensuring that African American rage and frustration knew no regional boundaries. Racial violence broke out in San Francisco, Tucson, and Phoenix, in 1966, in Houston and Seattle in 1967, and in Omaha (the birthplace of Malcolm X), Portland, Oakland, Las Vegas, Denver, Kansas City (Kansas), and Wichita by the end of the decade. There was nothing particularly "western" about these uprisings. If impoverished black communities in Denver, Seattle, or Los Angeles seemed less visually alienating than Harlem, South Side Chicago, or Southeast Washington, the underlying conditions were remarkably similar. Thus cultural or revolutionary nationalism that emerged on the streets of West Oakland and South Central Los Angeles found ready acceptance whether in Chicago, Atlanta, Boston, or New York.

Tens of thousands of African American westerners saw their lives improved by the pre-1965 civil rights movement. Employment and educational opportunities also grew during the black power era of the late 1960s. Yet after Watts there was a palpable decline in optimism among middle-class and working-class black westerners about the region's potential to offer them both opportunity and racial justice. Even the successful knew that thousands of other black people in South Central Los Angeles, Denver's Five Points, Seattle's Central District, or Houston's Fourth Ward faced a daunting task in overcoming the physical and psychological barriers constructed by centuries of racism and poverty, particularly in an era of declining sympathy for their condition. These westerners had finally abandoned the search for a racial "promised land." Instead they chose political and cultural struggle because for them the West was the "end of the line both socially and geographically. There was was no better place to go."[65]

Conclusion

❖ ❀ ❖ ❀ ❖

Make, of my past, a road to the light
Out of the darkness, the ignorance, the night.

Langston Hughes, son of the West, spoke these words from his poem "Negro Mother" at his NAACP-sponsored performance in Albuquerque, New Mexico, on February 7, 1946. They aptly describe the goal of this history of the African American West. By exploring the African American past in the region least identified with the black historical experience, *In Search of a Racial Frontier* has attempted to provide a light to understand the present and future. That future is full of numerous possibilities, as recent events have shown.

In April 1992 South Central Los Angeles exploded in a maelstrom of rage. Although Los Angeles is the largest metropolis in the West, those scenes of carnage, no less than the city itself, undermine the regional self-image most westerners prefer: placid valleys or broad vistas populated by proud, self-reliant citizens jealously guarding their individual rights and freedom "under an open sky." Yet African American western history, much like the Los Angeles uprising, intrudes itself onto our sensibilities and forces a reexamination of the imagined West. That history, with its examples of resistance, conflict, and cooperation between African Americans and other westerners, can be celebrated or critiqued, but it can no longer be ignored. It is no longer, as western regional historians and historians of African America have claimed, an interesting footnote to a story focused elsewhere.[1]

THE AFRICAN AMERICAN URBAN WEST, 1990
Western Cities with 50,000 or More
African American Populations

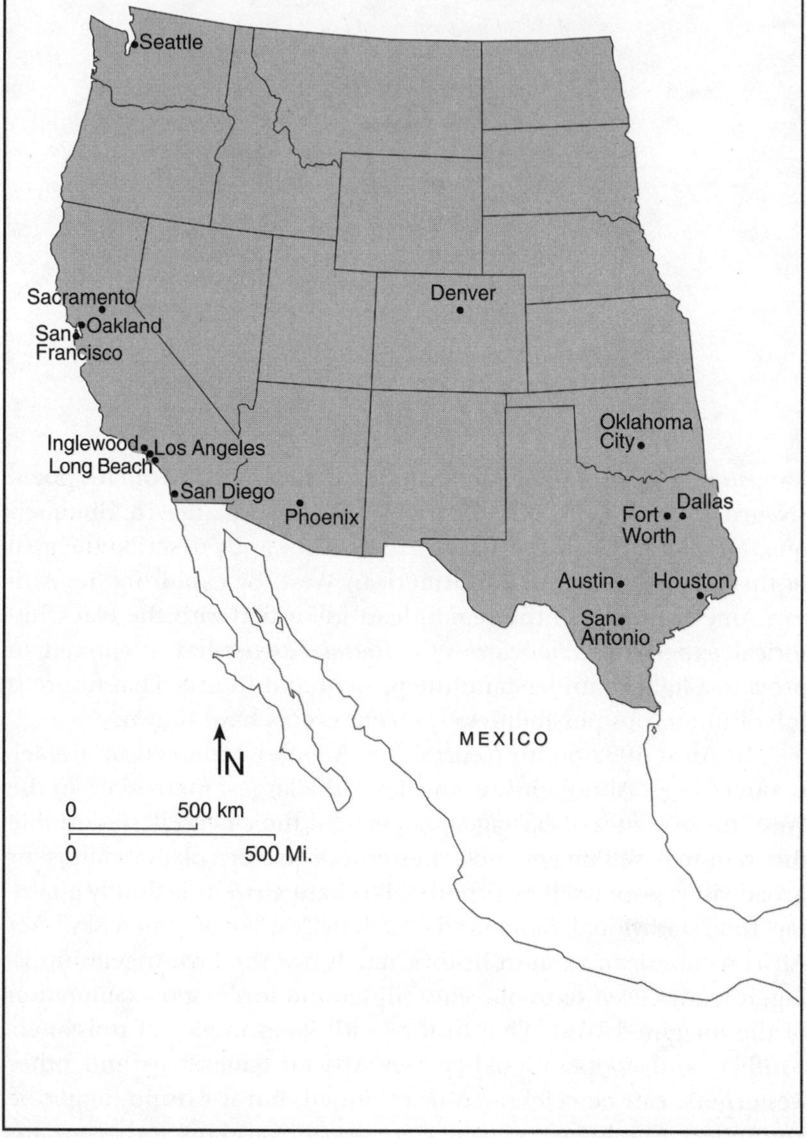

Seattle

Sacramento
San Oakland
Francisco

Denver

Inglewood Los Angeles
Long Beach

San Diego

Phoenix

Oklahoma
City

Fort Dallas
Worth

Austin Houston

San
Antonio

MEXICO

N

0   500 km

0   500 Mi.

The Los Angeles riot of 1992 made the nation aware of the complex relationships between Anglos and people of color in the modern urban West. It also highlighted divisions among people of color-class differences between Korean Americans and African Americans, political and economic rivalries between Latinos and Asians or between blacks and Latinos. Indeed Watts, the western black community whose name came to symbolize black "militancy" in the 1960s, is now populated mainly by people from Mexico and Central America. Social scientists and commentators describe the transformation of Watts and the growing rivalry between Latinos, Asians, and blacks throughout the West as a consequence of increasingly liberal post-1965 immigration laws that encouraged migration from Asia and Latin America. Yet the multiple sources of these conflicts are rooted in five centuries of encounter of racially and culturally diverse peoples as both individuals and distinct populations.[2]

The question asked at the beginning of this book still looms large. Was the West a racial frontier beyond which lay the potential for an egalitarian society? Even allowing for subregional, cultural, or gender differences and the presence of some Euro-Americans supportive of racial equality, those who have studied white western racial attitudes generally have claimed no. Two western historians writing in distinct periods and for different audiences arrived at that conclusion. J. W. Smurr in his 1957 discussion of nineteenth-century western racial thought argues: "The pioneer did not solve the problem of minority rights on the frontier. . . . He did not solve the problem in the West because he did not solve it in the East." Three decades later Richard White wrote much the same about the twentieth-century West. "Even newly arrived white westerners . . . regard native-born westerners with dark skin as aliens although their ancestors had been in the West for generations. . . . Segregation in most of the West . . . was just as real as in the South. . . . In coming west, African Americans had . . . voted with their feet against legal segregation and the South only to find themselves subject to de facto segregation in the West."[3]

Despite the evidence of racism all around them, many African Americans continued to believe the West did offer a chance for both economic opportunity and political freedom. Economic opportunity propelled hundreds of free blacks to enter Mexican Texas in the 1820s and thousands to gold rush California in the 1850s. In the 1890s tens of thousands came to homestead on Oklahoma Territory for "the last chance for a free home." Two hundred thousand Afri-

Western Cities with 50,000 or More African Americans, 1990

	Black Population	Total Population	Black % of Total Population
Los Angeles	487,674	3,485,398	13.9
Houston	457,990	1,630,553	28.0
Dallas	296,994	1,006,877	29.4
Oakland	163,335	372,242	43.8
San Diego	104,261	1,110,594	9.3
Fort Worth	98,532	447,619	22.0
San Francisco	79,039	723,959	10.9
Oklahoma City	71,064	444,719	15.9
San Antonio	65,844	935,933	7.0
Denver	60,046	467,610	12.8
Long Beach	58,761	429,433	13.6
Austin	57,868	465,622	12.4
Inglewood, CA	56,861	109,602	51.8
Sacramento	56,521	369,365	15.3
Seattle	51,948	516,259	10.0
Phoenix	51,053	983,403	5.1

Source: U.S. Census, 1990 Census of Population, General Characteristics by States (Washington, D.C.: Government Printing Office, 1992), table 6.

can Americans seeking similar opportunity migrated to West Coast shipyards and aircraft plants during World War II. The desire for freedom seemed centuries older than the quest for land. Isabel de Olvera's deposition to the alcalde of Querétaro in 1600 expressed concern about racially inspired discrimination: "I . . . fear that I may be annoyed by some individual since I am a mulatto." Her response, however—"it is proper to protect my rights. . . . I demand justice—"—illustrates a determination to challenge that discrimination and sets a contesting tone that continues for many African Americans to this day. In their own way black westerners who fought segregated Kansas schools from the 1870s to the 1950s, who refused to accept the boilermakers' discriminatory union plan in World War II, or who confront racial discrimination today through the courts or in direct action protests continue Olvera's legacy. They too demand justice.[4]

Ten years ago Patricia Limerick asked that all historians view the West through its complex, varied, paradoxical history rather than as a collage of stereotypes. The West was, and remains, as she reminds us, the home of "Indian, Hispanics, Asians, blacks and Anglos . . . who share the same region and its history, but wait to be introduced."[5] I hope *In Search of the Racial Frontier* begins that introduction for African American westerners. As that introduction evolves, African Americans can finally work out their shared destiny with the region's other westerners under that open sky.

Notes

◇ ✿ ◇ ✿ ◇

Introduction

1. See Duane A. Smith, " 'We Are Equal': Racial Attitudes in the West," *The Westerners Brand Book* (Chicago) 30:11 (January 1974), 82. See also Eugene Berwanger, *The West and Reconstruction* (Urbana: University of Illinois Press, 1981), introduction, ch. 1 and 2; Albert Broussard, *Black San Francisco: The Struggle for Racial Equality in the West, 1900–1954* (Lawrence: University Press of Kansas, 1993), ch. 8–13, and Quintard Taylor, *The Forging of a Black Community: Seattle's Central District from 1870 through the Civil Rights Era* (Seattle: University of Washington, 1994), ch. 6 and 7.

2. Richard White argues that the Anglo conquest had the ironic consequence of generating new "races" in the West by creating a group consciousness in its victims and introducing the tendency to confuse cultural and ethnic identity with racial status. See White, "Race Relations in the American West," *American Quarterly* 38:3 (1986), 396–99. See also Michael Omi and Howard Winant, *Racial Formation in the United States from the 1960s to the 1990s* (New York: Routledge, 1994), 82, 88–91, 107–12, for a contemporary assessment of the western racial model as increasingly the national paradigm. On the ability of white westerners to exchange and extend racial stereotypes from one group to another, see Dan Caldwell, "The Negroization of the Chinese Stereotype in California," *Southern California Historical Quarterly* 53:2 (June 1971); 123–31, and Luther Spoehr, "Sambo and the 'Heathen Chinee': Californians' Racial Stereotypes in the Late 1870s," *Pacific Historical Review* 42:2 (May 1975), 185–204.

3. See Roger W. Lotchin, "The Historians' War or the Home Front's War?: Some Thoughts for Western Historians," *Western Historical Quarterly* 26:2 (Summer 1995), 186.

4. Examples of this genre include Patricia Nelson Limerick, *The Legacy of Conquest: The Unbroken Past of the American West* (New York: W. W. Norton, 1987); Vicki L. Ruiz, *Cannery Women, Cannery Lives: Mexican Women, Unionization, and the California Food Processing Industry, 1930–1950* (Albuquerque: University of New Mexico Press, 1987); Peggy Pascoe, *Relations of Rescue: The Search for Female Moral Authority in the American West, 1874–1939* (New York: Oxford University Press, 1990); Richard White, *"It's Your Misfortune and None of My Own": A New History of the American West* (Norman: University of Oklahoma Press, 1991); and Clyde A. Milner II, ed., *A New Significance: Re-*

Envisioning the History of the American West (New York: Oxford University Press, 1996). For an early critique of New West historiography, see Michael P. Malone, "Beyond the Last Frontier: Toward a New Approach to Western American History," *Western Historical Quarterly* 20:4 (November 1989), 409–27.

5. Webb's quote appears in "The American West: Perpetual Mirage," *Harper's Magazine* (May 1957), 30. For an illuminating discussion of the necessity of challenging the "mythic West," see Limerick, *The Legacy of Conquest,* introduction and ch. 10.

6. See Lawrence B. de Graaf, "Recognition, Racism, and Reflections on the Writing of Western Black History," *Pacific Historical Review* 44:1 (February 1975), 22–51. De Graaf's critique of western black historiography remains compelling and persuasive. The quotation is from Kenneth W. Porter, *The Negro on the American Frontier* (New York: New York Times and Arno Press, 1969), p. 4. Other examples of the recognition school of western African American historiography include Philip Durham and Everett L. Jones, *The Negro Cowboys* (New York: Dodd, Mead, 1965); William H. Leckie, *Buffalo Soldiers: A Narrative of the Negro Calvary in the West* (Norman: University of Oklahoma Press, 1967); and William L. Katz's *The Black West* (Garden City, N. Y.: Doubleday, 1971 [reprinted Seattle: Open Hand Publishing, 1987]).

7. See W. Sherman Savage, *Blacks in the West* (Westport, Conn.: Greenwood Press, 1976). On the explosion of post-1976 literature on the African American West, see Quintard Taylor, "From Esteban to Rodney King: Five Centuries of African American History in the West," *Montana: The Magazine of Western History* 46:4 (Winter 1996), 18–23.

8. For the debate on black soldiers in the West, see Frank Schubert, "Black Soldiers on the White Frontier," *Phylon* 32:4 (Winter 1971), 410–15; Ronald Coleman, "The Buffalo Soldiers: Guardians of the Uintah Frontier, 1886–1901," *Utah Historical Quarterly* 47:4 (Fall 1979), 421–39; and de Graaf, "Recognition, Racism, and Reflections," 37. The role of African American soldiers as guardians of western industrial capital is explained in Jerry M. Cooper, *The Army and Civil Disorder: Federal Military Intervention in Labor Disputes, 1877–1900* (Westport, Conn. Greenwood Press, 1980), 172–78, 259–60; Clayton D. Laurie, "The United States Army and the Labor Radicals of the Coeur d'Alenes: Federal Military Intervention in the Mining Wars of 1892–1899," *Idaho Yesterdays* 37:2 (Summer 1993), 14–17; and Quintard Taylor, "A History of Blacks in the Pacific Northwest, 1788–1970" (Ph.D. dissertation, University of Minnesota, 1977), 118–23. For an early but still useful critique of the dilemmas posed by the writing of the "recognition school" historians, see Jack Forbes, *Afro-Americans in the Far West: A Handbook for Educators* (Berkeley: Far West Laboratory for Educational Research and Development, 1969), pp. 32–33.

9. See, for example, Lawrence B. de Graaf, "The City of Black Angels: The Emergence of the Los Angeles Ghetto, 1890–1930," *Pacific Historical Review* 39:3 (August 1970); Douglas Henry Daniels, *Pioneer Urbanites: A Social and Cultural History of Black San Francisco* (Philadelphia: Temple University Press, 1980); Emory J. Tolbert, *The UNIA and Black Los Angeles* (Los Angeles: Center for Afro-American Studies, 1980); Thomas C. Cox, *Blacks in Topeka: A Social History* (Baton Rouge: Louisiana State University Press, 1982); Howard Beeth and Cary D. Wintz, eds., *Black Dixie: Afro-Texas History and Culture in Houston* (College Station: Texas A&M University Press, 1992); Broussard, *Black San Francisco;* Bradford Luckingham, *Minorities in Phoenix: A Profile of Mexican American, Chinese American, and African American Communities, 1860–1992* (Tucson: University of Arizona Press, 1994); and Taylor, *Forging.* On small cities, see William Lang's "The Nearly Forgotten Blacks on Last Chance Gulch, 1900–1912," *Pacific Northwest Quarterly* 70:2 (April 1979), 50–51, which remains one of the best articles on small African American communities in the West. For other examples, see C. Robert Haywood, "No Less a Man: Blacks in Cow Town Dodge City, 1876–1886," *Western Historical Quarterly* 19:2 (May 1988), 161–82; Quintard Taylor, "The Emergence of Afro-American Communities in the Pacific Northwest, 1865–1910," *Journal of Negro History* 64:4 (Fall 1979), 342–51; and Quintard Taylor, "The Great Migration: The Afro-American Communities of Seattle and Portland during the 1940s," *Arizona and the West* 23:2 (Summer 1981), 109–26.

10. Quoted in Richard A. Garciá, *Rise of the Mexican American Middle Class: San Antonio, 1929–1941* (College Station: Texas A&M University Press, 1991), p. 23. For a discussion of San Antonio and Seattle, see Kenneth Mason, "Paternal Community: African

Americans and Race Relations in San Antonio, Texas, 1867–1937" (PhD. dissertation, University of Texas at Austin, 1994), and Taylor, *Forging,* ch. 1.

11. See, for example, Durham and Jones, *The Negro Cowboys;* Leckie, *Buffalo Soldiers;* and Katz, *The Black West.* For a discussion of the more slowly evolving but equally misleading image of the single African American frontier woman who strikes it rich doing laundry and investing profits in mines and real estate, see Susan H. Armitage and Deborah Gallacci Wilbert, "Black Women in the Pacific Northwest: A Survey and Research Prospectus," in Karen J. Blair, ed., *Women in Pacific Northwest History: An Anthology* (Seattle: University of Washington Press, 1988), p. 139. Information on the myriad roles of black western women can be found in Glenda Riley, "American Daughters: Black Women in the West," *Montana: The Magazine of Western History* 38:2 (Spring 1988), 14–27, and Lawrence B. de Graaf, "Race, Sex, and Region: Black Women in the American West, 1850–1920," *Pacific Historical Review* 49:1 (February 1980), 285–314.

12. Eugene Berwanger, "Hardin and Langston: Western Black Spokesmen of the Reconstruction Era," *Journal of Negro History* 64:2 (Spring 1979), 101–14.

1: Spanish Origins, 1528–1848

1. For a detailed discussion of Esteban's travels in Florida, Texas, and Mexico, see A. D. F. Bandelier, ed., *The Journey of Álvar Núñez Cabeza de Vaca* (New York: A. S. Barnes & Co., 1905), and George Parker Winship, "The Coronado Expedition, 1540–1542," Fourteenth Annual Report of the Bureau of Ethnology, Smithsonian Institution, 1892–93 (Washington, D.C.: Government Printing Office, 1896), 329–73. See also David J. Weber's introduction to Cleve Hallenbeck, ed., *The Journey of Fray Marcos de Niza* (Dallas: Southern Methodist University Press, 1987), xxvii–viii.

2. See Bandelier, ed., *Journey of Álvar Núñez Cabeza de Vaca,* 53–54, 65.

3. Ibid., pp. 72–73, 76–78, 87–94, 106–08, 180–84, and Winship, "The Coronado Expedition," pp. 346–48. For a discussion of Esteban's ability to serve as a linguistic and cultural interpreter, see Shirley Diane Ibrahim, "Estevan, the Moor of New Mexico: An Experiment in Point of View" (Ed.D. thesis, East Texas State University, 1978), ch. 2 and 3.

4. See Hallenbeck, ed., *Journey of Fray Marcos,* 15–18, 22, 30–32. For various accounts of Esteban's fatal encounter with the Zuni, see George P. Hammond and Agapito Rey, eds., *Narratives of the Coronado Expedition, 1540–1542* (Albuquerque: University of New Mexico Press, 1940), 63–81, 145, 160, 177–78, 197–99. See also Ramón A. Gutiérrez, *When Jesus Came, the Corn Mothers Went Away: Marriage, Sexuality, and Power in New Mexico, 1500–1846* (Stanford: Stanford University Press, 1991), 39–40, and Joe S. Sando, *Pueblo Nations: Eight Centuries of Pueblo Indian History* (Santa Fe: Clear Light Publishers, 1992), 43–46.

5. David J. Weber, *The Mexican Frontier, 1821–1846: The American Southwest under Mexico* (Albuquerque: University of New Mexico Press, 1982), xvi.

6. See Winship, "The Coronado Expedition," 379, 400; the quote appears on page 379. See also Caroll L. Riley, "Blacks in the Early Southwest," *Ethnohistory* 19:3 (Summer 1972), 252–57; Jack D. Forbes, "Blacks Pioneers: The Spanish-Speaking Afroamericans of the Southwest," *Phylon,* 27:3 (Fall 1966), 233–34; Oakah L. Jones, Jr., *Los Paisanos: Spanish Settlers on the Northern Frontier of New Spain* (Norman: University of Oklahoma Press, 1979), 40–41; and Alwyn Barr, *Black Texans: A History of Negroes in Texas, 1528–1971* (Austin: Jenkins Publishing Co., 1973), 3.

7. The Olvera statement and account appear in George P. Hammond and Agapito Rey, eds., *Don Juan de Oñate: Colonizer of New Mexico, 1595–1628* (Albuquerque: University of New Mexico Press, 1953), 560–62.

8. For slave importation figures for New Spain and British North America, consult Philip Curtin, *The Atlantic Slave Trade: A Census* (Madison: University of Wisconsin Press, 1969), 46, 72. See also Gonzalo Aguirre Beltrán, "The Integration of the Negro into the National Society of Mexico," in Magnus Morner, ed., *Race and Class in Latin America,* (New York: Columbia University Press, 1970), 27; Leslie B. Rout, Jr., *The African Experience in Spanish America: 1502 to the Present Day* (London: Cambridge

University Press, 1977), 126–34, and Patricia Seed, "Social Dimensions of Race: Mexico City, 1753," *Hispanic American Historical Review* 62:3 (November 1982), 569–602.

9. See Aguirre Beltrán, "The Integration of the Negro," 24–25, and Colin M. MacLachan and Jaime E. Rodríguez O., *The Forging of the Cosmic Race: A Reinterpretation of Colonial Mexico* (Berkeley: University of California Press, 1980), 217–22. For an opposing view of black assimilation into New Spain, see Colin Palmer, *Slaves of the White God: Blacks in Mexico, 1570–1650* (Cambridge: Harvard University Press, 1976), ch. 2.

10. The Labaquera quote appears in Charles E. Chapman, *A History of California: The Spanish Period* (New York: MacMillan, 1921), 203. See also Gerald E. Poyo and Gilberto M Hinojosa, eds., *Tejano Origins in Eighteenth-Century San Antonio* (Austin: University of Texas Press, 1991), 30–31, 33, and Aguirre Beltrán, "The Integration of the Negro," pp. 17–18. The fullest treatment of the black presence at the local level in northern New Spain is Vincent Mayer's account of the slaves and freedpeople in the silver-mining community of Parral in what is now the state of Chihuahua, Mexico. See Vincent Mayer, Jr., "The Black on New Spain's Northern Frontier: San José de Parral, 1631 to 1641," *Occasional Papers of the Center of Southwest Studies*, Paper No. 2 (November 1974), pp. 1–33.

11. See "Mestizaje: The First Census of Los Angeles, 1781," in David J. Weber, ed., *Foreigners in Their Native Land: Historical Roots of the Mexican Americans* (Albuquerque: University of New Mexico Press, 1973), 33–35; Forbes, "Black Pioneers," 235–42; Gloria E. Miranda, "Racial and Cultural Dimensions of *Gente de Razón* Status in Spanish and Mexican California," *Southern California Quarterly* 70:3 (Fall 1988), 265–78, and A. Odell Thurman, "The Negro in California before 1890," *Pacific Historian* 19:4 (Winter 1975), 324–25. Rudolph Lapp reminds us, however, that the first four blacks to land in California, three men and one woman, arrived with Sir Francis Drake when he reached the San Francisco Bay in 1579. See Lapp, *Blacks in Gold Rush California* (New Haven: Yale University Press, 1977), 2.

12. For a rich discussion of the role of blacks in the settlement of Los Angeles, see Antonio Ríos-Bustamante, "Los Angeles, Pueblo and Region, 1781–1850: Continuity and Adaptation on the North Mexican Periphery" (Ph.D. dissertation, UCLA, 1985), 56–59, 71–72, and Lonnie Bunch III, *Black Angelenos: The Afro-American in Los Angeles, 1850–1950* (Los Angeles: California Afro-American Museum, 1988), 10–12. Ríos-Bustamante describes the settlers' background in Sinola, including the reasons for the heavy concentration of mulattoes in the province. The list of original settlers can be found in Weber, *Foreigners in Their Native Land*, 34–35. See also Jones, *Los Paisanos*, 174.

13. Both Fray Antonio Olivares and Fray Juan Agustín Morfi are quoted in Jesús F. de La Teja, *San Antonio de Béxar: A Community on New Spain's Northern Frontier* (Albuquerque: University of New Mexico Press, 1995), 18, 24; see Chapter 2 for a discussion of the social integration of mulattoes and *lobos* (blacks and Indians) into eighteenth-century San Antonio society. See also Kenneth Mason, "Paternal Continuity: African Americans and Race Relations in San Antonio, Texas, 1867–1937" (Ph.D. dissertation, University of Texas, Austin, 1994), ch. 1, for background on blacks in eighteenth-century San Antonio. On Laredo's population, see Gilberto Miguel Hinojosa, *A Borderlands Town in Transition, Laredo, 1755–1870* (College Station: Texas A&M University Press, 1983), 17–18. See also Jones, *Los Paisanos*, 50–51, and Poyo and Hinojosa, *Tejano Origins in Eighteenth Century San Antonio*, 5, 33, 47.

14. The full account of Antonia Lusgardia Ernandes appears in Vicki Ruiz, "Gendered Histories: Interpreting Voice and Locating Power," in Clyde A. Milner II, ed., *A New Significance: Re-Envisioning the History of the American West* (New York: Oxford University Press, 1996), 98–99.

15. The first quote appears in Gutiérrez, *When Jesus Came*, p. 104, the second on page 103. Gutiérrez however cautions that the word *mulatto* in New Mexico did not always imply some African ancestry. For his discussion of race in colonial New Mexico, see pages 194–99. For the third quote, see Jack D. Forbes, ed., *The Indian in America's Past*, (Englewood Cliffs, N.J.: Prentice-Hall, 1964), 147. See also Jones, *Los Paisanos*, 132, 164. Unlike southern New Spain, or other frontier regions, some black and biracial New Mexico settlers identified with the Native Americans. From the mid-seventeenth

century mulattoes and *lobos* (black and Indian mixtures) joined the Pueblo, including, notably, the descendants of Mateo Naranjo, a free black servant who accompanied the Juan de Oñate expedition to New Mexico. See Fray Angélico Chávez, "Pohe-yemo's Representative and the Pueblo Revolt of 1680," *New Mexico Historical Review* 42:2 (April 1967), 85–126. See also J. Manuel Espinosa, *The Pueblo Indian Revolt of 1696 and the Franciscan Missions in New Mexico: Letters of the Missionaries and Related Documents* (Norman: University of Oklahoma Press, 1988), 11–13, 24–25. Stefanie Beniniato, however, challenges the assertion that the descendants of Naranjo were the leaders of the Pueblo revolt, but she recognizes their incorporation into the Indian community. See her "Pope, Pose-yemu, and Naranjo: A New Look at Leadership in the Pueblo Revolt of 1680," *New Mexico Historical Review* 65:4 (October 1990), 417–35.

16. See Dedra S. McDonald, "Slavery and Freedom in the Southwest: African Descendants in Spanish Colonial New Mexico" (unpublished paper in the author's possession), 1–34.

17. On Huizar, see de La Teja, *San Antonio,* p. 28. For background on both the official attitude toward, and the actual evolution of, racial miscegenation involving African slaves and their descendants in colonial Mexico, see Aguirre Beltrán, "The Integration of the Negro," 25–26; Magnus Morner, *Race Mixture in the History of Latin America* (Boston: Little, Brown, 1967), 30–31, 44–45; and Rout, *The African Experience in Spanish America,* ch. 5. For a discussion of this process in Spanish California, see Miranda, "Racial and Cultural Dimensions," 265–78.

18. See Forbes, "Black Pioneers," 238, 244; Barr, *Black Texans,* 3.

19. The Rodríguez quote appears in de La Teja, *San Antonio,* 27. See also Morner, *Race Mixture in the History of Latin America,* 56; Gutiérrez, *When Jesus Came,* 194–206. See Donald E. Chipman, *Spanish Texas, 1519–1821* (Austin: University of Texas Press, 1992), 188–89, and Miranda, "Racial and Cultural Dimensions of *Gente de Razón* Status," 266–67, 269–70, 272–76, for discussions of the importance of racial purity to Spanish-speaking settlers in northern New Spain.

20. For a history of the Mexican War of Independence, see Ramón Eduardo Ruíz, *Triumphs and Tragedy: A History of the Mexican People* (New York: W. W. Norton, 1992), ch. 8, and Michael C. Meyer and William L. Sherman, *The Course of Mexican History* (New York: Oxford University Press, 1995), ch. 16. On the image of Mexican freedom for English-speaking African Americans, see George Ruble Woolfolk, *The Free Negro in Texas, 1800–1860: A Study in Cultural Compromise* (Ann Arbor: University Microfilms International, 1976), 42, 78–79.

21. Woolfolk, *The Free Negro in Texas,* 22–23, 36–37, 153–55; the quotes appear on pages 22–23. For a discussion of free black English-speaking women in Texas during this period, see Ruthe Winegarten, *Black Texas Women: 150 Years of Trial and Triumph* (Austin: University of Texas Press, 1995), 2–4.

22. These black women are briefly described in Harold Schoen, "The Free Negro in the Republic of Texas: Origin of the Free Negro in the Republic," *Southwestern Historical Quarterly* 39:4 (April 1936), 301–02; and Winegarten, *Black Texas Women,* 8–9. On Goyens, see Diane Elizabeth Prince, "William Goyens, Free Negro on the Texas Frontier" (M.A. thesis, Stephen F. Austin State College, 1967), 1–2, 19–23, 29–30, and Victor H. Treat, "William Goyens: Free Negro Entrepreneur," in Alwyn Barr and Robert A. Calvert, eds., *Black Leaders: Texans for Their Times* (Austin: Texas State Historical Association, 1981), 20–47. Goyens's personal life reflected the ambiguous status of free blacks in Texas. He owned four slaves—three women and one man—but was himself kidnapped and enslaved in 1826 by Bele Yngles, who demanded one thousand pesos for his freedom. Goyens bought a black woman whom he exchanged for his own liberty. See Prince, pp. 24–26. For a discussion of other free blacks, see Paul Lack, *The Texas Revolutionary Experience: A Political and Social History, 1835–1836* (College Station: Texas A&M Press, 1992), 248.

23. Andrew Forest Muir, "The Free Negro in Jefferson and Orange Counties, Texas," *Journal of Negro History* 35:2 (April 1950), 183–205.

24. Quoted from Benjamin Lundy, *The Life, Travels and Opinions of Benjamin Lundy, Including His Journeys to Texas and Mexico* (Philadelphia: William D. Parrish, 1847), 48. See also Merton L. Dillon, *Benjamin Lundy and the Struggle for Negro Freedom* (Urbana: University of Illinois Press, 1966), 169, 176–83.

25. Quoted in Rosalie Schwartz, *Across the Rio to Freedom: U.S. Negroes in Mexico* (El Paso: Texas Western Press, 1975), 22.
26. See Randolph B. Campbell, *An Empire for Slavery: The Peculiar Institution in Texas, 1821–1865* (Baton Rouge: Louisiana State University Press, 1989), ch. 1 and 2, and Weber, *The Mexican Frontier,* ch. 9.
27. On black slavery in Texas before American settlement, see Chipman, *Spanish Texas,* 206–07.
28. Quoted in Campbell, *An Empire for Slavery,* 24. See also pages 18–23.
29. Ramón Músquiz and José María Viesca were two of the most prominent Mexican leaders who supported slavery in Texas. Músquiz, the chief politician at San Antonio, openly declared that Texas could not be developed "without the aid of the robust . . . negroes, and who, to their misfortune, suffer slavery." Governor Viesca of Coahuila and Texas agreed and appealed for an exemption of Texas from the 1829 emancipation decree of Mexican President Vicente Guerrero, despite its promulgation precisely because of the growth of slavery in the province. See Campbell, *An Empire for Slavery,* 25, and Weber, *The Mexican Frontier,* 176. Fred Robbins describes the activities of the Bowie brothers, John, Resin, and James, who were responsible for introducing fifteen hundred African slaves into the United States through smuggling activities in and around Galveston between 1818 and 1820. See Robbins, "The Origin and Development of the African Slave Trade in Galveston, Texas, and Surrounding Areas from 1816 to 1836," *East Texas Historical Journal* 9:2 (October 1971), 153–61.
30. Quoted in Campbell, *An Empire for Slavery,* 30. See also page 39.
31. Both quotes are from Lack, *The Texas Revolutionary Experience,* 244. For background on Santa Anna and the Texas independence campaign, see Ruiz, *Triumphs and Tragedy,* 205–11; Meyer and Sherman, *The Course of Mexican History,* 335–40; and Weber, *The Mexican Frontier,* 245–55. See also Paul Lack, "Slavery and the Texas Revolution," *Southwestern Historical Quarterly,* 89:2 (October 1985), 181–202. Randolph Campbell takes issue with Lack about the centrality of slavery in the Texas revolution; see his *An Empire for Slavery,* 48–49.
32. Quoted in Lack, *The Texas Revolutionary Experience,* 244.
33. See José Enrique de la Peña, *With Santa Anna in Texas: A Personal Narrative of the Revolution* (College Station: Texas A&M University Press, 1975), p. 175. See page 104 for Peña's account of black slaves who assisted the Mexican Army's crossing of the Colorado River. See also Lack, *The Texas Revolutionary Experience,* 245–46, and Schwartz, *Across the Rio to Freedom,* 24–26.
34. Quoted in Arnoldo De León, *They Called Them Greasers: Anglo Attitudes Toward Mexicans in Texas, 1821–1900* (Austin: University of Texas Press, 1983), 11. See also Lack, *The Texas Revolutionary Experience,* 241–43.
35. The Wharton quote appears in De León, *They Called Them Greasers,* 2. See also Billy D. Ledbetter, "White over Black in Texas: Racial Attitudes in the Ante-Bellum Period," *Phylon,* 34:4 (December 1973), 406.
36. Lack, *The Texas Revolutionary Experience,* 86.
37. Quoted in Woolfolk, *The Free Negro in Texas,* 54. The Austin quote appears in Lack, *The Texas Revolutionary Experience,* 14. See also Lack, "Slavery and the Texas Revolution," 188.
38. See Lack, *The Texas Revolutionary Experience,* 245–46. For a discussion of blacks fleeing to the Comanche, see J. W. Wilbarger, *Indian Depredations in Texas* (Austin: Stock Co., 1935), 217, and Kenneth W. Porter, "Negroes and Indians on the Texas Frontier, 1831–1876: A Study in Race and Culture," in Porter, ed., *The Negro on the American Frontier* (New York: Arno Press and the *New York Times,* 1971), 381–91.
39. See Harold Schoen, "The Free Negro in the Republic of Texas: The Free Negro and the Texas Revolution," *Southwestern Historical Quarterly* 40:1 (July 1936), 26–34; Prince, "William Goyens," 38–54; and Lack, *The Texas Revolutionary Experience,* 248.
40. See Harold Schoen, "The Free Negro in the Republic of Texas: Legal Status," *Southwestern Historical Quarterly* 40:3 (January 1937), 174–75, and Campbell, *An Empire for Slavery,* 46–47.
41. Quoted in Lack, *The Texas Revolutionary Experience,* 264.
42. For an account of Pico's life see Martin Cole and Henry Welcome, eds., *Don Pío Pico's Historical Narrative* (Glendale, Calif.: Arthur H. Clark Co., 1973), 12–15, 19–21.

43. Ibid., 42–53; Pico's description of Victoria appears on page 39. See also Weber, *The Mexican Frontier,* 243.
44. Richard H. Dana, *Two Years before the Mast* (New York: Macmillan, 1911), 72–73. See also Forbes, *Afro-Americans in the Far West,* 17.
45. Thurman, "The Negro in California before 1890," 325–26; Lapp, *Blacks in Gold Rush California,* 3–4.
46. Light moved to San Diego in the early 1840s but was last reported in the California gold country in the 1850s. See David J. Weber, "A Black American in Mexican San Diego: Two Recently Recovered Documents," *Journal of San Diego History* 20:2 (Spring 1974), 29–32; Lapp, *Blacks in Gold Rush California,* 4.
47. See Mary Lee Spence and Donald Jackson, eds., *The Expeditions of John Charles Frémont* (Urbana: University of Illinois Press, 1973), vol. 2, pp. xxv, 63. See also W. Sherman Savage, "The Influence of Alexander Liedesdorff on the History of California," *Journal of Negro History* 38:3 (July 1953), 322–32, and Lapp, *Blacks in Gold Rush California,* 9–11.
48. The Sutter quote appears in Albert Hurtado, *Indian Survival on the California Frontier* (New Haven: Yale University Press, 1988), 61.
49. Quoted in Hiram M. Chittenden, *The American Fur Trade of the Far West* (Stanford: Academic Reprints, 1954), vol. 1, p. 263.
50. For background on the fur trade in the West, see LeRoy R. Hafen, "A Brief History of the Fur Trade of the Far West," in Hafen, ed., *The Mountain Men and the Fur Trade of the Far West* (Glendale, Calif.: Arthur H. Clark Co., 1965), 21–72, and Robert V. Hine, *The American West: An Interpretive History,* (Boston: Little, Brown, 1973), 44–49. William H. Goetzmann offers an analysis of the Mountain Man "mystique" in *Exploration and Empire: The Explorer and the Scientist in the Winning of the American West* (New York: Alfred A. Knopf, 1966), 106–09.
51. See Reuben Thwaites, ed., *Original Journals of the Lewis and Clark Expedition* (New York: Antiquarian Press, 1959), vol. 1, p. 53; vol. 3, pp. 246–47; vol. 5, pp. 67, 72, 75. Robert B. Betts, *In Search of York: The Slave Who Went to the Pacific with Lewis and Clark* (Boulder: Colorado Associated University Press, 1985) provides the best book-length account of York. For York's impact on Native Americans, see James P. Ronda, *Lewis and Clark among the Indians* (Lincoln: University of Nebraska Press, 1984), 58–59, 64.
52. See John Charles Frémont, "A Report of the Exploring Expedition to Oregon and North California in the Years 1843–44," U.S. 28th Congress, 2d Session, *House Document 166,* December 2, 1844–March 3, 1845, 238–40, and Spence and Jackson, eds., *The Expeditions of John Charles Frémont,* vol. 1, pp. 427–28, 561; vol. 2, p. 330. On April 23, 1861, shortly after the outbreak of the Civil War, Dodson offered the services of "three hundred reliable colored free citizens" to the federal government in defense of Washington, D.C. See Herbert Aptheker, ed., *A Documentary History of the Negro People in the United States* (New York: Citadel Press, 1951), 459.
53. On Rose, see Willis Blenkinsop, "Edward Rose," in Hafen, ed., *The Mountain Men and the Fur Trade* (Glendale, Calif., Arthur H. Clark Co., 1972), vol. 9, pp. 338–41; Rose is listed as a member of the overland Astorians. See Kenneth W. Porter, "Roll of Overland Astorians," *Oregon Historical Quarterly* 34 (June 1933), 111.
54. See James P. Ronda, *Astoria and Empire* (Lincoln: University of Nebraska Press, 1990), 172–74.
55. Quoted in John C. Ewers, ed., *The Adventures of Zenas Leonard, Fur Trapper* (Norman: University of Oklahoma Press, 1959), 51–52.
56. See Thomas D. Bonner, ed., *Life and Adventures of James Beckwourth* (Lincoln: University of Nebraska Press, 1972), 98–99, 122–41; Delmont R. Oswald, "James P. Beckwourth," in LeRoy Hafen, ed., *The Mountain Men and the Fur Trade of the Far West* (Glendale, Calif.: Arthur H. Clark Co., 1968), vol. 6, pp. 37–60; and LeRoy R. Hafen, "The Last Years of James P. Beckwourth," *Colorado Magazine* 5:4 (August 1928), 134–39.
57. Smith, Beckwourth, and Walkara, the Ute Indian leader who led the band of thieves, made off in 1840 with twelve hundred horses from the Mission San Luis Obispo that they sold to Indians and other trappers. See Weber, *The Mexican Frontier,* 101–02; Bonner, *Life and Adventures,* 456–65; and Oswald, "James P. Beckwourth," 50–55.
58. See Bonner, *Life and Adventures,* 518–520; Hafen, "The Last Years of James P. Beck-

wourth," 138–39; and Oswald, "James P. Beckwourth," 43–46. Beckwourth's testimony on the Sand Creek Massacre appeared in "Report of the Secretary of War," 39th Congress, 2d Session, *Senate Executive Document No. 26*, 68–76. For a brief discussion of Beckwourth's California years, see Lapp, *Blacks in Gold Rush California*, 35.

2: Slavery in the Antebellum West, 1835–65

1. The "natural limits" of slavery debate has a long history and historiography. See, for example, Charles W. Ramsdell, "The Natural Limits of Slavery Expansion," *Mississippi Valley Historical Review* 16:2 (September 1929), 151–71; and Charles Desmond Hart, "The Natural Limits of Slavery Expansion: Kansas-Nebraska, 1854," *Kansas Historical Quarterly* 34:1 (Spring 1968), 32–50. Eugene Berwanger's *The Frontier against Slavery: Western Anti-Negro Prejudice and the Slavery Extension Controversy* (Urbana: University of Illinois Press, 1967) remains the starting point for any discussion of the race-slavery-politics nexus in the antebellum West, but see also Robert W. Johannsen, *Frontier Politics on the Eve of the Civil War* (Seattle: University of Washington Press, 1955) and James A. Rawley, *Race and Politics: "Bleeding Kansas" and the Coming of the Civil War* (Philadelphia: J. B. Lippincott, 1969) for localized studies.
2. See Randolph Campbell, *An Empire for Slavery: The Peculiar Institution in Texas, 1821–1865* (Baton Rouge: Louisiana State University Press, 1989), 55–56, 251. Campbell's monograph is the definitive study of slavery in Texas.
3. To get a sense of the extent of slavery in nominally free states and territories, see Rawley, *Race and Politics*, 87; James R. Harvey, "Negroes in Colorado" (M.A. thesis, University of Denver, 1941), 15–17; Quintard Taylor, "Slaves and Free Men: Blacks in the Oregon Country, 1840–1860," *Oregon Historical Quarterly* 83:2 (Summer 1982), 165–69; James D. Bish, "The Black Experience in Selected Nebraska Counties, 1854–1920" (M.A. thesis, University of Nebraska at Omaha, 1989), 5–7, 11, 19; Alvin R. Sunseri, "A Note on Slavery and the Black Man in New Mexico," *Negro History Bulletin*, 38:1 (October–November 1975), 58–59; Albert S. Broussard, "Slavery in California Revisited: The Fate of a Kentucky Slave in Gold Rush California," *Pacific Historian* 29:1 (Spring 1985), 17–21.
4. The quotes are from Campbell, *An Empire for Slavery*, 4, 213. See also James Smallwood, "Blacks in Antebellum Texas: A Reappraisal," *Red River Valley Historical Review* 2:4 (Winter 1975), 443–66.
5. Campbell, *An Empire for Slavery*, 56–58.
6. Ibid., 118–23.
7. For a background on the southern roots of Texas cattle ranching, see Forrest McDonald and Grady McWhiney, "The Antebellum Southern Herdsman: A Reinterpretation," *Journal of Southern History* 41:2 (May 1975), 147–66, and Terry G. Jordan, *Trails to Texas: Southern Roots of Western Cattle Ranching* (Lincoln: University of Nebraska Press, 1981), ch. 1. For a discussion of African participation in seventeenth-century South Carolina cattle raising, see Peter H. Wood, *Black Majority: Negroes in Colonial South Carolina from 1670 through the Stono Rebellion* (New York: W. W. Norton, 1974), 28–32, and Terry G. Jordan, *North American Cattle-Ranching Frontiers* (Albuquerque: University of New Mexico Press, 1993), 112–13, 117, 177–89. Indigenous African cattle herding is described in Philip D. Curtin, *Economic Change in Precolonial Africa: Senegambia in the Era of the Slave Trade* (Madison: University of Wisconsin Press, 1975), 18–21, 218–23. Black participation in the cattle ranching in New Spain is discussed in Vincent Mayer, Jr., "The Black on New Spain's Northern Frontier: San José de Parral, 1631 to 1641," *Occasional Papers of the Center of Southwest Studies*, Paper No. 2 (November 1974), pp. 2–3, and Jordan, *North American Cattle-Ranching Frontiers*, 92–93. Richard Slatta in his comparative study of cattle ranching in the Americas found extensive black slave involvement in Venezuela and Argentina as well as Mexico. See Slatta, *Cowboys of the Americas* (New Haven: Yale University Press, 1990), 95.
8. See Smallwood, "Blacks in Antebellum Texas," 448–49. See also Philip Durham and Everett L. Jones, *The Negro Cowboys* (New York: Dodd, Mead, 1965), 15–19; Alwyn Barr, *Black Texans: A History of Negroes in Texas, 1528–1971* (Austin: Jenkins Publishing Co., 1973), 19–20; Tamara Miner Haygood, "Use and Distribution of Slave Labor in Harris

County, Texas, 1836–60," in Howard Beeth and Cary D. Wintz, eds., *Black Dixie: Afro-Texan History and Culture in Houston* (College Station: Texas A&M University Press, 1992), 40; and Campbell, *An Empire for Slavery*, 124.

9. Randolph B. Campbell and Donald Pickens, "'My Dear Husband': A Texas Slave's Love Letter, 1862," *Journal of Negro History*, 65:4 (Fall 1980), 363. See also Smallwood, "Blacks in Antebellum Texas," 452, and Campbell, *An Empire for Slavery*, 159.

10. See Campbell, *An Empire for Slavery*, 193–96.

11. Kenneth W. Porter, "Negroes and Indians on the Texas Frontier, 1831–1876: A Study in Race and Culture," in Porter, ed., *The Negro on the American Frontier* (New York: Arno Press and the *New York Times*, 1971), 392–93. See also Campbell, *An Empire for Slavery*, 247. For a discussion of a group of blacks captured by the Comanche in north-central Texas in 1864, see Barbara A. Neal Ledbetter, *Fort Belknap Frontier Saga: Indians, Negroes and Anglo-Americans on the Texas Frontier* (Burnet, Texas: Eakin Press, 1982), 114–18, 135–37.

12. Quoted in Susan Jackson, "Slavery in Houston: The 1850s," *Houston Review* 2:2 (1980), 81. See also Paul D. Lack, "Urban Slavery in the Southwest," *Red River Valley Historical Review* 4:2 (Spring 1981), 14, and Barr, *Black Texans*, 24–25.

13. See Lack, "Slavery and Vigilantism in Austin, Texas, 1840–1860," *Southwestern Historical Quarterly* 85:1 (July 1981), 2, 12, and "Urban Slavery in the Southwest," 9, 16. See also Haygood, "Use and Distribution of Slave Labor," 35–38; Barr, *Black Texans*, 25; Campbell, *An Empire for Slavery*, 125–26.

14. Quoted in George P. Rawick, ed., *The American Slave: A Composite Autobiography* vol. 4, *The Texas Narratives* (Westport, Conn.: Greenwood Publishing Co., 1972), part 2, p. 132. See also Smallwood, "Blacks in Antebellum Texas," 460.

15. This remarkable Seminole-black colony lasted until 1861, when the Indians returned to the United States to fight with the Confederacy while the blacks remained in Mexico. Kenneth W. Porter provides the most detailed history of the Seminole-black colony in "The Seminole in Mexico," in *The Negro on the American Frontier*, 424–59. See also Kevin Mulroy, *Freedom on the Border: The Seminole Maroons in Florida, the Indian Territory, Coahuila, and Texas* (Lubbock: Texas Tech University Press, 1993), 54–60, and Susan A. Miller, "Wild Cat and the Origins of the Seminole Migration to Mexico," (M.A. thesis, University of Oklahoma, 1988), 151–76. For a discussion of the raid on the Seminole-black colony, see Ronnie C. Tyler, "The Callahan Expedition of 1855: Indians or Negroes?," *Southwestern Historical Quarterly* 70:4 (April 1967), 574–85. For a brief glimpse of the lives of fugitive slaves in Mexico, see Frederick Law Olmsted, *A Journey through Texas* (New York: Mason Brothers, 1859), 323–27, while Rosalie Schwartz, *Across the Rio to Freedom: U.S. Negroes in Mexico* (El Paso: Texas Western Press, 1975) discusses numerous pre–Civil War efforts of slaves to gain freedom south of the Rio Grande.

16. See Lack, "Urban Slavery in the Southwest," 21 and "Slavery and Vigilantism in Austin," 5–6, 9; Barr, *Black Texans*, 32–33; Campbell, *An Empire for Slavery*, 218–19. Campbell, however, absolved the Germans, another ethnic group long suspected of harboring abolitionist views. Although a few German immigrants, such as San Antonio newspaper editor Adolph Douai, publicly questioned slavery and some actually harbored fugitives, the vast majority of Texas's largest non-Anglo population embraced "the proslavery consensus." That Texas Germans owned few slaves could be attributed, according to Campbell, to their relative poverty rather than their philosophical opposition to the institution. See pages 215–17.

17. The Manning quote appears in Leon Litwack, *Been in the Storm So Long: The Aftermath of Slavery* (New York: Vintage Books, 1979), 33. See also Ira Berlin, ed., *The Black Military Experience* (New York: Cambridge University Press, 1982), 12, 15. Florida with 1,044 recruits was the Confederate state with the next lowest number of black enlistees in the Union army. The largest number, 24,052, came from Louisiana. See also James Marten, "Slaves and Rebels: The Peculiar Institution in Texas, 1861–1865," *East Texas Historical Journal* 28:1 (1990), 29–36.

18. Quoted in Barr, *Black Texans*, 37. See also Rawick, *The American Slave*, vol. 4, *The Texas Narratives*, part 2, pp. 133, 134, for the Haywood quotes.

19. See Theda Perdue, *Slavery and the Evolution of Cherokee Society, 1540–1866* (Knoxville: University of Tennessee Press, 1979), 47–49. Kenneth W. Porter has written extensively

on the black-Seminole relationship. See his "Negroes and the Seminole War, 1817–1818," "Negroes and the Seminole War, 1835–1842," and "Florida Slaves and Free Negroes in the Seminole War, 1835–1842," all in Porter, *The Negro on the American Frontier*, 205–337. See also Daniel F. Littlefield, Jr., *Africans and Creeks: From the Colonial Period to the Civil War* (Westport, Conn.: Greenwood Press, 1979), 13–15, and R. Halliburton, Jr., *Red over Black: Black Slavery among the Cherokee Indians* (Westport, Conn., Greenwood Press, 1977), 142.

20. See William G. McLoughlin, "Red Indians, Black Slavery and White Racism: America's Slaveholding Indians," *American Quarterly*, 26:4 (October 1974), 368; Perdue, *Slavery*, 36, 42; and Littlefield, *Africans and Creeks*, 21–22.

21. Although Indian slaveholders were drawn from the ranks of all social classes and backgrounds, it was often the descendants of the white traders or Indian warriors who had acquired or been awarded slaves by their British, French, or American allies who led in promoting plantation agriculture. Such slaveholders emerged as an economic and political elite in each of the nations except the Seminole. See Perdue, *Slavery*, 68–69, and Littlefield, *Africans and Creeks*, 27–28, 38. See also Daniel Littlefield, *The Chickasaw Freedmen: A People without a Country* (Westport, Conn.: Greenwood Press, 1980), 10–11. For census figures, see Halliburton, *Red over Black*, 27.

22. See William G. McLoughlin, *After the Trail of Tears: The Cherokees' Struggle for Sovereignty, 1839–1880* (Chapel Hill: University of North Carolina Press, 1993), 126–27; Grant Foreman, *Indian Removal: The Emigration of the Five Civilized Tribes of Indians* (Norman: University of Oklahoma Press, 1972), 111; Halliburton, *Red over Black*, 33–37, 57; Littlefield, *Africans and Creeks*, 84; and Janet Halliburton, "Black Slavery in the Creek Nation," *Chronicles of Oklahoma* 56:3 (Fall 1978), 303–06.

23. Not all the slaves moved from the East to Indian Territory. Some were confiscated by Georgians who took over Cherokee and Creek plantations and farms, while others made their escape during the preparation for the removal or en route to the West. According to Daniel Littlefield, the Creek lost more than two thirds of their slaves during removal. See Littlefield, *Africans and Creeks*, 116, and Halliburton, *Red over Black*, 58, 61. For background on the removal, see Angie Debo, *A History of the Indians of the United States* (Norman: University of Oklahoma Press, 1979), ch. 7; Foreman, *Indian Removal*, 44–104, 152–89, 206–26, 279–312, 342–70; and Perdue, *Slavery*, 62–69.

24. Quoted in Josiah Gregg, *Commerce of the Prairies*, ed. Max L. Morehead (Norman: University of Oklahoma Press, 1954), 400–01. See also Perdue, *Slavery and the Evolution of Cherokee Society*, 71–72, Halliburton, *Red over Black*, 54–55, Littlefield, *Africans and Creeks*, 111–16; and Foreman, *Indian Removal*, 142, 225.

25. The Thompson quotation appears in Mulroy, *Freedom on the Border*, 20–21. See also Miller, "Wild Cat," 19, 22–23, 85–87.

26. See Porter, "The Negro Abraham," in Porter, *The Negro on the American Frontier*, 295–337, and "John Caesar: Seminole Negro Partisan," ibid., 339–56. See also Foreman, *Indian Removal*, 324–26, 330, 347–49, 359, and Daniel F. Littlefield, Jr., and Mary Ann Littlefield, "The Beams Family: Free Blacks in Indian Territory," *Journal of Negro History* 61:1 (January 1976), 18. For a discussion of the Cherokee slaves who fled to the Seminole Nation, see Perdue, *Slavery and the Evolution of Cherokee Society*, 81–82.

27. See Littlefield, *Africans and Creeks*, 138, and McLoughlin, *After the Trail of Tears*, 129–31.

28. Quoted in Perdue, *Slavery*, 107. The Washington Irving visit is described on pages 106–07. For a detailed discussion of John Cowaya, see Miller, "Wild Cat," 80–83, 151, 161, 163.

29. Littlefield, *Africans and Creeks*, 46, 139, 141, and *The Chickasaw Freedmen*, 25.

30. See Henry Bibb, "Narrative of the Life and Adventures of Henry Bibb, an American Slave," in Gilbert Osofsky, ed., *Puttin' on Ole Massa* (New York: Harper and Row, 1969), 139–44. See also Littlefield, *The Chickasaw Freedmen*, 11, and Perdue, *Slavery*, 80–81.

31. The quotes appear in Halliburton, *Red over Black*, 62, 83.

32. See Daniel F. Littlefield, Jr., and Lonnie E. Underhill, "Slave 'Revolt' in the Cherokee Nation, 1842," *American Indian Quarterly* 3:2 (Summer 1977), 121–23, 126–27, and Theda Perdue, "Cherokee Planters, Black Slaves and African Colonization," *Chronicles of Oklahoma* 60:3 (Fall 1982), 327.

33. I have excluded from the count the approximately thousand blacks resident in the

Seminole Nation because, according to the census of 1860, the Seminole "hold no slaves." See Bureau of the Census, *Eighth Census of the U.S., 1860* (Washington, D.C.: Government Printing Office, 1864), xv, and Michael F. Doran, "Population Statistics of Nineteenth Century Indian Territory," *Chronicles of Oklahoma* 53:4 (Winter 1975), 501–02.

34. Chaney McNair's quote appears in George P. Rawick, ed., *The American Slave*, Supplement, Series 1, *The Oklahoma Narratives* (Westport, Conn.: Greenwood Press, 1979), vol. XII, pp. 224, 225. For background on slave recollections of the Civil War, see John C. Neilson, "Indian Masters, Black Slaves: An Oral History of the Civil War in Indian Territory," *Panhandle-Plains Historical Review* 65 (1992), 42–54. The authorization to recruit federal troops regardless of their color appeared in correspondence from Brigadier General James G. Blunt, commander of the department of Kansas, to Colonel William Weer, commander of the Indian Expedition, July 19, 1862. See *The War of the Rebellion: A Compilation of the Official Records of the Union and Confederate Armies* (Washington, D.C: Government Printing Office, 1900), series I, vol. 13, pp. 487–89. See also Lary C. Rampp and Donald L. Rampp, *The Civil War in the Indian Territory* (Austin: Presidial Press, 1975), 6–12, 20; W. Craig Gaines, *The Confederate Cherokees: John Drew's Regiment of Mounted Rifles* (Baton Rouge: Louisiana State University Press, 1989), 55–57, Littlefield, *Africans and Creeks*, 238–39; and Perdue, *Slavery and the Evolution of Cherokee Society*, 138–39.

35. The Ward quote appears in Rawick, ed., *The American Slave*, Supplement Series 1, vol. 7, p. 362. On the transfer of slaves to Texas and the Chickasaw and Choctaw nations, see Daniel Littlefield, *The Cherokee Freedmen: From Emancipation to American Citizenship* (Westport, Conn.: Greenwood Press, 1978), 15, and Perdue, *Slavery*, 138–40.

36. Flake's descendants are scattered throughout Utah and remain practicing Mormons. See Leonard J. Arrington and Davis Bitton, *The Mormon Experience: A History of the Latter-day Saints* (Urbana: University of Illinois Press, 1992), 100–01; Eugene E. Campbell, *Establishing Zion: The Mormon Church in the American West, 1847–1869* (Salt Lake City: Signature Books, 1988), 5–10; James B. Christensen, "Negro Slavery in Utah Territory," *Phylon* 18:3 (Third Quarter 1957), 298, 304; and Jack Beller, "Negro Slaves in Utah," *Utah Historical Quarterly* 2:4 (October 1929), 122–26.

37. See Newell G. Bringhurst, *Saints, Slaves, and Blacks: The Changing Place of Black People within Mormonism* (Westport, Conn.: Greenwood Press, 1981), 4–11, 20–21, 35–38, 41, 45, 87–95, for a discussion of the nexus of race, color, and religion among the Mormons before 1847. On the persecution of Mormons, see Arrington and Bitton, *The Mormon Experience*, 44–64. The growth of Mormonism in the slaveholding states is described in Leonard J. Arrington, "Mormon Beginnings in the American South," *Task Papers in LDS History*, No. 9 (Salt Lake City: Historical Department of the Church of Jesus Christ of Latter-day Saints, 1976), 2–6. See also Bringhurst, *Saints, Slaves and Blacks*, 41, 45, 94–95.

38. Ronald Coleman, "A History of Blacks in Utah, 1825–1910" (Ph.D. dissertation, University of Utah, 1980), 31–34.

39. Ibid., 35–36. Leonard Arrington counted 220 Mississippi Saints and their 40 black slaves in the Salt Lake Valley by 1848. Most of the "black Saints" had little choice in either their conversion or their migration to the Great Basin Zion. However one slave, Samuel W. Chambers, proved the exception. Chambers was born in 1831 in western Alabama and three years later was moved by his master to Noxubee County in eastern Mississippi. In 1844, at the age of thirteen, Chambers was converted to Mormonism, and despite his isolation and illiteracy, he kept informed of the affairs of the Mormons. After his emancipation in 1865 he sharecropped in Mississippi until he could earn enough money to migrate with his family to Utah. He arrived in Salt Lake City in 1870, and for the next fifty-nine years he was a highly regarded member of the Salt Lake City Mormon community. See Arrington, "Mormon Beginnings in the American South," 7, 11, and Arrington and Bitton, *The Mormon Experience,* 101–05. For a discussion of Biddy Mason's ordeal across the plains and Rockies to the Salt Lake Valley, see Dolores Hayden, "Biddy Mason's Los Angeles, 1851–1891," *California History* 68:3 (Fall 1989), 88.

40. Coleman, "A History of Blacks in Utah," 39–40.

41. Ibid., 40–41, 45–47.
42. See Bringhurst, *Saints, Slaves, and Blacks,* 68–69, and Arrington, "Mormon Beginnings in the American South, 15. Much of the text of the act appears in Coleman, "A History of Blacks in Utah," 50.
43. Coleman, "A History of Blacks in Utah," 50; Bringhurst, *Saints, Slaves, and Blacks,* 70.
44. For the Young quote, see the *Deseret News,* October 14, 1863, 4. Bankhead's comments appeared in Charles W. Nibley, *Reminiscences: 1849–1931* (Salt Lake City: Utah Family Society, 1934), 35–36. See also Coleman, "A History of Blacks in Utah," 55.
45. This girl was rescued by General James Shields, the U.S. military commander in the area who paid the debt and reunited her with her family. See Alvin R. Sunseri, *Seeds of Discord: New Mexico in the Aftermath of the American Conquest, 1846–1861* (Chicago: Nelson Hall, 1979), 39–41. For a discussion of the Spanish colonial origins of enslavement of Indians in New Mexico, see Ramón A. Gutiérrez, *When Jesus Came, the Corn Mothers Went Away: Marriage, Sexuality, and Power in New Mexico, 1500–1846* (Stanford: Stanford University Press, 1991), 104–05, 112–13, 152–55, 180–90.
46. The Calhoun quote appears in Sunseri, *Seeds of Discord,* 60. The best discussion of enslaved Native Americans in New Mexico can be found in James F. Brooks, "The Old Way Gave to Many a Pleasurable Excitement: Customary Justice and State Power in New Mexico, 1780–1880" (unpublished paper in author's possession), 1–38.
47. Apparently since the 1840s comanchero had brought to New Mexico runaway slaves they found on the plains. See Sunseri, *Seeds of Discord,* 59–63, and Brooks, "The Old Way," 20.
48. For a discussion of the difficulty of eliminating slavery and peonage in New Mexico, see Brooks, "The Old Way," 22–27, and Sunseri, *Seeds of Discord,* 42.
49. On Allen's claim, see Johannsen, *Frontier Politics,* 48–49. The Southworth and Taylor narratives are found in George P. Rawick, ed., *The American Slave: A Composite Autobiography,* supplement series 1, *Arkansas, Colorado, Minnesota, Missouri and Oregon and Washington Narratives* (Westport, Conn.: Greenwood Press, 1977), vol. 2, pp. 273–78. See also Fred Lockley, "Some Documentary Records of Slavery in Oregon," *Oregon Historical Quarterly,* 17:2 (June 1916), 107–15. For additional background on black slavery in Oregon, see Elizabeth McLagan, *A Peculiar Paradise: A History of Blacks in Oregon, 1788–1940* (Portland: Georgian Press, 1980), ch. 3, and Taylor, "Slaves and Free Men," 153–70.
50. See Fred Lockley, "The Case of Robin Holmes vs. Nathaniel Ford," *Oregon Historical Quarterly,* 23:2 (June 1922), 111–37; McLagan, *A Peculiar Paradise,* 33–36; and Taylor, "Slaves and Free Men," 167–68.
51. Quoted in Berwanger, *The Frontier against Slavery,* 82. Williams provides a detailed argument against slavery in Oregon in his "Free State Letter," originally published in the *Oregon Statesman,* July 28, 1867, and reprinted in the *Oregon Historical Review* 9:3 (September 1908), 254–73.
52. The estimate is from Rudolph Lapp, *Blacks in Gold Rush California* (New Haven: Yale University Press, 1977), 65. Givens is quoted on page 131.
53. Ibid., 120–21.
54. The Lester quote appears in the *Pennsylvania Freeman,* December 5, 1850, p. 2. The quote of the German observer is in Ruth Frye Ax, ed., *Bound for Sacramento* (Claremont, Calif.: Saunders Studio Press, 1938), 144. See also Lapp, *Blacks in Gold Rush California,* 137–39, 155–56.
55. On the rescue of the Berkeley slaves, see Marguerite Carleton Hussey, "The History of the Napoleon Byrne Family" (unpublished manuscript in the Byrne Family Papers), 35, Bancroft Library, University of California, Berkeley. On other abolitionist activity, see Lapp, *Blacks in Gold Rush California,* 119–21, 136–37.
56. See Hayden, "Biddy Mason's Los Angeles," 89–91, the quote appears on page 90. For background on the Perkins and Lee cases, see Ray R. Albin, "The Perkins Case: The Ordeal of Three Slaves in Gold Rush California," *California History* 67:4 (December 1988), 215–27, and William E. Franklin, "The Archy Case: The California Supreme Court Refuses to Free a Slave," *Pacific Historical Review* 32:2 (May 1963), 137–54.
57. Quoted in Hayden, "Biddy Mason," 91.

3: Freedom in the Antebellum West, 1835–65

1. See *Minutes and Proceedings of the Third Annual Convention For the Improvement of the Free People of Color in the United States* (New York: Published by Order of the Convention, 1833) in Howard Holman Bell, *Minutes of the Proceedings of the National Negro Conventions, 1830–64* (New York: Arno Press and the *New York Times,* 1969), 27–28. For a discussion of Mexican Texas as one destination considered by the convention, see Rosalie Schwartz, *Across the Rio to Freedom: U.S. Negroes in Mexico* (El Paso: Texas Western Press, 1975), 20–21.
2. The fullest discussion of "race" and California politics can be found in David Alan Johnson, *Founding the Far West: California, Oregon, and Nevada, 1840–1890* (Berkeley: University of California Press, 1992), 121–22, 125–27. For a survey of the various legislative measures enacted against free blacks throughout the West, see Eugene H. Berwanger, *The Frontier against Slavery: Western Anti-Negro Prejudice and the Slavery Extension Controversy* (Chicago: University of Illinois Press, 1967), 72, 76–77, 118–21; Leon Litwack, *North of Slavery: The Negro in the Free States, 1790–1860* (Chicago: University of Chicago Press, 1961), 70–71, 93; Malcolm Edwards, "The War of Complexional Distinction: Blacks in Gold Rush California and British Columbia," *California Historical Quarterly* 56:1 (Spring 1977), 36; James A Rawley, *Race and Politics: "Bleeding Kansas" and the Coming of the Civil War* (Philadelphia: J. B. Lippincott, 1969), pp. 95–96; K. Keith Richard, "Unwelcome Settlers: Black and Mulatto Oregon Pioneers" *Oregon Historical Quarterly* 84:1(Spring 1983), part 1, pp. 35–36. On Texas, see Harold Schoen, "The Free Negro in the Republic of Texas: Legal Status," *Southwestern Historical Quarterly* 40:3 (January 1937), 169–99.
3. Quoted in John Minto, "Reminiscences of Experiences on the Oregon Trail in 1844," *Oregon Historical Quarterly* 2:3 (September 1901), 212.
4. See Abner H. Francis to Frederick Douglass, October 1851, in C. Peter Ripley, *The Black Abolitionist Papers,* vol. 4, *The United States, 1847–1858* (Chapel Hill: University of North Carolina Press, 1991), 102–06.
5. Newby's letter to Douglass appears in ibid., 235. See also Rudolph Lapp, *Blacks in Gold Rush California* (New Haven: Yale University Press, 1977), 49, Lapp's study represents by far the most comprehensive survey of African Americans in antebellum California.
6. The Margaret Frink quote comes from her *Adventures of a Party of California Gold Seekers* (Oakland: privately printed, 1897), p. 92. Although most African American emigrants to California came overland, some slaves and free people also reached the state by ship. Anne Fuller, for example, worked as a stewardess on a passenger ship that sailed around Cape Horn to reach San Francisco. Two disparate groups were more likely to sail to California: black East Coast residents, usually New Englanders, New Yorkers, and Philadelphians, who embarked from their respective seaports, and the slaves of wealthy southern planters, who sailed usually from New Orleans. See Albert Broussard, "The New Racial Frontier: San Francisco's Black Community: 1900–1940" (Ph.D. dissertation, Duke University, 1977), 3, and Lapp, *Blacks in Gold Rush California,* 25, 29.
7. *New Bedford Mercury,* December 21, 1848, p.4
8. See *Frederick Douglass' Paper,* April 1, 1852, p. 3, and P. Brown to Alley Brown, December 1851, California-Oregon Collection, Missouri Historical Society, St. Louis, Missouri.
9. U.S. Census, *Seventh Census of the United States, 1850* (Washington, D.C.: Robert Armstrong, Public Printer, 1853), xxxiii; U.S. Bureau of the Census, *Eighth Census of the United States, 1860, Population* (Washington, D.C.: Government Printing Office, 1864), 33.
10. See J. S. Holliday, *The World Rushed In: The California Gold Rush Experience* (New York: Simon and Schuster, 1981), 41; Lapp, *Blacks in Gold Rush California,* 50–51.
11. Lapp, *Blacks in Gold Rush California* 52–53, 58, 61. Black and integrated mining groups, however, did occasionally encounter white resistance and intimidation, as at Hawkins Bar on the Tuolumne River in 1849, when armed southerners drove out a group of black and white New England miners, and in 1855, when white miners in Amador County drove out black miners. See Lapp, *Blacks in Gold Rush California,* 56, 59–60.

12. J. D. Borthwick, *Three Years in California* (Oakland: Biobooks, 1948), 134–35.
13. See Lynn M. Hudson, "A New Look, or 'I'm Not Mammy to Everybody in California': Mary Ellen Pleasant, a Black Entrepreneur," *Journal of the West* 32:3 (July 1993), 36; Douglas Daniels, *Pioneer Urbanites: A Social and Cultural History of Black San Francisco* (Philadelphia: Temple University Press, 1980), 20; and Lapp, *Blacks in Gold Rush California*, 96–99.
14. The report on black businesses appeared in the *Daily Alta Californian*, April 7, 1854, p. 2. See also Mifflin W. Gibbs, *Shadow and Light: An Autobiography* (New York: Arno Press and the *New York Times*, 1968), 44–4, and *Proceedings of the First State Convention of the Colored Citizens of the State of California* (Sacramento: Democratic State Journal Printer, 1855), 18.
15. See Lapp, *Blacks in Gold Rush California*, 103–04.
16. For a discussion of the crucial religious, cultural, and political role of antebellum African American churches in San Francisco, see Philip M. Montesano, "San Francisco Black Churches in the Early 1860s: Political Pressure Group," *California Historical Quarterly* 52:2 (Summer 1973), 145–52; Larry George Murphy, "Equality before the Law: The Struggle of Nineteenth Century Black Californians for Social and Political Justice," (Ph.D. dissertation, University of California at Berkeley, 1973), 3; and Lapp, *Blacks in Gold Rush California*, 160–61, 219, 232.
17. See *Proceedings of the First State Convention*, 60. William H. Newby, in an 1854 letter to Frederick Douglass, described in considerable detail the activities of the San Francisco Athenaeum Institute. See Ripley, *The Black Abolitionist Papers*, vol. 4, pp. 234–36.
18. See Lapp, *Blacks in Gold Rush California*, 108–11. For a discussion of white attitudes toward black San Franciscans, see Roger W. Lotchin, *San Francisco, 1846–1856: From Hamlet to City* (New York: Oxford University Press, 1974), 129–33.
19. Lapp, *Blacks in Gold Rush California*, 111–17, 163–65.
20. The Owens's only son, Charles, married Ellen, Biddy Mason's eldest daughter, a few weeks after the Mason trial. See Dolores Hayden, "Biddy Mason's Los Angeles, 1856–1891," *California History* 68:3 (Fall 1989), 89, 95. See also Lapp, *Blacks in Gold Rush California*, 118–19, and Lonnie Bunch III, *Black Angelenos: The Afro-American in Los Angeles, 1850–1950* (Los Angeles: California Afro-American Museum, 1988), 14.
21. For background on the National Negro Convention Movement, see Howard H. Bell, ed., *Minutes of the Proceedings of the National Negro Conventions, 1830–1864* (New York: Arno Press and the *New York Times*, 1969), i–vi.
22. James G. Barbadoes first appeared as a Massachusetts delegate to the national convention of 1831. David Ruggles represented New York in the convention of 1833 while Jonas H. Townsend of New York attended the 1843 national meeting. See *Minutes and Proceedings of the First Annual Convention of the People of Color* (Philadelphia: Published by the Convention, 1831), 8; *Minutes and Proceedings of the Third Annual Convention*, 4; and *Minutes and Proceedings of the National Convention of Colored Citizens* (New York: Piercy & Reed, Printers, 1843), 10. For a profile of one of black antebellum California's political spokespersons, see Rudolph Lapp, "Jeremiah B. Sanderson: Early California Negro Leader," *Journal of Negro History* 53:4 (October 1968), 321–32.
23. Mifflin Gibbs provides a detailed description of the caning incident in the Pioneer Boot and Shoe Emporium and of the immediate political response of some black Californians. See Gibbs, *Shadow and Light*, 46–47.
24. *Proceedings of the First State Convention*, 3–5, 12–16, 22, 26. The quotes appear on page 27.
25. See *Proceedings of the Second Annual Convention of the Colored Citizens of the State of California* (San Francisco: J. H. Udell and W. Handall, Printers, 1856), 61–69; For the tribute to black women, see page 60. On the 1857 convention, see Lapp, *Blacks in Gold Rush California*, 230–38. For a discussion of the exodus to British Columbia, see James W. Pilton, "Negro Settlement in British Columbia, 1858–1871" (M.A. thesis, University of British Columbia, 1951), 28–37; Crawford Kilian, *"Go Do Some Great Thing": The Black Pioneers of British Columbia* (Vancouver: Douglas & McIntyre, Publishers, 1978), 15–25, 35–52; and Edwards, "The War of Complexional Distinction," 36–45.
26. Robert J. Chandler provides a rich and fascinating account of Republican efforts to assist the black community during this period. See Chandler, "Friends in Time of Need, Republicans and Black Civil Rights in California during the Civil War Era,"

Arizona and the West 24:4 (Winter 1982), 319–40. See also James A. Fisher, "The Struggle for Negro Testimony in California, 1851–1863" *Southern California Quarterly* 51:4 (December 1969), 313–24; and Gerald Stanley, "Civil War Politics in California," *Southern California Quarterly* 64:2 (Summer 1982), 115–32. On the Franchise League, see James Fisher, "A History of the Political and Social Development of the Black Community in California, 1850–1950" (Ph.D. dissertation, State University of New York at Stony Brook, 1971), 95.

27. The Bowen and Brown cases were followed by other streetcar segregation cases involving Mary Ellen Pleasant and Emma J. Turner. In October 1866 Pleasant was removed from a Omnibus Railroad Company streetcar. She charged racial discrimination but later withdrew her claim when company officials assured her that "negroes would hereafter be allowed to ride on the car." Two years later Pleasant and Turner filed separate lawsuits against the North Beach and Mission Railroad Company and won in lower court. However, both women lost in appeal in the California Supreme Court. For background on the Pleasant cases, see the *Daily Alta California*, of San Francisco, October 18, 1866, 1; Hudson, "A New Look," 37; and Broussard, "The New Racial Frontier," 26–27. On Turner, see Chandler, "Friends in Time of Need," 332–34. California's 1893 antidiscrimination statute is profiled in Nathaniel S. Colley, "Civil Actions for Damages Arising out of Violations of Civil Rights," *Hastings Law Journal* 17 (December 1965), 190.

28. On Philip A. Bell, see John H. Telfer, "Philip Alexander Bell and the San Francisco Elevator," *San Francisco Negro Historical & Cultural Society Monograph*, no. 9 (August 1966), 1–11, and I. Garland Penn, *The Afro-American Press and Its Editors* (New York: Arno Press, 1969), 91–99. The long, bitter rivalry between Anderson and Bell is described in Broussard, "The New Racial Frontier," 47–54. Anderson is briefly profiled in the first issue of the *Pacific Appeal*, April 2, 1862, p. 1. On James Madison Bell's poem, see Broussard, "The New Racial Frontier," 6.

29. *Proceedings of the California State Convention of Colored Citizens* (San Francisco, Office of the *Elevator*, 1865), 76, 89, 92, 95.

30. See Richard B. Sheridan, "From Slavery in Missouri to Freedom in Kansas: The Influx of Black Fugitives and Contrabands into Kansas, 1854–1864," *Kansas History* 12:1 (Spring 1989), 30–31, 37, and Gunja SenGupta, "Servants for Freedom: Christian Abolitionists in Territorial Kansas, 1854–1858," *Kansas History* 16:3 (Autumn 1993), 200–13. See also Harrison Anthony Trexler, "Slavery in Missouri, 1804–1865," *Johns Hopkins University Studies in Historical and Political Science*, series 32, no. 2 (1914), 202–03, and Richard Cordley, *A History of Lawrence, Kansas, from the First Settlement to the Close of the Rebellion* (Lawrence: E. F. Caldwell, 1895), 163–69. Albert Castel and James Rawley argue, however, that Kansas's reputation as a western bulwark of abolitionist sentiment was greatly exaggerated by both pro and antislavery partisans. Abolitionists were a vocal, active, influential minority among a majority of white Kansans who were "frightened by the mere mention of . . . negro equality." See Castel, "Civil War Kansas and the Negro," *Journal of Negro History* 51:2 (April 1966), 125–26, and Rawley, *Race and Politics*, 96, 98.

31. Sheridan, "From Slavery in Missouri to Freedom in Kansas," 29–31. The Underground Railroad extended from Albany, Kansas Territory, through Nebraska City, Nebraska Territory, where fugitives were ferried across the Missouri River to Percival, Iowa, and on to Canada. See Nebraska Writers' Project (Works Projects Administration), *The Negroes of Nebraska* (Lincoln: Woodruff Printing Company, 1940), 11, and James D. Bish, "The Black Experience in Selected Nebraska Counties, 1854–1920" (M.A. thesis, University of Nebraska at Omaha, 1989), 8–9.

32. Quoted in H. D. Fisher, *The Gun and the Gospel: Early Kansas and Chaplain Fisher* (Chicago: Kenwood Press, 1896), 42–43. See also Dudley Taylor Cornish, *The Sable Arm: Black Troops in the Union Army, 1861–1865* (Lawrence: University Press of Kansas, 1987), 69–74, 78; Alvin Josephy, Jr., *The Civil War in the American West* (New York: Alfred A. Knopf, 1991), 350–51; and Wendell Holmes Stephenson, *The Political Career of General James H. Lane* (Topeka: Kansas State Historical Society, 1930), ch. 12. For an account of one slave family's liberation by Kansas troops, see William A. Dobak, "Civil War on the Kansas-Missouri Border: The Narrative of Former Slave Andrew Williams," *Kansas History* 6:4 (Winter 1983), 237–42.

33. For the Fisher quotation, see *Gun and the Gospel,* 156. See also Stephenson, *The Political Career of General James H. Lane,* 126–27; Daniel F. Littlefield, Jr., *Africans and Creeks: From the Colonial Period to the Civil War* (Westport, Conn.: Greenwood Press, 1979), 236–37; Cordley, *A History of Lawrence, Kansas,* 182–86; and Castel, "Civil War Kansas and the Negro," 128.

34. See Henry Clay Bruce, *The New Man: Twenty-nine Years a Slave, Twenty-nine Years a Free Man* (New York: Negro Universities Press, 1969), 108–09.

35. The quotations are from Sheridan, "From Slavery in Missouri to Freedom in Kansas," 39. See also Castel, "Civil War Kansas and the Negro," 129–30.

36. See Richard Cordley, *Pioneer Days in Kansas* (New York: Pilgrim Press, 1903), 137–38.

37. See Kathe Schick, "The Lawrence Black Community, 1860–1866" (unpublished manuscript, Watkins Community Museum, Lawrence, Kansas, n.d.), 13–17.

38. The quotes are from Cordley, *Pioneer Days in Kansas,* 150–51. See also Cordley, *A History of Lawrence, Kansas,* 185–86, and Schick, "The Lawrence Black Community," 30–31.

39. Sheridan, "From Slavery in Missouri to Freedom in Kansas," 42.

40. Ibid., 43.

41. For an account of this intraracial conflict, see Bruce, *The New Man,* 79–81. See also Marilyn Dell Brady, "Kansas Federation of Colored Women's Clubs, 1900–1930," *Kansas History* 9:1 (Spring 1986), 21; Schick, "The Lawrence Black Community," 12–13; and Sheridan, "From Slavery in Missouri to Freedom in Kansas," 39–40.

42. See *The War of the Rebellion: A Compilation of the Official Records of the Union and Confederate Armies* (Washington, D.C.: Government Printing Office, 1900), series 11, vol. 13, p. 489. The Lane quote appears in Stephenson, *The Political Career of General James H. Lane,* 125. See also Josephy, *The Civil War in the American West,* 351, 354, and Cornish, *The Sable Arm,* 69–70.

43. See Cornish, *The Sable Arm,* 75, and Sheridan, "From Slavery in Missouri to Freedom in Kansas," 44, for descriptions of Lane's recruiting tactics.

44. The Kansas Independent Colored Battery, with its three commissioned African American officers—First Lieutenant William D. Matthews, Second Lieutenant Patrick H. Minor, and Captain Douglas—was the only completely black unit then in the U.S. Army. See C. Peter Ripley, ed., *The Black Abolitionist Papers,* vol. 5, *The United States, 1859–1865* (Chapel Hill: University of North Carolina Press, 1992), 330–33.

45. Sheridan, "From Slavery in Missouri to Freedom in Kansas," 44, and Cornish, *The Sable Arm,* 76.

46. Lary C. Rampp and Donald L. Rampp, *The Civil War in the Indian Territory* (Austin: Presidial Press, 1975), 40–51, 88, 105–06.

47. *The War of the Rebellion: Official Records of the Union and Confederate Armies* (Washington, D.C.: Government Printing Office, 1880–1902), series 1, vol. XXII, part 1, pp. 449, 450. See also Rampp and Rampp, *The Civil War in the Indian Territory,* 20–29, for a detailed account of the Battle of Honey Springs. All quotes are from Rampp.

48. "Proceedings of the Kansas Convention," in Philip S. Foner and George E. Walker, eds., *Proceedings of the Black State Conventions, 1840–1865* (Philadelphia: Temple University Press, 1980), 230–39. The quotes appear on pages 232, 233, 237.

49. For a discussion of Crawford's leadership of black troops, see Mark A. Plummer, *Frontier Governor: Samuel J. Crawford of Kansas* (Lawrence: University Press of Kansas, 1971), 22–24.

4: Reconstruction in the West, 1865–75

1. *Pacific Appeal,* February 14, 1863, p. 2.

2. *San Francisco Elevator,* April 17, 1868, p. 2. See also Mifflin W. Gibbs, *Shadow and Light: An Autobiography* (New York: Arno Press and the *New York Times,* 1968), 85, 108–10, and C. Peter Ripley, ed., *The Black Abolitionist Papers, Vol. 4, The United States, 1847–1858* (Chapel Hill: University of North Carolina Press, 1991), 237–40.

3. Ironically, the state's black population grew by 283 percent between 1900 and 1910, suggesting that the decline was temporary.

4. Eugene H. Berwanger, *The West and Reconstruction* (Urbana: University of Illinois

Press, 1981), 10. For a discussion of the West and the federal government, see Patricia Limerick, *Legacy of Conquest: The Unbroken Past of the American West* (New York: W. W. Norton, 1987), 78–87; Donald Worster, *Under Western Skies: Nature and History in the American West* (New York: Oxford University Press, 1992), 233–34; and Richard White, *"It's Your Misfortune and None of My Own:" A New History of the American West* (Norman: University of Oklahoma Press, 1991), 57–59, 135, 155–56.

5. Berwanger, *The West and Reconstruction*, p. 25.
6. The quotations are from ibid., 26–27. For a discussion of the evolution of Deady's views on race, see Ralph James Mooney, "Matthew Deady and the Federal Judicial Response to Racism in the Early West," *Oregon Law Review* 63:4 (1984), 627–37.
7. See William L. Richter, *The Army in Texas during Reconstruction, 1865–1870* (College Station: Texas A&M University Press, 1987), 15–16.
8. Alton Hornsby, "The Freedmen's Bureau Schools in Texas, 1865–1870," *Southwestern Historical Quarterly* 76:4 (April 1973), 398, 415, 417. For background on the bureau's activity in postwar Texas, see Barry A. Crouch, *The Freedmen's Bureau and Black Texas* (Austin: University of Texas Press, 1992), especially ch. 2 and 3, and Richter, *The Army in Texas*, ch. 2.
9. The quotes are in James A. Smallwood, *Time of Hope, Time of Despair: Black Texans during Reconstruction* (Port Washington, N.Y.: Kennikat Press, 1981), 26, 35.
10. Quoted ibid., 28.
11. See also the *Houston Telegraph* article reprinted in the *Dallas Herald*, February 3, 1866, p. 2, and Leon F. Litwack, *Been in the Storm So Long: The Aftermath of Slavery,* (New York: Vintage Books, 1979), 184–85.
12. Smallwood, *Time of Hope, Time of Despair*, 54, 129–30.
13. As late as 1910 only 30 percent of rural Texas blacks owned their own farms. See U.S. Census, *Negro Population in the United States, 1790–1915* (Washington, D.C.: Government Printing Office, 1918), 587, 588. On railroad segregation, see Litwack, *Been in the Storm So Long*, 262. For a discussion of the various legal and extralegal strategies employed to prevent Texas blacks from acquiring land, see Smallwood, *Time of Hope, Time of Despair*, 36, 53.
14. Quoted in Smallwood, *Time of Hope, Time of Despair*, 54–58. For a discussion of the impact of the convict leasing system on black prisoners, see Donald R. Walker, *Penology for Profit: A History of the Texas Prison System, 1867–1912* (College Station: Texas A&M University, 1988), ch. 5; Lawrence D. Rice, *The Negro in Texas, 1874–1900* (Baton Rouge: Louisiana State University Press, 1971), 246–250; and Anne Butler, "Still in Chains: Black Women in Western Prisons, 1865–1910," *Western Historical Quarterly* 20:1 (February 1989), 26–29.
15. For a discussion of Ruby's career in Texas, see Carl H. Moneyhon, "George T. Ruby and the Politics of Expediency in Texas," in Howard N. Rabinowitz, ed., *Southern Black Leaders of the Reconstruction Era* (Urbana: University of Illinois Press, 1982), 363–92; Randall Woods, "George T. Ruby: A Black Militant in the White Business Community," *Red River Valley Historical Review* 1:3 (Autumn 1974), 269–80; and Merline Pitre, *Through Many Dangers, Toils and Snares: The Black Leadership of Texas, 1868–1900* (Austin: Eakin Press, 1985), ch. 10. On Ruby's post-Texas activities, see Robert G. Athearn, *In Search of Canaan: Black Migration to Kansas, 1879–80* (Lawrence: Regents Press of Kansas, 1978), 230–31.
16. For an account of Gaine's life and brief political career, see Ann Patton Malone, "Matt Gaines: Reconstruction Politician," in Alwyn Barr and Robert A. Calvert eds., *Black Leaders: Texans for Their Times* (Austin: Texas State Historical Association, 1981), 50–81.
17. The first Gaines quote appears in Carl Moneyhon, *Republicanism in Reconstruction Texas* (Austin: University of Texas Press, 1980), 139, and the second is from Malone, "Matt Gaines," 63; see also pages 60–61. The most detailed assessment of black Texas politicians during Reconstruction can be found in Pitre, *Through Many Dangers*, ch. 1–3.
18. On African American members of the Texas legislature, see Alwyn Barr, "Black Legislators of Reconstruction Texas," *Civil War History* 32:4 (December 1986), 340–52. Carl Moneyhon provides the most detailed treatment of Texas Unionists and the Republican party during the Reconstruction: see his *Republicanism in Reconstruction Texas*, ch.

2 and 4 and pp. 84–85. See also Pitre, *Through Many Dangers*, 35, and Richter, *The Army in Texas*, 131. On Davis and West Texans, see Moneyhon, *Republicanism in Reconstruction Texas*, 129–30, and Merline Pitre, "The Evolution of Black Political Participation in Reconstruction Texas," *East Texas Historical Journal* 26:1 (Spring 1981) 39, 41.
19. *San Antonio Daily Herald*, March 28, 1869, p. 2. See also Smallwood, *Time of Hope, Time of Despair*, 27, 124, 130, 146–147, and Moneyhon, *Republicanism in Reconstruction Texas*, ch. 5.
20. The fourteen members of the Twelfth Legislature (1871–73) were the largest number of blacks elected until well into the twentieth century. Virtually all represented the heavily African American counties between the Trinity and Colorado rivers that constituted the heart of Texas plantation country. See Pitre, *Through Many Dangers*, 21–36, and J. Mason Brewer, *Negro Legislators of Texas and Their Descendants* (Dallas: Mathis Publishing Company, 193), 125–28. The fullest accounts of Norris Wright Cuney's career are in Maude Cuney Hare, *Norris Wright Cuney: A Tribune of the Black People* (Austin: Steck-Vaughn Co., 1968) and Paul Douglas Casdorph, "Norris Wright Cuney and Texas Republican Politics, 1883–1896," *Southwestern Historical Quarterly* 68:4 (April 1965), 455–64.
21. Arrest statistics suggest that the Texas State Police was a highly effective law enforcement agency. In 1871 it made 3,602 arrests, far more than the total number of arrests made by local law officers for the seven years immediately following the Civil War. William Richter, however, argues that the Texas State Police, however creditably it performed its duty to preserve order, was opposed primarily for its political role of protecting black and white Republican voters from coercion and intimidation. On the police, see Ann Patton Baenziger, "The Texas State Police during Reconstruction: A Reexamination," *Southwestern Historical Quarterly* 72:4 (April 1969), 470–491, while the militia is described in Otis A. Singletary, "Texas Militia during Reconstruction," *Southwestern Historical Quarterly* 60:1 (July 1956), 23–35. See also Richter, *The Army in Texas*, 193.
22. See John Wesley Hardin, *The Life of John Wesley Hardin* (Norman: University of Oklahoma Press, 1961), 61–63; Rice, *The Negro in Texas*, 12; Smallwood, *Time of Hope, Time of Despair*, 156–58; and Moneyhon, *Republicanism in Reconstruction Texas*, 94–95. On Goldstein Dupree's assassination by the Klan, see Pitre, *Through Many Dangers*, 132. Richard Maxwell Brown focuses on the prevalence of violence and lawlessness in Texas and its roots in Reconstruction politics: see his *Strain of Violence: Historical Studies of American Violence and Vigilantism* (New York: Oxford University Press, 1975), 237–86.
23. See Barry A. Crouch, "The 'Cords of Love': Legalizing Black Marital and Family Rights in Postwar Texas," *Journal of Negro History* 79:4 (Fall 1994), 334–51, and Smallwood, *Time of Hope*, 113–16.
24. See Smallwood, *Time of Hope*, 97.
25. Ibid., 96–103.
26. Ibid., 116–18.
27. The careers of both of Texas's first black state senators suggest the extent of the removal of blacks from the state's political arena. Ruby did not stand for reelection in 1873 and left the state the following year to return to New Orleans, where he was employed by former Louisiana Governor P. B. S. Pinchback. Gaines won reelection but was denied his seat because of his conviction for a bigamy charge earlier that year that effectively ended his political career. He concentrated instead on leading a succession of small churches until his death in 1900. See Woods, "George T. Ruby," 279–80, and Malone, "Matt Gaines," 69–71. See also Smallwood, *Time of Hope*, 156–58, and Barr, *Black Texans*, 76–80.
28. Angie Debo, *And Still the Waters Run: The Betrayal of the Five Civilized Tribes* (Princeton: Princeton University Press, 1980), 12–14, 17.
29. The full text of Sanborn's first letter and a brief description of the second appear in M. Thomas Bailey, *Reconstruction in Indian Territory: A Story of Avarice, Discrimination, and Opportunism* (Port Washington, N.Y.: Kennikat Press, 1972), 47–51.
30. Ibid., 48, 49.
31. Donald Grinde and Quintard Taylor, "Red vs. Black: Conflict and Accommodation in the Post Civil War Indian Territory, 1865–1907," *American Indian Quarterly* 8:3 (Sum-

mer 1984), 212–13. See also Thomas F. Andrews, "Freedmen in Indian Territory: A Post-Civil War Dilemma," *Journal of the West* 4:3 (July 1965), 367–76, and Daniel F. Littlefield, Jr., *The Cherokee Freedmen: From Emancipation to American Citizenship* (Westport, Conn.: Greenwood Press, 1978), 8–10.

32. The Chickasaw and Choctaw argument against incorporation is presented in Andrews, "Freedmen in Indian Territory," 371. For a discussion of the ambiguous legal status of freedpeople in the two nations immediately after the war and of the black codes, see Daniel F. Littlefield, Jr., *The Chickasaw Freedmen: A People without a Country* (Westport, Conn.: Greenwood Press, 1980), 30–40. On antiblack violence in the nations, see Angie Debo, *The Rise and Fall of the Choctaw Republic* (Norman: University of Oklahoma Press, 1961), 109, and Littlefield, *The Chickasaw Freedmen,* 32–33.

33. Littlefield, *The Chickasaw Freedmen,* 45.

34. See Angie Debo, *The Road to Disappearance* (Norman: University of Oklahoma Press, 1941), 170; Jimmie Lewis Franklin, *Journey toward Hope: A History of Blacks in Oklahoma* (Norman: University of Oklahoma Press, 1982), 9–10; and Grinde and Taylor, "Red vs. Black," 214–215.

35. Quoted in Debo, *The Road to Disappearance,* 237; see also pages 185–96, 202, 221. I want to express my appreciation to Daniel F. Littlefield and Kevin Mulroy for determining the number of freedman representatives among the Creek, Cherokee, and Seminole nations.

36. For the Boudinot quote, see *Cherokee Advocate,* March 28, 1877, p. 2. The Johnson quote appears in a July 30, 1879, editorial on page 2. For a list of Cherokee freedman councilors, see Emmet Starr, *History of the Cherokee Indians and Their Legends and Folk Lore* (Millwood, N.Y.: Kraus Reprint Co., 1977), 277–83.

37. Quoted in *Cherokee Advocate,* September 9, 1876, p. 2. See also Littlefield, *The Cherokee Freedmen,* 75–76.

38. See *Cherokee Advocate,* editorial, July 30, 1879, p. 2. See also Littlefield, *The Cherokee Freedmen,* 80–81, 78–79.

39. Littlefield, *The Cherokee Freedmen,* 99–103. Attorney General Devin's ruling on intruders was an important victory that prompted Cherokee freedpeople to intensify their campaign to obtain what they considered an equitable share of tribal resources. In 1883 Congress gave the Cherokee three hundred thousand dollars for the sale of several million acres of tribal land west of the Arkansas River. When tribal leaders voted to limit the distribution of the money to full-blooded Cherokee, the freedpeople hired black Missouri attorney James Milton Turner to press their case. See Gary R. Kremer, *James Milton Turner and the Promise of America: The Public Life of a Post–Civil War Black Leader* (Columbia: University of Missouri Press, 1991), 131–38.

40. See Littlefield, *The Chickasaw Freedmen,* 57–60. The Overton quote appears on page 66. For a discussion of the increasing cultural integration of Indian freedpeople into African American society, see pages 77, 79, 86–88.

41. *San Francisco Elevator,* October 30, 1868, p. 2.

42. See J. W. Smurr, "Jim Crow Out West," in J.W. Smurr and K. Ross Toole, eds., *Historical Essays on Montana and the Northwest: In Honor of Paul C. Phillips* (Helena: Western Press, Historical Society of Montana, 1957), 157–59; Forrest G. Wood, *Black Scare: The Racist Response to Emancipation and Reconstruction* (Berkeley: University of California Press, 1970), 81; and Michael P. Malone, Richard B. Roeder, and William L. Lang, *Montana: A History of Two Centuries* (Seattle: University of Montana Press, 1991), 95.

43. *Olympia Commercial Age,* March 26, 1870, p. 2. For the Stanford and Stewart quotes, see Berwanger, *The West and Reconstruction,* 132–133. Obviously the views of Stewart and Stanford were not shared by conservative western Republican leaders, such as Nevadan Charles A. Sumner, editor of the *Gold Hill News,* who consistently opposed black suffrage, or Cornelius Hedges of Helena, Montana Territory, who wrote in 1867, "I cannot really say that I am in favor of letting all the negroes in the south vote. It is letting in too much ignorance. . . . I don't know that I have a much higher opinion of negroes than formerly but I think they are better than rebels. I wish all negroes could be returned to Africa, if they are not they will soon die out in this country. . . . I shall not mourn the result." Quoted in Berwanger, *The West and Reconstruction,* 133.

44. The Stephenson quotation appears in Elmer Rusco, *"Good Time Coming?". Black Nevadans in the Nineteenth Century* (Westport, Conn.: Greenwood Press, 1975), 75. Stephen-

son, who was born in Washington, D.C., in 1825, migrated to Sacramento in 1862 but the following year relocated to Virginia City, Nevada, where for the next seven years he was the only black physician in the state and its best-known black civil rights advocate. For background, see Rusco, *"Good Time Coming?,"* 141–42.

45. The quotes are from the *Kansas Tribune,* October 28, 1866, p. 2.
46. Daniel Wilder, *Annals of Kansas* (Topeka: G. W. Martin, 1875), 471.
47. See Berwanger, *The West and Reconstruction,* 144.
48. Quoted ibid., 145. See also Berwanger, "William J. Hardin: Colorado Spokesman for Racial Justice, 1863–1873," *Colorado Magazine* 52:1 (Winter 1975), 55–56. Hardin apparently lived in California and Nebraska before settling in Denver in 1863. For background on Hardin, see Eugene Berwanger, "Hardin and Langston: Western Black Spokesmen of the Reconstruction Era," *Journal of Negro History* 64:2 (Spring 1979), 108 and Howard Roberts Lamar, *The Far Southwest, 1846–1912: A Territorial History* (New Haven: Yale University Press, 1966), 254–261.
49. Berwanger, *The West and Reconstruction,* p. 146. Hardin also debated local white leaders opposed to equal suffrage, including Colorado's congressional candidates in 1865, James M. Cavanaugh and John M. Chivington. His speech was so effective that the predominantly white audience, although still opposed to black suffrage in principle, concluded that Hardin had earned the right to vote. Candidate Cavanaugh reversed his stand and pronounced himself in favor of impartial suffrage. See Berwanger, "William J. Hardin," 55.
50. President Johnson claimed a territory should have at least a population large enough to qualify for 1 congressional representative, approximately 125,000 people, and Colorado Territory at the time had only about one-fifth that number of inhabitants. See Robert G. Athearn, *The Coloradans* (Albuquerque: University of New Mexico Press, 1976), 80–82, and Berwanger, *The West and Reconstruction,* 67, 147–48.
51. Berwanger, *The West and Reconstruction,* pp. 149–50.
52. On the first Montana election, see Smurr, "Jim Crow Out West," 161–62, and Berwanger, *The West and Reconstruction,* 152–53. The South Pass City, Wyoming, episode is described in Sidney Howell Fleming, "Solving the Jigsaw Puzzle: One Suffrage Story at a Time," *Annals of Wyoming* 62:1 (Spring 1990), 60.
53. On black voter participation in post-1867, Colorado elections, see Berwanger, *The West and Reconstruction,* 155–56.
54. See *Journal of the Senate Proceedings of the Legislative Assembly of Oregon, 1870* (Salem: T. Patterson, State Printer, 1870), 654. Although their action was largely symbolic, the Oregon legislature finally ratified the Fifteenth Amendment on the hundredth anniversary of the state's admission to the Union (1959) while the California legislature voted for ratification only in 1962. See Elizabeth McLagan, *A Peculiar Paradise: A History of Blacks in Oregon, 1788–1940* (Portland: Georgian Press, 1980), 71, and Berwanger, *The West and Reconstruction,* 183. On Stewart's role in crafting the Fifteenth Amendment, see William M. Stewart, *Reminiscences of Senator William M. Stewart of Nevada,* ed. George Rothwell Brown (New York: Neale Publishing Co., 1908), 231–38, and William Gillette, *The Right to Vote: Politics and the Passage of the Fifteenth Amendment* (Baltimore: Johns Hopkins University Press, 1969), 54–78.
55. For background on Charles Langston, see *Report of the Proceedings of the Colored Convention, Held at Cleveland, Ohio* (Rochester: North Star Press, 1848), 3–4, 8, and John Mercer Langston, *From the Virginia Plantation to the National Capitol: An Autobiography* (Hartford, Conn.: American Publishing Co., 1894), 14–15, 75, 184–89.
56. See Wood, *Black Scare,* 94–97, for a discussion of Hartley's views and of the national debate on the simultaneous removal of racial and gender restrictions on suffrage.
57. Berwanger, *The West and Reconstruction,* 166–67.
58. Ibid., 168–70. The Brown quote appears on page 170.
59. The Langston quotations appear in ibid. 170 and 166 respectively. See also pages 171–73, 179.
60. See the *Elevator,* February 11, 1870, p. 2; *Helena Daily Herald,* April 15, 1870, p. 3; Rusco, *"Good Time Coming?,"* 98–99; *Portland Oregonian,* April 7, 1870, p. 2; K. Keith Richard, "Unwelcome Settlers: Black and Mulatto Oregon Pioneers," part II," *Oregon Historical Quarterly* 84:2 (Summer 1983), 183–84; and *Daily Rocky Mountain News,* February 20, 1867, p. 4.

61. For a discussion of Hardin's political career in Wyoming, see Roger D. Hardaway, "William Jefferson Hardin: Wyoming's Nineteenth Century Black Legislator," *Annals of Wyoming* 63:1 (Winter 1991), 2–13. On Waller's role as a U.S. diplomat in Madagascar, see Randall Bennett Woods, *A Black Odyssey: John Lewis Waller and the Promise of American Life, 1878–1900* (Lawrence: Regents Press of Kansas, 1981), ch. 7–9.

62. Thomas C. Cox, *Blacks in Topeka, Kansas, 1865–1915: A Social History* (Baton Rouge: Louisiana State University Press, 1982), 122.

5: Migration and Settlement, 1875–1920

1. The Stokes quote appears in *Proceedings of the First State Convention of the Colored Citizens of the State of California* (Sacramento: Democratic State Journal Print, 1855), 6. For a discussion of the Fort Benton area, see J. W. Smurr, "Jim Crow Out West," in J. W. Smurr and K. Ross Toole, eds., *Historical Essays on Montana and the Northwest* (Helena: Western Press, 1957), 159, and Christian McMillen, "Border State Terror and the Genesis of the African American Community in Deer Lodge and Chouteau Counties, Montana, 1870–1890," *Journal of Negro History* 79:2 (Spring 1994), 220–28. On Forts Huachuca and Davis, see Richard E. Harris, *The First Hundred Years: A History of Arizona Blacks* (Apache Junction, Ariz.: Relmo Publishers, 1983), 11, and Erwin N. Thompson, "The Negro Soldiers on the Frontier: A Fort Davis Case Study," *Journal of the West* 7:2 (April 1968), 217–35.

2. Rayner, the African American leader who symbolized both black Populism and the effort to build a permanent interracial political coalition based on economic interests, is profiled in Greg Cantrell, *Kenneth and John B. Rayner and the Limits of Southern Dissent* (Urbana: University of Illinois Press, 1993), ch. 11–13. For a discussion of the coalition and its failure, see Lawrence D. Rice, *The Negro in Texas, 1874–1900* (Baton Rouge: Louisiana State University Press, 1971), ch. 5, and Lawrence D. Goodwyn, "Populist Dreams and Negro Rights: East Texas as a Case Study," *American Historical Review* 76:4 (December 1971), 1435–56. The only other significant black participation in western Populism came in Kansas, where the most active spokespersons for the People's party were urbanites such as the Rev. Benjamin F. Foster of Topeka and Kansas City newspaper editor and former Democrat Charles H. J. Taylor. On Kansas black Populism, see William H. Chafe, "The Negro and Populism: A Kansas Case Study," *Journal of Southern History* 34:3 (August 1968), 402–19, and Randall B. Woods, "After the Exodus: John Lewis Waller and the Black Elite, 1878–1900," *Kansas Historical Quarterly* 43:2 (Summer 1977), 172–92. The black exodus to Texas is discussed in Leon F. Litwack, *Been in the Storm So Long: The Aftermath of Slavery* (New York: Vintage Books, 1979), 411, and Cantrell, *Kenneth and John B. Rayner,* 188–89.

3. For background on the Homestead Act and its consequences for western settlement, see Richard White, *"It's Your Misfortune and None of My Own": A History of the American West* (Norman: University of Oklahoma Press, 1991), 143–45.

4. The Louisianian's quote appears in Nell Irvin Painter, *Exodusters: Black Migration to Kansas after Reconstruction* (Topeka: University Press of Kansas, 1986), 159. See also Albert Castel, "Civil War Kansas and the Negro," *Journal of Negro History* 51:2 (April 1966), 135, and Randall B. Woods, "Integration, Exclusion, or Segregation? The 'Color Line' in Kansas, 1878–1900," *Western Historical Quarterly* 14:2 (April 1983), 196–97.

5. Quoted in Thomas C. Cox, *Blacks in Topeka Kansas, 1865–1915: A Social History* (Baton Rouge: Louisiana State University Press, 1982), 36. For an account of George Washington Carver's homesteading efforts in Ness County, Kansas, see Linda O. McMurry, *George Washington Carver: Scientist and Symbol* (New York: Oxford University Press, 1981), pp. 24–27.

6. See Painter, *Exodusters,* 109–13; Cox, *Blacks in Topeka,* 40; and Joseph V. Hickey, " 'Pap' Singleton's Dunlap Colony: Relief Agencies and the Failure of a Black Settlement in Eastern Kansas," *Great Plains Quarterly* 11:1 (Winter 1991), 24–26. Singleton has long been falsely credited with establishing another colony in Cherokee County, Kansas. For an analysis of the Cherokee colony myth, see Gary R. Entz, "Image and Reality on the Kansas Prairie: 'Pap' Singleton's Cherokee County Colony," *Kansas History* 19:2 (Summer 1996), 125–39.

7. Hickey, " 'Pap' Singleton's Dunlap Colony," 29–30.

8. Ibid., 30–31.

9. See also Glen Schwendemann, "Nicodemus: Negro Haven on the Solomon," *Kansas Historical Quarterly* 34:1 (Spring 1968), 10–13, and Kenneth W. Hamilton, *Black Towns and Profit: Promotion and Development in the Trans-Appalachian West, 1877–1915* (Urbana: University of Illinois Press, 1991), 5–10.

10. The Hickman quote appears in Schwendemann, "Nicodemus: Negro Haven on the Solomon," 14. Willianna Hickman's initial response to Nicodemus supports Anne Hyde's claim that women often viewed the West far differently from men. They saw far less economic opportunity and far greater danger and limits to a stable family existence. See Anne F. Hyde, "Cultural Filters: The Significance of Perception in the History of the American West," *Western Historical Quarterly* 24:3 (August 1993), 360–61.

11. The Scruggs quote appears in Schwendemann, "Nicodemus," 17. See also Claire O'Brien, " 'With One Mighty Pull': Interracial Town Boosting in Nicodemus, Kansas," *Great Plains Quarterly* 16:2 (Spring 1996), 119.

12. The first quote appears in the *Nicodemus Western Cyclone*, May 13, 1886, p. 2, and the second is in *Western Cyclone*, March 24, 1887, p. 2. The third quotation appears in Schwendemann, "Nicodemus," 28. See also Hamilton, *Black Towns and Profit*, 16, 25. See Craig Miner, *West of Wichita: Settling the High Plains of Kansas, 1865–1890* (Lawrence: University Press of Kansas, 1986), 84–85, and O'Brien, " 'With One Mighty Pull,' " 127–28, for a discussion of the varied responses of western Kansas white settlers to their African American neighbors.

13. See Martin Dann, "From Sodom to the Promised Land: E. P. McCabe and the Movement for Oklahoma Colonization," *Kansas Historical Quarterly* 40:3 (Autumn 1974), 371–72. See also Schwendemann, "Nicodemus," 24, 27.

14. See Norman L. Crockett, *The Black Towns* (Lawrence: Regents Press of Kansas, 1979), 8, and Hamilton, *Black Towns and Profit*, 30–35.

15. The first quote appears in Cox, *Blacks in Topeka*, 41–42. For the second quote, see the *St. Louis Globe-Democrat*, March 14, 1879, p. 8. See also Robert G. Athearn, *In Search of Canaan: Black Migration to Kansas, 1879–80* (Lawrence: Regents Press of Kansas, 1978), ch. 1–3. For a discussion of the conditions that prompted the Exodus, see Painter, *Exodusters*, ch. 3–5.

16. Quoted in Painter, *Exodusters*, 3–4.

17. All quotes are from Cox, *Blacks in Topeka*, 42, 47–48, 49.

18. Ibid., 57, 59, 69–71.

19. Quoted in Athearn, *In Search of Canaan*, 256. See also page 278, and Cox, *Blacks in Topeka*, 66.

20. Painter, *Exodusters*, 200. About four hundred Exodusters settled in Nebraska, primarily in Lincoln, where they encountered much the same response as did the Kansas migrants. Many of the state's Democratic politicians and newspapers condemned the migration as a Republican scheme to gain voters. However, one Nebraska farmer's request for black labor in a state desperately in need of workers suggests that whites could, under the right conditions, lay aside their prejudices. J. M. Snyder of Sherman County wrote Kansas Governor John St. John to request blacks as laborers. "We can furnish them work, pay them, give them good quarters, and eat at the table with them if they will keep themselves in a tidy condition." In June 1879 Nebraskans organized a Freedmen's Relief Association in Lincoln under the leadership of William NcNeil in preparation for the first forty-two Exodusters, who arrived in the city on July 1. The Snyder quote appears in Athearn, *In Search of Canaan*, 161. See also James D. Bish, "The Black Experience in Selected Nebraska Counties, 1854–1920" (M.A. thesis, University of Nebraska, Omaha, 1989), 47–62.

21. *Langston City Herald*, December 19, 1891, p. 2.

22. Quoted in Daniel F. Littlefield, Jr., and Lonnie Underhill, "Black Dreams and 'Free' Homes: The Oklahoma Territory, 1891–1894," *Phylon* 34:4 (December 1973), 342. See also Jimmie Lewis Franklin, *Journey toward Hope: A History of Blacks in Oklahoma* (Norman: University of Oklahoma Press, 1982), 11–12. William Eagleson's *American Citizen* was formerly the *Colored Citizen*.

23. Littlefield and Underhill, "Black Dreams and 'Free' Homes," 344.

24. Quoted in Martin Dann, "From Sodom to the Promised Land: E. P. McCabe and the Movement for Oklahoma Colonization," *Kansas Historical Quarterly* 40:3 (Autumn 1974), 376. Jere W. Roberson suggests that McCabe and his supporters never intended to control Oklahoma Territory, but they hoped to gain enough political power to ensure that black rights would be respected; see Roberson, "Edward P. McCabe and the Langston Experiment," *Chronicles of Oklahoma* 51:3 (Fall 1973), 344–46.
25. All quotes are from Roberson, "Edward P. McCabe," 346, 351. See also Franklin, *Journey toward Hope*, 13–15.
26. The McCabe quote appears in the *Langston City Herald*, June 11, 1892, p. 3. See also Littlefield and Underhill, "Black Dreams and 'Free' Homes," 344–45; Roberson, "Edward P. McCabe," 349; and Hamilton, *Black Towns and Profit*, 103–04.
27. See, for example, the *Langston City Herald*, February 6, 1892, p. 2. Langston City was unsuccessful in its bid to attract a railroad, but McCabe, using his political connections, was able to obtain for the city the Colored Agricultural and Normal School, which eventually became Langston University, the only publicly supported black educational institution in Oklahoma. See Hamilton, *Black Towns and Profit*, 112–14.
28. *Langston City Herald*, December 26, 1891, p. 2.
29. See Littlefield and Underhill, "Black Dreams and 'Free' Homes," 348–49.
30. Quoted in ibid., 352.
31. For a discussion of the Dawes Act and its consequences for Indians and freedpeople in Indian Territory, see Angie Debo, *And Still the Waters Run: The Betrayal of the Five Civilized Tribes* (Princeton: Princeton University Press, 1972), ch. 1–4, and Donald A. Grinde, Jr., and Quintard Taylor, "Red vs. Black: Conflict and Accommodation in the Post Civil War Indian Territory, 1865–1907," *American Indian Quarterly* 8:3 (Summer 1984), 220–25. See also Franklin, *Journey toward Hope*, 20–22, on settlement in territorial Oklahoma.
32. Franklin, *Journey toward Hope*, 23–25.
33. Gilbert C. Fite, "A Family Farm Chronicle," in Clyde A. Milner, ed., *Major Problems in the History of the American West* (Lexington, Mass.: D. C. Heath and Co., 1989), 431–32, and Franklin, *Journey toward Hope*, 22–23. Although Oklahoma blacks deserted farming primarily for economic reasons, a minority of black settlers, after witnessing the state's rapid embrace of racially discriminatory legislation, chose in 1914 to leave the United States for West Africa. See William E. Bittle and Gilbert Geis, *The Longest Way Home: Chief Alfred C. Sam's Back-to-Africa Movement* (Detroit: Wayne State University Press, 1964), ch. 3 and 4.
34. On the Africa quote, see William Loren Katz, *The Black West* (New York: Doubleday, 1971), 250. See also Hamilton, *Black Towns and Profit*, 2, 154. Hamilton omitted Dearfield, the all-black town in northeastern Colorado. On Dearfield and other Colorado settlements, see George H. Wayne, "Negro Migration and Colonization in Colorado," *Journal of the West* 15:1 (January 1976), 112–17. African Americans also started towns in Montana and Washington territories. For a brief description, see Quintard Taylor, "A History of Blacks in the Pacific Northwest, 1788–1970," Ph.D. dissertation, University of Minnesota, 1977, 102–05.
35. Hamilton, *Black Towns and Profit*, 120–31.
36. Booker T. Washington, "Boley, A Negro Town in the West," *Outlook* 88 (January 1908), 28, 31. For background on Boley, see Hamilton, *Black Towns and Profit*, 120–24.
37. Hamilton, *Black Towns and Profit*, 131–33. See also Franklin, *Journey toward Hope*, pp. 18–19. Although never as prominent as Boley or Langston City, Allensworth, California, also developed along the lines of Twin Territories cities. For a discussion of Allensworth, see Hamilton, *Black Towns and Profit*, 138–48.
38. See *Cleveland Gazette*, December 29, 1883, p. 2, and the *People's Advocate*, of Washington, D.C., January 19, 1884, p. 2. For a detailed discussion of black homesteaders in Nebraska, see Nebraska Writers' Project (Works Projects Administration), *The Negroes of Nebraska* (Lincoln: Woodruff Printing Co., 1940), 8–9, 12–14, and Bish, "The Black Experience in Selected Nebraska Counties," ch. 6. A brief account of an African American homesteading colony near Alexander, North Dakota, appears in William C. Sherman, *Prairie Mosaic: An Ethnic Atlas of Rural North Dakota* (Fargo: North Dakota Institute for Regional Studies, 1983), 14.

39. The quotes are from Ava Speece Day, "The Ava Speese Day Story," in Frances Jacobs Alberts, ed., *Sod House Memories* (Hastings, Neb.: Sod House Society, 1972), pp. 263–64 and 275. See also Bish, "The Black Experience in Selected Nebraska Counties," 157, 209–20.

40. The quotation appears in the *Denver Post,* June 8, 1909, p. 1. The best accounts of Dearfield are Melvin Edward Norris, Jr., "Dearfield, Colorado—The Evolution of a Rural Black Settlement: An Historical Geography of Black Colonization on the Great Plains" (Ph.D. thesis, University of Colorado, Boulder, 1980); Frederick P. Johnson, "Agricultural Negro Colony in Eastern Colorado," *Western Farm Life Journal* (May 11, 1915), pp. 11–12; Norris, "Dearfield, Colorado," ch. 6–8; and Karen Waddell, "Dearfield, a Dream Deferred," *Colorado Heritage,* issue 2 (1988), 2–12.

41. The Jackson quote appears in Johnson, "Agricultural Negro Colony," 11. See also Norris, "Dearfield, Colorado," ch. 7.

42. Quoted in Johnson, "Agricultural Negro Colony," 11.

43. The quotes appear in Norris, "Dearfield, Colorado," 157 and 162 respectively.

44. On the last years of Dearfield, see ibid., 171–212, and Waddell, "Dearfield," 7–10.

45. Oscar Micheaux, *The Conquest: The Story of a Negro Pioneer* (Lincoln: University of Nebraska Press, 1994), 53. See also Janis Hebert, "Oscar Micheaux: A Black Pioneer," *South Dakota Review* 11:4 (Winter 1973–74), 62–63. The Micheaux quotation appears on page 62.

46. Micheaux's accomplishments in film remain an impressive record to this day. His 1931 production *The Exile* was the first all-black feature-length movie, while his 1948 three-hour epic *The Betrayal* remained the longest black-produced motion picture until the 1970s. Paul Robeson made his motion-picture debut in the 1925 Micheaux film *Body and Soul,* but Micheaux's most celebrated actors were Edna Mae Harris and Robert Earl Jones, the father of James Earl Jones. See Thomas Cripps, *Slow Fade to Black: The Negro in American Film, 1900–1942* (New York: Oxford University Press, 1993), 183–202, and Cripps, *Making Movies Black: The Hollywood Message Movie from World War II to the Civil Rights Era* (New York: Oxford University Press, 1993), 104, 146–47. See also Chester J. Fontenot, Jr., "Oscar Micheaux, Black Novelist and Film Maker," in Virginia Faulkner with Frederick C. Luebke, eds., *Vision and Refuge: Essays on the Literature of the Great Plains* (Lincoln: University of Nebraska Press, 1982), 109–25, and Leathern Dorsey's introduction to the 1994 reprint of *The Conquest,* xi–xxi.

47. The quotes are from Robert Anderson, *From Slavery to Affluence: Memoirs of Robert Anderson, Ex-Slave* (Steamboat Springs, Colo.: Steamboat Pilot, Printer, 1967), 55, 58. See also pages 44–54, and Darold D. Wax, "Robert Ball Anderson, Ex-Slave, a Pioneer in Western Nebraska, 1884–1930," *Nebraska History* 64:2 (Summer 1983), 163–85, and Wax, "The Odyssey of an Ex-Slave: Robert Ball Anderson's Pursuit of the American Dream," *Phylon* 45:1 (Spring 1984), 67–79.

48. See Todd Guenther, " 'Y'all Call Me Nigger Jim Now, But Someday You'll Call Me Mr. James Edwards': Black Success on the Plains of the Equality State," *Annals of Wyoming* 61:2 (Fall 1989), 21–24.

49. Ibid., 39. For background information on black settlement in Wyoming, see Guenther, "At Home on the Range: Black Settlement in Rural Wyoming, 1850–1950" (M.A. thesis, University of Wyoming, 1988).

50. U.S. Bureau of the Census, *Population of the United States, 1890,* part 2 (Washington, D.C.: Government Printing Office, 1897), 532–626. For a discussion of the emergence of the cowboy as a cultural icon, see Richard Slatta, *Cowboys of the Americas* (New Haven: Yale University Press, 1990), 191–96.

51. See Bureau of the Census, *Population of the United States, 1890,* Part 2, 532–626; U.S. Bureau of the Census, *Negro Population, 1790–1915* (Washington, D.C.: Government Printing Office, 1918), 513–16; and Terry G. Jordan, *Trails to Texas: Southern Roots of Western Cattle Ranching* (Lincoln: University of Nebraska Press, 1981), 143. Historians' inflated estimates of the number of black cowboys stemmed from a loose interpretation of figures provided by Philip Durham and Everett L. Jones in 1965 and Kenneth W. Porter in 1969. Durham and Jones claimed 5,000 black cowboys rode out of Texas on cattle drives in the three decades following the Civil War. Porter, the first professional historian to investigate black participation in the cattle industry, while not

stating a specific figure, claimed that 25 percent of all western cowboys were African American. Durham and Jones as well as Porter based their projections on a 1925 estimate provided by George W. Saunders, president of the Texas Trail Drivers Association, although Porter also examined extant lists of trail herd outfits. Saunders claimed "35,000 men went up the trail with herds," and of this number, "about one-third were negroes and Mexicans," a statement that suggests there were 8,750 black cowboys. Most historians accepted Porter's figures or the Durham and Jones figure of 5,000 as representative of the entire West and particularly of Texas. Yet Saunders's estimate of the number of drovers and percentage of black and Chicano cowboys have not been verified by any other source. See Durham and Jones, *The Negro Cowboys* (New York: Dodd, Mead, 1965), 44–45, and Porter, "Negro Labor in the Western Cattle Industry, 1866–1900," *Labor History* 10:3 (Summer 1969), 346–74, reprinted in Porter, *The Negro on the American Frontier* (New York: Arno Press and the *New York Times*, 1971), 494–521. For Saunders's original estimate, see John Marvin Hunter, ed., *The Trail Drivers of Texas* (Nashville: Colesbury Press, 1925), 453.

52. See J. Frank Dobie, ed., *Legends of Texas* (Austin: Texas Folklore Society, 1924), 52–53. The first quote appears in Cordia Sloan Duke and Joe B. Frantz, *6,000 Miles of Fence: Life on the XIT Ranch of Texas* (Austin: University of Texas Press, 1961), 172; the second in Charles A. Siringo, *Riata and Spurs* (Boston: Houghton Mifflin, 1927), 8. On Bose Ikard, see James Evetts Haley, *Charles Goodnight, Cowman & Plainsman* (Norman: University of Oklahoma Press, 1949), 242. The Print Olive–James Kelly episode is recounted in Harry E. Chrisman, *The Ladder of Rivers: The Story of I. P. (Print) Olive* (Denver: Sage Books, 1962), 122, and Bish, "The Black Experience in Selected Nebraska Counties," pp. 204–05. See also Durham and Jones, *The Negro Cowboys*, which remains a leading source for background information on African Americans in the range cattle industry. Their book, followed in 1969 by Kenneth W. Porter's influential "Negro Labor in the Western Cattle Industry, 1866–1900," reintroduced the black cowboy to the twentieth-century American public. Despite the enormous popularity of the "black cowboy" image no scholars have built upon the foundation provided by these accounts.

53. R. C. Crane, ed., "D. W. Wallace ('80 John'): A Negro Cattleman on the Texas Frontier," *West Texas Historical Society Year Book* 28 (1952), 113–17.

54. See Hunter, ed., *The Trail Drivers of Texas*, 717, 400, 987, 113, 230–31, 378.

55. Quoted in John M. Hendrix, "Tribute Paid to Negro Cowmen," *Cattleman* (February 1936), 24, while the Poll Allen episode is detailed in William Joseph Alexander Elliot, *The Spurs* (Dallas: Texas Spur Co., 1939), 209.

56. See C. Robert Haywood, " 'No Less a Man': Blacks in Cow Town Dodge City, 1876–1886," *Western Historical Quarterly* 19:2 (May 1988), 161, and Porter, "Negro Labor in the Western Cattle Industry," 510–16.

57. See J. A. Comstock's description of the incident in the *Dodge City Daily Globe*, July 28, 1933, p. 4. See also Haywood, " 'No Less a Man,' " 162, 169–70.

58. On the Dakota Territory cowboy, see Lincoln A. Lang, *Ranching with Roosevelt* (Philadelphia: J. B. Lippincott, 1926), 286–88. On the Lincoln County range war, see William A. Keleher, *Violence in Lincoln County, 1869–1881: A New Mexico Item* (Albuquerque: University of New Mexico Press, 1957), 128, and John P. Wilson, *Merchants, Guns & Money: The Story of Lincoln County and Its Wars* (Santa Fe: Museum of New Mexico Press, 1987), 84. On McJunkin, see Monroe Billington, "Black History and New Mexico's Place Names," *Password* 29:3 (Fall 1984), 110. Battavia is described in Allen A. Erwin, *The Southwest of John Slaughter, 1841–1922* (Glendale, Calif.: Arthur H. Clark Co., 1965), 135, 143, 147–150. See also Edna B. Patterson, Louise A. Ulph, and Victor Goodwin, *Nevada's Northeast Frontier* (Sparks: Nev.: Western Printing and Publishing Co., 1969), 323, 382, 638, and Durham and Jones, *The Negro Cowboys*, 124–25, 134–35.

59. The first quote appears in *Trinidad Daily Advertiser*, June 2, 1883, p. 1, and the second in *Field and Farm*, July 23, 1887, p. 8. See also Haywood, " 'No Less a Man,' " 170, and Durham and Jones, *The Negro Cowboys*, 55–56, 65–66. Few extant studies have analyzed the two groups often described with black cowboys, African American outlaws or lawmen, with the sophistication and sensitivity of Richard Maxwell Brown's *No Duty to*

Retreat: Violence and Values in American History and Society (New York: Oxford University Press, 1991). However, the best treatments are Daniel F. Littlefield, Jr., and Lonnie Underhill, "Negro Marshals in the Indian Territory," *Journal of Negro History* 54:2 (April 1971), 77–87; Nudie Williams, "Black Men Who Wore the Star," *Chronicles of Oklahoma* 59:1 (Spring 1981), 83–90; Arthur T. Burton, *Black, Red and Deadly: Black and Indian Gunfighters of the Indian Territory, 1870–1907* (Austin: Eakin Press, 1991); and Jones and Durham, *The Negro Cowboys,* 172–88.

60. The Haywood family ranching activities are outlined in George P. Rawick, *The American Slave: A Composite Autobiography,* vol. 4, *Texas Narratives* (Westport, Conn.: Greenwood Publishing Co., 1972), part 2, p. 133, while the Kansas ranchers Peoples and Hilton are briefly described in Haywood, " 'No Less a Man,' " 167, 172. On the Dow brothers and Palmer, see Elmer Rusco, *"Good Time Coming?". Black Nevadans in the Nineteenth Century* (Westport, Conn.: Greenwood Press, 1975), 142–144. On Wallace, see Hertha Auburn Webb, "D. W. '80 John' Wallace: Black Cattleman, 1875–1939" (M.A. thesis, Prairie View A&M College, 1957).

61. Durham and Jones, *The Negro Cowboys,* 159. Ironically the rodeos, one of the early attempts to engage the West as "theater," had a significant black presence, including the legendary performers Bill Pickett of Oklahoma, Jesse Stahl of California, and Oregonian George Fletcher, who starred for years in the Pendleton Roundup. The roundup was founded in 1908 by eight cowboys, including Charles Buckner, an African American. For a survey of black rodeo performers through the twentieth century, see Clifford P. Westermeier, "Black Rodeo Cowboys," *Red River Valley Historical Review* 3:3 (Summer 1978), 4–27. Bill Pickett, the most famous of these performers, is profiled in Colonel Bailey C. Hanes, *Bill Pickett, Bulldogger: The Biography of a Black Cowboy* (Norman: University of Oklahoma Press, 1977).

62. Theodore Roosevelt, *Ranch Life and the Hunting Trail* (New York: Century Co., 1920), 11.

63. Joseph G. McCoy, *Historic Sketches of the Cattle Trade in the West and Southwest* (originally published, 1874; reprinted Washington: Rare Book Shop, 1932), 375.

64. George W. Pierson, *The Moving American* (New York: Alfred A. Knopf, 1973), 168.

6: Buffalo Soldiers in the West, 1866–1917

1. The Leckie and Forbes quotes are from Lawrence B. de Graaf, "Recognition, Racism, and Reflections on the Writing of Western Black History," *Pacific Historical Review* 44:1 (February 1975), 37, while McCombs's statement appears in Frank N. Schubert, ed., *On the Trail of the Buffalo Soldier: Biographies of African Americans in the U.S. Army, 1866–1917* (Wilmington, Del.: Scholarly Resources, 1995), p. xviii. In separate correspondence with the author (October 23, 1995) Schubert claims that twenty-five thousand black men served in the four units between 1866 and 1917.

2. See Schubert, *On the Trail of the Buffalo Soldier,* xiv. On the Civil War origins of the western black military units, see Dudley Taylor Cornish, *The Sable Arm: Black Troops in the Union Army, 1861–1865* (Lawrence: University Press of Kansas, 1987), 286–88.

3. Congress originally authorized forty-one infantry regiments, including four black units, with two in the South and two on the frontier. After the Army Reorganization Act of 1869, the total number of infantry units was reduced to twenty-five. The two southern regiments were sent to Louisiana and consolidated there as the 25th Infantry, while the two western units were collapsed in Texas into the new 24th Infantry. Some black soldiers served in the West prior to 1867. Companies of the 57th Infantry, organized in Little Rock and Helena, Arkansas, in 1864, were stationed at Fort Union and Fort Bascom, New Mexico Territory, until the regiment was disbanded on December 31, 1866. The 125th Infantry, organized in spring 1865 in Louisville, Kentucky, served in Kansas and New Mexico until disbanded on December 20, 1867, and the 38th Infantry, the only post–Civil War regiment of the three, was formed in 1866. The 38th was employed specifically to help with the defense of the Colorado and Indian territories and Kansas. See William H. Leckie, *The Buffalo Soldiers: A Narrative of the Negro Cavalry in the West* (Norman: University of Oklahoma Press, 1967), 6; Arlen L. Fowler, *The Black Infantry in the West, 1869–1891* (Westport, Conn.: Green-

wood Publishing Co., 1971), 4, 12; J. G. Randall and David Donald, *The Civil War and Reconstruction* (Boston: D. C. Heath and Co., 1961), 530; and Monroe Lee Billington, *New Mexico's Buffalo Soldiers, 1866–1900* (Niwot: University Press of Colorado, 1991), 4–5.

4. Troop K of the Ninth Cavalry was briefly assigned to Fort Myer, Virginia, just outside Washington, D.C., in April 1891, but no large-scale reassignment of black soldiers east of the Mississippi occurred until after 1898. See Jack D. Foner, *Blacks and the Military in American History: A New Perspective* (New York: Praeger, 1974), 69. The Auger quote appears on page 48. On black troop assignments in Texas, see William L. Richter, *The Army in Texas during Reconstruction, 1865–1870* (College Station: Texas A&M University Press, 1987), 17, 24.

5. See *Bellville Countryman*, August 18, 1865, p. 2. The Sheridan quote appears in Richter, *The Army in Texas*, 32. See also pages 55, 67, and 153 and James A. Smallwood, *Time of Home, Time of Despair: Black Texans during Reconstruction* (Port Washington, N.Y.: Kennikat Press, 1981), 39, 131.

6. For background on the commanding officers of the four all-black regiments, see William H. Leckie and Shirley A. Leckie, *Unlikely Warriors: Benjamin H. Grierson and His Family* (Norman: University of Oklahoma Press, 1984), ch. 3 and 4; Paul H. Carlson, *"Pecos Bill": A Military Biography of William R. Shafter* (College Station: Texas A&M University Press, 1989). On Pershing, see Frank E. Vandiver, *Black Jack: The Life and Times of John J. Pershing* (College Station: Texas A&M. University Press, 1977), vol. 1, pp. 137–38, 150–51, 171, 216, and Donald Smythe, S.J., "John J. Pershing at Fort Assiniboine," *Montana: The Magazine of Western History* 18:1 (Winter 1968), 19–20.

7. Flipper, Alexander, and Young were the only graduates of West Point until Benjamin O. Davis, Jr., in 1936. Benjamin O. Davis, Sr., had been an officer in the Eighth U.S. Volunteer Infantry during the Spanish-American War. He subsequently enlisted in the Ninth Cavalry to be eligible to take the officers' qualifying examination. Tutored by Lieutenant Charles Young while both were assigned to Fort Duchesne, Utah, Davis passed the examination and was assigned to the Tenth Cavalry. See Marvin Fletcher, *The Black Soldier and Officer in the United States Army, 1891–1917* (Columbia: University of Missouri Press, 1974), 72–74, 84, and Ronald Coleman, "The Buffalo Soldiers: Guardians of the Uintah Frontier, 1886–1901," *Utah Historical Quarterly* 47:4 (Fall 1979), 433–34.

8. The Allensworth quote appears in Fowler, *The Black Infantry in the West*, p. 136. See also Frank N. Schubert, *Buffalo Soldiers, Braves, and the Brass: The Story of Fort Robinson, Nebraska* (Shippensburg, Pa.: White Mane Publishing Co., 1993), 53–54. 130–31, and Earl F. Stover, "Chaplain Henry V. Plummer, His Ministry and His Courtmartial," *Nebraska History* 56:1 (Spring 1975), 21–50.

9. On Allensworth, see Fowler, *The Black Infantry in the West*, pp. 105–06. Flipper is profiled in Theodore D. Harris, ed., *Negro Frontiersman: The Western Memoirs of Henry O. Flipper, First Negro Graduate of West Point* (El Paso: Texas Western College Press, 1963), vii–ix. For discussions of other black officers, see Nellie Arnold Plummer, *Out of the Depths: or, The Triumph of the Cross* (Hyattsville, Md.: privately printed, 1927); Chaplain T. G. Steward, *The Colored Regulars in the United States Army* (Philadelphia: A.M.E. Book Concern, 1904); and William Seraile, *Voice of Dissent: Theophilus Gould Steward (1843–1924) and Black America* (Brooklyn: Carlson Publishing, 1991).

10. The Waller quote is in Reuben Waller, "History of a Slave Written by Himself at the Age of 89 Years," in John M. Carroll, ed., *The Black Military Experience in the West* (New York: Liveright, 1971), 194; the quote from Private Creek appears in Erwin N. Thompson, "The Negro Soldiers on the Frontier: A Fort Davis Case Study," *Journal of the West* 7:2 (April 1968), 226. See also William A. Dobak, "Black Regulars Speak," *Panhandle-Plains Historical Review* 47 (1974), 21; Frank N. Schubert, "The Violent World of Emanuel Stance, Fort Robinson, 1887," *Nebraska History* 55:2 (Summer 1974), 203–04; and Leckie, *Buffalo Soldiers*, p. 10. One soldier's life in the army is profiled in Thomas R. Buecker, "One Soldier's Service: Caleb Benson in the Ninth and Tenth Cavalry, 1875–1908," *Nebraska History* 74:2 (Summer 1993), 54–62.

11. Elizabeth B. Custer, *Tenting on the Plains, or General Custer in Kansas and Texas* (New York: Charles L. Webster & Co., 1889), 677–78.

12. The quote appears in Lonnie J. White, "Warpaths on the Southern Plains: The Battles of the Saline River and Prairie Dog Creek," *Journal of the West* 4:4 (October 1965), 498. For background on the experiences of the black troops at Fort Hays, see James N. Leiker, "Black Soldiers at Fort Hays, Kansas, 1867–1869: A Study in Civilian and Military Violence," *Great Plains Quarterly* 17:1 (Winter 1997), 3–17. Statistics indicate that black soldiers were less frequently involved in conflict with Native Americans than their numbers in the West would suggest. While they constituted approximately 20 percent of the effective strength of the army, the 1891 report of the adjutant general showed they were engaged in only 5.2 percent of the 2,704 Indian engagements between 1866 and 1891. The Ninth Cavalry participated in 68 engagements, the Tenth in 49, the Twenty-fourth in 9, and the Twenty-fifth in 15. See Thomas D. Phillips, "The Black Regulars," in Allan G. Bogue, Thomas D. Phillips, and James E. Wright, eds., *The West of the American People* (Itasca, Ill.: F. E. Peacock Publishers, 1970), 141.

13. The attack on the Kiowa camp is described in "Report of the Agent for the Kiowa, Comanche and Wichita Agency," *Annual Report of the Commissioner of Indian Affairs, 1879* (Washington, D.C.: Government Printing Office, 1879), 64. See also "Oklahoma," *Harper's Weekly Magazine,* 29:1475 (March 28, 1885), 199: Leckie, *Buffalo Soldiers,* 20, 28, 166–68, 246–51; and Coleman, "The Buffalo Soldiers," 430.

14. Paul H. Carlson, "William R. Shafter, Black Troops, and the Opening of the Llano Estacado, 1870–1875," *Panhandle-Plains Historical Review* 47(1974), 4–14, and Leckie, *Buffalo Soldiers,* 88–89, 217.

15. Born in Williamson County, Tennessee, George Jordan was a nineteen-year-old farmer when he joined the army in Nashville, Tennessee, in 1866. He retired from the army in 1897 in Crawford, Nebraska, and was buried in the post cemetery in 1904 near Fort Robinson. See Walter F. Beyer and Oscar F. Keydel, eds., *Deeds of Valor: How American Heroes Won the Medal of Honor* (Detroit: Perrien-Keydel Co., 1907), vol. 2, pp. 273–76, and Leckie, *Buffalo Soldiers,* 220–21.

16. For a full account of the incident, see Robert M. Utley, *Frontier Regulars: The United States Army and the Indian, 1866–1891* (New York: Macmillan, 1973), 402–11, and Utley, *The Last Days of the Sioux Nation* (New Haven: Yale University Press, 1963), ch. 7 and 12; Richard Jensen, R. Eli Paul, and John E. Carter, *Eyewitness at Wounded Knee* (Lincoln: University of Nebraska Press, 1991), ch. 1; and Schubert, *Buffalo Soldiers,* 25–31.

17. Prather's poem "The Indian Ghost Dance and War," appears in James Mooney, *The Ghost Dance Religion and the Sioux Outbreak of 1890* (Washington, D.C.: Government Printing Office, 1896), 882–883. On Prather's views toward the Indians, see Frank N. Schubert, *Black Valor: Buffalo Soldiers and the Medal of Honor, 1870–1898* (Wilmington, Del.: Scholarly Resources, 1997), 127–28. See also Utley, *Frontier Regulars,* 408–11, and Schubert, *Buffalo Solders,* pp. 29–31.

18. Organizational Returns, Tenth Cavalry, August 1881, quoted in Leckie, *Buffalo Soldiers,* 238; Grierson's report is cited on page 155. See also Billington, *New Mexico's Buffalo Soldiers,* 10–11, 23.

19. The Hatch quote appears in Leckie, *Buffalo Soldiers,* 190. The most complete discussion of the El Paso Salt War can be found in Mary Romero, "El Paso Salt War: Mob Action or Political Struggle?," *Aztlán: International Journal of Chicano Studies Research* 16:1–2 (1985), 119–43, and C. L. Sonnichsen, *The El Paso Salt War, 1877* (El Paso: Texas Western Press, 1961).

20. Quoted in Frank N. Schubert, "The Suggs Affray: The Black Cavalry in the Johnson County War," *Western Historical Quarterly* 4:1 (January 1973), 60.

21. Ibid., 60–64.

22. Ibid, 66–68.

23. On the Fort Hays incident, see James M. Leiker, "Black Soldiers at Fort Hays," 9–14. The Sturgis confrontation is described in Thomas R. Buecker, "Confrontation at Sturgis: An Episode in Civil-Military Race Relations, 1885," *South Dakota History* 14:3 (Fall 1984), 238–61.

24. *Sturgis Weekly Record,* September 25, 1885, p. 2, and *Black Hills Daily Times,* September 23, 1885, p. 1.

25. *Las Cruces Thirty-Four,* November 12, 1879, p. 2. One week later, after conversation

with Ninth Cavalry officers, the editor of the *Thirty-Four* published another editorial where he admitted he had "unintentionally done great injustice to the officers and men [of the Ninth] and then recalled the regiment's recently completed difficult campaign against Victorio's Apache warriors. After adding that "our faith in negro troops is not strong," the editorial concluded by calling on the community to "give the Ninth another chance," *Thirty-Four,* November 19, 1879, p. 1.

26. Leckie, *Buffalo Soldiers,* 99, 108–09, 164, 235–37.
27. The *Boston Evening Transcript* quote appears in Foner, *Blacks and the Military,* 74. Private Thomas's letter appears in the *Salt Lake City Tribune,* October 22, 1896, p. 4. For Young's speech, see the *Daily Palo Alto,* December 9, 1903, p. 1.
28. The McKibbin quote appears in Foner, *Blacks and the Military,* 83; see also page 82. For a detailed discussion of the Texas incidents, see Garna L. Christian, *Black Soldiers in Jim Crow Texas, 1899–1917* (College Station: Texas A&M University Press, 1995), 5–12, 30–45, 51–53, and Fletcher, *Black Soldier and Officer,* 113, 119.
29. See Christian, *Black Soldiers in Jim Crow Texas,* 17–20, 25, 27, 35. The quotes appear on pages 42 and 35 respectively.
30. Both quotes appear in Ann J. Lane, *The Brownsville Affair: National Crisis and Black Reaction* (Port Washington, N.Y.: Kennikat Press, 1971), 166, 16 respectively. Not all local citizens opposed the soldiers stationed there. Some businesses, such as the local drugstore, welcomed their trade. The response to black customers by the saloon proprietors adjourning Fort Brown reflected the varied attitudes. Of the four white-owned saloons, two excluded black troops, while the other two established separate bars at the backs of their businesses. The four saloons owned by Mexican American proprietors welcomed the soldiers without restriction. See Lane, *The Brownsville Affair,* 15. For background, see John D. Weaver, *The Brownsville Raid* (New York: W. W. Norton, 1970), ch. 2 and 3, and Fletcher, *Black Soldier and Officer,* 120–21.
31. Lane, *The Brownsville Affair,* 5; Weaver, *The Brownsville Raid,* ch. 5; and Fletcher, *Black Soldier and Officer,* 121–22.
32. The Roosevelt quote is from Fletcher, *Black Soldier and Officer,* 127. See Lane, *The Brownsville Affair,* 18–20.
33. Roosevelt's quote appears in Foner, *Blacks and the Military,* p. 79. On the national impact of the Brownsville raid and Roosevelt's response, see Lane, *The Brownsville Affair,* ch. 5–8; Louis R. Harlan, *Booker T. Washington: The Wizard of Tuskegee, 1901–1915* (New York: Oxford University Press, 1983), 309–13, 318; and David Levering Lewis, *W. E. B. Du Bois: Biography of a Race, 1868–1919* (New York: Henry Holt, 1993), pp. 331–32. The final chapter in the Brownsville saga came in December 1973, when Congress exonerated and voted a twenty-five-thousand-dollar pension to Dorsie Willis of Minneapolis, Minnesota, the only survivor among the 167 men. See Fletcher, *Black Soldier and Officer,* 146–47.
34. Robert V. Haynes, "The Houston Mutiny and Riot of 1917," *Southwestern Historical Quarterly* 74:4 (April 1973), 418–21. For background on Houston's separate white and black communities, see Robert V. Haynes, *A Night of Violence: The Houston Riot of 1917* (Baton Rouge: Louisiana State University Press, 1976), ch. 2.
35. The Chamber of Commerce quote appears in Haynes, *A Night of Violence,* 52. See also pages 83–89.
36. The Henry quote appears ibid., 126–27. Haynes's account of the development of the mutiny and riot is detailed in Chapters 4 and 5.
37. Sparks, who escaped the wrath of the soldiers, resumed his brutal behavior toward the black populace. Four days after the riot he shot and killed black Houstonian Wallace Williams. Sparks was indicted and brought to trial, but the jury took only "one minute" to acquit him. See Martha Gruening, "Houston: An NAACP Investigation," *Crisis* 15:1 (November 1917), 14–18; Haynes, *A Night of Violence,* ch. 6, and Christian, *Black Soldiers and Jim Crow Texas,* ch. 9.
38. President Woodrow Wilson commuted the sentences of 10 soldiers to life imprisonment after receiving an NAACP petition signed by 12,000 people requesting executive clemency for the condemned soldiers. See *Crisis* 15:6 (April 1918), 283; C. Calvin Smith, "On the Edge: The Houston Riot of 1917 Revisited," *Griot* 10:1 (Spring 1991), 3–12, and Haynes, *A Night of Violence,* 296. The NAACP continued to work for the exoneration of the other accused soldiers for the next two decades. In 1924 it pre-

sented a petition signed by 120,000 to President Calvin Coolidge. Finally, in 1938, President Franklin Roosevelt released the last prisoner. See Charles Flint Kellogg, *NAACP: A History of the National Association for the Advancement of Colored People,* vol. 1, *1909–1920* (Baltimore: Johns Hopkins University Press, 1967), 262. The Brownsville and Houston episodes were two of a long chronicle of violent response of black soldiers to racial bigotry by civilians. Besides the incidents previously described at San Angelo, Texas, in 1878, Suggs, Wyoming, in 1892, and El Paso in 1900, San Antonio in 1911 and 1916, and Del Rio, Texas, the same year, there were confrontations at Sturgis City, Dakota Territory (1885), Walla Walla, Washington (1891), Huntsville, Alabama (1898), Winnemucca, Nevada, and San Carlos Agency, Arizona Territory (1899), near Fort Niobrara, Nebraska, and Athens, Ohio (1904), Seattle (1912), and Iwilei, Hawaii (1915). See Haynes, "The Houston Mutiny," 437, footnote 74, and 438–39.

39. See Christian, *Black Soldiers in Jim Crow Texas,* 177–78.
40. Quoted in Fowler, *Black Infantry,* 21. Black soldiers seemed generally more pleased with their living quarters in Kansas, Dakota Territory, and Montana, but they took particular pride in Fort Sill, Indian Territory, which Tenth Cavalry troops built in 1869. See Leckie, *Buffalo Soldiers,* 47–49. For an example of the routine of black soldiers, see the Fort Cummings, New Mexico, daily schedule in Billington, *New Mexico's Buffalo Soldiers,* 115–16.
41. The Fort Washakie quote appears in Fletcher, *Black Soldier and Officer,* 79; the baseball quote is on page 101. See also Fowler, *Black Infantry,* 85; Billington, *New Mexico's Buffalo Soldiers,* 157–58; and Schubert, *Buffalo Soldiers,* 101–08, 119–20.
42. See Michael J. Clark, "Improbable Ambassadors: Black Soldiers at Fort Douglas, 1896–99," *Utah Historical Quarterly* 46:3 (Summer 1978), 282–85, 291–95.
43. Surgeon Jefferson Kean is quoted in Schubert, *Buffalo Soldiers,* 58. The paragraph's first quotation is from Virginia Scharff, "Gender and Western History: Is Anybody Home on the Range?", *Montana: The Magazine of Western History* 41:2 (Spring 1991), 62. Before 1878 only the wives of enlisted men who served as camp laundresses were allowed to reside in military housing. After that date even they were relegated to off-post housing. For a rich discussion of families and community at western military outposts, see Schubert, *Buffalo Soldiers,* ch. 5 and 12, and Billington, *New Mexico's Buffalo Soldiers,* ch. 8.
44. Schubert, *Buffalo Soldiers,* 62.
45. Quoted in ibid., 66. See also page 63 and Schubert, *On the Trail of the Buffalo Soldiers,* 9.
46. Quoted in Billington, *New Mexico's Buffalo Soldiers,* 132.
47. Quoted in Schubert, "The Violent World of Emanuel Stance," 211; see also pages 207–215. Tension between the soldiers and commissioned officers of the Ninth Cavalry Regiment were also an issue. In 1867 troops of the Ninth mutinied at San Pedro Springs, just outside San Antonio, over their treatment by lieutenant Edward M. Heyl. See Byron Price, "Mutiny at San Pedro Springs," *By Valor & Arms* 1:3 (Spring 1975), 31–34. See also Billington, *New Mexico's Buffalo Soldiers,* 39, 128, for a discussion of the problem in New Mexico Territory.
48. The *St. Louis Republic* editorial is quoted in Schubert, "The Suggs Affray," 67.
49. Barton C. Hacker, "The United States Army as a National Police Force: The Federal Policing of Labor Disputes, 1877–1898," *Military Affairs* 33:1 (April 1969), 260. See also Jerry M. Cooper, *The Army and Civil Disorder: Federal Military Intervention in Labor Disputes, 1877–1900* (Westport, Conn.: Greenwood Press, 1980), 259–60.
50. See the *Army and Navy Register* 13:51 (December 17, 1892), 816; T.G. Steward, "The Strike in Montana," *Independent* 46:2384 (August 9, 1894), 1017.
51. See U.S. Congress, Senate, *Federal Aid in Domestic Disturbances, 1787–1903,* S. Doc. 209, 57th Congress, 2d session, 1902–1903, part 10, pp. 222–25. See also Robert Wayne Smith, *The Coeur d'Alene Mining War of 1892: A Case Study of an Industrial Dispute* (Corvallis: Oregon State University Press, 1961), 74–79; Clayton D. Laurie, "The United States Army and the Labor Radicals of the Coeur d'Alenes: Federal Military Intervention in the Mining Wars of 1892–1899," *Idaho Yesterdays* 37:2 (Summer 1993), 14–17; John H. Nankivell, ed., *History of the Twenty-fifth Regiment United States Infantry, 1869–1926* (Denver: Smith-Brooks Printing Co., 1927), 51–53; and Cooper, *The Army and*

Civil Disorder, 165–70. For Siringo's account of his activities as a spy in the Coeur d'Alene district, see his *A Cowboy Detective: A True Story of Twenty-two Years with a World Famous Detective Agency* (Chicago: W. B. Conkey Co., 1912), 138.

52. *Spokane Spokesman Review,* July 29, 1892, p. 2, and Smith, *The Coeur d'Alene Mining War,* 90–91, 110–14.

53. See *Idaho Daily Statesman,* May 5, 1899, p. 1; *Federal Aid in Domestic Disturbances,* part 12, pp. 246–53; Cooper, *The Army and Civil Disorder,* 172–76; and Laurie, "The United States Army and the Labor Radicals," 24.

54. *Harper's Weekly,* 43:2213 (May 20, 1899), 498. See also Cooper, *The Army and Civil Disorder,* 176.

55. The quote by Attorney General Hayes appears in the *Idaho Daily Statesman,* May 9, 1899, p. 1. See also Cooper, *The Army and Civil Disorder,* 178. On December 30, 1905, retired Governor Steunenberg was killed by a bomb set to explode when he opened a gate at his Caldwell, Idaho, home. Although leaders of the Western Federation of Miners were tried for the assassination, none were convicted. See Laurie, "The United States Army and the Labor Radicals," 29.

56. May Arkwright Hutton, whose sympathies were clearly with the striking miners, provided a firsthand account that was published one year after martial law was declared. Even discounting her partisanship, her account depicts a charged political and military situation exacerbated by racial tension. She accused the black troopers of using conduct and language around white women that was "impossible to describe in print" and concluded that the "barbarity practiced by the negro soldiers . . . are a shame and disgrace to our civilization." See Hutton, *The Coeur d'Alenes or a Tale of the Modern Inquisition in Idaho* (Wallace, Ida.: May Arkwright Hutton, 1900), 144–58. See also "Herded in by Negro Troops," *Spokane Spokesman Review,* May 4, 1899, p. 1; Cooper, *The Army and Civil Disorder,* 182–83; and Laurie, "The United States Army and the Labor Radicals," 25–27.

57. See Vandiver, *Black Jack,* vol. 2, pp. 604–46, and Horace D. Nash, "Blacks on the Border: Columbus, New Mexico, 1916–1922" (M.A. thesis, New Mexico State University, 1988), 11–13.

58. Quoted in the *El Paso Morning Times,* June 30, 1916, p. 2. See also James N. Leiker, "Fracas at El Carrizal: The Intersection of Race and Nationalism in United States/ Mexico Relations, 1916," (unpublished paper in the author's possession), 17–18, 23–32; Captain Lewis S. Morey, "The Cavalry Fight at Carrizal," in John M. Carroll, *The Black Military Experience in the American West* (New York: Liveright, 1971), 497–503; Haldeen Braddy, *Pershing's Mission in Mexico* (El Paso: Texas Western Press, 1966), 47–58; and Vandiver, *Black Jack,* vol. 2, pp. 650–55.

59. See Leiker, "Fracas at El Carrizal," 35–37; and Vandiver, *Black Jack,* vol. 2, pp. 655–68.

60. Du Bois editorial, "Thirteen," *Crisis* 15:3 (January 1918), 114. The Mullins quote appears in Foner, *Blacks and the Military,* 53. The other quotes are from the *Langston City Herald,* October 15, 1892, p. 1, and Rayford W. Logan, *The Betrayal of the Negro from Rutherford B. Hayes to Woodrow Wilson* (London: Collier Books, 1965), 335.

7: The Black Urban West, 1870–1910

1. For a general discussion of the network of western cities, see Lawrence H. Larsen, *The Urban West at the End of the Frontier* (Lawrence: Regents Press of Kansas, 1978), ch. 1 and 2.

2. For a history of one Kansas African American community in the 1870s and 1880s, see Susan Greenbaum, *The Afro-American Community in Kansas City, Kansas: A History* (Kansas City: City of Kansas City, 1982), ch. 2 and 3. See also Eugene H. Berwanger, "Hardin and Langston: Western Black Spokesmen of the Reconstruction Era," *Journal of Negro History* 64:2 (Spring 1979), 102.

3. See U.S. Bureau of the Census, *Twelfth Census of the United States, 1900, Population* Part 1, (Washington, D.C.: U.S. Government Printing Office, 1901), cxix–xi, and Willard B. Gatewood, *Aristocrats of Color: The Black Elite, 1880–1920* (Bloomington: Indiana University Press, 1990), 129–38. For a discussion of one nineteenth-century western urban community, see Quintard Taylor, *The Forging of a Black Community: Seattle's Cen-*

tral District from 1870 through the Civil Rights Era (Seattle: University of Washington Press, 1994), ch. 1.

4. *Fort Scott Colored Citizen,* June 14, 1878, p. 1. For a detailed examination of the occupational and social structure of two nineteenth-century black western communities, see Thomas C. Cox, *Blacks in Topeka, Kansas, 1865–1915: A Social History* (Baton Rouge: Louisiana State University Press, 1982), ch 4, and Taylor, *Forging,* ch. 1. See also Willard Gatewood's appraisal of elites in western cities in *Aristocrats of Color,* 138.

5. The first quote is from a *Pacific Appeal* editorial, June 7, 1862, p. 2. The second appears in the *Montana Plaindealer,* May 24, 1907, p. 1. See also Douglas Henry Daniels, *Pioneer Urbanites: A Social and Cultural History of Black San Francisco* (Philadelphia: Temple University Press, 1980), 106.

6. On the Kansas and Puget Sound AME conferences, see Randall Bennett Woods, *A Black Odyssey: John Lewis Waller and the Promise of American Life, 1878–1900* (Lawrence: Regents Press of Kansas, 1981), 44, and Taylor, *Forging,* 37–38.

7. On the black western press, see Gayle Beradi and Thomas W. Segady, "Community Identification and Cultural Formation: The Role of African American Newspapers in the American West, 1880–1914," *Griot* 10:1 (Spring 1991), 13–19. For an analysis of the role of one black Kansas newspaper in defending African American political interests, see Teresa C. Klassen and Owen V. Johnson, "Sharpening of the *Blade:* Black Consciousness in Kansas, 1892–97," *Journalism Quarterly* 63:2 (Summer 1986), 298–304.

8. Daniels, *Pioneer Urbanites,* 106–07.

9. Throughout the late nineteenth century San Franciscans who were foreign-born or of foreign-born parentage constituted more than half the city's population and at times more than 70 percent. See William Issel and Robert W. Cherny, *San Francisco, 1865–1932: Politics, Power and Urban Development* (Berkeley: University of California Press, 1986), 55, and Daniels, *Pioneer Urbanites,* 17, 82.

10. The Idaho quote appears in the *Pacific Appeal,* July 18, 1863, p. 3. For a detailed discussion of the *Elevator–Pacific Appeal* rivalry, see Albert Broussard, "The New Racial Frontier: San Francisco's Black Community, 1900–1940" (Ph.D. dissertation, Duke University, 1977), pp. 49–54.

11. Mary Ellen Pleasant's role as a successful, foresighted entrepreneur who, more than any other African American of the era, moved easily among the city's elite is now well documented in the public record. However, her alleged occult powers are the products of myth and folklore. For a balanced, scholarly appraisal of Pleasant, see Lynn M. Hudson, "When 'Mammy' Becomes a Millionaire: Mary Ellen Pleasant, an African American Entrepreneur" (Ph.D. dissertation, Indiana University, 1996). See also Daniels, *Pioneer Urbanites,* 29–30, for a discussion of other prosperous San Francisco African Americans.

12. Daniels, *Pioneer Urbanites,* 15–17, 31.

13. See Issel and Cherny, *San Francisco,* 125–30, and Daniels, *Pioneer Urbanites,* 17.

14. Daniels, *Pioneer Urbanites,* 36.

15. *San Francisco Daily Alta California,* November 9, 1889, p. 1. See also Daniels, *Pioneer Urbanites,* 36–39.

16. The anonymous politico is quoted in the *San Francisco Daily Evening Post,* June 25, 1873, p. 1. The Pleasant quote appears in Lynn M. Hudson, "A New Look, or 'I'm Not Mammy to Everybody in California': Mary Ellen Pleasant, a Black Entrepreneur," *Journal of the West* 32:3 (July 1993), 37. For a discussion of Booth's victory, see James Adolphus Fisher, "A History of the Political and Social Development of the Black Community in California, 1850–1950" (Ph.D. dissertation, State University of New York at Stony Brook, 1972), 117–18; Booth's inaugural quote appears on page 118. On black San Francisco politics through 1910, see Albert S. Broussard, *Black San Francisco: The Struggle for Racial Equality in the West, 1900–1954* (Lawrence: University Press of Kansas, 1993), 92–94.

17. For a discussion of San Francisco politics during this period, see Issel and Cherny, *San Francisco,* ch. 6 and 7.

18. For the quote on the black women, see the *San Francisco Chronicle,* June 6, 1894, p. 5. On Jackson, see *San Francisco Call,* March 22, 1891, p. 8, and March 22, 1900, p. 4. See also Daniels, *Pioneer Urbanites,* 124–28, 132–40.

19. Powell is quoted in Daniels, *Pioneer Urbanites*, 119. See also Francis N. Lortie, *San Francisco's Black Community, 1870–1890: Dilemmas in the Struggle for Equality* (San Francisco: R and E Research Associates, 1973), 20–21.

20. On the lack of employment opportunities in the Bay Area, see Broussard, *Black San Francisco*, 38–39. Black Oakland is described in Lawrence P. Crouchett, Lonnie G. Bunch III, and Martha Kendall Winnacker, *Visions toward Tomorrow: The History of the East Bay Afro-American Community, 1852–1977* (Oakland: Northern California Center for Afro-American History and Life, 1989), 1–18. Shorey's life is detailed in E. Berkeley Tompkins, "Black Ahab: William T. Shorey, Whaling Master," *California Historical Quarterly* 51:1 (Spring 1972), 75–84.

21. See Lyle W. Dorsett, *The Queen City: A History of Denver* (Boulder: Pruett Publishing Co., 1977), 52–53; Lionel Dean Lyles, "An Historical-Urban Geographical Analysis of Black Neighborhood Development in Denver, 1860–1970" (Ph.D. dissertation, University of Colorado, 1977), 57–63; Stephen J. Leonard and Thomas J. Noel, *Denver: Mining Camp to Metropolis* (Niwot: University Press of Colorado, 1990), 23, Eugene Berwanger, "William J. Hardin: Colorado Spokesman for Racial Justice, 1863–1873," *Colorado Magazine* 52:1 (Winter 1975), 59; and Gatewood, *Aristocrats of Color*, 134–35.

22. For a brief account of Barney Ford, see Frank Hall, *History of the State of Colorado* (Chicago: Blakely Printing Co., 1895), vol. 4, pp. 440–41; the quote appears on page 441. See also Lyles, "An Historical-Urban Geographical Analysis," 58.

23. Quoted in *Colorado Statesman*, October 30, 1909, p. 3. See Lynda Faye Dickson, "The Early Club Movement among Black Women in Denver: 1890–1925" (Ph.D. dissertation University of Colorado, 1982), 72–84, and Moya Hansen, "Pebbles on the Shore: Economic Opportunity in Five Points, 1920–1950" (unpublished paper in author's possession), p. 7. See also Brian R. Werner, "Colorado's Pioneer Blacks: Migration, Occupations and Race Relations in the Centennial State" (M.A. thesis, University of Northern Colorado, 1979), 9–10, 27; see page 57 for an occupational chart of black Denver between 1870 and 1885. See also Dorsett, *The Queen City*, 104–05, and Lyles, "An Historical-Urban Geographical Analysis," 64–67.

24. On Walker, see her entry in Edward T. James, Janet Wilson James and Paul S. Boyer, eds., *Notable American Women, 1607–1950: A Biographical Dictionary* (Cambridge: Harvard University Press, 1971), vol. 3, pp. 533–35. For a discussion of black leisure activities in Denver, see Moya Hansen, "Entitled to Full and Equal Enjoyment: Leisure and Entertainment in the Denver Black Community, 1900 to 1930," *University of Colorado at Denver Historical Studies Journal* 10:1 (Spring 1993), 57–71.

25. For a description of the West Indian Emancipation Day celebration on August 1, 1865, see *Rocky Mountain News*, August 2, 1865, p. 4. See also William M. King, *Going to Meet a Man: Denver's Last Legal Public Execution, 27 July 1886* (Niwot: University Press of Colorado, 1990), 2, 4–5, 71; Dickson, "The Early Club Movement," 83–87; and Werner, "Colorado's Pioneer Blacks," 12–15.

26. If African colonization received scant support, some Denver blacks looked to resettlement schemes within the state, the most important of which was the all-black community of Dearfield, founded in Weld County, to remove blacks from the pressure of urban living. For a discussion of Dearfield, see George H. Wayne, "Negro Migration and Colonization in Colorado—1870–1930," *Journal of the West* 15:1 (January 1976), 110–18. See also Dorsett, *The Queen City*, 93, 114.

27. See Lawrence H. Larsen and Barbara J. Cottrell, *The Gate City: A History of Omaha* (Boulder: Pruett Publishing Co., 1982), ch. 3, pp. 121–23, and Nebraska Writers' Project (Works Progress Administration), *The Negroes of Nebraska* (Lincoln: Woodruff Printing Co., 1940), 10, 24.

28. Nebraska Writers' Project, *The Negroes of Nebraska*, pp. 20, 33, 38.

29. Ibid., p. 23.

30. See *Daily Nebraska State Journal* (Lincoln), October 11, 1891, p. 1, for Cushing quote. See also October 10, 1891, pp. 1–2, and October 11, 1891, p. 2, and *Omaha World-Herald* October 10, 1891, pp. 1–2. Omaha was to experience a far more horrific lynching on September 28, 1919, when more than one thousand rioters lynched William Brown, an itinerant packinghouse laborer, before twenty-five thousand spectators. The most detailed account of this episode can be found in Arthur V. Age, "The Omaha Riot of 1919" (M.A. thesis, Creighton University, 1964). The McCulloch quote

appears in Josie MaCague McCulloch, "Memories of Omaha: A Reminiscence," *Nebraska History* 35:4 (December 1954), 280.

31. Owens is described in F. H. Crumbly, "A Los Angeles Citizen," *Colored American Magazine* 9:3 (September 1905), 482–85, and Lonnie Bunch III, *Black Angelenos: The Afro-American in Los Angeles, 1850–1950* (Los Angeles: California Afro-American Museum, 1988), 17–19. See also Lawrence B. de Graaf, "The City of Black Angels: Emergence of the Los Angeles Ghetto, 1890–1930," *Pacific Historical Review* 39:3 (August 1970), 327; Dolores Hayden, "Biddy Mason's Los Angeles, 1856–1891" *California History* 68:3 (Fall 1989), 95–99; Charlotta A. Bass, *Forty Years: Memoirs from the Pages of a Newspaper* (Los Angeles: privately published, 1960), 8; and Gatewood, *Aristocrats of Color.* 132.

32. See J. Max Bond, "The Negro in Los Angeles" (Ph.D. dissertation, University of Southern California, 1936), 11–14; the Bond quote appears on page 13. See also Hayden, "Biddy Mason's Los Angeles," 86, 97, and Bunch, *Black Angelenos,* 19–20.

33. The Texas quote appears in de Graaf, "The City of Black Angels," 330. For the Rydall quote, see E. H. Rydall, "California for Colored Folk," *Colored American Magazine* 12:5 (May 1907), 386. For the interview of Tennessee migrants, see Bond, "The Negro in Los Angeles," 65. See also pp. 14–15 and de Graaf, "City of Black Angels," 330, 334–35. On Harrison Gray Otis and black Los Angeles, see Mikel Hogan García, "Adaptation Strategies of the Los Angeles Black Community, 1883–1919" (Ph.D. dissertation, University of California, Irvine, 1985), 33–36.

34. The Sojourner Truth Club quote appears in Lonnie G. Bunch, "A Past Not Necessarily Prologue: The African American in Los Angeles," in Norman M. Klein and Martin J. Schiesl, eds., *Twentieth-Century Los Angeles: Power, Promotion, and Social Conflict* (Claremont, Calif.: Regina Books, 1990), 108. The Women's Day Nursery Association, founded in January 1907 at the Wesley Chapel AME Church, was profiled in the *Los Angeles Times,* February 12, 1909, section 3, p. 4. On black politics in the first two decades of the twentieth century, see Douglas Flamming, "African Americans and the Politics of Race in Progressive-Era Los Angeles," in William Deverall and Tom Sitton, eds., *California Progressivism Revisited* (Berkeley: University of California Press, 1994), 203–28. On Neimore and the *Eagle,* see Fisher, "A History of the Political and Social Development of the Black Community," p. 163.

35. See the *Los Angeles Times,* February 12, 1909, section 3, p. 2, for an account of the history of the Forum. See also Emory J. Tolbert, *The UNIA and Black Los Angeles: Ideology and Community in the American Garvey Movement* (Los Angeles: Center for Afro-American Studies, 1980), 27, 33; E. Frederick Anderson, *The Development of Leadership and Organization Building in the Black Community of Los Angeles from 1900 through World War II* (Saratoga, Calif.: Century Twenty One Publishing, 1980), 59–60, 73; Garcia, "Adaptation Strategies," 85–86; Flamming, "African Americans and the Politics of Race in Progressive-Era Los Angeles," 205, 208; and Bunch, "A Past Not Necessarily Prologue," 107–08.

36. For representative discussions of blacks in western towns and small cities, see Michael Coray, "African-Americans in Nevada," *Nevada Historical Society Quarterly* 34:4 (Winter 1992), 242; C. Robert Haywood, " 'No Less a Man': Blacks in Cow Town Dodge City, 1876–1886," *Western Historical Quarterly* 19:2 (May 1988), 161–82; Nupur Chaudhuri, " 'We All Seem Like Brothers and Sisters': The African-American Community in Manhattan, Kansas, 1865–1940," *Kansas History* 14:4 (Winter 1991), 270–88; Quintard Taylor, "The Emergence of Black Communities in the Pacific Northwest, 1865–1910," *Journal of Negro History* 64:4 (Fall 1979), 342–54; Willard B. Gatewood, Jr., "Kate D. Chapman Reports on 'The Yankton Colored People,' 1889," *South Dakota History* 7:1 (Winter 1976), 28–35; Joseph Franklin, *All through the Night: The History of Spokane Black Americans* (Fairfield, Wash.: Ye Galleon Press, 1989); Marilyn T. Bryan, "The Economic, Political and Social Status of the Negro in El Paso," *Password* 13:3 (Fall 1968), 74–86; and Alwyn Barr, "Black Migration into Southwestern Cities, 1865–1900," in Garry W. Gallagher, ed., *Essays on Southern History Written in Honor of Barnes F. Lathrop* (Austin: General Libraries, University of Texas at Austin, 1980), 17–38.

37. The quote appears in Cary D. Wintz, "Blacks," in Fred R. von der Mehden, ed., *The Ethnic Groups of Houston* (Houston: Rice University Studies, 1984), 15. See also Wintz, "The Emergence of a Black Neighborhood: Houston's Fourth Ward, 1865–1915," in

Char Miller and Heywood T. Sanders, ed., *Urban Texas: Politics and Development* (College Station: Texas A&M University Press, 1990), 97–100. See Kenneth Mason, "Paternal Continuity: African Americans and Race Relations in San Antonio, Texas, 1867–1937" (Ph.D. dissertation, University of Texas, Austin, 1994), ch. 2, for a discussion of post–Civil War migration to San Antonio.

38. See Robert Prince, *A History of Dallas from a Different Perspective* (Dallas: Nortex Press, 1993), 31–41, and Beeth and Wintz, *Black Dixie,* pp. 21–25, 74–75.

39. See Howard Beeth and Cary D. Wintz, "Historical Overview," in Beeth and Wintz, eds., *Black Dixie: Afro-Texas History and Culture in Houston* (College Station: Texas A&M University Press, 1992), 87–92. See also Wintz, "The Emergence of a Black Neighborhood," 103–105; Prince, *A History of Dallas,* 42–55; Barr, "Black Migration into Southwestern Cities," 17–38, and Mason, "Paternal Continuity," 45–56. One west Texas city, El Paso, challenged the general pattern of race relations in the state. See Bryan, "The Economic, Political and Social Status of the Negro in El Paso," 74–86. For a discussion of the violence that underlay Texas segregation, see Bruce A. Glasrud, "Enforcing White Supremacy in Texas, 1900–1910," *Red River Valley Historical Review* 4:4 (Fall 1979), 65–74.

40. See Henry J. Wolfinger, "A Test of Faith: Jane Elizabeth James and the Origins of the Utah Black Community," in Clark Knowlton, ed., *Social Accommodation in Utah* (Salt Lake City: University of Utah Press, 1975), 126–72, and Ronald G. Coleman, "A History of Blacks in Utah, 1825–1910" (Ph.D. dissertation, University of Utah, 1980), 89–103.

41. See William L. Lang, "The Nearly Forgotten Blacks on Last Chance Gulch, 1900–1912," *Pacific Northwest Quarterly,* 70:2 (April 1979), 50–51.

42. For the Bass quote, see *Montana Plaindealer,* March 30, 1906, p. 1. See *Helena Colored Citizen,* October 29, 1894, pp. 2, 4, and November 5, pp. 1, 2, for the efforts of Ball to get Montana blacks to vote for Helena as the state capital. See also Lang, "The Nearly Forgotten Blacks," 52. For a discussion of the impact of Clore Street on white and black Helena, see William L. Lang, "Tempest on Clore Street: Race and Politics in Helena Montana, 1906," *Scratchgravel Hills* 3 (Summer 1980), 9–14.

43. The Bass quote on Jim Crow is in the *Plaindealer* front-page editorial, March 5, 1909. See also Lang, "The Nearly Forgotten Blacks," 55–57. By 1970 Helena had only 45 blacks out of a city population of 22,730. In 1990 the population figures were 55 and 24,569 respectively.

44. See Cox, *Blacks in Topeka,* 201.

45. See Woods, *A Black Odyssey,* 94, and Woods, "Integration, Exclusion, or Segregation,: The 'Color Line' in Kansas, 1878–1900," *Western Historical Quarterly* 14:2 (April 1983), 194. See also Cox, *Blacks in Topeka,* 1–2, 19–32.

46. For a discussion of the exodus to Topeka and the city's response, see Cox, *Blacks in Topeka,* 42–81.

47. See Woods, *A Black Odyssey,* 104, 120, and Cox, *Blacks in Topeka,* 82–83, 123–24, 145.

48. Cox, *Blacks in Topeka,* 97, 98, 129, 140, 152.

49. Ibid., 152–55, 174.

50. Ibid., 155–58.

51. Ibid., 154–55. The Kansas Industrial and Educational Institute was not the oldest or largest African American college in the state. Freedmen's University was founded in Quindaro, Kansas, in 1863 by the Reverend Eben Blatchley, a white Presbyterian minister. After his death in 1877 the Kansas AME. Conference assumed control of the school and in 1881 renamed it Western University. In 1899 the Kansas legislature granted an appropriation of ten thousand dollars with the stipulation that industrial education supplement the school's academic program. Western University educated black Kansans until it closed in 1943. See Susan G. Greenbaum, *The Afro-American Community in Kansas City, Kansas: A History* (Kansas City: City of Kansas City, 1982), 36–37, 69–76, 97, and Cox, *Blacks in Topeka,* 158–59.

52. The quote from the *Park City,* Utah, *Park Record,* March 18, 1882, appears in Duane A. Smith, *Rocky Mountain Mining Camps: The Urban Frontier* (Lincoln: University of Nebraska Press, 1967), 35.

53. Both quotes are from James C. Carper, "The Popular Ideology of Segregated Schooling: Attitudes toward the Education of Blacks in Kansas, 1854–1900," *Kansas History*

1:4 (Winter 1978), 257. See also Klassen and Johnson, "Sharpening of the *Blade,*" 298–304.

54. Quoted in Bernard D. Reams, Jr., and Paul E. Wilson, eds., *Segregation and the Fourteenth Amendment in the States: A Survey of State Segregation Laws, 1865–1953; Prepared for the United States Supreme Court in re: Brown vs. Board of Education of Topeka* (Buffalo: William S. Hein, Publishers, 1975), 183.

55. Woods, "Integration, Exclusion, or Segregation?," 186–87.

56. The teachers are quoted in Carper, "The Popular Ideology of Segregated Schooling," 258. The Martin quote appears on page 260. Those who opposed school desegregation are quoted on pages 261, 259, 262 respectively.

57. Quoted in the *Topeka Colored Citizen,* September 20, 1878, p. 4.

58. The "screen" quote appears in Bradford Luckingham, *Minorities in Phoenix: A Profile of Mexican American, Chinese American, and African American Communities, 1860–1992* (Tucson: University of Arizona Press, 1994), 143. On the *Reynolds* case, see Cox, *Blacks in Topeka,* 112–13. Topeka schools were apparently segregated as early as 1865. See Cox, *Blacks in Topeka,* 27. The Virginia City, Nevada, campaign is described in Elmer R. Rusco, *"Good Time Coming?": Black Nevadans in the Nineteenth Century* (Westport, Conn.: Greenwood Press, 1975), 80–92. On the Denver campaign, see Eugene H. Berwanger, "William J. Hardin: Colorado Spokesman for Racial Justice, 1863–1873," *Colorado Magazine* 52:1 (Winter 1975), 59, and Robert G. Athearn, *The Coloradans* (Albuquerque: University of New Mexico Press, 1976), 54. William M. King describes a comparable campaign in Central City, Colorado. See King, "Black Children, White Law: Black Efforts to Secure Public Education in Central City, Colorado, 1864–1869," *Essays and Monographs in Colorado History* (1984), 56–79. The long campaign of California's nineteenth-century African American leaders to desegregate that state's schools is profiled in Charles Wollenberg, *All Deliberate Speed: Segregation and Exclusion in California Schools, 1855–1975* (Berkeley: University of California Press, 1976), ch. 1. On Oklahoma and Texas, see Jimmie Lewis Franklin, *Journey toward Hope: A History of Blacks in Oklahoma* (Norman: University of Oklahoma Press, 1982), ch. 2, and Alwyn Barr, *Black Texans: A History of Negroes in Texas, 1528–1971* (Austin: Jenkins Publishing Co., 1973), 60–69. The rise of segregation in Arizona is profiled in Robert Kim Nimmons, "Arizona's Forgotten Past: The Negro in Arizona, 1539–1965" (M.A. thesis, Northern Arizona University, 1971), 105–06, 111–13, 116–17; and Luckingham, *Minorities in Phoenix,* 132–37.

59. The Wichita school segregation issue is described in Sondra Van Meeter, "Black Resistance to Segregation in the Wichita Public Schools, 1870–1912," *Midwest Quarterly* 20:3 (Autumn 1978), 64–67.

60. Ibid., 67–71. The quotes appear on pages 69–70.

61. Ibid., 72–77. For a discussion of successful desegregation efforts in Portland, Oregon, see Thomas Alexander Wood, "First Admission of Collored [*sic*]. Children to the Portland Public Schools" (unpublished manuscript, no. 37, Oregon Historical Society), 1–6; for the school official's quote, see page 1. See also Helen Marie Casey, *Portland's Compromise: The Colored School, 1867–1872* (Portland: Portland Public Schools, Public Information Department, 1980), 1–11. For background on the Portland African American community, see Quintard Taylor, "The Emergence of Afro-American Communities in the Pacific Northwest, 1865–1910," *Journal of Negro History* 64:4 (Fall 1979), 342–51. On similar successful desegregation efforts in Helena, Montana Territory, consult the *Helena Independent,* May 14, 1882, p. 3; J. W. Smurr, "Jim Crow Out West," in J. W. Smurr and K. Ross Toole, eds., *Historical Essays on Montana and the Northwest* (Helena: Western Press, Historical Society of Montana, 1957), 150–85, and Lang, "The Nearly Forgotten Blacks," 51.

62. Oklahoma's first state constitution, for example, contained provisions requiring segregated schools, in effect codifying a policy that had long existed in both Indian and Oklahoma territories. See Philip Mellinger, "Discrimination and Statehood in Oklahoma," *Chronicles of Oklahoma* 49:3 (Autumn 1971), 368, 372, and Franklin, *Journey toward Hope,* ch. 2. On Texas, see Barr, *Black Texans,* 98–104, for a discussion of black education in late-nineteenth-century Texas, and Robert Prince, *A History of Dallas from a Different Perspective* (Dallas: Nortex Press, 1993), 48, on the growth of one all-black high school.

63. The first quote appears in Lynda Faye Dickson, "The Early Club Movement among Black Women in Denver: 1890–1925" (Ph.D. dissertation, University of Colorado, 1982), 129. The second quote is from Marilyn Dell Brady, "Kansas Federation of Colored Women's Clubs, 1900–1930," Kansas History 9:1 (Spring 1896), 19. For background on the national women's club movement, see Paula Giddings, *When and Where I Enter: The Impact of Black Women on Race and Sex in America* (New York: William Morrow & Co., 1984), ch. 5 and 6.
64. Brady, "The Kansas Federation," 21; Ruthe Winegarten, *Black Texas Women: 150 Years of Trial and Triumph* (Austin: University of Texas Press, 1995), 189; Crouchett, *Visions toward Tomorrow,* 14; Stacey Shorter, "Forgotten Pioneers: African American Women's Community Formation in Cheyenne, Wyoming, 1867–1904" (unpublished paper in author's possession), 6; Dickson, "The Early Club Movement," 145; Taylor, *Forging,* 140.
65. See Charles H. Wesley, *The History of the National Association of Colored Women's Clubs, Inc.: A Legacy of Service* (Washington, D.C.: Associated Publishers, 1984), 406–519.
66. Brady, "The Kansas Federation," 19–23.

8: The Black Urban West, 1911–40

1. See *Crisis,* 6:3 July 1913), 130–32, 6:4 (August 1913), 192–95, and 6:5 (September, 1913), 237–40. For a discussion of the local response to Du Bois's visit in Los Angeles, San Francisco, and Seattle, see Lonnie G. Bunch, "A Past Not Necessarily Prologue: The Afro-American in Los Angeles," in Norman M. Klein and Martin J. Schiesl, eds., *20th Century Los Angeles: Power, Promotion, and Social Conflict* (Claremont, Calif: Regina Books, 1990), 101; Albert Broussard, *Black San Francisco: The Struggle for Racial Equality in the West, 1900–1954* (Lawrence: University Press of Kansas, 1993), 76; and Quintard Taylor, *The Forging of a Black Community: Seattle's Central District from 1870 through the Civil Rights Era* (Seattle: University of Washington Press, 1994), 79, 88.
2. Black Los Angeles's eclipse of the Bay Area communities is described in James Adolphus Fisher, "A History of the Political and Social Development of the Black Community in California, 1850–1950" (Ph.D. dissertation, State University of New York at Stony Brook, 1972), 161, 170–73. See also Emory J. Tolbert, *The UNIA and Black Los Angeles: Ideology and Community in the American Garvey Movement* (Los Angeles: Center for Afro-American Studies, UCLA, 1980), 72. On Omaha, see Lawrence H. Larsen and Barbara J. Cottrell, *The Gate City: A History of Omaha* (Boulder: Pruett Publishing Co., 1982), 166–68.
3. On the Tulsa riot, see Scott Ellsworth, *Death in a Promised Land: The Tulsa Race Riot of 1921* (Baton Rouge: Louisiana State University Press, 1982), 15–16, 57–70.
4. *Northwest Enterprise,* July 21, 1927, p. 4. See also Taylor, *Forging,* 61.
5. Dellums is quoted in Broussard, *Black San Francisco,* 40. The Bogle quotes are from E. Kimbark MacColl, *The Growth of a City: Power and Politics in Portland, Oregon, 1915 to 1950* (Portland: Georgian Press, 1980), 536.
6. For background on the concentration of the motion-picture industry in Southern California, see Thomas Cripps, *Slow Fade to Black: The Negro in American Film, 1900–1942* (New York: Oxford University Press, 1977), 90–94, 112.
7. Ibid., 108–09.
8. On the rise and fall of Stepin Fetchit, see Donald Bogle, *Toms, Coons, Mulattoes, Mammies and Bucks: An Interpretive History of Blacks in American Film* (New York: Viking Press, 1973), 38–44, and Cripps, *Slow Fade to Black,* 105–06.
9. Cripps, *Slow Fade to Black,* 99, 101–02, 241, 275, 360–66.
10. Lonnie Bunch III, *Black Angelenos: The Afro-American in Los Angeles, 1850–1950* (Los Angeles: California Afro-American Museum, 1988), 31. Central Avenue is described on pages 29 to 34 and in Ted Gioia, *West Coast Jazz: Modern Jazz in California, 1945–1960* (New York: Oxford University Press, 1992), 6–9. On the Hotel Somerville, see *Crisis* 35:9 (September 1928), 309, 317–318, while Chandler Owen's quote appears in Owen, "From Coast to Coast," *Messenger* 4:5 (May 1922), 409. On Houston businesses, see James M. SoRelle, "The Emergence of Black Business in Houston, Texas: A Study of Race and Ideology, 1919–45," in Howard Beeth and Cary D. Wintz, eds., *Black Dixie:*

Afro-Texan History and Culture in Houston (College Station: Texas A&M University Press, 1992), 103–15, and Cary D. Wintz, "Blacks," in Fred R. von der Mehden, ed., *The Ethnic Groups of Houston* (Houston: Rice University Studies, 1984), 23–25.

11. Cogwell's quote appears in Taylor, *Forging*, 74. For background on Asian-black business competition in Seattle, see pages 73–74. The most detailed comparative discussion of entrepreneurial activity among Asian American and African Americans can be found in Ivan H. Light, *Ethnic Enterprise in America: Business and Welfare among Chinese, Japanese and Blacks* (Berkeley: University of California Press, 1972), especially 10–18, 23–30.

12. *Colorado Statesman*, November 18, 1933, p. 1. See also U.S. Bureau of the Census, *Census of Unemployment, 1937. Final Report on Total and Partial Unemployment* (Washington, D.C.: Government Printing Office, 1938), vol. 1–3, Table 1; Randy J. Sparks, " 'Heavenly Houston' or 'Hellish Houston'?: Black Unemployment and Relief Efforts, 1929–1936," *Southern Studies* 25: (Winter 1986), 355, and Lawrence P. Crouchett, Lonnie G. Bunch III and Martha Kendall Winnacker, *Visions toward Tomorrow: The History of the East Bay Afro-American Community, 1852–1977* (Oakland: Northern California Center for Afro-American History and Life, 1989), 35.

13. Quoted in Elizabeth McLagan, *A Peculiar Paradise: A History of Blacks in Oregon, 1788–1940* (Portland: Georgian Press, 1980), 126–27. The Pittman quote appears in Broussard, *Black San Francisco*, 118. See also pages 117, 119. The Jackson quote appears in Taylor, *Forging*, 64.

14. See Bunch, *Black Angelenos*, 37; Luckingham, *Minorities in Phoenix*, 150; Sparks, " 'Heavenly Houston,' " 360; Crouchett, Bunch, and Winnacker, *Visions*, 35–36; and Moya Hansen, "Pebbles on the Shore: Economic Opportunity in Five Points, 1920–1950," (unpublished paper in author's possession), 23–24. The Jackson quote appears in Taylor, *Forging*, 63.

15. The Johnson quote appears in James Martin SoRelle, "The Darker Side of 'Heaven': The Black Community in Houston, Texas, 1917–1945" (Ph.D. dissertation, Kent State University, 1980), 139. The Hickok and *Houston Informer* quotes are from Sparks, " 'Heavenly Houston,' " 365. Much the same pattern held in Dallas and San Antonio, where the local political elite ensured that government assistance preferred to local blacks by New Deal agencies did not challenge patterns of segregation and discrimination. See Roger Biles, "The New Deal in Dallas, *Southwestern Historical Quarterly* 95:1 (July 1991), 15–19, and Kenneth Mason, "Paternal Continuity: African Americans and Race Relations in San Antonio, Texas, 1867–1937" (Ph.D. dissertation, University of Texas, Austin, 1994), 390–91. For a discussion of racial discrimination in New Deal programs in Los Angeles in 1935 by an African American government employee, see Floyd C. Covington, "Where the Color Line Chokes," *Sociology and Social Research* 20:3 (January–February 1936), 236–241. On discrimination nationally, see William H. Harris, *The Harder We Run: Black Workers since the Civil War* (New York: Oxford University Press, 1982), 101–06, and Harvard Sitkoff, *A New Deal for Blacks: The Emergence of Civil Rights as a National Issue* (New York: Oxford University Press, 1978), 47–57.

16. For an account of the future president's activities, see Christie L. Bourgeois, "Stepping over Lines: Lyndon Johnson, Black Texans, and the National Youth Administration, 1935–1937," *Southwestern Historical Quarterly* 91:2 (October 1987), 149–72. The quotes appear on pages 150, 166, 171 respectively.

17. For the quote on employment, see the *Colorado Statesman*, November 18, 1933, p. 1. On Phoenix, see Thomas E. Sheridan, *Arizona: A History* (Tucson: University of Arizona Press, 1995), 265.

18. On California, see Olen Cole, Jr., "Black Youth in the National Youth Administration in California, 1935–1943," *Southern California Quarterly* 73:4 (Winter 1991), 385–402, and Broussard, *Black San Francisco*, 120–27.

19. See Sparks, " 'Heavenly Houston,' " p. 361; Taylor, *Forging*, p. 99; Robert Kim Nimmons, "Arizona's Forgotten Past: The Negro in Arizona, 1539–1965" (M.A. thesis, Northern Arizona University, 1971), 166–68; Stephen J. Leonard and Thomas J. Noel, *Denver: Mining Camp to Metropolis* (Niwot: University Press of Colorado, 1990), 366–67; and Roy H. Williams and Kevin J. Shay, *Time Change: An Alternative View of the History of Dallas* (Dallas: To Be Publishing Co., 1991), 62.

20. On the activities of the federations in Washington and Oregon respectively, see Tay-

lor, *Forging*, pp. 88, 94, 104, and McLagan, *A Peculiar Paradise*, 126, 167. The Williams quote appears on p. 126 of McLagan.

21. On Augustus Hawkins, see Fisher, "The Black Community in California," 228–35. Ben Hooper is described in Lyle W. Dorsett, *The Queen City: A History of Denver* (Boulder: Pruett Publishing Co., 1977), p. 232.

22. For a discussion of Bellinger's history and role in San Antonio politics, see Neil Gary Sapper, "A Survey of the History of the Black People of Texas, 1930–1954" (Ph.D. dissertation, Texas Tech University, 1972), 36–54, 68–69, 102–03, and Mason, "Paternal Continuity," 184–91; the quotation on Bellinger appears on page 190 of Mason. Mason also describes African American participation in San Antonio machine politics in the pre-Bellinger years on pages 159–84. The Progressive Voters League is profiled in Marvin Dulaney, "The Progressive Voters League," *Legacies: A History Journal for Dallas and North Central Texas* 3:1 (Spring 1991), 27–35, while Maury Maverick's ambivalent relationship with black voters is described in Richard Henderson, *Maury Maverick: A Political Biography* (Austin: University of Texas Press, 1970), 185, 220–25. On Oklahoma, see Franklin, *Journey toward Hope*, 122–27.

23. The Sierra Madre advertisement is cited in Bunch, "A Past Not Necessarily Prologue," 103. On Eureka Villa, see *California Eagle*, October 31, 1924, p. 12; February 6, 1925, p. 3. For the McBeth quote, see the *California Eagle*, December 26, 1924, p. 1. The anonymous black landlord is quoted in J. Max Bond, "The Negro in Los Angeles" (Ph.D. dissertation, University of Southern California, 1936), 65. See also pages 33–34 and Lawrence B. de Graaf, "The City of Black Angels: Emergence of the Los Angeles Ghetto, 1890–1930," *Pacific Historical Review* 39:3 (August 1970), 345–47.

24. The Bontemps quote appears in Arna Bontemps, "Why I Returned," *The Old South: 'A Summer Tragedy' and Other Stories of the Thirties* (New York: Dodd, Mead, 1973), pp. 5–6. See also de Graaf, "City of Black Angels," 347; *Pittsburgh Courier*, September 29, 1923, p. 13; and Bunch, "A Past Not Necessarily Prologue," 103. For a history of Watts between its founding and annexation to Los Angeles, see MaryEllen Bell Ray, *The City of Watts, California: 1907 to 1926* (Los Angeles: Rising Publishing, 1985), ch. 4 and 5, and Patricia Rae Adler, "Watts: From Suburb to Black Ghetto" (Ph.D. dissertation, University of Southern California, 1977), 48–50, 309.

25. The first quote appears in Bond, "The Negro in Los Angeles," 35. The entire restrictive covenant affecting southwest Los Angeles appears in Charlotta A. Bass, *Forty Years: Memoirs from the Pages of a Newspaper* (Los Angeles: Charlotta A. Bass, 1960), 97. On the Garrett case, see E. Frederick Anderson, *The Development of Leadership and Organization Building in the Black Community of Los Angeles from 1900 through World War II* (Saratoga, Calif,: Century Twenty One Publishing, 1980), 39. On the Booker T. Washington, Jr., episode, see *Los Angeles Times*, February 17, 1924, part 2, p. 6. The long history of the Los Angeles black community campaign against housing discrimination is described in Bunch, "A Past Not Necessarily Prologue," 106–07, 114, 117–19, while Clement Vose's *Caucasians Only: The Supreme Court, the NAACP and the Restrictive Covenant Cases* (Berkeley: University of California Press, 1967) remains the best study of both restrictive covenants and the long and ultimately successful legal struggle against them; see especially ch. 1, 3, 8.

26. Omaha's restrictive covenants are discussed in Larsen and Cottrell, *The Gate City*, 158. The WPA quote on black Dallas appears in Gerald D. Saxon, ed., *The WPA Dallas Guide and History* (Dallas: Dallas Public Library, 1992), 291. For the long history of segregation in Dallas, see Sapper, "A Survey of the History of the Black People of Texas," 389–91, and Bruce Alan Glasrud, "Black Texans, 1900–1930: A History" (Ph.D. dissertation, Texas Tech University, 1969), 182–86. On Houston, see SoRelle, "The Darker Side of 'Heaven,' " 223–27, the Brownell quote is on page 217.

27. The Denver incidents are described in Leonard and Noel, *Denver*, 193, and Dorsett, *The Queen City*, 225, while Alfalfa Bill Murray's actions are detailed in Franklin, *Journey toward Hope*, 51.

28. The quotation on slum conditions in Phoenix appears in Sheridan, *Arizona*, 263. See also Lionel Dean Lyles, "An Historical-Urban Geographical Analysis of Black Neighborhood Development in Denver, 1860–1970" (Ph.D. dissertation, University of Colorado, 1977), 75. The *San Francisco Spokesman* quote appears in Broussard, *Black San Francisco*, 33.

29. See Bradford Luckingham, *Minorities in Phoenix: A Profile of Mexican American, Chinese American, and African American Communities, 1862–1992* (Tucson: University of Arizona Press, 1994), 152. On discrimination in intercollegiate athletic programs in the Big Six Conference, see Kristine M. McCusker, "The Forgotten Years' of America's Civil Rights Movement: Wartime Protests at the University of Kansas, 1939–1945" *Kansas History* 17:1 (Spring 1994), 29, 35; Nebraska Writers' Project (WPA), *The Negroes of Nebraska* (Lincoln: Woodruff Printing Co. 1940), 34: and Charles H. Martin, "Jim Crow in the Gymnasium: The Integration of College Basketball in the American South," *International Journal of the History of Sport* 10:1 (April 1993), 72–73.

30. Quote from Richard E. Harris, *The First 100 Years: A History of Arizona Blacks* (Apache Junction Ariz.: Relmo Publishers, 1983), 51. See also Sapper, "A Survey of the History of the Black People of Texas," 330. The number of lynchings of African Americans recorded per state between 1882 and 1968 were California 2, Colorado 3, Kansas 19, Montana 2, Nebraska 5, New Mexico 3, North Dakota, 3, Oklahoma 40, Oregon 1, Texas 352, Utah 2, Washington 1, and Wyoming 5. See W. Augustus Low and Virgil A. Clift, eds., *Encyclopedia of Black America* (New York: Da Capo Press, 1981), 542. Ironically the lynching that drew the largest number of spectators occurred in Omaha in 1919, when 25,000 people gathered to see the murder of William Brown. See Larsen and Cottrell, *The Gate City,* 168–74. For African American assessments of their most serious discriminatory challenges, see Taylor, *Forging,* ch. 2, Luckingham, *Minorities in Phoenix,* 142–44, 160–62; and Wintz, "Blacks," 20.

31. On the growth of the NAACP in the West, see NAACP, *Ninth Annual Report,* 1918, 86–87, cited in Melvin James Banks, "The Pursuit of Equality: The Movement for First Class Citizenship among Negroes in Texas, 1920–1950" (D.D.S., Syracuse University, 1962), 181; Alwyn Barr, *Black Texans: A History of Negroes in Texas, 1528–1971* (Austin: Jenkins Publishing Co., 1973), 144; Franklin, *Journey toward Hope,* 52; Taylor, *Forging,* 88; Leonard and Noel, *Denver,* 193; Quintard Taylor, "A History of Blacks in the Pacific Northwest, 1788–1970" (Ph.D. dissertation, University of Minnesota, 1977), 164; Richard Stephenson, "Race in the Cactus State," *Crisis* 61:4 (April 1954), 201; Nebraska Writers' Project, *The Negroes of Nebraska,* 29; Thomas A. Cox, *Blacks in Topeka, Kansas, 1865–1915: A Social History* (Baton Rouge: Louisiana State University Press, 1982), 154; Ronald Coleman, "Blacks in Utah History: An Unknown Legacy," in Helen Z. Papanikolas, ed., *The Peoples of Utah* (Salt Lake City: Utah Historical Society, 1976), 139; and Mamie O. Oliver, *Idaho Ebony: The Afro-American Presence in Idaho State History* (Boise: Idaho State Historical Society, 1990), 22. On Arizona, see Nimmons, "Arizona's Forgotten Past," 133–35.

32. E. Burton Ceruti and J. H. Shackleford to W. E. B. Du Bois, September 24, 1913, quoted in Tolbert, *The UNIA and Black Los Angeles,* 34. See also Anderson, *The Development of Leadership,* 38, and Charles Flint Kellogg, *NAACP: A History of the National Association for the Advancement of Colored People,* vol. 1, *1909–1920,* (Baltimore: Johns Hopkins University Press, 1967), 136–37.

33. Broussard, *Black San Francisco,* 76.

34. For a discussion of the significance of *The Birth of a Nation* as a film and a detailed description of the national protest it generated, see Richard Schickel, *D. W. Griffith: An American Life* (New York: Simon and Schuster, 1984), ch. 9 and 10, and Cripps, *Slow Fade to Black,* ch. 2. The national office's efforts to ban the film are described in Kellogg, *NAACP,* 142–45.

35. Broussard, *Black San Francisco,* 77–80.

36. Spingarn to Mary Childs Neary, secretary, NAACP, memo, March 9, 1915, quoted in Cripps, *Slow Fade to Black,* 53.

37. See W. E. B. Du Bois, "The Slanderous Film," *Crisis* (December 1915), 76–77. Some black entrepreneurs did in fact accept Du Bois's challenge to develop "race" movies. For examples, see Cripps, *Slow Fade to Black,* ch. 3. *The Birth of a Nation* opponents' greatest single success came in Kansas, where it was banned from 1915 to 1924. Kansas NAACP branch protests played a role in the ban, but it was also helped by the adamant opposition of Governor Arthur Capper and the politically powerful veterans' organization the Grand Army of the Republic. See Gerald R. Butters, Jr., "*The Birth of a Nation* and the Kansas Board of Review of Motion Pictures: A Censorship Struggle," *Kansas History* 14:1 (Spring 1991), 2–14. For a discussion of protests against

The Birth of a Nation in other western black communities, see Taylor, *Forging*, 89, and Luckingham, *Minorities in Phoenix*, 140.

38. Quote in Broussard, *Black San Francisco*, 86. On the Oklahoma City NAACP's role in *Guinn*, see Franklin, *Journey toward Hope*, 53–54, 113–14, and Kellogg, *NAACP*, 205–06.

39. The Love lawsuit was the first to reach the High Court but was dismissed because the primary election that inspired the legal action had already occurred. See Robert V. Haynes, "Black Houstonians and the White Democratic Primary, 1920–45," in Beeth and Wintz, eds., *Black Dixie*, 194–95.

40. The primary election law quotation appears in *General Laws of the State of Texas, 38th Legislature, Second Session*, 1923, ch. 32, pp. 74–75.

41. For background on Lawrence Nixon and his selection as the plaintiff in El Paso, see Conrey Bryson, *Dr. Lawrence A. Nixon and the White Primary* (El Paso: Texas Western Press, 1974), 5–7, 16–17, 31–37. The quotes appear on pages 17 and 23. See also Michael Lowery Gillette, "The NAACP in Texas, 1937–1957," (Ph.D. dissertation, University of Texas at Austin, 1984), 1–2.

42. See Darlene Clark Hine, "The Elusive Ballot: The Black Struggle against the Texas Democratic White Primary, 1932–1945," *Southwestern Historical Quarterly* 81:4 (April 1978), 371–74, and Richard Kluger, *Simple Justice: The History of Brown v. Board of Education and Black America's Struggle for Equality* (New York: Vintage Books, 1975), 122–23.

43. Hine, "The Elusive Ballot," 385–88; Sapper, "A Survey of the History of the Black People of Texas," 39–40.

44. Hine, "The Elusive Ballot," 390–92. In 1948 black Texans reached three political milestones. In Dallas black precinct election officials were employed for the first time in the twentieth century; in San Antonio George J. Sutton, benefiting from a Latino-black coalition, became the first African American elected official since 1898; and Lyndon Johnson was elected to the U.S. Senate from Texas (on a eighty-seven-vote margin) with considerable black support. By 1953 all organized opposition to black political participation had ceased, and African Americans voted without restraint in the primaries of both major political parties. See Sapper, "A Survey of the History of the Black People of Texas," 130–31, 139, 157, 167.

45. For background on the Urban League, including the number and location of western chapters, see Nancy J. Weiss, *The National Urban League, 1910–1940* (New York: Oxford University Press, 1974), 71–79. For similar background on the UNIA, see Tony Martin, *Race First: The Ideological and Organizational Struggles of Marcus Garvey and the Universal Negro Improvement Association* (Westport, Conn.: Greenwood Press, 1976), 6, 23–24, and Judith Stein, *The World of Marcus Garvey*, (Baton Rouge: Louisiana State University Press, 1986), ch. 2.

46. Weiss, *The National Urban League*, 165, 246. For a description of the Nebraska chapters, see Dennis Mihelich, "The Lincoln Urban League: The Travail of Depression and War," *Nebraska History* 70:4 (Winter 1989), 303–16; Mihelich, "The Formation of the Lincoln Urban League," *Nebraska History* 68:2 (Summer 1987), 63–73; and Mihelich, "World War II and the Transformation of the Omaha Urban League," *Nebraska History* 60:3 (Fall 1979), 401–23. The Seattle chapter is profiled in Taylor, *Forging*, 94–98.

47. See Martin, *Race First*, 361–68, for a listing of UNIA branches in the West. On the appeal of Garveyism in the small communities, see Tolbert, *The UNIA and Black Los Angeles*, 53, 58. Garveyism in Texas is described in Glasrud, "Black Texans," 325–27.

48. On Garvey's Los Angeles visit, see *California Eagle*, June 10, 1922, p. 1. Despite the prominent roles they initially played in the UNIA, Noah Thompson and John D. Gordon soon emerged as critics of Garvey's "irresponsible" business practices. Citing financial management of the UNIA's Black Star Steamship Line, Thompson resigned his position in 1921 and founded the Pacific Coast Negro Improvement Association, producing the earliest break in UNIA unity both locally and nationally. Although it never repudiated its support of racial nationalism or the redemption of Africa, the PCNIA concentrated on economic development projects and planned to purchase prime real estate on Central Avenue. By 1923 the PCNIA had transformed itself into the California Development Company, and Thompson himself helped organize the Commercial Council of Los Angeles to encourage blacks to engage in cooperative economics. See Tolbert, *The UNIA in Black Los Angeles*, 49–60, 62–72, 74, 81.

49. Proctor is quoted in Esther Hall Mumford, *Seven Stars and Orion: Reflections of the Past* (Seattle: Ananse Press, 1986), 43–44.
50. James W. Byrd, "Afro-American Writers in the West," J. Golden Taylor, ed., *A Literary History of the American West* (Fort Worth: Texas Christian University Press, 1987), 1140–41.
51. Quoted in Ralph L. Crowder, "John Edward Bruce & The Value of Knowing the Past: Politician, Journalist, and Self-Trained Historian of the African Diaspora, 1856–1924" (Ph.D. dissertation, University of Kansas, 1994), 291. See also pages 287–90.
52. See Langston Hughes, *The Big Sea: An Autobiography of Langston Hughes* (New York: Knopt, 1940), pp. 12–26. The poem "One Way Ticket" appears in Byrd, "Afro-American Writers in the West," 1142. For background on Hughes's Kansas childhood, see Mark Scott, "Langston Hughes of Kansas," *Kansas History* 3:1 (Spring 1980), 3–25, and Arnold Rampersad, *The Life of Langston Hughes* (New York: Oxford University Press, 1986), vol. 1, pp. 3–22.
53. See Dorothy Jean Palmer McIver, "Stepchild in Harlem: The Literary Career of Wallace Thurman" (Ph.D. dissertation, University of Alabama, 1983), 26–30, and Byrd, "Afro-American Writers in the West," 1143–46.
54. The phrase "Beale Street of the West" appears in Gilmore Millen's *Sweet Man* (New York: Grosset & Dunlap, 1930), 267. Millen, a white writer from Memphis, Tennessee, who migrated to Los Angeles, focused his efforts on describing black life in the city through his novel. See also Arna Bontemps, *God Sends Sunday* (New York: Harcourt, Brace, 1931); Bette Yarbrough Cox, *Central Avenue—Its Rise and Fall (1890–c.1955)* (Los Angeles: Beem Publications, 1996), 40; and Bunch, *Black Angelenos*, 32–33.
55. See Le Roi Jones, *Blues People: Negro Music in White America* (New York: William Morrow and Co., 1963), 109–121; Paul De Barros, *Jackson Street after Hours: The Roots of Jazz in Seattle* (Seattle: Sasquatch Books, 1993), viii–ix. It is important to note that jazz was not universally embraced by black westerners. Ralph Ellison, who grew up in Oklahoma City in the 1920s and who during that period tried unsuccessfully to "play what I heard and felt around me," recalled that jazz was regarded by "most of the respectable Negroes of the town as a backward, low-class form of expression, and . . . there was a marked difference between those who accepted it and lived close to their folk experience and those whose status stirrings led them to reject and deny it." See Ellison, *Shadow and Act* (New York: Random House, 1964), 190, 238.
56. On the evolution of jazz, see Thomas J. Hennessey, *From Jazz to Swing: African American Jazz Musicians and Their Music, 1890–1935* (Detroit: Wayne State University Press, 1994), ch. 1 and 2; Eileen Southern, *The Music of Black Americans: A History* (New York: W. W. Norton, 1971), pp. 389–90; and Tom Stoddard, *Jazz on the Barbary Coast* (Chigwell, England: Storyville Publications, 1982), 98, 126, 131–33. Stoddard argues that San Francisco's Barbary Coast during the first two decades of the twentieth century had most of the conditions that encouraged the rise of jazz in New Orleans's Storyville district, including an active (if smaller) cohort of African American musicians. George Morrison's discussion of early jazz appears in Gunther Schuller, *Early Jazz: Its Roots and Musical Development* (New York: Oxford University Press, 1968), 362–63. See also De Barros, *Jackson Street*, 9–10.
57. Williams is quoted in Nat Shapiro and Nat Hentoff, eds., *Hear Me Talkin' to Ya: The Story of Jazz by the Men Who Made It* (New York: Dover Publications, 1966), 287. See also David W. Stowe, "Jazz in the West: Cultural Frontier and Region during the Swing Era," *Western Historical Quarterly* 23:1 (February 1992), 53.
58. See Ross Russell, *Jazz Style in Kansas City and the Southwest* (Berkeley: University of California Press, 1971); 32; see also p. 72. The *Down Beat* quote appears in Stowe, "Jazz in the West," 56; see also pages 65–66.
59. Quoted in Neil Sapper, "Black Culture in Urban Texas: A Lone Star Renaissance," *Red River Valley Historical Review* 6:2 (Spring 1981), 66. See also Marc Rice, "Frompin' in the Great Plains: Listening and Dancing to the Jazz Orchestras of Alphonso Trent, 1925–44," *Great Plains Quarterly* 16:2 (Spring 1996), 108–10.
60. Walter Harrold is quoted in Stowe, "Jazz in the West," 66.
61. On Trent's band, see Henry Q. Rinne, "A Short History of the Alphonso Trent Orchestra," *Arkansas Historical Quarterly* 45:3 (Autumn 1986), 228–49, and Rice, "Frompin'

in the Great Plains," 107–15. See also Russell, *Jazz Style*, 53–64, and Franklin, *Journey toward Hope*, 166–70.

62. The Young quote appears in Hennessey, *From Jazz to Swing*, 117. See also pages 57–58 and Russell, *Jazz Style*, 66–87. On Morrison, see Schuller, *Early Jazz*, 362–65.

63. Stoddard, *Jazz*, 6, 143; Hennessey, *From Jazz to Swing*, 34–35, 58–59; and Cox, *Central Avenue*, 10–14.

64. Gioia, *West Coast Jazz*, 3–9; Hennessey, *From Jazz to Swing*, 58–60, 114–15; Cripps, *Slow Fade to Black*, 100–01; Bunch, *Black Angelenos*, 33–34; and Cox, *Central Avenue*, 30–36. For one black musician's experiences with the Hollywood studios, see Joe Darensbourg, *Jazz Odyssey: The Autobiography of Joe Darensbourg* (Baton Rouge: Louisiana State University Press, 1988), 61–63.

65. See Michael Austin, "Harlem of the West: The Douglas Hotel & Creole Palace Nite Club" (M.A. thesis, University of San Diego, 1994), 3–7.

66. Tom Stoddard reports black jazz musicians playing in Yokohama, Japan, as early as 1925, see Stoddard, *Jazz*, 140. See also De Barros, *Jackson Street*, 47–49.

67. The Wright quote appears in Taylor, *Forging*, 147. The Henson and Royal quotes appear in De Barros, *Jackson Street*, 37. See also Darensbourg, *Jazz Odyssey*, 56, 59, 63.

68. On black women, see De Barros, *Jackson Street*, 20–26.

9: World War II and the Postwar Black West, 1941–50.

1. In 1940 Texas, Oklahoma, and Kansas accounted for 86 percent of the West's blacks. Ten years later their share dropped to 67 percent. Conversely, the Pacific coast states—California, Oregon, and Washington—jumped from 10 to 28 percent. For specific population increases, see U.S. Bureau of the Census, *Sixteenth Census of the United States, 1940, Population*, vol. 2, *Characteristics of the Population* (Washington, D.C.: Government Printing Office, 1943), table 35; U.S. Bureau of the Census, *Seventeenth Census of the United States, 1950, Census of the Population*, vol. 2, *Characteristics of the Population* (Washington, D.C.: Government Printing Office, 1952), table 53.

2. The quote appears in Marilynn S. Johnson, *The Second Gold Rush: Oakland and the East Bay in World War II* (Berkeley: University of California Press, 1993), 58. Trotter posits that proletarianization first occurred in World War I with the waves of southern black migrants lured to northern industrial centers. For a full discussion of his thesis, see *Black Milwaukee: The Making of an Industrial Proletariat, 1915–45* (Urbana: University of Illinois Press, 1985), ch. 2, 7. Not all black laborers sought the industrial workplace. Hundreds of Jamaicans were recruited to the Pacific Northwest as braceros to assist in the agricultural harvests; their labor was considered crucial to the war effort. On Jamaicans in the Pacific Northwest, see Erasmo Gamboa, *Mexican Labor and World War II: Braceros in the Pacific Northwest, 1942–1947* (Austin: University of Texas Press, 1990), 63, 85, 108. Ida Rousseau Mukenge provides a detailed study of the wartime transformation of one community institution, the North Richmond Missionary Baptist Church; *The Black Church in Urban America: A Case Study in Political Economy* (Lanham, Md.: University Press of America, 1983), ch. 3–5.

3. The Archibald quote appears in Katherine Archibald, *Wartime Shipyard: A Study in Cultural Disunity* (Berkeley: University of California Press, 1947), 92. For a discussion of Executive Order 8802 and the Fair Employment Practices Committee it spawned, see Jervis Anderson, *A. Philip Randolph: A Biographical Portrait* (New York: Harcourt Brace Jovanovich, 1972), 241–61, and Richard M. Dalfuime, "The 'Forgotten Years' of the Negro Revolution," *Journal of American History* 55:1 (June 1968); 92–100. See Alonzo Nelson Smith, "Black Employment in the Los Angeles Area, 1938–1948" (Ph.D. dissertation, University of California at Los Angeles, 1978), ch. 4, for the impact of the FEPC on one western city.

4. The quote appears in Robert E. Colbert, "The Attitude of Older Negro Residents toward Recent Negro Migrants in the Pacific Northwest," *Journal of Negro Education* 15:4 (Fall 1946), 699. On western population statistics, see Shirley Ann Moore, "The Black Community in Richmond, California, 1910–1963" (Ph.D. dissertation, University of California, Berkeley, 1989), 76.

5. Quintard Taylor, *The Forging of a Black Community: Seattle's Central District from 1870*

through the Civil Rights Era (Seattle: University of Washington Press, 1994), 167–68.

6. For figures on overall black migration, see U.S. Department of Labor, *Negroes in the United States: Their Employment and Economic Status,* Bulletin 1119 (Washington, D.C.: Bureau of Labor Statistics, December 1952), 5–9; Keith E. Collins, *Black Los Angeles: The Maturing of the Ghetto, 1940–1950* (Saratoga, Calif.: Century Twenty One Publishing, 1980), 18; and Lawrence B. de Graaf, "Negro Migration to Los Angeles," 1930–1950" (Ph.D. dissertation, University of California, Los Angeles, 1962), 261–63.

7. See Collins, *Black Los Angeles,* 18; Johnson, *The Second Gold Rush,* 32–33. On Portland employment figures, see FEPC Headquarters Records, Reel 13, Documents. Microfilm No. 16335E, National Archives, Record Group 228, and Gerald D. Nash, *The American West Transformed: The Impact of the Second World War* (Bloomington: Indiana University Press, 1985), 103. On Seattle, see Taylor, *Forging,* 161.

8. See de Graaf, "Negro Migration to Los Angeles," 269; LeRoy E. Harris, "The Other Side of the Freeway: A Study of Settlement Patterns of Negroes and Mexican Americans in San Diego, California" (D.A. dissertation, Carnegie-Mellon University, 1974), 64; and Taylor, *Forging,* 161.

9. The Duncan quote appears in Taylor, *Forging,* 164. The second quote is in Moore, "The Black Community in Richmond," 79. See also Johnson, *The Second Gold Rush,* 37, 55–56.

10. The quote is from Johnson, *The Second Gold Rush,* 38. See also pages 52–54 and Moore, "The Black Community in Richmond," 78.

11. The quotation appears in Lynell George, *No Crystal Stair: African Americans in the City of Angels* (London: Verso Press, 1992), 1. See also Gretchen Lemke-Santangelo, *Abiding Courage: African American Migrant Women and the East Bay Community* (Chapel Hill: University of North Carolina Press, 1996), 66; Johnson, *The Second Gold Rush,* 52; Moore, "The Black Community in Richmond," 76; and Paul Spickard, "Work and Hope: African American Women in Southern California during World War II," *Journal of the West* 32:3 (July 1993), 71–72.

12. Quoted in Lemke-Santangelo, *Abiding Courage,* 65. For the Coleman account, see Delores Nason McBroome, "Parallel Communities: African-Americans in California's East Bay, 1850–1963" (Ph.D. dissertation, University of Oregon, 1991), 124–25.

13. Johnson, *The Second Gold Rush,* 63.

14. The Marshall quote appears in Amy Kesselman, *Fleeting Opportunities: Women Shipyard Workers in Portland and Vancouver during World War II and Reconversion* (Albany: State University of New York Press, 1990), 43. See also Johnson, *The Second Gold Rush,* 65.

15. The Williams quote appears in Kesselman, *Fleeting Opportunities,* 43. See also pages 41–42; Archibald, *Wartime Shipyard,* 60–61, 83–84; and Johnson, *The Second Gold Rush,* 63–65, 75.

16. The personnel director is quoted in Broussard, *Black San Francisco,* 157. See also Archibald, *Wartime Shipyards,* 88.

17. See William H. Harris, "Federal Intervention in Union Discrimination: FEPC and West Coast Shipyards during World War II," *Labor History* 22:3 (Summer 1981), 325–47; Herbert Hill, *Black Labor and the American Legal System,* vol. 1 *Race Work and the Law* (Washington, D.C.: Bureau of National Affairs, 1977), 192–95, 200. For a full discussion of the boilermakers' discriminatory practices in Portland and Los Angeles, see Alonzo Smith and Quintard Taylor, "Racial Discrimination in the Workplace: A Study of Two West Coast Cities during the 1940's," *Journal of Ethnic Studies* 8:1 (Spring 1980), 35–54.

18. The Washington quote appears in FEPC Headquarters Records, Reel 14. See also Harris, "Federal Intervention," 327–328, and Hill, *Black Labor,* 187.

19. Harris, "Federal Intervention," 332.

20. Quoted in Archibald, *Wartime Shipyard,* 99. See also *James et al. v. Marinship Corporation,* 25, 2d California Reports, 721 (1944); *Williams et al. v. International Brotherhood of Boilermakers, Iron Shipbuilders and Helpers of America,* 28, 2d California Reports, 568 (1946); and William H. Harris, *The Harder We Run: Black Workers since the Civil War* (New York: Oxford University Press, 1982), 120–21. See FEPC Headquarters Records, Reel 14, Documents, for a list of black workers in various auxiliary unions across the nation. See also Smith and Taylor, "Racial Discrimination," 39–40, 43–45; Hill, *Black Labor,* 204; and Moore, "The Black Community in Richmond," 96.

21. The Tuttle quotation appears in Robert C. Weaver, "Negro Employment in the Aircraft Industry," *Quarterly Journal of Economics* 59:4 (August 1945), 598. The quote from the North American Aviation President appears in de Graaf, "Negro Migration," 168.
22. On the demonstration by black women, see *California Eagle,* July 16, 1942, pp. 1-A, 8-B. For a general discussion of the transition to black labor among the companies, see Weaver, "Negro Employment," 608–13; de Graaf, "Negro Migration to Los Angeles," 173; and Taylor, *Forging,* 163–65.
23. Collins, *Black Los Angeles,* 60–61.
24. The two Christina Hill quotations appear in Sherma Berger Gluck, *Rosie the Riveter Revisited: Women, the War and Social Change* (Boston: Twayne Publishers, 1987), 43, 23 respectively. Comparative figures for the percentage of African Americans in the local population and percentages of employees in individual plants bear out de Graaf's argument of perceived opportunity outside the South. For example, Vultee Aircraft in Nashville in 1944 had a 4.9 percent black work force in a city that was 30 percent African American, while its plant in Los Angeles had a 3.2 percent work force when blacks constituted only 7.1 percent of the city's population. North American Aviation's work force in its Inglewood plant was 7.2 percent black in 1944, in contrast with its Dallas facility, which was 6.5 percent in a city where African Americans were 18 percent of the population. See Robert Weaver's 1945 national survey of the aircraft industry, "Negro Employment," 616, 620–22, and de Graaf, "Negro Migration to Los Angeles," pp. 208–11.
25. Both quotations appear in Roosevelt Fitzgerald, "The Demographic Impact of Basic Magnesium Corporation on Southern Nevada," *Nevada Public Affairs Review, Ethnicity and Race in Nevada* 2 (1987), 32. See also Michael Coray, "African-Americans in Nevada," *Nevada Historical Quarterly,* 35:4 (Winter 1992), 247–50. For a discussion of Carver Park, see Jamie Coughtry and R. T. King, eds., *Lubertha Johnson: Civil Rights Efforts in Las Vegas: 1940s–1960s* (Reno: University of Nevada Oral History Program, 1988), 13–30. For background on blacks in Las Vegas prior to World War II, see Perry Bruce Kaufman, "The Best City of Them All: A History of Las Vegas, 1930–1960" (Ph.D. dissertation, University of California, Santa Barbara, 1974), 325–39.
26. See *Las Vegas Review Journal,* October 20, 1943, p. 1; Jamie Coughtry and R. T. King, eds., *Woodrow-Wilson: Race, Community and Politics in Las Vegas, 1940s–1980s* (Reno: University of Nevada Oral History Program, 1990), 33–40; Fitzgerald, "The Demographic Impact of Basic Magnesium," 33–34; and Coray, "African-Americans in Nevada," 250.
27. *Houston Informer,* December 26, 1942, p. 19. See also the *Dallas Express,* May 15, 1943, p. 1. See Gary Sapper, "A Survey of the History of the Black People of Texas, 1930–1934" (Ph.D. dissertation, Texas Tech University, 1972), 265–76; Michael R. Botson, Jr., "Organized Labor at the Hughes Tool Company, 1918–1942: From Welfare to the Steel Workers Organizing Committee" (M.A. thesis, University of Houston, 1994), 7–8, 51; and James M. SoRelle, "The Darker Side of 'Heaven,' ": The Black Community in Houston, Texas, 1917–1945" (Ph.D. dissertation, Kent State University, 1980), 159–68. For a discussion of population change in Texas, see Larry H. Long, "Migration to, from, and within Texas and Its Metropolitan Areas for Selected Periods of Time between 1930 and 1960" (M.A. thesis, University of Texas, 1968), 101, 138. See Nash, *The American West Transformed,* 104–05, for a brief discussion of wartime Tucson.
28. Robert Franklin Jefferson, "Making the Men of the 93rd: African American Servicemen in the Years of the Great Depression and the Second World War, 1935–1947" (Ph.D. dissertation, University of Michigan, 1995), 231–32, 234, 243.
29. Ibid., 242.
30. For the role of black troops in constructing the Alcan Highway, see Heath Twichell, *Northwest Epic: The Building of the Alaska Highway* (New York: St. Martin's Press, 1992), ch. 7, 9, 10, and Lael Morgan, "Writing Minorities out of History: Black Builders of the Alcan Highway," *Alaska History* 7:2 (Fall 1992), 1–6. On the reaction to black service personnel in Hawthorne and Hastings, see Nash, *The American West Transformed,* 105–06, and Beverly Russell, "World War II Boomtown: Hastings and the Naval Ammunition Depot," *Nebraska History* 76:2 and 3 (Summer/Fall 1995), 76–80.
31. On the Salina incident see John Morton Blum, *V Was for Victory: Politics and American Culture during World War II.* (New York: Harcourt Brace Jovanovich, 1976), 190–91.

The El Paso incident is described in *Time* (July 10, 1944), 65. See also Lawrence B. de Graaf, "Significant Steps on an Arduous Path: The Impact of World War II on Discrimination against African Americans in the West," *Journal of the West* 35:1 (January 1996), 28–29. On the Fort Lawton riot: Taylor, *Forging*, 167.

32. Sapper, "A Survey of the History of the Black People of Texas," 368. On black troops in Hollywood, see Beth Bailey and David Farber, *The First Strange Place: Race and Sex in World War II Hawaii* (Baltimore: Johns Hopkins University Press, 1993), 138, 148–49, 161–65.

33. The black sailors killed and wounded at Port Chicago accounted for 15 percent of all African American naval casualties during World War II. See Robert L. Allen, *The Port Chicago Mutiny* (New York: Amistad Press, 1993), 56–64.

34. The first quote appears in ibid., 76, the second in Charles Wollenberg, "Blacks vs. Navy Blue: The Mare Island Mutiny Court Martial," *California History* 58:1 (Spring 1979), 68.

35. See Wollenberg, "Blacks vs. Navy Blue," 66, 70; Allen, *Port Chicago Mutiny*, 127–35, 145.

36. The Portland official is quoted in Stuart McElderry, "Boundaries and Limits: Housing Segregation and Civil Rights Activism in Portland, Oregon, 1930–1962" unpublished paper in the author's possession, 18. See also Hansen, "Pebbles on the Shore," 33; Dennis N. Mihelich, "World War II and the Transformation of the Omaha Urban League," *Nebraska History* 60:3 (Fall 1979), 401; and Sapper, "A Survey of the History of the Black People of Texas," 253–259.

37. The Holtezendorff quote appears in de Graaf, "Negro Migration," 189; the Caldwell quote in Nash, *The American West Transformed*, 94.

38. Carol Levene, "The Negro in San Francisco," *Common Ground* 9:1 (Spring 1949), 11–14; Broussard, *Black San Francisco*, 173–74.

39. The Royal Towns quote appears in Johnson, *The Second Gold Rush*, 95; see also pages 93–96.

40. Dorothy W. Baruch, "Sleep Comes Hard," *Nation*, 160:4 (January 27, 1945), 95–96.

41. Quoted in Arna Bontemps and Jack Conroy, *Anyplace but Here* (New York: Hill and Wang, 1966), 9. See also Patricia Rae Adler, "Watts: From Suburb to Black Ghetto" (Ph.D. dissertation, University of Southern California, 1977), 251, 262–65.

42. Harlan Dale Unrau, "The Double V Movement in Los Angeles during the Second World War: A Study in Negro Protest" (M.A. thesis, California State College, Fullerton, 1971), 30–38.

43. On Portland and Seattle, see Quintard Taylor, "The Great Migration: The Afro-American Communities of Seattle and Portland during the 1940s," *Arizona and the West* 23:2 (Summer, 1981), 109–26. For a discussion of San Diego, see Lawrence I. Hewes, *Intergroup Relations in San Diego: Some Aspects of Community Life in San Diego Which Particularly Affect Minority Groups* (San Francisco: American Council on Race Relations, 1946), 9, 13–15.

44. The San Franciscan is quoted in Broussard, *Black San Francisco*, 173. The facts of the Short house fire remained in dispute, with local authorities concluding the fire was an accident while blacks throughout the region considered it arson. See *California Eagle*, December 20, 1945, p. 1; January 3, 1946, pp. 1, 16; January 24, 1946, p. 1. See also Spickard, "Work and Hope," 76. The Maywood newspaper quote appears in *California Eagle*, March 26, 1942, p. 1-A.

45. The estimate of the housing unavailable to black residents appears in de Graaf, "Negro Migration," 284. Miller was the attorney in *Barrows v. Jackson*, the 1953 case in which the U.S. Supreme Court outlawed restrictive covenants. For background on the campaign against restrictive covenants, see Loren Miller, *The Petitioners: The Story of the Supreme Court of the United States and the Negro* (New York: Pantheon Books, 1966), 321–23, and Clement Vose, *Caucasians Only: The Supreme Court, the NAACP and the Restrictive Covenant Cases* (Berkeley: University of California Press, 1967), ch. 7. Two restrictive covenant challenges, the "Sugar Hill" lawsuit and the *Laws* family case, drew national attention. For a discussion of those cases, see *California Eagle*, December 6, 1945, pp. 1, 5, December 20, 1945, pp. 1, 28; Carey McWilliams, "Los Angeles: An Emerging Pattern," *Common Ground* 9:1 (Spring 1949), 5–6, and McWilliams, "The House on 92nd Street," *Nation* 162:25 (June 8, 1946), 690–91; Elizabeth J. De Kam, "A Home to Call One's Own: A Textual Analysis of the Story of Residential Racial-

Restrictive Covenants in the California *Eagle* and Los Angeles *Sentinel*" (M.A. thesis, California State University, 1993), 1–2, 99–104; Unrau, "The Double V Movement," 106–07; and Bass, *Forty Years*, 110–12.

46. The Stewart quote appears in Nash, *The American West Transformed*, 98. On this postwar segregation, see Johnson, *The Second Gold Rush*, 213–33.
47. For discussion of the Thanksgiving night riot, see Thomas E. Sheridan, *Arizona: A History* (Tucson: University of Arizona Press, 1995), 273–74, and Luckingham, *Minorities in Phoenix*, 157. For various examples of racial violence, see Ulysses G. Lee, *United States Army in World War II, Special Studies: The Employment of Negro Troops* (Washington, D.C.: Office of the Chief of Military History, 1966), 366–67; Bailey and Farber, *The First Strange Place*, 151–52; Johnson, *The Second Gold Rush*, pp. 168–69; Nash, *The American West Transformed*, 95–96; and Taylor, *Forging*, 167–68.
48. See James A. Burran, "Violence in an 'Arsenal of Democracy': The Beaumont Race Riot, 1943," *East Texas Historical Review* 14:1 (Spring 1976), 39–40, 41–48, and James S. Olson and Sharon Phair, "The Anatomy of a Race Riot: Beaumont, Texas, 1943," *Texana* 11:1 (Winter 1973); 64–72.
49. For a discussion of such efforts in one western city, see Quintard Taylor, "Blacks and Asians in a White City: Japanese Americans and African Americans in Seattle, 1890–1940," *Western Historical Quarterly* 22:4 (November 1991), 401–29.
50. See Kevin A. Leonard, " 'Brothers under the Skin'?: African Americans, Mexican Americans and World War II in California," (unpublished paper presented at The Impact of World War II on California Conference, San Marino, California, November 1995), 4–7.
51. Ibid., 8–12.
52. The first quotation appears in Beatrice Griffith, *American Me* (Boston: Houghton Mifflin, 1948), 41. The second quote is from George Lipsitz, "From Chester Himes to Nursery Rhymes: Local Television and the Politics of Cultural Space in Postwar Los Angeles," (unpublished paper in the author's possession, 1990), 9. See also Bruce Tyler, "Zoot-Suit Culture and the Black Press," *Journal of American Culture* 17:2 (Summer 1994), 21–33.
53. Maya Angelou, *I Know Why the Caged Bird Sings* (New York: Bantam Books, 1971), 177–79. For background on black-Japanese relations in San Francisco and Seattle respectively, see Thelma Thurston Gorham, "Negroes and Japanese Evacuees," *Crisis* 52:11 (November 1945), 314–16, 330–31, and Taylor, *Forging*, 126–28.
54. See Leonard, " 'Brothers under Skin' " 18–19. Two organizations instituted postwar programs to reduce tensions between Japanese Americans and African Americans. Pilgrim House, a settlement house established for black migrants in San Francisco's Little Tokyo in 1943, began a series of meetings in 1945 to promote interracial cooperation. In Seattle the Jackson Street Community Council also reduced interracial tensions between people of color by encouraging discussion of common issues and concerns. See Leonard, " 'Brothers under the Skin'," 19–20, and Taylor, *Forging*, 174–75.
55. Wilson Record, "Willie Stokes at the Golden Gate," *Crisis* 56:6 (June 1949), 177. On Portland's declining African American population, see *Portland Oregonian*, June 16, 1947, p. 8.
56. Broussard, *Black San Francisco*, 206–08.
57. Taylor, *Forging*, 175.
58. Quoted in Johnson, *The Second Gold Rush*, 206. See also pages 213–14.
59. Ibid., 215.
60. The Starks quote appears in Moore, "The Black Community in Richmond," 187. For a discussion of the group unity strategy in Richmond, see pages 159, 170. On the successful black-candidates, see James A. Atkins, *Human Relations in Colorado: A Historical Record* (Denver: Colorado Department of Education, 1968), 121; Lawrence P. Crouchett, *William Byron Rumford: The Life and Public Service of a California Legislator* (El Cerrito, Calif.: Downey Place Publishing House, 1984), 32–37; Taylor, *Forging*, 176; Hayzel Burton Daniels, "A Black Magistrate's Struggles," in Anne Hodges Morgan and Rennard Strickland, eds., *Arizona Memories* (Tucson: University of Arizona Press, 1984), 336. San Antonio's black-Latino coalition is described in Robert Garland Landolt, *The Mexican-American Workers of San Antonio, Texas* (New York: Arno Press, 1976),

268, and Sapper, "A Survey of the History of Black People of Texas," 167–68. On San Francisco, see Max Silverman, "Urban Redevelopment and Community Response: African Americans in San Francisco's Western Addition" (M.A. thesis, San Francisco State University, 1994), 66.

61. On the growing black influence in Western politics, see Broussard, *Black San Francisco,* 236–38; Johnson, *The Second Gold Rush,* 204–07; Lemke-Santangelo, *Abiding Courage,* 162–65, and Sapper, "A Survey of the Black People of Texas," 119, 131, 147, 157. The Patman quote appears in Richard Polenberg, *War and Society: The United States, 1941–1945* (Philadelphia: J. B. Lippincott, 1972), 112.

62. The Hawes quote appears in Hampton Hawes and Don Asher, *Raise Up off Me* (New York: Coward, McCann & Geoghegan, 1974), 29. The Willard quote is in Anthony Sweeting, "The Dunbar Hotel and Central Avenue Renaissance, 1781–1950" (Ph.D. dissertation, UCLA, 1992), 309–10; see also pages 311–22. Also, consult Gary Marmorstein, "Central Avenue Jazz: Los Angeles Black Music of the Forties," *Southern California Quarterly* 70:4 (Winter 1988), 415–26; Robert Gordon, *Jazz West Coast: The Los Angeles Jazz Scene of the 1950s* (London: Quartet Books, 1986), ch. 1 and 2; and Bette Yarbrough Cox, *Central Avenue—Its Rise and Fall (1890–c.1955)* (Los Angeles: Beem Publications, 1996), 65–70.

63. Quoted in Tom Mazzolini, "Interview with Bob Geddins," *Living Blues* 34 (September–October 1977), 20. On the rise of rhythm and blues and gospel music in post-1945 Los Angeles, see Ralph Eastman, "Central Avenue Blues: The Making of Los Angeles Rhythm and Blues, 1942–1947," *Black Music Research Journal* 9:1 (Spring 1989), 19–32, and Jacqueline Cogdell Djedje, "Gospel Music in the Los Angeles Black Community: A Historical Overview," *Black Music Research Journal* 9:1 (Spring 1989), 35–77. See also Johnson, *The Second Gold Rush,* 138–41, 240, on black music in the Bay Area, and Paul De Barros, *Jackson Street after Hours: The Roots of Jazz in Seattle* (Seattle: Sasquatch Books, 1993), ch. 4 and 5, on Seattle.

64. L. D. Reddick, "The New Race Relations Frontier," *Journal of Educational Sociology* 19:3 (November 1945), 143–45.

10: The Civil Rights Movement in the West, 1950–70

1. Steven F. Lawson, "Freedom Then, Freedom Now: The Historiography of the Civil Rights Movement," *American Historical Review,* 96:2 (April 1991), 456–59; Clayborne Carson, "Civil Rights Reform and the Black Freedom Struggle," in Charles Eagles, ed., *The Civil Rights Movement in America* (Jackson: University of Mississippi Press, 1986), 19–32; and Quintard Taylor, "The Civil Rights Movement in the Urban West: Black Protest in Seattle, 1960–1970," *Journal of Negro History* 80:1 (Winter 1995), 1–14. There is a growing body of literature on the civil rights movement in the West. See, for example, Allan A. Saxe, "Protest and Reform: The Desegregation of Oklahoma City" (Ph.D. dissertation, University of Oklahoma, 1969); Larry S. Richardson, "Civil Rights in Seattle: A Rhetorical Analysis of a Social Movement" (Ph.D. dissertation, Washington State University, 1975); W. Edwin Derrick and J. Hershel Barnhill, "With 'All' Deliberate Speed: Desegregation of the Public Schools in Oklahoma City and Tulsa, 1954 to 1972," *Red River Valley Historical Review* 6:2 (Spring 1981), 78–90; Robert A. Goldberg, "Racial Change on the Southern Periphery: The Case of San Antonio, Texas, 1960–1965," *Journal of Southern History* 49:3 (August 1983), 349–74; Mary Melcher, "Blacks and Whites Together: Interracial Leadership in the Phoenix Civil Rights Movement," *Journal of Arizona History* 32:2 (Summer 1991), 195–216; F. Kenneth Jensen, "The Houston Sit-In Movement of 1960–61," in Howard Beeth and Cary D. Wintz, eds., *Black Dixie: Afro-Texan History and Culture in Houston* (College Station: Texas A&M University Press, 1992), 211–22; and Ronald Walters, "The Great Plains Sit-in Movement, 1958–60," *Great Plains Quarterly* 16:2 (Spring 1996), 85–94. For an oral history of the civil rights movement in Nevada's largest city, see Jamie Coughtry, ed., *Woodrow Wilson: Race, Community and Politics in Las Vegas, 1940s–1980s* (Reno: University of Nevada Oral History Program, 1990).

2. The Mahoney quotation appears in Melcher, "Blacks and Whites Together," 198, while Nichols's is in W. J. Rorabaugh, *Berkeley at War: The 1960s* (New York: Oxford University Press, 1989), 53. The obvious optimism of Mahoney and Nichols in the 1950s was

tempered by the Cold War–era attacks on progressive left-labor coalitions. Such attacks allowed more moderate reformers to dominate the civil rights agenda for much of the decade. For a discussion of the decline of the postwar left generally, see Gerald Horne, *Communist Front? The Civil Rights Congress, 1946–1956* (Rutherford, N.J.: Fairleigh Dickinson University Press, 1988), ch. 10 and 11. For an analysis of the process in one city, see Quintard Taylor, *The Forging of a Black Community: Seattle's Central District from 1870 through the Civil Rights Era* (Seattle: University of Washington Press, 1994), 181–85.

3. See Hayzel Burton Daniels, "A Black Magistrate's Struggles," in Anne Hodges Morgan and Rennard Strickland, eds., *Arizona Memories* (Tucson: University of Arizona Press, 1984), 336–38; Richard E. Harris, *The First 100 Years: A History of Arizona Blacks* (Apache Junction, Ariz.: Relmo Publishers, 1983), 72; and Bradford Luckingham, *Minorities in Phoenix: A Profile of Mexican American, Chinese American, and African American Communities, 1860–1992* (Tucson: University of Arizona Press), 161–63; the Struckmeyer quote appears on page 162. On Goldwater's civil rights activity, see Robert Alan Goldberg, *Barry Goldwater* (New Haven: Yale University Press, 1995), 89–91. On the parallel Mexican American challenge to school segregation, see Gilbert G. González, *Chicano Education in the Era of Segregation* (Philadelphia: Balch Institute Press, 1990), ch. 7, and Robert R. Alvarez, Jr., "The Lemon Grove Incident: The Nation's First Successful Desegregation Court Case," *Journal of San Diego History* 32:2 (Spring 1986), 116–35. See also Luckingham, *Minorities in Phoenix*, 49–50.

4. Richard Kluger, *Simple Justice: The History of Brown v. Board of Education and Black America's Struggle for Equality* (New York: Vintage Books, 1977), 372–77. The Scott quote appears on page 376.

5. Ibid., 375, 382. Four Topeka desegregation cases preceded *Brown: Reynolds v. Board of Education,* 1903, *Thurman-Watts v. Board of Education,* 1924, *Wright v. Board of Education,* 1929, and *Graham v. Board of Education,* 1941. The last case was a victory for junior high school desegregation. For background on the seventy-year struggle to integrate Kansas schools, see Randall B. Woods, "Integration, Exclusion, or Segregation? The 'Color Line' in Kansas,—1878–1900," *Western Historical Quarterly* 14:2 (April 1983), 181–98, and Deborah Dandridge and others, *Brown vs. Board of Education: In Pursuit of Freedom and Equality: Kansas and the African American Public School Experience, 1855–1955* (Topeka: Brown Foundation for Educational Equity, Excellence and Research, 1993), 7.

6. The quote appears in Kluger, *Simple Justice,* 395. In an essay describing the significance of the *Brown* decision four decades later, Cheryl Brown Henderson, daughter of the Reverend Oliver Brown, concluded that sexism may have played a role in the naming of this historic case. Brown was not, as is often assumed, chosen because his name appeared first on the list of plaintiffs. Darlene Brown, another plaintiff, was listed ahead of Oliver Brown. See Cheryl Brown Henderson and Shariba Rivers, "The Legacy of *Brown* 40 Years Later," in Charles Teddlie and Kofi Lomotey, eds., *Forty Years after the Brown Decision: Implications of School Desegregation for U.S. Education* (New York: AMS Press, 1996), vol. 14, pp. 373–82.

7. Ironically Sumner School was first used exclusively for African American children until 1885, when it was turned over to white pupils. The school was named after Boston attorney and later Massachusetts Senator Charles Sumner, who in 1849 argued for the plaintiffs in the nation's first school desegregation case, *Roberts v. City of Boston.* For background on the controversy, see Cheryl Brown Henderson, "Landmark Decision: Remembering the Struggle for Equal Education," *Land and People* 6:1 (Spring 1994), 2–5, and Kluger, *Simple Justice,* 408–09.

8. Kluger, *Simple Justice,* 390, 400–11; the Fleming quotation is on page 411. See also Jack Greenberg, *Crusaders in the Courts: How a Dedicated Band of Lawyers Fought for the Civil Rights Revolution* (New York: Basic Books, 1994), ch. 10.

9. Kluger, *Simple Justice,* 411–24; the quote appears on page 424. For a discussion of the influence of expert testimony on the language of the U.S. Supreme Court decision, see Greenberg, *Crusaders in the Courts,* 131–32.

10. Henderson, "Landmark Decision," 5.

11. See August Meier and Elliott Rudwick, *CORE: A Study in the Civil Rights Movement, 1942–1968* (New York: Oxford University Press, 1973), 15, 27, 59–60, and Jeffrey Har-

rison Smith, "The Omaha De Porres Club" (M.A. thesis, Creighton University, 1967), ch. 3.

12. Kristine M. McCusker, " 'The Forgotten Years' of America's Civil Rights Movement: The University of Kansas, 1939–1961" (M.A. thesis, University of Kansas, 1994), 1–3, 128–34.

13. See George Long, "How Albuquerque Got Its Civil Rights Ordinance," *Crisis* 60:11 (November 1953), 521–22; all quotes are from the student boycott clause, which appears on page 522. See also Marc Simmons, *Albuquerque: A Narrative History* (Albuquerque: University of New Mexico Press, 1982), 371.

14. Long, "How Albuquerque Got Its Civil Rights Ordinance," 521–24, and Simmons, *Albuquerque,* 371.

15. On the Wichita sit-ins, see Ronald Walters, "Standing Up in America's Heartland: Sitting-in before Greensboro," *American Visions* 8:1 (February 1993), 20–23, and Walters, "The Great Plains Sit-In Movement," 87–88.

16. Carl R. Graves, "The Right to Be Served: Oklahoma City's Lunch Counter Sit-ins, 1958–1964," *Chronicles of Oklahoma* 59:2 (Summer 1981), 152–55.

17. The Oklahoma City ordinance was passed on the same day the 1964 Civil Rights Act went into effect. For a discussion of the Oklahoma City campaign, see Clara Luper, *Behold the Walls* (Oklahoma City: Jim Wire, 1979), 134–36, and Graves, "The Right to Be Served," 155–60.

18. The quotation appears in Taylor, *Forging,* 198. For the variety of examples of civil disobedience protests in the West, see Meier and Rudwick, *CORE,* 233–34, 242–43; Lawrence P. Crouchett, Lonnie G. Bunch III, and Martha Kendall Winnacker, *Visions toward Tomorrow: The History of the East Bay Afro-American Community, 1852–1977* (Oakland: Northern California Center for Afro-American History and Life, 1989), 57; F. Jensen, "The Houston Sit-In Movement of 1960–61," 211–22; Goldberg, "Racial Change on the Southern Periphery, 355–59; Stuart McElderry, "Boundaries and Limits: Housing Segregation and Civil Rights Activism in Portland, Oregon, 1930–1962" unpublished paper in the author's possession), 31–37; Michael Coray, "African-Americans in Nevada," *Nevada Historical Society Quarterly* 35:4 (Winter 1992), 251–53; Elmer Rusco, "Civil Rights Movement in Nevada," *Nevada Public Affairs Review: Ethnicity and Race in Nevada* (1987), 75–77; Jamie Coughtry and R. T. King, eds., *Lubertha Johnson: Civil Rights Efforts in Las Vegas: 1940s–1960s* (Reno: University of Nevada Oral History Program, 1988), 40; and Taylor, *Forging,* ch. 7.

19. Hugh Pearson, *The Shadow of the Panther: Huey Newton and the Price of Black Power in America* (Reading, Mass.: Addison-Wesley Publishing Co., 1994), 49–50, and Max Silverman, "Urban Redevelopment and Community Response: African Americans in San Francisco's Western Addition" (M.A. thesis, San Francisco State University, 1994), 50–51, 64, 84.

20. The Ussery quote appeared in the *San Francisco Sun-Reporter,* August 3, 1963, and is quoted in Silverman, "Urban Redevelopment," 92. On the Oakland protests, see Pearson, *The Shadow of the Panther,* 51–52.

21. *San Francisco Sun-Reporter,* May 23, 1963, quoted in Silverman, "Urban Redevelopment," 87.

22. Pearson, *The Shadow of the Panther,* 52–53.

23. The shop-in was a typical CORE protest tactic wherein demonstrators filled shopping carts and went to the checkout stands, waited for the costs to be tallied, then left the store without taking or paying for the items. See David Lance Goines, *The Free Speech Movement: Coming of Age in the 1960s* (Berkeley: Ten Speed Press, 1993), 85, for a description of a shop-in at a Lucky supermarket in 1964.

24. James Richardson, *Willie Brown: A Biography* (Berkeley: University of California Press, 1996), 86–87, and Pearson, *The Shadow of the Panther,* 57–59.

25. Quoted in Pearson, *The Shadow of the Panther,* 70. See also pages 59–60, 70.

26. Ibid., 71–73. The unidentified student quote is Rorabaugh, *Berkeley at War,* 20. For a detailed discussion of the Free Speech Movement and its roots in civil rights activism, see pages 18–37 and Goines, *The Free Speech Movement,* 161–36.

27. The quotations are from Goldberg, "Racial Change on the Southern Periphery," 362, 370.

28. Quoted in ibid., 362; see also pages 352, 362–63. On the role of Henry B. González in

civil rights efforts, see Juan Gómez-Quiñonez, *Chicano Politics: Reality and Promise, 1940–1990* (Albuquerque: University of New Mexico Press, 1990), 57–59. On the Mexican American civil rights movement in Texas and its relationship to the national black struggle, see Mario T. García, *Mexican Americans: Leadership, Ideology, & Identity, 1930–1960* (New Haven: Yale University Press, 1989), 46–59.

29. Taylor, *Forging,* 223.
30. Ibid., 224, 227. For a background discussion of Asian Americans in the civil rights era, see Sucheng Chan, *Asian Americans: An Interpretative History* (Boston: Twayne Publishers, 1991), 174–75.
31. The parent is quoted in the *San Francisco Sun-Reporter,* September 22, 1962. See Silverman, "Urban Redevelopment," 89.
32. The Texas public schools were established and segregated with the adoption of a new state constitution in 1876. This segregation extended to "Mexican" children, the vast majority of whom lived in south Texas. For background on Texas segregation, see William Henry Kellar, "Make Haste Slowly: A History of School Desegregation in Houston, Texas" (Ph.D. dissertation, University of Houston, 1994), 1, 5–6, 217.
33. Jensen, "The Houston Sit-In Movement," 213–17.
34. Kellar, "Make Haste Slowly," 299. On Tyronne Day, see page 322. There is now extensive literature on the role of business elites as reluctant supporters of desegregation. See, for example, Elizabeth Jacoway and David R. Colburn, *Southern Businessmen and Desegregation* (Baton Rouge: Louisiana State University Press, 1982) and W. Marvin Dulaney, "Whatever Happened to the Civil Rights Movement in Dallas, Texas?," in W. Marvin Dulaney and Kathleen Underwood, eds., *Essays on the American Civil Rights Movement* (College Station: Texas A&M University Press, 1993), 66–95.
35. Kellar, "Make Haste Slowly," 343–71.
36. The statement appears in Berkeley Unified School District, "Integration of the Berkeley Elementary Schools: A Report to the Superintendent" (Berkeley: Berkeley Unified School District, 1967), 1. See also Rorabaugh, *Berkeley at War,* 54–57.
37. Rorabaugh, *Berkeley at War,* 62.
38. Ibid., 62–63.
39. Ibid., 63.
40. See *Berkeley Citizens United Bulletin,* November 1964, p. 3, and Neil V. Sullivan, *Now Is the Time: Integration in the Berkeley Schools* (Bloomington: Indiana University Press, 1969), 32–33, 42–43, 64–65.
41. The quotations appear in Sullivan, *Now Is the Time,* 50, 88–90. The Berkeley desegregation plan is described in detail in Berkeley Unified School District, "Desegregation of the Berkeley Public Schools: Its Feasibility and Implementation," (Berkeley: Berkeley Unified School District, 1964), 13–29.
42. Rorabaugh, *Berkeley at War,* 69. For a positive assessment of Berkeley's desegregation, see Sullivan, *Now Is the Time,* ch. 8, 20.
43. All quotes are from Rorabaugh, *Berkeley at War,* 68. For a discussion of school desegregation in San Francisco, Seattle, Oklahoma City, and Tulsa, see Doris R. Fine, *When Leadership Fails: Desegregation and Demoralization in the San Francisco Schools* (New Brunswick, N.J.: Transaction Books, 1986), ch. 2, 3, 9; Doris Pieroth, "With All Deliberate Caution: School Integration in Seattle, 1954–1968," *Pacific Northwest Quarterly* 73:2 (April 1982), 50–61; and Derrick and Barnhill, "With All Deliberate Speed," 78–90.
44. See Gerald Horne, *Fire This Time: The Watts Uprising and the 1960s* (Charlottesville: University Press of Virginia, 1995), 96, and Jerry Cohen and William S. Murphy, *Burn, Baby, Burn! The Los Angeles Race Riot, August 1965* (New York: E. P. Dutton, 1966), 25–41, 146, 213, 232, 256. Although *Fire This Time* is the most comprehensive study of the uprising, the post-Watts literature also includes Paul Bullock, *Watts, the Aftermath: An Inside View of the Ghetto by the People of Watts, California* (New York: Grove Press, 1969); Robert Conot, *Rivers of Blood, Years of Darkness* (New York: Bantam Books, 1967); Bruce Michael Tyler, "Black Radicalism in Southern California, 1950–1982" (Ph.D. dissertation, UCLA, 1983); and Mark Baldassare, ed., *The Los Angeles Riots: Lessons for the Urban Future* (Boulder, Colo.: Westview Press, 1994). See also Richard M. Elman, *Ill-at-Ease in Compton* (New York: Pantheon Books, 1967).
45. Cohen and Murphy, *Burn, Baby, Burn!,* 44.

46. Patricia Rae Adler, "Watts, from Suburb to Black Ghetto" (Ph.D. dissertation, University of Southern California, 1977), 251–64.
47. The Bontemps quotation appears in Arna Bontemps and Jack Conroy, *Anyplace but Here* (New York: Hill and Wang, 1966), 9. For the Weaver quotation, see Robert C. Weaver, *The Negro Ghetto* (New York: Russell and Russell, 1948 [reprinted 1967]), 87. See also Adler, "Watts," 251, 255–65.
48. See Johnie Scott, "The Coming of the Hoodlum," in Budd Schulberg, ed., *From the Ashes: Voices of Watts* (New York: World Publishing Co., 1969), 98, and Adler, "Watts," 289, 291–94, 301, 303.
49. Eldridge Cleaver, *Soul on Ice* (New York: Dell Publishing Co., 1968), 27. On the educational and income levels of blacks in Watts in 1950 and 1960, see Sally Jane Sandoval, "Ghetto Growing Pains: The Impact of Negro Migration on the City of Los Angeles, 1940–1960" (M.A. thesis, California State University, Fullerton, 1974), ch. 5.
50. Raphael J. Sonenshein, *Politics in Black and White: Race and Power in Los Angeles* (Princeton: Princeton University Press, 1993), 43–46, 55–56, and Tyler, "Black Radicalism," 287.
51. Sonenshein, *Politics in Black and White*, 43–46.
52. On the Canton, Mississippi, speech, see Clayborne Carson, *In Struggle, SNCC and the Black Awakening of the 1960s* (Cambridge: Harvard University Press, 1967), ch. 14. On the origins of black power, see Stokely Carmichael and Charles V. Hamilton, *Black Power: The Politics of Liberation in America* (New York: Vintage, 1967), ch. 2, and William L. Van Deburg, *New Day in Babylon: The Black Power Movement and American Culture, 1965–1975* (Chicago: University of Chicago Press, 1992), 31–34. Finally see Taylor, *Forging*, 216–23, for a discussion of the transition of black political leadership in Seattle from nonviolence to black power.
53. Tyler, "Black Radicalism," 45, 221–22, and Horne, *Fire This Time*, 200–01.
54. John Gregory Dunne, "The Ugly Mood of Watts: Militant Leaders in Los Angeles' Negro Ghetto Are Trying to Win Power by Threatening Whites With Violence—and behind Their Threats Lies Hatred," *Saturday Evening Post* 239:15 (July 16, 1966), 85–86; Andrew Kopkind, "Watts—Waiting for D-Day," *New Republic* 154:24 (June 11, 1966), 15–17. See also Tyler, "Black Radicalism," 226.
55. Huey P. Newton, *Revolutionary Suicide* (New York: Harcourt Brace Jovanovich, 1973), 22. On Newton's background, see pages 11–18, 45–50, 67–72, 105–09. See also Bobby Seale, *Seize the Time: The Story of the Black Panther Party and Huey P. Newton* (New York: Vintage Books, 1968), 4–8; Rorabaugh, *Berkeley at War*, 5; and Pearson, *The Shadow of the Panther*, 2, 45–9.
56. Befitting their image as alliance-oriented revolutionaries, Newton and Seale received their first weapons from Richard Aoki, a self-styled Japanese American revolutionary, and later in 1966 sold *Quotations from Chairman Mao Tse-tung* on the campus of UC-Berkeley. The sales generated revenue for more guns and introduced the Panthers to white radical students eager to support black revolutionaries. See Pearson, *The Shadow of the Panther*, 112–13. The BPP ten-point program appears in Newton, *Revolutionary Suicide*, 116–19.
57. Newton, *Revolutionary Suicide*, 114–36, 145–51; Pearson, *The Shadow of the Panther*, 119, 123–31.
58. Newton, *Revolutionary Suicide*, 154–57; Rorabaugh, *Berkeley at War*, 110; and Pearson, *The Shadow of the Panther*, 148–50.
59. Pearson, *The Shadow of the Panther*, 156, 167, 169, 209. On the COINTELPRO campaign, see Ward Churchill and Jim Vander Wall, *Agents of Repression: The FBI's Secret Wars against the Black Panther Party and the American Indian Movement* (Boston: South End Press, 1988), ch. 2, 3.
60. *Los Angeles Times*, January 18, 1969, pp. 1, 17. See also Elaine Brown, *A Taste of Power: A Black Woman's Story* (New York: Pantheon Books, 1992), ch. 8. For the relationship between gangs and post-Watts militancy, see Mike Davis, *City of Quartz: Excavating the Future in Los Angeles* (New York: Vintage, 1992), 296–98, and Tyler, "Black Radicalism," 227–34.
61. See Jeffrey A. Scott "The Sixties Student Movement at San Francisco State College: A New Perspective," *Wazo Weusi Journal* 1:1 (Fall 1992), 58–60, and Dikran Karagueuzian, *Blow It Up! The Black Student Revolt at San Francisco State College and the Emergence*

of Dr. Hayakawa (Boston: Gambit, 1971), ch. 6–10. For a discussion of the Brown Berets and AIM, the largest of the 1960s-era ethnic defense organizations, see Rudolfo Acuna, *Occupied America: The Chicano's Struggle toward Liberation* (New York: Harper and Row, 1972), 231–33, and Russell Means, *Where White Men Fear to Tread: The Autobiography of Russell Means* (New York: St. Martin's Press, 1995), 148–55, 162–165.

62. On gender relations in the Black Panther Party, see Angela Darlean Brown, "Servants of the People: A History of Women in the Black Panther Party," (A.B. thesis, Harvard University, 1992), ch. 3, and Brown, *A Taste of Power*, 108–10, 307–10, 357, 367–68, 438–50.

63. Newton, *Revolutionary Suicide*, ch. 11, 12, 19, and Brown, *A Taste of Power*, 135–37.

64. The full editorial appears in *Los Angeles Sentinel*, January 23, 1969, pp. B-1 and B-5. One consequence was the rapid expansion of western street gangs by the early 1970s with the Los Angeles–based Crips and Bloods as a eighty-thousand-member core of two rival confederations that eventually spread as far north as Seattle and as far east as Kansas City. For two interpretations of their growth in the post-Watts era, see Davis, *City of Quartz*, 267–84, 296–99, and Horne, *Fire This Time*, 189–204.

65. Quoted in Taylor, *Forging*, 191.

Conclusion

1. See Quintard Taylor, "From Esteban to Rodney King: Five Centuries of African American History in the West," *Montana: The Magazine of Western History* 46:4 (Winter 1996), 3–4.

2. Ibid., 3–4, 16–17. On the Rodney King uprising, see Mark Baldassare, ed., *The Los Angeles Riots: Lessons for the Urban Future* (Boulder, C.: Westview Press, 1994).

3. See J. W. Smurr, "Jim Crow out West," in J. W. Smurr and K. Ross Toole, eds., *Historical Essays on Montana and the Northwest* (Helena: Western Press, Historical Society of Montana, 1957), 194, and Richard White, *"It's Your Misfortune and None of My Own": A History of the American West* (Norman: University of Oklahoma Press, 1991), 577, 589.

4. For the complete Olvera statement, see George P. Hammond and Agapito Rey, eds., *Don Juan de Oñate: Colonizer of New Mexico, 1595–1628* (Albuquerque: University of New Mexico Press, 1953), 560–62.

5. Quoted in Patricia Nelson Limerick, *The Legacy of Conquest: The Unbroken Past of the American West* (New York: W. W. Norton, 1987), 349.

Bibliography

◊ ✿ ◊ ✿ ◊

Books, Articles, Reports, Government Documents, Theses, and Dissertations

Acuña, Rodolfo. *Occupied America: The Chicano's Struggle toward Liberation.* New York: Harper and Row, 1972.

Adler, Patricia Rae. "Watts: From Suburb to Black Ghetto." Ph.D. dissertation, University of Southern California, 1977.

Age, Arthur V. "The Omaha Riot of 1919." M.A. thesis, Creighton University, 1964.

Aguirre Beltrán, Gonzalo. "The Integration of the Negro into the National Society of Mexico." In Magnus Morner, ed., *Race and Class in Latin America.* New York: Columbia University Press, 1970.

Albin, Ray R. "The Perkins Case: The Ordeal of Three Slaves in Gold Rush California." *California History* 67:4 (December 1988), 215–27.

Allen, Robert L. *The Port Chicago Mutiny.* New York: Amistad Press, 1993.

Alvarez, Robert R., Jr., "The Lemon Grove Incident: The Nation's First Successful Desegregation Court Case." *Journal of San Diego History* 32:2 (Spring 1986), 116–35.

Anderson, E. Frederick. *The Development of Leadership and Organization Building in the Black Community of Los Angeles from 1900 through World War II.* Saratoga, Calif.: Century Twenty One Publishing, 1980.

Anderson, Jervis. *A Philip Randolph: A Biographical Portrait.* New York: Harcourt Brace Jovanovich, 1972.

Anderson, Robert. *From Slavery to Affluence; Memoirs of Robert Anderson, Ex-Slave.* Steamboat Springs, Color.: Steamboat Pilot, Printer, 1967.

Andrews, Thomas F. "Freedmen in Indian Territory: A Post-Civil War Dilemma." *Journal of the West* 4:3 (July 1965), 367–76.

Angelou, Maya. *I Know Why the Caged Bird Sings.* New York: Bantam Books, 1971.

Aptheker, Herbert, ed. *A Documentary History of the Negro People in the United States.* New York: Citadel Press, 1951.

Archibald, Katherine. *Wartime Shipyard: A Study in Cultural Disunity.* Berkeley: University of California Press, 1947.

Armitage, Susan H., and Deborah Gallacci Wilbert. "Black Women in the Pacific Northwest: A Survey and Research Prospectus." In Karen Blair, ed., *Women in Pacific Northwest History: An Anthology.* Seattle: University of Washington Press, 1988.

Arrington, Leonard. "Mormon Beginnings in the American South." *Task Papers in LDS*

History, no. 9. Salt Lake City: Historical Department of the Church of Jesus Christ of Latter-day Saints, 1976.

———, and Davis Bitton. *The Mormon Experience: A History of the Latter-day Saints.* Urbana: University of Illinois Press, 1992.

Athearn, Robert. *The Coloradans.* Albuquerque: University of New Mexico Press, 1976.

———. *In Search of Canaan: Black Migration to Kansas, 1879–80.* Lawrence: Regents Press of Kansas, 1978.

Atkins, James A. *Human Relations in Colorado: A Historical Record.* Denver: Colorado Department of Education, 1968.

Austin, Michael. "Harlem of the West: The Douglas Hotel & Creole Palace Nite Club." M.A. thesis, University of San Diego, 1994.

Ax, Ruth Frye, ed. *Bound for Sacramento.* Claremont, Calif.: Saunders Studio Press, 1938.

Baenziger, Ann Patton. "The Texas State Police during Reconstruction: A Reexamination." *Southwestern Historical Quarterly* 72:4 (April 1969), 470–91.

Bailey, Beth, and David Farber. *The First Strange Place: Race and Sex in World War II Hawaii.* Baltimore: Johns Hopkins University Press, 1993.

Bailey, M. Thomas. *Reconstruction in Indian Territory: A Story of Avarice, Discrimination, and Opportunism.* Port Washington, N.Y.: Kennikat Press, 1972.

Baldassare, Mark, ed. *The Los Angeles Riots: Lessons for the Urban Future.* Boulder, Colo.: Westview Press, 1994.

Bandelier, F., ed. *The Journey of Álvar Nuñez Cabeza de Vaca.* New York: A. S. Barnes & Company, 1905.

Banks, Melvin James. "The Pursuit of Equality: The Movement for First Class Citizenship among Negroes in Texas, 1920–1950." D.S.S. dissertation, Syracuse University, 1962.

Barr, Alwyn. "Black Legislators of Reconstruction Texas." *Civil War History* 32:4 (December 1986), 340–52.

———. "Black Migration into Southwestern Cities, 1865–1900." In Garry W. Gallagher, ed., *Essays on Southern History Written in Honor of Barnes F. Lathrop.* Austin: General Libraries, University of Texas at Austin, 1980.

———. *Black Texans: A History of Negroes in Texas, 1528–1971.* Austin: Jenkins Publishing Co., 1973.

Baruch, Dorothy W. "Sleep Comes Hard." *Nation* 160:4 (January 27, 1945), 95–96.

Bass, Charlotta A. *Forty Years: Memoirs from the Pages of a Newspaper.* Los Angeles: privately published, 1960.

Beeth, Howard, and Cary D. Wintz, eds. *Black Dixie: Afro-Texan History and Culture in Houston.* College Station: Texas A&M University Press, 1992.

Bell, Howard H., ed. *Minutes of the Proceedings of the National Negro Conventions 1830–1864.* New York: Arno Press and the *New York Times*, 1969.

Beller, Jack. "Negro Slaves in Utah." *Utah Historical Quarterly* 2:4 (October 1929), 122–26.

Beniniato, Stefanie. "Pope, Pose-yemu, and Naranjo: A New look at Leadership in the Pueblo Revolt of 1680." *New Mexico Historical Review* 65:4 (October 1990), 417–35.

Beradi, Gayle, and Thomas W. Segady. "Community Identification and Cultural Formation: The Role of African American Newspapers in the American West, 1880–1914." *Griot* 10:1 (Spring 1991), 13–19.

Berkeley Unified School District. "Desegregation of the Berkeley Public Schools: Its Feasibility and Implementation." Berkeley: Berkeley Unified School District, 1964.

———. "Integration of the Berkeley Elementary Schools: A Report to the Superintendent." Berkeley: Berkeley Unified School District, 1967.

Berlin, Ira, ed. *The Black Military Experience.* New York: Cambridge University Press, 1982.

Berwanger, Eugene. *The Frontier against Slavery: Western Anti-Negro Prejudice and the Slavery Extension Controversy.* Urbana: University of Illinois Press, 1967.

———. "Hardin and Langston: Western Black Spokesmen of the Reconstruction Era." *Journal of Negro History* 64:2 (Spring 1979), 101–14.

———. *The West and Reconstruction.* Urbana: University of Illinois Press. 1981.

———. "William J. Hardin: Colorado Spokesman for Racial Justice, 1863–1873." *Colorado Magazine* 52:1 (Winter 1975), 52–65.

Betts, Robert B. *In Search of York: The Slave Who Went to the Pacific with Lewis and Clark.* Boulder: Colorado Associated University Press, 1985.

Beyer, Walter F., and Oscar F. Keydel, eds. *Deeds of Valor: How American Heroes Won the Medal of Honor.* Detroit: Perrien-Keydel Co., 1907. 2 vols.

Bibb, Henry. "Narrative of The Life and Adventures of Henry Bibb, an American Slave." In Gilbert, Osofsky, ed. *Puttin' on Ole Massa.* New York: Harper and Row, 1969.

Biles, Roger. "The New Deal in Dallas." *Southwestern Historical Quarterly* 95:1 (July 1991), 1–19.

Billington, Monroe. "Black History and New Mexico's Place Names." *Password* 29:3 (Fall 1984), 107–56.

———. *New Mexico's Buffalo Soldiers, 1866–1900.* Niwot: University Press of Colorado, 1991.

Bish, James D. "The Black Experience in Selected Nebraska Counties, 1854–1920." M.A. thesis, University of Nebraska at Omaha, 1989.

Bittle, William E., and Gilbert Geis. *The Longest Way Home: Chief Alfred C. Sam's Back-to-Africa Movement.* Detroit: Wayne State University Press, 1964.

Blenkinsop, Willis, "Edward Rose." In Le Roy Hafen, ed., *The Mountain Men and the Fur Trade of the Far West,* vol. 9. Glendale, Calif.: Arthur H. Clark Co., 1972.

Blum, John Morton. *V Was for Victory: Politics and American Culture during World War II.* New York: Harcourt Brace Jovanovich, 1976.

Bogle, Donald. *Toms, Coons, Mulattoes, Mammies and Bucks: An Interpretive History of Blacks in American Film.* New York: Viking Press, 1973.

Bond, J. Max. "The Negro in Los Angeles." Ph.D. dissertation, University of Southern California, 1936.

Bonner, Thomas D., ed. *Life and Adventures of James Beckwourth.* Lincoln: University of Nebraska Press, 1972.

Bontemps, Arna. *God Sends Sunday.* New York: Harcourt, Brace and Company, 1931.

———."Why I Returned." In Arna Bontemps, *The Old South: "A Summer Tragedy" and Other Stories of the Thirties.* New York: Dodd, Mead and Co., 1973.

———, and Jack Conroy. *Anyplace but Here.* New York: Hill and Wang, 1966.

Borthwick, J. D. *Three Years in California.* Oakland: Biobooks, 1948.

Botson, Michael R., Jr. "Organized Labor at the Hughes Tool Company, 1918–1942: From Welfare to the Steel Workers Organizing Committee." M.A. thesis, University of Houston, 1994.

Bourgeois, Christie L. "Stepping over Lines: Lyndon Johnson, Black Texans, and the National Youth Administration, 1935–1937." *Southwestern Historical Quarterly* 91:2 (October 1987), 149–72.

Braddy, Haldeen. *Pershing's Mission in Mexico.* El Paso: Texas Western Press, 1966.

Brady, Marilyn Dell. "Kansas Federation of Colored Women's Clubs, 1900–1930." *Kansas History* 9:1 (Spring 1986), 19–30.

Brewer, J. Mason. *Negro Legislators of Texas and Their Descendants.* Dallas: Mathis Publishing Company, 1935.

Bringhurst, Newell G. *Saints, Slaves, and Blacks: The Changing Place of Black People within Mormonism.* Westport, Conn.: Greenwood Press, 1981.

Brooks, James F. "The Old Way Gave to Many a Pleasurable Excitement": Customary Justice and State Power in New Mexico, 1780–1880." Unpublished paper in author's possession, 1994.

Broussard, Albert. *Black San Francisco: The Struggle for Racial Equality in the West, 1900–1954.* Lawrence: University Press of Kansas, 1993.

———. "The New Racial Frontier: San Francisco's Black Community: 1900–1940." Ph. D. dissertation, Duke University, 1977.

———. "Slavery in California Revisited: The Fate of a Kentucky Slave in Gold Rush California." *Pacific Historian* 29:1 (Spring 1985), 17–21.

Brown, Angela Darlean. "Servants of the People: A History of Women in the Black Panther Party." A.B. thesis, Harvard University, 1992.

Brown, Elaine, *A Taste of Power: A Black Woman's Story.* New York: Pantheon Books, 1992.

Brown, Richard Maxwell. *No Duty to Retreat: Violence and Values in American History and Society.* New York: Oxford University Press, 1991.

———. *Strain of Violence: Historical Studies of American Violence and Vigilantism.* New York: Oxford University Press, 1975.

Bruce, Henry Clay. *The New Man: Twenty-nine Years a Slave, Twenty-nine Years a Free Man.* New York: Negro Universities Press, 1969.

Bryan, Marilyn T. "The Economic, Political and Social Status of the Negro in El Paso." *Password* 13:3 (Fall 1968), 74–86.

Bryson, Conrey. *Dr. Lawrence A. Nixon and the White Primary.* El Paso: Texas Western Press, 1974.

Buecker, Thomas R. "Confrontation at Sturgis: An Episode in Civil-Military Race Relations, 1885." *South Dakota History* 14:3 (Fall 1984), 238–61.

———. "One Soldier's Service: Caleb Benson in the Ninth and Tenth Cavalry, 1875–1908." *Nebraska History* 74:2 (Summer 1993), 54–62.

Bullock, Paul. *Watts, the Aftermath: An Inside View of the Ghetto by the People of Watts, California.* New York: Grove Press, 1969.

Bunch, Lonnie, III. *Black Angelenos: The Afro-American in Los Angeles, 1850–1950.* Los Angeles: California Afro-American Museum, 1988.

———. "A Past Not Necessarily Prologue: The African American in Los Angeles." In Norman M. Klein and Martin J. Schiesl, eds., *20th Century Los Angeles: Power, Promotion, and Social Conflict.* Claremont, Calif.: Regina Books, 1990.

Burran, James A. "Violence in an 'Arsenal of Democracy': The Beaumont Race Riot, 1943." *East Texas Historical Review* 14:1 (Spring 1976), 39–51.

Burton, Arthur T. *Black, Red and Deadly: Black and Indian Gunfighters of the Indian Territory, 1870–1907.* Austin: Eakin Press, 1991.

Butler, Anne. "Still in Chains: Black Women in Western Prisons, 1865–1910." *Western Historical Quarterly* 20:1 (February 1989), 19–36.

Butters, Gerald R., Jr., "*The Birth of a Nation* and the Kansas Board of Review of Motion Pictures: A Censorship Struggle." *Kansas History* 14:1 (Spring 1991), 2–14.

Byrd, James W. "Afro-American Writers in the West." In J. Golden Taylor, ed., *A Literary History of the American West.* Fort Worth: Texas Christian University Press, 1987.

Caldwell, Dan. "The Negroization of the Chinese Stereotype in California." *Southern California Historical Quarterly* 53:2 (June 1971), 123–31.

California-Oregon Collection, Missouri Historical Society, St. Louis, Missouri.

Campbell, Eugene E. *Establishing Zion: The Mormon Church in the American West, 1847–1869.* Salt Lake City: Signature Books, 1988.

Campbell, Randolph, B. *An Empire for Slavery: The Peculiar Institution in Texas, 1821–1865.* Baton Rouge: Louisiana State University Press, 1989.

———. " 'My Dear Husband': A Texas Slave's Love Letter, 1862."*Journal of Negro History* 65:4 (Fall 1980), 361–64.

Cantrell, Greg. *Kenneth and John B. Rayner and the Limits of Southern Dissent.* Urbana: University of Illinois Press, 1993.

Carlson, Paul H. *"Pecos Bill": A Military Biography of William R. Shafter.* College Station: Texas A&M University Press, 1989.

———. "William R. Shafter, Black Troops, and the Opening of the *Llano Estacado,* 1870–1875." *Panhandle-Plains Historical Review* 47(1974), 1–18.

Carmichael, Stokely, and Charles V. Hamilton. *Black Power: The Politics of Liberation in America.* New York: Vintage, 1967.

Carper, James C. "The Popular Ideology of Segregated Schooling: Attitudes toward the Education of Blacks in Kansas, 1854–1900." *Kansas History* 1:4 (Winter 1978), 254–65.

Carson, Clayborne. "Civil Rights Reform and the Black Freedom Struggle." In Charles Eagles, ed., *The Civil Rights Movement in America.* Jackson: University of Mississippi Press, 1986.

———. *In Struggle, SNCC and the Black Awakening of the 1960s.* Cambridge: Harvard University Press, 1967.

Casdorph, Paul Douglas. "Norris Wright Cuney and Texas Republican Politics, 1883–1896." *Southwestern Historical Quarterly* 68:4 (April 1965), 455–64.

Casey, Helen Marie. *Portland's Compromise: The Colored School, 1867–1872.* Portland Ore.: Portland Public Schools, Public Information Department, 1980.

Castel, Albert. "Civil War Kansas and the Negro." *Journal of Negro History* 51:2 (April 1966), 125–38.

Chafe, William H. "The Negro and Populism: A Kansas Case Study." *Journal of Southern History* 34:3 (August 1968), 402–19.

Chan, Sucheng. *Asian Americans: An Interpretive History.* Boston: Twayne Publishers, 1991.

Chandler, Robert."Friends in Time of Need, Republicans and Black Civil Rights in California during the Civil War Era." *Arizona and the West* 24:4 (Winter 1982), 319–340.

Chapman, Charles E. *A History of California: The Spanish Period.* New York: Macmillan Co., 1921.

Chaudhuri, Nupur. "We All Seem Like Brothers and Sisters': The African-American Community in Manhattan, Kansas, 1865–1940." *Kansas History* 14:4 (Winter 1991), 270–88.

Chávez, Angélico Fray. "Pohe-yemo's Representative and the Pueblo Revolt of 1680." *New Mexico Historical Review* 42:2 (April 1967), 85–125.

Chipman, Donald E. *Spanish Texas, 1519–1821.* Austin: University of Texas Press, 1992.

Chittenden, Hiram M. *The American Fur Trade of the Far West.* Stanford: Academic Reprints, 1954. 2 vols.

Chrisman, Harry E. *The Ladder of Rivers: The Story of L. P. (Print) Olive.* Denver: Sage Books, 1962.

Christensen, James B. "Negro Slavery in Utah Territory," *Phylon* 18:3 (Third Quarter 1957), 298–305.

Christian, Garna L. *Black Soldiers in Jim Crow Texas, 1899–1917.* College Station: Texas A& M University Press, 1995.

Churchill, Ward, and Jim Vander Wall, *Agents of Repression: The FBI's Secret Wars against the Black Panther Party and the American Indian Movement.* Boston: South End Press, 1988.

Clark, Michael. "Improbable Ambassadors: Black Soldiers at Fort Douglas, 1896–99." *Utah Historical Quarterly* 46:3 (Summer 1978), 282–301.

Cleaver, Eldridge. *Soul on Ice.* New York: Dell Publishing Co., 1968.

Cohen, Jerry, and William S. Murphy. *Burn, Baby, Burn! The Los Angeles Race Riot, August 1965.* New York: E. P. Dutton & Co., 1966.

Colbert, Robert E. "The Attitude of Older Negro Residents toward Recent Negro Migrants in the Pacific Northwest." *Journal of Negro Education* 15:4 (Fall 1946), 695–703.

Cole, Martin, and Henry Welcome, eds. *Don Pío Pico's Historical Narrative.* Glendale, Calif.: Arthur H. Clark Co., 1973.

Cole, Olen, Jr. "Black Youth in the National Youth Administration in California, 1935–1943." *Southern California Quarterly* 73:4 (Winter 1991), 385–402.

Coleman, Ronald. "Blacks in Utah History: An Unknown Legacy." In Helen Z. Papanikolas, ed., *The Peoples of Utah.* Salt Lake City: Utah Historical Society, 1976.

———. "The Buffalo Soldiers: Guardians of the Uintah Frontier, 1886–1901." *Utah Historical Quarterly* 47:4 (Fall 1979), 421–39.

———. "A History of Blacks in Utah, 1825–1910." Ph.D. dissertation, University of Utah, 1980.

Colley, Nathaniel S. "Civil Actions for Damages Arising out of Violations of Civil Rights." *Hastings Law Journal* 17 (December 1965), 189–215.

Collins, Keith E. *Black Los Angeles: The Maturing of the Ghetto, 1940–1950.* Saratoga, Calif.: Century Twenty One Publishing, 1980.

Conot, Robert. *Rivers of Blood, Years of Darkness.* New York: Bantam Books, 1967.

Cooper, Jerry M. *The Army and Civil Disorder: Federal Military Intervention in Labor Disputes, 1877–1900.* Westport, Conn.: Greenwood Press, 1980.

Coray, Michael, "African-Americans in Nevada." *Nevada Historical Society Quarterly* 34:4 (Winter 1992), 239–57.

Cordley, Richard. *A History of Lawrence, Kansas from the First Settlement to the Close of the Rebellion.* Lawrence: E. F. Caldwell, 1895.

———. *Pioneer Days in Kansas.* New York: Pilgrim Press, 1903.

Cornish, Dudley Taylor. *The Sable Arm: Black Troops in the Union Army, 1861–1865.* Lawrence: University Press of Kansas, 1987.

Coughtry, Jamie, and R. T. King, eds. *Lubertha Johnson: Civil Rights Efforts in Las Vegas: 1940s–1960.* Reno: University of Nevada Oral History Program, 1988.

———. *Woodrow Wilson: Race, Community and Politics in Las Vegas, 1940s–1980s.* Reno: University of Nevada Oral History Program, 1990.

Covington, Floyd C. "Where the Color Line Chokes." *Sociology and Social Research* 20:3 (January–February 1936), 236–41.

Cox, Bette Yarbrough. *Central Avenue—Its Rise and Fall (1890–c.1955).* Los Angeles: Beem Publications, 1996.

Cox, Thomas C. *Blacks in Topeka: A Social History.* Baton Rouge: Louisiana State University Press, 1982.

Crane, R. C., ed. "D. W. Wallace ('80 John'); A Negro Cattleman on the Texas Frontier." *West Texas Historical Society Year Book* 28 (1952), 113–18.

Cripps, Thomas. *Making Movies Black: The Hollywood Message Movie from World War II to the Civil Rights Era.* New York: Oxford University Press, 1993.

———. *Slow Fade to Black: The Negro in America Film, 1900–1942.* New York: Oxford University Press, 1993.

Crockett, Norman L. *The Black Towns.* Lawrence: Regents Press of Kansas, 1979.

Crouch, Barry A. "The 'Cords of Love': Legalizing Black Marital and Family Rights in Postwar Texas," *Journal of Negro History* 79:4 (Fall 1994), 334–51.

———. *The Freedmen's Bureau and Black Texans.* Austin: University of Texas Press, 1992.

Crouchett, Lawrence P. *William Byron Rumford: The Life and Public Service of a California Legislator.* El Cerrito, Calif.: Downey Place Publishing House, 1984.

———, Lonnie G. Bunch III, and Martha Kendall Winnacker. *Visions toward Tomorrow: The History of the East Bay Afro-American Community, 1852–1977.* Oakland: Northern California Center for Afro-American History and Life, 1989.

Crowder, Ralph L. "John Edward Bruce & the Value of Knowing the Past: Politician, Journalist, and Self-Trained Historian of the African Diaspora, 1856–1924." Ph.D. dissertation, University of Kansas, 1994.

Crumbly, F. H. "A Los Angeles Citizen." *Colored American Magazine* 9:3 (September 1905), 482–85.

Curtin, Philip. *The Atlantic Slave Trade: A Census.* Madison: University of Wisconsin Press, 1969.

———. *Economic Change in Precolonial Africa: Senegambia in the Era of the Slave Trade.* Madison: University of Wisconsin Press, 1975.

Custer, Elizabeth B. *Tenting on the Plains, or General Custer in Kansas and Texas.* New York. Charles L. Webster & Co., 1889.

Dalfuime, Richard M. "The 'Forgotten Years' of the Negro Revolution." *Journal of American History* 55:1 (June 1968), 92–100.

Dana, Richard H. *Two Years before the Mast.* New York: Macmillan Co., 1911.

Dandridge, Deborah, and others. *Brown vs. Board of Education: In Pursuit of Freedom and Equality: Kansas and the African American Public School Experience, 1855–1955.* Topeka: Brown Foundation for Educational Equity, Excellence and Research, 1993.

Daniels, Douglas Henry. *Pioneer Urbanites: A Social and Cultural History of Black San Francisco.* Philadelphia: Temple University Press, 1980.

Daniels, Hayzel Burton. "A Black Magistrate's Struggles." In Anne Hodges Morgan and Rennard Stickland, eds., *Arizona Memories.* Tucson: University of Arizona Press, 1984.

Dann, Martin E. "From Sodom to the Promised Land: E. P. McCabe and the Movement for Oklahoma Colonization," *Kansas Historical Quarterly* 40:3 (Autumn 1974), 370–78.

Darensbourg, Joe. *Jazz Odyssey: The Autobiography of Joe Darensbourg.* Baton Rouge: Louisiana State University Press, 1988.

Davis, Mike. *City of Quartz: Excavating the Future in Los Angeles.* New York: Vintage, 1992.

Day, Ava Speece. "The Ava Speese Day Story." In Frances Jacobs Alberts, ed., *Sod House Memories.* Hastings, Nebraska: Sod House Society, 1972. 3 vols.

Debo, Angie. *And Still the Waters Run: The Betrayal of the Five Civilized Tribes.* Princeton: Princeton University Press, 1980.

———. *A History of the Indians of the United States.* Norman: University of Oklahoma Press, 1979.

———. *The Rise and Fall of the Choctaw Republic.* Norman: University of Oklahoma Press, 1961.

———. *The Road to Disappearance.* Norman: University of Oklahoma Press, 1941.

De Barros, Paul. *Jackson Street after Hours: The Roots of Jazz in Seattle.* Seattle: Sasquatch Books, 1993.

de Graaf, Lawrence B. "The City of Black Angels: The Emergence of the Los Angeles Ghetto, 1890–1930." *Pacific Historical Review* 39:3 (August 1970), 323–52.

———. "Negro Migration to Los Angeles, 1930–1950." Ph.D. dissertation, University of California, Los Angeles, 1962.

———. "Race, Sex, and Region: Black Women in the American West, 1850–1920." *Pacific Historical Review* 49:1 (February 1980), 285–314.

———. "Recognition, Racism, and Reflections on the Writing of Western Black History." *Pacific Historical Review* 44:1 (February 1975), 22–51.

———. "Significant Steps on an Arduous Path: The Impact of World War II on Discrimination against African Americans in the West." *Journal of the West* 35:1 (January 1996), 24–33.

De Kam, Elizabeth J. "A Home to Call One's Own: A Textual Analysis of the Story of Residential Racial-Restrictive Covenants in the California *Eagle* and Los Angeles *Sentinel.*" M.A. thesis, California State University, 1993.

de la Peña, José Enrique. *With Santa Anna in Texas: A Personal Narrative of the Revolution.* College Station: Texas A&M University Press, 1975.

de la Teja, Jesús. *San Antonio de Béxar: A Community on New Spain's Northern Frontier.* Albuquerque: University of New Mexico Press, 1995.

De León, Arnoldo. *They Called Them Greasers: Anglo Attitudes toward Mexicans in Texas, 1821–1900.* Austin: University of Texas Press, 1983.

Derrick, W. Edwin, and J. Hershel Barnhill. "With 'All' Deliberate Speed: Desegregation of the Public Schools in Oklahoma City and Tulsa, 1954 to 1972." *Red River Valley Historical Review* 6:2 (Spring 1981), 70–80.

Dickson, Lynda Faye. "The Early Club Movement among Black Women in Denver: 1890–1925." Ph.D. dissertation, University of Colorado, 1982.

Dillon, Merton L. *Benjamin Lundy and the Struggle for Negro Freedom.* Urbana: University of Illinois Press, 1966.

Djedje, Jacqueline Cogdell. "Gospel Music in the Los Angeles Black Community: A Historical Overview." *Black Music Research Journal* 9:1 (Spring 1989), 35–77.

Dobak, William A. "Black Regulars Speak." *Panhandle-Plains Historical Review* 47 (1974), 19–27.

———. "Civil War on the Kansas-Missouri Border: The Narrative of Former Slave Andrew Williams." *Kansas History* 6:4 (Winter 1983), 237–42.

Dobie, J. Frank, ed. *Legends of Texas.* Austin: Texas Folklore Society, 1924.

Doran, Michael F. "Population Statistics of Nineteenth Century Indian Territory." *Chronicles of Oklahoma* 53:4 (Winter 1975), 501–02.

Dorsett, Lyle W. *The Queen City: A History of Denver.* Boulder: Pruett Publishing Co., 1977.

Du Bois, W. E. B. "The Slanderous Film." *Crisis,* 11:2 (December 1915), 76–77.

———. "Thirteen." *Crisis* 15:3 (January 1918), 114.

Duke, Cordia Sloan, and Joe B. Frantz. *6,000 Miles of Fence: Life on the XIT Ranch of Texas.* Austin: University of Texas Press, 1961.

Dulaney, W. Marvin. "The Progressive Voters League." *Legacies: A History Journal for Dallas and North Central Texas* 3:1 (Spring 1991), 27–35.

———. "Whatever Happened to the Civil Rights Movement in Dallas, Texas?" In W. Marvin Dulaney and Kathleen Underwood, eds., *Essays on the American Civil Rights Movement.* College Station: Texas A&M University Press, 1993.

Dunne, John Gregory. "The Ugly Mood of Watts: Militant Leaders in Los Angeles' Negro Ghetto Are Trying to Win Power by Threatening Whites with Violence—and behind Their Threats Lies Hatred." *Saturday Evening Post* 239:15 (July 16, 1966), 85–86.

Durham, Philip, and Everett L. Jones, *The Negro Cowboys.* New York: Dodd, Mead and Co., 1965.

Eastman, Ralph. "Central Avenue Blues: The Making of Los Angeles Rhythm and Blues, 1942–1947." *Black Music Research Journal* 9:1 (Spring 1989), 19–32.

Edwards, Malcolm. "The War of Complexional Distinction: Blacks in Gold Rush California and British Columbia." *California Historical Quarterly* 56:1 (Spring 1977), 34–45.

Elliot, William Joseph Alexander. *The Spurs.* Dallas: Texas Spur Co., 1939.

Ellison, Ralph. *Shadow and Act.* New York: Random House, 1964.

Ellsworth, Scott. *Death in a Promised Land: The Tulsa Race Riot of 1921.* Baton Rouge: Louisiana State University Press, 1982.

Elman, Richard M. *III-at-Ease in Compton.* New York: Pantheon Books, 1967.

Entz, Gary R. "Image and Reality on the Kansas Prairie: 'Pap' Singleton's Cherokee County Colony." *Kansas History* 19:2 (Summer 1996), 124–39.

Erwin, Allen A. *The Southwest of John Slaughter, 1841–1922.* Glendale, Calif.: Arthur H. Clark Co., 1965.

Espinosa, Manuel J. *The Pueblo Indian Revolt of 1696 and the Franciscan Missions in New Mexico: Letters of the Missionaries and Related Documents.* Norman: University of Oklahoma Press, 1988.

Ewers, John C., ed. *The Adventures of Zenas Leonard, Fur Trapper.* Norman: University of Oklahoma Press, 1959.

Fair Employment Practices Committee, Headquarters Records, Reel 13–14, Documents. Microfilm No. 16335E, National Archives, Record Group 228.

Fine, Doris R. *When Leadership Fails: Desegregation and Demoralization in the San Francisco Schools.* New Brunswick, N.J.: Transaction Books, 1986.

Fisher, H.D. *The Gun and the Gospel: Early Kansas and Chaplain Fisher.* Chicago: Kenwood Press, 1896.

Fisher, James A. "A History of the Political and Social Development of the Black Community in California, 1850–1950." Ph.D. dissertation, State University of New York at Stony Brook, 1971.

———. "The Political Development of the Black Community in California, 1850–1950." *California Historical Quarterly* 50:3 (September 1971), 256–66.

———. "The Struggle for Negro Testimony in California, 1851–1863." *Southern California Quarterly* 51:4 (December 1969), 313–24.

Fite, Gilbert C. "A Family Farm Chronicle." In Clyde A. Milner, ed., *Major Problems in the History of the American West.* Lexington, Mass.: D. C. Heath and Co., 1989.

Fitzgerald, Roosevelt. "The Demographic Impact of Basic Magnesium Corporation on Southern Nevada." *Nevada Public Affairs Review, Ethnicity and Race in Nevada* 2 (1987), 29–35.

Flamming, Douglas. "African Americans and the Politics of Race in Progressive-Era Los Angeles." In William Deverall and Tom Sitton, eds., *California Progressivism Revisited.* Berkeley: University of California Press, 1994.

Fleming, Sidney Howell. "Solving the Jigsaw Puzzle: One Suffrage Story at a Time." *Annals of Wyoming* 62:1 (Spring 1990), 23–72.

Fletcher, Marvin. *The Black Soldier and Officer in the United States Army, 1891–1917.* Columbia: University of Missouri Press, 1974.

Foner, Jack D. *Blacks and the Military in American History: A New Perspective.* New York: Praeger, 1974.

Foner, Philip S., and George E. Walker, eds. *Proceedings of the Black State Conventions, 1840–1865.* Philadelphia: Temple University Press, 1980.

Fontenot, Chester J., Jr. "Oscar Micheaux, Black Novelist and Film Maker." In Virginia Faulkner with Frederick C. Luebke, eds., *Vision and Refuge: Essays on the Literature of the Great Plains.* Lincoln: University of Nebraska Press, 1982.

Forbes, Jack. *Afro-Americans in the Far West: A Handbook for Educators.* Berkeley: Far West Laboratory for Educational Research and Development, 1969.

———. "Black Pioneers: The Spanish-Speaking Afro-Americans of the Southwest." *Phylon* 27:3 (Fall 1966), 233–46.

———. *The Indian in America's Past.* Englewood Cliffs, N.J.: Prentice-Hall, 1964.

Foreman, Grant. *Indian Removal: The Emigration of the Five Civilized Tribes of Indians.* Norman: University of Oklahoma Press, 1972.

Fowler, Arlen L. *The Black Infantry in the West, 1869–1891.* Westport, Conn.: Greenwood Publishing Co., 1971.

Franklin, Jimmie Lewis. *Journey toward Hope: A History of Blacks in Oklahoma.* Norman: University of Oklahoma Press, 1982.

Franklin, Joseph. *All through the Night: The History of Spokane Black Americans.* Fairfield, Wash.: Ye Galleon Press, 1989.

Franklin, William E. "The Archy Case: The California Supreme Court Refuses to Free a Slave." *Pacific Historical Review* 32:2 (May 1963), 137–54.

Frémont, John Charles. "A Report of the Exploring Expedition to Oregon and North

California in the Years 1843–44." U.S. 28th Congress, 2d Session, *House Document 166,* December 2, 1844–March 3, 1845.

Frink, Margaret. *Adventures of a Party of California Gold Seekers.* Oakland, Calif.: privately printed, 1897.

Gaines, W. Craig. *The Confederate Cherokees: John Drew's Regiment of Mounted Rifles.* Baton Rouge: Louisiana State University Press, 1989.

Gamboa, Erasmo. *Mexican Labor and World War II: Braceros in the Pacific Northwest, 1942–1947.* Austin: University of Texas Press, 1990.

Garciá, Mario T. *Mexican Americans: Leadership, Ideology, & Identity, 1930–1960.* New Haven: Yale University Press, 1989.

Garciá, Mikel Hogan. "Adaptation Strategies of the Los Angeles Black Community, 1883–1919." Ph.D. dissertation, University of California, Irvine, 1985.

Garciá, Richard A. *Rise of the Mexican American Middle Class: San Antonio, 1929–1941.* College Station: Texas A&M University Press, 1991.

Gatewood, Willard B. *Aristocrats of Color: The Black Elite, 1880–1920.* Bloomington: Indiana University Press, 1990.

———. "Kate D. Chapman Reports on 'The Yankton Colored People,' 1889." *South Dakota History* 7:1 (Winter 1976), 28–35.

General Laws of the State of Texas, 38th Legislature, Second Session, 1923, ch. 32.

George, Lynell. *No Crystal Stair: African Americans in the City of Angels.* London: Verso Press, 1992.

Gibbs, Mifflin W. *Shadow and Light: An Autobiography.* New York: Arno Press and the *New York Times,* 1968.

Giddings, Paula. *When and Where I Enter: The Impact of Black Women on Race and Sex in America.* New York: William Morrow & Co.,1984.

Gillette, Michael Lowery. "The NAACP in Texas, 1937–1957." Ph.D. dissertation, University of Texas at Austin, 1984.

Gillette, William. *The Right to Vote: Politics and the Passage of the Fifteenth Amendment.* Baltimore: Johns Hopkins University Press, 1969.

Gioia, Ted. *West Coast Jazz: Modern Jazz in California, 1945–1960.* New York: Oxford University Press, 1992.

Glasrud, Bruce Alan. "Black Texans, 1900–1930: A History." Ph.D. dissertation, Texas Tech University, 1969.

———. "Enforcing White Supremacy in Texas, 1900–1910." *Red River Valley Historical Review* 4:4 (Fall 1979), 65–74.

Gluck, Sherma Berger. *Rosie the Riveter Revisited: Women, the War and Social Change.* Boston: Twayne Publishers, 1987.

Goetzmann, William H. *Exploration and Empire: The Explorer and the Scientist in the Winning of the American West.* New York: Alfred A. Knopf, 1966.

Goines, David Lance. *The Free Speech Movement: Coming of Age in the 1960s.* Berkeley: Ten Speed Press, 1993.

Goldberg, Robert Alan. *Barry Goldwater.* New Haven: Yale University Press, 1995.

———. "Racial Change on the Southern Periphery: The Case of San Antonio, Texas, 1960–1965." *Journal of Southern History* 49:3 (August 1983), 349–74.

Gómez-Quiñonez, Juan, *Chicano Politics: Reality and Promise, 1940–1990.* Albuquerque: University of New Mexico Press, 1990.

González, Gilbert G. *Chicano Education in the Era of Segregation.* Philadelphia: Balch Institute Press, 1990.

Goodwyn, Lawrence C. "Populist Dreams and Negro Rights: East Texas as a Case Study." *American Historical Review* 76:4 (December 1971), 1435–1456.

Gordon, Robert. *Jazz West Coast: The Lost Angeles Jazz Scene of the 1950s.* London: Quartet Books, 1986.

Gorham, Thelma Thurston. "Negroes and Japanese Evacuees." *Crisis* 52:11 (November 1945), 314–16, 330–31.

Graves, Carl R. "The Right to be Served: Oklahoma City's Lunch Counter Sit-ins, 1958–1964." *Chronicles of Oklahoma* 59:2 (Summer 1981), 152–66.

Greenbaum, Susan G. *The Afro-American Community in Kansas City, Kansas: A History.* Kansas City, Kan.: City of Kansas City, 1982.

Greenberg, Jack. *Crusaders in the Courts: How a Dedicated Band of Lawyers Fought for the Civil Rights Revolution.* New York: Basic Books, 1994.

Gregg, Josiah. *Commerce of the Prairies,* ed. Max L. Morehead. Norman: University of Oklahoma Press, 1954.

Griffith, Beatrice. *American Me.* Boston: Houghton Mifflin Co., 1948.

Grinde, Donald, and Quintard Taylor. "Red vs. Black: Conflict and Accommodation in the Post Civil War Indian Territory, 1865–1907." *American Indian Quarterly* 8:3 (Summer 1984), 211–29.

Gruening, Martha. " "Houston: An NAACP Investigation." *Crisis* 15:1 (November 1917), 14–18.

Guenther, Todd. "At Home on the Range: Black Settlement in Rural Wyoming, 1850–1950." M.A. thesis, University of Wyoming, 1988.

———. " 'Y'all Call Me Nigger Jim Now, but Someday You'll Call Me Mr. James Edwards': Black Success on the Plains of the Equality State." *Annals of Wyoming* 61:2 (Fall 1989), 20–40.

Gutiérrez, Ramón A. *When Jesus Came, the Corn Mothers Went Away: Marriage, Sexuality, and Power in New Mexico, 1500–1846.* Stanford: Stanford University Press, 1991.

Hacker, Barton C. "The United States Army as a National Police Force: The Federal Policing of Labor Disputes, 1877–1898." *Military Affairs* 33:1 (April 1969), 255–64.

Hafen, LeRoy R. "A Brief History of the Fur Trade of the Far West." In LeRoy Hafen, ed., *The Mountain Men and the Fur Trade of the Far West,* vol. 1. Glendale, Calif.: Arthur H. Clark Co., 1965. 10 vols.

———. "The Last Years of James P. Beckwourth." *Colorado Magazine* 5:4 (August 1928), 134–39.

Haley, James Evetts. *Charles Goodnight, Cowman & Plainsman.* Norman: University of Oklahoma Press, 1949.

Hall, Frank. *History of the State of Colorado.* Chicago: Blakely Printing Co., 1895. 4 vols.

Hallenbeck, Cleve, ed. *The Journey of Fray Marcos de Niza.* Dallas: Southern Methodist University Press, 1987.

Halliburton, R., Jr. *Red over Black: Black Slavery among the Cherokee Indians.* Westport, Conn.: Greenwood Press, 1977.

Hamilton, Kenneth W. *Black Towns and Profit: Promotion and Development in the Trans-Appalachian West, 1877–1915.* Urbana: University of Illinois Press, 1991.

Hammond, George P., and Agapito, Rey, eds. *Don Juan de Oñate: Colonizer of New Mexico, 1595–1628.* Albuquerque: University of New Mexico Press, 1953.

———. *Narratives of the Coronado Expedition, 1540–1542.* Albuquerque: University of New Mexico Press, 1940.

Hanes, Colonel Bailey C. *Bill Pickett, Bulldogger: The Biography of a Black Cowboy.* Norman: University of Oklahoma Press, 1977.

Hansen, Moya. "Entitled to Full and Equal Enjoyment: Leisure and Entertainment in the Denver Black Community, 1900 to 1930." *University of Colorado at Denver Historical Studies Journal* 10:1 (Spring 1993), 57–71.

———. "Pebbles on the Shore: Economic Opportunity in Five Points, 1920–1950." Unpublished paper in author's possession, 1994.

Hardaway, Roger D. "William Jefferson Hardin: Wyoming's Nineteenth Century Black Legislator." *Annals of Wyoming* 63:1 (Winter 1991), 2–13.

Hardin, John Wesley. *The Life of John Wesley Hardin.* Norman: University of Oklahoma Press, 1961.

Hare, Maude Cuney. *Norris Wright Cuney: A Tribune of the Black People.* Austin: Steck-Vaughn Co., 1968.

Harlan, Louis R. *Booker T. Washington: The Wizard of Tuskegee, 1901–1915.* New York: Oxford University Press, 1983.

Harris, LeRoy E. "The Other Side of the Freeway: A Study of Settlement Patterns of Negroes and Mexican Americans in San Diego, California." D. A. dissertation, Carnegie-Mellon University, 1974.

Harris, Richard E. *The First Hundred Years: A History of Arizona Blacks.* Apache Junction, Ariz.: Relmo Publishers, 1983.

Harris, Theodore, ed. *Negro Frontiersman: The Western Memoirs of Henry O. Flipper, First Negro Graduate of West Point.* El Paso: Texas Western College Press, 1963.

Harris, William H. "Federal Intervention in Union Discrimination: FEPC and West Coast Shipyards during World War II." *Labor History* 22:3 (Summer 1981), 325–47.
———. *The Harder We Run: Black Workers since the Civil War.* New York: Oxford University Press, 1982.
Hart, Charles Desmond. "The Natural Limits of Slavery Expansion: Kansas-Nebraska, 1854." *Kansas Historical Quarterly* 34:1 (Spring 1968), 32–50.
Harvey, James R. "Negroes in Colorado." M.A. thesis, University of Denver, 1941.
Hawes, Hampton, and Don Asher. *Raise Up off Me.* New York: Coward, McCann & Geoghegan, 1974.
Hayden, Dolores. "Biddy Mason's Los Angeles, 1851–1891." *California History* 68:3 (Fall 1989), 86–99.
Haygood, Tamara Miner. "Use and Distribution of Slave Labor in Harris County, Texas, 1836–60." In Howard Beeth and Cary D. Wintz, eds., *Black Dixie: Afro-Texan History and Culture in Houston.* College Station: Texas A&M University Press, 1992.
Haynes, Robert V. "Black Houstonians and the White Democratic Primary, 1920–45." In Howard Beeth and Cary D. Wintz, eds., *Black Dixie: Afro-Texan History and Culture in Houston.* College Station: Texas A&M University Press, 1992.
———. "The Houston Mutiny and Riot of 1917." *Southwestern Historical Quarterly* 74:4 (April 1973), 418–40.
———. *A Night of Violence: The Houston Riot of 1917.* Baton Rouge: Louisiana State University Press, 1976.
Haywood, Robert. "No Less a Man: Blacks in Cow Town Dodge City, 1876–1886." *Western Historical Quarterly* 19:2 (May 1988), 161–182.
Hebert, Janis. "Oscar Micheaux: A Black Pioneer." *South Dakota Review* 11:4 (Winter 1973–74), 62–69.
Henderson, Cheryl Brown. "Landmark Decision: Remembering the Struggle for Equal Education." *Land and People* 6:1 (Spring 1994), 2–5.
———, and Shariba Rivers. "The Legacy of *Brown* 40 Years Later." In Charles Teddlie and Kofi Lomotey, eds., *Forty Years after the Brown Decision: Implications of School Desegregation for U.S. Education,* vol. 14. New York: AMS Press, 1996.
Henderson, Richard. *Maury Maverick: A Political Biography.* Austin: University of Texas Press, 1970.
Hendrix, John M. "Tribute Paid to Negro Cowmen." *Cattleman* (February 1936), 24–26.
Hennessey, Thomas J. *From Jazz to Swing: African American Jazz Musicians and Their Music, 1890–1935.* Detroit: Wayne State University Press, 1994.
Hewes, Lawrence I. *Intergroup Relations in San Diego: Some Aspects of Community Life in San Diego Which Particularly Affect Minority Groups.* San Francisco: American Council on Race Relations, 1946.
Hickey, Joseph V. " 'Pap' Singleton's Dunlap Colony: Relief Agencies and the Failure of a Black Settlement in Eastern Kansas." *Great Plains Quarterly* 11:1 (Winter 1991), 23–36.
Hill, Herbert. *Black Labor and the American Legal System,* vol. I, *Race, Work, and the Law.* Washington, D.C.: Bureau of National Affairs, 1977.
Hine, Darlene Clark. "The Elusive Ballot: The Black Struggle against the Texas Democratic White Primary, 1932–1945." *Southwestern Historical Quarterly* 81:4 (April 1978), 371–92.
Hine, Robert V. *The American West: An Interpretive History.* Boston: Little, Brown and Co., 1973.
Hinojosa, Gilberto Miguel. *A Borderlands Town in Transition: Laredo, 1755–1870.* College Station: Texas A&M University Press, 1983.
Holliday, J. S. *The World Rushed In: The California Gold Rush Experience.* New York: Simon and Schuster, 1981.
Horne, Gerald. *Communist Front? The Civil Rights Congress, 1946–1956.* Rutherford, N.J.: Fairleigh Dickinson University Press, 1988.
———. *Fire This Time: The Watts Uprising and the 1960s.* Charlottesville: University Press of Virginia, 1995.
Hornsby, Alton. "The Freedman's Bureau Schools in Texas, 1865–1870." *Southwestern Historical Quarterly* 76:4 (April 1973), 397–417.
Hudson, Lynn M. "A New Look, or 'I'm Not Mammy to Everybody in California': Mary

Ellen Pleasant, a Black Entrepreneur." *Journal of the West* 32:3 (July 1993), 35–40.

———. "When 'Mammy' Becomes a Millionaire: Mary Ellen Pleasant, an African American Entrepreneur." Ph.D. dissertation, Indiana University, 1996.

Hughes, Langston. *The Big Sea: An Autobiography of Langston Hughes.* New York: A. A. Knopf, 1940.

Hunter, John Marvin, ed. *The Trail Drivers of Texas.* Nashville: Colesbury Press, 1925.

Hurtado, Albert. *Indian Survival on the California Frontier.* New Haven: Yale University Press, 1988.

Hussey, Marguerite Carleton. "The History of the Napoleon Byrne Family." Unpublished manuscript in the Byrne Family Papers, n.d., Bancroft Library, University of California, Berkeley.

Hutton, May Arkwright. *The Coeur d'Alenes or a Tale of the Modern Inquisition in Idaho.* Wallace, Idaho: May Arkwright Hutton, 1900.

Hyde, Anne F. "Cultural Filters: The Significance of Perception in the History of the American West." *Western Historical Quarterly* 24:3 (August 1993), 351–74.

Ibrahim, Shirley Diane. "Estevan, the Moor of New Mexico: An Experiment in Point of View." Ed. D. thesis, East Texas State University, 1978.

Issel, William, and Robert W Cherny. *San Francisco, 1865–1932: Politics, Power and Urban Development.* Berkeley: University of California Press, 1986.

Jackson, Susan. "Slavery in Houston: The 1850s." *Houston Review* 2:2 (1980), 66–82.

Jacoway, Elizabeth, and David R. Colburn. *Southern Businessmen and Desegregation.* Baton Rouge: Louisiana State University Press, 1982.

James, Edward T., Janet Wilson James, and Paul S. Boyer, eds. *Notable American Women, 1607–1950: A Biographical Dictionary.* Cambridge: Harvard University Press, 1971. 3 vols.

James v. Marinship Corporation, 25 Cal.2d 721 (1944).

Jefferson, Robert Franklin. "Making the Men of the 93rd: African American Servicemen in the Years of the Great Depression and the Second World War, 1935–1947." Ph.D. dissertation, University of Michigan, 1995.

Jensen, F. Kenneth. "The Houston Sit-In Movement of 1960–61." In Howard Beeth and Cary D. Wintz, eds., *Black Dixie: Afro-Texan History and Culture in Houston.* College Station: Texas A&M University Press, 1992.

Jensen, Richard, R. Eli Paul, and John E. Carter. *Eyewitness at Wounded Knee.* Lincoln: University of Nebraska Press, 1991.

Johannsen, Robert W. *Frontier Politics and the Sectional Conflict: The Pacific Northwest on the Eve of the Civil War.* Seattle: University of Washington Press, 1955.

Johnson, David Alan. *Founding the Far West: California, Oregon, and Nevada, 1840–1890.* Berkeley: University of California Press, 1992.

Johnson, Frederick P. "Agricultural Negro Colony in Eastern Colorado." *Western Farm Life Journal* (May 11, 1915), 5, 12.

Johnson, Marilynn. *The Second Gold Rush: Oakland and the East Bay in World War II.* Berkeley: University of California Press, 1993.

Jones, LeRoi. *Blues People: Negro Music in White America.* New York: William Morrow and Co., 1963.

Jones, Oakah L., Jr. *Los Paisanos: Spanish Settlers on the Northern Frontier of New Spain.* Norman: University of Oklahoma Press, 1979.

Jordan, Terry G. *North American Cattle-Ranching Frontiers.* Albuquerque: University of New Mexico Press, 1993.

———. *Trails to Texas: Southern Roots of Western Cattle Ranching.* Lincoln: University of Nebraska Press, 1981.

Josephy, Alvin M., Jr. *The Civil War in the American West.* New York: Alfred A. Knopf, 1991.

Journal of the Senate Proceedings of the Legislative Assembly of Oregon, 1870. Salem: T. Patterson, State Printer, 1870.

Karagueuzian, Dikran. *Blow It Up! The Black Student Revolt at San Francisco State College and the Emergence of Dr. Hayakawa.* Boston: Gambit, 1971.

Katz, William Loren. *The Black West.* Garden City, N.Y.: Doubleday and Co., 1971. Reprinted Seattle: Open Hand Publishing, 1987.

Kaufman, Perry Bruce. "The Best City of Them All: A History of Las Vegas, 1930–1960." Ph.D. dissertation, University of California, Santa Barbara, 1974.

Keleher, William A. *Violence in Lincoln County, 1869–1881: A New Mexico Item.* Albuquerque: University of New Mexico Press, 1957.

Kellar, William Henry. "Make Haste Slowly: A History of School Desegregation in Houston, Texas." Ph.D. dissertation, University of Houston, 1994.

Kellogg, Charles Flint. *NAACP: A History of the National Association for the Advancement of Colored People.* vol. 1, *1909–1920.* Baltimore: Johns Hopkins University Press, 1967.

Kesselman, Amy. *Fleeting Opportunities: Women Shipyard Workers in Portland and Vancouver during World War II and Reconversion.* Albany: State University of New York Press, 1990.

Kilian, Crawford. *"Go Do Some Great Thing": The Black Pioneers of British Columbia.* Vancouver: Douglas & McIntyre, Publishers, 1978.

King, William M. "Black Children, White Law: Black Efforts to Secure Public Education in Central City, Colorado, 1864–1869." *Essays and Monographs in Colorado History* (1984), 56–79.

———. *Going to Meet a Man: Denver's Last Legal Public Execution, 27 July 1886.* Niwot: University Press of Colorado, 1990.

Klassen, Teresa C., and Owen V. Johnson. "Sharpening of the *Blade:* Black Consciousness in Kansas, 1892–97." *Journalism Quarterly* 63:2 (Summer 1986), 298–304.

Kluger, Richard. *Simple Justice: The History of Brown v. Board of Education and Black America's Struggle for Equality.* New York: Vintage Books, 1975.

Kopkind, Andrew. "Watts—Waiting for D-Day." *New Republic* 154:24 (June 11, 1966), 15–17.

Kremer, Gary R. *James Milton Turner and the Promise of America: The Public Life of a Post–Civil War Black Leader.* Columbia: University of Missouri Press, 1991.

Lack, Paul. "Slavery and the Texas Revolution." *Southwestern Historical Quarterly,* 89:2 (October 1985), 181–202.

———. "Slavery and Vigilantism in Austin, Texas, 1840–1860." *Southwestern Historical Quarterly* 85:1 (July 1981), 1–20.

———. *The Texas Revolutionary Experience: A Political and Social History, 1835–1836.* College Station: Texas A&M University Press, 1992.

———. "Urban Slavery in the Southwest." *Red River Valley Historical Review* 4:2 (Spring 1981), 1–20.

Lamar, Howard Roberts. *The Far Southwest 1846–1912: A Territorial History.* New Haven: Yale University Press, 1966.

Landolt, Robert Garland. *The Mexican-American Workers of San Antonio, Texas.* New York: Arno Press, 1976.

Lane, Ann J. *The Brownsville Affair: National Crisis and Black Reaction.* Port Washington, N.Y.: Kennikat Press, 1971.

Lang, Lincoln. *Ranching with Roosevelt.* Philadelphia: J. B. Lippincott Co., 1926.

Lang, William. "The Nearly Forgotten Blacks on the Last Chance Gulch, 1900–1912." *Pacific Northwest Quarterly* 70:2 (April 1979), 50–51.

———. "Tempest on Clore Street: Race and Politics in Helena, Montana, 1906." *Scratchgravel Hills* 3 (Summer 1980), 9–14.

Langston, John Mercer. *From the Virginia Plantation to the National Capitol: An Autobiography.* Hartford, Conn.: American Publishing Co., 1894.

Lapp, Rudolph. *Afro-Americans in California.* San Francisco: Boyd & Fraser Publishing Co., 1986.

———. *Blacks in Gold Rush California.* New Haven: Yale University Press, 1977.

———. "Jeremiah B. Sanderson: Early California Negro Leader." *Journal of Negro History* 53:4 (October 1968), 321–32.

Larsen, Lawrence H. *The Urban West at the End of the Frontier.* Lawrence: Regents Press of Kansas, 1978.

Larsen, Lawrence H. and Barbara J. Cottrell. *The Gate City: A History of Omaha.* Boulder: Pruett Publishing Co., 1982.

Larson, T. A. "The Woman Suffrage Movement in Washington." *Pacific Northwest Quarterly* 67:2 (April 1976), 49–62.

Laurie, Clayton D. "The United States Army and the Labor Radicals of the Coeur d'Alenes: Federal Military Intervention in the Mining Wars of 1892–1899." *Idaho Yesterdays* 37:2 (Summer 1993), 12–29.

Lawson, Steven F. "Freedom Then, Freedom Now: The Historiography of the Civil Rights Movement." *American Historical Review* 96:2 (April 1991), 456–71.

Leckie, William H. *Buffalo Soldiers: A Narrative of the Negro Cavalry in the West* Norman: University of Oklahoma Press, 1967.

———, and Shirley A. Leckie. *Unlikely Warriors: Benjamin H. Grierson and His Family*. Norman: University of Oklahoma Press, 1984.

Ledbetter, Barbara A. Neal. *Fort Belknap Frontier Saga: Indians, Negroes and Anglo-Americans on the Texas Frontier*. Burnet, Texas: Eakin Press, 1982.

Ledbetter, Billy D. "White over Black in Texas: Racial Attitudes in the Ante-Bellum Period." *Phylon* 34:4 (December 1973), 406.

Lee, Ulysses G. *United States Army in World War II, Special Studies: The Employment of Negro Troops*. Washington, D.C.: Office of the Chief of Military History, 1966.

Leiker, James N. "Black Soldiers at Fort Hays, Kansas, 1867–1869: A Study in Civilian and Military Violence." *Great Plains Quarterly* 17:1 (Winter 1997), 3–17.

———. "Fracas at El Carrizal: The Intersection of Race and Nationalism in United States/Mexico Relations, 1916." Unpublished paper in the author's possession, 1995.

Lemke-Santangelo, Gretchen. *Abiding Courage: African American Migrant Women and the East Bay Community*. Chapel Hill: University of North Carolina Press, 1996.

Leonard, Kevin A. "Brothers under the Skin'? African Americans, Mexican Americans and World War II in California," unpublished paper presented at The Impact of World War II on California Conference, San Marino, Calif., November 1995.

Leonard, Stephen J., and Thomas J. Noel. *Denver: Mining Camp to Metropolis*. Niwot: University Press of Colorado, 1990.

Levene, Carol. "The Negro in San Francisco." *Common Ground* 9:1 (Spring 1949), 10–17.

Lewis, David Levering. *W. E. B. Du Bois: Biography of a Race, 1868–1919*. New York: Henry Holt and Co., 1993.

Light, Ivan H. *Ethnic Enterprise in America: Business and Welfare among Chinese, Japanese and Blacks*. Berkeley: University of California Press, 1972.

Limerick, Patricia Nelson. *The Legacy of Conquest: The Unbroken Past of the American West*. New York: W. W. Norton, 1987.

Lipsitz, George. "From Chester Himes to Nursery Rhymes: Local Television and the Politics of Cultural Space in Postwar Los Angeles," Unpublished paper in the author's possession, 1990.

Littlefield, Daniel F., Jr. *Africans and Creeks: From the Colonial Period to the Civil War*. Westport, Conn.: Greenwood Press, 1979.

———. *The Cherokee Freedmen: From Emancipation to American Citizenship*. Westport, Conn.: Greenwood Press, 1978.

———. *The Chickasaw Freedmen: A People without a Country*. Westport, Conn.: Greenwood Press, 1980.

———, and Mary Ann Littlefield. "The Beams Family: Free Blacks in Indian Territory." *Journal of Negro History* 61:1 (January 1976), 17–35.

———, and Lonnie E. Underhill. "Black Dreams and 'Free' Homes: The Oklahoma Territory, 1891–1894." *Phylon* 34:4 (December 1973), 342–57.

———, and ———. "Negro Marshals in the Indian Territory." *Journal of Negro History* 54:2 (April 1971), 77–87.

———, and ———. "Slave 'Revolt' in the Cherokee Nation, 1842." *American Indian Quarterly* 3:2 (Summer 1977), 121–23.

Litwack, Leon. *Been in the Storm So Long: The Aftermath of Slavery*. New York: Vintage Books, 1979.

———. *North of Slavery: The Negro in the Free States, 1790–1860*. Chicago: University of Chicago Press, 1961.

Lockley, Fred. "The Case of Robin Holmes vs. Nathaniel Ford." *Oregon Historical Quarterly* 23:2 (June 1922), 111–37.

———. "Some Documentary Records of Slavery in Oregon." *Oregon Historical Quarterly* 17:2 (June 1916), 107–115.

Logan, Rayford W. *The Betrayal of the Negro from Rutherford B. Hayes to Woodrow Wilson*. London: Collier Books, 1965.

Long, George. "How Albuquerque Got Its Civil Rights Ordinance." *Crisis* 60:11 (November 1953), 521–25.

Long, Larry H. "Migration to, from, and within Texas and Its Metropolitan Areas for Selected Periods of Time between 1930 and 1960." M.A. thesis, University of Texas, 1968.

Lortie, Francis N. *San Francisco's Black Community, 1870–1890: Dilemmas in the Struggle for Equality.* San Francisco: R and E Research Associates, 1973.

Lotchin, Roger W. "The Historians' War or the Home Front's War?: Some Thoughts for Western Historians." *Western Historical Quarterly.* 26:2 (Summer 1995), 185–86.

————. *San Francisco, 1846–1856: From Hamlet to City.* New York: Oxford University Press, 1974.

Low, Augustus, and Virgil A. Clift, eds. *Encyclopedia of Black America.* New York: Da Capo Press, 1981.

Luckingham, Bradford. *Minorities in Phoenix: A Profile of Mexican American Chinese American, and African American Communities, 1860–1992.* Tucson: University of Arizona Press, 1994.

Lundy, Benjamin. *The Life, Travels and Opinions of Benjamin Lundy, Including His Journeys to Texas and Mexico.* Philadelphia: William D. Parrish, 1847.

Luper, Clara. *Behold the Walls.* Oklahoma City: Jim Wire, 1979.

Lyles, Lionel Dean. "An Historical-Urban Geographical Analysis of Black Neighborhood Development in Denver, 1860–1970." Ph.D. dissertation, University of Colorado, 1977.

MacColl, E. Kimbark. *The Growth of a City: Power and Politics in Portland, Oregon 1915 to 1950.* Portland, Ore.: Georgian Press, 1980.

MacLachan, Colin M. and Jaime E. Rodríguez O. *The Forging of the Cosmic Race: A Reinterpretation of Colonial Mexico.* Berkeley: University of California Press, 1980.

Malone, Ann Patton. "Matt Gaines: Reconstruction Politician." In Alwyn Barr and Robert A. Calvert, eds., *Black Leaders: Texans for Their Times.* Austin: Texas State Historical Association, 1981.

Malone, Michael P. "Beyond the Last Frontier: Toward a New Approach to Western American History." *Western Historical Quarterly* 20:4 (November 1989), 409–27.

————. Richard B. Roeder, and William L. Lang. *Montana: A History of Two Centuries.* Seattle: University of Washington Press, 1991.

Marmorstein, Gary. "Central Avenue Jazz: Los Angeles Black Music of the Forties." *Southern California Quarterly* 70:4 (Winter 1988), 415–26.

Marten, James. "Slaves and Rebels: The Peculiar Institution in Texas, 1861–1865." *East Texas Historical Journal* 28:1 (1990), 29–36.

Martin, Charles H. "Jim Crow in the Gymnasium: The Integration of College Basketball in the American South." *International Journal of the History of Sport* 10:1 (April 1993), 68–86.

Martin, Tony. *Race First: The Ideological and Organizational Struggles of Marcus Garvey and the Universal Negro Improvement Association.* Westport, Conn.: Greenwood Press, 1976.

Mason, Kenneth. "Paternal Community: African Americans and Race Relations in San Antonio, Texas, 1867–1937." Ph.D. dissertation, University of Texas at Austin, 1994.

Mayer, Vincent, Jr. "The Black on New Spain's Northern Frontier: San José de Parral, 1631 to 1641." *Occasional Papers of the Center of Southwest Studies.* Paper no. 2 (November 1974), 1–33.

Mazzolini, Tom. "Interview with Bob Geddins." *Living Blues* 34 (September–October 1977), 19–30.

McBroome, Delores Nason. "Parallel Communities: African-Americans in California's East Bay, 1850–1963." Ph.D. dissertation, University of Oregon, 1991.

McCoy, Joseph G. *Historic Sketches of the Cattle Trade in the West and Southwest.* Originally published, 1874. Reprinted Washington: Rare Book Shop, 1932.

McCulloch, Josie MaCague. "Memories of Omaha: A Reminiscence." *Nebraska History* 35:4 (December 1954), 277–303.

McCusker, Kristine M. " 'The Forgotten Years' of America's Civil Rights Movement: Wartime Protests at the University of Kansas, 1939–1945." *Kansas History* 17:1 (Spring 1994), 26–37.

McDonald, Dedra S. "Slavery and Freedom in the Southwest: African Descendants in Spanish Colonial New Mexico." Unpublished paper in the author's possession, 1995.

McDonald, Forrest, and Grady McWhiney. "The Antebellum Southern Herdsman: A Reinterpretation." *Journal of Southern History* 41:2 (May 1975), 147–66.

McElderry, Stuart. "Boundaries and Limits: Housing Segregation and Civil Rights Activism in Portland, Oregon, 1930–1962." Unpublished paper in the author's possession, 1994.

McIver, Dorothy Jean Palmer. "Stepchild in Harlem: The Literary Career of Wallace Thurman." Ph.D. dissertation, University of Alabama, 1983.

McLoughlin, William G. *After the Trail of Tears: The Cherokees' Struggle for Sovereignty, 1839–1880.* Chapel Hill: University of North Carolina Press, 1993.

———. "Red Indians, Black Slavery and White Racism: America's Slaveholding Indians." *American Quarterly.* 26:4 (October 1974), 367–85.

McLagan, Elizabeth. *A Peculiar Paradise: A History of Blacks in Oregon, 1788–1940.* Portland, Ore.: Georgian Press, 1980.

McMillen, Christian. "Border State Terror and the Genesis of the African American Community in Deer Lodge and Chouteau Counties, Montana, 1870–1890." *Journal of Negro History* 79:2 (Spring 1994), 212–14.

McMurry, Linda O. *George Washington Carver: Scientist and Symbol.* New York: Oxford University Press, 1981.

McWilliams, Carey. "The House on 92nd Street." *Nation* 162:25 (June 8, 1946), 690–91.

———. "Los Angeles: An Emerging Pattern." *Common Ground* 9:1 (Spring 1949), 3–10.

Means, Russell. *Where White Men Fear to Tread: The Autobiography of Russell Means.* New York: St. Martin's Press, 1995.

Meier, August, and Elliott Rudwick. *CORE: A Study in the Civil Rights Movement, 1942–1968.* New York: Oxford University Press, 1973.

Melcher, Mary. "Blacks and Whites Together: Interracial Leadership in the Phoenix Civil Rights Movement." *Journal of Arizona History* 32:2 (Summer 1991), 195–216.

Mellinger, Philip. "Discrimination and Statehood in Oklahoma." *Chronicles of Oklahoma* 49:3 (Autumn 1971), 340–378.

Meyer, Michael, and William Sherman. *The Course of Mexican History.* New York: Oxford University Press, 1995.

Micheaux, Oscar. *The Conquest: The Story of a Negro Pioneer.* Lincoln: University of Nebraska Press, 1994.

Mihelich, Dennis. "The Formation of the Lincoln Urban League." *Nebraska History* 68:2 (Summer 1987), 63–73.

———. "The Lincoln Urban League: The Travail of Depression and War." *Nebraska History* 70:4 (Winter 1989), 303–16.

———. "World War II and the Transformation of the Omaha Urban League." *Nebraska History* 60:3 (Fall 1979), 401–23.

Millen, Gilmore. *Sweet Man.* New York: Grosset & Dunlap, 1930.

Miller, Loren. *The Petitioners: The Story of the Supreme Court of the United States and the Negro.* New York: Pantheon Books, 1966.

Miller, Susan A. "Wild Cat and the Origins of the Seminole Migration to Mexico." M.A. thesis, University of Oklahoma, 1988.

Milner, Clyde A., II, ed. *A New Significance: Re-Envisioning the History of the American West.* New York: Oxford University Press, 1996.

Miner, Craig. *West of Wichita: Setting the High Plains of Kansas, 1865–1890.* Lawrence: University Press of Kansas, 1986.

Minto, John. "Reminiscences of Experiences on the Oregon Trail in 1844." *Oregon Historical Quarterly* 2:3 (September 1901), 209–54.

Minutes and Proceedings of the First Annual Convention of the People of Color. Philadelphia: published by the convention, 1831.

Minutes and Proceedings of the Third Annual Convention for the Improvement of the Free People of Color in the United States. New York: published by order of the convention, 1833. In Howard Holman Bell, ed., *Minutes of the Proceedings of the National Negro Conventions, 1830–1864.* New York: Arno Press and the *New York Times,* 1969.

Minutes of the National Convention of Colored Citizens. New York: Piercy & Reed, Printers, 1843.

Miranda, Gloria E. "Racial and Cultural Dimensions of *Gente de Razón* Status in Spanish and Mexican California." *Southern California Quarterly* 70:3 (Fall 1988), 265–78.

Moneyhon, Carl. "George T. Ruby and the Politics of Expediency in Texas." In Howard N. Rabinowitz, ed., *Southern Black Leaders of the Reconstruction Era.* Urbana: University of Illinois Press, 1982.
———. *Republicanism in Reconstruction Texas.* Austin: University of Texas Press, 1980.
Montesano, Philip M. "San Francisco Black Churches in the Early 1860s: Political Pressure Group." *California Historical Quarterly* 52:2 (Summer 1973), 145–52.
Mooney, James. *The Ghost Dance Religion and the Sioux Outbreak of 1890.* Washington, D. C.: Government Printing Office, 1896.
Mooney, Ralph James. "Matthew Deady and the Federal Judicial Response to Racism in the Early West." *Oregon Law Review* 63:4 (1984), 561–637.
Moore, Shirley Ann. "The Black Community in Richmond, California, 1910–1963." Ph.D. dissertation, University of California, Berkeley, 1989.
Morey, Captain Lewis S. "The Cavalry Fight at Carrizal." In John M. Carroll, ed., *The Black Military Experience in the West.* New York: Liveright, 1971.
Morgan, Anne Hodges, and Rennard Strickland, eds. *Arizona Memories.* Tucson: University of Arizona Press, 1984.
Morgan, Lael. "Writing Minorities out of History: Black Builders of the Alcan Highway." *Alaska History* 7:2 (Fall 1992), 1–13.
Morner, Magnus. *Race Mixture in Latin American.* Boston: Little, Brown and Co., 1967.
Muir, Andrew Forest. "The Free Negro in Jefferson and Orange Counties, Texas." *Journal of Negro History* 35:2 (April 1950), 183–205.
Mukenge, Ida Rousseau. *The Black Church in Urban America: A Case Study in Political Economy.* Lanham, Md.: University Press of America, 1983.
Mulroy, Kevin. *Freedom on the Border: The Seminole Maroons in Florida, the Indian Territory, Coahuila, and Texas.* Lubbock: Texas Tech University Press, 1993.
Mumford, Esther Hall. *Seven Stars and Orion: Reflections of the Past.* Seattle: Ananse Press, 1986.
Murphy, Larry George. "Equality before the Law: The Struggle of Nineteenth Century Black Californians for Social and Political Justice." Ph.D. dissertation, University of California, Berkeley, 1973.
Nankivell, John H., ed. *History of the Twenty-fifth Regiment United States Infantry, 1869–1926.* Denver: Smith-Brooks Printing Co., 1927.
Nash, Gerald D. *The American West Transformed: The Impact of the Second World War.* Bloomington: Indiana University Press, 1985.
Nash, Horace D. "Blacks on the Border: Columbus, New Mexico, 1916–1922." M.A. thesis, New Mexico State University, 1988.
Nebraska Writers' Project (Works Progress Administration). *The Negroes of Nebraska.* Lincoln: Woodruff Printing Co., 1940.
Neilson, John C. "Indian Masters, Black Slaves: An Oral History of the Civil War in Indian Territory." *Panhandle-Plains Historical Review* 65 (1992), 42–55.
Newton, Huey P. *Revolutionary Suicide.* New York: Harcourt Brace Jovanovich, 1973.
Nibley, Charles W. *Reminiscences: 1849–1931.* Salt Lake City: Utah Family Society, 1934.
Nimmons, Robert Kim. "Arizona's Forgotten Past: The Negro in Arizona, 1539–1965," M.A. thesis, Northern Arizona University, 1971.
Norris, Melvin Edward, Jr., "Dearfield, Colorado—The Evolution of a Rural Black Settlement: An Historical Geography of Black Colonization on the Great Plains." Ph.D. dissertation, University of Colorado, Boulder, 1980.
O'Brien, Claire, " 'With One Mighty Pull': Interracial Town Boosting in Nicodemus, Kansas." *Great Plains Quarterly* 16:2 (Spring 1996), 117–30.
Oliver, Mamie O. *Idaho Ebony: The Afro-American Presence in Idaho State History.* Boise: Idaho State Historical Society, 1990.
Olmsted, Frederick Law. *A Journey through Texas.* New York: Mason Brothers, 1859.
Olson, James S., and Sharon Phair. "The Anatomy of a Race Riot: Beaumont, Texas, 1943." *Texana* 11:1 (Winter 1973), 64–72.
Omni, Michael, and Howard Winant. *Racial Formation in the United States from the 1960s to the 1990s.* New York: Routledge, 1994.
Oswald, Delmont R. "James P. Beckwourth." In LeRoy Hafen, ed., *The Mountain Men and the Fur Trade of the Far West.* Glendale, Calif.: Arthur H. Clark Co., 1965.
Owen, Chandler. "From Coast to Coast." *Messenger* 4:5 (May 1922), 407–10.

Painter, Nell Irvin. *Exodusters: Black Migration to Kansas after Reconstruction.* Topeka: University Press of Kansas, 1986.

Palmer, Colin. *Slaves of the White God: Blacks in Mexico, 1570–1650.* Cambridge: Harvard University Press, 1976.

Pascoe, Peggy. *Relations of Rescue: The Search for Female Moral Authority in the American West, 1874–1939.* New York: Oxford University Press, 1990.

Patterson, Edna B., Louise A. Ulph, and Victor Goodwin. *Nevada's Northeast Frontier.* Sparks, Nev.: Western Printing and Publishing Co., 1969.

Pearson, Hugh. *The Shadow of the Panther: Huey Newton and the Price of Black Power in America.* Reading, Mass.: Addison-Wesley Publishing Co., 1994.

Penn, I. Garland. *The Afro-American Press and Its Editors.* New York: Arno Press, 1969.

Perdue, Theda. "Cherokee Planters, Black Slaves and African Colonization." *Chronicles of Oklahoma* 60:3 (Fall 1982), 322–31.

———. *Slavery and the Evolution of Cherokee Society, 1540–1866.* Knoxville: University of Tennessee Press, 1979.

Phillips, Thomas D. "The Black Regulars." In Allan G. Bogue, Thomas D. Phillips, and James E. Wright, eds., *The West of the American People.* Itasca, Ill.: F. E. Peacock Publishers, 1970.

Pieroth, Doris. "With All Deliberate Caution: School Integration in Seattle, 1954–1968." *Pacific Northwest Quarterly* 73:2 (April 1982), 50–61.

Pierson, George W. *The Moving American.* New York: Alfred A. Knopf, 1973.

Pilton, James W. "Negro Settlement in British Columbia, 1858–1871." M.A. thesis, University of British Columbia, 1951.

Pitre, Merline. "The Evolution of Black Political Participation in Reconstruction Texas." *East Texas Historical Journal* 26:1 (Spring 1981), 36–45.

———. *Through Many Dangers, Toils and Snares: The Black Leadership of Texas, 1868–1900.* Austin: Eakin Press, 1985.

Plummer, Mark A. *Frontier Governor: Samuel J. Crawford of Kansas.* Lawrence: University Press of Kansas, 1971.

Plummer, Nellie Arnold. *Out of the Depths; or, The Triumph of the Cross.* Hyattsville, Md.: privately printed, 1927.

Polenberg, Richard. *War and Society: The United States, 1941–1945.* Philadelphia: J. B. Lippincott Co., 1972.

Porter, Kenneth W. "John Caesar: Seminole Negro Partisan." In Kenneth W. Porter, ed., *The Negro on the American Frontier.* New York: Arno Press and the *New York Times,* 1971.

———. "The Negro Abraham." Ibid. 1971.

———. "Negro Labor in the Western Cattle Industry, 1866–1900." in Ibid.

———. "Negroes and Indians on the Texas Frontier, 1831–1876: A Study in Race and Culture." Ibid.

———. "Roll of Overland Astorians." *Oregon Historical Quarterly* 34 (June 1933), 103–12.

Poyo, Gerald E., and Gilberto M. Hinojosa, eds. *Tejano Origins in Eighteenth-Century San Antonio.* Austin: University of Texas Press, 1991.

Price, Byron. "Mutiny at San Pedro Springs." *By Valor & Arms* 1:3 (Spring 1975), 31–34.

Prince, Diane Elizabeth. "William Goyens, Free Negro on the Texas Frontier." M.A. thesis, Stephen F. Austin State College, 1967.

Prince, Robert. *A History of Dallas from a Different Perspective.* Dallas: Nortex Press, 1993.

Proceedings of the California State Convention of Colored Citizens. San Francisco: Office of the *Elevator,* 1865.

Proceedings of the First State Convention of the Colored Citizens of the State of California. Sacramento: Democratic State Journal Printer, 1855.

Proceedings of the Second Annual Convention of the Colored Citizens of the State of California. San Francisco: J. H. Udell and W. Handall, Printers, 1856.

Rampersad, Arnold. *The Life of Langston Hughes.* New York: Oxford University Press, 1986. 2 vols.

Rampp, Lary C., and Donald L. Rampp. *The Civil War in the Indian Territory.* Austin: Presidial Press, 1975.

Ramsdell, Charles W. "The Natural Limits of Slavery Expansion." *Mississippi Valley Historical Review* 16:2 (September 1929), 151–71.

Randall, J. G., and David Donald. *The Civil War and Reconstruction*. Boston: D. C. Heath and Co., 1961.

Rawick, George P., ed. *The American Slave: A Composite Autobiography*, vol. 4, *The Texas Narratives*. Westport, Conn.: Greenwood Publishing Co., 1972.

———. *The American Slave: A Composite Autobiography*, supplement, series 1, vol. 2, *Arkansas, Colorado, Minnesota, Missouri and Oregon and Washington Narratives*. Westport, Conn.: Greenwood Publishing Co., 1977.

———. *The American Slave*, supplement, series 1, vol. 12, *The Oklahoma Narratives*. Westport, Conn.: Greenwood Press, 1979.

Rawley, James A. *Race and Politics: "Bleeding Kansas" and the Coming of the Civil War*, Philadelphia: J. B. Lippincott Co., 1969.

Ray, MaryEllen Bell. *The City of Watts, California: 1907 to 1926*. Los Angeles: Rising Publishing, 1985.

Reams, Bernard D., Jr., and Paul E. Wilson, eds. *Segregation and the Fourteenth Amendment in the States: A Survey of State Segregation Laws, 1865–1953; Prepared for the United States Supreme Court in re, Brown vs. Board of Education of Topeka*. Buffalo: William S. Hein, Publishers, 1975.

Record, Wilson. "Willie Stokes at the Golden Gate." *Crisis* 56:6 (June 1949), 175–79.

Reddick, L. D. "The New Race Relations Frontier." *Journal of Educational Sociology* 19:3 (November, 1945), 129–45.

"Report of the Agent for the Kiowa, Comanche and Wichita Agency." In *Annual Report of the Commissioner of Indian Affairs, 1879*. Washington, D.C.: Government Printing Office, 1879.

Report of the Proceedings of the Colored Convention, Held at Cleveland, Ohio. Rochester, N.Y.: North Star Press, 1848.

"Report of the Secretary of War." 39th Congress, 2d Session, *Senate Executive Document No. 26*.

Rice, Lawrence D. *The Negro in Texas, 1874–1900*. Baton Rouge: Louisiana State University Press, 1971.

Rice, Marc. "Frompin' in the Great Plains: Listening and Dancing to the Jazz Orchestras of Alphonso Trent, 1925–44." *Great Plains Quarterly* 16:2 (Spring 1996), 107–15.

Richard, K. Keith. "Unwelcome Settlers: Black and Mulatto Oregon Pioneers," Part 1. *Oregon Historical Quarterly* 84:1 (Spring 1983), 35–36.

Richardson, James. *Willie Brown: A Biography*. Berkeley: University of California Press, 1996.

Richardson, Larry S. "Civil Rights in Seattle: A Rhetorical Analysis of a Social Movement." Ph.D. dissertation, Washington State University, 1975.

Richter, William L. *The Army in Texas during Reconstruction, 1865–1870*. College Station: Texas A&M University Press, 1987.

Riley, Caroll L. "Blacks in the Early Southwest." *Ethnohistory* 19:3 (Summer 1972), 252–57.

Riley, Glenda. "American Daughters: Black Women in the West." *Montana: The Magazine of Western History* 38:2 (Spring 1988), 14–27.

Rinne, Henry Q. "A Short History of the Alphonso Trent Orchestra." *Arkansas Historical Quarterly* 45:3 (Autumn 1986), 228–49.

Ríos-Bustamante, Antonio. "Los Angeles, Pueblo and Region, 1781–1850: Continuity and Adaptation on the North Mexican Periphery." Ph.D. dissertation, University of California, Los Angeles, 1985.

Ripley, C. Peter. *The Black Abolitionist Papers*, vol. 4, *The United States, 1847–1858*. Chapel Hill: University of North Carolina Press, 1991.

Robbins, Fred. "The Origin and Development of the African Slave Trade in Galveston, Texas, and Surrounding Areas from 1816 to 1836." *East Texas Historical Journal* 9:2 (October 1971), 153–61.

Roberson, Jere W. "Edward P. McCabe and the Langston Experiment." *Chronicles of Oklahoma* 51:3 (Fall 1973), 343–55.

Romero, Mary. "El Paso Salt War: Mob Action or Political Struggle?" *Aztlán: International Journal of Chicago Studies Research* 16:1–2 (1985), 119–43.

Ronda, James P. *Astoria and Empire*. Lincoln: University of Nebraska Press, 1990.

———. *Lewis and Clark among the Indians*. Lincoln: University of Nebraska Press, 1984.

Roosevelt, Theodore. *Ranch Life and the Hunting Trail*. New York: Century Co., 1920.

Rorabaugh, W. J. *Berkeley at War: The 1960s*. New York: Oxford University Press, 1989.

Rout, Leslie B., Jr. *The African Experience in Spanish America: 1502 to the Present Day.* London: Cambridge University Press, 1977.

Ruiz, Ramón Eduardo. *Triumphs and Tragedy: A History of the Mexican People.* New York: W. W. Norton, 1992.

Ruiz, Vicki. *Cannery Women, Cannery Lives: Mexican Women, Unionization, and the California Food Processing Industry, 1930–1950.* Albuquerque: University of New Mexico Press, 1987.

———. "Gendered Histories: Interpreting Voice and Locating Power." In Clyde A. Milner II, ed., *A New Significance: Re-Envisioning the History of the American West.* New York: Oxford University Press, 1996.

Rusco, Elmer. "Civil Rights Movement in Nevada." *Nevada Public Affairs Review: Ethnicity and Race in Nevada* 2 (1987), 75–81.

———. *"Good Time Coming?" Black Nevadans in the Nineteenth Century.* Westport, Conn.: Greenwood Press, 1975.

Russell, Beverly. "World War II Boomtown: Hastings and the Naval Ammunition Depot." *Nebraska History* 76:2 and 3 (Summer/Fall 1995), 75–83.

Russell, Ross. *Jazz Style in Kansas City and the Southwest.* Berkeley: University of California Press, 1971.

Rydall, E. H. "California for Colored Folk." *Colored American Magazine* 12:5 (May 1907), 386–88.

Sando, Joe S. *Pueblo Nations: Eight Centuries of Pueblo Indian History.* Santa Fe: Clear Light Publishers, 1992.

Sandoval, Sally Jane. "Ghetto Growing Pains: The Impact of Negro Migration on the City of Los Angeles, 1940–1960." M.A. thesis, California State University, Fullerton, 1974.

Sapper, Gary. "Black Culture in Urban Texas: A Lone Star Renaissance." *Red River Valley Historical Review* 6:2 (Spring 1981), 56–77.

———. "A Survey of the History of the Black People of Texas, 1930–1954." Ph.D. dissertation, Texas Tech University, 1972.

Savage, W. Sherman, *Blacks in the West.* Westport, Conn.: Greenwood Press, 1976.

———. "The Influence of Alexander Liedesdorff on the History of California." *Journal of Negro History* 38:3 (July 1953), 322–32.

Saxe, Allan A. "Protest and Reform: The Desegregation of Oklahoma City." Ph.D. dissertation, University of Oklahoma, 1969.

Saxon, Gerald D., ed. *The WPA Dallas Guide and History.* Dallas: Dallas Public Library, 1992.

Scharff, Virginia. "Gender and Western History: Is Anybody Home on the Range?" *Montana: The Magazine of Western History* 41:2 (Spring 1991), 62–65.

Schick, Kathe. "The Lawrence Black Community, 1860–1866." Unpublished manuscript, Watkins Community Museum, Lawrence, Kans., n.d.

Schickel, Richard. *D. W. Griffith: An American Life.* New York: Simon and Schuster, 1984.

Schoen, Harold. "The Free Negro in the Republic of Texas: The Free Negro and the Texas Revolution." *Southwestern Historical Quarterly* 40:1 (July 1936), 26–34.

———. "The Free Negro in the Republic of Texas: Legal Status." *Southwestern Historical Quarterly* 40:3 (January 1937), 169–99.

———. "The Free Negro in the Republic of Texas: Origin of the Free Negro in the Republic." *Southwestern Historical Quarterly* 39:4 (April 1936), 298–308.

Schubert, Frank. "Black Soldiers on the White Frontier: Some Factors Influencing Race Relations." *Phylon* 32:4 (Winter 1971), 410–15.

———. *Black Valor: Buffalo Soldiers and the Medal of Honor, 1870–1898.* Wilmington, Del.: Scholarly Resources, 1997.

———. *Buffalo Soldiers, Braves, and the Brass: The Story of Fort Robinson, Nebraska.* Shippensburg, Pa.: White Mane Publishing Co., 1993.

———, ed. *On the Trail of the Buffalo Soldier: Biographies of African Americans in the U.S. Army, 1866–1917.* Wilmington, Del.: Scholarly Resources, 1995.

———. "The Suggs Affray: The Black Cavalry in the Johnson County War." *Western Historical Quarterly* 4:1 (January 1973), 57–68.

———. "The Violent World of Emanuel Stance, Fort Robinson, 1887." *Nebraska History* 55:2 (Summer 1974), 203–20.

Schuller, Gunther. *Early Jazz: Its Roots and Musical Development.* New York: Oxford University Press, 1968.

Schwartz, Rosalie. *Across the Rio to Freedom: U.S. Negroes in Mexico.* El Paso: Texas Western Press, 1975.

Schwendemann, Glen. "Nicodemus: Negro Haven on the Solomon." *Kansas Historical Quarterly* 34:1 (Spring 1968), 10–31.

Scott, Jeffrey A. "The Sixties Student Movement at San Francisco State College: A New Perspective." *Wazo Weusi Journal* 1:1 (Fall 1992), 48–63.

Scott, Johnie. "The Coming of the Hoodlum." In Budd Schulberg, ed., *From the Ashes: Voices of Watts.* New York: World Publishing Co., 1969.

Scott, Mark. "Langston Hughes of Kansas." *Kansas History* 3:1 (Spring 1980), 3–25.

Seale, Bobby. *Seize the Time: The Story of the Black Panther Party and Huey P. Newton.* New York: Vintage Books, 1968.

Seed, Patricia. "Social Dimensions of Race: Mexico City, 1753." *Hispanic American Historical Review* 62:3 (November 1982), 569–602.

SenGupta, Gunja. "Servants for Freedom: Christian Abolitionists in Territorial Kansas, 1854–1858." *Kansas History* 16:3 (Autumn 1993), 200–13.

Seraile, William. *Voice of Dissent: Theophilus Gould Steward (1843–1924) and Black America.* Brooklyn: Carlson Publishing, 1991.

Shapiro, Nat, and Nat Hentoff, eds. *Hear Me Talkin' to Ya: The Story of Jazz by the Men Who Made It.* New York: Dover Publications, 1966.

Sheridan, Richard B. "From Slavery in Missouri to Freedom in Kansas: The Influx of Black Fugitives and Contrabands into Kansas, 1854–1864." *Kansas History* 12:1 (Spring 1989), 28–47.

Sheridan, Thomas E. *Arizona: A History.* Tucson: University of Arizona Press, 1995.

Sherman, William C. *Prairie Mosaic: An Ethnic Atlas of Rural North Dakota.* Fargo: North Dakota Institute for Regional Studies, 1983.

Shorter, Stacey. "Forgotten Pioneers: African American Women's Community Formation in Cheyenne, Wyoming, 1867–1904." Unpublished paper in author's possession, 1995.

Silverman, Max. "Urban Redevelopment and Community Response: African Americans in San Francisco's Western Addition." M.A. thesis, San Francisco State University, 1994.

Simmons, Marc. *Albuquerque: A Narrative History.* Albuquerque: University of New Mexico Press, 1982.

Singletary, Otis A. "The Texas Militia during Reconstruction." *Southwestern Historical Quarterly* 60:1 (July 1956), 23–35.

Sitkoff, Harvard. *A New Deal for Blacks: The Emergence of Civil Rights as a National Issue.* New York: Oxford University Press, 1978.

Siringo, Charles A. *A Cowboy Detective: A True Story of Twenty-two Years with a World Famous Detective Agency.* Chicago: W. B. Conkey Co., 1912.

———. *Riata and Spurs.* Boston: Houghton Mifflin Company, 1927.

Slatta, Richard. *Cowboys of the Americas.* New Haven: Yale University Press, 1990.

Smallwood, James. "Blacks in Antebellum Texas: A Reappraisal." *Red River Valley Historical Review* 2:4 (Winter 1975), 443–66.

———. *Time of Hope, Time of Despair: Black Texans during Reconstruction.* Port Washington, N.Y.: Kennikat Press, 1981.

Smith, Alonzo Nelson. "Black Employment in the Los Angeles Area, 1938–1948." Ph.D. dissertation, University of California, Los Angeles, 1978.

———, and Quintard Taylor. "Racial Discrimination in the Workplace: A Study of Two West Coast Cities during the 1940's." *The Journal of Ethnic Studies* 8:1 (Spring 1980), 35–54.

Smith, Calvin C. "On the Edge: The Houston Riot of 1917 Revisited." *Griot* 10:1 (Spring 1991), 3–12.

Smith, Duane A. *Rocky Mountain Mining Camps: The Urban Frontier.* Lincoln: University of Nebraska, 1967.

———. " 'We Are Equal': Racial Attitudes in the West." *Westerners Brand Book* (Chicago) 30:11 (January 1974), 81–82.

Smith, Jeffrey Harrison. "The Omaha De Porres Club." M.A. thesis, Creighton University, 1967.

Smith, Robert Wayne. *The Coeur d'Alene Mining War of 1892: A Case Study of an Industrial Dispute.* Corvallis: Oregon State University Press, 1961.

Smurr J. W. "Jim Crow out West." In J. W. Smurr and K. Ross Toole, eds., *Historical Essays on Montana and the Northwest: In Honor of Paul C. Phillips.* Helena: Western Press, Historical Society of Montana, 1957.

Smythe, Donald, S.J. "John J. Pershing at Fort Assiniboine." *Montana: The Magazine of Western History* 18:1 (Winter 1968), 19–23.

Sonenshein, Raphael J. *Politics in Black and White: Race and Power in Los Angeles.* Princeton: Princeton University Press, 1993.

Sonnichsen, C. L. *The El Paso Salt War, 1877.* El Paso: Texas Western Press, 1961.

SoRelle, James M. "The Darker Side of 'Heaven': The Black Community in Houston, Texas, 1917–1945." Ph.D. dissertation, Kent State University, 1980.

———. "The Emergence of Black Business in Houston, Texas: A Study of Race and Ideology, 1919–45." In Howard Beeth and Cary D. Wintz, eds., *Black Dixie: Afro-Texan History and Culture in Houston.* College Station: Texas A&M University Press, 1992.

Southern, Eileen. *The Music of Black Americans: A History.* New York: W. W. Norton, 1971.

Sparks, Randy J. " 'Heavenly Houston' or 'Hellish Houston'? Black Unemployment and Relief Efforts, 1929–1936." *Southern Studies* 25:4 (Winter 1986), 353–66.

Spence, Mary Lee, and Donald Jackson, eds. *The Expeditions of John Charles Frémont.* Urbana: University of Ilinois Press, 1973. 2 vols.

Spickard, Paul. "Work and Hope: African American Women in Southern California during World War II." *Journal of the West* 32:3 (July 1993), 70–79.

Spoehr, Luther. "Sambo and the 'Heathen Chinee': Californians' Racial Stereotypes in the Late 1870s." *Pacific Historical Review* 42:2 (May 1975), 185–204.

Stanley, Gerald. "Civil War Politics in California." *Southern California Quarterly* 64:2 (Summer 1982), 115–32.

Stein, Judith. *The World of Marcus Garvey.* Baton Rouge: Louisiana State University Press, 1986.

Stephenson, Richard. "Race in the Cactus State." *Crisis* 61:4 (April 1954), 197–203.

Stephenson, Wendell Holmes. *The Political Career of General James H. Lane.* Topeka: Kansas State Historical Society, 1930.

Steward, T. G., *The Colored Regulars in the United States Army.* Philadelphia: A.M.E. Book Concern, 1904.

———. "The Strike in Montana." *Independent* 46:2384 (August 9, 1894), 1017

Stewart, William M. *Reminiscences of Senator William M. Stewart of Nevada.* George Rothwell Brown ed. New York: Neale Publishing Co., 1908.

Stoddard, Tom. *Jazz on the Barbary Coast.* Chigwell, England: Storyville Publications, 1982.

Stover, Earl F. "Chaplain Henry V. Plummer, His Ministry and His Courtmartial." *Nebraska History* 56:1 (Spring 1975), 21–50.

Stowe, David W. "Jazz in the West: Cultural Frontier and Region during the Swing Era." *Western Historical Quarterly* 23:1 (February 1992), 53–73.

Sullivan, Neil V. *Now Is the Time: Integration in the Berkeley Schools.* Bloomington: Indiana University Press, 1969.

Sunseri, Alvin R. "A Note on Slavery and the Black Man in New Mexico." *Negro History Bulletin* 38:1 (October–November 1975), 457–59.

———. *Seeds of Discord: New Mexico in the Aftermath of the American-Conquest, 1846–1861.* Chicago: Nelson Hall, 1979.

Sweeting, Anthony. "The Dunbar Hotel and Central Avenue Renaissance, 1781–1950." Ph.D. dissertation, University of California, Los Angeles, 1992.

Taylor, Quintard. "Black Urban Development—Another View: Seattle's Central District, 1910–1940." *Pacific Historical Review* 58:4 (November 1989), 429–48.

———. "Blacks and Asians in a White City: Japanese Americans and African Americans in Seattle, 1890–1940." *Western Historical Quarterly* 22:4 (November 1991), 401–29.

———. "The Civil Rights Movement in the Urban West: Black Protest in Seattle, 1960–1970." *Journal of Negro History* 80:1 (Winter 1995), 1–14.

———. "The Emergence of Afro-American Communities in the Pacific Northwest 1865–1910." *Journal of Negro History* 64:4 (Fall 1979), 342–51.

———. *The Forging of a Black Community: Seattle's Central District from 1870 through the Civil Rights Era.* Seattle: University of Washington Press, 1994.

———. "From Esteban to Rodney King: Five Centuries of African American History in the West." *Montana: The Magazine of Western History* 46:4 (Winter 1996), 2–23.

———. "The Great Migration: The Afro-American Communities of Seattle and Portland during the 1940s." *Arizona and the West* 23:2 (Summer 1981), 109–26.

———. "A History of Blacks in the Pacific Northwest, 1788–1970." Ph.D. dissertation, University of Minnesota, 1977.

———. "Slaves and Free Men: Blacks in the Oregon Country, 1840–1860." *Oregon Historical Quarterly* 83:2 (Summer 1982), 165–69.

Telfer, John H. "Philip Alexander Bell and the *San Francisco Elevator.*" *San Francisco Negro Historical & Cultural Society Monograph*, no. 9 (August 1966).

Thompson, Erwin N. "The Negro Soldiers on the Frontier: A Fort Davis Case Study." *Journal of the West* 7:2 (April 1968), 217–35.

Thurman, Odell A. "The Negro in California before 1890." *Pacific Historian* 19:4 (Winter 1975), 324–25.

Thwaites, Reuben, ed. *Original Journals of the Lewis and Clark Expedition.* New York: Antiquarian Press, 1959. 8 vols.

Tolbert, Emory J. *The UNIA and Black Los Angeles.* Los Angeles: Center for Afro-American Studies, 1980.

Tompkins, E. Berkeley. "Black Ahab: William T. Shorey, Whaling Master." *California Historical Quarterly* 51:1 (Spring 1972), 75–84.

Treat, Victor H. "William Goyens: Free Negro Entrepreneur." In Alwyn Barr and Robert A. Calverts, eds., *Black Leaders: Texans for Their Times.* Austin: Texas State Historical Association, 1981.

Trexler, Harrison Anthony. "Slavery in Missouri, 1804–1865." *Johns Hopkins University Studies in Historical and Political Science* series 32, no. 2 (1914), 202–03.

Trotter, Joe William. *Black Milwaukee: The Making of an Industrial Proletariat, 1915–45.* Urbana: University of Illinois Press, 1985.

Twichell, Heath. *Northwest Epic: The Building of the Alaska Highway.* New York: St. Martin's Press, 1992.

Tyler, Bruce. "Black Radicalism in Southern California, 1950–1982." Ph.D. dissertation, University of California, Los Angeles, 1983.

———. "Zoot-Suit Culture and the Black Press." *Journal of American Culture* 17:2 (Summer 1994), 21–33.

Tyler, Ronnie C. "The Callahan Expedition of 1855: Indians or Negroes?" *Southwestern Historical Quarterly* 70:4 (April 1967), 574–85.

Unrau, Harlan Dale. "The Double V Movement in Los Angeles during the Second World War: A Study in Negro Protest." M.A. thesis, California State College, Fullerton, 1971.

U.S. Bureau of the Census, *Census of Unemployment, 1937. Final Report on Total* and Partial Unemployment. Washington, D.C.: Government Printing Office, 1938.

———. *Census of Population, 1950,* vol. 2, *Characteristics of the Population.* Washington, D.C.: Government Printing Office, 1953.

———. *Census of Population, 1960,* vol. I, *Characteristics of the Population.* Washington, D.C.: Government Printing Office, 1963.

———. *Eighth Census of the U.S., 1860.* Washington, D.C.: Government Printing Office, 1864.

———. *Negro Population in the United States, 1790–1915.* Washington, D.C.: Government Printing Office, 1918.

———. *Population of the United States, 1890.* Washington, D.C.: Government Printing Office, 1897.

———. *Seventeenth Census of the United States, 1950 Census of the Population,* vol. 2, *Characteristics of the Population,* Washington D.C.: Government Printing Office, 1952.

———. *Seventh Census of the United States, 1850.* Washington: Robert Armstrong, Public Printer, 1853.

———. *Sixteenth Census of the United States, 1940, Population,* vol. 2, *Characteristics of the Population.* Washington, D.C.: Government Printing Office, 1943.

———. *Twelfth Census of the United States, 1900, Population,* part 1, Washington, D.C.: Government Printing Office, 1901.

————. *1970 Census of Population,* vol. I, *Characteristics of the Population.* Washington, D.C.: Government Printing Office, 1973.

U.S. Congress, Senate, *Federal Aid in Domestic Disturbances, 1787–1903.* S. Doc. 209, 57th Congress, 2d session, 1902–03.

U.S. Department of Labor. *Negroes in the United States: Their Employment and Economic Status.* Washington, D.C.: Bureau of Labor Statistics, December 1952.

Utley, Robert M. *Frontier Regulars: The United States Army and the Indian, 1866–1891.* New York: Macmillan, 1973.

————. *The Last Days of the Sioux Nation.* New Haven: Yale University Press, 1963.

Van Deburg, William L. *New Day in Babylon: The Black Power Movement and American Culture, 1965–1975.* Chicago: University of Chicago Press, 1992.

Vandiver, Frank E. *Black Jack: The Life and Times of John J. Pershing.* College Station: Texas A&M University Press, 1977. 2 vols.

Van Meeter, Sondra. "Black Resistance to Segregation in the Wichita Public Schools, 1870–1912." *Midwest Quarterly* 20:3 (Autumn 1978), 64–77.

Vose, Clement. *Caucasians Only: The Supreme Court, the NAACP and the Restrictive Covenant Cases.* Berkeley: University of California Press, 1967.

Waddell, Karen. "Dearfield, a Dream Deferred." *Colorado Heritage,* issue 2 (1988), 2–12.

Walker, Donald R. *Penology for Profit: A History of the Texas Prison System, 1867–1912.* College Station: Texas A&M University Press, 1988.

Waller, Reuben. "History of a Slave Written by Himself at the Age of Eighty-Nine Years." In John M. Carroll, ed., *The Black Military Experience in the West.* New York: Liveright, 1971.

Walters, Ronald. "The Great Plains Sit-in Movement, 1958–60." *Great Plains Quarterly* 16:2 (Spring 1996), 85–94.

————. "Standing Up in America's Heartland: Sitting-in before Greensboro." *American Visions* 8:1 (February 1993), 20–23.

The War of the Rebellion: A Compilation of the Official Records of the Union and Confederate Armies. Washington, D.C.: Government Printing Office, 1900. 129 vols.

Washington, Booker T. "Boley, a Negro Town in the West," *Outlook* 88 (January 1908), 28–31.

Wax, Darold D. "The Odyssey of an Ex-Slave: Robert Ball Anderson's Pursuit of the American Dream." *Phylon* 45:1 (Spring 1984), 67–79.

————. "Robert Ball Anderson, Ex-Slave, a Pioneer in Western Nebraska, 1884–1930." *Nebraska History* 64:2 (Summer 1983), 163–92.

Wayne, George H. "Negro Migration and Colonization in Colorado." *Journal of the West* 15:1 (January 1976), 102–20.

Weaver, John D. *The Brownsville Raid.* New York: W. W. Norton, 1970.

Weaver, Robert C. "Negro Employment in the Aircraft Industry." *Quarterly Journal of Economics* 59:4 (August 1945), 597–625.

————. *The Negro Ghetto.* New York: Russell and Russell, 1948.

Webb, Hertha Auburn. "D. W. '80 John' Wallace: Black Cattleman, 1875–1939." M.A. thesis, Prairie View A&M College, 1957.

Webb, Walter Prescott. "The American West: Perpetual Mirage." *Harper's Magazine* (May 1957).

Weber, David J. "A Black American in Mexican San Diego: Two Recently Recovered Documents." *Journal of San Diego History* 20:2 (Spring 1974), 29–32.

————. "Mestiazje: The First Census of Los Angeles, 1781." In Weber, *Foreigners in Their Native Land: Historical Roots of the Mexican Americans.* Albuquerque: University of New Mexico Press, 1973.

————. *The Mexican Frontier, 1821–1846: The American Southwest under Mexico.* Albuquerque: University of New Mexico Press, 1982.

Weiss, Nancy J. *The National Urban League, 1910–940.* New York: Oxford University Press, 1974.

Werner, Brian R. "Colorado's Pioneer Blacks: Migration, Occupations and Race Relations in the Centennial State." M.A. thesis, University of Northern Colorado, 1979.

Wesley, Charles H. *The History of the National Association of Colored Women's Clubs, Inc.: A Legacy of Service.* Washington: Associated Publishers, 1984.

Westermeier, Clifford P. "Black Rodeo Cowboys." *Red River Valley Historical Review* 3:3 (Summer 1978), 4–27.

White, Lonnie J. "Warpaths on the Southern Plains: The Battles of the Saline River and Prairie Dog Creek." *Journal of the West* 4:4 (October 1965), 485–03.

White, Richard. *"It's Your Misfortune and None of My Own:" A New History of the American West*. Norman: University of Oklahoma Press, 1991.

———. "Race Relations in the American West." *American Quarterly* 38:3 (1986), 394–416.

Wilbarger, J. W. *Indian Depredations in Texas*. Austin: Stock Co., 1935.

Wilder, Daniel. *Annals of Kansas*. Topeka: G. W. Martin, 1875.

Williams v. International Brotherhood of Boilermakers, Iron Shipbuilders and Helpers of America, 28 Cal.2d 568 (1946).

Williams, Nudie. "Black Men Who Wore the Star." *Chronicles of Oklahoma* 59:1 (Spring 1981), 83–90.

Williams, Roy H., and Kevin J. Shay. *Time Change: An Alternative View of the History of Dallas*. Dallas: To Be Publishing Co., 1991.

Wilson, John P. *Merchants, Guns & Money: The Story of Lincoln County and Its Wars*. Santa Fe: Museum of New Mexico Press, 1987.

Winegarten, Ruthe. *Black Texas Women: 150 Years of Trial and Triumph*. Austin: University of Texas Press, 1995.

Winship, George Parker. "The Coronado Expedition, 1540–1542." *Fourteenth Annual Report of the Bureau of Ethnology*. Smithsonian Institution, 1892–93, Washington, D.C.: Government Printing Office, 1896.

Wintz, Cary D. "Blacks." In Fred R. von der Mehden, ed., *The Ethnic Groups of Houston*. Houston: Rice University Studies, 1984.

———. "The Emergence of a Black Neighborhood: Houston's Fourth Ward, 1865–1915." In Char Miller and Heywood T. Sanders, eds., *Urban Texas: Politics and Development*. College Station: Texas A&M University Press, 1990.

Wolfinger, Henry J. "A Test of Faith: Jane Elizabeth James and the Origins of the Utah Black Community." In Clark Knowlton, ed., *Social Accommodation in Utah*. Salt Lake City: University of Utah Press, 1975.

Wollenberg, Charles. *All Deliberate Speed: Segregation and Exclusion in California Schools, 1855–1975*. Berkeley: University of California Press, 1976.

———. "Blacks vs. Navy Blue: The Mare Island Mutiny Court Martial." *California History* 58:1 (Spring 1979), 62–75.

Wood, Forrest G. *Black Scare: The Racist Response to Emancipation and Reconstruction*. Berkeley: University of California Press, 1970.

Wood, Peter H. *Black Majority: Negroes in Colonial South Carolina from 1670 through the Stono Rebellion*. New York: W. W. Norton, 1974.

Wood, Thomas Alexander. "First Admission of Collored [*sic*] Children to the Portland Public Schools." Unpublished manuscript, no. 37, Oregon Historical Society.

Woods, Randall B. "After the Exodus: John Lewis Waller and the Black Elite, 1878–1900." *Kansas Historical Quarterly* 43:2 (Summer 1977), 172–92.

———. *A Black Odyssey: John Lewis Waller and the Promise of American Life, 1878–1900*. Lawrence: Regents Press of Kansas, 1981.

———. "George T. Ruby: A Black Militant in the White Business Community." *Red River Valley Historical Review* 1:3 (Autumn 1974), 269–80.

———. "Integration, Exclusion, or Segregation? The 'Color Line' in Kansas, 1878–1900." *Western Historical Quarterly* 14:2 (April 1983), 181–98.

Woolfolk, George Ruble. *The Free Negro in Texas, 1800–1860: A Study in Cultural Compromise*. Ann Arbor: University Microfilms International, 1976.

Worster, Donald. *Under Western Skies: Nature and History in the American West*. New York: Oxford University Press, 1992.

Newspapers and Magazines

Bellville Countryman, 1865.
Berkeley Citizens United Bulletin, 1964.
Black Hills Daily Times, 1885.

Boise Idaho Daily Statesman, 1899.
Cleveland Gazette, 1883.
Crisis, 1913, 1918, 1928
Dallas Express, 1943.
Dallas Herald, 1866.
Denver Colorado Statesman, 1933.
Denver Daily Rocky Mountain News, 1867.
Denver Field and Farm, 1887.
Denver Post, 1909.
Denver Rocky Mountain News, 1865.
Dodge City Daily Globe, 1933.
El Paso Morning Times, 1916.
Fort Scott Colored Citizen, 1878.
Harper's Weekly, 1885–99.
Helena Colored Citizen, 1894.
Helena Daily Herald, 1870.
Helena Independent, 1882.
Helena Montana Plaindealer, 1906–09.
Houston Informer, 1942.
Lawrence Kansas Tribune, 1866.
Langston City Herald, 1891–92.
Las Cruces Thirty-four, 1879.
Las Vegas Review Journal, 1943.
Lincoln Daily Nebraska State Journal 1891.
Los Angeles California Eagle, 1922–46.
Los Angeles Sentinel, 1969.
Los Angeles Times, 1909–69.
New Bedford Mercury, 1848.
Nicodemus Western Cyclone, 1886–87.
Olympia Commercial Age, 1870.
Omaha World-Herald, 1891.
Palo Alto Daily Palo Alto, 1903.
Park City, Utah, *Park Record,* 1882.
Philadelphia Pennsylvania Freeman, 1850.
Pittsburgh Courier, 1923.
Portland Oregonian, 1870–1947.
Rochester Frederick Douglass' Paper, 1852.
St. Louis Globe Democrat, 1879.
Salem Oregon Statesman, 1867.
Salt Lake City Deseret News, 1863.
Salt Lake City Tribune, 1896.
San Antonio Daily Herald, 1869.
San Francisco Call, 1891.
San Francisco Chronicle, 1894.
San Francisco Daily Alta California, 1854–89.
San Francisco Daily Evening Post, 1873
San Francisco Elevator, 1868–70.
San Francisco Pacific Appeal, 1862–63.
Seattle Daily Intelligencer 1879.
Seattle Northwest Enterprise, 1927.
Spokane Spokesman Review, 1892–99.
Sturgis Weekly Record, 1885.
Time Magazine, 1944.
Tahlequah Cherokee Advocate, 1876–79.
Topeka Colored Citizen, 1878.
Trinidad Daily Advertiser, 1883.
Washington, D.C., *People's Advocate,* 1884.
Washington, D.C., *The Army and Navy Register,* 1892.

Index

◊ ✿ ◊ ✿ ◊